Carrying on the Anatomical Studies

Left to right: Thorstein Veblen, Joseph Schumpeter, John Maynard Keynes, and Alfred Marshall.

THE ECONOMIC PROBLEM

PRENTICE-HALL, INC.

Englewood Cliffs, New Jersey

ROBERT L. HEILBRONER

The
Economic
Problem

SECOND EDITION

For Adolph Lowe

13-226985-6
Library of Congress Catalog Card No.: 72-101151
Current printing (last number): 10 9 8 7 6 5 4 3 2 1

LONDON   PRENTICE-HALL INTERNATIONAL, INC.
SYDNEY   PRENTICE-HALL OF AUSTRALIA, PTY. LTD.
TORONTO   PRENTICE-HALL OF CANADA, LTD.
NEW DELHI   PRENTICE-HALL OF INDIA PRIVATE LTD.
TOKYO   PRENTICE-HALL OF JAPAN, INC.

PREFACE

The trouble with economics is that it will not stand still. Issues change, ideas change, understanding changes. Even the past does not look exactly the same from one year to the next, and the present is apt to alter almost out of all recognition.

Change is the main reason for this revised edition. In the three years since the text was written, in the two years since galleys were read and last-minute improvements squeezed in, large-scale changes have taken place in the American economic picture. Conglomerates are here. Inflation is a much more important subject. The role of money is appraised somewhat differently. The balance of payments has emerged as a major problem. The decentralization of the East European economies has proceeded apace.

All this would be reason enough to recast many chapters of the original text—just as, no doubt, similar changes will require another recasting three years or so hence. But there is a second reason for a new edition. This is simply the personal experience that I have had in teaching with *The Economic Problem,* plus the vicarious experience I have gained through the letters and suggestions sent to me by economics instructors in innumerable colleges and universities. It is on the basis of their recommendations, as well as that of my own experience, that other changes have been introduced: T accounts in the chapter on banking, new diagrams and explanations with regard to liquidity preference, Phillips curves, growth, and correction of errors that slyly creep into textbooks when an author's back is turned. I am grateful for the criticism that I have received, and pleased that the basic text has served its purpose well enough to warrant a new version.

After so much accent on change, let me in conclusion emphasize continuity. *The Economic Problem* was originally written to represent a point of view and to serve a specific teaching purpose: a point of view that stressed the inextricable element of history behind and within economics, and a teaching purpose that sought to concentrate the energies of the text on a relatively few central concepts rather than dissipating them over issues and problems that were essentially secondary in importance. That point of view and that teaching aim remain as the chief identificatory marks of this handsome new edition of *The Economic Problem,* as they did within the old. If the book should ever warrant a future edition, I can assure the reader that they will continue to be there as well.

ROBERT L. HEILBRONER

INTRODUCTION
FOR INSTRUCTORS

The cry in the land is "economic literacy," and there is much head-shaking as to whether a nation of economic illiterates can long survive. I must confess that I am more than a little suspicious of this cry when it resounds from quarters that teach a kind of economic patriotism; and I look askance at some of the presumed cures for our condition, which have included attempts to interest elementary school children in the stock market. Nonetheless, there is an apparent core of good sense beneath the nonsense. We do live in an age in which the importance of economic policy bulks very large, and there is no doubt that we must rely on the informed opinion of our citizenry to distinguish between those policies that will cause the nation to prosper and those that will cause it to decline.

There was a time, not too terribly long ago, when such choices were relatively easy to make, even for citizens who had never taken a course in economics. Until the Great Depression, the prevailing ideas of economists, right or wrong, were not at great variance with those of the public at large. Thrift and enterprise, balanced budgets, laissez faire, and a few like tenets provided the scholar and the ordinary citizen with their "principles" of economics. As a result, the issue of economic illiteracy never arose, save on those few occasions, mainly having to do with the tariff, when the ideas of economists and of the business and working community diverged.

I need hardly labor the point that things are not the same today. Economics has not only become infinitely more refined and complicated than it was only a generation ago, but its fundamental ideas are no longer such that they command the unthinking approval of the economically untaught. Every economist is aware, of course, that a central conception of modern economic policy—the use of the government budget as a stabilizing and compensating mechanism—is a notion that goes squarely against the grain of untutored common sense. But no less perplexing are other problems that emerge increasingly to the fore as political issues—problems having to do with automation or with the alleviation of poverty or with assistance to the underdeveloped nations. Here, too, an easy reliance on "common sense" may give results quite different from those expected or desired by an electorate guided only by the prevailing wisdom.

How are we to guard against this danger? The answer is that eternal hope and despair of a democracy: education. Not that formal schooling alone will dispel economic illiteracy—in very important part, the necessary understanding will have to be gained from books and television programs and the speeches of Presidents and other prominent national figures. But in the end, the most enduring and cumulative contribution undoubtedly must come through the gradual creation of an adult population that has received formal economic training for at least some portion of its educational career. I retain my skepticism that stock market analysis at the elementary school level will create a generation of economic sophisticates. But I am hopeful about the results of teaching economics in high school, and still more hopeful about its being taught at the junior college and four-year college level. In 1970, some 750,000 students enrolled in at least an introductory course in economics. Moreover, if present trends continue, we can expect that number to rise to 900,000 within a decade.

This is an enormous opportunity, but it is also a considerable problem. As every teacher of the subject knows, economics is not a subject that can be taught in a few lessons, and only a small minority of students will go on into intermediate or advanced courses. Thus, for most students there is only the space of a few months in which the subject can be mastered—stored up for the rest of adult life, not merely grasped until the exams, after which it immediately begins to melt away.

Is this too much to expect from a single exposure to economics? I do not think so, provided that the course is focused on essentials, cleared of all distractions and needless difficulties, and not afraid to repeat the main points in various contexts. But what are the "essentials" that we would wish to teach in one course, hopefully for a lifetime? I think they are three—perhaps three-and-a-half.

First, I would emphasize a broad understanding of *economic history* —not, of course, to learn names and dates, but to gain a sense of the evolution of the economic system, of the internal changes that have gradually altered the setting of economic life, and of the trajectory of economic evolution. The substantive issues of growth, or stability, or the operation of the market mechanism—all matters that must subsequently be carefully studied and technically conquered—are not likely to be approached with genuine interest until they are first understood in the dramatic context of history. When I wrote in *The Worldly Philosophers** that "A man who thinks that economics is only a matter for professors forgets that this is the science that has sent men to the barricades," I did not envision an economic textbook that would read like a revolutionary tract. But the undercurrent of social tension beneath all of economics should not be lost to sight even in the necessarily dispassionate analysis of economic relationships and techniques. Accordingly, the purpose of the long historical introduction and conclusion of this text is not only to teach some economic fundamentals of the greatest importance, but to provide a springboard from which to take off with enthusiasm into the more demanding intellectual tasks to follow.

Second, the economically literate adult must understand the basic elements of *macroeconomics*. This is so generally accepted that I will not linger to argue the case. I would only emphasize that in my view, such an understanding involves above all the income-expenditure-employment relationship and the use of the public budget as a stabilizing or growth-promoting device. The finer details of the operation of the system are not essential at the first level and may even obscure the central issues that must be completely clear.

Hence the text does not hesitate to compress some problems drastically and to expand some others. A student will not learn the Hicks-Hansen synthesis in these pages. On the other hand, he should emerge with a really solid grasp of the intersectoral relations that establish the moving level of GNP, and he will find a much longer treatment than elsewhere of that forbidden but critical subject, the relationship between technology and unemployment.

Third, I think that an economically literate adult must understand

---

* On the front endpapers of the book, the reader will find a gallery of those sometimes very worldly and sometimes out-of-this worldly characters drawn by Bernarda Bryson. I am grateful to the *Scientific American* for permission to use one of Miss Bryson's drawings.

the *essentials of microeconomics*. Why? Because it introduces him to the market mechanism that is the foundation on which the entire economic society rests. Note that I stress *essentials*. Microeconomics is a treacherous subject because it leads so easily into so many fascinating by-paths. These are explored, however, at the risk of losing one's central conception of the market as a mechanism for social allocation. I have tried valiantly to stay on this main avenue (with only a glance or two right or left).

But there is another reason for including a section on microeconomics. It is that a study of price theory takes a student into the very heart of economic reasoning in a way that macroanalysis does not. A student who has never struggled and then come to be familiar with the meaning of supply and demand or with the conditions and consequences of market structures or with the behavior of the firm under pure and restricted competition has surely missed something of great value in learning to think like an economist. Even after the fine points of microanalysis have been forgotten, a memory of the process of economic reasoning itself should linger. Hence there is perhaps more than the ordinary emphasis on the meaning and assumptions of economic thinking, in addition to the familiar apparatus of price theory.

Therewith my three candidates for the elements of economic literacy. I mentioned another half: foreign trade, of course. One cannot very well get introduced to economics without some awareness that even so vast an economic system as the United States is affected by a still vaster world system of economic forces. In part, this is covered at the conclusion in a resumption of the historical portion of the text, but the subject first needs special attention in a small technical section of its own. (It is small only because international trade and finance is too vast a topic to be very thoroughly covered in the first year. Thus the "half.") What I have attempted to do is to take a few aspects of the problem, such as comparative advantage and the balance of payments, treat them carefully (rather than skim over the whole field rapidly) and thereafter set the whole international problem into a global perspective in the final chapter of the book.

I refrain from offering suggestions about how best to teach the respective sections of the text. Everyone has his favorite way of presenting micro- and macroeconomics, and ideally a text should supplement and support the instructor's style, rather than force him to hew to a mold that suits him ill. I will, however, add a word about the initial section of the book, since I believe that many instructors may not have experienced the problems of teaching economic history. At various times I have used economic history in an introductory course in three ways: (1) I have simply assigned chapters seriatim and worked through the text, talking about the various historical epochs and their economic problems as a general background for the macro and micro work to follow; (2) I have lectured on the general problems of economic growth and on the relation between comparative economic systems and their economic characteristics, allowing the text to serve as a kind of backdrop to my remarks; (3) I have simply assigned the reading to be completed before the end of the course, and turned the classwork immediately to the problems of macroanalysis. All these approaches have had their usefulness, and my choice among them is dictated partly by the amount of time I feel like devoting to macro-or microproblems, partly by my assessment of the class and its needs, and partly by my predilections of the moment.

A final word about the text. As some readers may recognize, much of two parts of the book—history and macrotheory—have been previously published as independent books, *The Making of Economic Society* and *Understanding Macroeconomics.* Although this longer volume was originally conceived as it now stands, it has been a very long while in the writing, and the first two sections, when they were completed, seemed capable of standing on their own feet and of serving a useful purpose. Here they are integrated into their originally intended whole, improved by many helpful comments I have received from instructors, satisfied and otherwise.

Finally, I should like to take this opportunity to thank the people who, at various stages in this enterprise, have given me their time and advice. Harry Johnson and Hans Neisser read the macro section in its original version and both provided an indispensable critique. Goran Ohlin was the initial reader of the history section and strengthened it immeasurably with comments. Richard Attiyeh, Wylie Logan Jones, John M. Kuhlman, Paul Phillips, Richard O'Rourke, Peter John, David Borfeld, Abraham Falick, Don Kline, and above all, John Hannaford read all or parts of the text and benefited me with their suggestions and comments. But my special debt is reserved for three individuals. One of these is Al Goodyear. As my editor at Prentice-Hall, he suggested this book and then tactfully and patiently helped me bring it to eventual fruition. The second is Peter Bernstein, who has read the entire text with scrupulous care. There are very few economists of his versatility and I am fortunate to have had his abilities in my service. And third is, of course, Adolph Lowe. I say "of course" since every book that I have written has paid its last and best tribute to this remarkable man who has been called by Kenneth Boulding "one of the few people in the world today who deserves the title of economic philosopher." It is an honor to dedicate this book to him.

About the author

Robert L. Heilbroner wrote *The Worldly Philosophers* while he was still a graduate student and was foolish enough not to use it as a dissertation. As a compensation, it has sold more than a million copies and has become standard fare for high school seniors and college freshmen. After receiving his doctoral degree at the New School for Social Research, Dr. Heilbroner joined that institution, where he is now a Professor and Chairman of the Economics Department of the Graduate Faculty. In the course of writing *The Economic Problem*, two further books were born: *The Making of Economic Society* and *Understanding Macroeconomics*, both here integrated into the originally conceived whole. Dr. Heilbroner has lectured widely on university campuses and before business and professional groups, as well as on television. He is currently at work on a history of the industrial transformation of America. Dr. Heilbroner, his wife, and their two sons live in New York City and Chilmark, Massachusetts.

Other books by Robert L. Heilbroner

THE WORLDLY PHILOSOPHERS
THE FUTURE AS HISTORY
THE GREAT ASCENT
THE MAKING OF ECONOMIC SOCIETY
UNDERSTANDING MACROECONOMICS
THE LIMITS OF AMERICAN CAPITALISM
UNDERSTANDING MICROECONOMICS

CONTENTS

Introduction for students   1

PART
one

The Emergence of Modern Economic Society

The setting of the problem · The individual and society · Division of
labor · Economics and scarcity · Economics and social organization · The
production and distribution problems · Mobilizing effort · Allocating
effort · Distributing output · The three solutions to the economic
problem · Tradition · Command · The market · Economics and the market
system

1
THE
ECONOMIC PROBLEM 7

THE PRE-MARKET ECONOMY 24

The economic organization of antiquity · Agricultural foundation of ancient societies · Economic life of the cities · Slavery · Wealth and power · "Economics" and social justice in antiquity · Economic society in the Middle Ages · Manorial organization of society · Economics of manorial life · Town and fair · Guilds · Medieval economics · Prerequisites of change

THE EMERGENCE OF THE MARKET SOCIETY 48

The itinerant merchant · Urbanization · The Crusades · Growth of national power · Exploration · Change in religious climate · Breakdown of the manorial system · Appearance of the economic aspect of life · Labor, land, and capital come into being · Enclosures · Factors of production · Rise of the "profit motive" · The workings of competition · The market system and the rise of capitalism

THE INDUSTRIAL REVOLUTION 72

Pace of technical change · England in 1750 · Rise of the New Men · The industrial entrepreneur · Industrial and social repercussions · Early capitalism and social justice · The industrial revolution in the perspective of theory · Capital and productivity · Capital and saving · Growth in early capitalism · Incentives for growth · The market as a capital-building mechanism

THE IMPACT OF INDUSTRIAL TECHNOLOGY 95

Impact of one invention · General impact of technology · Distribution of the labor force · Rise of unionism · Economies of large-scale production · The great entrepreneurs

Change in competition • Limitation of competition • The threat of economic feudalism • Rise of antitrust legislation • Structure of the national market: periphery and center • Conglomerates and the marketplace • Stability of market shares • Causes of stabilization: antitrust • The new corporate executive • Oligopoly and market behavior • Challenge to consumer sovereignty • The pressure on prices • Unresolved problem of economic power

THE CHANGE IN MARKET STRUCTURE 110

America in 1929 • The Great Crash • The Great Depression • Causes of the Depression: speculation • Weakness on the farm • Weakness in the factory • Maldistribution of income • Critical role of capital formation • Effects of falling investment

THE GREAT DEPRESSION 131

The New Deal • The farm problem • The attempt to control markets • Countering the Depression • The economy fails to respond • Compensatory government spending • Impact of the war • Aftermath of the war: inflation • Instruments of policy • Redistribution of income • Growth of the government sector • The New Economics • Remaining problems • A final prospect

THE EVOLUTION OF GUIDED CAPITALISM 146

PART
two

Prosperity and Recession—The Economics of the Macro System

The macroeconomic perspective • National wealth • Capital • Wealth and claims • The flow of production • Wealth and output • Inputs and outputs • The consumption flow • The investment flow • Gross and net investment • Consumption and investment • Gross national product • Stocks and flows • Cautions about GNP

WEALTH AND OUTPUT 169

10

OUTPUT AND INCOME 188

Output and demand • An economic model • Cost and output • Costs and incomes • Factor costs and national income • Factor costs and household incomes • Costs of materials • Tax costs • Indirect vs. direct taxes • Depreciation • Another view of costs and incomes • The three streams of expenditure • The crucial role of expenditures • The complete circuit • GNP as a sum of costs and a sum of expenditures • NNP and national income • The circular flow

11

SAVING AND INVESTMENT 207

The meaning of saving • The demand gap • The dilemma of saving • The offset to savings • Claims • Public and private claims • Completed act of offsetting savings • Intersectoral offsets • Real and money saving • Transfer payments and profits • Transfer payments and taxes • Profits and demand • Saving, investment, and growth

12

THE CONSUMPTION SECTOR 222

The household sector • Subcomponents of consumption • Consumption and GNP • Saving in historic perspective • Long-run savings behavior • Short-run vs. long-run savings behavior • The consumption-income relationship • Propensity to consume • The average propensity to consume • Marginal propensity to consume • A diagram of the propensity to consume • Propensity to consume, in simple mathematics • Passivity of consumption

13

THE INVESTMENT SECTOR 239

The investment sector in profile • Categories of investment • Investment in historic perspective • Importance of investment • The multiplier • Continuing impact of respending • Marginal propensity to save • Basic multiplier formula • Leakages • The downward multiplier • The multiplier and investment

The motivation of investment • Expectations • Induced and autonomous investment • The acceleration principle • A model of the acceleration principle • Autonomous investment • The determinants of investment • Rate of interest • Marginal efficiency of capital • Saving and investment • An investment model • Interplay of saving and investment • Consumption diagram re-examined • The complete schedule diagrammed • The determination of equilibrium • A change in equilibrium • Another approach to the equilibrium problem • Two diagrams, one solution • The idea of equilibrium • The paradox of thrift • A note on exports, injections, and leakages • Impact of foreign trade • Leakages and injections

14

INVESTMENT AND EQUILIBRIUM 255

Government in the expenditure flow • Government sector in historical perspective • Composition of public spending • Classifying public expenditure • Character of the public sector • Fiscal policy • Taxes, expenditures, and GNP • Automatic stabilizers • A diagram of government spending • Another view of equilibrium • **Deficit spending** • **Deficits and losses** • Debts and assets • Real corporate debts • Total business debts • Government deficits • Sales vs. taxes • Internal and external debts • Problems of a national debt • Expenditures vs. tax cuts • Perpetual public debts • Real burdens • Indirect effects • Personal debts and public debts • The public sector again in perspective • Public and private assets • Political problems • Political vs. economic judgments

15

THE GOVERNMENT SECTOR 280

The supply of money • Currency • Bookkeeping money • Federal Reserve System • The banks' bank • Fractional reserves • Loans and investments • Inside the banking system • Assets and liabilities • T accounts • Excess reserves • Making a loan • The loan is spent • Expanding the money supply • The expansion of the money supply • Limits on the expansion • Why banks must work together • Overlending • Investments and interest • Controlling the money supply • The role of the Federal Reserve • Monetary control mechanisms • Paper money and gold • The gold cover • Gold and money • Money and belief

16

MONEY 307

The quantity theory of money • Quantity equation • Quantity theory • Changes in V • Changes in T • Output and prices • Inflation and public finance • Full employment vs. underemployment • Money and sticky prices • The problem of inflation • Bottlenecks and wage pressures • The unemployment–inflation relation • Inflation vs. unemployment • The Phillips curve • Inflation as a way of life • Money and expenditure • The case for the quantity theory • Money and interest rates • Liquidity and interest rates • Financial demand for money • Liquidity preference • Liquidity preference and interest rates • A market out of equilibrium • The argument in review • The art of monetary management • Shifting liquidity preferences • Fiscal policy and monetary policy • Monetary policy in perspective

17

MONEY AND THE MACRO SYSTEM 331

18

EMPLOYMENT AND OUTPUT   354

Employment in perspective • Participation in the labor force • Short-run changes • Meaning of unemployment • Shifting demands for labor • Impact of technology • Influence of demand • Evolution of demand • Employment, demand, and leisure • Importance of the tertiary sector • The generation of employment • Age groups irregularly distributed • New technology • New demands • Employment and investment • Inventions build industries • Inventions reduce cost • Incomes vs. employment • Impact of automation • Unemployment in the U.S. • Combatting unemployment • The long-run prospect

19

THE PROBLEM OF GROWTH   380

Structural requirements of growth • Capital formation • The historical record: stability and cycles • Business cycles • Reference cycles • Causes of cycles • Mechanism of business fluctuation • The anatomy of growth • Actual vs. potential GNP • Demand vs. capacity • Marginal capital—output ratio • Income vs. output • Balanced growth • Policy for balanced growth • Importance of growth rates • The causes of growth • Extensive investment • Productivity • Causes of improved productivity • Changing patterns of growth • Value of growth

PART

three   **Microeconomics—Anatomy of a Market System**

20

INTRODUCTION TO THE MICROECONOMY   405

Micro- and macroeconomics • System in micro perspective • The market as a system • The tasks of the market • Production-possibility curve • More production possibilities • The law of increasing cost • From production possibilities to market actualities • Circular flow again • The two markets

21

THE MARKET FOR GOODS   415

Behavior and prices • Conditions of supply and demand • Marginal utility • Quantities and schedules • Individual and collective demand • Balancing supply and demand • Emergence of the equilibrium price • Function of equilibrium prices • The role of competition • Prices and allocation • Price vs. nonprice rationing • Shortages and surpluses

Shifts in demand and supply · Price changes · Elasticity · Elasticities, expenditures, and receipts · Behind elasticities of demand · Marginal utility again · Necessities and elasticity · Other influences on demand · Importance of time · Substitution and demand · Complements · Individual and collective demand, again · The market as a self-correcting mechanism · Stability and instability · Unstable situations · Destabilizing expectations · Predictive and normative price theory

THE MARKET IN
MOVEMENT 433

Distribution of income · Land, labor, and capital · The supply curves of factors · The supply curve of labor · Elasticities and mobility · Time and technical specificity · Rents and incomes · Quasi rents · Quasi rents and incomes · Supply curves and prices · Income differences · Direct demand for factors · Comparative earnings · Causes of income disparity · Property income · Derived demand

THE MARKET
FOR FACTORS 455

Economics of the firm · The problem of scale · Factor mix · Law of variable proportions · Productivity curve: increasing returns · Diminishing returns · Total, average, and marginal product · The law reviewed · Diminishing returns and increasing cost · Marginal revenue and marginal cost · Productivity and profit · Choice among factors · Bidding for factors · Factor pricing · The market solution to distribution · Minimum wages · Marginal productivity and social justice

THE FIRM IN THE
FACTOR MARKET 474

Inside the firm: fixed and variable cost · Per unit cost · Fixed and variable costs per unit · Total cost per unit · The cost profile · Average and marginal costs · From cost to revenue · From supply to demand · Average and marginal revenue · Marginal revenue and marginal cost · Entry and exit · Long-run equilibrium · Profits and equilibrium · Long run and short run · Economies of scale · Increasing or decreasing long-run costs · The competitive environment · Pure competition defined · Competition in fact and theory

EQUILIBRIUM OF
THE FIRM 496

Monopoly • "Pure" monopolies • Limits of monopoly • Cost curves for the monopolist • Monopoly revenues • Equilibrium for the monopoly • Monopoly vs. competitive prices • Oligopoly • The maximizing assumption • Oligopolistic indeterminancy • Imperfect competition • Equilibrium in monopolistic competition • Extent of market imperfection

COMPETITION IN THE
REAL WORLD 519

Strengths of the market • Weaknesses of the market • Waste • Advertising • Product differentiation • Gains from advertising and differentiation • Monopoly and inefficiency • Gains from monopoly • Waste and the market's operation • Size and instability • The market in perspective • The issue of power • Deeper weaknesses of the market system • The market as a social instrument • Historical perspective on the market system

THE MARKET SYSTEM
IN REVIEW 536

PART
four   **The Economics of International Gain and Loss**

The bias of nationalism • Source of the difficulty • Gains from trade • Gains from specialization • Unequal advantages • Trade-off relationships • Comparative advantage • Opportunity cost • The role of prices • The case for free trade • Classical argument for free trade • The case for tariffs • Mobility • Full employment • National self-sufficiency • Infant industries • The basic argument

THE GAINS
FROM TRADE 551

Foreign exchange • Mechanism of exchange • The supply of, and demand for, foreign exchange • Nonmerchandise items • Balance of payments on current account • U.S. balance of payments on current account • Rate of exchange and the balance of payments • Appreciation and depreciation of foreign exchange • Process of adjustment • Fixed vs. flexible exchange rates • Problems of flexible exchange rates • Fixed exchange rates • More on the balance of payments • Government transactions • Foreign aid in the balance of payments • Capital movements • Gold and reserves • Dollar reserves • Balancing the balance of payments • Meaning of balance of payments deficit • The gold problem • The gold crisis of 1968 • Balance of payments in 1968 • Lessons of 1968 • Curing the balance of payments deficit • Devaluation • Strengthening the IMF • International vs. interregional trade • Addendum: a note on the gold standard

29

THE PROBLEM OF
INTERNATIONAL
TRANSACTIONS 572

The Challenge to the Market System

PART
five

Trials of capitalism abroad • European capitalism: feudal heritage and national rivalry • Crucial role of European trade • Breakdown of international trade • European socialism • Recovery of European capitalism • The Common Market • Socialism and modern European capitalism • Conservative planning • Europe and America • Socialist planning in the U.S.S.R. • The drive to total planning • The planning mechanism • The plan in action • Planning and efficiency • Plans for reform

30

THE DRIFT OF
EUROPEAN ECONOMIC
HISTORY 609

Background to underdevelopment • Conditions of backwardness • Social inertia • Further problems: population growth • Role of imperialism • Engineering of development • Problem of equipment • Trade problems • Limitations on private foreign investment • The crucial avenue of aid • Economic possibilities for growth • Social and political problems • Collectivism and underdevelopment • Political implications • Challenge to the West

31

THE UNDERDEVELOPED
WORLD 632

32

THE TRAJECTORY OF ECONOMIC SOCIETY 654

The stages of economic development • Inception of growth • Economies in mid-development • High consumption economies • Convergence of systems • Changing nature of the economic problem • Problem of abundance • Problem of work • Beyond the making of economic society

STATISTICAL APPENDIX 666

INDEX 670

INTRODUCTION
FOR STUDENTS

I can hardly imagine a student not reading the pages addressed to his professors, so I will begin by assuming that the main purposes of this book, as they are set forth in the preceding Introduction, are already clear. Yet, before the actual text begins and I drop the first person pronoun for the decent anonymity of textbook prose, there is a personal word that I would like to address to the students (and to their teachers who will no doubt be trespassing in these pages).

The question that I have found uppermost in my own students' minds as they approach their first course in economics is "How difficult will it be?" I don't believe in waving this question aside with airy reassurances. Economics *is* difficult in a special way for certain people, and it is wise to face this fact at the beginning. At the same time, it is important to understand the reasons for the difficulties that the subject sometimes presents. They do not lie, I believe, in its inherent complexity. Economics, at least on the level of this book, presents no undue strains on anyone's powers of memory or computation or creative ability; and even in its most technically involved parts, where graphs and a few simple equations come into use, it is far from forbidding.

What is the nature of the difficulty then? I believe there are two causes, one relatively easily overcome and the second not so easily. The first is simply the need to acquire a new vocabulary when you speak or write economics. Like every technical discipline, from engineering to psychology, economics seeks to define its concerns as precisely as possible, and this necessitates creating words and phrases that have an unambiguous meaning, but that are unfamiliar in ordinary talk. To become an economist you have to learn at least a dozen words that have meanings different from those they have in daily use—I think of *capital, investment, consumption,* or *demand,* for instance—and another dozen phrases that come at first awkwardly to the tongue (and sometimes not at all to the mind): *marginal propensity to consume, average variable cost,* and some others.

In economics as in French, some people acquire new words and phrases easily, and some do not; and in economics as in French, until you can say things correctly, you are apt to say things very wrongly. So when the text says *gross domestic private investment,* those are the words that should be learned and not just any combination of three of them because they seem to mean almost the same thing. Fortunately, the necessary economic vocabulary is a good deal smaller than French, and the long and awkward phrases get shorter and easier as you say them a few times.

Economics is not really a hard language to learn. The second and more fundamental difficulty is that it is a hard language to think. This is because of an attribute of economics that comes as a surprise to many students. It is the *abstractness* of the subject. By *abstractness,* I most emphatically do not mean dullness, for economics is anything but dull. I mean that the matters with which economics is concerned— unemployment, monopoly, inflation—undergo a curious fading as they come under the economic lens. The color, the variety, the passion of life is bleached out, and what remains for investigation is schematized, as in a blueprint.

There is a very good reason for this blueprinting process. It is that economics is not primarily interested in the *description* of social happenings, but in the *analysis* of their causes and effects. If you want a rollicking account of the late 1920's, for example, you must go to the books of a social historian, such as Frederick Lewis Allen's *Only Yesterday,* and not to a book of economics that deals with the same period, such as Joseph Schumpeter's *Business Cycles.* Allen is trying to reconstitute in the reader's mind what it was like to live in those times; Schumpeter is interested in discovering the subterranean forces that were at work during the period and that eventually blew it up like a great volcano. Thus economics tries to go to the root of things. It tries to establish the long-lasting causes of, and connections among, events that emerge on the surface of life—the *reasons* for prosperity and depression rather than the characteristics of either; the *reasons* for unemployment or inflation rather than the injustices of both.

The point is, then, that it takes a special effort of mind to learn to think of or to view things as an economist does, and this is not a turn of mind that everyone has. Further, the very injustices and failures about which economics *is* ultimately concerned often get in the way of putting a certain distance between ourselves and the problem at hand. The capacity to think in the generalizing fashion of economics, rather than in the individualizing fashion of daily life, is a gift that is distributed unevenly among people. Some take to this unaccustomed but powerful mode of thought as a duck to water; others have to swim for their lives. For the latter, I have no lifesaver ready at hand; but it may at least be helpful for a student who finds himself sinking to know what the trouble may be.

Finally, I must offer a word of advice to all students, easy swimmers or not. Accompanying the text you will find questions and problems, some at the end of chapters, others in a very skillfully prepared workbook by Dr. John Hannaford. *Do them.* Economics is not a subject that will just "sink in" by reading about it. It has to be learned by working in and with it. Even economic history, unlike the lists of kings or Presidents we all once learned, cannot simply be memorized, but must be thought about, for it is essentially explanatory and not merely narrative history. And certainly the operation of the economy as a whole, in Part Two, or of its constituent parts, in Part Three, cannot be learned by merely reading or listening to the instructor, no matter how attentively. The relationships that economics seeks to clarify must be figured out by yourself, by drawing your own diagrams (without looking at the text) or by calculating your own answers to the problems in the workbook. If you are like most students, you will find that when you sit down to reproduce a "simple" diagram, you will not get it quite right the first time, or your calculations will somehow go astray. It is only by making mistakes and then discovering what went wrong that what the psychologist calls the "Aha!" sensation will come.

After these possibly discouraging words, I feel I should redress the balance with a last paragraph. People study economics for a variety of reasons: to learn something about the public issues of our day, to prepare for a career in business, or simply to fill a curriculum requirement. Whatever their motives, it would be a shame if all these students of economics did not also feel something of the excitement of the subject. I said before that if economics is abstract, it is certainly not dull. Let me now go on to say that I think it is the most audacious and even dangerous of all the social sciences. No other branch of social study is so daring in its willingness to risk predictions about the outcome of a process in which millions of participants play their unsupervised roles; none so disastrous when its facts or its logic are wrong.

But then, too, no other branch of study holds such possibilities for the improvement of the human condition in a world that is, in the main, still brutally poor. I do not mean that the rescuers of mankind must be economists, although I myself believe that the appeal of economics is greatest to those who feel affronted by the miseries and inequities of the human spectacle. But I am certain that if would-be rescuers are to be effective, they will at least have to listen to economists. For if the final appeal of economics is to the heart, the whole point of the study of economics is to marry heart and head.

one

THE EMERGENCE OF
MODERN ECONOMIC SOCIETY

THE ECONOMIC PROBLEM *1*

Economics is a large subject, and the first problem that confronts us is how to approach it, how to get hold of the thing.

There are several ways this can be done. One can fly over the economic continent, so to speak, and observe how the system generates its immense output and what brings about changes in the flow of output. Or one can enter the continent on foot and reconnoiter the subject by studying at close range the individuals and firms whose activities, in the aggregate, *are* "the system." Or finally, one can take a third route into economics—a route whose approach is, to continue our metaphor, geological. This is an approach that focuses our initial attention on the question of how the continent came to be there in the first place and on what forces have shaped, and continue to shape, its massive landscape.

The first two approaches are the usual ways of making a first contact with economics, and each has much to recommend it. The flight over the economy brings us immediately to issues of tremendous importance—prosperity and recession, unemployment, inflation. The tour on foot, although less dramatic at first, soon comes to issues no less charged with the public interest—competition and monopoly, labor unions and corporations. Yet, for all their intrinsic interest, both routes share a common disadvantage for a first reconnaissance. The trouble is that they both plunge us into the problems of the contemporary economic world before we have had a chance to see that world in perspective. It is difficult to debate the issues of prosperity and recession, for instance, before we have become familiar with the long ground swell of economic growth on whose advancing front our prosperity or recession is being carried. In the same way, it is premature to get exercised about labor unions or corporations, competition or monopoly, before we have a picture of the changing structure of our society and some understanding of how and why that structure has changed.

Hence, in this book we shall follow the third approach to the study of economics, and begin to grasp what it is all about by studying the *historical evolution* of the system. As we trace our economic development, we will also be learning a good deal about the economy from "above" and from "within," so that when we pursue the standard routes in parts Two and Three, their subject matter should already be generally familiar to us. But our first objective is not to learn about economics just as a series of contemporary problems; it is to see economic activity as an ongoing central concern of mankind with whose obdurate difficulties it is now our turn to struggle.

THE SETTING OF THE PROBLEM

Having decided on our tour of exploration, it would be convenient if we could immediately begin to examine our economic past. But not quite yet. Before we can retrace economic history, we need to know what economic history *is*. And that, in turn, requires us to take a moment to clarify what we mean by economics and by the economic problem itself.

The answer is not a complicated one. Economics is essentially the study of a process we find in all human societies—"the" economic problem is simply *the process of providing for the material well-being of society*. In its simplest terms, economics is the study of how man earns his daily bread.

This hardly seems like a particularly stimulating subject for historical scrutiny. Indeed, when we look back over the pageant of what is usually called "history," the humble matter of bread hardly strikes the eye at all. Power and glory, faith and fanaticism, ideas and ideologies are the aspects of the human chronicle that crowd the pages of history books. If the simple quest for bread is a moving force in human destiny, it is well concealed behind what one philosopher historian has called "that history of international crime and mass murder which has been advertised as the history of mankind."[1]

Yet, if man does not live by bread alone, it is obvious that he cannot live without bread. Like every other living thing, the human being must eat—the imperious first rule of continued existence. And this first prerequisite is less to be taken for granted than at first appears, for the human organism is not, in itself, a highly efficient mechanism for survival. From each hundred calories of food it consumes, it can deliver only about twenty calories of mechanical energy. On a decent diet, man can produce just about one horsepower-hour of work daily, and with that he must replenish his exhausted body. With what is left over, he is free to build a civilization.

As a result, in many countries, the sheer continuity of human existence is far from assured. In the vast continents of Asia and Africa, in the Near East, even in some countries of South America, brute survival is the problem that stares humanity in the face. Millions of human beings have died of starvation or malnutrition in our present era, as countless hundreds of millions have died over the long past. Whole nations are acutely aware of what it means to face hunger as a condition of ordinary life; it has been said, for example, that the Egyptian fellah, from the day he is born to the day he dies, never knows what it is to have a full stomach. In many of the so-called underdeveloped nations, the life span of the average person is less than half of ours. Not many years ago, an Indian demographer made the chilling calculation that of one hundred Asian and one hundred American infants, more Americans would be alive at age sixty-five than Indians at age *five!* The statistics, not of life but of premature death throughout most of the world, are overwhelming and crushing.

Thus we can see that economic history must focus on the central problem of survival and on how man has solved that problem. For most Americans, this may make economics seem very remote. None of us is conscious of anything resembling a life-or-death struggle for existence. That it might be possible for us to experience severe want, that we might ever know in our own bodies the pangs of hunger experienced by an Indian villager or a Bolivian peon is a thought nearly impossible for us to entertain seriously.

Short of a catastrophic war, it is highly unlikely that any of us ever will know the full meaning of the struggle for existence. Nonetheless,

THE
INDIVIDUAL
AND SOCIETY

[1] Karl Popper, *The Open Society and Its Enemies,* 3rd ed. (London: Routledge & Kegan Paul, Ltd., 1957), II, 270.

even in our prosperous and secure society, there remains, however unnoticed, an aspect of life's precariousness, a reminder of the underlying problem of survival. *This is our helplessness as economic individuals.*

For it is a curious fact that as we leave the most impoverished peoples of the world, where the human being with his too few calories scratches out for himself a bare subsistence, we find the economic insecurity of the individual many times multiplied. The solitary Eskimo, Bushman, Indonesian, Nigerian, left to his own devices, will survive a considerable time. Living close to the soil or to his animal prey, such an individual can sustain his own life, at least for a while, singlehanded. With a community numbering only a few hundred, he can live indefinitely. Indeed, a very large percentage of the human race today lives in precisely such fashion—in small, virtually self-contained peasant communities that provide for their own survival with a minimum of contact with the outside world. This large portion of mankind suffers great poverty, but it also knows a certain economic independence. If it did not, it would have been wiped out centuries ago.

When we turn to the New Yorker or the Chicagoan, on the other hand, we are struck by exactly the opposite condition, by a prevailing ease of material life coupled with an extreme *dependence* on others. We can no longer envisage the solitary individual or the small community surviving unaided in the great metropolitan areas where most Americans live, unless they loot warehouses or stores for food and necessities. The overwhelming majority of Americans have never grown food, caught game, raised meat, ground grain into flour, or even fashioned flour into bread. Faced with the challenge of clothing themselves or building their own homes, they would be hopelessly untrained and unprepared. Even to make minor repairs in the machines which surround them, they must call on other members of the community whose business it is to fix cars or repair plumbing or whatever. Paradoxically, perhaps, the richer the nation, the more apparent is this inability of its average inhabitant to survive unaided and alone.

DIVISION OF LABOR

There is, of course, an answer to the paradox. We survive in rich nations because the tasks we cannot do ourselves are done for us by an army of others on whom we can call for help. If we cannot grow food, we can buy it; if we cannot provide for our needs ourselves, we can hire the services of someone who can. This enormous *division of labor* enhances our capacity a thousandfold, for it enables us to benefit from other men's skills as well as our own.

Along with this invaluable gain, however, comes a certain risk. It is a sobering thought, for example, that we depend on the services of less than 150,000 men—only one out of every five hundred people working in the nation—to provide us with that basic commodity, coal.

An even smaller number of workers—only one third as many—are responsible for running the locomotives that haul all the nation's rail freight and passenger service. A still smaller number—under 15,000—comprises our total commercial aircraft pilot crew. A failure of any one of these very small groups to perform its functions would cripple us: in the case of airplane pilots, slightly; in the case of locomotive engineers, badly; in the case of coal miners, perhaps disastrously. As we know, when from time to time we face a bad strike, our entire economic machine may falter because a strategic group ceases to perform its accustomed tasks.

Thus along with the abundance of material existence as we know it goes a hidden vulnerability: our abundance is assured only insofar as the organized cooperation of huge armies of people is to be counted upon. Indeed, our continuing existence as a rich nation hinges on the tacit precondition that the mechanism of social organization will continue to function effectively. *We are rich, not as individuals, but as members of a rich society, and our easy assumption of material sufficiency is actually only as reliable as the bonds that forge us into a social whole.*

Strangely enough, then, we find that man, not nature, is the source of most of our economic problems, at least above the level of subsistence. To be sure, the economic problem itself—that is, the need to struggle for existence—derives ultimately from the *scarcity* of nature. If there were no scarcity, goods would be as free as air, and economics —at least in one sense of the word—would cease to exist as a social preoccupation.

And yet if the scarcity of nature sets the stage for the economic problem, it does not impose the only strictures against which men must struggle. For scarcity, as a felt condition, is not solely the fault of nature. If Americans today, for instance, were content to live at the level of Mexican peasants, all our material wants could be fully satisfied with but an hour or two of daily labor. We would experience little or no scarcity, and our economic problems would virtually disappear. Instead, we find in America—and indeed in all industrial societies—that as the ability to increase nature's yield has risen, so has the reach of human wants. In fact, in societies such as ours, where relative social status is importantly connected with the possession of material goods, we often find that "scarcity" as a psychological experience and goad becomes more pronounced as we grow wealthier: our desires to possess the fruits of nature race out ahead of our mounting ability to produce goods.

Thus the "wants" that nature must satisfy are by no means fixed. But, for that matter, nature's yield itself is not a constant. It varies over a wide range, depending on the social application of human energy and skill. Scarcity is therefore not attributable to nature alone but to "human nature" as well; and economics is ultimately concerned not merely with the stinginess of the physical environment, but equally with the appetite of the human being and the productive capability of the community.

Hence we must begin a systematic analysis of economics by singling out the functions that social organization must perform to bring human nature into social harness. And when we turn our attention to this fundamental problem, we can quickly see that it involves the solution of two related and yet separate elemental tasks:

1. *A society must organize a system to assure the production of enough goods and services for its own survival.*
2. *Society must also arrange the distribution of the fruits of its production so that more production can take place.*

These two tasks of economic continuity are, at first look, very simple.* But it is a deceptive simplicity. Much of economic history, as we shall see, is concerned with the manner in which various societies have sought to cope with these elementary problems; and what strikes us in surveying their attempts is that most of them were partial failures. (They could not have been total failures, or society would not have survived.) Hence it behooves us to look more carefully into the two main economic tasks, to see what hidden difficulties they may conceal.

THE PRODUCTION AND
DISTRIBUTION PROBLEMS

What are the obstacles that a society encounters in organizing a system to produce the goods and services it needs?

Since nature is usually stingy, it would seem that the production problem must be essentially one of applying engineering or technical skills to the resources at hand, of avoiding waste and utilizing social effort as efficaciously as possible.

This is indeed an important task for any society, and a great deal of formal economic thought, as the word itself suggests, is devoted to

---

* In Chapter 20, we will return to the Economic Problem in a somewhat more technical perspective. There we will note that the production problem is itself a twofold task, involving both a choice of different *ends* to which effort may be put and also of different *methods* by which those ends may be sought. Here, where the challenge of social organization is emphasized, we combine these two tasks into a single overarching concern.

economizing. Yet this is not the core of the production problem. Long before a society can even concern itself about using its energies "economically," it must first marshal the energies to carry out the productive process itself. That is, *the basic problem of production is to devise social institutions that will mobilize human energy for productive purposes.*

This basic requirement is not always so easily accomplished. For example, in the United States in 1933, the energies of nearly thirteen million people—one-quarter of our work force—were not directed into the production process at all. Although these unemployed men and women were eager to work, although empty factories were available for them to work in, despite the existence of pressing wants, somehow a terrible and mystifying breakdown short-circuited the production process, with the result that an entire third of our previous annual output of goods and services simply disappeared.

We are by no means the only nation that has, on occasion, failed to find work for willing workers. In the very poorest nations, where production is most desperately needed, we frequently find that unemployment is a chronic condition. The streets of the Asian cities are thronged with people who cannot find work. But this, too, is not a condition imposed by the scarcity of nature. There is, after all, an endless amount of work to be done, if only in cleaning the filthy streets or patching up the homes of the poor, building roads, or digging ditches. Yet, what seems to be lacking is a social mechanism to put the unemployed to work.

Both these examples point out to us that the production problem is not solely a physical and technical struggle with nature. On these "scarcity" aspects of the problem will depend the speed with which a nation may forge ahead and the level of well-being it can reach with a given effort. But the original mobilization of productive effort itself is a challenge to its social organization, and on the success or failure of that social organization will depend the volume of the human effort that can be directed to nature.

But putting men to work is only the first step in the solution of the production problem. Men must not only be put to work; they must be put to work *in the right places.* They must produce the goods and services that society needs. Thus, *in addition to assuring a large enough quantity of social effort, the economic institutions of society must also assure a viable allocation of that social effort.*

In a nation such as India or Bolivia, where the great majority of the population is born in peasant villages and grows up to be peasant cultivators, the solution to this problem offers little to vex our understanding. The basic demands of society—food and fiber—are precisely the goods that its peasant population "naturally" produces. But in an industrial society, the proper allocation of effort becomes an enormously

ALLOCATING EFFORT

complicated task. People in the United States demand much more than bread and cotton. They need, for instance, such things as automobiles. Yet no one "naturally" produces an automobile. On the contrary, in order to produce one, an extraordinary spectrum of special tasks must be performed. Some people must make steel; others must make rubber. Still others must coordinate the assembly process itself. And this is but a tiny sampling of the far from "natural" tasks that must be performed if an automobile is to be produced.

As with the mobilization of its total production effort, society does not always succeed in the proper allocation of its effort. It may, for instance, turn out too many cars or too few. Of greater importance, it may devote its energies to the production of luxuries while large numbers of its people are starving. Or it may even court disaster by an inability to channel its productive effort into areas of critical importance. In the early 1950's, for instance, the British suffered a near economic collapse because they were unable to get enough of their workers to mine coal.

Such allocative failures may affect the production problem quite as seriously as a failure to mobilize an adequate quantity of effort, for a viable society must produce not only goods, but the right goods. And the allocative question alerts us to a still broader conclusion. It shows us that the act of production, in and of itself, does not fully answer the requirements for survival. Having produced enough of the *right* goods, society must now *distribute* those goods so that the production process can go on.

DISTRIBUTING
OUTPUT

Once again, in the case of the peasant who feeds himself and his family from his own crop, this requirement of adequate distribution may seem simple enough. But when we go beyond the most primitive society, the problem is not always so readily solved. In many of the poorest nations of the East and South, urban workers have often been unable to deliver their daily horsepower-hour of work because they have not been given enough of society's output to run their human engines to capacity. Worse yet, they have often languished on the job while granaries bulged with grain and the well-to-do complained of the ineradicable laziness of the masses. At the other side of the picture, the distribution mechanism may fail because the rewards it hands out do not succeed in persuading people to perform their necessary tasks. Shortly after the Russian Revolution, some factories were organized into communes in which managers and janitors pooled their pay, and from which all drew equal allotments. The result was a rash of absenteeism on the part of the previously better-paid workers and a threatened breakdown in industrial production. Not until the old unequal wage payments were reinstituted did production resume its former course.

As was the case with failures in the production process, distributive failures need not entail a total economic collapse. Societies can exist— and indeed, in the majority of cases, do exist—with badly distorted productive and distributive efforts. It is only rarely, as in the instances above, that maldistribution actively interferes with the actual ability of a society to staff its production posts. More frequently, an inadequate solution to the distribution problem reveals itself in social and political unrest or even in revolution.

Yet this, too, is an aspect of the total economic problem. For if society is to insure its steady material replenishment, it must parcel out its production in a fashion that will maintain not only the capacity but the willingness to go on working. And thus again we find the focus of economic inquiry directed to the study of human institutions. For a viable economic society, we can now see, is not only one which can overcome the stringencies of nature, but one which can contain and control the intransigence of human nature.

THE THREE SOLUTIONS TO THE ECONOMIC PROBLEM

Thus to the economist, society presents itself in what is to us an unaccustomed aspect. He sees it essentially as an elaborate mechanism for survival, a mechanism for accomplishing the complicated tasks of production and distribution necessary for social continuity.

But the economist sees something else as well, something that at first seems quite astonishing. Looking not only over the diversity of contemporary societies, but back over the sweep of all history, he sees that man has succeeded in solving the production and distribution problems in but three ways. That is, within the enormous diversity of the actual social institutions that guide and shape the economic process, the economist divines but three overarching *types* of systems which separately or in combination enable humankind to solve its economic challenge. These great systemic types can be called economies run by *Tradition,* economies run by *Command,* and economies run by the *Market.* Let us briefly see what is characteristic of each.

Perhaps the oldest and, until a very few years ago, by far the most generally prevalent way of solving the economic challenge has been that of tradition. It has been a mode of social organization in which both production and distribution were based on procedures devised in

TRADITION

15

the distant past, rigidified by a long process of historic trial and error, and maintained by heavy sanctions of law, custom, and belief.

Societies based on tradition solve the economic problems very manageably. First, they deal with the production problem—the problem of assuring that the needful tasks will be done—by assigning the jobs of fathers to their sons. Thus a hereditary chain assures that skills will be passed along and jobs will be staffed from generation to generation. In ancient Egypt, wrote Adam Smith, the first great economist, "every man was bound by a principle of religion to follow the occupation of his father and was supposed to commit the most horrible sacrilege if he changed it for another."[2] And it was not merely in antiquity that tradition preserved a productive orderliness within society. In our own Western culture, until the fifteenth or sixteenth centuries, the hereditary allocation of tasks was also the main stabilizing force within society. Although there was some movement from country to town and from occupation to occupation, birth usually determined one's role in life. One was born to the soil or to a trade; and on the soil or within the trade, one followed in the footsteps of one's forebears.

Thus tradition has been the stabilizing and impelling force behind a great repetitive cycle of society, assuring that society's work would be done each day very much as it had been done in the past. Even today, among the less industrialized nations of the world, tradition continues to play this immense organizing role. In India, for example, until very recently, one was born to a caste which had its own occupation. "Better thine own work is, though done with fault," preached the Bhagavad-Gita, the great philosophic moral poem of India, "than doing other's work, even excellently."

Tradition not only provides a solution to the production problem of society, but it also regulates the distribution problem. Take, for example, the Bushmen of the Kalahari Desert in South Africa who depend for their livelihood on their hunting prowess. Elizabeth Marshall Thomas, a sensitive observer of these peoples, reports on the manner in which tradition solves the problem of distributing their kill.

The gemsbok has vanished . . . Gai owned two hind legs and a front leg, Tsetchwe had meat from the back, Ukwane had the other front leg, his wife had one of the feet and the stomach, the young boys had lengths of intestine. Twikwe had received the head and Dasina the udder.

It seems very unequal when you watch Bushmen divide the kill, yet it is their system, and in the end no person eats more than any other. That day Ukwane gave Gai still another piece because Gai was his relation, Gai gave meat to Dasina because she was his wife's mother . . . No one, of course, contested

---

[2] *The Wealth of Nations* (New York: Modern Library, Inc., 1937), p. 62.

Gai's large share, because he had been the hunter and by their law that much belonged to him. No one doubted that he would share his large amount with others, and they were not wrong, of course; he did.[3]

The manner in which tradition can divide a social product may be, as the illustration shows, very subtle and ingenious. It may also be very crude and, by our standards, harsh. Tradition has often allocated to women, in nonindustrial societies, the most meager portion of the social product. But however much the end-product of tradition may accord with, or depart from, our accustomed moral views, we must see that it is a workable *method* of dividing society's production.

Traditional solutions to the economic problems of production and distribution are most commonly encountered in primitive agrarian or nonindustrial societies where, in addition to serving an economic function, the unquestioning acceptance of the past provides the necessary perseverance and endurance to confront harsh destinies. Yet even in our own society, tradition continues to play a part in solving the economic problem. It plays its smallest role in determining the distribution of our own social output, although the persistence of such traditional payments as tips to waiters, allowances to minors, or bonuses based on length of service are all vestiges of old traditional ways of distributing goods, as is the differential between men's and women's pay for equal work.

More important is the continued reliance on tradition, even in America, as a means of solving the production problem—that is, in allocating the performance of tasks. Much of the actual process of selecting an employment in our society is heavily influenced by tradition. We are all familiar with families in which sons follow their fathers into a profession or a business. On a somewhat broader scale, tradition also dissuades us from certain employments. Sons of American middle-class families, for example, do not usually seek factory work, even though factory jobs may pay better than office jobs, because "blue-collar employment" is not in the middle-class tradition.

Thus, even in our society—clearly not a "traditional" one—custom provides an important mechanism for solving the economic problem. But now we must note one very important consequence of the mechanism of tradition. *Its solution to the problems of production and distribution is a static one.* A society that follows the path of tradition in its regulation of economic affairs does so at the expense of large-scale rapid social and economic change.

Thus the economy of a Bedouin tribe or a Burmese village is in few essential respects changed today from what it was a hundred or even a thousand years ago. The bulk of the peoples living in tradition-bound societies repeat, in the daily patterns of their economic life, much of

[3] *The Harmless People* (New York: Alfred A. Knopf, Inc., 1959), pp. 49–50.

17

the routine that characterized them in the distant past. Such societies may rise and fall, wax and wane, but external events—war, climate, political adventures and misadventures—are mainly responsible for their changing fortunes. Internal, self-generated economic change is but a small factor in the history of most tradition-bound states. *Tradition solves the economic problem, but it does so at the cost of economic progress.*

COMMAND

A second manner of solving the problem of economic continuity also displays an ancient lineage. This is the method of imposed authority, of economic command. It is a solution based not so much on the perpetuation of a viable system by the changeless reproduction of its ways, as on the organization of a system according to the orders of an economic commander-in-chief.

Not infrequently we find this authoritarian method of economic control superimposed upon a traditional social base. Thus the Pharaohs of Egypt exerted their economic dictates above the timeless cycle of traditional agricultural practice on which the Egyptian economy was based. By their orders, the supreme rulers of Egypt brought into being the enormous economic effort that built the pyramids, the temples, the roads. Herodotus, the Greek historian, tells us how the Pharaoh Cheops organized the task.

[He] ordered all Egyptians to work for himself. Some, accordingly, were appointed to draw stones from the quarries in the Arabian mountains down to the Nile, others he ordered to receive the stones when transported in vessels across the river. . . . And they worked to the number of a hundred thousand men at a time, each party during three months. The time during which the people were thus harassed by toil lasted ten years on the road which they constructed, and along which they drew the stones; a work, in my opinion, not much less than the Pyramid.[4]

The mode of authoritarian economic organization was by no means confined to ancient Egypt. We encounter it in the despotisms of medieval and classical China which produced, among other things, the colossal Great Wall, or in the slave labor by which many of the great public works of ancient Rome were built. Of course, we find it today in the dictates of the communist economic authorities. In less drastic form we find it also in our own society; for example, in the form of taxes—that is, in the preemption of part of our income by the public authorities for public purposes.

Economic command, like tradition, offers solutions to the twin prob-

---

[4] *Histories,* trans. Cary (London: 1901), Book II, p. 124.

lems of production and distribution. In times of crises, such as war or famine, it may be the only way in which a society can organize its manpower or distribute its goods effectively. Even in America, we commonly declare martial law when an area has been devastated by a great natural disaster. On such occasions we may press people into service, requisition homes, impose curbs on the use of private property such as cars, or even limit the amount of goods a family may consume.

Quite aside from its obvious utility in meeting emergencies, command has a further usefulness in solving the economic problem. Unlike tradition, the exercise of command has no inherent effect of slowing down economic change. Indeed, the exercise of authority is the most powerful instrument society has for *enforcing economic change.* Authority in modern China or Russia, for example, has effected radical alterations in the systems of production and distribution. But again, even in our own society, it is sometimes necessary for economic authority to intervene into the normal flow of economic life, to speed up or bring about change. The government may, for instance, utilize its tax receipts to lay down a network of roads that will bring a backwater community into the flux of active economic life. It may undertake an irrigation system that will dramatically change the economic life of a vast region. It may deliberately alter the distribution of income among social classes.

To be sure, economic command which is exercised within the framework of a democratic political process is very different from that which is exercised by a dictatorship: there is an immense social distance between a tax system controlled by Congress and outright expropriation or labor impressment by a supreme and unchallengeable ruler. Yet whilst the means may be much milder, the *mechanism* is the same. In both cases, command diverts economic effort toward goals chosen by a higher authority. In both cases it interferes with the existing order of production and distribution, to create a new order ordained from "above."

This does not in itself serve to commend or condemn the exercise of command. The new order imposed by the authorities may offend or please our sense of social justice, just as it may improve or lessen the economic efficiency of society. Clearly, command can be an instrument of a democratic as well as of a totalitarian will. There is no implicit moral judgment to be passed on this second of the great mechanisms of economic control. Rather, it is important to note that no society—certainly no modern society—is without its elements of command, just as none is devoid of the influence of tradition. *If tradition is the great brake on social and economic change, so economic command can be the great spur to change.* As mechanisms for assuring the successful solution to the economic problem, both serve their purposes, both have their uses and their drawbacks. Between them, tradition and command have accounted for most of the long history of man's economic efforts to cope with his environment and with himself. The fact that human society has survived is testimony to their effectiveness.

THE MARKET

But there is also a third solution to the economic problem, a third way of maintaining socially viable patterns of production and distribution. This is the *market organization of society*—an organization that, in truly remarkable fashion, allows society to insure its own provisioning with a minimum of recourse either to tradition or command.

Because we live in a market-run society, we are apt to take for granted the puzzling—indeed, almost paradoxical—nature of the market solution to the economic problem. But assume for a moment that we could act as economic advisers to a society that had not yet decided on its mode of economic organization. Suppose, for instance, that we were called on to act as consultants to one of the new nations emerging on the continent of Africa.

We could imagine the leaders of such a nation saying, "We have always experienced a highly tradition-bound way of life. Our men hunt and cultivate the fields and perform their tasks as they are brought up to do by the force of example and the instruction of their elders. We know, too, something of what can be done by economic command. We are prepared, if necessary, to sign an edict making it compulsory for many of our men to work on community projects for our national development. Tell us, is there any other way we can organize our society so that it will function successfully—or better yet, more successfully?"

Suppose we answered, "Yes, there is another way. Organize your society along the lines of a market economy."

"Very well," say the leaders. "What do we then tell people to do? How do we assign them to their various tasks?"

"That's the very point," we would answer. "In a market economy, no one is assigned to any task. In fact, the main idea of a market society is that each person is allowed to decide for himself what to do."

There is consternation among the leaders. "You mean there is no assignment of some men to mining and others to cattle raising? No manner of designating some for transportation and others for weaving? You leave this to people to decide for themselves? But what happens if they do not decide correctly? What happens if no one volunteers to go into the mines, or if no one offers himself as a railway engineer?"

"You may rest assured," we tell the leaders, "none of that will happen. In a market society, all the jobs will be filled because it will be to people's advantage to fill them."

Our respondents accept this with uncertain expressions. "Now look," one of them finally says, "let us suppose that we take your advice and allow our people to do as they please. Let's talk about something specific, like cloth production. Just how do we fix the right level of cloth output in this 'market society' of yours?"

"But you don't," we reply.

"We don't! Then how do we know there will be enough cloth produced?"

"There will be," we tell him. "The market will see to that."

"Then how do we know there won't be *too much* cloth produced?" he asks triumphantly.

"Ah, but the market will see to that too!"

"But what is this market that will do these wonderful things? Who runs it?"

"Oh, nobody runs the market," we answer. "It runs itself. In fact there really isn't any such *thing* as 'the market.' It's just a word we use to describe the way people behave."

"But I thought people behaved the way they wanted to!"

"And so they do," we say. "But never fear. They will want to behave the way you want them to behave."

"I am afraid," says the chief of the delegation, "that we are wasting our time. We thought you had in mind a serious proposal. What you suggest is inconceivable. Good day, sir."

Could we seriously suggest to such an emergent nation that it entrust itself to a market solution of the economic problem? That will be a problem to which we shall return at the very end of our book. But the perplexity which the market idea would rouse in the mind of someone unacquainted with it may serve to increase our own wonderment at this most sophisticated and interesting of all economic mechanisms. How does the market system assure us that our mines will find miners, our factories workers? How does it take care of cloth production? How does it happen that in a market-run nation each person can indeed do as he wishes and, withal, fulfill needs that society as a whole presents?

Economics, as we commonly conceive it and as we shall study it in much of this book, is primarily concerned with these very problems. Societies that rely primarily on tradition to solve their economic problems are of less interest to the professional economist than to the cultural anthropologist or the sociologist. Societies that solve their economic problems primarily by the exercise of command present interesting economic questions, but here the study of economics is necessarily subservient to the study of politics and the exercise of power.

It is a society that solves its economic problems by the market process that presents an aspect especially interesting to the economist. For here, as we shall see, economics truly plays a unique role. Unlike the case with tradition and command, where we quickly grasp the nature of the economic mechanism of society, when we turn to a market society we are lost without a knowledge of economics. For in a market society it is not at all clear that the problems of production and distribution will be solved by the free interplay of individuals without guidance from tradition or command.

In subsequent parts of this book we shall analyze these puzzling questions in more detail. But the task of our initial exploration must now be clear. As our imaginary interview with the leaders of an emergent nation has suggested, the market solution appears very strange to someone brought up in the ways of tradition or command. Hence the question arises: how did the market solution itself come into being? Was it imposed, full-blown, on our society at some earlier date? Or did it arise spontaneously and without forethought? This is the focusing question of economic history to which we now turn, as we retrace the evolution of our own market system out of the tradition and authority dominated societies of the past.

SUMMARY

1. Economics is the study of how man assures his material sufficiency, of how societies arrange for their *material provisioning*.

2. Economic problems arise because the wants of most societies exceed the gifts of nature, giving rise to the general condition of *scarcity*.

3. Scarcity, in turn (whether it arises from nature's stinginess or man's appetites) imposes two severe tasks on society:

   a) It must mobilize its energies for *production*—producing not only enough goods, but the right goods, and

   b) It must resolve the problem of *distribution*, arranging a satisfactory solution to the problem of Who Gets What?

4. These problems exist in all societies, but they are especially difficult to solve in advanced societies in which there exists a far-reaching *division of labor*. Men in wealthy societies are far more socially interdependent than men in simple societies.

5. Over the course of history, there have evolved three types of solutions to the two great economic problems. These are *Tradition*, *Command*, and the *Market System*.

6. Tradition solves the problems of production and distribution by enforcing a continuity of tasks and rewards through social institutions such as the caste system. *Typically, the economic solution imposed by Tradition is a static one*, in which little change occurs over long periods of time.

7. Command solves the economic problem by imposing allocations of effort or reward by *governing authority*. Command can be a means for achieving rapid and far-reaching economic *change*. It can take extreme totalitarian or mild democratic forms.

8. The market system is a complex mode of organizing society in which order and efficiency emerge ''spontaneously'' from a seemingly uncontrolled society. We shall investigate the market system in great detail in the chapters to come.

1. If everyone could produce all the food he needed in his own backyard, and if technology were so advanced that we could all make anything we wanted in our basements, would an "economic problem" exist?

2. Suppose that everyone were completely versatile—able to do everyone else's work just as well as his own. Would a division of labor still be useful in society? Why?

3. Modern economic society is sometimes described as depending on "organization men" who allow their lives to be directed by the large corporations for which they work. Assuming that this description has some glimmer of truth, would you think that modern society should be described as one of Tradition, Command, or the Market?

4. In what way do your own plans for the future coincide with or depart from the occupations of your parents? Do you think that the so-called generational split is observable in all modern societies?

5. Economics is often called the science of scarcity. How can this label be applied to a society of considerable affluence such as our own?

6. What elements of Tradition and Command do you think are indispensable in a modern industrial society? Do you think that modern society could exist without any dependence on Tradition or without any exercise of Command?

7. Much of production and distribution involves the creation or the handling of *things*. Why are production and distribution *social* problems rather than engineering or physical problems?

8. Do you consider man's wants to be insatiable? Does this imply that scarcity must always exist?

2 THE PRE-MARKET ECONOMY

"Nobody ever saw a dog make a fair and deliberate exchange of one bone for another with another dog," wrote Adam Smith in *The Wealth of Nations.* "Nobody ever saw one animal by its gestures and natural cries signify to another, this is mine, that yours; I am willing to give this for that."[1]

Smith was writing about "a certain propensity in human nature. . . ; the propensity to truck, barter, and exchange one thing for another." That such a propensity exists as a universal characteristic of humankind is perhaps less likely than Smith believed, but he was certainly not mistaken in putting the act of exchange at the very center of his scheme of economic life. For there can be no doubt that exchange, buying and selling, lies at the very heart of a market society such as he was describing. And so, as we now begin to study the rise of the market society,

[1] Smith, *op. cit.,* p. 13.

what could be more natural than to commence by tracing the pedigree of markets themselves?

It comes as something of a surprise, perhaps, to discover how very ancient is that pedigree. Men have traded with one another at least as far back as the last Ice Age. We have evidence that the mammoth-hunters of the Russian steppes obtained Mediterranean shells in trade, as did also the Cro-Magnon hunters of the central valleys of France. In fact, on the moors of Pomerania in northeastern Germany, archeologists have come across an oaken box, replete with the remains of its original leather shoulder strap, in which were a dagger, a sickle head, and a needle—all of Bronze Age manufacture. According to the conjectures of experts, this was very likely the sample kit of a prototype of the traveling salesman, an itinerant representative who collected orders for the specialized production of his community.[2]

And as we proceed from the dawn of civilization to its first organized societies, the evidences of trade and of markets increase rapidly. As Miriam Beard has written:

Millennia before Homer sang, or the wolf suckled Romulus and Remus, the bustling damkars (traders) of Uruk and Nippur . . . were buckling down to business. Atidum the merchant, in need of enlarged office facilities, was agreeing to rent a suitable location from Ribatum, Priestess of Shamash, for one and one-sixth shekels of silver per year—so much down and the rest in easy installments. Abu-wakar, the rich shipper, was delighted that his daughter had become Priestess of Shamash and could open a real estate office near the temple. Ilabras was writing to Ibi: "May Shamash and Marduk keep thee! As thou knowest, I had issued a note for a female slave. Now the time to pay is come."[3]

Thus at first glance it seems as if we can discover evidences of a market society deep in the past. But these disconcerting notes of modernity must be interpreted with caution. If markets, buying and selling, even highly organized trading bodies were well-nigh ubiquitous features of ancient society, they must not be confused with the equally ubiquitous presence of a *market society*. Trade existed as an important adjunct to society from earliest times, but the fundamental impetus to production, or the basic allocation of resources among different uses, or the distribution of goods among social classes was largely divorced from the marketing process. That is, *the markets of antiquity were not the means by which those societies solved their basic economic problems*. They were subsidiary to the great processes of production and distribution rather than integral to them; they were "above" the critical economic

---

[2] *Cambridge Economic History of Europe* (London: Cambridge University Press, 1952), II. 4.

[3] *A History of the Business Man* (New York: The Macmillan Company, 1938), p. 12.

machinery rather than within it. As we shall see, between the deceptively contemporary air of many markets of the distant past and the reality of our contemporary market economy lies an immense distance over which society would take centuries to travel.

THE ECONOMIC
ORGANIZATION OF ANTIQUITY

We must ourselves traverse that distance if we are to understand how contemporary market society came into being and, indeed, if we are to understand what it is. For only by immersing ourselves in the societies of the past, only by seeing how they did, in fact, solve their economic problems, can we begin to understand clearly what is involved in the evolution of the market society which is our own environment.

Needless to say, it would make an enormous difference which of the many pre-market societies of the past we visited as general observers. To trace economic history from the monolithic temple-states of Sumer and Akkad to the "modernity" of classical Greece or Rome is to undertake a cultural journey of fantastic distance. Yet, traveling only as economic historians, we will find that it makes much less difference in which of the societies of antiquity we light. For as we examine these societies, we can see that underlying their profound dissimilarities of art or political rule or religious belief, there are equally profound similarities of economic structure, similarities we call to mind less frequently because they are in the "background" of history and rarely adorn its more exciting pages. But these identifying characteristics of economic organization are the ones that now interest us as we turn our gaze to the past. What is it that we see?

**AGRICULTURAL
FOUNDATION
OF ANCIENT
SOCIETIES**

The first and perhaps the most striking impression is the overwhelmingly agricultural aspect of all these economies.

In a sense, of course, all human communities, no matter how industrialized, live off the soil: all that differentiates the "agricultural" society from the "industrial" is the number of the nonagricultural population that its food growers can support. Thus an American farmer, working a large acreage with abundant equipment, maintains perhaps thirty nonfarmers; while an Asian peasant, tilling his tiny plot with little more than a stick-plow, is often hard pressed to sustain his own family.

Over all of antiquity the capacity of the agricultural population to sustain a nonfarming population was very limited. Exact statistics are unavailable, but we can project backwards to the situation that prevailed in all these ancient nations by looking at the underdeveloped regions of the world today where the levels of technique and the productivity of agriculture bear a close—too close—resemblance to antiquity. Thus in India, in Egypt, in the Philippines, Indonesia, Brazil, Colombia, Mexico, we find that it takes two farm families to support one nonfarm family, while in tropical Africa, a recent survey tells us: "the productivity of African agriculture is still so low that it takes anywhere from two to ten people—men, women, and children—to raise enough food to supply their own needs and those of *one* additional—non-food-growing—adult."[4]

Antiquity was not *that* badly off; indeed at times it produced impressive agricultural outputs. But neither was it remotely comparable to American farm productivity with its enormous capacity to support a nonagricultural population. All ancient economic societies were basically rural economies. This did not preclude, as we shall see, a very brilliant and wealthy urban society nor a far-flung network of international trade. Yet the typical economic personage of antiquity was neither trader nor urban dweller. He was a tiller of the soil, and it was in his rural communities that the economies of antiquity were ultimately anchored.

But this must not lead us to assume that economic life was therefore comparable to that of a modern agricultural community like Denmark or New Zealand. Contemporary farmers, like businessmen, are very much bound up in the web of transactions characteristic of a market society. They sell their output on one market; they buy their supplies on another. The accumulation of money, and not of wheat or corn, is the object of their efforts. Books of profit and loss regularly tell them if they are doing well or not. The latest news of agricultural technology is studied and put into effect if it is profitable.

None of this properly describes the "farmer" of ancient Egypt, of antique Greece or Rome, or of the great Eastern civilizations. With few exceptions, the tiller of the soil was a peasant, and a peasant is a social creature very different from a farmer. He is not technologically alert but, on the contrary, clings with stubborn persistence—and often with great skill—to his well-known ways. He must, since a small error might mean starvation. He does not buy the majority of his supplies but, to a large extent, fashions them himself; similarly, he does not produce for a "market," but principally for himself. Finally, he is often not even free to consume his own crop, but typically must hand over a portion—a tenth, a third, half, or even more—to the owner of his land.

For in the general case, the peasant of antiquity did not own his land. We hear of the independent citizen—farmers of classical Greece and

[4] George H. T. Kimble, *Tropical Africa* (New York: Twentieth Century Fund, 1960), I, 572. (Italics added.)

republican Rome, but these were exceptions to the general rule in which peasants were but tenants of a great lord. And even in Greece and Rome, the independent peasantry tended to become swallowed up as the tenantry of huge commercial estates. Pliny mentions one such enormous estate or latifundium (literally: broad farm) with a quarter of a million livestock and a population of 4,117 slaves.

Hence the peasant, who was the bone and muscle of the economies of antiquity, was in himself a prime example of the nonmarket aspect of these economies. Although some cultivators freely sold a portion of their own crop in the city marketplaces, the great majority of agricultural producers scarcely entered the market at all. For many of these producers—especially when they were slaves—this was, accordingly, an almost cashless world, where a few coppers a year, carefully hoarded and spent only for emergencies, constituted the only link with a world of market transactions.*

Thus, whereas the peasant's legal and social status varied widely in different areas and eras of antiquity, in a broad view the tenor of his economic life was singularly constant. Of the web of transactions, the drive for profits of the modern farmer, he knew little or nothing. Generally poor, tax-ridden and oppressed, prey to nature's caprices and to the exploitation of war and peace, bound to the soil by law and custom, the peasant of antiquity—as the peasant today who continues to provide the agricultural underpinnings to the civilizations of the East and South—was dominated by the economic rule of tradition. His main stimulus for change was command—or, rather, obedience. Labor, patience, and the incredible endurance of the human being were his contributions to civilization.

ECONOMIC LIFE OF THE CITIES

The basic agricultural cast of ancient society and its typical exclusion of the peasant-cultivator from an active market existence makes all the more striking another common aspect of economic organization in antiquity. This is the diversity, vitality, and ebullience of the economic life of the cities.

Whether we turn to ancient Egypt, classical Greece, or Rome, we cannot help but be struck by this contrast between the relatively static countryside and the active city. In Greece, for example, a whole panoply of goods passed across the docks of the Piraeus: grain from Italy, metal from Crete and even Britain, books from Egypt, perfume from still more distant origins. Isocrates, in the *Panegyricus,* boasts: "The articles which it is difficult to get, one here, one there, from the rest of the world; all these it is easy to buy in Athens." So, too, Rome developed a thriving

---

*This is not, let us note, only an ancient condition. Traveling in Morocco, John Gunther reported of the local peasant-serfs: "formerly they got no wages—what would they need money for—but this is changing now." *Changing now—in 1953!* (*Inside Africa.* New York: Harper & Row, 1955, p. 104.)

foreign and domestic commerce. By the time of Augustus, 6,000 loads of ox-towed barges were required to feed the city annually,[5] while in the city forum a crowd of speculators converged as on "an immense stock exchange."[6]

Thus something which at least superficially approximated our own society was visible in many of the larger urban centers of antiquity. And yet we must not be beguiled into the conclusion that this was a market society similar to our own. In at least two respects the differences were profound.

The first of these was the essentially restricted character and scope of the market function of the city. Unlike the modern city, which is not only a receiver of goods shipped in from the hinterlands but also an important exporter of goods and services back to the countryside, the cities of antiquity tended to assume an economically parasitic role vis-à-vis the rest of the economy. Much of the trade that entered the great urban centers of Egypt, Greece, and Rome (over and above the necessary provisioning of the city masses) was in the nature of luxury goods for its upper classes, rather than raw materials to be worked and then sent out to a goods-consuming economy. The cities were the vessels of civilization; but as centers of economic activity, a wide gulf separated them from the country, making the cities enclaves of economic life rather than nourishing components of integrated rural-urban economies.

Even more important was a second difference between the ancient city economies and a contemporary market society. This was their reliance on *slave labor*.

For slavery on a massive scale was a fundamental pillar of nearly every ancient economic society. In Greece, for instance, the deceptively modern air of the Piraeus masks the fact that much of the purchasing power of the Greek merchant was provided by the labor of 20,000 slaves who labored under sickening conditions in the silver mines of Laurentium. At the height of "democratic" Athens, it is estimated that at least one-third of its population were slaves. In Italy of 30 B.C., some 1,500,000 slaves—on the latifundia, in the galleys, the mines, the "factories," the shops—provided a major impetus in keeping the economic machinery in motion.[7] Seneca even tells us that a proposal that they wear special dress was voted down lest recognizing their own number, they might know their strength.

Slaves were not, of course, the only source of labor. Groups of free artisans and workmen, often banded together in *collegia* or fraternal

[5] *Cambridge Economic History of Europe,* II, 47.
[6] W. C. Cunningham, *An Essay on Western Civilization* (New York: 1913), p. 164.
[7] K. J. Beloch, *Die Bevölkerung der Griechisch-Römischen Welt* (Leipzig: 1886), p. 478.

bodies, also serviced the Roman city, as did similar free workmen in Greece and elsewhere. In many cities, especially latter-day Rome, a mass of unemployed (but not enslaved) laborers provided a source of casual work. Yet, without the motive power of the slave, it is doubtful if the brilliant city economies of the past could have been sustained. And this brings us to the central point. It is that the flourishing market economy of the city rested atop an economic structure run by tradition and command. Nothing like the free exercise and interplay of self-interest guided the basic economic effort of antiquity. If an astonishingly modern urban market structure greets our eye, we must not forget that its merchants are standing on the shoulders of innumerable peasants and slaves.

WEALTH AND POWER

The presence of great agglomerations of urban wealth amid a far poorer rural setting alerts us to another characteristic of ancient economic society. This is the special relationship between its wealth and its underlying economic organization.

In any society, wealth implies that a *surplus* has been wrung from nature, that a social organization has not alone solved its economic production problem but has achieved a margin of effort above that required for its own existence. Perhaps what first astonishes us when we regard the civilizations of the ancient world is the size of surplus which could be got from a basically poor peasant population. The temples of the ancient Assyrian kings, the extraordinary treasures of the Aztecs, the pyramids and pleasure craft of the Pharaohs of Egypt, the Acropolis of Athens, and the magnificent roads and architecture of Rome all testify to the ability of an essentially agricultural civilization to achieve a massive surplus, to pry considerable amounts of labor loose from the land, support it at whatever low level, and put it to work building for posterity.

But the stupendous achievements of the past testify as well to something else. The surplus productive potential which society manages to achieve (whether by technology or by adroit social organization) can be applied in many directions. It can be directed to agricultural improvements, such as irrigation ditches or dams, where it is apt to increase the bounty of the harvest still further. It can be applied to the tools and equipment of the city workman, where it is apt to raise his ability to produce. Or the surplus may be used to support a large standing army, or a nonworking religious order, or a class of courtiers and idle nobility.

Thus the social form taken by the accumulation of wealth reveals a great deal about any society. "To whom does the surplus accrue?" is a question which invariably sheds important light on the structure of power within that society.

To whom did the wealth of antiquity accrue? At first glimpse it seems impossible to answer in a phrase. Emperors, nobles, religious orders, merchant traders—all enjoyed the wealth of antiquity at one time or another. But at second look, an interesting and significant generalization becomes possible: most wealth did not go to those who played a strictly *economic* role. Although there are records of clever slaves in Egypt and Rome who became wealthy, and although rich merchants and bankers are visible throughout the annals of antiquity, theirs was not the primary route to wealth. Rather, *in ancient civilization wealth was generally the reward for political, military, or religious power or status, and not for economic activity.*

There was a reason for this. Societies tend to reward most highly the activities they value most highly; and in the long and turbulent centuries of antiquity, political leadership, religious tutelage, and military prowess were unquestionably more necessary for social survival than trading *expertise*. In fact, in many of these societies, economic activity itself was disdained as essentially ignoble. As Aristotle wrote in his *Politics,* "in the best-governed polis . . . the citizens may not lead either the life of craftsmen or of traders, for such a life is devoid of nobility and hostile to perfection of character." It was a theme on which Cicero would later expand in his essay *De Officiis* (Book I).

The toil of a hired worker, who is paid only for his toil and not for artistic skill, is unworthy of a free man and is sordid in character. For in his case, money is the price of slavery. Sordid too is the calling of those who buy wholesale in order to sell retail, since they would gain no profits without a great deal of lying. . . . Trade on a small retail scale is sordid, but if it is on a large wholesale scale including the import of many wares from everywhere and their distribution to many people without any misrepresentation, it is not to be too greatly censured. . . .

Especially, added the great lawyer, "if those who carry on such trade finally retire to country estates, after being surfeited or at least satisfied with their gains."

Over and above the lesser social function of the merchant compared with the general, the consul, or the priest, this disdain of wealth obtained from "ignoble" economic activity reflected an economic fact of great importance: society had not yet integrated the production of wealth with the production of goods. Wealth was still a surplus to be seized by conquest or squeezed from the underlying agricultural population; it was not yet a natural adjunct of a system of continuously increasing production in which some part of an expanding total social output might accrue to many classes of society.

And so it would be for many centuries. Until the smallest as well as the largest activities of society would receive their price tag, until purchases and sales, bids and offers would penetrate down to the lowest orders of society, the accumulation of wealth would always remain more a matter of political, military, or religious power than of economics. To sum it up: *in premarket societies, wealth tended to follow power; not until the market society would power tend to follow wealth.*

"ECONOMICS" AND SOCIAL JUSTICE IN ANTIQUITY

Before we move on to view the economic system of antiquity in transition and evolution, we must ask one more question. What did contemporary economists think of it?

The answer we find is an interesting one: there were no contemporary "economists." Historians, philosophers, political theorists, writers on manners and morals abounded during the long span of history we here call "antiquity," but economists, as such, did not exist. The reason is not far to seek. The economics of society—that is, the mode by which society organized itself to meet the basic tasks of economic survival— were hardly such as to provoke the curiosity of a thoughtful man. There was little or no "veil" of money to pierce, little or no complexity of contractual relationship in the marketplace to unravel, little or no economic rhythm of society to interpret. As the harvest flourished, as the justice or injustice of the tax gathering system varied, as the fortunes of war and politics changed, so went the lot of the peasant proprietor, the slave, the petty craftsman, and trader. As relative military strength rose or fell, as individual merchants fared luckily or otherwise, as the arts prospered or declined, so went the pulse of trade. As his prowess in war or politics permitted, as his chance at ransoms, local monopolies, or marriage dictated, so fared the individual acquisitor of wealth. In all of this there was little to tax the analytic powers of social observers.

If there was a problem of economics—aside from the eternal problems of poor harvests, fortunes of war, etc.—it was inextricably mingled with the problem of social justice. As far back as the early Assyrian tablets, we have records of reformers who sought to alleviate taxes on the peasantry, and throughout the Bible—indeed, down through the Middle Ages—a strain of primitive communism, of egalitarian sharing, runs through the background of religious thought. In the Book of Leviticus, for example, there is mentioned the interesting custom of the *jubilee* year, one year in each fifty, in which the Israelites were to "return to each man unto his possession." * But despite the fact that religion was concerned with riches and poverty, and thus with the distributive problem of economics, the span of antiquity saw little or no systematic inquiry into the *social system* which produced riches or poverty. If riches were an affront, this was due to the personal failings of greedy men; and if social justice were to be obtained, it must be achieved by personal redistribution, by alms and charity. The idea of

---

* That is, lands which had been forfeited in debt, etc., were to be restored to their original owners. The wrath of the later prophets such as Amos indicates that the injunction must have been observed largely in the breach.

an "economic" study of society, as contrasted with a political or moral one, was conspicuous largely by its absence.

There was, however, one exception which we should note. Aristotle, the great pupil of Plato, turned his powerful scrutiny to economic affairs, and with him the systematic study of economics, as such, truly begins. Not that Aristotle, any more than the majority of the Church fathers, was a radical social reformer. Much is summed up in his famous sentence: "From the hour of their birth, some are marked out for subjection, others for rule."[8] But the student of the history of economic thought turns first to Aristotle for questions whose treatment he can subsequently trace down through the present time: questions such as "What is value?" "What is the basis of exchange?" "What is interest?"

We will not linger here over Aristotle's formulations of these ideas. But one point we might note, for it accords with what we have already seen of the attitude of antiquity to economic activity itself. When Aristotle examined the economic process, he differentiated it into two branches—not production and distribution, as we have done, but *use* and *gain*. More specifically, he differentiated between *oeconomia*—whence "economics," and *chrematistike*, from which we have no precise derivative term. By *oeconomia* the Greek philosopher meant the art of household management, the administration of one's patrimony, the careful husbanding of resources. *Chrematistike*, on the other hand, implied the use of nature's resources or of human skill for acquisitive purposes: *chrematistike* was trade for trade's sake, economic activity that had as its motive and end not use, but profit. Aristotle approved of *oeconomia* but not of *chrematistike*, and within the scope of the essentially limited market structure of antiquity, where the city trader all too frequently exploited the country peasant, it is not hard to see why. The much more difficult problem of whether a market society, in which *everyone* strives for gain, might warrant approval or disapproval never appears in Aristotle's writings, as it never appeared in ancient history. The market society with its genuinely perplexing questions of economic order and economic morality had yet to come into being. Until it did, the philosophy needed to rationalize that order was understandably lacking.

ECONOMIC SOCIETY IN THE MIDDLE AGES

Our conspectus of economic organization has thus far scanned only the great civilizations of antiquity. Now we must turn in somewhat closer

[8] *Politics,* Book I.

focus to a society far nearer in time and, what is more important, immediately precedent to ours in terms of social evolution. This is the vast expanse of history we call the Middle Ages, an expanse which stretches over and describes the Western world, from Sweden to the Mediterranean, "beginning" with the fall of Rome and "ending" with the Renaissance.

Modern scholarship emphasizes more and more the diversity which characterizes that enormous span of time and space, a diversity not alone of social appearance from century to century but of contrast from locality to locality within any given period. It is one thing to speak of "life" in the Middle Ages if one has in mind a tenth century peasant community in Normandy where, it is estimated, the average inhabitant probably never saw more than two hundred or three hundred persons in his lifetime or commanded a vocabulary of more than six hundred words),[9] and another if we mean the worldly city of Florence about which Boccaccio wrote so engagingly.

Even more relevant for our purposes is the need to think of the Middle Ages in terms of economic variety and change. The early years of feudal economic life are very different from the middle or later years, particularly insofar as general well-being is concerned. The commencement of feudalism coincided with a period of terrible retrenchment, deprivation, depopulation. During the fifth century the population of Rome actually fell from 1,500,000 to 300,000. But by the twelfth century, towns had again expanded (after 600 years!) to the limits of their old Roman walls and even spilled out beyond; and by the beginning of the fourteenth century, a very considerable prosperity reigned in many parts of Europe.* Then came a series of catastrophes: a ghastly two-year famine in 1315; thereafter, in 1348, the Black Death, which carried off between one-third and two-thirds of the urban population; a century-long devastating struggle between England and France and among the petty principalities of Germany and Italy. All of these misfortunes pulled back the level of economic existence to dreadful depths. Neither stasis nor smooth linear progress, but enormous and irregular secular tides mark the long history of feudalism, and they caution us against a simplistic conception of its development.

Our purpose, however, is not to trace these tides, but rather to form a generalized picture of the *economic structure* which, beneath the swings of fortune, marks the feudal era as a unique way-station of Western economic history. And here we can begin by noting the all-important development which underlay the genesis of that economic structure. *This was the breakdown of large-scale political organization.*

[9] George G. Coulton. *Medieval Village, Manor and Monastery* (New York: Harper & Row, Torchbooks, 1960), p. 15.
*There is some evidence that in England around the year 1500, real wages for common laborers achieved a level that they would not again surpass for at least three centuries. (*Economica,* November 1956, pp. 296–314.)

For as Rome "fell" and as successive raids and invasions from north, east, and south tore apart the European countryside, the great administrative framework of law and order was replaced by a patchwork quilt of small-scale political entities. Even in the ninth century, when Charlemagne's Holy Roman Empire assumed such impressive dimensions on the map, beneath the veneer of a unified "state" there was, in fact, political chaos: neither a single language nor a coordinated central government nor a unified system of law, coinage, or currency nor, most important, any consciousness of "national" allegiance bound the statelets of Charlemagne's day into more than temporary cohesion.

We note this striking difference between antiquity and the Middle Ages to stress the tremendous economic consequences that came with political dissolution. As safety and security gave way to local autarky and anarchy, long voyages of commodities became extremely hazardous, and the once vigorous life of the great cities impossible. As a common coin and a common law disappeared, merchants in Gaul could no longer do business with merchants in Italy, and the accustomed network of economic connections was severed or fell into disuse. As disease and invasion depopulated the countryside, men turned of necessity to the most defensive forms of economic organization, to forms aimed at sheer survival through self-sufficiency. A new need arose, a need to compress the viable organization of society into the smallest possible compass. For centuries this insularity of economic life, this extreme self-reliance would be the economic hallmark of the Middle Ages.

The need for self-sufficiency brought with it a new basic unit of economic organization: the *manorial estate*.

What was such an estate like? Typically, it was a large tract of land, often including many thousands of acres, which was "owned" by a feudal lord, spiritual or temporal.* The word "owned" is properly in quotation marks, for the manor was not first and foremost a piece of economic property as such. Rather, it was a social and political entity in which the lord of the manor was not only landlord, but protector, judge, police chief, administrator. Although himself bound into a great hierarchy in which each lord was some other lord's servant (and even the pope was *servus servorum Dei*), the feudal noble was, within the confines of his own manor, quite literally "lord of the land." He was also undisputed owner and master of many of the people who lived on the land, for the serfs (or villeins) of a manor, although not slaves, were in many respects as much the property of the lord as were his (or their) houses, flocks, or crops.

---

*That is, the lord might be the abbot or the bishop of the locality, or he might be a secular personage, a baron who came into his possessions by inheritance or by being made a knight and given lands for exceptional service in battle or for other reasons.

At the focal point of the estate was the lord's homestead, a great manor house, usually armed against attack from marauders, walled off from the surrounding countryside, and sometimes attaining the stature of a genuine castle. In the enclosed courtyard of the manor were workshops in which cloth might be spun or woven, grapes pressed, food stored, simple ironwork or blacksmithing work performed, coarse grain ground. Extending out around the manor was a patchwork of fields, typically subdivided into acre or half-acre "strips," each with its own cycle of crops and rest. Half or more of all of these belonged directly to the lord; the remainder "belonged," in various senses of that legal term, to the hierarchy of free, half-free, and unfree families who made up an estate.

The exact meaning of the word "belonged" hinged on the obligations and rights accruing to a serf, a freeman, or whatever other category one might be born into. Note however that even a freeman who "owned" his land could not sell it to another feudal lord. At best, his ownership meant that he could not himself be displaced from his land short of extraordinary circumstances. A lesser personage than a freeman did not even have this security. A typical serf was literally tied to "his" plot of land. He could not, without specific permission and, usually, without specific payment, leave his homestead for another, either within the domain of the manor or within that of another. With his status came, as well, a series of obligations which lay at the very core of the manorial economic organization. These consisted of the necessity to perform labor for the lord—to till his fields, to work in his shops, to provide him with a portion of one's own crop. From manor to manor, and from age to age, the labor-dues varied: in some localities they amounted to as much as four or even five days of labor a week, which meant that only by the labor of a serf's wife or children could his own fields be maintained. And finally, the serfs owed small money-payments: head taxes, like the *chevage;* death-duties, like the *heriot;* or *merchet,* a marriage fee, or dues to use the lord's mill or his ovens.

There was, however, an extremely important *quid pro quo* for all of this. If the serf gave the lord his labor and much of the fruits of his toil, in exchange the lord provided some things which the serf alone could not have obtained.

The most important of these was a degree of physical security. It is difficult for us to reconstruct the violent tenor of much of feudal life, but one investigator has provided a statistic which may serve to make the point. Of the sons of English dukes born in 1330–1479, *46 per cent* died violent deaths. Their life expectancy when violent death was excluded was 31 years; when violent death was included, it was but 24 years.[10] The peasant, although not a warrior and therefore not

---

[10] T. H. Hollingsworth, "A Demographic Study of the British Ducal Families," *Population Studies,* XI (1957–58). I am indebted to Dr. Goran Ohlin for this reference.

occupationally exposed to the dangers of continual combat, assassination, etc., was pre-eminently fair prey for the marauding lord, defenseless against capture, unable to protect his poor possessions against destruction. Hence we can begin to understand why even free men become serfs by "commending" themselves to a lord who, in exchange for their economic, social, and political subservience, offered them in return the invaluable cloak of his military protection.

In addition, the lord offered a certain element of *economic* security. In times of famine, it was the lord who fed his serfs from the reserves in his own manorial storehouses. And, although he had to pay for it, the serf was *entitled* to use the lord's own beasts and equipment in cultivating his own strips as well as those of the lord himself. In an age when the average serf possessed almost no tools himself, this was an essential boon.[11]

These facts should not incline us to an idyllic picture of feudal life. The relation between lord and serf was often and even usually exploitative in the extreme. Yet we must see that it was also mutually supportive. Each provided for the other services essential for existence in a world where over-all political organization and stability had virtually disappeared.

Despite the extreme self-sufficiency of manorial life, there is much here that resembles the economic organization of antiquity.

ECONOMICS OF MANORIAL LIFE

To begin with, like those earlier societies, this was clearly a form of economic society organized by tradition. Indeed, the hand of custom —the famous "ancient customs" of the medieval manor court which served frequently as the counsel for the otherwise undefended serf—was never stronger. Lacking strong unified central government, even the exercise of command was relatively weak. As a result, the pace of economic change, of economic development, although by no means lacking, was extremely slow during the early years of the medieval period.

Second, even more than with antiquity, this was a form of society which was characterized by a striking absence of money transactions. Unlike the latifundium of Rome, which sold its output to the city, the manor supplied only itself, and perhaps a local town. No manorial estate was ever quite so self-sufficient that it could dispense with monetary links with the outside world; even serfs bought a few commodities and sold a few eggs; and the lord, on occasion, had to buy considerable supplies which he could not produce for himself. But on the whole,

---

[11] For a picture of life among the various classes in medieval Europe, one might turn to Eileen Power's *Medieval People* (Garden City, N.Y.: Doubleday & Co., Inc., Anchor Books, 1954), a scholarly but charming account of the reality of human existence which lies behind history. For a sense of the violent tenor of the times, see J. Huizinga, *The Waning of the Middle Ages* (Garden City, N.Y.: Doubleday & Co., Inc., Anchor Books, 1954), Chap. I.

very little money changed hands. As Henri Pirenne, an authority on medieval economic history, has put it:

> . . . the tenants paid their obligations to their lord in kind. Every serf . . . owed a fixed number of days of labour and a fixed quantity of natural products or of goods manufactured by himself, corn, eggs, geese, chickens, lambs, pigs, and hempen, linen or woollen cloth. It is true that a few pence had also to be paid, but they formed such a small proportion of the whole that they cannot prevent the conclusion that the economy of the domain was a natural economy . . . since it did not engage in commerce it had no need to make use of money. . . .[12]

TOWN AND FAIR

It would, however, be a misrepresentation of medieval life to conclude that cash and cash transactions and the bargaining of a market society were wholly foreign to it. Rather, as was the case with antiquity, we must think of medieval economic society as consisting of a huge, static, virtually moneyless foundation of agricultural production atop which flourished a considerable variety of more dynamic activities.

For one thing, in addition to manors, there also existed the shrunken descendants of Roman towns (and as we shall later see, the nuclei of new towns) and these small cities obviously required a network of markets to serve them. Every town had its stalls to which peasants brought some portion of their crop for sale. More important, towns were clearly a different social unit from manors, and the laws and customs of the manors did not apply to their problems. Even when towns fell under manorial protection, townspeople little by little won for themselves freedom from feudal obligations of labor and, more important, from feudal obligations of law.* In contrast to the "ancient customs" of the manor, a new, evolving "law of merchants" regulated much of the commercial activity within the town walls.

Another locus of active economic life was the fair. The fair was a kind of traveling market, established in fixed localities for fixed dates, in which merchants from all over Europe conducted a genuine international exchange. Held usually but once a year, the great fairs were tremendous occasions, a mixture of social holiday, religious festival, and a time of intense economic activity. At some fairs, like those at Champagne in France or Stourbridge in England, a wide variety of merchandise was brought for sale: silks from the Levant, books and parchments, horses, drugs, spices. Anyone who has ever been to the Flea

---

[12] *Economic and Social History of Medieval Europe* (New York: Harcourt, Brace & World, Inc., Harvest Books, 1956), p. 105.

* Hence the saying "City air makes men free"; for the serf who escaped to a city and remained there a year and a day was usually considered to have passed from the jurisdiction of his lord to that of the city burghers.

Market, the famous open-air bazaar outside Paris, or to a country fair in New England or the Middle West has savored something of the atmosphere of such a market. One can imagine the excitement which fairs must have engendered in the still air of medieval life.

And finally, within the towns themselves, we find the tiny but highly important centers of medieval "industrial" production. For even at its grandest, the manor could not support every craft needed for its maintenance, much less its extension. The services or products of glaziers and masons, expert armorers and metalworkers, fine weavers and dyers had to be bought when they were needed, and typically they were to be found in the medieval institutions as characteristic of town life as the manors themselves were of life in the country.

These institutions were the *guilds*—trade, professional, and craft organizations of Roman origins. Such organizations were the "business units" of the Middle Ages; in fact, one could not usually set oneself up in "business" unless one belonged to a guild. Thus the guilds were a kind of exclusive union, but not a union of workers so much as of managers. The dominant figures in the guild were the guildmasters—independent manufacturers, working in their own houses and banding together to elect their own guild government which then laid down the rules concerning the internal conduct of affairs. Under the master guildsmen were their few journeymen (from the French *journée* or day), who were paid by the day, and their half-dozen or so apprentices, ten to twelve years old, who were bound to them for periods of three to twelve years as their legal wards. In time, an apprentice could become a journeyman and then, at least in medieval romance, graduate to the status of a full-fledged guildmaster on completion of his "masterpiece."

Any survey of medieval town life delights in the color of guild organization: the broiders and glovers, the hatters and scriveners, the shipwrights and upholsterers, each with its guild hall, its distinctive livery, and its elaborate set of rules. But if life in the guilds and at the fairs provides a sharp contrast with the stodgy life on the manor, we must not be misled by surface resemblances into thinking that it represented a foretaste of modern life in medieval dress. It is a long distance from the guild to the modern business firm, and it is well to fix in mind some of the differences.

In the first place, the guild was much more than just an institution for organizing production. While most of its regulations concerned wages and conditions of work and specifications of output, they also dwelt at length on "noneconomic" matters: on the charitable contributions expected from each member, on his civic role, on his appropriate dress, and even on his daily deportment. Guilds were the regulators not only of production but of social conduct: when one member of the mercer's guild in London "broke the hed" of another in an argument over some merchandise, both were fined £10 and bonded for £200 not to repeat the disgrace. In another guild, members who engaged in a brawl were fined a barrel of beer, to be drunk by the rest of the guild.

But between guild and modern business firm there is a much more profound gulf than this pervasive paternalism. *Unlike a modern firm, the purpose of a guild was not first and foremost to make money.* Rather, it was to preserve a certain orderly way of life—a way which envisaged a decent income for its master craftsmen but which was certainly not intended to allow any of them to become a "big" businessman or a monopolist. On the contrary, guilds were specifically designed to ward off any such outcome of an uninhibited struggle among their members. The terms of service, the wages, the route of advancement of apprentices and journeymen were all fixed by custom. So, too, were the terms of sale: a guild member who cornered the supply of an item was guilty of *forestalling,* for which rigorous penalties were invoked, and one who bought wholesale to sell at retail was similarly punished for the faults of *engrossing* or *regrating.* Thus competition was strictly limited and profits were held to prescribed levels. Advertising was forbidden, and even technical progress in advance of one's fellow guildmen was considered disloyal.

In the great cloth guilds of Florence in the fourteenth century, for instance, no merchant was permitted to tempt a buyer into his shop or to call out to a customer standing in another's doorway, nor even to process his cloth in a manner different from that of his brethren. Standards of cloth production and processing were subject to the minutest scrutiny. If a scarlet dye, for instance, were found to be adulterated, the perpetrator was condemned to a crushing fine and, failing payment, to loss of his right hand.[13]

Surely the guilds represent a more "modern" aspect of feudal life than the manor, but the whole temper of guild life was still far removed from the goals and ideals of modern business enterprise. There was no free play of price, no free competition, no restless probing for advantage. Existing on the margin of a relatively moneyless society, the guilds perforce sought to take the risks out of their slender enterprises. Their aim was not increase, but preservation, stability, orderliness. As such, they were as drenched in the medieval atmosphere as the manors.

MEDIEVAL ECONOMICS

Beyond even these differences, we must note a still deeper chasm between medieval economic society and that of a market economy. This is the gulf between a society in which economic activity is still inextricably mixed with social and religious activity, and one in which economic life has, so to speak, emerged into a special category of its

---

[13] G. Renard, *Histoire du Travail à Florence* (Paris: 1913), pp. 190 ff.

own. In our next chapter we shall be talking about the ways in which a market society creates a special sphere of economic existence. But as we complete our introduction to medieval economic society, the main point to which we should pay heed is that no such special sphere then existed. *In medieval society, economics was a subordinate and not a dominant aspect of life.*

And what was dominant? The answer is, of course, that in economic matters as in so many other facets of medieval life, the guiding ideal was religious. It was the Church, the great pillar of stability in an age of disorder, that constituted the ultimate authority on economics, as on most other matters.

But the economics of medieval Catholicism was concerned not with the credits and debits of successful business operation so much as with the credits and debits of the souls of business operators. As R. H. Tawney, one of the great students of the problem, has written:

. . . the specific contributions of medieval writers to the technique of economic theory were less significant than their premises. Their fundamental assumptions, both of which were to leave a deep imprint on social thought of the sixteenth and seventeenth centuries, were two: that economic interests are subordinate to the real business of life, which is salvation; and that economic conduct is one aspect of personal conduct, upon which, as on other parts of it, the rules of morality are binding. Material riches are necessary . . . since without them men cannot support themselves and help one another . . . But economic motives are suspect. Because they are powerful appetites men fear them, but they are not mean enough to applaud them. Like other strong passions, what they need, it is thought, is not a clear field, but repression. . . .[14]

Thus what we find throughout medieval religious thought is a pervasive uneasiness with the practices of economic society. Essentially, the Church's attitude toward trade was wary and nicely summed up in the saying: "Homo mercator vix aut numquam Deo placere potest"—the merchant can scarcely or never be pleasing to God.

We find such a suspicion of business motives in the Church's concern with the idea of a "just price." What was a just price? It was selling a thing for what it was worth, and no more. "It is wholly sinful," wrote Thomas Aquinas, "to practise fraud for the express purpose of selling a thing for more than its just price, inasmuch as a man deceives his neighbor to his loss."[15]

But what *was* a thing "worth"? Presumably, what it cost to acquire it or make it. Suppose, however, that a seller had himself paid too much for an article—then what was a "just price" at which he might resell

[14] *Religion and the Rise of Capitalism* (New York: Harcourt, Brace & World, Inc., 1947), p. 31.

[15] A. E. Monroe, ed., "Summa Theologica," in *Early Economic Thought* (Cambridge, Mass.: Harvard University Press, 1924), p. 54.

it? Or suppose a man paid too little—was he then in danger of spiritual loss, offsetting his material gain?

These were the questions over which the medieval "economist-theologians" mulled, and they testify to the mixture of economics and ethics, characteristic of the age. But they were not merely theoretical questions. We have records of the dismay that economic theology brought to actual participants in the economic process. One St. Gerald of Aurillac in the tenth century, having bought an ecclesiastical garment in Rome for an unusually low price, learned from some itinerant merchants that he had picked up a "bargain"; instead of rejoicing, he hastened to send to the seller an additional sum, lest he fall into the sin of avarice.[16]

St. Gerald's attitude was no doubt exceptional. Yet if the injunction to charge fair prices did not succeed in staying men's appetites for gain, it did stay their unbridled enthusiasm. Men in ordinary business frequently stopped to assess the condition of their moral balance sheets. Whole towns would, on occasion, repent of usury and pay a heavy amend, or merchants like Gandouîle le Grand would, on their death-beds, order restitution made to those from whom interest had been extracted. Men of affairs in the twelfth and thirteenth centuries occasionally inserted codicils in their wills urging their sons not to follow their footsteps into the snares of trade, or they would seek to make restitution for their commercial sins by charitable contributions. One medieval merchant of London founded a divinity scholarship with £14 "forasmoche as I fynde myn conscience aggrugged that I have deceived in this life divers persons to that amount."[17]

Thus the theological cast of suspicion injected a wholly new note into the moneymaking process. For the first time it associated the making of money with *guilt*. Unlike the acquisitor of antiquity who unashamedly reveled in his treasures, the medieval profiteer counted his gains in the knowledge that he might be imperiling his soul.

Nowhere was this disapproval of moneymaking more evident than in the Church's horror of usury—lending money at interest. Money-lending had, since Aristotle's day, been regarded as an essentially parasitic activity, an attempt to make a "barren" commodity, money, yield a return. But what had always been a vaguely disreputable and unpopular activity became, under Church scrutiny, a deeply evil one. Usury was decreed to be a *mortal* sin. At the Councils of Lyons and Vienne in the thirteenth and fourteenth centuries, the usurer was declared a pariah of society, to whom no one, under pain of excommunication, might rent a house, whose confession might not be heard,

[16] Henri Pirenne, *Economic and Social History of Medieval Europe* (New York: Harcourt, Brace & World, Inc., Harvest Books, 1956), p. 27.

[17] S. L. Thrupp, *The Merchant Class in Medieval London* (Chicago: University of Chicago Press, 1948), p. 177. Also Renard, *op. cit.,* pp. 220 ff.

whose body might not have Christian burial, whose very will was invalid. Anyone even defending usury was to be suspected of heresy.

These powerful churchly sentiments were not produced merely by theological scruples. On the contrary, many of the Church's injunctions against both usury and profiteering arose from the most secular of realities. Famine, the endemic scourge of the Middle Ages, brought with it the most heartless economic gouging; loans commanded 40 and 60 per cent—for bread. Much of the dislike of profit seeking and interest taking rose from its identification with just such ruthless practices, with which medieval times abounded.

Finally, another, perhaps even more fundamental, reason underlay the disrepute of gain and profit. This was the essentially static organization of economic life itself. Let us not forget that that life was basically agricultural and that agriculture, with its infinite complexity of peasant strips, was far from efficient. To quote once more from Henri Pirenne:

. . . the whole idea of profit, and indeed the possibility of profit, was incompatible with the position occupied by the great medieval landowner. Unable to produce for sale owing to the want of a market, he had no need to tax his ingenuity in order to wring from his men and his land a surplus which would merely be an encumbrance, and as he was forced to consume his own produce, he was content to limit it to his needs. His means of existence was assured by the traditional functioning of an organization which he did not try to improve.[18]

What was true of the country was also true of the city. The idea of an *expanding* economy, a *growing* scale of production, an *increasing* productivity was as foreign to the guildmaster or fair-merchant as to the serf and lord. Medieval economic organization was conceived as a means of reproducing, but not enhancing, the material well-being of the past. Its motto was perpetuation, not progress. There is little wonder that in such a static organization, profits and profitseeking were viewed as essentially disturbing rather than welcome economic phenomena.

PREREQUISITES OF CHANGE

We have traced the broad outlines of the economic organization of the West roughly up to the tenth or twelfth century. Once again it is wise

[18] *Op. cit.,* p. 63.

to emphasize the diversity of currents concealed within a landscape we have too often been forced to treat as undifferentiated. At best, our journey into antiquity and the Middle Ages can give us a few glimpses of the prevailing flavor of the times, a sense of the ruling economic climate, of the main institutions and ideas by which men organized their economic efforts.

But one thing is certain. We are very far from the temper and tempo of modern economic life. The few stirrings we have witnessed in the slow world of the manor and the town are but the harbingers of a tremendous change which, over the course of the next centuries, would dramatically alter the basic form of economic organization itself, replacing the old ties of tradition and command with new ties of market transactions.

We shall have to wait until our next chapter to witness the actual process of change itself. But perhaps it will help us put into focus both what we have already seen and what we are about to witness if we anticipate our line of advance. We now have an idea of a pre-market society, a society in which markets exist but which does not yet depend on a market mechanism to solve the economic problem. What changes will be required to transform such a society into a true market economy?

1. *A new attitude toward economic activity will be needed.*

For such a society to function, men must be free to seek gain. The suspiciousness and unease which surrounded the ideas of profit, of change, of social mobility must give way to new ideas which would encourage those very attitudes and activities. In turn this meant, in the famous words of Sir Henry Maine, that the *society of status* must give way to the *society of contract,* that the society in which men were born to their stations in life must give way to a society in which they were free to define those stations for themselves.

Such an idea would have seemed to the medieval mind without any possible rationale. The idea that a general free-for-all should determine men's compensations, with neither a floor to prevent them from being ground down nor a ceiling to prevent them from rising beyond all reason, would have appeared senseless—even blasphemous. If we may listen again to R. H. Tawney:

To found a science of society upon the assumption that the appetite for economic gain is . . . to be accepted, like other natural forces . . . would have appeared to the medieval thinker as hardly less irrational or less immoral than to make the premise of social philosophy the unrestrained operation of such necessary human attributes as pugnacity or the sexual instinct.[19]

Yet some such freeing of the quest for economic gain, some such

---

[19] *Op. cit.,* pp. 31–32.

aggressive competition in the new contractual relationship of man to man would be essential for the birth of a market society.

2. *The monetization of economic life will have to proceed to its ultimate conclusion.*

One prerequisite of a market economy should by now be clear: such an economy must involve the process of exchange, of buying and selling, at every level of society. But for this to take place men must have the wherewithal to enter a market; that is, they must have cash. And, in turn, if society is to be permeated with cash, men must earn money for their labors. In other words, *for a market society to exist, nearly every task must have a monetary reward.*

Even in our highly monetized society we do not pay for every service: most conspicuously not for the housekeeping services of a wife. But all through the pre-market era, the number of unpaid services—the amount of work performed by law without monetary compensation— was vastly larger than in our society. Slave labor was, of course, unpaid. So was most serf labor. Even the labor of apprentices was remunerated more in kind, in food and lodging, than in cash. Thus probably 70 to 80 per cent of the actual working population of an ancient or medieval economy labored without anything resembling full payment in money.

Clearly, in such a society the possibilities for a highly involved exchange economy were limited. But a still more important consequence must be noted. The absence of a widespread monetization of tasks meant the absence of a widespread *market for producers.* Nothing like the flow of "purchasing power" which dominates and directs our own productive efforts could be forthcoming in a society in which money incomes were the exception rather than the rule.

3. *The pressures of a free play of market "demand" will have to take over the regulation of the economic tasks of society.*

All through antiquity and the Middle Ages, as we have seen, tradition or command solved the economic problem. These were the forces that regulated the distribution of social rewards. But in a market society, another means of control must rise to take their place. *An all-encompassing flow of money demand, itself stemming from the total monetization of all economic tasks, must become the great propulsive mechanism of society.* Men must go to their tasks not because they are ordered there, but because they will make money there; and producers must decide on the volume and the variety of their output not because the rules of the manor or the guild so determine, but because there is a market demand for particular things. From the top to the bottom of society, in other words, a new marketing orientation must take over the production and distribution tasks. The whole replenishment, the steady provisioning, the very progress of society must now be subject to the guiding hand of a universal demand for labor and goods.

What forces would ultimately drive the world of medieval economic organization into a world of money, of universal markets, of profit-seeking? The stage is now set for us to attempt to answer this profoundly important and difficult question. Let us turn to a consideration of the causes capable of effecting so vast a change.

SUMMARY

1. We must differentiate between markets, which have a very ancient pedigree, and market societies, which do not. *In a market society, the economic problem itself—both production and distribution—is solved by means of a vast exchange between buyers and sellers.* Many ancient societies had markets, but these markets did not organize the fundamental activities of these societies.

2. The economic societies of antiquity had several features in common, which contrast sharply with those of modern market economies:
   • They rested on an agricultural base of *peasant farming.*
   • Their cities were—from an economic point of view—parasitic *centers of consumption, not active centers of production.*
   • *Slavery* was a common and very important form of labor.

3. As a result, in the economic societies of antiquity we find the economic side of life subservient to the political side. Priest, warrior, and statesman were superior to merchant or trader; *wealth followed power,* not—as in market societies to come—the other way around.

4. Medieval economic life emerged from the catastrophic disorganization that followed the decline of Roman law and order. It was characterized by a unique form of organization called the *manorial* system in which:
   • *Local lords were the centers of political, military, economic, and social power.*
   • *Most peasants were bound as serfs to a particular lord, for whom they were required to work and to whom they owed both labor and taxes or dues.*
   • *Physical security against brigands or other lords was provided by the lord, as well as some economic security in times of distress.*

5. *The manorial system,* particularly in its earlier days (sixth to tenth centuries), *was a static economic system,* in which monetary payments played only a minor role. Self-sufficiency was the main purpose and the most outstanding characteristic of the manor.

6. Side by side with the manor existed the economic life of the *towns.* Here monetary exchange always played a more important role, as did the organization of a more active economic life in the institution of *fairs.*

7. The *guild* was the main form of organizing production in the towns and cities. *Guilds were very different from modern-day businesses,* insofar as they discouraged competition or profit seeking and sought to impose general rules on the methods of production, rates of pay, practices of marketing, and so on.

8. All through medieval times the church—the main social organization of the age—was suspicious of buying and selling activity. In part this reflected a dislike of the exploitative practices of the times, in part it was a consequence of an ancient contempt for moneymaking (remember Aristotle's dislike of *chrematistike*) and especially for moneylending (usury). The religious leaders of the day worried about "just" prices, and did not admit that unregulated buying and selling gave rise to just prices.

9. Three profound and pervasive changes would be needed to convert medieval society into a market society:

- *A new attitude toward moneymaking* as a legitimate activity would have to replace the medieval suspicion of profit seeking.
- *The web of monetization would have to expand* beyond its narrow confines—that is, buying and selling would have to control the output of all products and the performance of nearly all tasks.
- *The flux of "demand" and "supply" would have to be allowed to take over the direction of economic activity* from the dictates of lords and the usages of custom.

1. What differences, if any, characterize the economic attitudes and behavior of the American farmer and the American businessman? Can this comparison also describe the behavior and attitude of the Egyptian peasant and the Egyptian merchant? What accounts for the difference between the two societies?

2. Julius Caesar and J. P. Morgan were both wealthy and powerful men. What is the difference in the origins of their wealth and their power? Does power still follow wealth in modern economic societies? Does wealth still follow power in nonmarket societies? If not, why not?

3. To what uses was the surplus of society put in ancient Rome? In feudal society? In modern America? In the U.S.S.R.? What significance attaches to these different uses? What do they tell us about the structure of these societies?

4. What do you think of the validity of Aristotle's distinction between economic activity for *use* and *gain?*

5. In what ways is a serf a different *economic* creature from a modern farm worker? How is a slave different from an industrial worker?

6. What changes would have to take place within a guild before it resembled a modern business?

7. The Bible has numerous hostile references to moneymaking—"It is easier for a camel to go through the eye of a needle than for a rich man to enter into the kingdom of God." How do you account for this ancient churchly antipathy toward wealth? Is religion today still suspicious of moneymaking? Why?

8. Is the idea of a "just" price (or a "just" wage) still encountered in our own society? What is usually meant by these terms? Do you think these ideas are compatible with a market system?

9. The manorial system persisted for nearly 1,000 years. Why do you think change was so slow in coming?

10. Ancient Greece and Rome are a great deal more "modern" in their temper than feudal Europe. Yet neither was remotely a modern economic system. Why not?

3

THE EMERGENCE OF
THE MARKET SOCIETY

Tradition, changelessness, order—these were the key concepts of economic society in the Middle Ages, and our preceding chapter introduced us to this unfamiliar and static way of economic life. But our purpose in this chapter is different. It is no longer to describe those factors which preserved the economic stability of medieval society, but to identify those forces which eventually burst it asunder.

Once again we need to begin with a word of caution. Our chapter spans an immense variety of historical experience. We must beware of thinking that the forces of change which dominate this chapter were identical from region to region or from century to century, or that the transition which they effected was uniform throughout the broad expanse of Europe. On the contrary, the great evolution which we will witness in these pages was not sharp and clear, but muddy and irregular. At the same time that the first evidences of a truly modern market society were beginning to manifest themselves in the medieval cities of Italy or Holland, the most archaic forms of feudal relationship still persisted in the agricultural sectors of these nations, and indeed in the city life of other nations. We must bear in mind that the historic processes of this chapter extended from the tenth to the seventeenth (and even eighteenth and nineteenth) centuries and manifested themselves in no two countries in precisely the same way.

With these cautions in mind, now let us turn to the great evolution itself. What agents were powerful enough to effect the major historic changes needed to bring about a market society?

THE ITINERANT MERCHANT

We meet the first of these forces of change in an unexpected guise. It is a small irregular procession of armed men, jogging along one of the rudimentary roads of medieval Europe: standard-bearer with colors in the lead, then a military chief, then a group of riders carrying bows and swords, and finally a caravan of horses and mules laden with casks and bales, bags and packs.

Someone unacquainted with medieval life might easily take such a troop for part of the baggage train of a small army. But he would be mistaken. These were not soldiers but merchants, the traveling merchants whom the English of the twelfth century called "pie-powers," from *pieds poudreux,* dusty feet. No wonder they were dusty; many of them came immense distances along routes so bad that we know of one instance where only the intervention of a local ecclesiastical lord prevented the "road" from being plowed up as arable land. In their bags and packs were goods which had somehow made a perilous journey across Europe, or even all the way from Arabia or India, to be sold from town to town, or from halt to halt, as these merchant adventurers wound their way across the medieval countryside.

And adventurers they were indeed. For in the fixed hierarchies of the great manorial estates of Europe there was no natural place for these unlanded peddlers of goods, with their unfeudal attributes of calculation and (often very crude) bookkeeping and their natural insistence on trade in money. The traveling merchants ranked very low in society. Some of them, without doubt, were the sons of serfs, or even runaway serfs themselves. Yet since no one could prove their bondage, they had, if only by default, the gift of "freedom." It is no wonder that in the eyes of the nobility, the merchants were upstarts and a disturbing element in the normal pattern of things.

Yet no one would have dispensed with their services. To their brightly canopied stalls at the fairs flocked the lords and ladies of the manors as well as the Bodos and Ermentrudes of the fields. After all, where else could one buy pepper, or purple dye, or acquire a guaranteed splinter from the Cross? Where else could one buy the marvelous cloths woven in Tuscany or learn such esoteric words, derived from the Arabic, as "jar" or "syrup"? If the merchant was a disturbing leaven in the mix of medieval life, he was also the pinch of active ingredient without which the mixture would have been very dull indeed.

We first note the traveling merchant in Europe in the eighth and ninth century, and we can follow his progress until the fourteenth and fifteenth century. By this time, largely through the merchants' own efforts, commerce was sufficiently organized so that it no longer required these itinerant journeyers.* For what these travelers brought, together with their wares, was the first breath of commerce and commercial intercourse to a Europe which had sunk to an almost tradeless and self-sufficient manorial stagnation. Even to towns as minuscule and isolated as Forcalquier in France—a dot on the map without so much as a road to connect its few hundred souls to the outer world—these hardy traders beat their path: we know from a primitive book of accounts that in May, 1331, thirty-six itinerant merchants visited Forcalquier to transact business at the home and "shop" of one Ugo Teralh, a notary.[1] And so, in a thousand isolated communities, did they slowly weave a web of economic interdependence.

URBANIZATION   An important by-product of the rise of the itinerant merchant was the slow urbanization of medieval life, the creation of new towns and villages. When the traveling merchants stopped, they naturally chose the protected site of a local castle or burg, or of a church. And so we find growing up around the walls of advantageously situated castles—in the *foris burgis,* whence *faubourg,* the French word for "suburb"—more or less permanent trading places, which in turn became the inner core of small towns. Nestled close to the castle or cathedral wall for protection, the new burgs were still not "of" the manor. The inhabitants of the burg—the burgesses, burghers, bourgeois—had at best an anomalous and insecure relation to the manorial world within. As we have seen, there was no way of applying the time-hallowed rule of "ancient customs" in adjudicating their disputes, since there *were* no ancient customs in the commercial quarters. Neither were there clear-cut rules for their taxation or for the particular degrees of fealty they owned their local masters. Worse yet, some of the growing towns began to surround themselves with walls. By the twelfth century, the commercial burg of Bruges, for example, had already swallowed up the old fortress like a pearl around a grain of sand.

    Curiously, it was this very struggle for existence in the interstices of feudal society which provided much of the impetus for the development of a new social and economic order within the city. In all previous

---

*Records of an order for goods placed on the occasion of a funeral of a Swedish nobleman in 1328 include saffron from Spain or Italy, caraway seed from the Mediterranean, ginger from India, cinnamon from Ceylon, pepper from Malabar, anise from southern Europe, and Rhine and Bordeaux wines. The order was placed for immediate delivery from one local merchant, despite the fact that Sweden was then a laggard and even primitive land. Cf. Fritz Rorig, *Mittelalterliche Weltwirtschaft* (Jena: 1933), p. 17. (I am again indebted to Dr. Goran Ohlin for this reference.)
[1] *Cambridge Economic History of Europe,* II, 325–26.

civilizations, cities had been the outposts of central government. Now, for the first time, they existed as independent entities outside the main framework of social power. As a result, they were able to define for themselves—as they *had* to define for themselves—a code of law and social behavior and a set of governing institutions which were eventually to displace those of the feudal countryside.

The process was long drawn out, for the rate of growth of towns was often very slow. In the nearly two centuries between 1086 and 1279, for example, the town of Cambridge, England, added an average of but one house *per year.*[2] One important reason for this almost imperceptible rate of expansion was the difficulty of moving men or materials over the terrible roads. Not the least consequence of the decline of Roman power had been the decay of its once magnificent system of highways, the very stones of which were pilfered for building materials during the years of worst social disorganization. Until the roads recovered, economic movement was perforce limited and limping. And it is worth remarking that in many parts of Europe, a system of transportation as efficient as that of ancient Rome was not enjoyed until the eighteenth or even nineteenth centuries.

Yet if growth was slow, it was steady; and in some locales it was much faster than in Cambridge. During the 1,000 years of the Middle Ages nearly 1,000 towns were fathered in Europe, a tremendous stimulus to the commercialization and monetization of life, for each town had its local marts, its local toll gates, often its local mint; its granaries and shops, its drinking places and inns, its air of "city life" which contrasted so sharply with that of the country. The slow, spontaneous growth of urban ways was a major factor in introducing a marketing flavor to European economic life.

THE CRUSADES

The rise of the itinerant merchant and the town were two great factors in the slow evolution of a market society out of medieval economic life; a third factor was the Crusades.

It is an ironic turn to history that the Crusades, the supreme religious adventure of the Middle Ages, should have contributed so much toward the establishment of a society to which the Church was so vigorously opposed. If we consider the Crusades, however, not from the point of view of their religious impulse, but simply as great expeditions of exploration and colonization, their economic impact becomes much more understandable.*

The Crusades served to bring into sudden and startling contact two

---

[2] George Gordon Coulton, *Medieval Panorama* (London: Meridian Books, Ltd., 1955), p. 285.

*We might note here some of the complex interaction of the process we are watching. For the Crusades were not only a cause of European economic development, but also a *symptom* of the development which had previously taken place.

very different worlds. One was the still slumbering society of European feudalism with all its rural inertia, its aversion to trade, and its naïve conceptions of business; the other was the brilliant society of Byzantium and Venice, with its urban vitality, its unabashed enjoyment of money-making, and its sophisticated business ways. The Crusaders, coming from their draughty castles and boring manorial routines, thought they would find in the East only untutored heathen savages. They were astonished to be met by a people far more civilized, infinitely more luxurious, and much more money-oriented than they.

One result was that the simple-minded Crusaders found themselves the pawns of commercial interests which they little understood. During the first three Crusades, the Venetians, who provided ships, gulled them as shamelessly as country bumpkins at a fair. The fact that they were fleeced, however, did not prevent the Crusaders from reaching the Holy Land, albeit with inconclusive results. But in the notorious Fourth Crusade (1202–1204) Dandolo, the wily 94-year-old Doge of Venice, managed to subvert the entire religious expedition into a gigantic plundering operation for Venetian profit.

First Dandolo held up the voyagers for an initial transportation price of 85,000 silver marks, an enormous sum for the unmoneyed nobility to scrape up. Then, when the funds had been found, he refused to carry out his bargain until the Crusaders agreed first to attack the town of Zara, a rich commercial rival of Venice. Since Zara was a *Christian*, not an "infidel" community, Pope Innocent III was horrified and suggested that the attack be directed instead against heathen Egypt. But Egypt was one of Venice's best customers, and this horrified Dandolo even more. The Crusaders, stranded and strapped, had no choice: Zara soon fell—after which, at Dandolo's urging, Christian Constantinople was also sacked. The "heathen" Orient was never reached at all, but Venice profited marvelously.

It was not only Venice which gained, however. The economic impact on the Crusaders themselves was much more formidable than the religious. On many this impact was disastrous, as knights who had melted down their silver plate to join the Crusades came back penniless to their ruined manor houses. To others, however, the Crusades brought a new economic impetus. When in 1101, for example, the Genoese raided Caesarea, a Palestinian seaport, 8,000 soldiers and sailors reaped a reward of some forty-eight *solidi* each, plus two pounds of pepper —and thus were 8,000 petty capitalists born.[3] And in 1204 when Constantinople fell, not only did each knight receive twenty marks in silver as his share of the booty, but even the squires and archers were rewarded with a few marks each.

Thus the Crusades provided an immense fertilizing experience for Europe. The old, landed basis of wealth came into contact with a new

[3] *Cambridge Economic History of Europe,* II, 306.

moneyed basis which proved much more powerful. Indeed, the old conception of life itself was forcibly revised before a glimpse of an existence not only wealthier, but gayer and more vital. As a means of shaking a sluggish society out of its rut, the Crusades played an immense role in speeding along the economic transformation of Europe.

Yet another factor in the slow commercialization of economic life was the gradual amalgamation of Europe's fragmented economic and political entities into larger wholes. As the disintegration of economic life following the break-up of the old Roman Empire had shown, a strong economic society requires a strong and broad political base. Hence as political Europe began its slow process of reknitting, once again its economic tempo began to rise.

One of the most striking characteristics of the Middle Ages, and one of its most crippling obstacles to economic development, was the medieval crazy quilt of compartmented, isolated areas of government. Over a journey of a hundred miles, a traveling merchant might fall under a dozen different sovereignties, each with different rules, regulations, laws, weights, measures, money. Worse yet, at each border there was apt to be a toll station. At the turn of the thirteenth and fourteenth centuries there were said to be more than thirty toll stations along the Weser River and at least thirty-five along the Elbe; along the Rhine, a century later, there were more than sixty such toll stations, mostly belonging to local ecclesiastical princes: Thomas Wykes, an English chronicler, described the system as "the raving madness of the Teutons." But it was not only a German disease. There were so many toll stations along the Seine in France in the late fifteenth century that it cost half its final selling price to ship grain 200 miles down the river.[4] Indeed, among the European nations, England alone enjoyed an internally unified market during the middle and late Middle Ages. This was one powerful contributory factor to England's emergence as the first great European economic power.

The amalgamation of Europe's fragmented markets was essentially a political as well as an economic process; it followed the gradual centralization of power which changed the map of Europe from the infinite complexity of the tenth century to the more or less "modern" map of the sixteenth. Here, once again, the burgeoning towns played a central and crucial role. It was the city burghers who became the allies of the nascent monarchies, thereby disassociating themselves still further from their local feudal lords while, in turn, supplying the shaky monarchs with an absolutely essential prerequisite for kingship: cash.

Thus monarch and bourgeois combined to bring about the slow growth of centralized governments, and from centralized government,

[4] *Ibid.*, pp. 134–35.

in turn, came not alone a unification of law and money but a direct stimulus to the development of commerce and industry as well. In France, for example, manufacturing was promoted by royal patronage of the famous Gobelin tapestry and Sèvres porcelain works, and business was created for innumerable craftsmen and artisans by the demands of the royal palaces and banquet halls. In other fields, growing national power also imparted a new encouragement: navies had to be built, armies had to be equipped, and these new "national" armed forces, many of whom were mercenaries, had to be paid. All this set into faster motion the pumps of monetary circulation.

EXPLORATION

Another economic impetus given by the gradual consolidation of political power was the official encouragement of exploration. All through the long years of the Middle Ages a few intrepid adventurers, like Marco Polo, had beat their way to remote regions in search of a short route to the fabled riches of India; and as a matter of fact, by the early fourteenth century the route to the Far East was well enough known so that silk from China cost but half the price of that from the Caspian area, only half the distance away.

Yet the network of all these hazardous and brave penetrations beyond Europe formed only the thinnest of spider webs. There still remained the systematic exploration of the unknown, and this awaited the kingly support of state adventurers. Columbus and Vasco da Gama, Cabral and Magellan did not venture on their epoch-making journeys as individual merchants (although they all hoped to make their fortunes thereby) but as adventurers in fleets bought with, and equipped by, royal money, bearing the royal mark of approval, and sent forth in hope of additions to the royal till.

The economic consequences of those amazing adventures were incalculably great. For one thing, they opened up an invigorating flow of precious metals into Europe. Gold and silver, coming from the great Spanish mines in Mexico and Peru, were slowly redistributed to other nations as Spain paid in gold specie for goods it bought abroad. As a result, prices rose throughout Europe—between 1520 and 1650 alone, it is estimated that they increased 200 to 400 per cent, bringing about both stimulus and stress to industry, but setting in motion a great wave of speculation and commerce.

In addition, of course, the longer-run results of exploration brought an economic stimulus of still greater importance. The establishment of colonies in the sixteenth and seventeenth centuries and the subsequent enjoyment of trade with the New World provided a tremendous boost in propelling Europe into a bustling commercial society. The discovery of the New World was, from the beginning, a catalytic and revolutionizing influence on the Old.

The forces of change that we have thus far summarized were actually visible. At any time during the long transition from a nonmarket into a market society we could have witnessed with our own eyes the traveling merchants, the expanding towns, the Crusades, the evidences of a growing national power. Yet these were not the only forces that undermined the feudal system and brought into being its commercial successor. There were, as well, powerful but invisible currents of change, currents which affected the intellectual atmosphere, the beliefs, and attitudes of Europe. One of these, of special importance, was a change in the religious climate of the times.

In our last chapter we saw how deeply the Catholic church was imbued with theological aversions to the principle of gain—and especially to interest taking or usury. An amusing story of the times sums up the position of the Church very well. Humbertus de Romanis, a monk, tells of someone who found a devil in every nook and cranny of a Florentine cloister, although in the marketplace he found but one. The reason, Humbertus explains, was that it took only one to corrupt a marketplace, where every man harbored a devil in his own heart.[5] In such a disapproving climate, it was hard for the commercial side of life to thrive.

To be sure, for all its fulminations against gain and usury, the Church itself grew in time to a position of commanding economic importance. Through its tithes and benefices it was the largest collector and distributor of money in all of Europe; and in an age in which banks and safe deposit boxes did not exist, it was the repository of much feudal wealth. Some of its sub-orders, such as the Knights Templar, became immensely wealthy and served as banking institutions, lending to needy monarchs on stiff terms. Nonetheless, all of this faintly disreputable activity was undertaken despite, and not because of, the Church's deepest convictions. For behind the ecclesiastical disapproval of wealth seeking was a deep-seated theological conviction, a firm belief in the transient nature of this life on earth and the importance of preparing for the Eternal Morrow. The Church lifted its eyes and sought to lift the eyes of others above the daily struggle for existence. It strove to minimize the importance of life on earth and to denigrate the earthly activities to which an all too weak flesh succumbed.

What changed this dampening influence on the zest of wealth making? According to the theories of the German sociologist Max Weber and the English economic historian R. H. Tawney, the underlying cause lay in the rise of a new theological point of view contained in the teachings of the Protestant reformer John Calvin (1509–1564).

Calvinism was a harsh religious philosophy. Its core was a belief in *predestination*, in the idea that from the beginning God had chosen the

[5] Beard, *A History of the Business Man*, p. 160.

saved and the damned, and that nothing man could do on earth could alter that inviolable writ. Furthermore, according to Calvin, the number of the damned exceeded by a vast amount the number of the saved, so that for the average person the chances were great that this earthly prelude was but the momentary grace given before eternal Hell and Damnation commenced.

Perhaps only a man of Calvin's iron will could have borne life under such a sentence. For we soon find that in the hands of his followers in the Lowlands and England, the inexorable and inscrutable quality of the original doctrine began to be softened. Although the idea of predestination was still preached, it was now allowed that in the tenor of one's worldly life there was a *hint* of what was to follow. Thus the English and Dutch divines taught that whereas even the saintliest-seeming man might end in Hell, the frivolous or wanton one was certainly headed there. Only in a blameless life lay the slightest chance of demonstrating that Salvation was still a possibility.

And so the Calvinists urged a life of rectitude, severity and, most important of all, diligence. In contrast to the Catholic theologians who tended to look upon worldly activity as vanity, the Calvinists sanctified and approved of endeavor as a kind of index of spiritual worth. Indeed in Calvinist hands there grew up the idea of a man *dedicated* to his work: "called" to it, as it were. Hence the fervid pursuit of one's calling, far from evidencing a distraction from religious ends, came to be taken as evidence of a dedication to a religious life. The energetic merchant was, in Calvinist eyes, a *Godly* man, not an ungodly one; and from this identification of work and worth, it was not long before the notion grew up that the more successful a man, the more worthy he was. Calvinism thus provided a religious atmosphere which, in contrast to Catholicism, encouraged wealth seeking and the temper of a business-like world.

Perhaps even more important than its encouragement in seeking wealth was the influence of Calvinism on the *use* of wealth. By and large the prevailing attitude of the prosperous Catholic merchants had been that the aim of worldly success was the enjoyment of a life of ease and luxury, while Catholic nobility displayed on occasion a positively grotesque disdain for wealth. In an orgy of gambling that gripped Paris at the end of the seventeenth century, a prince who sent his mistress a diamond worth 5,000 *livres* had it pulverized and strewn over her reply when she rejected it as being too small. The same prince eventually gambled away an income of 600,000 *livres* a year. A *maréchal* whose grandson turned up his nose at a gift of a purse of gold threw it into the street: "Let the street cleaner have it then." [6]

The Calvinist manufacturer or trader had a very different attitude

[6] Werner Sombart, *Luxury and Capitalism* (New York: Columbia University Press, 1938), pp. 120ff. Also Thirion, *La Vie Privée des Financiers au XVIIIe Siècle* (Paris: 1895), p. 292.

toward wealth. If his religion approved of diligence, it most emphatically did not approve of indulgence. Wealth was to be accumulated and put to good use, not frittered away.

Calvinism promoted an aspect of economic life of which we have hitherto heard very little: *thrift*. It made saving, the conscious abstinence from the enjoyment of income, a virtue. It made investment, the use of saving for productive purposes, an instrument of piety as well as profit. It even condoned, with various *quids* and *quos,* the payment of interest. In fact, Calvinism fostered a new conception of economic life. In place of the old ideal of social and economic stability, of knowing and keeping one's "place," it brought respectability to an ideal of struggle, of material improvement, of economic growth.

Economic historians still debate the precise degree of influence which may properly be attributed to "the Protestant Ethic" in bringing about the rise of a new gain-centered worldly philosophy. After all, there was nothing much that a Dutch Calvinist would have been able to teach an Italian Catholic banker about the virtues of a businesslike approach to life. Yet, looking back on the subsequent course of economic progress, it is striking that without exception it was the Protestant countries with their "Puritan streak" of work and thrift which forged ahead in the economic race. As one of the powerful winds of change of the sixteenth and seventeenth centuries, the new religious outlook must be counted as a highly favorable stimulus for the evolution of the market society.

The enumeration of all these currents does not exhaust the catalog of forces bearing against the old fixed economic order in Europe. The list could be expanded and greatly refined.* Yet, with all due caution we can now begin to comprehend the immense coalition of events —some as specific as the Crusades, some as diffuse as a change in religious ideals—that jointly cooperated to destroy the medieval framework of economic life and to prepare the way for a new dynamic framework of market transactions.

One important aspect of this profound alteration was the gradual *monetization of feudal obligations*. In locality after locality we can trace the conversion of the old feudal payments in *kind*—the days of labor or chickens or eggs which a lord received from his tenants—into payments of *money* dues and money rents with which they now discharged their obligations to him.

BREAKDOWN OF THE MANORIAL SYSTEM

---

*An extremely important influence (to which we will specifically turn in our next chapter) was the rise of a new interest in technology, founded on scientific inquiry into natural events. Another important causative factor was the development of modern business concepts and techniques. The German economic historian Werner Sombart has even said that if he were forced to give a single date for the "beginning" of modern capitalism he would choose 1202, the year in which appeared the *Liber Abaci,* a primer of commercial arithmetic. Similarly, the historian Oswald Spengler has called the invention of double-entry bookkeeping in 1494 an achievement worthy of being ranked with that of Columbus or Copernicus.

A number of causes lay behind this commutation of feudal payments. One was the growing urban demand for food, as town and city populations began to swell. In concentric circles around the town, money filtered out into the countryside, at one and the same time raising the capacity of the rural sector to buy urban goods and whetting its desire to do so. At the same time, in a search for larger cash incomes to buy a widening variety of goods, the nobility looked with increasing favor on receiving its rents and dues in money rather than in kind. In so doing, however, it unwittingly set into motion a cause for the further serious deterioration of the manorial system. Usually, the old feudal services were converted into *fixed* sums of money payments. This temporarily eased the cash position of the lord, but soon placed him in the squeeze which always hurts the creditor in times of inflation. And even when dues were not fixed, rents and money dues lagged sufficiently behind the growing monetary needs of the nobility, so that still further feudal obligations were monetized to keep the lord in cash. But as prices rose and the monetized style of life expanded still further, these too failed to keep him solvent.

The result was that the rural nobility, which now depended increasingly on rents and dues for its income, steadily lost its economic power.* Indeed, beginning in the sixteenth century we find a new class coming into being—the *impoverished* nobility. In the year 1530 in the Gevaudan district of France, we find that 121 lords had an aggregate income of 21,400 *livres,* but one of these seigneurs accounted for 5,000 *livres* of the sum, another for 2,000—and the rest averaged but a mean 121 *livres* apiece.[7] In fact, the shortage of cash afflicted not only the lesser nobility but even the monarchy itself. Maximilian I, Emperor of the Holy Roman Empire, on occasion lacked the cash to pay for even the overnight lodgings of his entourage on tour; and when two of his grandchildren married children of the King of Hungary, all the trappings of the weddings—2,000 caparisoned horses, jewels, and gold and silver plate—were borrowed from merchant bankers to whom Maximilian had written wheedling letters begging them not to forsake him in his moment of need.

Clearly, the manorial system was incompatible with a cash economy; for while the nobility was pinched between rising prices and costs and static incomes, the merchant classes, to whom cash naturally gravitated, steadily increased their power. In the Gevaudan district, for example, where the richest lord had his income of 5,000 *livres,* the richest town merchants had incomes up to 65,000 *livres.* In Germany, while Maximilian scratched for cash, the great banking families of Augsburg

---

*This process of economic decline was considerably enhanced by the ineptitude of the nobility as managers of their estates. The descendants of the Crusaders were not much more businesslike than their ancestors.

[7] *Cambridge Economic History of Europe,* I, 557–58.

commanded incomes far larger than Maximilian's entire kingly revenue. In Italy, the Gianfigliazzi of Florence, who began as "nobodies" lending money to the Bishop of Fiesole, ended up stripping him of his possessions and leaving him a pauper; while in Tuscany, the lords who looked down their noses at usurers in the tenth century lost their estates to them in the twelfth and thirteenth. All over Europe men of mean social standing turned the monetary economy to good account. One Jean Amici of Toulouse made a fortune in English booty during the Hundred Years War; Guillaume de St-Yon grew rich by selling meat at rapacious prices to Paris; and Jacques Coeur, the most extraordinary figure of all, rose from merchant to King's coiner, then to King's purchasing agent, then to financier not for, but *of,* the King, during the course of which he accumulated a huge fortune estimated at 27 million *écus.**

APPEARANCE OF THE ECONOMIC ASPECT OF LIFE

Behind all of these profoundly disturbing events we can discern an immense process of change that literally revolutionized the economic organization of Europe. Whereas in the tenth century, cash and money transactions were only peripheral to the solution of the economic problem, by the sixteenth and seventeenth centuries cash and transactions were already beginning to provide the very molecular force of economic cohesion.

But over and above this general monetization of life, another and perhaps even more profound change was taking place. This was the emergence of a separate *economic* sphere of activity visible within, and separable from, the surrounding matrix of social life. It was the creation of a whole aspect of society which had never previously existed, but which was thenceforth to constitute a commanding facet of human existence.[8]

In antiquity and feudal times, as we have seen, one could not easily separate the economic motivations or even the economic actions of the great mass of men from the normal round of existence itself. The peasant following his immemorial ways was hardly conscious of acting according to "economic" motives; indeed, he did not: he heeded the orders of his lord or the dictates of custom. Nor was the lord himself economically oriented. His interests were military or political or reli-

*Note, however, that Coeur eventually fell from power, was imprisoned, and died in exile. The counting house was not yet fully master of the castle.

[8] The following section owes much to the insights of Karl Polanyi's famous *The Great Transformation* (Boston: Beacon Press, Inc., 1957, paperback ed.), Part II.

gious, and not basically oriented toward the idea of gain or increase. Even in the towns, as we have seen, the conduct of ordinary business was inextricably mixed with non-economic concerns. The undeniable fact that men were acquisitive, not to say avaricious, did not yet impart its flavor to life in general; the making of money, as we have been at some pains to indicate, was a tangential rather than a central concern of ancient or medieval existence.

LABOR, LAND, AND CAPITAL COME INTO BEING

With the ever-widening scope of monetization, however, a genuinely new element of life came slowly to the fore. Labor, for example, emerged as an activity quite different from the past. No longer was "labor" part of an explicit social relationship in which one man (serf or apprentice) worked for another (lord or guildmaster) in return for at least an assurance of subsistence. Labor was now a mere quantum of effort, a "commodity" to be disposed of on the marketplace for the best price it could bring, quite devoid of any reciprocal responsibilities on the part of the buyer, beyond the payment of wages. If those wages were not enough to provide subsistence—well, that was not the buyer's responsibility. He had bought his "labor," and that was that.

This emergence of "pure" labor—labor as a quantity of effort detached from a man's life and bought on the market in fixed amounts—had a parallel in two other main elements of economic life. One of these was land. Formerly conceived as the territory of a great lord, as inviolable as the territory of a modern nation-state, land was now also seen in its economic aspect as something to be bought or leased for the economic return it yielded. An estate which was once the core of political and administrative power became a "property" with a market price, available for any number of uses, even as a site for a factory. The dues, the payments in kind, the intangibles of prestige and power which once flowed from the ownership of land gave way to the single return of *rent;* that is, to a money return derived from putting land to *profitable* use.

The same transformation became true of property. As it was conceived in antiquity and throughout most of the Middle Ages, property was a sum of tangible wealth, a hoard, a treasury of plate, bullion, or jewels. Very logically, it was realized in the form of luxurious homes, in castles and armaments, in costly robes and trappings. But with the monetization and commercialization of society, property, too, became expressible in a monetary equivalent: a man was now "worth" so many *livres,* or *écus,* or pounds, or whatever. Property became *capital,* manifesting itself no longer in specific goods, but as an abstract sum of infinitely flexible use whose "value" was its capacity to earn *interest* or *profits.*

None of these changes, it should be emphasized, was planned, clearly foreseen, or for that matter, welcomed. It was not with equanimity that the feudal hierarchies saw their prerogatives nibbled away by the mercantile classes. Neither did the tradition-preserving guildmaster desire his own enforced metamorphosis into a "capitalist," a man of affairs guided by market signals and beset by competition. But perhaps for no social class was the transition more painful than for the peasant, caught up in a process of history that dispossessed him from his livelihood and made him a landless laborer.

This process, which was particularly important in England, was the *enclosure movement,* a by-product of the monetization of feudal life. Starting as early as the thirteenth century, the landed aristocracy, increasingly squeezed for cash, began to view their estates not merely as the ancestral fiefs, but as potential sources of cash revenue. In order to raise larger cash crops, they therefore began to "enclose" the pasture which had previously been deemed "common land." Communal grazing fields, which had in fact always belonged to the lord despite their communal use, were now claimed for the exclusive benefit of the lord and turned into sheepwalks. Why sheepwalks? Because a rising demand for woolen cloth was making sheep-raising a highly profitable occupation. The medieval historian Eileen Power writes:

The visitor to the House of Lords, looking respectfully upon that august assembly, cannot fail to be struck by a stout and ungainly object facing the throne—an ungainly object upon which in full session of Parliament, he will observe seated the Lord Chancellor of England. The object is a woolsack, and it is stuffed as full of pure history as the office of the Lord Chancellor itself. . . The Lord Chancellor of England is seated upon a woolsack because it was upon a woolsack that this fair land rose to prosperity.[9]

The enclosure process in England proceeded at an irregular pace over the long centuries; not until the late eighteenth and early nineteenth centuries did it reach its engulfing climax.* By its end, some ten million acres, nearly *half* the arable land of England, had been "enclosed"—in its early Tudor days by the more or less high-handed conversion of the "commons" to sheep-raising; in the final period, by the forcible consolidation of strips and plots into tracts suitable for commercial farming, for which tenants presumably received "fair compensation."

From a strictly economic point of view, the enclosure movement was unquestionably salutary in that it brought into productive employment

---

[9] *Medieval People* (Garden City, N.Y.: Doubleday & Co., Inc., Anchor Books, 1954), p. 125.
*In other European nations an enclosure process also took place, but at a much slower pace. In France, Italy, and southern Germany the small-holder peasant persisted long after he had virtually ceased to exist in England; in northeastern Germany, on the other hand, the small peasant was deprived of his holdings and turned into a landless proletarian.

land which had hitherto yielded only a pittance. Indeed, particularly in the eighteenth and nineteenth centuries, enclosure was the means by which England "rationalized" its agriculture and finally escaped from the inefficiency of the traditional manorial strip system. But there was another, crueler side to enclosure. As the common fields were enclosed, it became ever more difficult for the tenant to support himself. In the fifteenth and sixteenth centuries, when the initial enclosure of the commons reached its peak, as many as three-fourths to nine-tenths of the tenants of some estates were simply turned off the farm. Whole hamlets were thus wiped out. Sir Thomas More described it savagely in Book I of his *Utopia*.

Your sheep that were wont to be so meek and tame, and so small eaters, now, as I hear say, be become so great devourers and so wild, that they eat up and swallow down the very men themselves. They consume, destroy and devour whole fields, houses and cities. For look in what parts of the realm doth grow the finest, and therefore dearest wool, there noblemen and gentlemen, yea and certain abbots, holy men Got wot, not contenting themselves with the yearly revenues and profits that were wont to grow to their forefathers and predecessors of their land . . . leave no ground for tillage, they enclose all into pastures, they throw down houses, they pluck down towns and leave nothing standing, but only the church to make of it a sheep house . . .

The enclosure process provided a powerful force for the dissolution of feudal ties and the formation of the new relationships of a market society. By dispossessing the peasant, it "created" a new kind of labor force—landless, without traditional sources of income, however meager, impelled to find work for wages wherever it might be available.

Together with this agricultural proletariat, we begin to see the emergence of an urban proletariat, partly brought about by a gradual transformation of guilds into more "business-like" firms, partly by the immigration into the cities of some of the new landless peasantry. And then to exacerbate the whole situation, from the middle of the eighteenth century a rising population (itself traceable in large measure to the increase in food output resulting from the enclosures) began to pour growing numbers onto the labor market. As a result of this complicated interplay of causes and effects, we find England plagued with the problem of the "wandering poor." One not untypical proposal of the eighteenth century was that they be confined in what a reformer candidly termed "Houses of Terror."

Thus did the emergence of a market-oriented system grind into being a "labor force," and though the process of adjustment for other classes of society was not so brutal, it, too, exacted its social price. Tenaciously the guildmasters fought against the invasion of their protected trades by manufacturers who trespassed on traditional preserves or who upset established modes of production with new machinery. Doggedly the landed nobility sought to protect their ancient privileges against the encroachment of the moneyed *nouveaux riches.*

Yet the process of economic enlargement, breaking down the established routines of the past, rearranging the power and prestige of all social classes, could not be stopped. Ruthlessly it pursued its historic course and impartially it distributed its historic rewards and sacrifices. Although stretched out over a long period, it was not an evolution but a slow revolution which overtook European economic society. Only when that society had run its long gauntlet, suffering one of the most wrenching dislocations of history, would the world of transactions appear "natural" and "normal" and the categories of "land," "labor," and "capital" become so matter-of-fact that it would be difficult to believe they had not always existed.

Yet, as we have seen, it was not at all "natural" and "normal" to have free, wage-earning, contractual labor or rentable, profit-producing land or fluid, investment-seeking capital. They were *creations* of the great transformation of a pre-market into a market society. Economics calls these creations the *factors of production,* and much of economics is concerned with analyzing the manner in which these three basic constituents of the productive process are combined by the market mechanism.

What we must realize at this stage of our inquiry, however, is that "land," "labor," and "capital" do not exist as eternal categories of *social* organization. Admittedly, they are categories of *nature,* but these eternal aspects of the productive process—the soil, human effort, and the artifacts which can be applied to production—do not take on, in every society, the specific separation that distinguishes them in a market society. In pre-market economies, land, labor, and capital are inextricably mixed and mingled in the figure of slave and serf, lord and guildmaster—none of whom enters the production process as the incarnation of a specific economic function offered for a price. The slave is not a "worker," the guildmaster is not a "capitalist," nor is the lord a "landlord." Only when a social system has evolved in which labor is sold, land is rented, and capital is freely invested do we find the categories of economics emerging from the flux of life.

Modern economics thus describes the manner in which a certain kind of society, with a specific history of acculturation and institutional evolution, solves its economic problems. It may well be that in another era there will no longer be "land," "labor," and "capital". If, for example, a pure communist society ever evolves, the method by which the social product will be assured or distributed need not bear any more relation to our present system of wage payments or rental incomes or profit-shares than our own system bears to its feudal predecessor. In that case, "economics" as we know it will have to be revised to correspond to the new social relationships by which the production and distribution problems will be solved.

But the emergence of a market society, with its new factors of production, was not yet the only creation of the forces of change we have examined in this chapter. Along with the new relationships of man to man in the marketplace, there arose a new form of *social control* to take over the guidance of the economy from the former aegis of tradition and command.

RISE OF
THE "PROFIT
MOTIVE"

What was this new form of control? Essentially, it was a pattern of social behavior, of normal, everyday action that the new market environment imposed on society. And what was this pattern of behavior? In the language of the economist, it was the drive to *maximize one's income* (or to minimize one's expenditures) by concluding the best possible bargains on the marketplace. In ordinary language, it was the drive to buy cheap and sell dear, or in business terminology, the *profit motive*.

The market society had not, of course, invented this motive. Perhaps it did not even intensify it. But it did make it a *ubiquitous* and *necessitous* aspect of social behavior. Although men may have *felt* acquisitive during the Middle Ages or antiquity, they did not enter en masse into market transactions for the basic economic activities of their livelihoods. And even when, for instance, a peasant sold his few eggs at the town market, rarely was the transaction a matter of overriding importance for his continued existence. Market transactions in a fundamentally nonmarket society were thus a subsidiary activity, a means of supplementing a livelihood which, however sparse, was largely independent of buying or selling.

With the monetization of labor, land, and capital, however, transactions became *universal* and *critical* activities. Now everything was for sale, and the terms of transactions were anything but subsidiary to existence itself. To a man who sold his labor on a market, in a society that assumed no responsibility for his upkeep, the price at which he concluded his bargain was all-important. So it was with the landlord and the budding capitalist. For each of these a good bargain could spell riches—and a bad one, ruin. Thus the pattern of economic maximization was generalized throughout society and given an inherent urgency which made it a powerful force for shaping human behavior.

The new market society did more than merely bring about an environment in which men were forced to follow their economic self-interest. It brought into being at the same time a social environment in which men could be *controlled* in their economic activities. With the emergence of a generalized drive to maximize income, it now became possible to steer the application of men's energies in various directions by raising or lowering the rewards offered for different tasks. If more effort was needed in the making of shoes, the market mechanism could attract that effort by raising the rewards for land, labor, and capital employed in shoe manufacture. Or if society wished to diminish the amount of social energy employed in making hats, it had but to lower the market rewards—wages, rents, profits—of hat manufacture, and there would ensue an exodus of the factors of the production from hat-making toward other, more profitable fields. Thus, in the universalized presence of a drive toward income maximization, society possessed a powerful tool for *allocating its resources.*

Note, however, that this regulatory device required more than just the profit motive. Equally necessary was a *mobility of the factors of production.* To the extent that labor was tied to its manorial estates or to its guild establishments, or that guildmasters were forbidden to expand their scales of operation or to venture into new endeavors, the control mechanism would not work. In that case, raising rewards for shoes or lowering rewards for hats could only increase or decrease the incomes of those already engaged in the field, but could not bring about any substantial increase or decrease in the quantity of social effort put into each pursuit.

An essential part of the evolution of the market society was thus not only the monetization of life but the mobilization of life—that is, the dissolution of those ties of place and station which were the very cement of feudal existence. And this essential requirement of mobility leads to a further point. Mobility meant that any job or activity was now open to all comers. *Competition appeared.* The traditional compartmented division of feudal labor had to give way to a universal rivalry among employments. No longer was each employment a protected haven for apprentice and guildmaster alike. Now any worker and any employer could be displaced from his task by a competitor who would do the job more cheaply.

For those who *were* displaced, the institution of competition must have seemed a harsh and unjust one; but for society as a whole, it provided an essential safeguard. Having freed the drive of economic self-interest from the limitations of feudalism, society seemed in danger of being endlessly gouged by profiteering merchants or demanding workmen—the very fear of the medieval social philosopher. What competition did, however, was to *contain* the economic drive. By pitting seller against seller, it made it difficult for any single participant to gain a strategic position for his own advantage. Even though every seller in a competitive market would *like* to charge monopolistic prices, the presence of a crowd of eager competitors at his elbow, each ready to steal away the lucrative business of the next by shading his price, assured society that ultimate selling prices would be no more than the minimum required to make continued production possible.

THE WORKINGS
OF
COMPETITION

Competition not only prevented the seller from using his economic power to general social disadvantage, but it also assured a similar restraint on the buyer. No single purchaser could force prices below the cost of production, for other eager buyers would quickly outbid him. And this competitive mechanism worked not only in the market for commodities but in the market for factors, as well. Clearly, no laborer could ask for more than the "going" wage if he wanted to secure employment. But neither would he have to take less from any single wage-cutting employer, for he could always find better wages elsewhere.

Even if all employers in, say, the shoe trade paid lower wages than employers in the hat trade, again competition would provide the remedy. For labor would then leave the shoe trade for the hat trade, thereby bringing about a shortage of workers in the shoe plants and a surplus in hats. Wages would therefore rise in the shoe trade as manufacturers sought to bid labor back into their plants, and they would decline in hats.

Now we begin to see the complex nature of the price control mechanism provided by the competitive struggle. Across the market, buyer and seller faced one another in a contest wherein every buyer sought to pay as little as possible and every seller sought to gain as much as possible. By itself this would be merely a tug of war about the outcome of which one could say very little. But because sellers on one side of the tug of war were themselves engaged in a contest with one another, and because buyers at the other end of the rope were engaged in a similar contest, the outcome of the contest was quite predictable. While prices of goods might sway back and forth in the short run, the interaction of supply and demand operated to bring them always back toward *costs of production* in the long run. And while incomes of factors in different employments might fluctuate temporarily upward or downward, again the competitive mechanism operated always to bring the rewards for similar tasks into a common alignment.

We shall investigate this process more carefully in Part Three. Now, only one final point should be noted. We have seen how a competitive market economy operated to fulfill the wants of society. But who was to say what its wants were?

In pre-market economies, such a question did not pose subtle problems. The "wants" of such societies were either codified by ageless tradition or specifically formulated by its rulers. But in a market society, the specification of wants suddenly takes on a new dimension. It now consists of the demands of everyone who has the wherewithal to enter the market. *The "wants" of society are thus expressed by millions of daily orders placed on the market by an entire community.* As these orders enter the marketplace they affect the prices at which goods sell. Thus shifts in prices become, in effect, signals to producers: rising prices betokening an increase in demand and an actual or prospective increase in rewards; falling prices signaling the opposite.

In this way the market society catapults the consumer into a position of extraordinary importance. On his ability and willingness to buy hinges the panoply of demands which confront society's producers. If consumers do not want a good or service, or if they do not wish to buy it at its offered price, that good or service will go unsold. In that case, the production effort needed to supply it will not pay for itself and will soon terminate. *In a market society, the consumer is the ultimate formulator of the pattern of economic activity.* He is now the sovereign of the economic process—sovereign not as an individual, but as a member of an entire society which collectively guides and controls its on-going productive effort through a market mechanism.

Does the market really work as this first introduction to it suggests? Much of the rest of this book will be devoted to that very question—that is, to what extent the outcome of the market process in actuality corresponds with its outcome in a "pure" market system. But we are not yet ready to consider that problem. We have so far traced the market only to its first half-formed appearance when the "theory" of a market was still far from formulated in men's minds. Let us therefore return to our historical narrative as the market system begins to evolve into capitalism itself. For the slow evolution of the market system cannot be considered merely as the rise of a new mechanism of social control. It must also be seen as the evolution of a new socio-economic organization of society, a new structure of law, of political organization, of social institutions, of ideas.

For example, a market society could not coexist with a form of legal organization that did not recognize the freedom of the individual to contract for employment as he wished. Nor could it exist under a code of law that barely recognized "private property" as we know it. Neither could it flourish under a political system in which privilege accrued to birth rather than to achievement, or in which the landed nobility by law and usage possessed the main power to regulate society's affairs. Feudalism as a legal, political, and social organization had to give way to another form of society with a very different set of laws, customs, and political institutions.

We call that other form of society *capitalism*, and the long process of change which we have studied in its economic aspects can be given a wider interpretation as the evolution (and revolution) of feudalism into capitalism. The student of government notes the growth of political representation on the part of the middle classes, a growth most dramatically symbolized in the overthrow of feudal power in the French Revolution, but most fully realized in the long rise of parliamentary power in England. So, too, a student of law notes the rise of the law of contract, or the decline of the legal restrictions of serfdom or in the legal prerogatives of the aristocracy. Without a study of these changes, we cannot fully comprehend the manner in which capitalism arose from feudalism. Yet without an understanding of the deeper-seated economic changes which took place, so to speak, spontaneously and without conscious human intervention, the accompanying legal and political changes cannot themselves be understood.

Many of those necessary changes did not take place until the sixteenth and seventeenth centuries, or even later. After all, serfdom was not formally abolished in France until 1789; and in Germany, not until a half century later. Certainly by 1700, the market society had not yet reached a stage in which capitalism had achieved full legal and political status. Although "land," "labor," and "capital" had come into being, although a highly monetized society characterized France and England and Holland, although the merchant classes were strong and rich, there was still lacking a final achievement of economic "freedom," a final throwing off of traditional bonds and restrictions on labor and capital, a final loosening of controls and commands from above. In England in the late 1700's, for example, no master hatter could employ more than two apprentices, or no master cutler more than one, and these and similar guild regulations did not vanish until the medieval Statute of Artificers was repealed in 1813. Likewise in France, an immense web of regulations bound the would-be capitalist. Rules and edicts, many of them seeking to standardize production, laid down the exact number of threads to be woven into the cloths of the French textile manufacturers, and to disregard these laws was to risk pillorying—first for the cloth, then for the manufacturer.

Thus in the decades before the opening of the eighteenth century—indeed, well into that century—we find the great revolution of the market still incomplete; or rather, we find the nearly complete process of monetization and commercialization contained uncomfortably within a frame of legal and social organization not yet fully adapted to it.

We call this stage of pre-capitalism *mercantilism,* but we must not think of mercantilism solely as a time in which a nascent capitalism was held back by an outmoded social and economic order. On the contrary, it was also a time when the final achievement of capitalism was powerfully stimulated and accelerated. For the policies of mercantilism were devoted to building up national economic strength—in part by subsidy, in part by urging the rising manufacturer to expand. In France, Colbert, finance minister to Louis XIV, told the butterfly court of Versailles that the greatness of the country depended on its wealth, its wealth on its work, and its work on the encouragement of those industrial, commercial, and agricultural producers who were, in the main, regarded with supercilious disdain. With this end in mind he struggled to encourage the rising *bourgeoisie* and to promote the interests of manufacture and commerce in general.

He did so in a curiously self-defeating way, with a web of regulations, tariffs, and ordinances which suffocated the entrepreneurial impulse at the same time that it sought to foster it; and the social benefits of his economic policy were largely vitiated by the necessity to abide by a feudal system of taxation which was harsh, iniquitous, and corrupt. Yet, as in no previous period, the seeds for subsequent growth were deliberately sown all through the mercantile era by the royal patronage of shipyards and porcelain factories, tapestry works and arsenals. It is curious that the zest for expansion was often more notable on the part of the monarch than the manufacturer: Frederick the Great complained in the margin of one of his edicts that his commoners had to be dragged to their profits "by their noses and ears."[10]

And one significant anomaly is also to be remarked. Despite the multiplicity of regulations which mercantilism imposed, it was also during these years—perhaps because of the very difficulties of regulation—that the idea of a totally free and unhampered market began to gain acceptance. "Que faut–il faire pour vous aider?" (How may we help you?) wrote Colbert to the merchant Legendre. "Nous laissez faire" (Leave us alone) was the answer. Colbert scarcely heeded the advice, but soon it would become the slogan of the new capitalist world.

A full-scale review of economic history must study European mercantilism at length, for it is a critical era of economic history, an era in which industrial growth was first launched as a deliberate act of national economic policy. Yet it was, so to speak, a position of unstable rest, not fully emancipated from the past, not fully entrant upon the future. The basic elements of capitalism had been created and waited for a full trial. The trial was soon to come, first in England, later throughout Europe and in the United States. We shall soon watch this major chapter of economic history unfold.

[10] Lowe, *Economics and Sociology* (London: George Allen & Unwin, 1935), p. 23.

SUMMARY

1. *Powerful forces of change* were operative within European feudalism, and served gradually to introduce the structure of a market society. Primary among these forces were:
   - The role of *the itinerant merchant* in introducing trade, money, and the acquisitive spirit into feudal life.
   - The *process of urbanization* as a source of economic activity, and as the locus of a new, trade-centered seat of power.
   - *The Crusades* as a force for the disruption of feudal life and the introduction of new ideas.
   - The rise of unifying, commerce-supporting *national states*.
   - The stimulus of the *Age of Exploration* and of the *gold* it brought into Europe.
   - The emergence of *new religious ideas* more sympathetic to business activity than Catholicism had been.
   - The *monetization of dues* within the manorial system.

2. As a consequence of these forces, we begin to see *the separation of economic from social life*. The processes of production and distribution were no longer indistinguishably melded into the prevailing religious, social, and political customs and practices, but now began to form a sharply distinct area of life in themselves.

3. With the rise of the economic aspect of life, we see *deep-seated transformations* taking place. The peasant-serf is no longer bound to the land, but becomes a free, mobile laborer; the guildmaster is no longer hobbled by guild rules but becomes an independent entrepreneur; the lord of the land becomes (in the modern sense of the word) a landlord. The transformation was a long and often violent one, especially in the complex case of the enclosures.

4. The advent of free laborers, capitalists, and landlords, each selling his services on the market for land and capital and labor, made it possible to speak of the *"factors of production."* By this was implied two things: the *physical categories* of land, labor, and capital as distinguishable agents in the production process, and the *social categories* of laborers, landowners, and capitalists as distinct groups or classes entering the marketplace.

5. The emergence of the factors of production signaled the entrance of the full-fledged *market system*. Its earmarks were:
   - The appearance of the *"profit motive"* as a guide for economic behavior.
   - The greatly increased legal and social *mobility* of the factors of production.
   - A widespread *competition* among all individuals in their economic activities.
   - The *appearance of "demand"*—the amounts that consumers were willing and able to spend—as the new regulator of production.
   - The *elevation of the consumer*, en masse, to a new position of economic control.

6. The market system required not alone the economic innovations of the market process, but a whole panoply of *legal and political changes* as well. The freedom and independence of the economic person, an idea quite incompatible with feudalism, was an essential precondition for a fluid market system.

7. The transformation was not achieved in one bound. The evolution of feudalism into a free market system led to a transitional stage called *mercantilism*. Mercantilism was characterized by an effort to regulate commerce and production in great detail, while at the same time supporting and encouraging it.

8. The complexities and difficulties of mercantilist regulation gave rise to the slogan that was to be the rallying cry of the new philosophy of *capitalism: laissez faire* (leave us alone).

1. What was so disruptive to feudal life about the activities of the merchant? Are business activities today also the causes of social stress?

2. The underdeveloped nations today often resemble the economies of antiquity or of the Middle Ages, at least insofar as their poverty and stagnation is concerned. Discuss what relevance, if any, the forces of change mentioned in this chapter have on the modernization of these areas. Are there new forces of change?

3. The leading nations in the world, so far as per capita income is concerned, are the U.S., New Zealand and Australia, and the Scandanavian states. Among the less affluent Western nations are Ireland, Spain, Portugal, and Italy. Do you think this proves the validity of the Weber-Tawney thesis as to the importance of the Protestant ethic in economic growth? Does the addition of Latin America change the argument? Asia?

4. The process of monetization and commercialization was often a violent one in Europe. Do you think the Civil War, which ended slavery and displaced the southern semifeudal plantation system, could be considered as part of the same transformation in America?

5. Is economic life distinctly separate from social and political life in America?

6. Do you think most people in the United States obey the profit motive? Are most people mobile in the United States? Do you know anyone who has changed his residence because of economic considerations? His profession?

7. Profit-making is certainly as old as man. Do you think we can speak of the origins of capitalism as being equally old?

8. How would you define *feudalism? Mercantilism? Capitalism?*

9. What legal and political changes were necessary to change feudalism into a market system?

4 THE INDUSTRIAL REVOLUTION

Heretofore, in our survey of economic history, we have concentrated almost entirely on two main currents of economic activity: agriculture and commerce. Yet there was, from earliest days, a third essential source of economic wealth—industry—which we have purposely let slip by unnoticed. For in contrast to agriculture and commerce, industrial manufacture did not leave a major imprint on economic society itself. As a peasant, a serf, a merchant, or a guildsman, the actors in the economic drama directly typified the basic activities of their times, but this would not have been true of someone in industry. Such a person as a "factory worker"—indeed, the very idea of an *industrial* "proletarian"—was singularly absent from the long years before the late seventeenth century.

Let us note as well that the "industrial capitalist" was also lacking. Most of the moneymakers of the past gained their fortunes by trading, or transporting, or lending—not by making. It is amusing—more than amusing: instructive—to mark the best ways of getting rich enumerated by Leon Battista Alberti, a fifteenth-century architect, musician, and courtier. They are: (1) wholesale trade; (2) seeking for treasure trove; (3) ingratiating oneself with a rich man to become his heir; (4) usury; (5) the rental of pastures, horses, and the like. A seventeenth-century commentator adds to this: royal service, soldiering, and alchemy. Manufacturing is conspicuously absent from both lists.[1]

Granted, in ancient Greece, Demosthenes had an armor and a cabinet "factory"; and from long before his time, in ancient Egypt we even have the attendance record of workers in "factories" for the production of cloth. Yet it is clear that this form of production was far less important than either agriculture or commerce in shaping the economic texture of the times. For one thing, the typical scale of manufacture was small. Note that the very word "manufacture" (from the Latin *manus,* hand, and *facere,* to make) implies a system of hand, rather than machine, technology. Demosthenes' enterprises, for example, employed no more than fifty men. It is true that from time to time we do come across quite large manufacturing operations; already in the second century A.D. a Roman brickworks employed forty-six foremen; and by the time we reach the seventeenth century, enterprises with several hundred workers are not unheard of. Yet such operations were the exception rather than the rule. In 1660, for instance, a steelmaker in France needed no more than three tons of pig iron a year for his output of swords or sickle blades or artistic cutlery. Similarly, most guild operations, as we have seen, were small. As late as 1843, a Prussian census showed only sixty-seven working people for every hundred masters.[2] In the past—as today in the East and Near East—most "industry" was carried on in the backs of small shops or the dim cellars of houses, in sheds behind bazaars, or in the scattered homes of workers to whom materials would be supplied by an organizing "capitalist."

In addition to the smallness of the scale of industry, another aspect of the times delayed industrial manufacture from making known its social presence. This was the absence of any sustained interest in the development of an *industrial technology.* Throughout antiquity and the Middle Ages, little of society's creative energy was directed toward a systematic improvement of manufacturing techniques. It is indicative of the disinterest attached to productive technology that so simple and important an invention as the horse collar had to await the Middle Ages

[1] Werner Sombart, *The Quintessence of Capitalism* (New York: E. P. Dutton & Co., Inc., 1915), pp. 34–35.

[2] *Cambridge Economic History of Europe,* II, 34; John U. Nef, *Cultural Foundations of Industrial Civilization* (New York: Harper & Row, Torchbooks, 1960), p. 131; R. H. Tawney, *Equality,* 4th ed. (London: Macmillan & Co., Ltd., 1952), p. 59.

for discovery: the Egyptians, Greeks, and Romans, who were capable of a magnificent technology of architecture, were simply not fundamentally concerned with the techniques of everyday production itself.[3] Even well into the Renaissance and Reformation, the idea of industrial technology hardly attracted serious thought. Leonardo da Vinci, for example, whose fecund mind played with inventions of the most varied kind, was primarily interested in machines for war or for amusement. His profound excursions into technology were neither motivated by, nor put to, practical use.

There was good reason for this prevailing indifference: in the societies of the pre-market world, the necessary economic base for any large-scale industrial manufacture was totally lacking. In economies sustained by the labor of peasants, slaves, and serfs, economies in which the stream of money was small and the current of economic life, accidents of war and nature aside, relatively changeless from year to year, who could dream of a process in which avalanches of goods would be turned out? The very idea of industrial production on the large scale was inconceivable in such an unmonetized, static setting.*

For all these reasons, the pace of industrialization was slow. It is a question whether Europe in the year 1200 was significantly more technologically advanced than it had been in the year 200 B.C. The widespread use of waterpower in industry, for instance, did not appear until the fifteenth century, and it would be still another century before windmills provided a common means of tapping the energy of nature. The mechanical clock dates from the thirteenth century, but not for 200 years would significant improvements be made in instruments for navigation, surveying, or measuring. Movable type, that indispensable forerunner of mass communication, did not appear until 1450.

In short, despite important pockets of highly organized production, notably in the thirteenth-century Flanders cloth industry and in Northern Italian towns, not until the late sixteenth century can we discern the first signs of a general ground swell of industrial technology, and even in that day it would have been impossible to foresee that one day industry would be the dominant form of productive organization. As a matter of fact, as late as the eighteenth century, when manufacturing had already begun to reach respectable proportions as a form of social endeavor, it was not generally thought of as inherently possessing any but secondary importance. Agriculture, of course, was the visible foundation of the nation itself. Trading was regarded as useful insofar as it brought a nation gold. But, at best, industry was seen as a hand-

---

[3] E. M. Jope, in *History of Technology,* eds. Charles J. Singer *et al.* (New York: Oxford University Press, 1956), II, 553. There was, however, considerable improvement in mining techniques, especially for silver and copper.

*Even today, one sees the difficulties of the unmonetized, static, underdeveloped societies in finding an industrial-minded, rather than commercial-minded, entrepreneurial group.

maiden of the others, providing the trader with the goods to export, or serving the farmer as a secondary market for the products of the earth.*

What finally conspired to bring manufacturing into a position of overwhelming prominence?

It was a complex concatenation of events that finally brought about the eruption we call the industrial revolution. As with the Commercial Revolution and the Mercantile era which preceded it and formed its indispensable preparation, it is impossible in a few pages to do justice to the many currents which contributed to that final outburst of industrial technology. But if we cannot trace the process in detail, we can at least gain an idea of its impetus and of the main forces behind it if we turn now to England around 1750. Here, for the first time, industrial manufacture as a major form of economic activity began to work its immense social transformations. Let us observe the process as it took place.

Why did the industrial revolution originally take place in England and not on the Continent? To answer the question we must look at the background factors which distinguished England from most other European nations in the eighteenth century.

The first of these factors was simply that England was relatively wealthy. In fact, a century of successful exploration, slave trading, piracy, war, and commerce had made her the richest nation in the world. Even more important, her riches had accrued not merely to a few nobles, but to a large upper-middle stratum of commercial *bourgeoisie*. England was thus one of the first nations to develop, albeit on a tiny scale, a prime requisite of an industrial economy: a "mass" consumer market. As a result, a rising pressure of demand inspired a search for new techniques. Very typically, the Society for the Encouragement of Arts and Manufactures (itself a significant child of the age) offered a prize for a machine that would spin six threads of cotton at one time, thus enabling the spinner to keep up with the technologically more advanced weaver. It was this which led, at least in part, to Arkwright's spinning jenny, of which we shall hear more shortly.

Second, England was the scene of the most successful and thoroughgoing transformation of feudal society into commercial society. The process of enclosures was a significant clue to a historic change that sharply marked off England from the Continent. It was that in England

---

*It was in the mid-eighteenth century that the French doctor François Quesnay propounded one of the first systematic explanations of economic production and distribution. It is noteworthy that in his system (called *Physiocracy*) only the farmer was regarded as a producer of net worth; and the manufacturer, while his utility was not ignored, was nonetheless relegated to the "sterile" (i.e., non-wealth-producing) classes.

alone the aristocracy had made its peace with (and more than that, found its profits in) commerce. Although sharp conflicts of interest remained between the "old" landed power and the "new" monied power, by 1700 the ruling orders in England had decisively opted for adaptation rather than resistance to the demands of the market economy.[4]

Third, England was the locus of a unique enthusiasm for science and engineering. The famous Royal Academy, of which Newton was an early president, was founded in 1660 and was the immediate source of much intellectual excitement. Indeed, a popular interest in gadgets, machines, and devices of all sorts soon became a mild national obsession: *Gentlemen's Magazine,* a kind of *New Yorker* of the period, announced in 1729 that it would henceforth keep its readers "abreast of every invention"—a task which the mounting flow of inventions soon rendered quite impossible. No less important was an enthusiasm of the British landed aristocracy for scientific farming: English landlords displayed an interest in matters of crop rotation and fertilizer which their French counterparts would have found quite beneath their dignity.

Then there were a host of other background causes, some as fortuitous as the immense resources of coal and iron ore on which the British sat; others as purposeful as the development of a national patent system which deliberately sought to stimulate and protect the act of invention itself.* And then, as the Revolution came into being, it fed upon itself. The new techniques (especially in textiles) simply destroyed their handicraft competition around the world and thus enormously increased their own markets. But what finally brought all these factors into operation was the energy of a group of New Men who made of the latent opportunities of history a vehicle for their own rise to fame and fortune.

RISE OF
THE NEW MEN

One such, for instance, was John Wilkinson. The son of an old-fashioned small-scale iron producer, Wilkinson was a man possessed by the technological possibilities of his business. He invented a dozen

[4] See Barrington Moore, *Social Origins of Dictatorship and Democracy* (Boston: Beacon Press, Inc., 1966), Chap. I.

*Phyllis Deane, in *The First Industrial Revolution* (paperback ed., Cambridge University Press, 1965) ascribes the onset of industrialism in England to a somewhat different set of causes: a rise in population, better food-producing techniques, a boom in foreign trade, and a vast improvement in transportation. There is no doubt that these were also indispensable elements in the process. I mention Miss Deane's book so that a student will not think that there is only one "right" way of accounting for very complex historical transformations. For yet another exceedingly good general account of the process, one might turn to the fascinating chapter by David Landes, "Technological Change and Development in Western Europe" in the *Cambridge Economic History* (Cambridge University Press, 1965), VI, esp. pp. 274–350, where the emphasis is focused on the process of technological advance, and in particular on the strategic inventions of steam power, and textile machinery.

things: a rolling mill and a steam lathe, a process for the manufacture of iron pipes, and a design for machining accurate cylinders. Typically, he decided that the old-fashioned leather bellows used in the making of iron itself were not efficient, and so he determined to make iron ones. "Everybody laughed at me," he later wrote. "I did it and applied the steam engine to blow them and they all cried: 'Who could have thought of it?'"

He followed his success in production with a passion for application: everything must be made of iron: pipes, bridges, even ships. After a ship made of iron plates had been successfully launched, he wrote a friend: "It answers all my expectations, and has convinced the unbelievers, who were nine hundred and ninety-nine in a thousand. It will be a nine-days wonder, and afterwards, a Columbus' egg."[5]

But Wilkinson was only one of many. The most famous was, of course, James Watt, who, together with Matthew Boulton, formed the first company for the manufacture of steam engines. Watt was the son of an architect, shipbuilder, and maker of nautical instruments. At thirteen he was already making models of machines, and by young manhood he was an accomplished artisan. He planned to settle in Glasgow, but the guild of hammermen objected to his making mathematical instruments—the last remnants of feudalism thus coming into an ironic personal conflict with the man who, more than any other, would create *the* invention that would destroy guild organization. At any rate, Watt found a haven at the university and there, in 1764, had his attention turned to an early and very unsatisfactory steam engine invented by Newcomen. In his careful and systematic way, Watt experimented with steam pressures, cylinder designs, and valves, until by 1796 he had developed a truly radical and (by the standards of those days) extraordinarily powerful and efficient engine. Interestingly, Watt could never have done so well with his engines had not Wilkinson perfected a manner of making good piston-cylinder fits. Previously, cylinders and pistons were made of wood and rapidly wore out. Typically, too, it was Wilkinson who bought the first steam engine to be used for purposes other than pumping: it worked the famous iron bellows.

There was needed, however, more than Watt's skill. The new engines had to be produced and sold, and the factory that made them had to be financed and organized. Watt at first formed a partnership with John Roebuck, another iron magnate, but it shortly failed. Thereafter luck came his way. Matthew Boulton, already a wealthy and highly successful manufacturer of buttons and buckles, took up Roebuck's contract with Watt, and the greatest combination of technical skill and business acumen of the day was born.

[5] Paul Mantoux, *The Industrial Revolution in the Eighteenth Century,* 2nd ed. (New York: Harcourt, Brace & World, Inc., 1928), pp. 313 n., 315.

Even then the firm did not prosper immediately. Expenses of development were high, and the new firm was not out of debt for twelve years. Yet from the beginning, interest was high. By 1781 Boulton was able to claim that the people of London, Birmingham, and Manchester were all "steam mill mad"; and by 1786, when two steam engines were harnessed to fifty pairs of millstones in the largest flour mill in the world, all of London came to see and marvel.

The steam engine was the greatest single invention, but by no means the sole mainstay, of the industrial revolution. Hardly less important were a group of textile inventions, of which the most famous was Arkwright's jenny, or water frame, as it was called to distinguish it from other hand-operated spinning jennies.*

Arkwright's career is, in itself, interesting. A barber, he plied his trade near the weaving districts of Manchester and so heard the crying need for a machine that would enable the cottage spinners to keep up with the technically more advanced weavers. Good fortune threw him into contact with a clockmaker named John Kay, whom he hired to perfect a machine that Kay had already begun with another employer-inventor. What happened thereafter is obscure: Kay left the business accused of theft and embezzlement, and Arkwright appeared as the "sole inventor" of a spinning jenny in 1769.

He now found two rich hosiers, Samuel Need and Jedediah Strutt, who agreed to set up business with him to produce water frames, and in 1771 the firm built its own spinning mill. It was an overnight success; by 1779 it had several thousand spindles, more than 300 workmen, and ran night and day. Within not many years Arkwright had built an immense fortune for himself and founded an even more immense textile industry for England. "O reader," wrote Carlyle, looking back on his career, "what a historical phenomenon is that bag-cheeked, pot-bellied, much enduring, much inventing barber! . . . It was this man that had to give England the power of cotton." [6]

THE INDUSTRIAL ENTREPRENEUR

It is interesting, as we watch the careers of these New Men to draw a few generalizations concerning them. For these were an entirely new class of economically important persons. Peter Onions, who was one of the inventors of the puddling process, was an obscure foreman; Arkwright was a barber; Benjamin Huntsman, the steel pioneer, was originally a maker of clocks; Maudslay, who invented the automatic

*Essentially what the water frame did was to enable cotton thread of much greater strength to be produced. As a result, for the first time it was possible to use cotton thread instead of linen thread for the warp (the vertical threads that take most of the strain in weaving) as well as for the weft. Not until Arkwright's invention was "cotton cloth" made wholly of cotton. The new cloth was incomparably superior to the old and instantly enjoyed a huge demand.

[6] Mantoux, *op. cit.*, p. 225.

screw machine, was a bright young mechanic at the Woolwich Arsenal. None of the great industrial pioneers came of noble lineage; and with few exceptions, such as Matthew Boulton, none even possessed money capital. In agriculture, the new revolutionary methods of scientific farming enjoyed aristocratic patronage and leadership, especially from the famous Sir Jethro Tull and Lord Townshend; but in industry, the lead went to men of humble origin and descent.

Let us note, therefore, that this required a social system flexible enough to permit the rise of such obscure "adventurers." It is not until we see the catalytic effect of unleashing and harnessing the energies of talented men in the lower and middle ranks of the social order that we begin to appreciate the immense liberating effect of the preceding economic and political revolutions. In the medieval hierarchy the meteoric careers of such New Men would have been unthinkable. In addition, the New Men were the product of the unique economic preparation of England itself. They were, of course, the beneficiaries of the rising demand and the technical inquisitiveness of the times. Beyond that, many of the small manufacturers were, themselves, former small proprietors who had been bought out during the late period of the enclosure movement and who determined to use their tiny capital in the promising area of manufacture.

Many of these New Men made great sums of money. A few, like Boulton and Watt, were modest in their wants. Despite an iron-clad patent, they charged for their engines only the basic cost of the machine and installation plus one-third the saving in fuel which the customer got. Some, like Josiah Wedgwood, founder of the great china works, actually refused, on principle, to take out patents. But most of them did not display such fine sensibilities. Arkwright retired a multi-millionaire living in ostentatious splendor; Huntsman, Wilkinson, Samuel Walker (who began life as a nailsmith and stole the secret of cast steel)—all went on to roll up huge fortunes.* Indeed, Wilkinson's iron business became a minor industrial state with a credit stronger than many German and Italian principalities. It even coined its own money, and its copper and silver tokens (with a profile and legend of John Wilkinson, Ironmaster) were much in use between 1787 and 1808.

Beyond mere avarice, the manufacturers have been described by the economic historian, Paul Mantoux, as

tyrannical, hard, sometimes cruel: their passions and greeds were those of upstarts. They had the reputation of being heavy drinkers and of having little regard for the honour of their female employees. They were proud of their newly

---

*In contrast to the manufacturers, the inventors did not usually fare successfully. Many of them, who did not have Watt's good fortune in finding a Boulton, died poor and neglected, fruitlessly suing for stolen inventions, unpaid royalties, ignored claims.

acquired wealth and lived in great style with footmen, carriages and gorgeous town and country houses.[7]

Pleasant or unpleasant, the personal characteristics fade beside one overriding quality. These were all men interested in expansion, in growth, in investment for investment's sake. All of them were identified with technological progress, and none of them disdained the productive process. An employee of Maudslay once remarked, "It was a pleasure to see him handle a tool of any kind, but he was *quite splendid* with an 18-inch file."[8] Watt was tireless in experimenting with his machines; Wedgwood stomped about his factory on his wooden leg scrawling, "This won't do for Jos. Wedgwood," wherever he saw evidence of careless work. Richard Arkwright was a bundle of ceaseless energy in promoting his interests, jouncing about England over execrable roads in a post chaise driven by four horses, pursuing his correspondence as he traveled.

"With us," wrote a French visitor to a calico works in 1788, "a man rich enough to set up and run a factory like this would not care to remain in a position which he would deem unworthy of his wealth."[9] This was an attitude entirely foreign to the rising English industrial capitalist. His work was its own dignity and reward; the wealth it brought was quite aside. Boswell, on being shown Watt and Boulton's great engine works at Soho, declared that he never forgot Boulton's expression as the latter declared, "I sell here, sir, what all the world desires to have—Power."[10]

The New Men were first and last *entrepreneurs*—enterprisers. They brought with them a new energy, as restless as it proved to be inexhaustible. In an economic, if not a political, sense, they deserve the epithet "revolutionaries," for the change they ushered in was nothing short of total, sweeping, and irreversible.

INDUSTRIAL AND SOCIAL REPERCUSSIONS

The first and most striking element of that change was a sharp rise in the output of the newly industrialized industries. The import of raw cotton for spinning weighed 1 million pounds in 1701; 3 million pounds in 1750; 5 million in 1781. That was a respectable rate of increase. But then came the sudden burst in textile technology. By 1784 the figure was over 11 million pounds; by 1789 it was three times greater yet, and still it grew: to 43 million pounds in 1799; 56 million in 1800; 60

---

[7] Mantoux, *op. cit.,* p. 397.

[8] Lewis Mumford, *Technics and Civilization* (New York: Harcourt, Brace & World, Inc., 1934), p. 210.

[9] Mantoux, *op. cit.,* p. 404.

[10] H. R. Fox Bourne, *English Merchants* (London: 1866), p. 119.

million in 1802.[11] So was it with much else where the new technology penetrated. The output of coal increased tenfold in forty years; that of pig iron leaped from 68,000 tons in 1788 to 1,347,000 tons in 1839.[12]

Thus, the first impact of the industrial revolution was an immense quickening of the pace of production in the new industrial sector of the economy, an effect which we find repeated in every nation which goes through an "industrial revolution." In France, for example, the impact of industrial techniques did not make its influence felt until about 1815: between that date and 1845, the French output of pig iron grew fivefold; her coal production, sevenfold; her rate of importation, tenfold.[13]

The industrial revolution, itself, did not immediately exert a comparable leverage on the *over-all* increase of output. The industrial sector, to begin with, was small; and the phenomenal rates of increase in those industries where its leverage was first and most fruitfully applied were by no means mirrored in every industry. What is of crucial importance, however, is that the industrial revolution ushered in the technology by which large-scale, sustained growth was eventually to take place. This is a process into which we must look more carefully at the end of this chapter.

But first we must pay heed to another immediate and visible result of the industrial revolution in England. We can describe it as the transformation of an essentially commercial and agricultural society into one in which industrial manufacture became the dominant mode of organizing economic life. To put it more concretely, the industrial revolution was characterized by *the rise of the factory to the center of social as well as economic life.* After 1850, the factory was not only the key economic institution of England, but it was the economic institution that shaped its politics, its social problems, the character of its daily life, just as decisively as the manor or the guild had done a few centuries earlier.

It is difficult for us today to realize the pace or the quality of change which this rise of factory work brought about. Until the mid-eighteenth century, Glasgow, Newcastle, and the Rhondda Valley were mostly waste or farm land, and Manchester in 1727 was described by Daniel Defoe as "a mere village." Forty years later there were a hundred integrated mills and a whole cluster of machine plants, forges, leather and chemical works in the area. A modern industrial city had been created.

[11] Mantoux, *op. cit.*, p. 258.
[12] J. L. and B. Hammond, *The Rise of Modern Industry* (New York: Harcourt, Brace & World, Inc., 1937), p. 160.
[13] A. Dunham, *The Industrial Revolution in France, 1815–48* (New York: Exposition Press, 1955), p. 432.

Already by the 1780's the shape of the new environment was visible. A French mineralogist visiting England in 1784 wrote:

[The] creaking, the piercing noise of the pulleys, the continuous sound of hammering, the ceaseless energy of the men keeping all this machinery in motion, presented a sight as interesting as it was new . . . The night is so filled with fire and light that when from a distance we see, here a glowing mass of coal, there darting flames leaping from the blast furnaces, when we hear the heavy hammers striking the echoing anvils and the shrill whistling of the air pumps, we do not know whether we are looking at a volcano in eruption or have been miraculously transported to Vulcan's cave . . .[14]

The factory provided not merely a new landscape but a new and uncongenial social habitat. In our day, we have become so used to urban-industrial life that we forget what a wrench is the transition from farm to city. For the peasant, this transfer requires a drastic adjustment. No longer does he work at his own pace, but at the pace of a machine. No longer are slack seasons determined by the weather, but by the state of the market. No longer is the land, however miserable its crop, an eternal source of sustenance close at hand, but only the packed and sterile earth of the industrial site.

It is little wonder that the English laborer, still more used to rural than urban ways, feared and hated the advent of the machine. Throughout the early years of the industrial revolution workmen literally attacked the invading army of machinery, burning and wrecking factories. During the late eighteenth century, for instance, when the first textile mills were built, whole hamlets rose in revolt rather than work in the mills. Headed by a mythical General Ludd, the Luddites constituted a fierce but fruitless opposition to industrialism. In 1813, in a mass trial which ended in many hangings and transportations, the movement came to an end.*

Distasteful as was the advent of the factory itself, even more distasteful were the conditions within it. Child labor, for instance, was commonplace and sometimes began at age four; hours of work were generally dawn to dusk; abuses of every kind were all too frequent. A Committee of Parliament appointed in 1832 to look into conditions gives this testimony from a factory overseer.

Q. At what time in the morning, in the brisk time, did these girls go to the mills?

---

[14] Mantoux, *op. cit.*, p. 313.

*Even in our day, however, we use the word "Luddite" to describe an attempt to "fight back" at the threat of machinery.

A. In the brisk time, for about six weeks, they have gone at three o'clock in the morning and ended at ten or nearly half past at night.

Q. What intervals were allowed for rest and refreshment during those nineteen hours of labour?

A. Breakfast a quarter of an hour, and dinner half an hour, and drinking a quarter of an hour.

Q. Was any of that time taken up in cleaning the machinery?

A. They generally had to do what they call dry down; sometimes this took the whole time at breakfast or drinking.

Q. Had you not great difficulty in awakening your children to the excessive labour?

A. Yes, in the early time we had to take them up asleep and shake them.

Q. Had any of them any accident in consequence of this labour?

A. Yes, my eldest daughter . . . the cog caught her forefinger nail and screwed it off below the knuckle.

Q. Has she lost that finger?

A. It is cut off at the second joint.

Q. Were her wages paid during that time?

A. As soon as the accident happened the wages were totally stopped.[15]

It was a grim age. The long hours of work, the general dirt and clangor of the factories, the lack of even the most elementary safety precautions, all combined to give early industrial capitalism a reputation from which, in the minds of many people of the world, it has never recovered. Worse yet were the slums to which the majority of workers returned after their travail. A government commissioner reports in 1839 on one such workers' quarter in Glasgow called "the wynds."

The wynds . . . house a fluctuating population of between 15,000 and 30,000 persons. This district is composed of many narrow streets and square courts and in the middle of each court there is a dunghill. Although the outward appearance of these places was revolting, I was nevertheless quite unprepared for the filth and misery that were to be found inside. In some bedrooms we visited at night we found a whole mass of humanity stretched on the floor. There were often 15 to 20 men and women huddled together, some being clothed and others naked. There was hardly any furniture there and the only thing which gave these holes the appearance of a dwelling was fire burning on the hearth. Thieving and prostitution are the main sources of income of these people.[16]

[15] Tawney, Bland, and Brown, *English Economic History, Selected Documents* (London: George Bell & Sons, Ltd., 1914), p. 510.

[16] Quoted in F. Engels, *The Condition of the Working Class in England* (New York: The Macmillan Company, 1958), p. 46.

Without question, the times were marked by tremendous social suffering. But it is well, in looking back on the birth years of industrial capitalism, to bear several facts in mind:

1. *It is doubtful if the poverty represented a deterioration in life for the masses in general.*

In at least some sections of England, industrialism brought immediate benefits. Wedgwood (an exceptionally good employer, it is true) used to tell his employees to ask their parents for a description of the country as *they* first knew it and to compare their present state. So, too, the twelve-hour day in Arkwright's mills was a two-hour *improvement* over previous Manchester standards. Furthermore, the existing poverty was not by any means new. As we know from Hogarth's etchings, long before the industrial revolution, "Gin Lane" already sported its pitiful types. As one reformer of the mid-nineteenth century wrote, those whose sensibilities were revolted by the sight of suffering factory children thought "how much more delightful would have been the gambol of free limbs on the hillside; the sight of the green mead with its spangles of buttercups and daisies; the song of the bird and the humming of the bee . . . [but] we have seen children perishing from sheer hunger in the mud hovel or in the ditch by the wayside."[17]

2. *Much of the harsh criticism to which early industrial capitalism was subjected derived not so much from its economic but from its political accompaniments.*

For coincident with the rise of capitalism, and indeed contributory to it, was a deep-seated change in the vantage point of political criticism. New ideas of democracy, of social justice, of the "rights" of the individual charged the times with a critical temper of mind before which *any* economic system would have suffered censure.

To be sure, the political movements by which capitalism was carried to its heights were not working-class movements, but middle-class, bourgeois movements: the rising manufacturers in England and France had little "social conscience" beyond a concern for their own rights and privileges. But the movement of political liberalism which they set into motion had a momentum beyond the narrow limits for which it was intended. By the first quarter of the nineteenth century, the condition of the working classes, now so exposed to public view in the new factory-slum environment, had begun to curry public sympathy.

Thus, one of the unexpected consequences of the industrial revolution was a sharp reorientation of political ideas. In the creation of an industrial working class and an industrial environment, the revolution be-

[17] Friedrich Hayek, ed., *Capitalism and the Historians* (Chicago: University of Chicago Press, 1954), p. 180.

queathed a new economic framework to politics. Karl Marx and Friedrich Engels were to write in 1848 that "all history" was the history of class struggle, but never did that struggle emerge so nakedly into the open as after the industrial environment had been brought into being.

Equally important was that the rise of political liberalism not only roused feelings of hostility toward the prevailing order, but initiated the slow process of amelioration. *From the outset, a reform movement coincided with capitalism.* In 1802, pauper apprentices were legally limited to a twelve-hour day and barred from night work. In 1819, the employment of children under nine was prohibited in cotton mills; in 1833, a 48- to 69-hour week was decreed for workers under eighteen (who comprised about 75 per cent of all cotton mill workers), and a system of government inspection of factories was inaugurated; in 1842, children under ten were barred from the coal mines; in 1847 a 10-hour daily limit (later raised to $10\frac{1}{2}$) was set for children and women.

The nature of the reforms is itself eloquent testimony to the conditions of the times, and the fact that the reforms were bitterly opposed and often observed in the breach is testimony to the prevailing spirit. Yet capitalism, unlike feudalism, was from the beginning subject to the corrective force of democracy. Karl Marx, drawing on the material of the 1830's, drew a mordant picture of the capitalist process in all its economic squalor, but he overlooked (or shrugged off) this countervailing force whose power was steadily to grow.

3. *The most important effect of the industrial revolution we have left for last: its long-term leverage on economic well-being.*

The ultimate impact of the industrial revolution was to usher in a rise of living standards on a mass scale unlike anything that the world had ever known before.

This did not happen overnight. In 1840, according to the calculations of Arnold Toynbee, Sr., the wage of an ordinary laborer came to eight shillings a week, which were six shillings less than he needed to buy the bare necessities of life.[18] He made up the deficit by sending his children or his wife, or both, to work in the mills. If, as we have noted, some sections of the working class gained from the early impact of industrialization, others suffered a *decline* from the standard of living enjoyed in 1795 or thereabouts. A Committee of Parliament in the 1830's, for example, discovered that a hand weaver at that earlier date could have bought more than three times as many provisions with his wages as at the later date. Although not every trade suffered equally, the first flush of the industrial revolution brought its hardships to bear full force, while its benefits were not as immediately noticeable.

By 1870, however, the long-run effects of the industrial revolution

[18] *The Industrial Revolution* (Boston: Beacon Press, Inc., 1956), p. 113.

were beginning to make themselves felt. The price of necessaries had by then risen to fifteen shillings, but weekly earnings had crept up to meet and even exceed that sum. Hours were shorter, too. At the Jarrow Shipyards and the New Castle Chemical Works, the workweek had fallen from 61 to 54 hours; and even in the notoriously long-worked textile mills, the stint was down to "only" 57 hours. It was still a far cry from an abundant society, much less an "affluent" one, but the corner had been turned.

THE INDUSTRIAL REVOLUTION IN THE PERSPECTIVE OF THEORY

We have reviewed very briefly the salient historic features of the rise of industrial capitalism. Now we must reflect back on the great economic and social changes we have witnessed and ask a pertinent economic question: *How did the process of industrialization raise material well-being?* To answer the question, we must turn to economic theory to elucidate systematically what we have thus far only described.

Let us begin by asking what is necessary for a rise in the economic well-being of a society. The answer is not difficult. If we are to enjoy a greater material well-being, generally speaking, we must produce more. This is particularly true when we begin at the stage of scarcely-better-than-subsistence which characterized so much of Europe before the industrial revolution. For such a society to raise the standard of living of its masses, the first necessity is unquestionably higher production. Despite all the inequities of distribution which attended the society of serf and lord, capitalist and child-employee, underlying the meanness of the times was one overriding reality: the sheer inadequacy of output. There was simply not enough to go around, and if somewhat less lopsided distributive arrangements might have lessened the moral indignity of the times, they would not have contributed much to a massive improvement in basic economic well-being. Even assuming that the wage of the city laborer and the income of the peasant could have been doubled had the rich been deprived of their share—and this is a wildly extravagant assumption—still, the characteristic of rural and urban life would have been its poverty.

We must add only one important qualification to this emphasis on increased output as the prerequisite of economic improvement. Over-all living standards will not improve if a country's population is growing even faster than its increased output. The production of goods and services must rise *faster* than population if individual well-being is to improve.

How does a society raise its *per capita* output?

We will not fully analyze this problem until we study growth in Chapter 19. But the industrial revolution enables us to understand a great deal about the problem. For clearly, *the key to higher output lies in enhancing the human energies of the community with the leverage of industrial capital.* Our analytic understanding of the growth must begin by looking further into this extraordinary power which capital possesses.

We have already frequently used the word "capital," but we have not yet defined it. We can see that in a fundamental sense, capital consists of anything which can enhance man's power to perform economically useful work. An unshaped stone is capital to the cave man who can use it as a hunting implement. A hoe is capital to a peasant; a road system is capital to the inhabitants of a modern industrial society. Knowledge is capital, too—indeed, perhaps the most precious part of society's stock of capital.

When economists talk of capital, however, they usually confine their meaning to *capital goods*—the stock of tools, equipment, machines, and buildings which society produces in order to expedite the production process.* All these capital goods have one effect in common on the productive process: they all operate to make human labor more productive. They make it possible for a worker to produce more goods in an hour (or a week, or a year) than he could produce without the aid of that capital. Capital is therefore a method of raising per capita *productivity,* which is an individual's output in a given span of time. For example, in a forty-hour week a typical modern worker using power-driven mechanical equipment can physically outproduce three men working seventy hours a week with the simpler tools of a half-century ago. To put it differently, in one day a modern worker will turn out as much output as his counterpart of 1900 in a full week—not because the modern worker works harder, but because he has at his command thousands of dollars worth of capital equipment rather than the few hundred dollars worth available to a worker in 1900.

Why does capital make labor so much more productive?

The most important reason is that capital goods enable man to use principles and devices such as the lever and the wheel, heat and cold, combustion and expansion in ways that the unaided body cannot.

---

* Is money capital? It certainly is to the individual who possesses it. But it is not capital for society as a whole. For money only represents *claims* to society's real wealth, which is its goods and services. If an individual's money disappears, he loses his claim on those goods and services, and we can indeed say that he has lost his "capital." But if *all* money disappeared, we could not say that society had lost its claim on its own wealth. It would only have to devise another system of tickets. More about this, too, in Part Two.

Capital gives men mechanical and physicochemical powers of literally transhuman dimensions. They magnify enormously his muscular strength; they refine his powers of control; they endow him with endurance and resilience far beyond those of the flesh and bone. In using capital, man utilizes the natural world as a supplement to his own feeble capacities.

Another reason for the augmentation of production lies in the fact that capital facilitates the *specialization of man's labor.* A team of men working together, each man tending to one job alone in which he is expert, can usually far outproduce the same number of men, each of whom does a variety of jobs. The prime example is, of course, the auto production line in which a thousand men cooperate to produce an immensely larger output of cars than could be achieved if each man built a car by himself. Auto assembly lines, of course, use prodigious quantities of capital in the overhead conveyor belts, the inventories of parts on hand, the huge factory with its power system, and so on. And while not all specialization of labor depends on capital, capital is usually necessary for the large-scale industrial operations in which specialization becomes most effective.

In our next chapter we will return to these important matters in the context of the development of modern industry. But while we are still discussing the basic question of the rise of industry itself, there is a fundamental problem to be disposed of. This is the question of how capital is made in the first place, of how a society generates the capital equipment it needs in order to grow.

CAPITAL
AND SAVING

This brings us for the first time to a relationship that we will encounter many more times in our study of economics, both in a perspective of history and from a later vantage point of theory. The relationship is between the creation of those physical artifacts we call capital, and the inescapable prior act that we call *saving.*

When we think of saving, we ordinarily picture it in financial terms; that is, as a decision not to spend part of our income. Behind this financial act, however, lies a "real" act that we must now clearly understand. *When we save money we also abstain from using a certain quantity of goods and services we might have bought.* To be sure, our money savings represent a claim on goods and services, a claim that we may later exercise. Until we do, however, we have freed resources which would otherwise have been used to satisfy our immediate wants. From these freed resources, society builds its capital or, in more technical language, carries out the act of *investment.*

In the simplest example, we can see this real meaning of saving in the case of a primitive hunter who abstains from a full meal today, so that he will not have to hunt tomorrow. By saving half of today's kill, he frees the resource of (his own) labor: instead of hunting, tomorrow, he will make a better spear. In a much more indirect and complex fashion, when we save money we are also giving up a potential meal (or some other consumption good), so that society can then make capital out of the goods and services we would otherwise have consumed.

Thus the acts of saving and investment are inextricably linked: saving is the releasing of resources from consumption; investment is the employment of these resources in making capital. Indeed, from society's point of view, saving and investment are only two sides of the same coin. Why do we then separate them in economic discourse? The reason is that different people may perform the saving and investing functions, especially in modern societies. We are no longer hunters and spear makers. Those who release the resources of society are usually not the same individuals as those who gather up those resources for investment purposes. Nonetheless, we can see that every act of investment, no matter who performs it, requires the presence of released resources.*

This does not mean that investment necessarily entails a *diminution* of consumption. A rich society does not feel its normal, recurrent saving as a "pinch" on its spending. A society with unemployed factors can put its idle resources to work building capital without diminishing its expenditure on consumption. (It is still saving, of course, insofar as it is not using those newly employed resources to make consumption goods.) But—and this is a crucial point—when a *fully employed* society builds more capital, it *must* curtail its consumption. In this case, there is nowhere whence the needed capital-building resources can come but from their erstwhile consumption employments.

Let us go on still further. We can now see that the *rate* at which an economy can invest—that is, the size of the yearly addition it can make to its stock of capital goods—depends on its capacity to save. If its living standards are already close to the margin of existence, it will not be able to transfer much labor from consumption effort to capital-building effort. However badly it may wish for more tools, however productive those tools would prove to be, it cannot invest beyond the point at which its remaining consumption activity would no longer be adequate to maintain subsistence. At the other extreme, if a society is well-to-do, it may be able to abstain from a great deal of current consumption effort to provide for the future. Accordingly, its growth will be fast. *It is a hard economic reality that the amount of construction for the future can never exceed the amount of resources and effort which are unused, or which can be released from consumption in the present.*

---

*Note, however, that an act of saving—i.e., an abstention from consumption—does not *automatically* bring about an act of purposive investment. This leads to serious problems to which we shall turn in Chapter 7, and in still greater detail in Part Two.

This seems to imply that the process of economic growth must perforce be very slow in a poor economy. And so it is. In England, as we have already seen, nearly three-quarters of a century elapsed before the new process of industrialization brought about an increase in productivity sufficiently large to be felt as a general improvement in the lot of the workingman. In the underdeveloped nations, as we shall see in Part Four, the prospect is equally or even more sluggish. At its best, growth is a gradual and cumulative, rather than an "instant" phenomenon; and where the initial level of savings is low because of poverty, the rate of advance is correspondingly slower.

Perhaps we can better appreciate this over-all determinant of the pace of growth if we now examine the actual social circumstances under which saving arose in early nineteenth-century England.

For who did the saving? Who abstained from consumption? Well-to-do agriculturalists and manufacturers (for all their ostentatious ways) were certainly important savers who plowed substantial sums into more new capital investments. Yet the savers were not just the manufacturers or the gentry but also another class—the industrial workers. Here, in the low level of industrial wages, a great sacrifice was made—not voluntarily, by any matter of means, but made just the same. From the resources the workers could have consumed was built the industrial foundation for the future.

We can also see something which is perhaps even more significant. This is the fact that England *had* to hold down the level of its working class consumption in order to free productive effort for the accumulation of capital goods. In point of historic actuality, the "holding-down" was accomplished largely by the forces of the market place—with a liberal assist, to be sure, from the capitalists and from a government quick to oppose the demands of labor in the interests of its upper classes. But social inequities aside, the hard fact remains that had industrial wages risen very much, a vast demand for consumers' goods would have turned the direction of the English economy away from capital-building, toward the satisfaction of current wants. This would certainly have redounded to the immediate welfare of the English worker (although the increase in per capita consumption would have been small). At the same time, however, it would have *postponed* the day when society's over-all productive powers were capable of generating an aggregate output of very large size.

This bitter choice must be confronted by every industrializing society, capitalist or socialist, democratic or totalitarian. To assuage the needs of today or to build for tomorrow is *the* decision which a developing society must make. As we shall see in Part Four, it is a decision which lies behind much of the political and economic agony of a large part of the world today.

There remains but one last question. We have gained some insight into the mechanics of growth, but we have not yet answered the question: how are these mechanics brought about? How does society arrange the reallocation of its factors of production to bring about the creation of the capital it needs?

This query brings us again to a consideration of our original division of economic societies into three types: traditional, command, and market. It also leads to some very important conclusions.

The first of these is obvious: it is that tradition-bound societies are not apt to grow. In such societies there is *no* direct social means of inducing the needed reallocation of factors. Worse yet, there are often strong social and religious barriers which create obstacles to the needed shifts in employment.

The situation is very different, however, when we turn to command societies. We have seen a striking use of command as the industrializing-agency in modern times. In at least one country, the Soviet Union, command has been the principal mechanism for a dramatic transition from peasanthood into industrialization, and in many other collectivist economies, command is now trying to bring into effect such a transition.

In Part Four we shall return to the Russian experience. Meanwhile, let us not forget that command was also one of the principal ways by which Europe began its industrialization. In the state-directed establishment of shipyards and armories, the construction of royal palaces and estates, tapestry works and chinaware factories, a very important organizing impetus was given to the creation of an industrial sector in the mercantilist era. True, of course, that in those days, command was never so ruthlessly applied nor so widely directed as with the Communist states. But however much milder the dosage, the medicine was in essence the same: the *initial* transfer of labor from the traditional pursuits of the land to the new tasks of the factory depended on a commanding authority which ordered the new pattern into being.*

But command was by no means the main agency for the final industrialization of the West. Rather, the organizing force which put men to work in making capital equipment was the market.

How did the market bring about this remarkable transformation? It

---

*As Barbara Ward has written in *India and the West:* "A developing society must at some point begin to save, even though it is still poor. This is the tough early stage of growth which Marx encountered in Victorian England and unfortunately took to be permanent. It is a difficult phase in any economy—so difficult that most societies got through it by *force majeure* . . . No one asked the British laborers moving into the Manchester slums whether they wanted to save. . . . The Soviet workers who came to Sverdlovsk and Magnitogorsk from the primitive steppes had no say in the scale or the condition of their work. Nor have the Chinese in their communes today."

achieved its purposes by the lure of monetary rewards. It was the hope of *profits* that lured manufacturers into turning out more capital goods. It was the attraction of better *wages* (or sometimes of *any* wages) that directed workers into the new plants. It was the signal of rising prices that encouraged, and falling prices that discouraged, the production of this or that particular capital good.

And what, we may next ask, opened the prospect of profits large enough to induce entrepreneurs to risk their savings in new capital goods? The answer brings us full circle to the focal point of this chapter. For the answer is to be found primarily in the body of technological advance constituting the core of the industrial revolution.

Not that every new invention brought with it a fortune for its pioneering promoters, or that every new product found a market waiting for it. The path of technical advance is littered with inventions born "too soon" and with enterprises founded with great hopes and closed down six months later. But looking back over the vast process of capital accumulation which, beginning in the late eighteenth century, lifted first England and then America into the long flight of industrial development, there is little doubt that the impelling force was the succession of inventions and innovations that successively opened new aspects of nature to human control. Steam power, the cheap and efficient spinning and weaving of cloth, the first mass production of iron, and later steel—these were the great breakthroughs of industrial science that opened the way for the massive accumulation of capital. And once the great inventions had marked out the channel of advance, secondary improvements and subsidiary inventions took on an important supporting role. To the enterpriser with a cost-cutting innovation went the prize of a market advantage in costs and a correspondingly higher profit. More than that, once one pioneer in a field had gained a technical advantage, competition quickly forced everyone else in the field to catch up as quickly as they could. Most of the cost-cutting innovations involved adding machinery to the production process—and this in turn boosted the formation of capital.

Capitalism as a whole proved an unparalleled machine for the accumulation of capital. In its development we find the first economic system in history in which economic growth became an *integral* part of daily life. As Marx and Engels were to write in the *Communist Manifesto:* "The bourgeoisie, during its scarce one hundred years, has created more massive and more colossal productive forces than have all preceding generations together." And the compliment, all the more meaningful coming from the two archenemies of its social order, was true.

1. The industrial revolution is *a great turning period* in history, during which manufacturing and industrial activity become primary forms of social production.

2. The industrial revolution began in England in the mid- to late eighteenth century (although its roots are far deeper). There are numerous reasons why it occurred there and then:

   • England was *a wealthy trading nation* with a well-developed middle class.
   • England's *aristocracy was much more commerce-minded* than the aristocracies of the Continent.
   • England was the home of a widespread vogue of *scientific investigation* and of ''gentlemen farmers'' interested in *agricultural innovation*.
   • England's relatively *open social structure* permitted the rise of New Men, such as Watt or Wilkinson, who brought to manufacturing a burst of new social energies.
   • Many other causes could be cited as well. The industrial revolution was a *many-sided, complex chain* of events.

3. The revolution brought with it changes of the greatest importance in society.

   • It ushered in a slow, but cumulative *rise in output* that was eventually to lift the industrial world out of an age-old poverty.
   • It brought the *factory* (and the *industrial slum*) as a new environment for work and life.
   • It gave rise to new kinds of *social abuses* and greatly sharpened the general *awareness of economic conditions*.

4. The industrial revolution was essentially a *capital-building process* (machines, buildings, canals, railways), as a result of which the productivity of labor was greatly increased.

5. *Capital generally enhances productivity* because it gives man far greater physical and chemical capabilities than he enjoys with unaided labor alone. It also enables men to combine and *specialize* their labor, as in modern factory production lines.

6. *Capital-building requires saving*. Capital can be built only if society has the use of resources normally used for filling its consumption needs. Saving releases these resources; investing puts them to use.

7. Society cannot devote more resources or energies to capital-building than those it releases from other uses (or those it has available as unemployed resources). Hence, by and large, *saving regulates the pace at which investment can proceed*. Poor societies, in which it is difficult to give up consumption, accordingly have great problems in amassing enough resources for investment.

8. The saving necessary for investment can come from agriculture, manufacturing enterprises, and many other sources. In poor nations, it must also often be wrung from workers or peasants by denying them the use of all the nation's economic potential to fill their consumption needs.

9. Hence *saving in poor nations is usually an involuntary process*. Capital-building in many developing nations today, particularly those under collectivist regimes, is accomplished by the agency of command. In the industrial revolution, it was accomplished in part by command, but mainly by the market system. The remarkable inventions of the industrial revolution served as sources of profits that resulted in great accumulations of capital.

1. It is interesting to note that technical improvements in agriculture or manufacturing have generally been slow to arise in countries that have relied on slave labor. Can you think of a reason why this might be so?

2. What forces do you think would be necessary to bring a new "industrial revolution" to the underdeveloped world today? Is an industrial revolution there apt to resemble that in England in the eighteenth century?

3. Industrialization in England was marked by a sharp growth of bitter political feeling on the part of the new factory proletariat. Do you think this must be an accompaniment of industrialization everywhere, or was it a particular product of early capitalism?

4. How does capital help human productivity? Discuss this in relation to the following kinds of labor: farm labor, office help, teaching, government administration.

5. When General Motors devotes a billion dollars to new investment (building new factories, warehouses, offices, etc.), who does the saving that is required? Stockholders? Workers? The public? Buyers of cars?

6. It is estimated that the value of the capital structures and equipment in the U.S. is some $2 trillion (Chap. 9). Assume that half of it were wiped out in some catastrophe. What would happen to U.S. productivity? To average U.S. well-being? How could the damage be repaired?

7. Does all investment require saving? Why?

8. Is capital-building in the U.S. today directed by the market alone? Does the government accumulate capital? Does public capital improve productivity as well as private capital?

9. Is building a school "investment"? Is building a hospital? A sports stadium? A housing project? A research lab? What do you think distinguishes investment, in general, from consumption?

THE IMPACT OF
INDUSTRIAL TECHNOLOGY 5

With this chapter, we enter a new major period of economic history. Formerly we have dealt largely with the past, giving only an occasional glance to later echoes of the problems we have encountered. Commencing with this chapter, our focus turns toward and into the actual present. We have reached the stage of economic history whose nearest boundary is our own time. Simultaneously, our point of geographic focus shifts. As economic history enters the mid-nineteenth century, the dynamic center of events comes increasingly to be located in the United States. Not only do we now begin to enter the modern world, but the economic trends in which we will be interested take us directly into our own society.

What will be the theme of this chapter? Essentially it will be a continuation of a motif we began with the industrial revolution—the impact of technology on economic society. Looking back, we can see that the burst of inventions which marked "the" revolution was not in any sense the completion of an historic event. Rather, it was merely the inception of a process of technological change which would continually accelerate down to the present time.

We can distinguish three or even four stages of this continuous process. The "first" industrial revolution was largely concentrated in new textile machinery, improved methods of coal production and iron manufacture, revolutionary agricultural techniques, and steam power. It was succeeded in the middle years of the nineteenth century by a "second" industrial revolution: a clustering of industrial inventions centering on steel, railroad and steamship transportation, agricultural machinery, and chemicals. By the early years of the twentieth century there was a third wave of inventions: electrical power, automobiles, the gasoline engine. In our own time there is a fourth: the revolution of electronics, air travel, automation, and, of course, nuclear energy.

It is difficult, perhaps impossible, to exaggerate the impact of this continuing industrial revolution. Now advancing rapidly, now slowly; now on a broad front, now on a narrow salient; now in the most practical of inventions, again in the purest of theoretical discoveries, the cumulative application of science and technology to the productive process was *the* great change of the nineteenth and twentieth centuries. The initial industrial revolution was thus in retrospect a kind of discontinuous leap in human history; a leap as important as that which had lifted the first pastoral settlements above the earlier hunting communities. We have already noted that in the factory the new technology brought a new working place for man, but its impact was vastly greater than that alone. The enormously heightened powers of transportation and communication, the far more effective means of wresting a crop from the soil, the hugely enhanced ability to apply power for lifting, hauling, shaping, binding, cutting—all this conspired to bring about a literal remaking of the human environment, and by no means an entirely benign one.

IMPACT
OF ONE
INVENTION

In this book we cannot do more than inquire into some of the economic consequences of the incursion of industrial technology into modern society, but it may help us gain some insight into the dimensions of that penetrative process if we follow for a short distance the repercussions of a single invention.

Let us therefore look in on the Paris Exposition of 1867, where curious visitors are gathered around an interesting exhibit: a small engine in which illuminating gas and air are introduced into a combustion chamber and ignited by a spark. The resulting explosion pushes a piston; the piston turns a wheel. There is but one working stroke in every four, and the machine requires a large flywheel to regularize its movement, but as the historian Allan Nevins writes, the effect of the machine "was comparable to the sudden snapping on of an electric globe in a room men had been trying to light with smoky candles."[1] It was the world's first internal combustion engine.

It was not long before the engine, invented by Dr. N. A. Otto of Germany, was a regular feature of the American landscape. Adapted to run on gasoline, a hitherto uninteresting by-product of kerosene manufacture, it was an ideal stationary power plant. Writes Nevins, "Soon every progressive farm, shop, and feed-mill had its one-cylinder engine chugging away, pumping water, sawing wood, grinding meal, and doing other small jobs."[2] By 1900 there were more than 18,500 internal combustion engines in the United States; and whereas the most powerful model in the Chicago World's Fair in 1893 was 35 horsepower, at the Paris Exposition seven years later it was 1,000 horsepower.

The internal combustion engine was an extraordinary means of increasing, diffusing, and giving mobility to a basic requirement of material progress: power. And soon the new engine opened the way for a yet more startling advance. In 1886, Charles E. Duryea of Chicopee, Massachusetts had already decided that the gasoline engine was a far more promising power source than steam for a self-propelling road vehicle. By 1892 he and his brother had produced the first gas-powered "automobile," a weak and fragile toy. The next model in 1893 was a better one, and by 1896 the Duryea brothers actually sold thirteen cars. In that same year, a thirty-two-year-old mechanic called Henry Ford sold his first "quadricycle." The history of the automobile industry had begun.

Its growth was phenomenal. By 1905 there were 121 establishments making automobiles, and 10,000 wage earners were employed in the industry. By 1923 the number of plants had risen to 2,471, making the industry the largest in the country. In 1960 its annual payroll was as large as the national income of the United States in 1890. Not only that, but the automobile industry had become the single greatest customer for sheet steel, zinc, lead, rubber, leather. It was the buyer of one out of every three radios produced in the nation. It absorbed twenty-five billion pounds of chemicals a year. It was the second largest user of engineering talent in the country, bowing only to national defense. It was the source of one-sixth of all the patents issued in the nation and the object of one-tenth of all consumer spending in the country. In fact, it has been estimated that no less than one job out of every seven and one business out of every six owed their existences directly or indirectly to the car.

Even this impressive array of figures by no means exhausts the impact of the internal combustion engine and its vehicular mounting. Roughly eight out of every ten families today own a car; nearly six out of ten

---

[1] *Ford, the Times, the Man, the Company* (New York: Charles Scribner's Sons, 1954), I, 96.
[2] *Study in Power, John D. Rockefeller* (New York: Charles Scribner's Sons, 1953), II, 109.

own two or more cars. As a result, some fifty thousand towns managed to flourish without rail or water connections, an erstwhile impossibility; and seven out of ten workers no longer live within walking distance of their places of employment but drive to work. To an extraordinary extent, in other words, our entire economy has become "mobilized"— which is to say, dependent for its very functioning on the existence of wheeled, self-propelled transportation. If by some strange occurrence our automotive fleet were put out of commission—say by a spontaneous change in the nature of the gasoline molecule, rendering it incombustible—the effect would be as grave and as socially disastrous as a catastrophic famine in the Middle Ages.

GENERAL IMPACT OF TECHNOLOGY

We dwell on the impact of the car, not because it is the most significant of technological changes. Before the car, there was the startling economic transformation caused by the train, and after it came the no less totally transforming effects of electrical communication. Rather, we touch on the profound economic implications of the automobile to illustrate the diffuse effects of all industrial technology—effects which economics often cannot measure and which exceed its normal area of study but which must, nonetheless, be borne in mind as the ever-present and primary reality of the technological revolution itself. Let us mention a few of these general effects on the society in which we live.

The first has been a *vast increase in the degree of urbanization of society.* To an extraordinary extent (as we shall see in our next chapters) technology has enhanced the ability of the farmer to support the nonfarmer. As a result, society has more and more taken on the aspects and problems of the city rather than the country. In 1790 only twenty-four towns and cities in all of the United States had a population of more than 2,500, and together they accounted for only 6 per cent of the total population. By 1860 the 392 biggest cities held 20 per cent of the population; by the late 1960's, 168 great metropolitan areas from Boston through Washington, D.C., along the eastern seaboard had become virtually one huge, loosely connected city with over 60 per cent of the nation's people. Industrial technology has literally refashioned the human environment, bringing with it all the gains—and all the terrible problems—of city life on a mass scale.

Second, *the steady growth of industrial technology has radically lessened the degree of economic independence of the average citizen.* In our opening chapter we noted the extreme vulnerability of the "unsupported" inhabitant of a modern society, dependent on the work of a thousand others to sustain his own existence. This, too, we can now trace to the effect of the continuing industrial revolution. Technology has not only moved men off the soil and into the city, but has vastly increased the specialized nature of work. Unlike the "man of all trades" of the early nineteenth century—the farmer who could perform so many of his necessary tasks himself—the typical factory worker or office worker is trained and employed to do only one small part of a social operation which now achieves staggering complexity. Technology has vastly increased the degree of economic interdependence of the modern community and has made the solution of the economic problem hinge on the smooth coordination of an ever-widening network of delicately connected activities.

Third, *the expansion of industrial technology has radically altered the character of work.* For the greater part of man's history, work has been a strenuous physical activity, largely carried on alone or in small groups in the open air, requiring considerable dexterity to match human strength to the infinite variations of the natural environment, and culminating in an end product as unambiguously identifiable as the grain in the field or the cloth on a loom.

The industrial revolution profoundly altered these attributes of work. Work now consisted more and more of repetitive movements which, however exhausting after a full day, rarely involved more than a fraction of a man's full muscular ability. In place of the judgments and aptitudes required to meet the variations of nature, it demanded only the ability to repeat a single task adapted to a changeless work surface. No longer alone in nature, the worker performed his job in vast sheds with regiments like himself. And most wrenching of all, in place of "his" product, what he saw emerging from the factory was an object in which he could no longer locate, much less appreciate, his own contribution.

A worker in an automobile plant reports:

I work on a small conveyor which goes around in a circle. We call it a "merry-go-round." I make up zigzag springs for front seats. Every couple of feet on the conveyor there is a form for the pieces that make up the seat springs. As that form goes by me, I clip several pieces together, using a clip gun. I then put the pieces on the form, and it goes around to where other men clip more pieces together. . . . The only operation I do is work the clip gun. It takes just a couple of seconds to shoot six or eight clips into the spring and I do it as I walk a few steps. Then I start right over again. . . .[3]

What has been the effect on workers of this basic alteration in the pace and pattern of labor? Looking around us at factories (and offices), we find that industrial technology often subjects men to a stultifying and enervating discipline—that it makes work a singularly joyless and meaningless process to which they must subordinate their individual personalities. This is an aspect of technology that has disturbed observers since Adam Smith commented, two hundred years ago, that a

[3]Charles R. Walker and Robert H. Guest, *The Man on the Assembly Line* (Cambridge: Harvard University Press, 1952), p. 46.

man who endlessly performed the same task "generally becomes as stupid and ignorant as it is possible for a human creature to become."[4] Later, Karl Marx wrote with passion and perception about the terrible effects of industrial capitalism in divorcing the worker from the fruits of his own toil; and since Marx, writers in socialist as well as in capitalist nations have articulated the feelings of impotence and estrangement experienced by the individual in a vast, mechanized environment.

Is industrial technology in fact the cause of a pervasive "alienation" of man? We do not really know. Man today is certainly as much the servant as the master of his industrial apparatus. Yet we must guard against too easy an indictment of technology as the great dehumanizer. Let us not forget the terrible toll on the human personality of pre-industrial labor, with its exhausted peasants and its brutalized common laborers. Further, let us bear in mind that if the repressive and disciplinary aspects of technology predominate in our time, it may be because we are still only in the inception of the industrial history of humankind. In a longer perspective, this same technology holds forth at least the promise of an eventual emancipation of man, as machinery gradually takes over his onerous, monotonous tasks.

DISTRIBUTION OF THE LABOR FORCE

To this long-run promise of technology we will return again at the very conclusion of Part Four. But meanwhile we must pay heed to another important aspect of the technological invasion. This is the striking alteration it has brought about in the tasks of social provisioning. It is obvious that the inventory of work-skills that we possessed in 1800 would never suffice to operate the social machine of the 1960's. But even in the much shorter span since 1900, the required distribution of skills has significantly changed, as Table 5-1 shows.

Note how different is our profile of occupations today from the not too distant past. We have already commented on the sharp drop in the number of people needed to feed the nation, but we can also see a shift within the "blue collar" group from unskilled to skilled and semiskilled jobs, as more people labor with capital equipment than with their hands. In addition, as the sharp increase in the number of managers and clerical workers indicates, a swifter and more complex production process requires ever more people to coordinate and oversee the actual making of goods. In 1899 there was one nonproduction worker for every thirteen production workers in manufacturing; in 1964, one for three.

RISE OF UNIONISM

Before we leave this discussion of the general impact of technology on economic society, we must briefly look into one last attribute of

[4] *The Wealth of Nations* (Modern Library ed.), p. 734.

TABLE 5 · 1

| | Per cent of labor force | |
	1900	1968
Managerial and professional		
Professional and technical workers	4.1	14.1
Managers, officials, and proprietors (nonfarm)	5.9	10.4
White-collar		
Clerical workers	3.1	16.9
Sales workers	4.8	6.1
Blue-collar		
Skilled workers and foremen	10.3	12.9
Semiskilled workers	12.8	18.4
Unskilled workers	12.4	4.2
Household and other service workers	8.9	12.5
Farm		
Farmers and farm managers	20.0	2.6
Farm laborers	17.6	2.1

Source: 1900 figures calculated from *Historical Statistics of the United States*, Series D 72–122, p. 74; 1968 figures from *Statistical Abstract 1968*, p. 225. Totals do not add to 100 per cent, owing to rounding.

industrialism—the rise of labor unions within the market system during the late nineteenth and early twentieth centuries.

Actually we can trace the origins of trade unionism back to early Roman times, when some workmen joined into semifraternal orders. But unionism as an important social institution obviously had to await the creation of a free labor force, and that, as we know, did not occur until relatively recent times. And even after labor had been pried loose from its feudal status and thrown upon the market for survival, unionism still awaited as a final stimulus the advent of an industrial technology that brought masses of men together in the insecure and impersonal environment of the factory.

Thus, all through the nineteenth century, as industrial technology entered nation after nation, we also find a strong impetus toward union organization. In nearly every nation, it should also be noted, these movements were met at first with determined and often ferocious resistance: under the so-called Conspiracy Doctrine and the Combination Laws (1800) of Great Britain, for example, thousands of workmen were punished for combining to raise wages—although in no case were employers punished for combining to lower them. Indeed, for a quarter of a century, British unionists were treated as rebels or common criminals, as they also were, for that matter, in France or Germany.

In America, trade union progress was also slow. The strong American belief in "rugged individualism"—a belief shared by many workers as well as by their bosses—a reliance on docile immigrant labor in the heavy industries, and the use of every legal and many illegal weapons on the part of employers kept American unionism largely limited to the skilled crafts long after the union movement had finally gained acceptance and some measure of power in Europe.

During the 1920's, for example, union membership *dropped* some 30 per cent, partly as a result of an all-out attack by the National Association of Manufacturers; partly as a consequence of labor's own indifference to unionism. By 1929 less than one nonagricultural worker in five belonged to a union, and not a single industrial union of consequence had yet organized a mass production industry.*

The coming of industrial unionism in America was compressed into a few dramatic years in the mid-1930's. Then, under the combined impetus of the New Deal and the newly-formed Congress for Industrial Organization (CIO), the long pent-up pressures of labor frustration finally broke the barriers of corporate resistance. In a series of dramatic strikes, the CIO won contracts from Ford and General Motors, United States Steel and Bethlehem Steel, all bastions of antilabor resistance. It was not the terms of the contracts that mattered so much as the fact that in signing any contract at all, the companies *for the first time* recognized the unions as bargaining agents for their workers regarding wages, hours, and working conditions.

As a result unionism boomed. By 1940 the number of the unionized had jumped from less than 4 million to over 8 million, and big business resistance to union was effectively finished.

It is difficult today to reconstruct that era, not so very long past, when Walter Reuther was thrown down a flight of concrete stairs and kicked by the hired strongmen of the Ford Motor Company, when coal miners carried rifles to fight the local police, or when strikers actually seized and occupied General Motors and Chrysler plants. The tumultuous history of this turning point in labor history has today given way to a much calmer era, in which tensions and conflicts continue to mark the relations of business and labor (as they always will in a market society), but the attitudes and actions of the antilabor past already seem to be ancient history.

We cannot trace here the full story of American unionism, (including the very important and checkered history of its efforts at self-government), but one point seems worth making before we return to our main narrative. It is that a high point in union membership seems to have been reached in the late 1950's when just over 18 million workers, or about 32 per cent of all nonagricultural employment, belonged to

---

*Craft unions seek to organize the workers of a particular skill (regardless of where they work) into one union; examples are the Newspaper Guild and the carpenters' or the plumbers' unions. Industrial unions, on the other hand, join all the members of a given industry (regardless of their craft or level of skill); examples are the Steelworkers and the United Auto Workers.

affiliates of the AFL-CIO or to independent unions. Since then there has been a stagnation in union growth, all the more noticeable against a rising total labor force.

Why has the union movement ceased to grow? The single, most cogent reason seems to lie in the very shift in the job spectrum we have already examined. Blue-collar jobs, where trade unionism has traditionally been strongest, are now a static or perhaps slowly declining fraction of the work force. Conversely, the fastest growing area of employment is in the service and white-collar sectors, where the antipathy to unionism has always been greatest.

Out of this shift in occupations may come a new era in labor relations—and in labor problems. It is unlikely, as we have seen, that industrial unionism will experience much further dynamic growth. But this does not mean that the power of organized labor is therefore on the wane. For the stability or shrinkage in industrial unionism has been compensated in recent years by a sudden rise of union strength in the service and white-collar areas, particularly in the public sector. Strikes of sanitation workers and teachers can be very disruptive and, more important, may be difficult to settle without large wage increases. Unlike the case of a union dealing with a corporation, a union dealing with a municipality or a state does not have to temper its demands to the ability of its adversary to pay wages out of its *sales*. Instead, wage increases are ultimately limited only by the amount of additional *tax revenues* that the union can force the public authority to allocate to its members. Thus, restraints on public wages are very hard to impose.

There is a second and even more cogent reason for labor's gain in the balance of power between employer and worker. Traditionally, the employer has held the whip hand over the union, because in all labor disputes, sooner or later, the pressure of sheer need would compel the union to agree to the employer's offer. But this inherent inequality is changing as technology increases the general affluence of the economy. When workers' bank balances and union treasuries are full, and when it is easy for strikers to find temporary employment, the traditional pressures on the union to "settle" lose much of their effect.

All this implies that considerable labor problems may lie ahead, for which there are no simple solutions. What is necessary is to recognize that these problems, which we tend to blame on this union leader or on that company or public official, have their roots in a much deeper change of situation—indeed, that they ultimately spring, as we have said, from the power of technology to increase productivity and to alter the occupational mix. Another way of putting it is that technology has rearranged the priorities of society, lessening the pressing nature of the production problem and exacerbating that of the distribution problem; and while such reflections do not help us solve our problems, at least they enable us to understand them better.

Thus far we have examined some of the diffuse effects of industrial technology on the life-ways of society. Now we must turn back to a more technical aspect of the industrial process—but one that in many ways underlies the larger and more general effects we have been studying. This is the development of a new method of industrial production first visible after the 1860's, although not fully realized until the turn of the twentieth century. This is the method of *mass production*.

Allan Nevins has described what mass production techniques looked like in the early Ford assembly lines.

Just how were the main assembly lines and lines of component production and supply kept in harmony? For the chassis alone, from 1,000 to 4,000 pieces of each component had to be furnished each day at just the right point and right minute; a single failure, and the whole mechanism would come to a jarring standstill. . . . Superintendents had to know every hour just how many components were being produced and how many were in stock. Whenever danger of shortage appeared, the shortage chaser—a familiar figure in all automobile factories—flung himself into the breach. Counters and checkers reported to him. Verifying in person any ominous news, he mobilized the foreman concerned to repair deficiencies. Three times a day he made typed reports in manifold to the factory clearing-house, at the same time chalking on blackboards in the clearing-house office a statement of results in each factory-production department and each assembling department.[5]

Such systematizing in itself resulted in astonishing increases in productivity. With each operation analyzed and subdivided into its simplest components, with a steady stream of work passing before stationary men, with a relentless but manageable pace of work, the total time required to assemble a car dropped astonishingly. Within a single year, the time required to assemble a motor fell from 600 minutes to 226 minutes; to build a chassis, from 12 hours and 28 minutes to 1 hour and 33 minutes. A stop-watch man was told to observe a 3-minute assembly in which men assembled rods and piston, a simple operation. The job was divided into three jobs, and half the men turned out the same output as before.[6]

But what interests us in the context of our study are not the technical achievements of mass production as much as its economic results. For increases in productivity bring reductions in cost. Even though the machinery needed for mass production is extremely expensive, output increases so fast that costs *per unit* of output drop dramatically.

Imagine, for instance, a small plant turning out 1,000 items a day with the labor of ten men and a small amount of equipment. Suppose each man is paid $10, each item before manufacture costs 10¢, and

[5] *Ford, the Times, the Man, the Company,* I, 507.
[6] *Ibid.,* pp. 504, 506.

the daily amount of "overhead"—that is, the daily share of costs such as rent, plant maintenance, office salaries, and wear-and-tear on equipment—comes to $100. Then our total daily cost of production is $300 per day ($100 of payroll, $100 of raw material cost, and $100 of overhead). Divided among 1,000 items of output, our cost per item is 30¢.

Now imagine that our product lends itself to mass production techniques. Our payroll may then jump to $1,000 and with our much larger plant and equipment, our daily overhead to $5,000. Nevertheless, mass production may have boosted output as much as 100 times. Then our total daily cost of production will be $16,000 ($1,000 of payroll, $5,000 of overhead, and $10,000 of raw material costs). Divided among our 100,000 items of output, our cost per item has fallen to 16¢. Despite a quintupling of over-all expense, our cost per unit has almost halved.

This is not a far-fetched example of what economists call *the economies of large-scale production*. A glance at Table 5-2 shows how mass production techniques did, in fact, boost output of Ford cars by more than one hundred times while reducing their cost by seven-eighths.

TABLE 5 · 2

Year	Unit sales, Ford cars	Price of typical model (touring)	
1907–1908	6,398	$2,800 (Model K)	
1908–1909	10,607	850	
1909–1910	18,664	950	
1910–1911	34,528	780	
1911–1912	78,440	690	
1912–1913	168,304	600	Model T
1913–1914	248,307	550	
1914–1915	221,805 (10 mos.)	490	
1915–1916	472,350	440	
1916–1917	730,041	360	

Compiled from Nevins, *Ford, the Times, the Man, the Company*, pp. 644, 646–47.

Nor do the dynamics of the industrial process come to a halt with these formidable economies of large-scale production. For this technological achievement brings into the market system itself a new element of primary importance. That element is *size*.

It is not difficult to see why. Once a firm—by virtue of adroit management, improved product, advantages of location, or whatever other reason—steps out decisively in front of its competitors in size, *the economies of large-scale production operate to push it out still further in front*. Bigger size usually means lower cost, at least for a young expanding industry. Lower cost means bigger profits. Bigger profits mean the ability to grow to still larger size. Thus the techniques of large-scale manufacture bring about a situation threatening to alter the whole meaning of competition. From a mechanism that prevents any single firm from dominating the market, competition now becomes a force that may drive an ever-larger share of the market into the hands of the largest and most efficient producer.

We shall have much more to say about the economics of the drive to bigness when we study the market system in Part Three. Yet, it may be helpful if we look once again at the actual historic scene in which this internal growth took place. For the processes of economic change described in this chapter did not occur in a vacuum. They were brought about by a social "type" and a business milieu which powerfully accelerated and abetted the process of industrial enlargement, much as the New Men had speeded along the initial industrializing process in England in the late eighteenth century.

The agents of change during the late nineteenth century in America were very much the descendants of their industrial forebears a century earlier. Like Arkwright and Watt, many of the greatest American entrepreneurs were men of humble origin endowed with an indomitable drive for business success. There was Carnegie in steel, Harriman in railroads, Rockefeller in oil, Frick in coke, Armour and Swift in meat packing, McCormick in agricultural machinery—to mention but a few. To be sure, the *typical* businessman was very different from these Horatio Alger stereotypes of the business hero. Economic historians, such as F. W. Taussig, looking back over the careers of the business leaders of the late nineteenth century, have discovered that the average entrepreneur was not a poor, industrious immigrant lad, but the son of well-circumstanced people often in business affairs themselves. Nor was the average businessman nearly so successful as a Carnegie or a Rockefeller.

Yet in nearly every line of business, at least *one* "captain of industry" appeared who dominated the field by his personality and ability. Though few achieved their supreme degree of pecuniary success, the number who climbed into the "millionaire class" was impressive. In 1880 it had been estimated that there were 100 millionaires in the country. By 1916 the number had grown to 40,000.

Interesting and significant differences distinguish these nineteenth century business leaders from those of a century earlier. The American captains of industry were not typically men whose leadership rested on inventive or engineering skills. With the growth of large-scale production, the engineering functions became the province of salaried production experts, of second-echelon plant managers. What was required now was the master touch in guiding industrial strategy, in making or breaking alliances, choosing salients for advance, or overseeing the logistics of the whole operation. More and more the great entrepreneurs were concerned with the strategy of finance, of competition, of sales, rather than with the cold technics of production itself.

Then, too, we must make note of the entrepreneurial tactics and tone of the period. In a phrase that has stuck, Matthew Josephson once called the great men of business in this era "the robber barons." In many ways, they did indeed resemble the predatory lords of the medieval era. For example, in the 1860's a small group of California entrepreneurs under the guiding hand of Collis Huntington performed the astonishing feat of building a railroad across the hitherto impassible Rockies and Sierras. Aware that Huntington and his associates would thereby have a monopolistic control of all rail traffic to California, the Congress authorized the construction of three competing lines. But the legislators had not taken the measure of the wily pioneers. Before their own line was completed, they secretly bought the charter of one competitive line; and when the second proved somewhat harder to buy out, they simply built it out, recklessly flinging their lines into its territory until it, too, was forced to surrender. Thereafter it was no great trick to buy out the third, having first blocked it at a critical mountain pass. Only one competitive source of transportation remained: the Pacific Mail Steamship Company. Fortunately, this was owned by the obliging Jay Gould, a famous robber baron in his own right; and for the payment of a proper tribute, he agreed to eliminate San Francisco as a cargo port. There was now *no* way of bringing goods across the nation into southern California except those which the Huntington group controlled. Counting the smaller lines and subsidiaries which passed into their grasp, *nineteen* rail systems, in all, came under their domain. It was not surprising that to the residents of California the resulting unified system was known as "the Octopus" and that its average freight rate was the highest in the nation.

And it was not just the railroad industry that used economic power to create a monopoly position. In whisky and in sugar, in tobacco and cattlefeed, in wire nails, steel hoops, electrical appliances, tin plate, in matches and meat there was an octopus similar to that which fastened itself on California. One commentator of the late 1890's pictured the American citizen born to the profit of the Milk Trust and dying to that of the Coffin Trust.

If the robber barons milked the public as consumers (and to an even greater extent bilked them as stockholders), they also had no compunctions about cutting each other down to size. In the struggle for financial control of the Albany and Susquehanna Railroad, for instance, James Fisk and J. P. Morgan found themselves in the uncomfortable position of each owning a terminal at the end of a single line. Like their feudal prototypes, they resolved the controversy by combat, mounting locomotives at each end and running them full tilt into each other—after which the losers still did not give up, but retired, ripping up the line and tearing down trestles as they went. In similar spirit, the Huntington group that built the Central Pacific hired General David Colton to run a subsidiary enterprise for them, and the General wrote to his employers:

I have learned one thing. We have got *no true* friends outside of us five. We cannot depend upon a human soul outside of ourselves, and hence we must all be good-natured, stick together, and keep to our own counsels.

whereupon he proceeded to swindle his friends out of several millions.

With this buccaneering went as well another identifying mark of the times: what the economist Thorstein Veblen was to call Conspicuous Consumption. One repentant member of the gilded age recalled in his memoirs parties at which cigarettes were wrapped in money for the sheer pleasure of inhaling wealth; a dog that was presented with a $15,000 diamond collar; an infant, resting in a $10,000 cradle, attended by four doctors who posted regular bulletins on the baby's (excellent) health; the parade of fabulous chateaux stuffed with fabulous and not-so-fabulous works of art on New York's Fifth Avenue; and the collection of impecunious European royalty as sons-in-law of the rich.

The age was a rollicking, sometimes cruel, but always dynamic one. Yet what interests us here is not to recount its colorful social history as much as to understand its deeper economic consequences. It is impossible to consider the period with which we have been concerned without taking into account the social type of the robber baron and the milieu in which he operated. Bold, aggressive, acquisitive, competitive, the great entrepreneur was the natural agent to speed along the process for which the technology of the day prepared the way. But as yet we have only begun to sketch out the changes wrought by the joint impact of strong men and ever-more complex machinery. Now we must look more carefully into the effect that this combination produced.

SUMMARY

1. The industrial revolution brought not one but *successive waves of technical progress* and economic advance.

2. In studying the impact of these industrial discoveries, we must broaden our lens to look beyond the effect on productivity alone (although that was no doubt the single most important result). Industrialization brought:

   • A vast increase in *urbanization*.
   • A cumulative rise in the degree of *economic interdependence* of individuals within society.
   • A new climate for and character of work, including *the disturbing problems of monotonous industrial work* (alienation).
   • A *sweeping redistribution of occupations* away from unskilled toward semi-skilled, technical, and managerial labor.
   • The rise of *unionism*.

3. The new technology brought as well a change in the character of both production and competition. Production became more and more a process of highly integrated subassemblies, making possible the *mass production* of goods. The large amounts of capital required for mass production led to very great *economies of scale*.

4. With the advent of mass production, *the nature of competition also changed radically*. Economies of scale led to situations in which a leading firm could undersell all competitors and thus dominate a market.

5. The dynamic potential of the new technology was given further impetus by the *aggressive "robber baron" era* of business leadership.

1. Describe the social, as well as economic, repercussions of the following inventions: the typewriter, the jet airplane, television, penicillin. Which do you think is greater in each case—the social or economic impact?

2. The philosopher Karl Jaspers has claimed that modern technology brings an "immense joylessness." Do you agree? Is factory work unpleasant, to your mind? Office work, in a very large organization such as an insurance company? Do you think the nature of industrial work can be basically changed?

3. White-collar jobs have always proved harder to unionize than so-called blue-collar (factory floor) jobs. Why do you think this is so? Do you think it might change?

4. Suppose that you have a business in which you hire five men, to whom you pay $2 an hour; suppose further that you have overhead costs of $100 a day and that you pay $1 in materials cost for each item that your business manufactures. Assuming that you keep all five men, what is your average cost per unit of output if your plant turns out 10 items per 8-hour day? 100 items? 1,000?

5. Which is more economical, a plant with a payroll of $400 a week, with $100 of overhead a week, and with an output of 100 units per week, or a plant with a payroll of $80,000 a week, an overhead of $100,000 a week, and with an output of 50,000 units per week?

6. How do you explain economies of large-scale production? Why do certain businesses, such as cigarette manufacture, seem to enjoy them, whereas other businesses, such as barbering, do not?

6 THE CHANGE IN MARKET STRUCTURE

So far we have investigated the impact of the new technology of mass production mainly insofar as it exerted its pervasive influence on "social" life, and we have only glanced at its effects on the workings of the economic system proper. Now we must look more carefully into this latter problem. For under the joint impetus of the drive of bold entrepreneurs and the self-feeding tendencies of economies of large-scale production dramatic changes began to appear in many sectors of the economy by the end of the nineteenth century. A system originally characterized by large numbers of small enterprises was starting to give way to one in which production was increasingly concentrated in the hands of a relatively few, very big and very powerful business units.

By 1900, for example, the number of textile mills, although still large, had dropped by a third from the 1880's; over the same period, the number of manufacturers of agricultural implements had fallen by 60 per cent, and the number of leather manufacturers by three-quarters. In the locomotive industry, two companies ruled the roost in 1900, contrasted with nineteen in 1860. The biscuit and cracker industry changed from a scatter of small companies to a market in which one producer had 90 per cent of the industry's capacity by the turn of the century. Meanwhile in steel there was the colossal U.S. Steel Corporation, which alone turned out over half the steel production of the nation. In oil, the Standard Oil Company tied up between 80 to 90 per cent of the nation's output. In tobacco, the American Tobacco Company controlled 75 per cent of the output of cigarettes and 25 per cent of cigars. Similar control rested with the American Sugar Company, the American Smelting and Refining Company, the United Shoe Machinery Company, and dozens more.

From an over-all view, the change was even more impressive. In the early 1800's, according to the calculations of Myron W. Watkins, no single plant controlled as much as 10 per cent of the output of a manufacturing industry. By 1904, 78 enterprises controlled over half the output of their industries, 57 controlled 60 per cent or more, and 28 controlled 80 per cent or more. From industry to industry, this degree of "concentration" varied—from no significant concentration at all in printing and publishing, for instance, to the highly concentrated market structure of industries like copper or rubber. But there was no mistaking the over-all change. In 1896, railroads excepted, there were not a dozen $10 million companies in the nation. By 1904, there were over 300 of them with a combined capitalization of over $7 billion. Together, these giants controlled over two-fifths of the industrial capital of the nation and affected four-fifths of its important industries.[1]

Clearly something akin to a major revolution in market structure had taken place. Let us examine more closely the course of events which led up to it.

The initial impact of the trend to big business was an unexpected one. Rather than diminishing the degree of competitiveness of the market structure, it extended and intensified it. In the largely agricultural, handicraft, and small factory economy of the early nineteenth century, "the" market consisted mainly of small, localized markets, each insulated from the next by the high cost of transportation and each supplied by local producers who had neither the means nor the motivation to invade the market on anything resembling a national scale.

The rise of mass production radically changed this fragmented market structure and, with it, the type of competition within the market. As canals and railroads opened the country and as new manufacturing techniques vastly increased output, the parochial quality of the market

[1]John Moody, *The Truth about Trusts* (Chicago: Moody Publishing Co., 1904). See also Ralph Nelson, *Merger Movements in American Industry, 1895–1956* (Princeton, N.J.: National Bureau of Economic Research, 1959).

system changed. More and more, one unified and interconnected market bound together the entire nation, and the petty semimonopolies of local suppliers were invaded by products from large factories in distant cities.

Quickly, a second development followed. As the new production techniques gained momentum, aggressive businessmen typically not only built, but overbuilt. "As confident entrepreneurs raced to take advantage of every ephemeral rise in prices, of every advance in tariff schedules, of every new market opened by the railroads and puffed up immigration," write Thomas Cochran and William Miller in a history of these industrializing times, "they recklessly expanded and mechanized their plants, each seeking the greatest share of the new melon."[2]

The result was a phenomenal burst in output but, simultaneously, a serious change in the nature of competition. Competition now became not only more extensive, but more *expensive*. As the size of the plant and the complexity of equipment grew, so did the "fixed charges" of a business enterprise—the interest on borrowed capital, the depreciation of capital assets, the cost of administrative staff, the rent of land, and "overhead," generally. These costs tended to remain fairly constant, regardless of whether sales were good or bad. Unlike the payment of wages to a working force, which dropped when men were fired, there was no easy way to cut down the steady drain of payments for these fixed expenditures. The result was that the bigger the business, the more vulnerable was its economic health when competition cut into its sales.

The ebullience of the age, plus the steady growth of a technology that required massive investments, made competition increasingly drastic. As growing giant businesses locked horns, railroad against railroad, steel mill against steel mill, each sought to assure the coverage of its fixed expenses by gaining for itself as much of the market as it could. The outcome was the emergence of "cutthroat competition" among massive producers, replacing the more restricted, local competition of the small business, small market world. In 1869, for example, the New York–Chicago railway freight rate on a hundredweight of grain crashed from $1.80, on February 4, to 40¢ twenty days later, climbed back to $1.88 in July, and then plummeted to 25¢ in August when another "war" broke out. In the oil fields, the coal fields, among the steel and copper producers, similar price wars repeatedly occurred as producers sought to capture the markets they needed to achieve a profitable level of production. All this was unquestionably favorable to the consumer, as indeed competitive situations always are, but it threatened literal bankruptcy for the competing enterprises themselves— and furthermore, bankruptcy on a multimillion dollar scale.

[2] *The Age of Enterprise* (New York: Harper & Row, Torchbooks, rev. ed., 1961), p. 139.

In these circumstances, it is not difficult to understand the next phase of economic development. The giants decided not to compete.

But how were they to avoid competition? Since common law invalidated any contract binding a competitor to fixed prices or production schedules, there seemed no alternative but voluntary cooperation: trade associations, "gentleman's agreements," or "pools," informal treaties to divide the market. By the 1880's there were a cordage pool and a whiskey pool, a coal pool, a salt pool, and endless rail pools, all calculated to relieve the individual producers from the mutually suicidal game of all-out competition. But to little avail. The division of the market worked well during good times; but when bad times approached, the pools broke down. As sales fell, the temptation to cut prices was irresistible, and thus began again the old, ruinous game of competition.

The robber baron ethics of the day contributed to the difficulties. "A starving man will usually get bread if it is to be had," said James J. Hill, a great railway magnate, "and a starving railway will not maintain rates."[3] Typically, at a meeting of rail heads called to agree upon a common freight schedule, the president of one road slipped out, during a brief recess, to wire the new rates to his road, so that it might be the first to undercut them. (By chance, his wire was intercepted, so that when the group next met it was forced to recognize that even among thieves there is not always honor.)

During the 1880's, a more effective device for control became available. In 1879, Samuel Dodd, lawyer for the new Standard Oil Company, had a brilliant idea for regulating the murderous competition that regularly wracked the oil industry. He devised the idea of a trust. Stockholders of companies that wished to join in the Standard Oil Trust were asked to surrender their actual shares to the board of directors of the new trust. Thereby they would give up working control over their companies, but in return they would get "trust certificates" which entitled them to the same share in the profits as their shares earned. In this way, the Standard Oil directors wielded control over all the associated companies, while the former stockholders shared fully in the profits.

Eventually, as we shall see, the trusts were declared to be illegal. But by that time, still more effective devices were created. In 1888 the New Jersey legislature passed a law allowing a corporation chartered in the state to buy stock in another corporation. This was a privilege that had not previously been available to corporations chartered anywhere in the United States. The result was the rapid appearance of the corporate merger, the coming together of two corporations to form a new, bigger one. In manufacturing and mining, alone, there were 43 mergers in 1895 (affecting $41 million dollars worth of corporate assets);

---

[3] Cochran and Miller, *op. cit.*, p. 141.

26 mergers in 1896, 69 mergers in 1897. Then in 1898 there were 303—and finally in 1899 a climactic *1,208 mergers combined some $2.26 billion in corporate assets.*[4] Another great wave of mergers occurred in the 1920's. In all, from 1895 to 1929, some $20 billion of industrial corporate wealth were merged into larger units.*

Another effective means of limiting competition was the *holding company.* Having passed a law permitting its corporations to buy stock in one another, New Jersey now allowed its corporations to do business in any state. Thus the legal foundation was laid for a central corporation which could control subsidiary enterprises by the simple means of buying a controlling share of their stock. By 1911, when the Standard Oil combine was finally dissolved, Standard Oil of New Jersey had used this device to acquire direct control over seventy companies and indirect control over thirty more.

Yet we must not think that it was only the movement toward trustification and merger that brought about the emergence of the giant firm with its ability to limit—or eliminate—competition. Equally, perhaps more, important was simply the process of internal growth. Ford and General Motors, General Electric and A.T.&T., DuPont and Carnegie Steel (later to be the core of U.S. Steel) grew essentially because their market was expanding and they were quick, able, efficient, and aggressive enough to grow faster than any of their competitors. All of them gobbled up some small businesses along the way, and most of them benefited from agreements not to compete. But their gradual emergence to a position of dominance within their industries was not, in the last analysis, attributable to these facts. It was the dynamism of their own business leadership, coupled with a production technique which made enormous size both possible and profitable.

THE THREAT OF ECONOMIC FEUDALISM

Certainly, size became enormous. By the end of the nineteenth century, some business units were already considerably larger than the states in which they were located. Charles William Eliot pointed out in 1888 that a single railway with headquarters in Boston not only employed three times as many people as the entire government of the Commonwealth of Massachusetts, but enjoyed gross receipts nearly six

---

[4] *Historical Statistics of the United States* (Washington, D. C.: U.S. Bureau of the Census), Series V, pp. 30–31.

*We must take a footnote to call attention to a development that deserves a chapter in itself. This is the importance of the *corporation,* as a marvelously adaptive legal form of organizing production, in spurring on the growth of the economy. Unlike the personal proprietorship or partnership, the corporation existed quite independently of its owners, survived their deaths, and could enter into binding contracts in "its" own name. Further, by limiting the liability of its owners to the value of the stock they had bought, it protected a capitalist against limitless loss. Much has been written, quite rightly, about the abuses of corporations, but it is important to recognize how valuable was this ingenious legal innovation in encouraging the accumulation of capital and in creating the organizational means to supervise and direct that capital into production.

times that of the state government which had created it. But by comparison with the findings of the Pujo Committee of the U.S. Senate, not quite twenty-five years later, the railway was still small. The committee pointed out that the Morgan banking interests held 341 directorships in 112 corporations whose aggregate wealth exceeded by three times the value of *all* the real and personal property of New England. And not only was the process of trustification eating away at the competitive structure of the market, but the emergence of enormous financially controlled empires posed as well a political problem of ominous portent. As Woodrow Wilson declared: "If monopoly persists, monopoly will always sit at the helm of government. I do not expect to see monopoly restrain itself. If there are men in this country big enough to own the government of the United States, they are going to own it."[5]

Not surprisingly, from many quarters the trend to bigness was vehemently opposed. From the 1880's on, a series of state laws strove to undo the trusts which squeezed their citizens. Louisiana sued the Cottonseed Oil Trust; New York, the Sugar Trust; Ohio, the Oil Trust—but to little avail. When one state, like New York, clamped down on its trusts, other states, seeing the revenue available from a change in corporate headquarters, virtually invited the trust to set up business there. When the Supreme Court ruled that corporations, as "persons," could not be deprived of property without "due process of law," state regulation became almost totally useless.

It was soon clear that if something further were to be done, the federal government would have to do it. "Congress alone can deal with the trusts," said Senator Sherman in 1890, "and if we are unwilling or unable, there will soon be a trust for every production and a master to fix the price for every necessity of life."[6]

The result was the Sherman Antitrust Act, an act which, on its surface, was an effective remedy for the problem. "Every contract, combination . . . or conspiracy, in restraint of trade" was declared to be illegal. Violators were subject to heavy fines and jail sentences, and triple damages could be obtained by persons who proved economic injury because of unfair price rigging.

Indeed, under the Sherman Act a number of trusts were prosecuted; and in a famous action in 1911, the great Standard Oil Trust was ordered dissolved. Yet, despite the break-up of a few trusts, the act was singularly weak. Fines for violations were too small to be effective, and in any case, few were levied: not until Franklin Roosevelt's time would

RISE OF
ANTITRUST
LEGISLATION

[5] Richard Hofstadter, *The Age of Reform* (New York: Alfred A. Knopf, Inc., 1955), p. 231.
[6] Cochran and Miller, *op. cit.,* p. 171.

the Antitrust Division of the Department of Justice have as much as a million dollars with which to investigate and control the affairs of a multi-billion dollar economy. In fact, during the first fifty years of its existence, only 252 criminal actions were instituted under the Sherman law. And then too, the prevailing judicial opinion of the 1890's and early 1900's was not much in sympathy with the act. The Supreme Court early dealt it a severe blow by finding, in the American Sugar Refining case, that manufacturing was not "commerce," and therefore the American Sugar Refining Company, which had bought controlling stock interests in its four largest competitors, was not to be considered as acting "in restraint of trade." It is not surprising that the concentration of business was hardly slowed in such a climate of opinion. As a humorist of the times put it: "What looks like a stone wall to a layman is a triumphal arch to a corporation lawyer."

These weaknesses led to further acts in 1914: primarily, the Clayton Antitrust Act, prohibiting specific kinds of price discrimination and mergers by the acquisition of stock in competing corporations; and the Federal Trade Commission, which sought to define and prevent "unfair" business practices. As we shall see later, these acts were not without their effect. Yet, undermining the entire antitrust movement there remained one critical and vitiating fact. The purpose of antitrust was essentially to restore competitive conditions to markets which were in danger of becoming "monopolized" by giant firms. Against this tendency, antitrust legislation could pose a deterrent only insofar as the monopolization process resulted from the outright *combination* of erstwhile competitors. Against a much more fundamental condition—the ability of large businesses to enjoy decisive advantages in finance, merchandising, and research over small businesses—it could offer no remedy. While antitrust effort concentrated its fire against collusion or amalgamation, it was powerless against the fact of spontaneous internal growth.

And therefore growth continued. Through most of the first quarter of the twentieth century, the biggest corporations not only grew, but grew much *faster* than their smaller competitors. As Adolf Berle and Gardiner Means pointed out in a famous study in 1932, between 1909 and 1928 the 200 largest nonfinancial corporations increased their gross assets over 40 percent more rapidly than all nonfinancial corporations.[7] Looking into the future, Berle and Means concluded:

Just what does this rapid growth of the big companies promise for the future? Let us project the trend of the growth of recent years. If the wealth of the large corporations and that of all corporations should each continue to increase for the next twenty years at its average annual rate for the twenty years from

[7] *The Modern Corporation and Private Property* (New York: The Macmillan Company, 1948), p. 36.

1909 to 1929, 70 per cent of all corporate activity would be carried on by two hundred corporations in 1950. If the more rapid rates of growth from 1924 to 1929 were maintained for the next twenty years 85 per cent of corporate wealth would be held by two hundred huge units. . . . If the indicated growth of the large corporations and of the national wealth were to be effective from now until 1950, half of the national wealth would be under the control of big companies at the end of that period.[8]

Indeed, warned the authors, if the trend of the past continued unchecked, it was predictable that in 360 years all the corporate wealth in the nation would have become fused into one gigantic enterprise which would then have an expected life span equal to that of the Roman Empire.

Has the Berle and Means project come true? The question brings to a climax our long survey of the changing market structure. We have been concerned with gathering up the various forces that created and shaped the market as a great system of economic control. Now we must see what the outcome of that process has been.

Let us begin by looking at the market system in the United States today. Immediately, we notice one thing: there is not one market system in America, but two. One of them, with which we are all familiar at firsthand, consists of the millions of small enterprises that make up the large stratum of the population known as "small-business men." Here are the stores we pass every day on the avenues, the columns of names in the yellow pages of the phone books.

There are roughly 10 million "small" businesses in America, counting every one from the newsstand through the farm (4 million farms) up to enterprises that employ several hundred people and count their dollar volume in tens of millions.* Among these 10 million business units, corporations number only about one million, but these one million corporations do *five times* as much business as all the small proprietorships and partnerships. In turn, however, most of the million corporations are small, even when measured by a small-business yardstick. Well over half do less than $100,000 a year in sales, with the result that the whole group of little corporations accounts for only 2 per cent of all corporate sales.

Thus, in terms of sales (or assets), little business is little indeed. Yet, by virtue of its numbers, the small businesses of America are by no means unimportant in the national economic picture. Small business

STRUCTURE OF THE NATIONAL MARKET: PERIPHERY AND CENTER

---

[8] *Ibid.,* pp. 40–41.

*Just to get an idea of scale, the 500th largest American industrial corporation in 1967 was Itek, with sales of $131 million and 5,749 employees. The biggest industrial corporation was General Motors, with sales of $20 billion and 728,198 employees.

collectively employs roughly 40 per cent of the American labor force. (This compares with 35 per cent of the labor force that works for the "not-for-profit" sector—state, local, and federal government, hospitals, social services agencies, clubs, etc.—and with 25 per cent that works for big business.) Millions of small entrepreneurs constitute the very core of the American "middle class," and thus give a characteristic small-business view to much of American political and social life.

Yet it must be emphasized that even as a collectivity, the 10 million minibusinesses do not begin to match the economic power of a tiny number of giant enterprises at the other end of the scale. In the apt phrase of Robert Averitt, small business constitutes the Periphery, but the giants constitute the Center.[9] For here, in a few hundred large industrial corporations, is an economy within an economy, a "system" unto itself. All by itself, this very small core of corporations—500 at the most—accounts for a third of all industrial sales, and within that core there is an inner core that by itself produces the main flow of industrial production on which the economy rests.

Table 6-1 gives us an introduction to the strategic position of the giant company.

The table speaks for itself. Note that nearly 200 giant corporations owned one-half of all the assets of the entire group and that in the vital manufacturing sector, fewer than 100 corporations owned over 40 per cent of all the plant and equipment, cash and other wealth of their group.

TABLE 6 · 1

GIANT CORPORATIONS (1955)

RELATIVE SHARES IN VARIOUS SECTORS OF U.S. ECONOMY

Sector	All corporations		Corporations with assets of $250 million or more	
	Number	Total assets ($ billion)	Number	Per cent of all corporation assets
Manufacturing	124,200	$201.4	97	42
Mining[a]	9,700	13.3	(19)	(32)
Public Utilities	4,800	62.9	56	72
Transportation	21,900	43.5	30	61
Total	**160,600**	**321.1**	**192**	**50**

[a] Figures in parentheses show number and share of corporations with assets of $100 million or more.

Source: *The Corporation in Modern Society*, Edward S. Mason, ed. (Cambridge: Harvard University Press, 1959), p. 87. (The last row has been calculated from the above.)

[9] Robert T. Averitt, *The Dual Economy* (New York: W. W. Norton & Company, Inc., 1968).

These figures, however, fail to indicate the full extent of concentration today. For recently there has been a burst of merger activity, which has still further raised the share of total corporate assets in the hands of the biggest companies. Between 1950 and 1961, one-fifth of the top 1,000 corporations disappeared—absorbed within the remaining four-fifths. As a result of this and other growth, by 1967 the 100 largest corporations owned nearly 50 per cent of all manufacturing assets in the nation—*almost the same share as the 200 largest corporations had owned in 1948.*[10] And in 1968 alone, according to the Federal Trade Commission, an all-time record of between $11 billion and $12 billion in assets were acquired by the biggest companies through mergers—more than twice the figure for 1967.

Here is a trend that seems to confirm the worst fears of Berle and Means. Does the conclusion that they feared also follow? For in *The Modern Corporation and Private Property* they wrote: "a society in which production is governed by blind market forces is being replaced by one in which production is carried on under the ultimate control of a handful of individuals."[11] In the light of our historical study, we can rephrase that conclusion very simply. It meant that the market as the basic control mechanism within capitalism was about to be replaced by another system, akin to a new economic feudalism. Is that the conclusion to which the statistics on corporate size now force us?

Surprisingly, that does not seem to be the case. For despite the massing of wealth in the hands of the giant corporations, concentration does not appear to be worsening in the area that is of critical importance for the control mechanism—the marketplace.

How can that seemingly contradictory state of affairs exist? How can corporations be getting bigger and not be increasingly monopolistic? The answer is that the merger wave that has so dramatically boosted the figures for the national concentration of business wealth has taken place largely by the rise of so-called *conglomerates*—corporations that have grown by merging with other corporations not *within* a given market but in a *different* market. Consider the case of International Telephone and Telegraph, now the 17th largest industrial corporation in the nation. Originally a much smaller company wholly engaged in running foreign communications systems, ITT has become a mammoth enterprise because it now also rents cars (Avis), operates motels and hotels (Sheraton), builds homes (Levitt & Sons), bakes bread (Continental), produces glass, makes consumer loans, manages mutual funds, and processes data.

[10] "Industrial Structure and Competition Policy," Study Paper No. 2, *Studies by the Staff of the Cabinet Committee on Price Stability* (Washington, January, 1969), p. 45.
[11] *Op. cit.,* p. 46.

We do not yet know what may be the long-term consequences of the rise of such giant, diversified companies. Many of them have been put together more with an eye to realizing the profits that could be had from exchanges of shares than with any careful consideration of operating efficiencies, and they may come unglued in the next heavy rain. Others may indeed prove to be efficient combinations of diverse activities that will enjoy the advantages of access to a central pool of capital and a topflight supermanagement. Still others may run afoul of antitrust laws and may be forced to dissolve.

STABILITY OF
MARKET
SHARES

But as matters now stand, it seems unlikely that the conglomerates will be adding to their size by buying up *competitors*. Hence it is likely that the structure of the individual markets in which they operate will show no more change than they have in the past. And here, in the critical area of the marketplace, we discover a truly surprising long-run stability. For more than half a century, now, there has been no substantial increase in "monopoly" in the nation's markets, considered as a whole. Going back to 1901, we find some industries—tobacco, chemicals, stone, clay and glass, transportation equipment—where industrial concentration has risen; but in others, no less important—food, textiles, pulp and paper, petroleum and coal products, rubber, machinery—concentration has fallen since 1901.

The same conclusion holds for more recent years. If we take the four largest companies in any industry between 1947 and 1958 (the latest year for which figures are available) and compare the value of their total shipments to the value of all shipments in the industry, we find a similar mixed trend. In a few instances, such as the automobile industry, where some early postwar competitors were shaken out, the concentration ratio has increased appreciably: in the case of autos, from 55 per cent in 1947 to 75 per cent in 1958. In the majority of industries, however, the movement toward concentration was imperceptible; and in a substantial number, concentration actually declined.

Perhaps most convincing of all is a recent government study that shows the degree of concentration within 213 industrial markets to be virtually unchanged between 1947 and 1966. In 1947, the average share of all markets going to the top four firms was 41.2 per cent; in 1966 it was 41.9 per cent. Moreover, the number of highly concentrated industries—where the top four firms did three-quarters or more of all sales—showed a sharp drop during the period.[12]

CAUSES OF
STABILIZATION:
ANTITRUST

What has produced this stabilization of concentration within industry? Two reasons suggest themselves.

[12] *The New York Times,* January 26, 1969.

120

The first is the *restraining effect of antitrust legislation.* At the point at which we left our historical narrative, we had seen only the ineffectiveness of early antitrust legislation. But beginning in the 1930's under Franklin Roosevelt, a much stronger enforcement of the various antitrust laws began to gain favor. A vigorous campaign to block the drift toward concentration resulted in a number of suits brought against major corporations for restraint of trade. No less important was a change in the prevailing judicial view, which now construed much less narrowly the powers of the Constitution to impose social controls over business enterprise. In more recent years, new amendments to the antitrust acts and a growing stringency of Justice Department rulings have made the marriage of competitive firms increasingly difficult.

One result of these obstacles in the way of direct "concentration-affecting" mergers is that corporations have been forced to seek acquisitions in fields considerably removed from their original base of operations. This is one source of that trend toward conglomerates we noted above. What interests us here is that this process of diversification has put many large corporations into fields in which they are not the dominant companies by any means. One study shows that in a thousand different product markets, the 100 biggest firms are not even among the four biggest sellers in almost half these markets.[13] By way of illustration, in 1965 the Radio Corporation of America acquired Random House, a book publisher. In its manufacturing activities, RCA is a large producer in a moderately concentrated field (the top four companies make just over one-quarter of all radios); in its broadcasting activities, as the owner of NBC, it is one of three great broadcasting networks; but as a book publisher it will have to swim in a highly competitive sea.

A second reason for the stabilization within markets is more diffuse, but no less significant. It lies in a decisive *change in the character of business management.*

We have already noticed a certain change in the evolution of the great entrepreneur, from the production-oriented industrialist of the early nineteenth century to the sales and strategy-oriented "captain of industry" of the late nineteenth. Yet throughout the first century of rapid corporate expansion, one characteristic marked both types of business leaders. Both were the direct owners of their enterprises. The men who ran the corporations were themselves the men who had put up the capital or who owned large blocks of stock in the enterprises. The Carnegie Steel Company, the Standard Oil Company, the Ford Motor Company were all extensions of the personalities of Carnegie, Rockefeller, and Ford. This personal direction of affairs was the case in the

---

[13] A. D. H. Kaplan, *Big Enterprise in a Competitive System* (Washington, D.C.: The Brookings Institution, 1964), p. 286.

overwhelming majority of the other large and small enterprises of the day.

But with time, a significant change set in. As the original founders of the great businesses died, their stock was inherited by heirs who often did not have business ability and who receded into the background. In addition, the widening dispersion of stock ownership among more and more small investors made it unnecessary for any group to own an actual majority of the stock to exercise control over a company. In 1928, for example, the board of directors of U.S. Steel (which included two of the largest stockholders in the company) held only 1.4 per cent of the company's stock. In that year, the biggest stockholder in A.T.&T. held but seven-tenths of 1 per cent of the company's total stock and the biggest shareowners of the Pennsylvania Rail Road held less than 3 per cent of the firm's stock.

The result was that the active direction of the big firms passed from owner-capitalists to a new group of "managers" who ruled the corporation by virtue of their *expertise* rather than because they owned it. The new management was different in many ways from its predecessors. In 1900, for example, half the top executives of the biggest corporations had followed paths to the top that could be described as "entrepreneurial" or "capitalist"—that is, half had built their own businesses or had risked their own capital as the means to business preeminence. By 1925 only a third of the top corporate executives had followed this path, and in 1960 *less than 3 per cent* had done so. More and more, the route to success lay through professional skills, whether in law or engineering or science, or in the patient ascent of the corporate hierarchical ladder. Significantly there was a visible change as well as a marked change in the educational background of the top corporate officials. As recently as the 1920's, a majority of the topmost corporate leaders had not gone to college; today over 90 per cent have college degrees and a third hold graduate degrees.[14]

The new management brought important changes in its wake. The affairs of big companies increasingly became matters to be handled in systematized, "professional" ways, rather than in the often highly personal, Haroun-al-Raschid mode of the founders. A certain bureaucratization thus crept into the conduct of business life, at the very time that the business community was waxing most vocal about the dangers of bureaucracy in government. More important, the new management now adopted a new strategy for corporate growth—or rather, abandoned an older one. Advances in technology, changes in product design, vigorous advertising, the wooing of businesses to be acquired in other fields—all these provided ample outlets for the managerial impulse toward expansion. But one mode of growth—the mode that the founders of the great enterprises had never hesitated to use—was now ruled out:

---

[14] Mabel Newcomer, *The Big Business Executive* (New York: Columbia University Press, 1955), pp. 61–63; and Jay Gould, *The Technical Elite* (New York: Augustus Kelley, 1966), pp. 160–71.

growth was no longer to be sought by the direct head-on competition of one firm against another in terms of *price*.

Thus, the evolution of a more "statesmanlike" attitude in business affairs brought a significant change in business tactics. But the change cannot be ascribed solely to a new outlook on the part of big-business men. Behind that new outlook was *a change in the market environment.*

We call this new kind of market situation *oligopoly,* meaning a market shared by a few sellers. Note that it is not *monopoly,* which is a market entirely served by one seller. Neither is it "pure competition," such as we envisaged when we first looked into the theory of a market economy.

What is the essential difference? We cannot investigate it thoroughly until Part Three, but the main points of the contrast are not difficult to grasp. Classical competition implies a situation in which there are so many firms (of roughly the same order of size) that no one of them by itself can directly influence market prices. This is the case—more or less—within much of the Periphery. In oligopoly, by way of contrast, the numbers of firms are few enough (or the disparity in size among the few large ones and the host of smaller ones is so great) that the large firms cannot help affecting the market situation. Here is the typical situation at the Center. As a result, whereas in classical competition firms must accept whatever prices the market thrusts upon them, in oligopolistic markets, prices can be "set," at least within limits, by the direct action of the leading firms.

In many of the most important industrial markets, as we have seen, it is oligopoly rather than pure competition that is the order of things today. In industry after industry, economies of large-scale production have brought about a situation in which a few large producers divide the market among themselves. Often these markets are dominated by one very large firm that serves as "price leader," raising or lowering its prices as general economic conditions warrant, and being followed up or down by everyone else in the field. U.S. Steel in the steel industry, General Motors in the auto field, Corn Products Refining in the cornstarch industry have more or less consistently "led" their industries in this fashion. By and large, as we would expect, these prices are considerably higher than the prices that a pure competitive market would enforce. General Motors, for instance, "targets" its prices to attain a 15 to 20 per cent return after taxes, *calculating its costs on the assumption that it will use only 60 to 70 per cent of its total plant capacity.* U.S. Steel sets its prices high enough so that it can earn a small profit *even if it operates only two days out of five.* In fact "target pricing" has come to be the established procedure for many leading manufacturing firms.[15]

---

[15] *Study of Administered Prices in the Steel Industry* and *Study of Administered Prices in the Automobile Industry,* Senate Report 1387, 85th Cong., 2nd sess.; see also R. F. Lanzillotti, "Pricing Objectives of Large Companies," *American Economic Review,* December 1958, pp. 921–40.

Prices set by leading firms, rather than by the interplay of competition among many firms, are called *administered prices*. This does not mean that in each of these industries firms do not vie with one another. On the contrary, if you ask a General Motors or a U.S. Steel executive, he will tell you of vigorous competition. He may show you that Ford had edged out General Motors in such-and-such a line, or that Bethlehem Steel has captured some of U.S. Steel's business. The point, however, is *that the competition among oligopolists typically utilizes every means except one: price cutting.* The tactics of lowering price to secure a rival's business is not regarded as "fair play," although once in a while it breaks out, just as it did in the days of cutthroat competition of the 1880's.* But what was common practice then is rare now. Competition among oligopolists today means winning business away from another by advertising, customer service, or product design—but not by "chiseling" on price. Everyone recognizes that it is to his advantage not to disturb the market. There have been few instances in steel, or oil, or automobiles, or chemicals, or cigarettes when out-and-out price "warfare" has taken the place of nonprice "competition."

CHALLENGE TO CONSUMER SOVEREIGNTY

Our inquiry has led us from the emergence of the giant corporation— a process that we have seen to be still going on—to a consideration of the change in corporate tactics within industrial markets. Now we must stand back a pace and once again look at the operation of the market system as a whole, seeking an answer to the questions we posed at the outset. What is the consequence of the giant corporation for American society? What are its effects on the operation of a market economy?

The second question is easier to cope with than the first. We will remember that a distinguishing feature of the market system was that the *power of control was vested in the consumer*. There were two aspects of this power. First, a market society enabled consumers to have the ultimate decision as to the allocation of the factors of production. *Their* desires arranged the productive pattern of society, not the desires of society's rulers, its keepers of traditions, or its producers. Second, the market society assured the consumer that he would be able to buy the output of society at the lowest price compatible with a continued flow of production. While producers might wish to make exorbitant profits from consumers, they would be prevented from doing so by the pressure of competition from other producers.

---

* On occasion, the administered prices in an oligopoly are maintained by out-and-out collusive agreement, which is strictly illegal. This was the case when General Electric, Westinghouse, and a number of smaller manufacturers were discovered in 1959 to be rigging prices and sharing the market for heavy electrical equipment. A number of top executives in the main concerns were sent to jail, heavy fines were imposed, and the purchasers of the equipment sued for triple damages. More frequently, however, oligopolistic prices are maintained simply by tacit consent.

Does the consumer still exercise this economic sovereignty? In a general sense he does. If the consumer does not choose to buy the goods produced by giant concerns, those concerns have no choice but to curtail the production of those goods. For example, in the mid-1950's the Ford Motor Company poured nearly a quarter of a billion dollars into the production of a new car, the Edsel. The car was rejected by consumers, and after a few years its production was quietly discontinued. Familiar, too, is the effect of a swing in consumer tastes. From the mid-1950's on, imports of foreign sports and small cars rose steadily—from 57,000 vehicles in 1955 to 668,000 in 1959. With the exception of American Motors, the major car manufacturers insisted that the trend to compacts was only a fad and that Americans "wanted" bigger cars. But there was no brooking the contrary opinion of consumers themselves. Eventually, all the major manufacturers were *forced* into the production of small cars.

What then is the difference between this state of affairs and that of the "ideal" market system? One major difference lies in the fact that the great corporations today do not merely "fill" the wants of consumers. They themselves help to *create* these wants by massive efforts to interest the public in buying the products they manufacture. In 1968, for example, business spent some $15 billion on advertising its products—an expenditure that is not far below our total expenditures for public elementary and secondary education. By way of contrast, in 1867 we spent only $50 million on advertising; and in 1900, only $542 million. So it is that while consumers still move the factors of production to satisfy their "wants," these wants are themselves increasingly influenced by the producers. In contrast to the ideal market where producers hasten at the beck of an imperious consumer demand, in the new market, consumers are to some extent themselves at the beck of an imperious producer demand.

We might note, for instance, that no sooner was the first small Ford placed on the market than the company announced a "luxury" small car, and this example was quickly followed by other producers. It may very well be that consumers prefer a large spectrum of sizes and shapes of automobiles. But it is difficult to square the original image of serving the consumers' uninfluenced wants with the process by which new models are designed and touted. We shall have a further word to say about this at the conclusion of our chapter.

The second main attribute of the ideal market was that consumers' interests were satisfied as cheaply as possible because prices were forced down to the average cost of producing goods. Is this still true?

We have already seen that prices in oligopolistic industries are considerably higher than they would be under competitive conditions. Yet they are not wholly without controls. If a direct price struggle is conspicuously lacking within oligopolistic industries, there are other pressures that nonetheless enforce a certain degree of price discipline.

One of these pressures has been called by John Kenneth Galbraith "countervailing power." [16] By this, Galbraith means that in an oligopolistic world the opposition of interests across the market provides some compensation for the absence of a contest of interests on each side of the market. Today, powerful corporate sellers often face equally powerful corporate *buyers*. The giant raw materials producer who faces little or no competition within his industry must sell to the giant chemical or other processing plant; the giant steel mill to the giant auto firm; the giant canner to the giant supermarket chain. Not least important, the large firm no longer bargains with the individual employee, but with large and powerful unions. This kind of neutralization of economic power does not hold true in every market nor in every situation, but, Galbraith contends, it is true in enough markets and in enough situations to constitute a powerful restraining force on the unhindered exercise of oligopolistic power.

A second restraining force is the competition among different *products*. Even if all steel prices are kept at "administered" levels, steel as a whole must compete with aluminum. Nor does the competition end here. What we find, indeed, is an immense chain of interproduct competition—steel against aluminum, aluminum against glass, glass against plastics, plastics against wood, wood against concrete, concrete against steel. And this competition is without doubt effective. Note that automobile engines are now made of cast aluminum as well as of steel; that buildings are now sheathed in glass as well as brick or concrete; that cooking utensils are made of glass as well as of aluminum; that drinking "glasses" are often made of plastic.

Thus prices are not *wholly* free from control. That does not mean that they are therefore adequately controlled. Oligopoly does not mean *arbitrarily* high prices, but it does mean a price structure considerably higher than those which a more competitive system might enjoy. "What few will question," writes Gardiner Means in a study of steel pricing, "is that the after-tax target rates of 16 and 20 per cent and the actual earnings in excess of these targets are well above a competitive rate of return. Prices set to achieve these targets must involve substantial premiums over costs, taxes and a legitimate rate of return. To this extent, the public interest is not served. . . ." [17]

UNRESOLVED
PROBLEM OF
ECONOMIC
POWER

How shall we summarize this complicated situation with its pluses and minuses?

[16] Cf. John K. Galbraith, *American Capitalism, the Concept of Countervailing Power* (Boston: Houghton Mifflin Company, 1952), pp. 115ff.
[17] *Pricing Power and the Public Interest* (New York: Harper & Row, 1962), p. 268.

Without doubt, many of the aspects of a system of giant oligopoly are disquieting departures from the rationale of a market economy as the *servant* of the consumer. Yet it would be erroneous to conclude that the emergence of these new attributes is nothing but a threat to the market system. On the contrary, in part at least, they can also be seen as new functional mechanisms for the *support* of that system.

Take first the phenomenon of advertising and the manipulation of consumers' wants. This seems at first glance a direct assault upon a prime principle of the market system—the sovereignty of consumers' wants. Yet, before we jump to that conclusion, we must note that the wants themselves have changed. In the nineteenth century, consumer wants were essentially focused on the basic requirements of simple existence: food, clothing, shelter. In the rich nation of the mid-twentieth century, however, these basic wants have been largely satisfied. Consumer demand is no longer driven to essentials, but hesitates before a whole range of possible luxuries and semiluxuries.

Thus the fact that producers can create and manipulate these wants testifies to the much more important fact that *the wants themselves are now amorphous and vague and susceptible to influence.* Curiously, then, we can view the rise of advertising as an attempt to introduce an orderliness and regularity of demand into a society where purely "spontaneous" demand would no longer firmly indicate which patterns of economic activity producers should follow.

In similar vein, we cannot conclude that the price-setting power of oligopolistic firms has no economic function. For the achievement of a certain market stability, which is the purpose of administered pricing, is not without its benefits to the economy. Indeed, a return to the uninhibited price competition of the nineteenth century might very well lead to a resumption of cutthroat tactics from which would emerge not a nicely balanced competitive market, but an array of triumphant monopolies.

And then, too, it has often been pointed out that the most "ideally" competitive industries, such as agriculture, are typically those which offer the worst wages and which display the least progressive economic characteristics. On the other hand, in those industries where oligopoly has permitted larger than competitive profits to accrue, we tend to find not only higher wages and more "social conscience," but the most forward-looking (and expensive) commitment to research and expansion. As Galbraith has written in a wry commentary on this situation: "The showpieces (of the economy) are, with rare exceptions, the industries which are dominated by a handful of large firms. The foreign visitor, brought to the United States . . . visits the same firms as do attorneys of the Department of Justice in their search for monopoly."[18]

---

[18] *Op. cit.*, p. 96.

Thus the changing market structure has its uses as well as its abuses. We must see in it not only a departure from the ideal market system, but also an attempt to find an accommodation within the real market system for a powerful new technology which impels all organizations—labor and government, as well as private industry—toward large-scale operations.* We must understand that if oligopoly undermines the market system in some regards, it strengthens it in others.

Beyond this mixed economic judgment, there are, however, other considerations that return us to the basic question of the relation between giant business and society at large. For in the end, the strictly economic consequences of oligopoly may be less important than the social and political consequences of business giantism. The deliberate endless titillation of the consumer is not a pretty spectacle for those who see in man something more than a voracious consumer of goods. Neither is the emergence within a democratic society of a fortress of well-nigh impregnable economic power a wholly reassuring political sight. When we contemplate the enormous corporations of the Center in whose unsupervised hands rests so much of the economic future of this nation, we cannot but feel that here is a structure of power that is simply immune to our normal processes of community control. As Professor Berle has said, "Some of these corporations can be thought of only in somewhat the way we have heretofore thought of nations." [19] Unlike nations, however, their power has not been rationalized in law, fully tested in practice, or well defined in philosophy. Unquestionably, the political and social influence of the great corporations poses problems with which capitalism will have to contend for many years to come.

---

* We should note that the situation is not peculiar to America. In every industrial market society, a similar concentration of production has occurred. Studies of concentration in England, France, Italy, Japan, Canada, Holland, and Scandanavia reveal that in most cases it has proceeded further than in the United States. See Andrew Schonfield, *Modern Capitalism* (New York: Oxford University Press, 1965), p. 241 n.

[19] *Op. cit.,* p. 15.

1. A combination of aggressive entrepreneurship and the economies of scale typical of industrial technology brought about a *concentration of economic power* in many markets in the late nineteenth and early twentieth centuries.

2. The emergence of large firms with massive capital structures led to "cutthroat" competition that was exceedingly dangerous for the firms concerned. Hence there were *many attempts to stabilize the competitive struggle* by means of pools, trusts, holding companies, and mergers.

3. As the great trusts and combines rose to power, there was a "countervailing" thrust of political *antitrust legislation,* culminating in the Sherman Antitrust Act (1890), later in the Clayton Antitrust Act (1914), and in subsequent amendments designed to make mergers more difficult.

4. None of these laws prohibited or interfered with *internal growth.* As a result, large businesses continued to expand. A famous survey by Berle and Means in 1933 predicted that if the rate of growth of the top 200 nonfinancial corporations continued, they would soon own virtually the entire economy.

5. This prediction has been partly borne out, especially in the recent rise of the *conglomerates*—enormous diversified corporations—that have dramatically increased the concentration of all manufacturing wealth held by the top 100 corporations. At the same time, the very diversification of these enterprises has precluded any marked change in concentration within industrial markets.

6. This stability within markets can be traced to several causes:

   * More effective *antitrust* legislation.
   * The *diffusion of corporate growth* into new, competitive markets.
   * The *bureaucratization* of business management.
   * The rise of *more stable market structures.*

7. We call the new market structures *oligopoly,* meaning few sellers. *The outstanding difference between oligopoly and traditional competition is that oligopolistic firms can set the levels of their prices more or less at their own discretion, whereas competitive firms have no alternative but to meet the "going" price of the market.*

8. The effect of oligopoly is twofold. First, it greatly *reduces the role of price competition.* Second, it opens the consumer to the *influence of advertising.*

9. The shift of power from consumer to producer is not total. Consumer tastes, however influenced, cannot be shaped at will or ignored. And *competition among products* still exercises an important restraint on firms.

10. The great corporation is at best only partially disciplined by the market. The presence of oligopoly poses *an unresolved problem* for capitalism.

1. Can you name the chief corporate executives of the top ten industrial firms in the U.S. (General Motors, Standard Oil of New Jersey, Ford, General Electric, Socony, U.S. Steel, Chrysler, Texaco, Gulf, Western Electric)? How many names of leading businessmen do you know? What does this suggest as to the character of business leadership today contrasted with the 1890's?

2. Why does heavy overhead cost lead to "cutthroat competition"? Why is this kind of competition dangerous?

3. Suppose Congress decided to foster a return to classical competition in the United States. What changes would have to be wrought in the American business scene? Do you think this is a practical possibility?

4. Compare the situation of a farmer selling fruit on a roadside stand and an executive of a large auto company selling a new model. How much latitude does each have in pricing his product?

5. Do you believe that tastes are ever created by advertising? Have your own been?

6. What do you consider to be the most desirable characteristic of bigness in business? The most undesirable?

7. Suppose you wanted to measure concentration in an industry. What attributes of the firms in that industry would interest you: their respective sales? their assets? their number of employees? Might different measures give different concentration ratios?

8. What are the important differences between "pure" competition and oligopoly as regards the position of the consumer? The producer? On net balance which do you think is preferable? Why?

THE GREAT DEPRESSION 7

In our last chapter we concentrated on important aspects of the developing industrial economy—the swift rise in productivity, the impact of mass production, the thickening texture of the market. But we purposely ignored one effect of technology which, in retrospect, towers over the others. This was the tremendous impetus it gave to the process of economic growth.

In our chapter on the industrial revolution, we commented on the importance of technology for growth. Prior to that time, a chart of the well-being of the average person in Europe would have shown a distressingly horizontal profile, rising in some years or even centuries, falling in others, perhaps tilted slightly upward as a whole, but certainly displaying nothing like a steady year-by-year increase in the output of goods and services available per capita. Even with the initial introduction of the new technology we noted that the standard of living did not immediately improve. But starting in the third quarter of the nineteenth century, the accumulations of capital and the accretion of

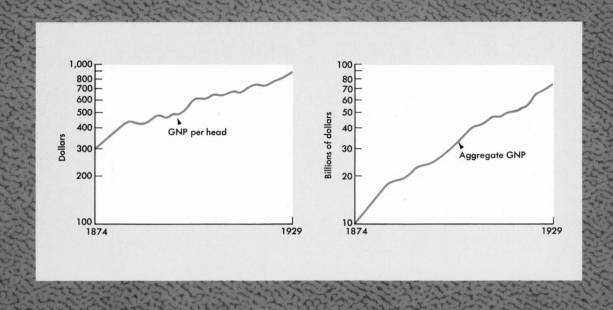

FIG. 7-1 **REAL GROSS NATIONAL PRODUCT
(1929 PRICES) AGGREGATE AND PER HEAD**

expertise began to display their hidden powers. In nearly every industrializing country, and most dramatically in the United States, the profile of economic well-being now began to show that steady and regular improvement that has become the very hallmark of modern economic times.

Figure 7-1 shows us the general path of this growth in the United States from the 1870's, when the process was in full swing, to 1929 when it reached a dramatic peak, to which we will shortly return. If we draw a line through the irregularly upward-moving graph to express the average rate of growth taking good years and bad together, we find it to be about 3.5 per cent (with all price changes eliminated), which means that the total volume of output was doubling about every 22 years. Since the number of mouths was also doubling, although more slowly, *per capita* shares in this mounting volume of goods obviously grew more slowly. Roughly, we can estimate that individuals improved their lot at a rate of about $1\frac{1}{2}$ to 2 per cent a year, doubling their real incomes every 40 years on the average. In Chapter 9 we will learn to interpret these growth figures with a certain caution. But there is no doubt that the period as a whole was one of unprecedented progress and improvement. How strange then that it should have ended in the greatest disaster in the history of the market system—one that very nearly spelled the end of capitalism and that permanently altered the system in ways that we must now learn about.

We in America today are nearer to the final triumph over poverty than ever before in the history of any land. The poorhouse is vanishing from among us. We have not yet reached the goal, but, given a chance . . . we shall soon with the help of God be in sight of the day when poverty will be banished from this nation.

Thus spoke Herbert Hoover in November 1928, and indeed by 1929 the American economy had shown extraordinary progress. Population had grown from 76 million in 1900 to over 121 million, while ten years had been added to the expectation of life at birth for whites and thirteen for nonwhites. To hold and feed and sustain its growing numbers, the nation had built up two new cities to a million each, five to over half a million, nearly 1,500 from rural to urban classification; $75 billion worth of homes, $9 billion worth of new farm structures; over $30 billion worth of new industrial equipment. Meanwhile, there were jobs for 48 million people—all save 3.2 per cent of the labor force in 1929. Furthermore, these job holders had seen average weekly hours of work in manufacturing drop from nearly 60 in 1900 to 44. Average hourly earnings rose from 20 cents in 1909 to 56 cents, while consumer prices lagged sufficiently behind to allow a rise in real wages of some 10 to 20 per cent. It was not surprising, then, that an atmosphere of optimism gripped America in 1929 and that President Hoover's official words only reflected an informal sentiment throughout the nation.

Certainly few Americans suspected that a major economic calamity might be just around the corner. On the contrary, most people were concerned with quite another prospect of the American economy, and a highly attractive one. This was the great stock market boom—a boom which by 1929 had pulled perhaps 10,000,000 people into "the market," where they had the pleasure of watching their money painlessly and effortlessly grow. As Frederick Lewis Allen, the social historian of the Twenties, described it:

The rich man's chauffeur drove with his ears laid back to catch the news of an impending move in Bethlehem Steel; he held fifty shares himself on a twenty point margin. The window cleaner at the broker's office paused to watch the ticker, for he was thinking of converting his laboriously accumulated savings into a few shares of Simmons. Edwin Lefevre (an articulate reporter on the market at this time who could claim considerable personal experience) told of a broker's valet who made nearly a quarter of a million in the market, of a trained nurse who cleaned up thirty thousand following the tips given her by her grateful patients; and of a Wyoming cattleman, thirty miles from the nearest railroad, who bought or sold a thousand shares a day.[1]

It was, of course, admittedly speculative, and yet the risks seemed eminently justified. Someone who had put $1,000 each year, from 1921 on, into a group of representative stocks would have found himself worth over $6,000 in 1925, almost $9,000 in 1926, well over $11,000 in 1927, and an incredible $20,000 in 1928. And that was just the beginning: during June and July of 1929 industrial stock averages went up nearly as much as they had during the entire year of 1928, which had been, in its time, a year of unprecedented rise. By August 1929, the three-months' summer spurt had already outdistanced the entire 1928 rise. In those three months alone, an investor who had bought 100 shares of Westinghouse would have almost doubled his money; even a buyer of staid A.T.&T. would have been richer by a third. It seemed that everyone had but to beg or borrow money to buy shares in order to get rich.

THE GREAT CRASH

What pricked the bubble? No one knows exactly what final event was to blame. But when the boom did break, it was as if an enormous dam had suddenly crumbled. All the frenzy that had stretched out over two years in sending stocks up was concentrated in a few incredible weeks beating them down. On Tuesday, October 29, 1929 an avalanche of selling crushed the exchanges. On occasion there were *no* offers to buy stock at all—just to sell it. Goldman Sachs, a much sought-after investment trust, lost almost half its quoted value on this single day. By the end of the trading session (the ticker, lagging behind, stretched out the agony two-and-a-half hours longer than the actual market transactions) 16,410,000 shares of stock had been dumped. In a single day, the rise in values of the entire preceding year had been wiped out. A few weeks later, $30 billion of "wealth" had vanished in thin air. Millions who had counted their paper gains and thought themselves well off discovered they were poor.

The great crash is in itself a fascinating chapter in the "madness of crowds." At first it seemed unconnected with anything bigger. In fact, the early weeks after the crash were regularly marked with expressions of confidence: the general cliché of the day was that things were "fundamentally sound." Yet things were *not* fundamentally sound. The terrifying Crash ushered in the much more terrifying Depression.

[1] *Only Yesterday* (New York: Bantam Books, Inc., 1946), p. 349.

Frederick Lewis Allen wrote:

> It was an oddly invisible phenomenon, this Great Depression. If one observed closely, one might note that there were fewer people on the streets than in former years, that there were many untenanted shops, that beggars and panhandlers were much in evidence; one might see breadlines here and there, and "Hoovervilles" in vacant lots at the edge of town (groups of tar-paper shacks inhabited by homeless people); railroad trains were shorter, with fewer Pullmans; and there were many factory chimneys out of which no smoke was coming. But otherwise there was little to see. Great numbers of people were sitting home, trying to keep warm.[2]

However invisible to the casual observer, the Depression was far from being a mere figment of the imagination. To begin with, gross national product—the measure of the nation's total output—fell precipitously from $104 billion in 1929 to $56 billion in 1933. Almost one dollar's worth of final output out of every two simply disappeared. As a result, unemployment soared. In 1929, the unemployed had numbered 1.5 million. By 1933 the number had risen eightfold until *one person out of every four in the entire labor force was without a job.* In the nation as a whole, residential construction fell by 90 per cent: there were virtually no houses built. Nine million savings accounts were lost as banks closed their doors. Eighty-five thousand businesses failed. In Pennsylvania in 1932, it was reported by the State Department of Labor that wages had fallen to 5 cents an hour in sawmills, 6 cents in brick and tile manufacturing, 7.5 cents in general contracting. In Tennessee, women in mills were paid as little as $2.39 for a 50-hour week. In Kentucky, miners ate the weeds that cows ate; in West Virginia, people began to rob stores for food. In California, a child starved to death and was discovered to have been living on refuse.[3]

How did this tragedy come about?

An immediate, precipitating cause was, of course, the speculative fever that had engulfed the economy by 1929. The mania was not just confined to Wall Street. Throughout the nation, a get-rich-quick philosophy had destroyed normal business and banking caution. Foreign bonds of the most dubious validity were eagerly (and sometimes ruthlessly) pushed by the banks into investors' hands or, worse folly, put into their own portfolios.* In addition, huge pyramided structures of

[2] *The Big Change* (New York: Harper & Row, 1952), p. 248.

[3] Arthur Schlesinger, Jr., *The Crisis of the Old Order* (Boston: Houghton Mifflin Company, 1957), pp. 249–50.

*Many of these deals were unsavory to the point of malfeasance. The son of the President of Peru, for instance, was paid $450,000 by the securities affiliate of the National City Bank for his services in connection with a $50 million bond issue which the bank's affiliate then floated for Peru. The President's son's "services" consisted almost entirely of an agreement not to block the deal. Eventually, of course, the bonds went into default. (John K. Galbraith, *The Great Crash, 1929.* Boston: Houghton Mifflin Company, 1955, p. 186.)

investment trusts and holding companies erected a house of cards atop the operating base of enterprise. For instance, Georgia Power & Light Company was controlled by the Seaboard Public Service Corporation, which was controlled by the Middle West Utilities Company, which was controlled by Insull Utility Investments, Inc., which was controlled by the Corporation Securities Company of Chicago (which was controlled, in turn, by Insull Utility Investments, which presumably *it* controlled). Of these companies, only one—Georgia Power—actually produced electricity. The rest produced only profits and speculative opportunities. And the Insull empire was only one of *twelve* holding companies that owned 75 per cent of all the utility operating plants in the country.

All these manipulative activities helped to pave the way for the Depression. When the stock market finally crashed, it brought down with it an immense flimsy structure of credit. Individual investors who had borrowed to the hilt to buy securities had their stock sold out from under them to meet their indebtedness to brokers. Banks and financial institutions, loaded with dubious foreign bonds, were suddenly insolvent. Meanwhile, to compound the terrible panic, the monetary authorities pursued policies that unwittingly weakened the banking system still further.[4]

WEAKNESS ON THE FARM

In the vulnerability of an economy bound up with a rickety and speculative financial superstructure we have located one reason for the Great Depression—or, more specifically, one reason why the Wall Street Crash pulled down with it so much business activity. But we have far from exhausted the explanations for the Depression itself. For the Crash, after all, might have been no worse than many previous speculative disasters. Why was it protracted into a chronic and deep-rooted ailment?

The question turns our attention away from the spectacular misfortunes of 1929 to a consideration of the state of the economy as a whole in the years preceding the collapse. We have already characterized the first quarter of the twentieth century as a time of unprecedented expansion. Could it be, however, that behind the over-all figures of rising output and incomes there were concealed pockets of trouble?

There was no question that one such worrisome sector existed. This was the farm sector, especially the all-important grains. All through the 1920's, the farmer was the "sick man" of the American economy. Each year saw more farmers going into tenantry, until by 1929 four out of ten farmers in the nation were no longer independent operators. Each year the farmer seemed to fall further behind the city dweller in terms of relative well-being. In 1910 the income per worker on the

[4] See Milton Friedman and Anna Schwartz, *The Great Contraction* (Princeton, N.J.: Princeton University Press, 1965).

farm had been not quite 40 per cent of the nonfarm worker; by 1930, it was just under 30 per cent.

Part of this trouble on the farm, without question, stemmed from the difficult heritage of the past. Beset now by drought, now by the exploitation of powerful railroad and storage combines, now by his own penchant for land speculation, the farmer was proverbially an ailing member of the economy. In addition, the American farmers had been traditionally careless of the earth, indifferent to the technology of agriculture. Looking at the average individual farmer, one would have said that he was poor because he was unproductive. Between 1910 and 1920, for instance, while nonfarm output per worker rose by nearly 20 per cent, output per farm worker actually fell. Between 1920 and 1930, farm productivity improved somewhat, but not nearly so fast as productivity off the farm. For the great majority of the nation's agricultural producers the trouble appeared to be that they could not grow or raise enough to make a decent living.

If we had looked at farming as a whole, however, a very different answer would have suggested itself. Suppose that farm productivity *had* kept pace with that of the nation. Would farm income as a whole have risen? The answer is disconcerting. The *demand* for farm products was quite unlike that for manufactured products generally. In the manufacturing sector, when productivity rose and costs accordingly fell, the cheaper prices of manufactured goods attracted vast new markets, as with the Ford car. Not so with farm products, however. When food prices fell, people did not tend to increase their actual consumption very greatly. Increases in over-all farm output resulted in much lower prices but not in larger cash receipts for the farmer. Faced with what is called an *inelastic demand*—a demand that does not respond in proportion to price changes—a flood of output only leaves sellers *worse* off than before, as we shall see in Chapter 22.

That is very much what happened during the 1920's. From 1915 to 1920, the farmer prospered because World War I greatly increased the demand for his product. Prices for farm output rose, and his cash receipts rose as well; in fact, they more than doubled. But when European farms resumed their output following the war, the American farmers' crops simply glutted the market. Although prices fell precipitously (40 per cent in the single year 1920–1921), the purchases of farm products did not respond in anything like equal measure. As a result, the cash receipts of the farmer toppled almost as fast as prices. Meanwhile, his taxes were up by some 70 per cent, and his mortgage payments and his cost of living in general had approximately doubled. Matters improved somewhat during the later 1920's but not enough to bring the crop farmers back to substantial prosperity.

There is a lesson here in economics as well as history. Had farmers constituted an oligopolistic market, the decline in farm income might have been limited. A few producers, facing an inelastic demand for their products, can see the sense in mutually curtailing output. Rather than flooding a market which does not want their product, they can agree, tacitly or otherwise, to hold back production to some amount which the market will absorb at a reasonable price. But the individual farmer is about as far from an oligopolist as one can imagine. When the price for his crop falls, it gains the individual farmer nothing to decrease his output. On the contrary, in his highly competitive situation, the best that he can do is to rush to sell as much as he can before things get worse—thereby unwittingly *making* things worse.

As its core, the trouble with the farm sector was that the market mechanism in this particular case did not yield a satisfactory result.* That might not have been so serious, had it not been for another development: while agriculture remained static and stagnant, the manufacturing sector was growing by leaps and bounds. Yet its growth was undermined because a fifth of the nation—the agricultural sector— was unable to match the growing volume of production with a growing volume of purchasing power. As the farmers' buying power lagged, it pulled down the demand for tractors, cars, gasoline and electric motors, and manufactured consumers' goods, generally. Weakness on the farm was thus symptomatic of a weakness throughout the economy, a failure of purchasing power across the whole lower stratum of the nation to keep up with the tempo of national industrial production.

WEAKNESS IN THE FACTORY

Most economists of the 1920's, as we have said, would have agreed that there was a source of potential trouble on the farm. Had we suggested that there might be another potential breeding ground for trouble in the factory or the mine, however, few would have given their assent. Most people's eyes, during the 1920's, were fixed on only one aspect of the industrial sector—production—and here there was surely little reason for complaint.

Yet had scrutiny penetrated a bit deeper, very serious signs might well have been spotted in this presumably most buoyant section of the economy. For while production was steadily rising, *employment* was not. In manufacturing, for example, physical output in 1929 was up 49 per cent over 1920, whilst employment was precisely unchanged. In mining, output was up 43 per cent, while employment had shrunk some 12 per

---

*In theory, we will remember (pp. 65–67) there was a cure for situations in which the producers of one commodity were undercompensated relative to other pursuits: producers would leave the undercompensated field for more lucrative occupations. Indeed, the American farmer tried this cure. It has been estimated that 20 farmers left the soil to seek city work for every urban worker who came to the land. Unfortunately, the cure did not work fast enough. While the agricultural sector steadily diminished in relative size, it could not shrink its absolute numbers significantly. From 1910 to 1930 approximately 10 million farmers remained "locked" on the farm, perhaps half of them barely contributing to national output beyond their own meager livelihoods.

cent. In transportation and in the utility industry again output was higher—slightly in transportation, spectacularly in utility's electrical output—and again employment had actually declined.

Over-all employment had not, of course, declined. It was significantly up in construction, in trade and finance, in the service industries, and in government. But note that all these employment-absorbing industries were characterized by one common denominator: they were all relatively devoid of technological advance. Or to put it the other way around, all the employment-static or declining industries were singularly characterized by rapid technological advance. In other words, pressing against the over-all upward tendency of the economy was an undertow of *technological displacement.*

Heretofore in our frequent consideration of technology, we have never stopped to inquire what its effects might be on employment. Rather, we have implicitly assumed those effects to be positive, as we dwelt on the capacity of industrial technology to increase output. Yet it is not difficult to see that technology need not always be favorable for employment. When a new invention creates a new industry, such as the automobile, it is clear that its employment-creating effect can be enormous. Yet, even in such an instance there is an undertow, albeit a small one, as the growing automobile industry crowds out the old carriage industry. When we turn to inventions that do not create new *demands* but merely make an established industry more productive, it is clear that the initial impact of technical change can generate serious unemployment.

How are such technologically displaced workers re-employed? We will return to this question later in our chapter and again in more detail in Chapter 18. At this juncture, however, we want to examine still further the effect of rapid technological change in the "displacing industries" themselves, during the 1920's. And here we see an interesting fact. As production soared and employment sagged, the output per man-hour rose rapidly; in fact, between 1920 and 1929 it increased over 30 per cent in transportation, over 40 per cent in mining, and over 60 per cent in manufacturing.* This much larger flow of production per hour meant that wages *could have* been raised substantially or prices cut sharply. But this is not what we find to have been the case. Only on the unionized railroads did wage rates rise (by about 5 per cent). In mining, hourly earnings fell by nearly 20 per cent, and in manufacturing they remained steady. Since the hours of work per week were also declining, the average annual earnings of employees in these industries were far from keeping pace with the rise in their productivity. In mining, average yearly earnings fell from $1,700 to $1,481. In trans-

*These productivity indexes cannot be computed from our previous output and employment figures, since weekly hours changed. For the original figures, see *Historical Statistics of the United States,* Series W.

portation and manufacturing, yearly earnings fell from 1920 through 1922 and did not regain 1920 levels until 1928 and 1929.

Thus the gains from higher productivity were not passed along to the industrial worker in terms of higher wages. Were they passed along via lower prices? Yes, to some extent. The over-all cost of living between 1920 and 1929 fell by about 15 per cent. Part of this reduction, as we have seen, was due to falling food prices. Nonfood goods fell sharply in price from 1920 postwar peaks to 1921; thereafter they, too, declined by about 15 per cent up to 1929, but the fall was not enough to distribute all the gains from industrial technology. How do we know this? Because the *profits* of large manufacturing corporations soared between 1920 and 1929. From 1916 through 1925, profits for these companies had averaged around $730-odd million a year; from 1926 through 1929, they averaged $1,400 million. Indeed, in the year 1929, profits were triple those of 1920.[5]

MALDISTRIBUTION OF INCOME

Now we can generalize from what we have just discovered about the trend of wages and profits, to state one further reason for the sudden weakness which overcame the economy, beginning in 1929. Income was distributed in such a way as to make the system vulnerable to economic shocks.

This does *not* mean that somehow the American economy was failing to generate "enough" purchasing power to buy its own output. An economy always creates enough *potential* buying power to purchase what it has produced (for reasons we shall investigate very carefully in Chapters 20–22).

There can, however, be a very serious *maldistribution* of the income payments arising from production. For not all the proceeds arising from production may be placed in the hands of people who will *exercise* their purchasing power. Incomes paid out to the lower-paid strata of the labor force do, indeed, return to the stream of purchasing power, for the workingman tends to spend his wages quickly. But incomes which take the form of profits, or business accruals, or as very high individual compensations may not quickly turn over as purchasing power. Profits or high incomes may be saved. They may eventually return to the great stream of purchasing demand, but income which is saved does not "automatically" return via the route of consumption expenditure. Instead, it must find a different route—the route of investment, of capital-building.

Returning to the economy in 1929, we can now see as well what was perhaps the deepest-seated reason for its vulnerability: the fact that its income payments were not going in sufficient volume to those

[5] *Historical Statistics of the United States,* V, 236.

who would surely spend them. We have already understood why farmers and working men, who were indeed possessed of a "limitless" desire to consume, were pinched in their *ability* to buy. Now we must complete the picture by seeing how the failure to distribute the gains of productivity to the lower-income groups swelled the incomes of those who were potential *non*spenders.

TABLE 7 · 1

TOP INCOMES

PERCENTAGE SHARES OF TOTAL INCOME RECEIVED BY THE TOP 1 PER CENT AND TOP 5 PER CENT OF TOTAL POPULATION *		
Year	Top 1 per cent	Top 5 per cent
1919	12.2	24.3
1923	13.1	27.1
1929	18.9	33.5

*The table shows the "disposable income variant": i.e., income after payment of taxes and receipt of capital gains.
Source: *Historical Statistics of the United States*, G135-6.

What we see here is an extraordinary, and steadily worsening, concentration of incomes. By 1929, the 15,000 families or individuals at the apex of the national pyramid, with incomes of $100,000 or more each, probably received as much income as 5 to 6 million families at the bottom of the pyramid. And more was involved here than just a matter of moral equity. It meant that the prosperity of the Twenties—and for the majority of the nation it *was* a prosperity of hitherto unequalled extent—in fact covered over an economic situation of grave potential weakness. For *if* the nation's on-going momentum should be checked, in this lopsided distribution of purchasing power lay a serious problem. So long as the high profits and salaries and dividends continued to be returned to the income stream, all was well. But what if they should not be?

CRITICAL ROLE OF CAPITAL FORMATION

The question brings us to a critical relationship that has gradually been emerging throughout these pages as the central dynamic process in determining the level of activity in a market society. The relationship is that between the savings that a society desires to make on the one hand, and its opportunities for profitable investment, on the other. Much of the next section of this book—Part Two on macroeconomics—will be devoted to investigating that relationship in some detail. But we cannot explain the main events of the Great Depression unless we have a general grasp of the problem now.

Actually we have already understood half the saving-investment relationship. In our chapter on the industrial revolution we saw that saving was an indispensable prerequisite for capital formation. Now we must complete our understanding by adding the next step in the growth process. *Unless we make large enough capital expenditures to absorb our saving, we will not be able to keep the economy moving forward.* If saving is essential for investment, investment is essential for prosperity.

Indeed, because investment expenditure is the way we return savings to the income flow, we can see that the rate at which we add to our stock of capital equipment will have a deep effect on our over-all economic well-being. When spending for investment is sluggish, bad times are upon us. When spending for capital formation quickens, good times are again at hand. In other words, *the rate of capital formation is really the key to prosperity or recession.*

That does not yet tell us why the rate of capital expenditure should fluctuate. But a moment's reflection makes the answer clear enough. Spending for consumption purposes tends to be a reliable and steady process. Most consumer goods are quickly used up and must be replaced. The desire to maintain a given standard of living is not subject to sudden shifts or changes. As consumers, we are all to a considerable extent creatures of habit.

Not so with capital expenditures. Unlike consumer goods, most capital goods are durable and their replacement can therefore easily be postponed. Again in contrast to consumer goods, capital goods are not bought out of habit or for personal enjoyment. They are bought only because they are expected to yield a *profit* when put to use. We commonly hear it said that a new store, a new machine, or an additional stock of inventory must "pay for itself." And so it must. New investment increases output and that additional output must have a profitable sale. If for any reason a profit is not anticipated, the investment will not be made.

This enables us to see that the *expectation* of profit (which may be greater or less than profits actually being realized at the moment) plays a crucial role in the rate of capital formation. But why—and this is the last and obviously the key question—should a profit not be expected from a new investment good?

The answers all bring us back to our point of departure in the early 1930's. One answer may be that a speculative collapse, such as the Great Crash, destroys "confidence" or impairs financial integrity and leads to a period of retrenchment while financial affairs are put in order. Another reason may be that costs shoot up and monetary troubles impede the boom: the banks may become loaned up and money for new capital projects may suddenly become "tight" and dear. Still another reason may be that consumption expenditures are sluggish, owing perhaps to a maldistribution of income, such as that of the late 1920's, thereby discouraging plant expansion. Or the rate of population growth or of family formation may decline, bringing a slowdown in the demand for housing. Or the boom may simply die a "natural death"—that is, the wave of technological advance on which it rode may peter out, the great investments needed to build up a tremendous industry may be completed, and no second wave of equal capital-attracting magnitude may immediately rise to take its place.

Many of these reasons, as we have seen, served to bring capital formation to a halt in the Great Depression. The Crash itself, with its terrible blow to confidence and to the solvency of banks and holding companies, the weakness of the agricultural sector, the drag of technological displacement, and the maldistribution of income, all combined to bring about a virtual cessation of economic growth. The figures in Table 7-2 for gross private domestic investment—the proper nomenclature for private capital formation—tell their own grim story.

TABLE 7 · 2

GROSS PRIVATE
DOMESTIC
INVESTMENT

	BILLIONS OF CURRENT DOLLARS			
Year	Residential nonfarm construction	Other construction	Producers' durable equipment	Change in inventories
1929	$3.6	$5.1	$5.9	$+1.7
1932	.6	1.2	1.6	−2.6

Thus the Great Depression can be characterized essentially as a tremendous and long-lasting collapse in the rate of capital formation. In housing, in manufacturing plant and equipment, in commercial building, in the accumulation of inventories, a paralysis afflicted the economy. Between 1929 and 1933 investment goods output shrank by 88 per cent in real terms—that is, after allowances for price changes. Although the capital goods industries employed only one-tenth of the total labor force in 1929, by 1933 one-third of total unemployment had been caused by the shrinkage of these critical industries.

Here is a major key to the Depression. But the trouble did not end there. When savings are not returned to active purchasing power because of inadequate investment, the fall in buying begins to spread. Let us say that a steelworker is laid off because of the slump in building. He will certainly pare his family's budget to the bone. But this in turn will create a further loss in income for the businesses where the steelworker's family ordinarily spent its income. Others will lose their jobs or have their wages reduced. In this way a kind of snowball effect, or to use the proper term, a *multiplier effect,* is brought about.

This helps us understand the mechanism of the Great Depression. As capital expenditures fell during the early 1930's, they pulled down consumption expenditures with them; and because of the multiplier effect, by an even larger amount than the fall in investment. From 1929 to 1933, consumption declined from $79 to $49 billion, nearly twice as large a drop as the absolute fall in investment. And the fall of consumption, in turn, pulled down still further the flow of capital expenditures.

To be sure, the process works the other way around, as well. When capital expenditures again begin to mount, consumption expenditures typically climb by an even larger amount. For example, President Truman pointed out in a radio address in 1949 that $1 billion of new public expenditures, which gave initial income to some 315,000 people, also added to the incomes of some 700,000 more. In expansion as well as in contraction, there is a typical *cumulative* pattern to economic activity, as success breeds further success, and failure breeds further failure.

Our brief excursion into the theory of economic fluctuations comes to an end at this point, to be pursued at much greater length in the macroeconomic portion of the text to follow. But the understanding we have gained enables us to see the Great Depression not only as an historical phenomenon, but as an instance of a more endemic problem of a market society. We have seen how that society paved the way for the Great Depression by its malfunctions in the 1920's. Now let us follow the struggles of the economy in the 1930's as it sought to escape from the deepest and most destructive depression it had ever known.

1. The outstanding economic fact of the hundred years prior to 1929 was the long trend of *economic growth*—a trend that doubled per capita incomes in the United States roughly every forty years and that brought U.S. prosperity in 1929 to unprecedented heights.

2. The long trend of growth came to a disastrous stop—for nearly a decade—with the advent of the *Great Depression*. The causes of the Depression were many:
   - A *speculative and shaky credit structure* that was demolished by the *stock market crash of 1929*, and by *inept monetary policy*.
   - A *steady deterioration of farm purchasing power* aggravated by the inelastic demand for farm products.
   - A considerable undertow of *technological unemployment*.
   - A bad and *worsening distribution of income*.

3. The joint effect of these causes was a tremendous *collapse in capital formation*. Between 1929 and 1933 investment (in real terms) declined by 88 per cent.

4. A *fall in investment is a prime cause of a fall in national income*, because investment is the route over which savings return to the flow of national spending. When investment fails to return savings, recession begins.

5. Investment is thus a critical element in determining the level of prosperity. It is, however, a highly volatile element, since *investment spending depends on expected profits*. When expectations are not optimistic, new capital will not be built.

6. A relatively small decline in investment spending can spread through the economy. This is called the *multiplier effect*.

1. Discuss the causes of the Great Depression in terms of what you know about the economy today. Do you think another Great Depression is possible? Another stock market crash?

2. Among the families you know, how many work for companies that provide goods or services for capital formation—that is, for investment purposes rather than for consumption?

3. Suppose that you were a businessman who intended to build a plant to turn out a promising new item—say, a pencil that would last twice as long as present kinds. What sorts of developments might discourage you from making this investment? How much would your final decision hinge on what you anticipated for the future, compared with what you knew to be the situation today?

4. How can the money you put into a savings bank get back into someone's hands as his income? The money you put into a newly-formed business? The money you put into insurance?

5. If your income (or your parents') was suddenly reduced to half, by how much would your expenditures fall? What sorts of businesses would be hit by your reduced spending? Would they in turn curtail their expenditures?

6. Why is investment so critical in determining the level of prosperity?

8 THE EVOLUTION OF GUIDED CAPITALISM

"This nation asks for action, and action now. . . . We must act and act quickly."

The words are from the inaugural address of the incoming President Franklin Delano Roosevelt. It is hard today to reconstruct the urgency, the sense of desperation, against which the words were addressed on March 4, 1933. A few hours before the actual inauguration ceremony, every bank in America had locked its doors. The monetary system was at the point of collapse. Nearly thirteen million Americans were without work. A veterans' march on Washington, 15,000 strong, in the previous year had been dispersed with tear gas, tanks, and bayonets. On the farms, mortgage-lifting parties, at which a noose was tactfully displayed, served as powerful deterrents to any representatives of insurance companies or banks who might be thinking of bidding in foreclosed land. Meanwhile, a parade of business leaders before the Senate Finance Committee had produced a depressing sense of impotence. Said the president of a great railroad: "The only way to beat the depression is to hit the bottom and then slowly build up." "I have no solution," said the president of one of New York's biggest banks. "I have no remedy in mind," testified the president of U.S. Steel. "Above all we must balance the budget," urged a long string of experts.[1] The crisis was a deep and genuine one; it is doubtful if the United States has ever stood closer to economic collapse and social violence.

The new President's response was immediate and vigorous: in the three months after Roosevelt's inauguration, writes Arthur Schlesinger, "Congress and the country were subjected to a presidential barrage of ideas and programs unlike anything known to American history." This was the famous Hundred Days of the New Deal—the days in which, half by design, half by accident, the foundation was laid for a new pattern of government relationship to the private economy, a pattern that was to spell a major change in the organization of American capitalism.

We begin to trace its general outline in the main measures of the Hundred Days. In all, some fifteen major bills were passed: the Emergency Banking Act, which reopened the banks under what amounted to government supervision; the establishment of the Civilian Conservation Corps to absorb at least some of the young unemployed; the Federal Emergency Relief Act to supplement the exhausted relief facilities of states and cities; the Emergency Farm Mortgage Act, which loaned four times as much to farmers in seven months as all federal loans in the previous four years; the Tennessee Valley Authority Act, setting up TVA, a wholly new venture into government enterprise; the Glass-Steagall Banking Act, divorcing commercial banks from their stock-and-bond floating activities and guaranteeing bank deposits; the first of the Securities Acts aimed at curbing stock speculation and reckless corporate pyramiding.

The Hundred Days only inaugurated the New Deal; it did not by any means complete it. Social Security, housing legislation, the National Recovery Act, the dissolution of public utility holding companies, the establishment of a Federal Housing Authority were yet to be passed. So was the Wagner Act. Indeed, it would not be until 1938 that the New Deal would be "completed" with the passage of the Fair Labor Standard Acts, establishing minimum wages and maximum hours and banning child employment for interstate commerce.

It would take us beyond the boundaries of our survey of general economic history to investigate the content of each of these important pieces of legislation, but we can gain an over-all view of the New Deal

[1] See Arthur Schlesinger, Jr., *The Crisis of the Old Order* (Boston: Houghton Mifflin Company, 1957), pp. 457–58.

by summarizing its achievements against the backdrop of the problems and issues of economic history that we have already encountered. Then we can see that the New Deal is important as marking a genuine change in the development of the market economy itself. With its advent we begin to trace the evolution of a new kind of capitalism, different in significant ways from that which we have heretofore studied. We must understand the nature of this evolution if we are to bring our survey of general economic history to its contemporary terminus in our own society.

THE
FARM
PROBLEM

One general problem that confronted the New Deal, we have noted earlier in this chapter. It was the severe misfunction of the market mechanism in agriculture.

The problem, we will remember, arose in large part from two causes: the nature of the inelastic demand for farm products, and the highly competitive, "atomistic" structure of the agricultural market itself. The New Deal could not alter the first cause, the inelasticity of demand, for this arose from the nature of the consumers' desire for food. But it could change the condition of supply which hurled itself, self-destructively, against an unyielding demand. Hence, one of the earliest pieces of New Deal legislation—the Agricultural Adjustment Act—sought to establish machinery by which farmers, as a group, could accomplish what they could not as competitive individuals: curtailment of output.

The curtailment was sought by offering payments to farmers who agreed to cut back their acreage or in other ways hold down their output. In the first year of the act, there was no time to cut back acreage, so that every fourth row of growing cotton had to be plowed under, and six million pigs were slaughtered. In a nation still hungry and ill-clad, such a spectacle of waste aroused sardonic and bitter comment. And yet, if the program reflected an appalling inability of a society to handle its distribution problem, its attack on over-production was not without results. In both 1934 and 1935 more than thirty million acres were taken out of production in return for government payments of $1.1 billion. Farm prices rose as a result. Wheat, which had slumped to 38¢ a bushel in 1932, rose to $1.02 in 1936. Cotton doubled in price, hog prices tripled, and the net income of the American farmer climbed from the fearful low of $2.5 billion in 1932 to $5 billion in 1936.

We need not here retrace the many later developments in the agricultural programs of the New Deal and its successors. Suffice it rather to make the point that the *central idea* of the AAA has remained. Farmers' incomes no longer reflect the extreme fluctuations characteristic of an inelastic demand, but are cushioned by government payments earned by adhering to some form of crop limitation. The uncontrolled competitive struggle to market crops has given way to a continuing effort to achieve a balance between supply and demand by limiting supply itself.

Has the idea worked well? It might have, but for one thing. Belatedly, technology caught up with American agriculture. Starting in the years before World War II and continuing thereafter with accelerating effect, productivity on the farm began to soar—in fact, it rose faster than productivity in industry. Hence, despite the limitation of *acreage,* the actual output of *crops* increased steadily: between 1940 and the mid-1960's, for instance, the amount of harvested acreage declined by *10 per cent,* but the yield per acre increased by *more than 50 per cent.* The result was a flood of output, huge quantities of which had to be purchased and stored by the government under its support programs. Only the gradual distribution of these surpluses to the underdeveloped lands during the 1960's prevented the surplus problem from becoming a permanent national embarrassment.*

At best, the attempt to solve the farm problem has been but a partial success. It has not, for instance, succeeded in much improving the economic status of the two million least productive small farmers, for these farmers are not able to raise enough crops to benefit substantially from crop supports. Nor has it succeeded in bringing about a sufficient reduction in farm output, so that the normal interplay of supply and demand would lift crop prices above their support levels and relieve the government of its purchase obligations.

Yet the attempt to improve the farm picture must not be brushed aside as ineffective. Without doubt, agriculture, as an income-producing activity, has benefited substantially—especially for the two million successful farmers who produce 90 per cent of our marketed farm products. Between 1940 and 1959 the farm operator families enjoying the use of electricity increased from 33 per cent to over 95 per cent; telephones increased from 25 per cent to 65 per cent; refrigerators from 15 per cent to over 90 per cent. In the West, Midwest, and Northeast, the independent farm operator is today, as he was never before, at a close parity to the urban middle class in terms of living standards.

Our primary interest, however, is not to assess the relative success or failure of the farm programs from early New Deal days to the present. It is, rather, to note that all of the programs spelled a fundamental change in the role of the government in a market society. *The*

---

*Actually, technology had been catching up with—and creating problems for—the farmer for a long time. One of the reasons for the overproduction of the 1920's was that we were steadily cutting back on the acreage needed to sustain horses and mules, as tractors came into general use. Before World War I, we used to devote over a quarter of our cropland to sustaining draft animals. After 1940, this fell to just over 10 per cent. Much of the land not needed for animals went into production for the market, thereby adding its load of straw to the camel's back. I am indebted to Professor Eldon Weeks for this point.

essence of that change was that the government sought to alter the structure of certain markets to allow the competitive process to produce socially acceptable results.

For it was not only in the agricultural sector that the government tried to ameliorate the functioning of the competitive process. In the industrial sector, as well, a new policy of active intervention tried to bring about a better working of the economic mechanism.

In industry as in agriculture, during the first years of acute economic distress, intervention mainly took the form of an attempt to limit supply. Under the provisions of the National Industrial Recovery Act (NIRA) passed in 1933, business was permitted to make sweeping price-and-production agreements (in return for wage agreements designed to better the incomes of the poorest paid). In other words, recovery was aimed at by legalizing the partial oligopolization of business.

The NIRA was greeted with great enthusiasm, and nearly 800 industrial "codes" were elaborated under it. But as the demoralized markets of the early 1930's regained some degree of orderliness, a new source of complaint arose. Smaller producers within many industries claimed that the codes favored the large producer. By the time the experiment was declared unconstitutional by the Supreme Court in 1935, it had already become apparent that the problem was not too much competition, but too little.

There arose a radical shift in policy signaled by the vigorous prosecution of the antitrust laws, a development we traced in Chapter 6. Yet, although the angle of attack had changed completely, the objective was much the same: *to make the market work.*

To what extent can the government make markets work? The answer, as we have seen, is far from clear-cut. Against the powerful forces of oligopoly on the one hand, and the self-defeating competition of "atomistic" industries on the other, the market-shaping powers of government may well prove to be inadequate. But in the formulation of the aim itself is evidence of a profoundly important change in the philosophy of the market society. No longer does laissez faire constitute the ideal relationship between government and economy. Slowly there has arisen the conception of active public intervention to insure the orderly operation of the system.

COUNTERING THE DEPRESSION

But the market system had broken down in a much more important way than was revealed in the farm glut or even in the troubles of the manufacturing sector. Its real collapse in the 1930's was its inability to solve the basic production problem itself—its inability to put together human beings, capital, and land, in order to produce a satisfactory level of output for the nation.

It is curious that the Roosevelt administration had little clear idea of how to remedy this situation when it first took office. Neither, as we have seen, did the business community. Indeed, for nearly everyone, economists included, the only "remedy" for the Depression was thought to be a balanced budget for the government.

Yet there were emergencies to be faced that could not be deferred, even if they unbalanced the budget. Many of the unemployed were literally at the brink of starvation, and the resources of private, state, and local charities were in most instances exhausted. President Roosevelt, unlike his predecessor, did not believe that the receipt of federal relief would "demoralize" the unemployed any more than the receipt of federal loans from the Reconstruction Finance Corporation had "demoralized" business. By May of the inaugural year, a relief organization had been established; and a year later, nearly one out of every seven Americans was receiving relief. In nine states, one out of five families—in one state one out of three families—was dependent on public support. Not that relief did much more than keep these unfortunate families from starvation—the average grant per family was less than $25 per month—but it did provide an economic floor, no matter how rickety.

The immediate aims of relief were humanitarian. Shortly, however, they were followed by thoughts of the *useful* possibilities of relief expenditures. Soon the great bulk of relief spending was being paid for public works of various sorts: schools, roads, parks, hospitals, slum clearance—and even federal art, theater, and writing projects.

As the public-works program grew, however, the finances of the federal government took a turn for the worse, until, by the mid-1930's, it was clear that something like a chronic deficit of $2 to $3 billion a year had been achieved. Each year the government spent more than it took in through taxes—not only for relief, but for conservation, farm subsidies, veterans' bonuses, public housing, aid to the states. To meet its bills it borrowed the necessary money from the public through the sale of government bonds to private individuals, to corporations, and to the commercial banks. Obviously, as the total amount of bonds outstanding grew each year, so did the total debt of the nation. In 1929, the national debt totaled $16.9 billion. By 1935 it had risen to $28.7 billion, and each year it steadily rose: to $36 billion in 1937, to $40 billion in 1939, to $42 billion in 1940.

At first the heavy spending of the federal government was greeted with wary acceptance by the business and banking communities as a necessary temporary expedient. Before long, however, even within the administration itself, the mounting deficit was regarded with considerable misgivings. The recurrent excess of government expenditure over tax receipts was thereupon apologized for as "pump priming"—as an injection of government fuel which would, so to speak, start up the

THE ECONOMY
FAILS TO
RESPOND

stalled motor of private expenditures, making further injections unnecessary. Thus, a few billions of government spending, it was hoped, would set into motion an upward spiral of spending and job expansion by the business sector.

But the upward spiral did not materialize. After 1933, helped by government spending, *consumption* expenditures began to rise, but private capital expenditures lagged behind. Although they, too, improved after 1933, by 1938 they were still 40 per cent below 1929.

Why did private investment fail to rise? The answer lies partly in the fact that the very government deficits that were supposed to cure the Depression only frightened business into a condition of economic paralysis that prolonged it. Coupled with the reform legislation of the New Deal, the new presence of government's large-scale economic activity caused business to lose its former "confidence." The businessman felt uncomfortable and ill-at-ease in a changing economic and political climate and was in no mood to plan ahead boldly for the future. The general outlook stressed caution rather than promise; cycles rather than growth; safety rather than gain. And then behind the psychological factors, real forces were also at work. A much slower rate of population growth in the 1930's depressed the important housing market. Even more serious, no major industry-creating technological breakthrough, comparable to the railway or the automobile, held sufficient promise of profitable growth to tempt private capital into a major capital-building boom of its own.

Thus, for many reasons, the new federal expenditures did not prime the pump. Private investment did not spontaneously rise to take over its traditional propulsive function, now "temporarily" carried out by the government. This did not mean, however, that the economic influence of government was therefore relegated to a minor role. On the contrary, the failure of pump priming—conceived as an emergency measure—caused a widening in the conception of the government's role. Government now began to be envisioned as a *permanent stabilizing and growth-promoting agency for the market economy as a whole.*

COMPENSATORY GOVERNMENT SPENDING

The idea was slow in taking form and did not, in fact, receive its full-dress exposition until the middle 1930's.* As is often the case with new ideas, it seemed at first complicated and difficult, and even among professional economists its basic concepts were the subject of murky discussion for a number of years. Yet in retrospect, it appears as a very simple argument.

---

*The most influential book setting forth the concept—albeit, in highly technical terms—was John Maynard Keynes' *General Theory of Employment, Interest and Money* published in 1936. Few books have roused such controversy or left so permanent a mark. We shall learn more about it; beginning with the next chapter.

The key to prosperity or depression, it had become increasingly evident, lay in the *total volume of expenditure* that a market society laid out for its goods and services. When that volume was high, employment and incomes were high; when it declined, output and employment declined as well. And what determined the volume of expenditure? As we have seen, the stream of consumption spending tended to be a passive factor, rising when individuals' incomes rose and diminishing when they fell. The volatile item, as both history and theory made clear, was the stream of capital expenditure.

From this starting point it is not difficult to take the next step. If lagging private capital expenditures were responsible for lagging employment and output, why could not the government step in to make up whatever deficiencies arose from private expenditure? There had always been, after all, a fairly regular flow of public expenditure, much of it for capital-creating purposes, such as roads or schools. Why could not this flow of public spending be deliberately enlarged when the occasion demanded, to maintain the needed total volume of expenditure? True, this required the government to borrow and spend and thereby increase its debt. But did not much private capital spending also result in corporate debts? And why could not the debt, itself, be handled as corporate debts which were never "paid off" in the aggregate but refunded, with new bond issues being sold to take the place of those coming due? *

To the economists of the Roosevelt administration, the answers to these questions seemed plain enough. The government not only could, but should, use its spending powers as an economic instrumentality for securing full employment. By this, they did not have in mind a "radical" revision of capitalism. Rather, they envisaged the evolution of a new form of *guided* capitalism—a market society in which the all-important levels of employment and output would no longer be left to the vagaries of the market but would be protected against decline and stimulated toward growth by public action.

This was not how matters appeared to many members of the nation, however, and especially to the business community. They saw government spending as inherently "wasteful," and the mounting debt as evidence that we would spend ourselves into "bankruptcy." Beneath these arguments there lurked a deeper suspicion, a suspicion that government spending, whatever the protestations to the contrary, was the entering wedge for socialism or worse.

The controversy raged through 1940. But in a sense, it was an empty debate. At its peak, the annual deficit never touched $4 billion, and federal government purchases never contributed more than 6 per cent to gross national product. Judged by the importance of government in

---

In Chap. 15, we will look very carefully into the arguments for and against deficit spending.

the economy, probably no industrial nation in the world was *less* socialist than the United States. Yet, if the fears of the conservatives were hardly realistic, neither were the hopes of the liberals. For in the prevailing atmosphere of distrust, the remedy of government spending could never be more than half-heartedly applied. Deficit spending in the 1930's was a holding operation and not an operation of growth. By 1939, although conditions had improved considerably over the levels of 1932, there were still 9.5 million people—17 per cent of the labor force—without work.

IMPACT OF
THE WAR

 In the end, it was not theory that settled the history of compensatory government spending, but history that settled the theory. With the outbreak of World War II came a tremendous forced expansion in government outlays. Year by year, spending for war purposes rose, until in 1944 federal expenditures totaled just over $100 billion, and with this unprecedented rise in expenditure came an equally swift rise in GNP. By 1945, our gross national product had risen by 70 per cent in real terms over 1939, and unemployment had dwindled to the vanishing point. The demonstration that public spending could indeed impel the economy forward—indeed, could lift it beyond all previously imagined bounds—was unmistakable. So was the fact that a government could easily carry an enormously much larger debt, a debt that now towered over $250 billion, provided that its gross national product was also much larger.

 And then, with the war had come a marked change in attitude both toward the government and to the economy in general. After four years of unprecedented effort, the American people looked to massive government action with a more accustomed eye; so, too, after four years of record output, they looked back upon the days of mass unemployment with a new feeling of shame. Perhaps most important of all, they looked ahead to the postwar period with considerable trepidation. Virtually every economist, contemplating the huge cutback in spending consequent upon a termination of hostilities, feared the rise of a vast new army of the unemployed. Even the most conservative opinion was uneasy at the political possibilities of such a return to the 1930's.

 The upshot of the change in attitude was the passage of the Employment Act of 1946, one of the truly historic pieces of American economic legislation. The act recognized (although in carefully circumspect terms) that it was "the continuing policy and responsibility of the Federal Government . . . to promote maximum employment, production, and purchasing power." It was, as we shall see, one thing to write such an act and another thing to implement it; but without question, the Employment Act marked the end of an era. The idea that the best thing the government could do to promote recovery was to do nothing, the belief that a balanced budget was in all cases the goal for government fiscal policy, and beyond that the trust in the blind forces of the market as inherently conducive to prosperity—all these once firmly held ideas of the past had been abandoned. The debate within capitalism was no longer whether or not government should undertake the responsibility for the over-all functioning of the market system; only the specific means were questioned: how best to achieve that end.

The war ended in 1945; within a year, federal spending dropped by $40 billion, and the nation waited tensely for the expected fall in employment, incomes, and prices.

Instead, it found itself confronting the least anticipated of all eventualities: a rousing inflationary boom. It is true that unemployment doubled, rising to two million, but this was still less than 4 per cent of the labor force. Meanwhile, the number of people at work showed a steady rise: 54 million jobs in 1945; 57 million in 1946; 60 million in 1947; 63 million in 1950. Industrial production, after a brief postwar dip, was buoyant: by 1953 it would surpass its wartime peak with no sign of more than momentary turndown. Most striking of all was what happened to prices. Year by year, the cost of living rose: up a third between 1945 and 1948, up another 10 per cent between 1948 and 1952, up still another 7 per cent from then to 1957. In all, the purchasing power of the dollar declined by more than a third in the first twelve postwar years.

What was the cause of this totally unforeseen turn of events?

There was no one single cause, but several. To begin with, the end of the war found America in a situation of "classic" inflationary potential: too much money and too little goods. The too little goods was, of course, the result of four years of wartime shortage; the too much money was the result of having added $150 billion to liquid savings during those same years of high incomes and consumer scarcity. With the end of the war, Americans lost no time in entering upon a mammoth spending spree. In fact, it was this unexpected surge of consumption that was the main reason why the gloomy postwar economic forecasts were not fulfilled. Meanwhile, the nation's supply of money itself, in the form of bank deposits, was also high, owing to wartime financing. Banks and other credit institutions were all too happy to supply loans to consumers or corporations. Thus an enormous pressure of pent-up demand, financed out of past savings and current incomes, exerted its pressure on the price level.

A second reason for the inflationary boom was that spending was high in the nonconsumer areas. Government expenditures ceased falling in 1947 and sparked by rising state and local needs, began to increase again, augmented in 1950, when the Korean War added its fillip to federal expenditures. High exports and Marshall aid to Europe provided another stimulus. Perhaps more significant was that private capital expenditures proved themselves unexpectedly strong. Encouraged by the avalanche of consumer buying, by a host of new inventions and industries stemming from the war, by a new impetus toward research and development, the longest and steadiest period of capital accumulation in American history added its expenditures to the flow of purchasing power.

And then there was a third cause of the inflationary trend. In "pattern-setting" areas of industry, such as automobiles or steel, powerful unions succeeded in winning sharp wage increases. That, in itself, was not so unusual; but in these years of "easy money," there was nothing to prevent corporations from passing along the increases in terms of higher prices. What made matters still worse was that the wage increases (particularly in the mid-1950's) were often in excess of productivity increases, while the corporation price boosts (especially in the critical case of steel) were in excess of the wage boosts. Easy money, strong labor unions, and oligopolistic industry all combined to create inflationary pressure points at strategic locations of the economy.

INSTRUMENTS
OF POLICY

It was a very different situation from that which the advocates of compensatory government spending had envisioned in the late 1930's. All through the 1950's it was the problem of inflation that occupied the authorities—and without much more success than had attended their efforts to curb mass unemployment twenty years earlier. Yet the confrontation with the problem of inflation was not without results; for out of the debate which it created, there emerged for the first time a general consensus on the nature of the mechanisms the government was entitled to use in seeking to affect the over-all operation of the system.

In our next section, on macroeconomics, we will look into these mechanisms in a technical way. Here, however, we need only to grasp the general nature of the three main devices of control.

The first were *monetary controls,* mainly centered in the Federal Reserve banking system. By easing or tightening the reserve requirements which all banks had to maintain behind their deposits, the Federal Reserve was able to encourage or discourage lending, the source of much economic activity. In addition, by buying or selling government bonds, the Federal Reserve was able to make the whole banking system relatively flushed with funds, when these were needed, or relatively short of funds when money seemed in excess supply.

The second were *tax adjustments.* The pressure of consumer buying during the postwar boom served as a reminder of the fact that the largest fraction of the volume of total expenditure was always consumption spending. By raising or lowering taxes, particularly income taxes, the government could quickly increase or diminish this broad flow of purchasing power.

The third was *the federal budget.* By the 1950's, the great debate over the virtues of a balanced government budget had virtually come to an end. Among academic groups and in a widening circle of business leaders, the budget was recognized as a tool for regulating total national expenditure. In inflationary times, a budget surplus would serve to "mop up" part of the inflationary purchasing flow. In depressed times, a budget deficit (covered by borrowing) was a mechanism for generating a desired increase in that flow.

The idea of monetary controls was not new, but the general consensus on the use of taxes and budgets as deliberate instruments of economic policy to counter boom and recession *was* new. Once again, as in the case with government spending, it was not the force of theoretical argument which had won this historic agreement. Rather, it was the fact of historic change which had placed theory in a new light. For essentially what commended the new means of influence over the market system were profound changes in the structure of that system. Let us see what those changes were.

In our concentration on the functional problems of the economy in its years of depression, war, and inflation, we have omitted one very significant development. This was a marked movement away from the extreme inequalities of reward which so vividly marked the capitalism of the past.

In part, this was brought about by a decline in unemployment, in part by aiding lower income groups through the support of trade unions, through the enactment of minimum wage floors, and through the passage of welfare legislation. The change was not entirely due to public policy, however. The occupational shifts which we noted at the commencement of our previous chapter also played a powerful role, as workers shifted out of low-paid agricultural and unskilled labor into the semiskilled and skilled categories of the factory.

However varied the causes, the results were striking.

Note in Table 8-1 that the lowest and second fifths benefited almost

REDISTRIBUTION OF INCOME

PER CENT INCREASE IN PRE-TAX AVERAGE INCOME (1950 DOLLARS)	
	1935–36 to 1962
Lowest fifth	120%
Second fifth	136
Third fifth	131
Fourth fifth	115
Highest fifth	74
Top 5 per cent	47
All groups	98

Source: *Statistical Abstract of the United States*, 1965, p. 340.

TABLE 8 · 1

INCREASED INCOME

twice as much as the highest fifth and almost three times as much as the top 5 per cent. While the bottom was moving up, owing to a variety of causes, the top was coming down—in large part owing to the pressure of higher tax rates. For beginning with the New Deal, then receiving an even stronger impetus from the war, stiffer tax schedules and stricter enforcement had borne down upon the relative affluence of upper income groups. Table 8-2 gives us some idea of the change.

TABLE 8 · 2

RELATIVE AFFLUENCE

PER CENT SHARES OF TOTAL INCOME RECEIVED BY TOP 1 PER CENT AND TOP 5 PER CENT OF TOTAL POPULATION				
	1929	1941	1946	1966
Top 1% (after tax)	19.1%	9.9%	7.7%	n.a.
Top 5% (before tax)	30.0	24.0	21.3	18.0

Source: *Historical Statistics of the United States,* G135, 105 (1929–1946). Figures for 1966 estimated from data, *Statistical Abstract,* 1968, p. 324.

What had happened was quite extraordinary. The share of income going to the top 1 per cent had been cut by over 60 per cent. That going to the top 5 per cent had been cut by more than one-third.

To be sure, we must exercise a good deal of caution in viewing these figures. They do not show large flows of personal receipts which are legally exempted from tax, such as tax-exempt interest, stock option rights, expense accounts, and the like. We do not know the extent to which such new tax-induced ways of "smuggling" income reduce the reliability of the figures, but it may be by a fairly substantial amount. In addition, we must note that there is little if any evidence that the ownership of *wealth*—bank accounts, stocks and bonds, and the like—has changed much despite the change in incomes. Wealth in the United States is still highly concentrated in the topmost groups of the population; for instance, it is estimated that the top 1 per cent of all "spending

TABLE 8 · 3

INCOME DISTRIBUTION IN 1929 AND 1963

Income levels 1963	Per cent of all households with this actual income in 1963	Per cent of all households with equivalent of this income in 1929
Less than $2000	11%	30%
2000–3999	18	38
4000–5999	20	16
6000–7999	18	7
8000–9999	12	3
10,000+	21	6

Source: *Survey of Current Business,* April 1964, Table 2, p. 4.

units" own at least 65 per cent of all corporate stock and that the wealthiest one-tenth of 1 per cent owns 35 per cent of it.[2]

Nonetheless, with all these cautions, it is undeniable that the years following the New Deal ushered in a remarkable over-all redistribution of income. If we look back from a recent date to 1929, the change is undeniably great.*

But now it is time to return to our main theme. For what we have here is not only a mass escalation in the income stratification of the nation—a development noteworthy in itself from the point of view of welfare. We see, as well, the development of a "middle-income" society *in which increases or decreases in income taxation provide a powerful mechanism of economic influence.*

TABLE 8 · 4

IMPACT OF INDIVIDUAL INCOME TAXES

Year	Number of taxable returns (millions)	Total income tax paid ($ billions)	Total income tax as % of total consumption	Income tax liability of median family ($)
1929	2.5	$ 1.0	1%	$ 17
1940	7.4	1.4	2	101 (1941)
1966	69.9	56.5	12	809

Source: *Statistical Abstract,* 1968, p. 389; *Historical Statistics,* Series Y 292, 299, 303, 307.

As we can see, the upward shift in the economic center of gravity of the nation has brought about a situation in which, for the first time, a change in income taxes can directly affect *mass* purchasing power.

[2] See J. K. Butters *et al., Effects of Taxation: Investment of Individuals* (Cambridge: 1960). p. 25. Cf., also, R. Lampman, *Changes in the Share of Wealth Held by Top Wealth Holders, 1922–56.* NBER Paper 71, 1960.

*How "fair" is income distribution in the United States today? Clearly, enormous disparities still characterize the division of income in this country: at the time of the last census (1959), the top 1 per cent of all families received almost as much income as did the poorest 31 per cent of all families. This meant that half a million fortunate families with incomes over $50,000 got almost as much income as 14 million unfortunate families with incomes of under $4,000. This is better than 1929, but it hardly satisfies most people's idea of "fairness." On the other hand, it must also be said that income distribution in the United States is more egalitarian than in most of the industrialized capitalist societies (and much more egalitarian than is the case in the underdeveloped countries). In an international ranking of capitalist nations, only the Scandanavian nations, the Netherlands, and the non-Arab population of Israel have more equal income distributions than we do, and not by much. It is difficult to make comparisons with the socialist nations. The absence of property incomes in Russia, China, and Cuba removes the upper extreme of wealth that characterizes all capitalist countries to some degree. In addition, none of the socialist nations has an economic group at the bottom comparable to our migrant workers or southern tenant farmers. On the other hand, the spread between high and low *earned* incomes—between janitors and factor managers—is probably greater in the Soviet Union than here (although this is not the case in Cuba and China). More important, the difference between *average* agricultural incomes and *average* industrial incomes is probably greater in the socialist countries than in the capitalist ones. (See Herman P. Miller, *Rich Man, Poor Man.* (New York: Thomas Y. Crowell Company, 1964, pp. 5, 13.)

The redistribution of income thus provides us with an understanding of the rationale behind one of the new instruments of economic manipulation. An insight into the second of our new instruments is provided if we examine another structural alteration in the economy: the change in the relative size of the government contribution to gross national product.

Table 8-5 gives us the magnitude of the change.

TABLE 8 · 5

**GROWTH
OF THE PUBLIC
SECTOR
(current dollars)**

Year	GNP (billions)	Gov't purchases of goods and services (billions)		All gov't purchases as per cent of GNP
		Federal	State & local	
1929	$104.4	$ 1.3	$ 7.2	8.1%
1940	100.6	6.2	7.9	14.0
1967	789.7	90.6	87.8	22.5

SOURCE: *Historical Statistics,* Series F, 67, 81, 86; *Economic Indicators: Survey of Current Business,* Dec., 1968, p. 7.

It is clear from the table that a major shift has taken place. Whereas in 1929 less than one dollar in ten of national production owed its origin to government purchasing, today about one dollar in five of all goods and services produced is sold to some branch of the government.

Here, too, lies a source of the new agreement on the mechanisms of influence. Today the government is in a position of such commanding economic strength that it cannot *avoid* influencing the trend of total expenditure, even by relatively modest changes in its budgetary balance. For example, a 10 per cent fall in government receipts and a 10 per cent rise in expenditures will add to total GNP expenditures an amount equal to one-and-a-half times all manufacturing investment; in 1929, a similar change in the budget position would have contributed new purchasing power equal to only one-tenth of all manufacturing investment.

Does the existence of these government "stabilizers" and the general consensus on the mechanisms of influence mean that economic fluctuations such as the Great Depression cannot recur?

It is certainly unlikely in the extreme that the terrible experience of the early 1930's will be repeated. Many of its causes, as we noted, were rooted in particular excesses of the times, and these, to a very large extent, have been corrected. The flimsiness of the banking structure, the extreme maldistribution of income—and perhaps most important of all, the barrier of inadequate economic understanding—have all been removed or much improved. Although history teaches us the virtues of caution in announcements of this kind, it seems fair to state that we now understand, as we never did before, the economic policies required to avoid or cure severe economic depressions.

In this regard the Kennedy tax cut proposed in 1962 is an interesting example of the New Economics in action. There had been a mild recession in 1960 from which the nation had not fully recovered by mid-1962, and President Kennedy's advisers were much concerned about the mounting level of unemployment in the country at large. To cure this unemployment, all agreed, the economy's rate of growth would have to increase, and this in turn required a major economic stimulus. But where was the stimulus to come from? Relying on the New Economics, the President's advisers recommended that taxes be cut across the board, despite mounting federal expenditures, so that a "deficit" in the nation's budget would be *deliberately* incurred.

As was to be expected, voices of disaster were raised. "At the heart of our national finances," declared Representative Cannon, Chairman of the House Appropriations Committee, "is a simple inescapable fact, easily grasped by anyone. It is that our government—any government—like individuals and families—cannot spend and continue to spend more than they take in without inviting disaster."

What Representative Cannon did not seem to grasp, however, was that the government was not proposing to spend more than it took in. It was proposing to spend more than it took in *in taxes, borrowing the rest from the nation's savings.* This was an operation that was, economically speaking, in no way different from the nation's business sector which in a normal year of growth took in, in sales, less than it spent for its running expenses plus its capital investments, and which regularly borrowed the difference.

Thus at its core the so-called New Economics proposed that the government be considered not as an individual "household," but as a full economic *sector,* no different from the business sector in its operation, except that it was subject to deliberate public control and could thus be used to help move the economy in a desired direction. This is a central aspect of modern economic policy to which we will turn in detail in Part Two.

After much debate, the controversial tax cut was finally passed in early 1964. Was it a success? As is often the case in economics, we cannot produce laboratory proof. Certainly the economy responded vigorously and unemployment fell after the tax cut. But by then other factors were also at work, including higher spending for the Vietnam war. Indeed, by the end of 1965, spending on Vietnam had already strained the economy to the point that the President's advisers recommended a tax *increase* to dampen inflationary pressures.

Hence we can only say that economists *think* the New Economics works. Perhaps more important, it is increasingly clear that business thinks so too and bases its plans on the assumption that government will no longer "let" depressions go unchecked. It is perhaps too early to be absolutely certain that the suspicions and misunderstandings of the 1930's have been overcome. Yet it seems likely that the graduates of the colleges and business schools who now play an important part in the direction of corporate affairs are not so likely to be panicked by government action to cure a slump as were their fathers thirty years ago. There is a hypothesis that should cheer the despairing instructor of economics!

REMAINING PROBLEMS

This general reassurance should not lead us to the easy assumption that economic fluctuations of considerable severity and unemployment of uncomfortable magnitude are not still possibilities. The basic cause of instability in the market system remains; and so long as anticipated profit is the critical link between savings and investment, it will continue to remain. Irregular bursts of capital formation and recurrent downward revisions of profit anticipations are virtually inseparable from an economic system in which the process of technical change and its conversion into real capital are left to the unguided impulses of individual business firms.

To be sure, we now possess powerful instruments of economic compensation against the *cumulative effects* of these shocks—protections we have never enjoyed (or understood) before. But the mere existence of these instruments does not guarantee that they will, in fact, be used. Lingering fears of an unbalanced budget may delay or even prevent the use of compensatory government expenditure. Then, too, nearly half our present total government expenditure (and 85 per cent of our *federal* expenditure) goes for defense purposes. The effective use of a compensatory mechanism in a truly *peacetime* economy might be much more difficult than in an economy where a large defense sector offers a politically acceptable area for public spending. Finally, we must remember that the New Economics is designed to be an instrument of restraint as well as one of stimulus—that it is meant to be used against inflation as well as recession. But to translate restraint into effective political action is a more difficult policy than expansion. The political problems of raising taxes, for example, are well-known.

There is, in addition, at least one weakness of the 1920's that we have not corrected. This is the trend toward technological displacement—a trend that in our day has assumed disturbing dimensions with the new technology of automation. For example, between 1950 and 1964, automobile output rose by 16 per cent while auto employment in the factories fell by 31 per cent. Over the same years, textile mill output rose by 37 per cent while textile mill production workers decreased by over 30 per cent.[3] In the manufacturing sector as a whole, the index of physical output jumped some 75 per cent during this period, while employment on the factory floor (so-called production workers) remained unchanged. In more recent years, manufacturing employment has again begun to rise, but the rate of increase in employment is only half the rate of increase in output, and it seems to be concentrated among nonproduction workers. Thus in important areas, an undercurrent of technological displacement has eaten into our job supply, and all the more seriously as a bulge in young job seekers has begun to swell our labor force.

We will have a chance to look more closely into automation and its meaning when we return to the problem of employment in our macroeconomic studies to come. But it is well to remind ourselves, as we close this section on our economic history, that we have not yet solved the basic production problem of society with sufficient dependability to write off the danger of unemployment and recession. The problems of using our economic tools courageously, of adapting them to the needs of a genuinely peacetime economy, of coping with the undertow of technological displacement are far from overcome.

Nor have we, for all our gains in income distribution, yet achieved a solution to the basic distribution problem of which we can be inordinately proud. In the nation as a whole, about 12 per cent of all persons live in "poor" households; another 6 per cent in "near-poor" households.* This is an encouraging drop from an incidence of poverty that was twice as high twenty years ago. But the remaining victims of poverty are very unequally distributed among the population. For example, over one-third of households headed by elderly persons fall within the category of poverty, mainly because Social Security benefits are still too low to make possible an acceptable standard of life. No less important, one-third of all nonwhite families are afflicted with poverty, compared with one-seventh of all white families, mainly because racial discrimination has systematically excluded nonwhite Americans from an even start in life or a fair chance at a job.

Thus, much poverty is associated with disadvantages that have little to do with the operation of the marketplace. That is why the spread of prosperity throughout the nation has disappointingly little effect on

[3] *Statistical Abstract*, 1968, pp. 717, 718.

*How do we define "poverty"? The Council of Economic Advisors takes into account both the number of members in a household, and the rural or urban location of that household. For a single individual, aged 65 and living in the city, poverty begins at about $1,700 (in 1968 prices); near-poverty begins at $2,000; for his counterpart in the country, the figure is $1,200 and $1,400. For a family of 4 in the city, poverty starts at about $3,500; near-poverty at $4,500. In the country the equivalent is about $2,400 and $3,100.

the low-lying strata of poverty. For instance, the Annual Report of the Council of Economic Advisors for 1968, commenting on the improvement in general well-being associated with the long boom of the 1960's, tells us that if the reduction in the number of poor between 1961 and 1968 could be continued for another ten years, poverty could be entirely eliminated. Unfortunately, the report goes on to say, this rate of improvement cannot be expected to continue. Almost 60 per cent of poor households today are headed by children or disabled or elderly persons who will not be drawn into the labor market even if the boom goes on. In addition, embolisms of terrible poverty are to be found in rural backwaters and in the city slums, where a whole culture of poverty has destroyed contact between the victims of indifference and the economy around them. To cure poverty for these groups will take more than the trickle-down effect of a buoyant economy. It will require the deliberate redistribution of income, whether by a system of family allowances or a guaranteed income or a negative income tax or some other such means.

But can we afford such a redistribution of income? How much would it cost to bring the poor up to the level of minimum decency? The council estimates that the cost of the poverty gap in 1967 was $9.7 billion; that is, the redistribution of little more than 1 per cent of our GNP would effectively eliminate poverty from our midst. Alternatively, if the 85 per cent of households that are not poor would consent to have the *growth* in their real incomes reduced by 2.5 per cent a year and if this differential of about $2.8 billion were transferred to those in poverty, we could close up the gap in about 4 years. Thus it is clear beyond doubt that we *can* eliminate poverty in America, as it has already been virtually eliminated in Sweden and Denmark and Norway, all countries "poorer" than we are. The question is not whether we can; it is whether we will.

It is important to remind ourselves of these failures. And yet, the magnitude of the over-all achievement must not be underrated on this account. For the first time in history, something approaching a society of "average" well-being has been won. If the sweep of economic history which has given us this society is maintained, the future may well see the advent of the first society in which the economic problem, for all intents and purposes, is solved. By 1980, if our trend of growth of the last thirty years is maintained, average family incomes will have risen well over $9,000, allowing for population increase and calculating in terms of today's prices. If our population continues to grow at about 1.5 per cent a year and our GNP increases only 3 per cent a year (which is lower than the historic trend of growth rates), our *per capita* GNP by the year 2000 will exceed $6,100. Making adjustments for the fact that not all of gross national output becomes household income, as we shall see in Chapter 10, we would have *family* income of almost $20,000 in terms of today's purchasing power. It would be unwise to take such projections as anything but a general forecast of *potentialities,* but the fact is that the potentialities are there.

Will we in fact realize the prospect of universal abundance? Or will our present economy, partly affluent, partly poor, continue to constitute the environment of the year 2000? The answer depends on many factors, not all of them within our control, for the American economy, rich as it is, is inextricably entangled in a world in which the great majority of human beings are still desperately poor. These problems we shall take up in Part Four of our text.

In part, however, the realization of the prospect of abundance does lie within our control, and to a large extent this control reflects how well we grasp the nature of our economic mechanism. Hence it is well that we now turn, at the point where history becomes big with the future, toward a much more detailed examination of how our economy actually operates. Our study of economic history has prepared the way for an understanding that only economic theory can give us.

SUMMARY

1. *The New Deal* was a major effort to reverse the downward spiral of the Great Depression. A many-pronged attack, it sought both to correct the failures of the economy, and to strengthen its workings.

2. The New Deal *interfered with the structure of markets* to a greater extent than had been tried by an American government before. Not only agricultural, but many industrial markets were regulated in an effort to bring about an orderly economic recovery. Although many of these efforts failed or were declared unconstitutional, the heritage of the New Deal has been a new concept of *government intervention* and an effective end to the philosophy of laissez faire.

3. The most important of the New Deal policies was the deliberate initiation of *government spending,* first for relief, then for public works, as a means of stimulating private investment—so-called priming the pump. Owing to the small scale of the public spending and the prevailing business attitude of fear and suspicion to government intervention, the pump priming did not work.

4. Out of the New Deal experience evolved a new conception of how the economy operated, and of how government might counteract depression. The key was now recognized to be the *total volume of expenditure.* And the new conception urged that whenever private expenditure was insufficient to maintain full employment, the government should add *compensatory spending* of its own.

5. The war provided convincing evidence that public expenditure could indeed bring about a high level of employment and output. After the war, the *Employment Act of 1946* recognized the role of the government in promoting "maximum employment."

6. Postwar experience brought inflation, rather than the generally expected recession. But the period also saw the formulation of a general consensus on the tools of the *New Economics:*

   • *Monetary controls* to encourage or discourage private spending.

- *Tax adjustments* to induce or to dampen consumer and business spending.
- The use of the *federal budget* as a balance wheel in the economy.

7. These new tools were made more workable by a considerable *redistribution of income* that had taken place and by *the enlargement of the public sector.*

8. The New Economics is by no means a cure for all economic ills, but it does hold the promise of *greater economic stability* than in the past.

QUESTIONS

1. What do you think is the prevailing attitude of big businessmen to government today? Of little businessmen? Farmers? Students?

2. "Even if the Hoover administration had wanted to take a more active role in combatting the Depression, it would have been difficult in those times for it to do so." Why?

3. Do you consider inflation to be as dangerous a condition as depression?

4. The farm problem will always be difficult to solve as long as agriculture is a highly competitive industry, faced with an inelastic demand and with a technology that continuously increases productivity. Explain why.

5. Do you think that all government spending is wasteful? Some? All private spending? Some? How does one measure "waste"?

6. In what ways has history provided the testing ground for the theory of government spending? Was the war such a test? Was it conclusive? What would invalidate the theory that government spending can properly supplement private investment to cure a depression?

two

PROSPERITY AND RECESSION

THE ECONOMICS OF THE MACRO SYSTEM

WEALTH AND OUTPUT 9

We have completed much of our "geological" survey of the economic system. Now we are about to survey the continent from another vantage point—that of macroeconomics. Our focus on history will not be entirely lost, but it will be relegated to the background, and our attention will be concentrated mainly on the very recent past and the present. Perhaps we can better describe the changed perspective of this section by saying that we are now using an X-ray rather than a camera. Our purpose is no longer to construct a narrative that explains the present in terms of the past, but to penetrate beneath the "story" of events to processes and relationships that only a knowledge of macroeconomic theory will reveal.

Through our study of the Great Depression and its consequences, we are, in a sense, familiar with the broad outlines of macroeconomics. Prosperity and recession, inflation and deflation, unemployment and growth are the great problems of macroeconomic inquiry, and we learned a good deal about them in chapters 7 and 8, when we followed the development of modern capitalism. Yet, as we shall see, there is much more to learn before we understand the causes of the phenomena that interest us. That is what we shall set out to do in the pages that follow.

THE MACROECONOMIC PERSPECTIVE

But what is "macroeconomics"? The word derives from the Greek *macro* meaning "big," and the implication is therefore that it is concerned with bigger problems than in microeconomics (*micro* = small). Yet as we shall see in Part Three, microeconomics wrestles with problems that are quite as large as those of macroeconomics. The difference is really not one of scale. It is one of approach, of original angle of incidence. *Macroeconomics begins from a viewpoint that initially draws our attention to aggregate economic phenomena and processes,* such as gross national product or saving and investment. Microeconomics begins from a vantage point that first directs our analysis to the individual constituents of economic behavior, mainly the actions of individuals and firms. Both views, as we shall see by the end of Part Three, are needed to comprehend the economy as a whole, just as it takes two different lenses to make a stereophoto jump into the round. But we can learn only one view at a time, and it is well to begin with the exciting spectacle of the entire national economy as it unfolds to the macroscopic gaze.

What does the economy look like from this perspective? The view is not unlike that from a plane. What we see first is the fundamental tableau of nature—the fields and forests, lakes and seas, with their inherent riches; then the diverse artifacts of man—the cities and towns, the road and rail networks, the factories and machines, the stocks of half-completed or unsold goods; and finally the human actors themselves with all their skills and talents, their energies, their social organization.

Thus our perspective shows us a vast panorama from which we single out for our special attention those elements and activities having to do with our worldly well-being, with our capacity to provide ourselves with the necessaries and luxuries of material life. It need hardly be said that this is at best only a partial view of society. An economist does not examine the flux of social goings-on, the quality of intellectual life, the spirituality or crassness of a community. Initially, at any rate, he concerns himself with only those aspects of society that bear on its *material provisioning,* and even here he often limits himself to things that he can measure in some fairly objective way.

Let us, then, begin to set our first economic impressions in order by directing our attention to an attribute of the landscape below us that is clearly important in the provisioning process, and that should be subject to roughly accurate measurement—our national wealth. By our wealth, we mean the very objects—or at least many of them—that have already caught our eye. Table 9-1 is an estimate made of the national wealth of the United States for the year 1967.

	Billions of dollars, rounded
Structures	
Residential	$ 721
Business	373
Government	347
Equipment	
Producers (machines, factories, etc.)	331
Consumers durables (autos, appliances)	325
Inventories, business	206
Monetary gold and silver	17
Land	
Farm	147
Residential	136
Business	105
Public	62
Net foreign assets	54
Total	**2828**

TABLE 9 · 1

U. S. NATIONAL WEALTH 1967 VALUE

Rather than encumber each table with sources that are, for the most part, identical, I have added the source only if the figures might be difficult to find or if they are the result of considerable arithmetical manipulation. All unidentified figures will be found in one or more of the following basic sourcebooks: *Historical Statistics of the United States* and *Statistical Abstract of the United States,* 1968, both published by the Bureau of the Census, Washington, D.C., and the National Income and Product Tables reported in *Survey of Current Business* (July, 1968), Department of Commerce, and in subsequent *Economic Indicators,* Joint Economic Committee.

Let us note immediately that this is not a full valuation of the riches of our society. No monetary worth is put on our human skills or even on the presence of so many head of population. Nor does this table pretend to embrace, much less measure, all our material possessions. Such immense economic treasures as the contents of the Library of Congress or the Patent Office cannot be accurately valued. Nor can works of art, nor military equipment—neither of which is included in the total. Much of our public land is valued at only nominal amounts. Hence at best this is the roughest of estimates. Nonetheless, it gives us an idea of the magnitude of the economic endowment that we have at our disposal.

It would perhaps be a much more meaningful idea if we could now compare our own national wealth with that of a poor nation, such as India, or more precisely, compare the *per capita* value of our wealth—that is, the share of our wealth that is available to each of us—to the *per capita* wealth of India. Alas, as is so often the case with the less developed countries, these measurements do not exist for India. But a few statistics that are available (Fig. 9-1) give us a glimmering of what such a comparison might show.

FIG. 9-1

COMPARATIVE WEALTH OF INDIA AND U.S., RECENT YEARS

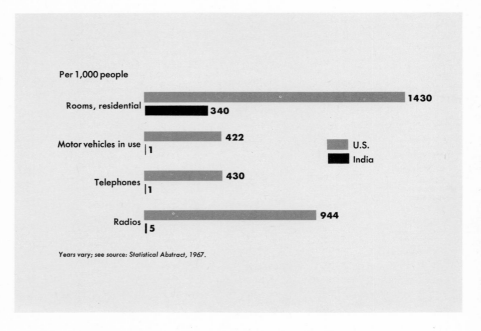

Per 1,000 people

	U.S.	India
Rooms, residential	1430	340
Motor vehicles in use	422	1
Telephones	430	1
Radios	944	5

Years vary; see source: Statistical Abstract, 1967.

It is clear enough that if we could total up all the items in both nations, the scales would tilt overwhelmingly in favor of the United States. That this has an immense significance for the relative well-being of the two countries is apparent. However, let us defer a consideration of exactly what that significance is, until we look a little more closely into the nature of national wealth itself.

CAPITAL

One portion of the endowment of a nation's wealth has a special significance. This is its national *capital*—the portion of its productive wealth that is *man-made* and therefore *reproducible*. If we look back at the table, we can see that our own national capital in 1967 consisted of the sum total of all our structures, our producers' equipment and our consumer durables, our inventories, our monetary gold and silver, and our foreign assets—$2378 billions in all.

We can think of this national capital as consisting of whatever has been preserved out of the sum total of everything that has ever been produced from the very beginning of the economic history of the United States up to a certain date—here December 31, 1967. Some of that capital—inventories for example—might be used up the very next day. On the other hand, inventories might also be increased. In fact, our national capital changes from date to date, as we do add to our inventories or to our stocks of equipment or structures, etc., or, more rarely, as we consume them and do not replace them. But at any date, our capital still represents *all that the nation has produced*—yesterday or a century ago—*and that it has not used up or destroyed.*

The reason that we identify our national capital within the larger frame of our wealth is that it is constantly changing and usually growing. Not that a nation's inheritance of natural resources is unimportant; indeed, the ability of a people to build capital depends to no small degree on the bounties or obstacles offered by its geography and geology—think of the economic limitations imposed by desert and ice on the Bedouin and the Eskimo. But the point in singling out our capital is that it represents the portion of our total national endowment over which we have the most immediate control. As we shall later see, much of a nation's current economic fortunes is intimately related to the rate at which it is adding to its capital wealth.

There remains to be noted one more thing before we leave the subject of wealth. In our table of national wealth, two items are missing that would be the very first to be counted in an inventory of our personal wealth: our bank accounts and our financial assets, such as stocks or bonds or deeds or mortgages. Why are these all-important items of personal wealth excluded from our summary of national wealth?

The answer to this seeming paradox is not hard to find. We have already counted the *things*—the houses, factories, machines, etc.,—that constitute the real assets behind stocks, bonds, deeds, and the like. Indeed these certificates tell us only who *owns* the various items of our national capital. Stocks and bonds and mortgages and deeds are *claims* on assets, but they are not those assets in themselves. The reality of General Motors is its physical plant and its going organization, not the shares of stock that organization has issued. If by some curious mischance all its shares disintegrated, General Motors would still be there; but if the plants and the organization disintegrated instead, the shares would not magically constitute for us another enterprise.

So, too, with our bank accounts. The dollars we spend or hold in our accounts are part of our personal wealth only insofar as they command goods or services. The value of coin or currency as "objects" is much less than their official and legal value as money. But most of the goods over which our money exerts its claims (although not, it must be admitted, the services it also buys) are already on our balance sheet. To count our money as part of national wealth would thus be to count a claim as if it were an asset, much as in the case of stocks and bonds.

Why, then, do we have an item for monetary gold and silver (mainly gold) in our table of national wealth? The answer is that under existing international arrangements, foreigners will accept gold in exchange for their own real assets (whereas they are not bound to accept our dollar bills) and that, therefore, monetary gold gives us a claim against *foreign* wealth.* In much the same way, the item of *net foreign assets* represents the value of all real assets located abroad that are owned by U.S. citizens, less the value of any real wealth located in the United States and owned by foreigners.

Thus we reach a very important final conclusion. *National wealth is not quite the same thing as the sum of personal wealth.* When we add up our individual wealth, we include first of all our holdings of money or stocks or bonds—all items that are excluded from our national register of wealth. The difference is that as individuals we properly consider our own wealth to be the *claims* we have against one another, whereas as a society we consider our wealth to be the stock of material *assets* we possess, and the only claims we consider are those that we may have against other societies. National wealth is thus a *real* phenomenon, the tangible consequence of past production. Financial wealth, on the other hand—the form in which individuals hold their wealth—is only the way the claims of ownership are established vis-à-vis the underlying real assets of the community. The contrast between the underlying, slow-changing reality of national wealth and the overlying, sometimes fast-changing financial representation of that wealth is one of the differences between economic life viewed from the vantage point of the economist and that same life seen through the eyes of a participant in the process. We shall encounter many more such contrasts as our study proceeds.

THE FLOW OF PRODUCTION

WEALTH
AND OUTPUT

But why is national wealth so important? Exactly what is the connection between the wealth of nations and the well-being of their citizens?

* Gold has, of course, a value in itself—we can use it for jewelry and for dentistry. However, in the balance sheet of our national wealth, we value the gold at its international exchange price, rather than merely as a commodity.

174

The question is not an idle one, for the connection between wealth and well-being is not a matter of direct physical cause and effect. After all, India has the largest inventory of livestock in the world, but its contribution to Indian living standards is far less than that of our livestock wealth. Or again, our national capital in 1933 was not significantly different from that in 1929, but one year was marked by widespread misery and the other by booming prosperity. Clearly then, the existence of great physical wealth by itself does not guarantee—it only holds out the possibility of—a high standard of living. It is only insofar as wealth interacts with the working population that it exerts its enormous economic leverage, and this interaction is not a mechanical phenomenon that we can take for granted, but a complex *social* process, whose motivations we must explore.

As the example of Indian livestock indicates, local customs and beliefs can effectively sterilize the potential physical benefits of wealth. Perhaps we should generalize that conclusion by observing that the political and social system will have a primary role in causing an effective or ineffective use of existing wealth. Compare the traditional hoarding of gold or gems in many backward societies with the possibility of their disposal to produce foreign exchange for the purchase of machinery.

In a modern industrial society, we take for granted some kind of effective social and political structure. Then why do we at times make vigorous use of our existing material assets and at other times seem to put them to little or no use? Why do we have "good times" and "bad times"? The question directs our attention back to the panorama of society to discover something further about its economic operation.

INPUTS AND OUTPUTS

This time, our gaze fastens on a different aspect of the tableau. Rather than noticing our stock of wealth, we note the result of our use of that wealth, a result we can see emerging in the form of a *flow of production*.

How does this flow of production arise? We can see that it comes into being as man combines his energies with his natural and man-made environment. We have already traced the long and painful history of his social and technical attempts to combine those energies and the environment successfully, and we take for granted, in our scrutiny of the production process, the very things that interested us in the first part of this book—the development of a "climate" of enterprise, the rise of an industrial technology, the underpinning of a vast capital equipment. Our gaze now focuses only on the growing edge of history, the present, where men gifted with the fruits of their past labors continue to cope with the material world.

Hence we take for granted the fact that men organize their struggle with nature according to the rules of a market process whose evolution was the main subject matter of Part One. Later, in Part Three, we shall go back to examine in greater detail the interactions of the actors on the marketplace. But right now we want to know what happens to the flow of output emerging under our eyes from thousands of enterprises as their entrepreneurs hire the factors of production and combine their services as inputs to yield a saleable output.*

It may help us picture the flow as a whole if we imagine that each and every good and service that is produced—each loaf of bread, each nut and bolt, each doctor's call, each theatrical performance, each car, ship, lathe, or bolt of cloth—can be identified in the way that a radio-active isotope allows us to follow the circulation of certain kinds of cells through the body. Then if we look down on the economic panorama, we can see the continuous combination of land, labor, and capital giving off a continuous flow of "lights" as goods and services emerge in their saleable form.

Where do these lights go? Many, as we can see, are soon extinguished. The goods or services they represent have been incorporated into other products to form more fully finished items of output. Thus from our aerial perspective we can follow a product such as cotton from the fields to the spinning mill, where its light is extinguished, for there the cotton disappears into a new product: yarn. In turn, the light of the yarn traces a path as it leaves the spinning mill by way of sale to the textile mill, there to be doused as the yarn disappears into a new good: cloth. And again, the cloth leaving the textile mill lights a way to the factory where it will become part of an article of clothing.

THE
CONSUMPTION
FLOW

And what of the clothing? Here at last we have what the economist calls a *final* good. Why "final"? Because once in the possession of its ultimate owner, the clothing passes out of the active economic flow. As a good in the hands of a consumer, it is no longer an object on the marketplace. Its light is now extinguished permanently—or if we wish to complete our image, we can imagine it fading gradually as the clothing "disappears" into the use and pleasure, the so-called *utility,* of the consumer. In the case of consumer goods like food, or of consumer services like recreation, the light goes out faster, for these items are literally "consumed" when they reach their final destination.

We shall have a good deal to learn in later chapters about the behavior of consumers. What we should notice in this first macroeconomic view is the supreme importance of this flow of production into consumers' hands. This is the vital process by which the population

*It is well to remember two things about the factors of production from Part One (see pp. 60 f.). The factors are both a representation of different *physical* elements of the production process (land and natural resources, man-made capital, and labor of all sorts); and also the incarnation of *social functions* (renting land, lending or risking capital, selling labor services) that must be combined if production is to be carried on.

replenishes or increases its energies and ministers to its wants and needs; it is a process that, if halted for very long, would cause a society to perish. That is why we speak of consumption as the ultimate end and aim of all economic activity.

Nevertheless, for all the importance of consumption, if we look down on the illuminated flow of output we see a surprising thing. Whereas the greater portion of the final goods and services of the economy is bought by the human agents of production for their consumption, we also find that a lesser but still considerable flow of final products is not. What happens to it?

If we follow an appropriate good, we may find out. Let us watch the destination of the steel that leaves a Pittsburgh mill. Some of it, like our cotton cloth, will become incorporated into consumers' goods, ending up as cans, automobiles, or household articles of various kinds. But some steel will not find its way to a consumer at all; instead, it will end up as part of a machine or an office building or a railroad track.

Now in a way, these goods are not "final," for they are used to produce still further goods or services—the machine producing output of some kind, the building producing office space, the rail track producing transportation. Yet there is a difference between such goods, used for production, and consumer goods, like clothing. The difference is that the machine, the office building, and the track are goods that are used by business enterprises as part of their productive equipment. As a result, they are usually carefully maintained and replaced as they wear out. In terms of our image, these goods slowly lose their light-giving powers as their services pass into flows of production, but usually they are replaced with new goods before their light is totally extinguished. That is why we call them *capital goods* in distinction to consumers' goods. As part of our capital, they will be preserved, maintained, and renewed, perhaps indefinitely. Hence *the stock of capital, like consumers, constitutes a final destination for output.**

We call the great stream of output that goes to capital *gross investment*. The very word *gross* suggests that it conceals a finer breakdown; and looking more closely, we can see that the flow of output going to capital does indeed serve two distinct purposes. Part of it is used to replace the capital—the machines, the buildings, the track, or whatever—

---

* We might note that some products, like automobiles, possess characteristics of both consumption goods and capital goods. We call such goods *consumer durables;* and unlike ordinary goods (such as clothing) held by consumers, we include them in our inventory of national wealth (see Table 9-1, p. 171).

that has been used up in the process of production. Just as the human agents of production have to be replenished by a flow of consumption goods, so the material agents of production need to be maintained and renewed if their contribution to output is to remain undiminished. We call the part of gross investment, whose purpose is to keep society's stock of capital intact, *replacement investment,* or simply *replacement.*

Sometimes the total flow of output going to capital is not large enough to maintain the existing stock—for instance, if we allow inventories (a form of capital) to become depleted, or if we simply fail to replace worn-out equipment or plant. This running-down of capital, we call *disinvestment,* meaning the very opposite of investment: instead of building up capital, we are literally consuming it.

Not all gross investment is used for replacement purposes, however. Some of the flow may *increase* the stock of capital, by adding buildings, machines, track, inventory, and so on.* If the total output consigned to capital is sufficiently great not only to make up for wear and tear, but to increase the capital stock, we say there has been *new* or *net investment,* or *net capital formation.*

Sometimes it helps to have a homely picture in mind to keep things straight. The difference between replacement and net investment is made clear by using as an example the paving of streets. Each year some streets wear out, and we have to repave them to keep them passable. This is clearly *investment,* but it does not add to our ability to enjoy surface transportation. Hence it is solely *replacement* investment. Only when we built *additional* streets do we undertake new or net investment. Also, sometimes we build a new street but allow an old one to deteriorate beyond usability. Here we have to offset the new investment with the *disinvestment* in our now unpassable road. Whether or not we have any net investment in street building as a whole depends on whether we have added or subtracted from street capacity when we consider the net investment and the disinvestment together.

One last important point. Who normally buys these additions to our capital wealth? As our example above shows, the government is one such buyer. But in the main, the purchasers of new capital goods are business firms who seek to increase their holdings of machines and buildings and equipment of various kinds. Since additions to business capital are additions to our nation's wealth, and since with more wealth we would expect to be able to produce still more goods and services, the act of business investment immediately stands out as a key element in the study of macroeconomics. In fact, as we shall see, in many ways the process and the problems of business investment will be a central point of focus in macroeconomic analysis.

---

*Note carefully that *increased* inventory is a form of investment. In Chapter 10, this will take on a special importance.

A simple diagram may help us picture the flows of output we have been discussing.

Figure 9-2 calls to our attention three important attributes of the economic system.

FIG. 9-2

THE CIRCULAR FLOW, VIEW I

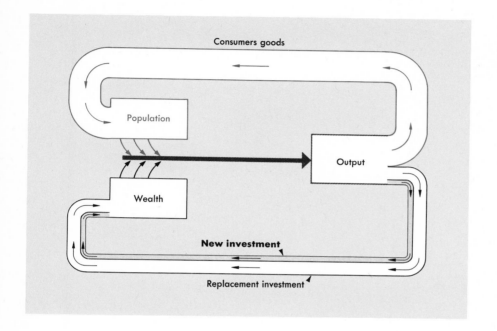

1. It emphasizes the essential *circularity,* the self-renewing, self-feeding nature of the production flow. This circularity is a feature of the macroeconomic process to which we will return again and again.

2. It illumines a basic choice that all economic societies must make: *a choice between consumption and investment.* For the split flow of production reveals that any good entering the capital stream cannot also be in the consumption stream. At any given level of output, consumption and investment are, so to speak, rivals for the current output of society.

3. Finally, it makes clear that *society can invest* (that is, add to its capital) *only the output that it refrains from consuming.* We call this relinquishing of consumption *saving,* and saving thus becomes an economic act located at the very core of the wealth-creation process. For the economic meaning of saving, as our diagram shows, is to release resources from consumption so that they can be used for the building of capital. Whether they *will* be so used is a matter that will occupy us through many subsequent chapters.

There remains but one preliminary matter before we proceed to a closer examination of the actual determinants of the flow of production. We have seen that the annual output of the nation is a revealing measure of its well-being, for it reflects the degree of interaction between the population and its wealth. Later we shall also find output to be a major determinant of employment. Hence it behooves us to examine the nature and general character of this flow and to become familiar with its nomenclature and composition.

We call the dollar value of the total annual output of final goods and services in the nation its gross national product. The gross national product (or GNP as it is usually abbreviated) is thus nothing but the dollar value of the total output of all consumption goods and of all investment goods produced in a year. As such we are already familiar with its general meaning. At this juncture, however, we must define GNP a little more precisely.

1. *GNP includes only final goods.*

We are interested, through the concept of GNP, in measuring the value of the *ultimate* production of the economic system—that is, the total value of all goods and services *enjoyed by its consumers or accumulated as new or replacement capital.* Hence we do not count the intermediate goods we have already noted in our economic panorama. To go back to an earlier example, we do not add up the value of the cotton *and* the yarn *and* the cloth *and* the final clothing when we compute the value of GNP. That kind of multiple counting might be very useful if we wanted certain information about our total economic activity, but it would not tell us accurately about the final value of output. For when we buy a shirt, the price we pay already includes the cost of the cloth to the shirtmaker; and in turn, the amount the shirtmaker paid for his cloth already included the cost of the yarn; and in turn, again, the seller of yarn included in his price the amount he paid for raw cotton. Embodied in the price of the shirt, therefore, is the value of all the intermediate products that went into it. Thus in figuring the value for GNP, we add only the values of all final goods, both for consumption and for investment purposes. Note as well that GNP only includes a given year's production of goods and services. Therefore sales of used car dealers, antique dealers, etc., are not included, because the value of these goods was picked up in GNP of the year they were produced.

2. *There are four categories of final goods.*

In our first view of macroeconomic activity we divided the flow of output into two great streams: consumption and gross investment. Now, for purposes of a closer analysis, we impose a few refinements on this basic scheme.

First we must pay heed to a small flow of production that has previously escaped our notice. This is the net flow of goods or services that leaves this country; that is, the total flow going abroad minus the flow that enters. This international branch of our economy will play a relatively minor role in our analysis for quite a while; we will largely ignore it until Chapter 14, then until Part Four. But we must give it its proper name: *net exports*. Because these net exports are a kind of investment (they are goods we produce but do not consume), we must now rename the great bulk of investment that remains in this country. We will henceforth call it *gross private domestic investment*.

The word *private* brings us to a second refinement. It concerns a subflow of goods and services within both the great consumption stream and the investment branch of activity. These are the goods and services bought or produced by the government (as contrasted with consumers or businesses). Some of these may be consumers' goods—policemen's services, say—and some may be investment goods, such as roads or schools or dams. Conventionally, however, we include all public purchases, whether for consumption or investment purposes, in a category called *government purchases of goods and services*.

This gives us four streams of "final" output, each going to a final purchaser of economic output. Therefore we can speak of gross national product as being the sum of consumption goods and services, gross private domestic investment, government purchases, and net exports, or (to abbreviate a long sentence) we can write that

$$GNP = C + I + G + E.$$

This is a descriptive equation that should be remembered.

It helps, at this juncture, to look at GNP over the past decades. In Figure 9-3 we show the long irregular upward flow of GNP from 1929

FIG. 9-3 GNP AND COMPONENTS, 1929–1968

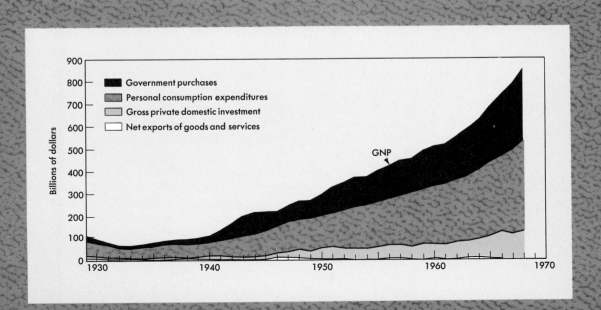

to the present, with the four component streams of expenditures visible. Later we will be talking at length about the behavior of each stream, but first we need to be introduced to the over-all flow itself. (Note that there is a Statistical Appendix following Chapter 32, where the actual figures for these and other series can be looked up as desired.)

STOCKS
AND FLOWS

One final point should be made about our basic equation. All through our discussion of GNP we have talked about *flows* of output. We do so to distinguish GNP, a "flow concept," from wealth or capital (or any asset) that is a *stock,* or a sum of wealth that exists at any given time.

A moment's reflection may make the distinction clear. When we speak of a stock of business capital or of land or structures, we mean a sum of wealth that we could actually inspect on a given date. GNP, however, does not "exist" in quite the same way. If our gross national product for a year is, say, $900 billion, this does not mean that on any day of that year we could actually discover this much value of goods and services. Rather, GNP tells us the average annual rate, for that year, at which production was carried out; so that if the year's flow of output had been collected in a huge reservoir without being consumed, at the end of the year the volume in the reservoir would indeed have totaled $900 billion. GNP is, however, constantly being consumed as well as produced. Hence the $900 billion figure refers to the value of the *flow of production over the year,* and should not be pictured as constituting a given sum of wealth at any moment in time.

CAUTIONS
ABOUT GNP

GNP is an indispensable concept in dealing with the performance of our economy, but it is well to understand the weaknesses as well as the strengths of this most important single economic indicator. There are four of them.

1. *GNP deals in dollar values, not in physical units.*

That is, it does not tell us how many goods and services were produced, but only what their sales value was. Trouble then arises when we compare the GNP of one year with that of another, to determine whether or not the nation is better off. For if prices in the second year are higher, GNP will appear higher, even though the actual volume of output is unchanged.

We can correct for this price change very easily when all prices have moved in the same degree or proportion. Then it is easy to speak of "real" GNP—that is, the current money value of GNP adjusted for price changes—as reflecting the actual rise or fall of output. The price problem becomes more difficult, however, when prices change in different degrees or even in different directions, as they often do. Then a

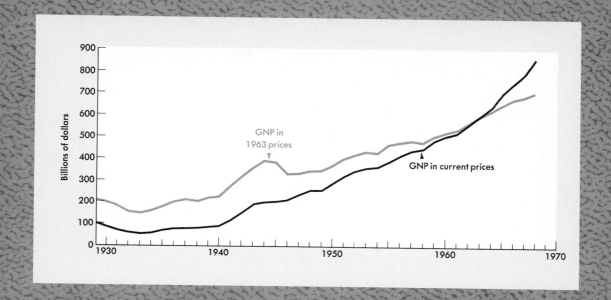

FIG. 9-4 GNP IN CONSTANT AND CURRENT PRICES, 1929–1968

comparison of "real" GNP from one year to the next, and especially over a long span of years, is unavoidably arbitrary to some extent.*

Figure 9-4 shows us the previous totals for GNP corrected as best we can for price changes. In this chart, 1963 is used as the "base," and the GNP's of other years are raised or lowered so that price changes are eliminated to the greatest possible extent. One can, of course, choose any year for a base. Although the basic dollar measuring rod will then change, the profile of "real" changes year to year will be the same.

2. *GNP does not reflect changes in the quality of output.*

The second weakness of GNP also involves its inaccuracy as an indicator of "real" trends over time. This time the difficulty revolves around the changes in the utility (or use and pleasure-producing capabilities) of goods and services. In a technologically advancing society, goods are usually improved from one decade to the next, or even more rapidly; and in an urbanizing, increasingly high-density society, the utility of other goods may be lessened over time. An airplane trip today, for example, is certainly highly preferable to one taken twenty or thirty

*A student who is unsure about how price indexes work should study Questions 5 and 6 at the end of this chapter.

years ago; a subway ride is not. Thus, to the extent that the quality of most goods and services improve, and as some deteriorate, GNP misrepresents the true value of output, especially over long stretches of time.

3. *GNP does not reflect the purpose of production.*

A third difficulty with GNP lies in its blindness to the ultimate use of production. If in one year GNP rises by a billion dollars owing to an increase in expenditure on education, and in another year it rises by the same amount because of a rise in cigarette purchases, the figures in each case show the same amount of "growth" of GNP. Even output that turns out to be wide of the mark or totally wasteful—such as the famous Edsel car that no one wanted or military weapons that are obsolete from the moment they appear—all are counted as part of GNP.

Thus, changes in GNP give us only a very rough indication of changes in the *quality* of life. That is why comparisons of GNP today and fifty or one hundred years ago—comparisons that show Americans today enjoying a vastly greater output than did their forebears—should not be interpreted to mean that life is therefore that much "better."

4. *GNP does not include most goods and services that are not for sale.*

Presumably GNP tells us how large our final output is. Yet it does not include one of the most important kinds of work and sources of consumer pleasure—the labor of wives in maintaining their households. Yet, curiously, if this labor were paid for—that is, if we engaged cooks and maids and babysitters instead of depending on our wives for these services, GNP *would* include their services as final output, since they would be purchased on the market. But the labor of wives being unpaid, it is excluded from GNP.*

The difficulty here is that we are constantly moving toward purchasing "outside" services in place of home services—laundries, bakeries, restaurants, etc., all perform work that used to be performed at home. Thus the process of *monetizing* activity gives an upward trend to GNP statistics which is not fully mirrored in actual output.

A related problem is that some parts of GNP are paid for by some members of the population and not by others. Rent, for example, measures the services of landlords for homeowners and is therefore included in GNP, but what of the man who owns his own home and pays no rent? Similarly, what of the family that grows some part of its food at home, and therefore does not pay for it? In order to include

---

*This gives rise to an amusing anomaly. Every time a man marries his cook, GNP declines by the amount of the wages he formerly paid her, even though her cooking may continue. Even if he pays her an allowance as large as her wages, GNP still declines, since allowances are not presumed to cover "productive services" and therefore are not picked up in GNP.

such items of "free" consumption into GNP, the statisticians of the Commerce Department add an "imputed" value figure to include goods and services like these not tallied on a cash register.

These problems lead economists to treat GNP in a gingerly fashion. We should remember that comparisons between GNP's are more trustworthy for two close years than for two distant ones (prices and qualities are not apt to have changed so much in the shorter span of time); and that GNP is, at best, an imperfect measure of real final output and a still less dependable indicator of ultimate well-being.

Consider, for example, that whereas U.S. per capita GNP is almost 50 per cent higher than that of Sweden, Sweden has virtually no slums, has almost twice as many hospital beds as we have per 100,000 population, and an infant mortality rate at least 40 per cent lower than ours. In the face of these figures, does our superior GNP enable us to proclaim that the United States' standard of living is really higher than that of Sweden?

Sobering comparisons such as these have led many economists in recent years to look beyond GNP toward development of more sensitive indices of real well-being. The Department of Health, Education and Welfare drew up the first such analysis of social indicators in 1968; the document, *Toward a Social Report* (1969) is well worth reading. But GNP is still our best single, simple way of summarizing the over-all performance of the economy. Gross national product today is a yardstick of economic activity used by every nation in the world. It has become a term familiar to every congressman and editorial writer, although not many of them could describe very clearly exactly what it means. Hence, let us turn to a closer study of this critical economic concept by examining how GNP is actually generated and maintained.

SUMMARY

1. Macroeconomics is not a separate part of economics, but an *approach to economic problems* through the study of certain aggregate processes.

2. We begin the study of macroeconomic processes by observing how a *flow of output* comes from human resources interacting with our national wealth (the most important part of which is our *capital*).

3. We note that capital consists of *real things*, and *not of the financial claims* against those things.

4. The flow of output shows us *the circular nature of the process of production*. From the interaction of population and wealth emerges a stream of goods going back to replenish consumers (consumption goods) and a stream to replenish and add to our capital wealth (gross investment).

5. A study of the flow of output and its division into consumption and investment emphasizes the essential choice that must be made between these *two basic uses of output*.

6. The investment flow can be subdivided into two: one flow *replaces or renews capital* that has been worn out or used up. This is *replacement investment*. The other flow *adds to the stock of capital wealth,* and is called *new* or *net capital* or *investment*. The two flows together are called *gross investment*.

7. The name for the total flow of output is *gross national product*. It is divided into four major categories:
   - *Consumption* (C), or the goods and services going to consumers.
   - *Gross private domestic investment* (I), or that portion of output going to private businesses as replacements for, and additions to, their real domestic capital.
   - *Government purchases* (G), or those goods and services (both consumers' and capital) bought by all public agencies.
   - *Net exports* (E), the net outflow of goods and services to other countries.
   - The formula $GNP = C + I + G + E$ conveniently summarizes these four subdivisions.

8. Note that GNP counts only the dollar value of *final goods and services* in each of these categories. Intermediate goods or services are not counted, since their value is included in the value of final goods.

9. GNP is an indispensable concept in macroeconomics. Nonetheless, it must be used with caution.
   - GNP deals in *dollar values, not physical units*. This can lead to problems in adjusting price changes from year to year so that GNP accurately reflects changes in output.
   - GNP does not show changes in the *quality* of output.
   - GNP does not reveal the *composition* of output.
   - GNP figures do not include *output* that is *not for sale*.
   Thus, comparisons from year to year should be made with caution, especially when the years are very far apart.

QUESTIONS

1. Why is capital so important a part of national wealth? Why is money not considered capital?

2. What is meant by the "circularity" of the economic process? Does it have something to do with the output of the system being returned to it as fresh inputs?

3. What is meant by net investment? by gross investment? What is the difference?

4. Write the basic formula for GNP and state *carefully* the exact names of each of the four constituents of GNP.

5. Suppose we had an island economy with an output of 100 tons of grain, each ton selling for $90. If grain is the only product sold, what is the value of GNP? Now suppose that production stays the same but that prices rise to $110. What is the value of GNP now? How could we "correct" for the price rise? If we didn't, would GNP be an accurate measure of output from one year to the next?

6. Now suppose that production rose to 110 tons but that prices fell to $81. The value of GNP, in terms of current prices, has fallen from $9,000 to $8,910. Yet, actual output, measured in tons of grain, has increased. Can you devise a price index that will show the change in real GNP?*

7. Presumably, the quality of most products improves over time. If their price is unchanged, does that mean that GNP understates or overstates the real value of output?

8. When more and more consumers buy "do-it-yourself" kits, does the value of GNP (which includes the sale price of these kits) understate or overstate the true final output of the nation?

9. Do you think that we should develop measures other than GNP to indicate changes in our basic well-being? What sorts of measures?

10. What is an intermediate good, and why are such goods not included in the value of GNP? Is coal sold to a utility company an intermediate good? Coal sold to a consumer? Coal sold to the army? What determines whether a good will or will not be counted in the total of GNP?

---

* The answer is not difficult. Let us use 100 as the price in the original year, to serve as the "base" for an index that will measure percentage changes in price. If 100 represents the actual price of $90, what index number will represent $81? Elementary algebra gives us the answer:

$$\$81 \text{ is to } \$90 \text{ as } X \text{ is to } 100$$

or

$$\frac{81}{90} = \frac{X}{100}$$

Solving by cross multiplying, we get

$$90X = 8,100$$
$$X = 90$$

Now we have a price index with which to compute real GNP, as follows:

Year	GNP in current prices	Price index	Real GNP (GNP in current prices divided by the price index)
1	100 tons $\times$ $90 = $9,000	100	($9,000 $\div$ 100) $\times$ 100 = $9,000
2	110 tons $\times$ 81 = 8,910	90	(8,000 $\div$ 90) $\times$ 100 = 9,900

Real GNP now shows a rise from $9,000 to $9,900, or 10 per cent. This is, of course, exactly the percentage by which the tonnage output of grain rose. Matters get a good deal more complicated when we deal with more than one good (although the principle is the same). For an introduction to this subject, see the Special Assignment in Professor Hannaford's *Student's Guide* to this book.

10 OUTPUT AND INCOME

So far, we have talked about output as it emerges from the interaction of wealth and labor, but we have not inquired very deeply into the manner in which that interaction takes place. Yet the output of our economy does not spring forth "automatically" by the pursuit of changeless tradition, as is the case in simple preindustrial societies. Nor is it brought into being because the labor force is more or less forcibly combined with material resources, as is the case in collectivized economics. Rather, in our kind of society, output results from innumerable activities and decisions on the marketplace where men buy and sell, largely as they wish. What we must now understand is precisely how this daily activity of the marketplace gives rise to the flow of gross national product.

OUTPUT AND DEMAND

How does the market actually bring output into existence? How does it effect the combination of land, labor, and capital under the guidance of an entrepreneur? Any businessman will give you the answer. He will tell you that the crucial factor enabling him to perform his economic task (or in his language, "to run a business") is *demand* or *purchasing power;* that is, the presence of buyers who are willing and able to buy some good or service at the price for which he is willing to sell it.

But how does demand or purchasing power come into existence? If we ask any buyer, he will tell us that his dollars come to him because they are part of his *income* or his cash receipts.

But where, in turn, do the dollar receipts or incomes of buyers come from? If we inquire again, most buyers will tell us that they have money in their pockets because in one fashion or another they have contributed to the process of production; that is, because they have helped to make the output that is now being sold.

Thus our quest for the motive force behind the flow of production leads us in a great circle through the market system. We can see this in Fig. 10-1.

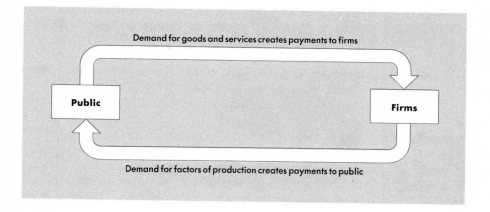

FIG. 10-1

THE CIRCULAR FLOW, VIEW II

At the top of the circle we see payments flowing from the public to firms, thereby creating the demand that brings forth production. At the bottom of the circle, we see more payments, this time flowing from firms back to the public, as businesses hire the services of the various factors in order to carry out production. Thus we can see that there is a constant regeneration of demand as money is first spent by the public on the output of firms, and then in turn spent by firms for the services of the public.

189

We must examine this chain of payments and receipts in great detail, for it contains the key to the operation of our economic system. First, however, we need a reminder about our method of inquiry. It must be obvious that it is impossible to depict the flux of buying and selling as it actually occurs on the marketplace of the nation. It would require us to fix in our minds more details than can be reported on all the financial pages of all the newspapers in the nation every day. Hence, to comprehend the basic processes of the economy, we must use a special method of reducing its confusion to understandable dimensions. This we do by extracting from the actual happenings of economic life those aspects that experience and analysis have taught us to regard as central and critical. From these crucial links and processes we then create an imaginary *model* of an economy that exhibits, in its operation, all the essential movements of its real-life counterpart. We shall find our model to be an indispensable guide to the complicated reality of economic life around us.

Our model, to begin with, will be a very simple one. We must, of course, exclude from it all the variety of life itself: the differences in personality of one man and another, the peculiar ways that one market differs from another, the distinctions that separate one firm from its competitor. We reduce our economy, in other words, to a colorless and abstract reproduction of life in which we can speak of general *kinds* of relationships without having to qualify each and every statement to accommodate each and every existing situation. Thus our model will call upon our capacity to think in that abstract manner which is so much a part of economic reasoning.

But our model will be simple not only in its disregard of "life." We must also simplify it, at first, by ruling out some of the very events to which we will later turn as the climax of our study. For instance, we shall ignore changes in *people's tastes,* so that we can assume that everyone will regularly buy the same kinds of goods. We shall ignore differences in the *structure of firms* or *markets,* so that we can forget about differences in competitive pressures. We shall rule out *population growth* and, even more important, *inventive progress,* so that we can deal with a very stable imaginary world. For the time being, we will exclude even *saving* and *net investment* (although of course we must permit replacement investment), so that we can ignore growth. Later, of course, we are to be deeply concerned with just such problems of dynamic change. But we shall not be able to come to grips with them until we have first understood an economic world as "pure" and changeless as possible.

The very abstract model we have created may seem too far removed from the real world to tell us much about its operation. But if we now go back to the circle of economic activity, in which payments to firms and factors become their incomes, and in turn reappear on the marketplace as demand, our model will enable us to explain a very important problem. *It is how an economy that has produced a given GNP is able to buy it back.*

This is by no means a self-evident matter. Indeed, one of the most common misconceptions about the flow of economic activity is that there will not be enough purchasing power to buy everything we have produced—that somehow we will fail to generate enough demand to keep up with the output of our factories. So it is well to understand once and for all how an economy can sustain a given level of production through its purchases on the market.

We start, then, with an imaginary economy in full operation. We can, if we wish, imagine it as having just produced its year's output, which is now sitting on the economic front doorstep looking for a buyer. What we must now see is whether it will be possible to *sell* this gross national product to the people who have been engaged in producing it. In other words, *we must ask whether there is enough income or receipts generated in the process of production to buy back all the products themselves.*

How does production create income? Businessmen do not think about "incomes" when they assemble the factors of production to meet the demand for their product. They worry about *cost.* All the money they pay out during the production process is paid under the heading of *cost,* whether it be wage or salary cost, cost of materials, depreciation cost, tax cost, or whatever. Thus it would seem that the concept of cost may offer us a useful point of entry into the economic chain. For *if we can show how all costs become incomes,* we will have taken a major step toward understanding whether our gross national product can in fact be sold to those who produced it.

COSTS AND INCOMES

It may help us if we begin by looking at the kinds of costs incurred by business firms in real life. Here is a hypothetical expense summary of General Manufacturing, which will serve as an example typical of all business firms, large or small. (If you will examine the year-end statements of any business, you will find that their costs all fall into one or more of the cost categories below.)

Wages, salaries, and employee benefits	$100,000,000
Rental, interest, and profits payments	5,000,000
Materials, supplies, etc.	50,000,000
Taxes other than income	15,000,000
Depreciation	20,000,000

TABLE 10 · 1

GENERAL MANUFACTURING COST SUMMARY

Some of these costs we recognize immediately as payments to factors of production. The item for "wages and salaries" is obviously a payment to the factor *labor*. The item "interest" (perhaps not so obviously) is a payment to the factor *capital*—that is, to those who have lent the company money in order to help it carry on its productive operation. The item for rent is, of course, a payment for the rental of *land* or natural resources from their owners.

Note that we have included profits with rent and interest. In actual accounting practice, profits are not shown as an expense; for our purposes, however, it will be quite legitimate and very helpful to regard profits as a special kind of factor cost going to entrepreneurs for their risk-taking function. In our next chapter, we shall go more thoroughly into the matter of profits.

Two things strike us about these factor costs. First, it is clear that they represent payments that have been made to secure production. In more technical language, they are payments for factor inputs that result in commodity outputs. All the production actually carried on within the company, all the value it has added to the economy, has been compensated by the payments the company has made to land, labor, and capital. To be sure, the company has incurred other costs, for materials and taxes and depreciation, and we shall soon turn to these. But whatever production, or assembly, or distribution the company itself has carried out during the course of the year has required the use of land, labor, or capital. Thus *the total of its factor costs represents the value of the total new output that General Manufacturing by itself has given to the economy.*

From here it is but a simple step to add up *all* the factor costs paid out by *all* the companies in the economy, in order to measure the total new *value added* by all productive efforts in the year. This measure is called *national income* (or sometimes national income at factor cost).* As we can see, it is less than gross national product, for it does not include other costs of output; namely, certain taxes and depreciation.

A second fact that strikes us is that *all factor costs are income payments.* The wages, salaries, interest, rents, etc., that were costs to the company were income to its recipients. So are the profits, which will accrue as income to the owners of the business.

Thus, just as it sounds, national income means the total amount of earnings of the factors of production within the nation. If we think of these factors as constituting the households of the economy, we can see that *factor costs result directly in incomes to the household sector.*

---

*It might be well to add that not all production (and therefore not all national income) originates with companies. Governments also produce value, such as the output of firemen's services or of roads, and private individuals, like farmers or doctors, produce output as "proprietorships." For the purposes of exposition, however, we can think of government units or individual proprietorships as "companies" since they incur exactly the same kinds of costs.

Thus, if factor costs were the only costs involved in production, the problem of buying back the gross national product would be a very simple one. We should simply be paying out to households, as the cost of production, the very sum needed to buy GNP when we turned around to sell it. But this is not the case, as a glance at the General Manufacturing expense summary shows. There are other costs, besides factor costs. How shall we deal with them?

The next item on the expense summary is puzzling. Called payments for "materials, supplies, etc.," it represents all the money General Manufacturing has paid, not to its own factors, but to other companies for other products it has needed. We may even recognize these costs as payments for those intermediate products that lose their identity in a later stage of production. How do such payments become part of the income available to buy GNP on the marketplace?

Perhaps the answer is already intuitively clear. When the General Manufacturing sends its checks to, let us say, U.S. Steel, or General Electric, or to a local supplier of stationery, each of these recipient firms now uses the proceeds of General Manufacturing's checks to pay its own costs. (Actually, of course, they have probably long since paid their own costs and now use General Manufacturing's payment only to reimburse themselves. But if we want to picture our model economy in the simplest way, we can imagine U.S. Steel and other firms sending their products to General Manufacturing and waiting until checks arrive to pay their own costs.)

And what are those costs? What must U.S. Steel or all the other suppliers now do with their checks? The answer is obvious. They must now reimburse their own factors and then pay any other costs that remain.

Figure 10-2 may make the matter plain. It shows us, looking back

FIG. 10-2

HOW
MATERIALS
COSTS BECOME
OTHER COSTS

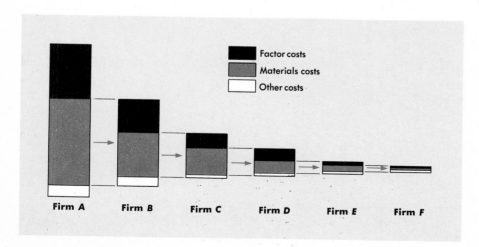

Factor costs
Materials costs
Other costs

Firm A   Firm B   Firm C   Firm D   Firm E   Firm F

down the chain of intermediate payments, that what constitutes material costs to one firm is made up of factor and other costs to another. Indeed, as we unravel the chain from company to company, it is clear that all the contribution to new output must have come from the contribution of factors somewhere down the line, and that all the costs of new output—all the value added—must ultimately be resolvable into payments to land, labor, and capital.

Another way of picturing the same thing is to imagine that all firms in the country were bought up by a single gigantic corporation. The various production units of the new supercorporation would then ship components and semifinished items back and forth to one another, but there would not have to be any payment from one division to another. The only payments that would be necessary would be those required to buy the services of factors—that is, various kinds of labor, or the use of property or capital—so that at the end of the year, the supercorporation would show on its expense summary only items for wages and salaries, rent, and interest (and as we shall see, taxes and depreciation) but it would have no item for materials cost.

We have come a bit further toward seeing how our gross national product can be sold. To the extent that GNP represents new output made during the course of the year, the income to buy back this output has already been handed out as factor costs, either paid at the last stage of production or "carried along" in the guise of materials costs. But a glance at the General Manufacturing expense summary shows that entrepreneurs incur two kinds of costs that we have still not taken into account: taxes and depreciation. Here are costs employers have incurred that have not been accounted for on the income side. What can we say about them?

TAX COSTS

Let us begin by tracing the taxes that General Manufacturing pays, just as we have traced its materials payments. In the first instance, its taxes will go to government units—federal, state, and local. But we need not stop there. Just as we saw that General Manufacturing's checks to supplier firms paid for the suppliers' factor costs and for still further interfirm transactions, so we can see that its checks to government agencies pay for goods and services that these agencies have produced—goods such as roads, buildings, or defense equipment; or services such as teaching, police protection, and the administration of justice. General Manufacturing's tax checks are thus used to help pay for factors of production—land, labor, and capital—that are used in the *public sector*.

In many ways, General Manufacturing's payments to government units resemble its payments to other firms for raw materials. Indeed, if the government *sold* its output to General Manufacturing, charging for the use of the roads, police services, or defense protection it affords the company, there would be *no* difference whatsoever. The reason we differentiate between a company's payment to the public sector and its payments for intermediate products is important, however, and worth looking into.

The first reason is clearly that, with few exceptions, the government does *not* sell its output. This is partly because the community has decided that certain things the government produces (education, justice, or the use of public parks, for instance) should not be for sale but should be supplied to all citizens without charge. In part, it is also because some things the government produces, such as defense or law and order, cannot be equitably charged to individual buyers, since it is impossible to say to what degree anyone benefits from—or even uses—these communal facilities. Hence General Manufacturing, like every other producer, is billed, justly or otherwise, for a share of the cost of government.

There is also a second reason why we consider the cost of taxes as a new kind of cost, distinct from factor payments. It is that when we have finished paying the factors we have not yet paid all the sums that employers must lay out. Some taxes, in other words, are an addition to the cost of production.

These taxes—so-called *indirect taxes*—are levied on the productive enterprise itself or on its actual physical output. Taxes on real estate, for instance, or taxes that are levied on each unit of output, regardless of whether or not it is sold (such as excise taxes on cigarettes), or taxes levied on goods sold at retail (sales taxes) are all payments that entrepreneurs must make as part of their costs of doing business.

INDIRECT VS. DIRECT TAXES

Note that not all taxes collected by the government are costs of production. Many taxes will be paid, not by the entrepreneurs as an expense of doing business, but by the *factors* themselves. These so-called *direct* taxes (such as income taxes) are *not* part of the cost of production. When General Manufacturing adds up its total cost of production, it naturally includes the wages and salaries it has paid, but it does not include the taxes its workers or executives have paid out of their incomes. Such direct taxes transfer income from earners to government, but they are not a cost to the company itself.

In the same way, the income taxes on the profits of a company do *not* constitute a cost of production. General Manufacturing does not pay income taxes as a regular charge on its operations, but waits until a year's production has taken place, and then pays income taxes on the profits it makes *after* paying its costs. If it finds that it has lost money over the year, it will not pay any income taxes—although it will have paid other costs, including indirect taxes. Thus direct taxes are not a cost that is paid out in the course of production and must be recouped, but a payment made by factors (including owners of the business) from the incomes they have earned through the process of production.

Thus we can see two reasons why taxes are handled as a separate item in GNP and are not telescoped into factor costs, the way materials costs are. One reason is that taxes are a payment to a *different sector* from that of business and thus indicate a separate stream of economic activity. But the second reason, and the one that interests us more at this moment, is that *certain taxes*—indirect taxes—*are an entirely new kind of cost of production, not previously picked up.* As an expense paid out by entrepreneurs, over and above factor costs (or materials costs), these tax costs must be part of the total selling price of GNP.

Will there be enough incomes handed out in the process of production to cover this item of cost?

We have seen that there will be. The indirect tax costs paid out by entrepreneurs will be received by government agencies who will use these tax receipts to pay incomes to factors working for the government. Thus the new item of tax costs will eventually become income to factors working in the public sector, and will be available, together with all other factor incomes, to create demand on the marketplace.

DEPRECIATION

But there is still one last item of cost. At the end of the year, when the company is totting up its expenses to see if it has made a profit for the period, its accountants do not stop with factor costs, material costs, and indirect taxes. If they did, the company would soon be in serious straits. In producing its goods, General Manufacturing has also used up a certain amount of its assets—its buildings and equipment—and a cost must now be charged for this wear and tear if the company is to be able to preserve the value of its physical plant intact. If it did not make this cost allowance, it would have failed to include all the resources that were used up in the process of production, and it would therefore be overstating its profits.

Yet, this cost has something about it clearly different from other costs that General Manufacturing has paid. Unlike factor costs or taxes or materials costs, depreciation is not paid for by check. When the company's accountants make an allowance for depreciation, all they do is make an entry on the company's books, stating that plant and equipment are now worth a certain amount less than in the beginning of the year.

At the same time, however, General Manufacturing *includes* the amount of depreciation in the price it intends to charge for its goods. As we have seen, part of the resources used up in production was its own capital equipment, and it is certainly entitled to consider the depreciation as a cost. Yet, it has not paid anyone a sum of money equal to this cost! How, then, will there be enough income in the marketplace to buy back its product?

The answer lies in the fact that we are not dealing with a single company but with a vast assemblage of companies, all of which are depreciating their assets—that is, adding to their costs sums equal to the wear and tear on their equipment—and *some of which are also busy replacing their equipment as it becomes completely worn out.*

Suppose we had 10 companies, each with machines worth $1,000 that deteriorated at a rate of $100 a year. If these companies originally bought their machines in different years, then we can see that each year the sum of depreciation costs would be $1,000 (10 companies each adding $100 to their costs), but that this would be nicely offset by the actual expenditure of $1,000 as, each year, one company bought itself a new machine to take the place of the unit that had finally worn out. Ten companies might not space their replacement expenditures so evenly. But when we deal with the thousands of companies in the economy and with the widely varying lifetimes of their equipment, we can make the quite realistic assumption that there will be a steady flow of replacement spending.*

This enables us to see that insofar as there is a steady stream of replacement expenditures going to firms that make capital goods, there will be payments just large enough to balance the addition to costs due to depreciation. As with all other payments to firms, these replacement expenditures will, of course, become incomes to factors, etc., and thus can reappear on the marketplace.

ANOTHER VIEW OF COSTS AND INCOMES

Because it is very important to understand the relationship between the "selling price" of GNP and the amount of income available to buy it back, it may help to look at the matter from a different point of view.

This time let us approach it by seeing how the economy arranges things so that consumers and government and business, the three great sectors of final demand, are each provided with enough purchasing power to claim the share of GNP they need. Suppose, to begin with, that the economy paid out income only to its factors and priced its goods and services accordingly. In that case, consumers could purchase the entire value of the year's output, but business and government would be unable to purchase any portion of that output for themselves.

This would obviously lead to serious trouble. Hence we must arrange for business and government to have a claim on the total output by taking a portion of the factors' purchasing power and transferring it to these two sectors. One means of doing this is by taxation. Direct (income) taxes simply transfer money directly from factors' pockets to

---

* But wait, some bright student will object. Suppose one of the 10 companies decides not to replace its machine, but to junk it, or suppose it decides to go out of business or to go into some other line. Then there won't be a flow of replacement spending equal to depreciation costs! Our student is quite right. But that brings us ahead of ourselves to consider a highly dynamic economy. In our calm model, we just ignore such complexities of the actual economic world. Furthermore, we are not too unrealistic in doing so. Save for the most severely depressed years, the economy as a whole *does* replace its depreciated assets.

the government, thereby lowering consumers' purchasing power. Indirect taxes accomplish the same thing by pricing goods above their factor costs, thus making it impossible for factors to claim the entire output.

In exactly the same way, business also reserves a claim on output by pricing its products to include a charge for depreciation. By so doing, it again reduces the ability of consumers to buy back the entire output of the economy, while it gives business the purchasing power to claim the output it needs (just as taxes give purchasing power to government). Now, after paying direct and indirect taxes and depreciation, the consumer is finally free to spend all the remainder of his income without danger of encroaching on the output that must be reserved for public activity and for the replacement of capital.

In other words, we can look at taxes and depreciation not merely as "costs" that the consumer has to pay, or as "incomes" that accrue to government and business, but also as the means by which the output of the economy is made available to two important claimants besides the public.

THE THREE STREAMS OF EXPENDITURE

Our analysis is now essentially complete. Item by item, we have traced each element of cost into an income payment, so that we now know there is enough income paid out to buy back our GNP at a price that represents its full cost.

Perhaps this was a conclusion we anticipated all along. After all, ours would be an impossibly difficult economy to manage if somewhere along the line purchasing power dropped out of existence, so that we were always faced with a shortage of income to buy back the product we made. But our analysis has also shown us a more unexpected thing. We are accustomed to thinking that all the purchasing power in the economy is received and spent through the hands of "people"—by which we usually mean households. Now we can see that this is not true. There is not only one, but there are *three* streams of incomes and costs, all quite distinct from one another.

1. Factor cost—Household—Consumers goods

2. Tax—Government agency—Government goods

3. Depreciation—Business—Replacement

To help visualize these three flows, imagine for an instant that our money comes in colors (all of equal value): black, orange, and gray. Now suppose that firms always pay their factors in black money, their taxes in orange money, and their replacement expenditures in gray money. In point of fact, of course, the colors would soon be mixed. A factor that is paid in black bills will be paying some of his black income for taxes; or a government agency will be paying out orange money as factor incomes; or firms will be using gray dollars to pay taxes or factors, and orange or black dollars to pay for replacement capital.

But at least in our mind we could picture the streams being kept quite separate. An orange tax dollar paid by General Manufacturing to the Internal Revenue Service for taxes could go from the government to another firm, let us say in payment for office supplies, and we can think of the office supply firm keeping these orange dollars apart from its other receipts, to pay its taxes with. Such an orange dollar could circulate indefinitely, from government agencies to firms and back again, helping to bring about production but never entering a consumer's pocket! In the same way, a gray replacement expenditure dollar going from General Manufacturing to, let us say U.S. Steel, could be set aside by U.S. Steel to pay for *its* replacement needs; and the firm that received this gray dollar might, in turn, set it aside for its own use as replacement expenditure. We could, that is, imagine a circuit of expenditures in which gray dollars went from firm to firm, to pay for replacement investment, and never ended up in a pay envelope or as a tax payment.

There is a simple way of explaining this seemingly complex triple flow. Each stream indicates the existence of a *final taker* of gross national product: consumers, government, and business itself.* Since output has final claimants other than consumers, we can obviously have a flow of purchasing power that does not enter consumers' or factors' hands.

THE CRUCIAL ROLE OF EXPENDITURES

The realization that factors do not get paid incomes equal to the total gross value of output brings us back to the central question of this chapter: can we be certain that we will be able to sell our GNP at its full cost? Has there surely been generated enough purchasing power to buy back our total output?

We have thus far carefully analyzed and answered half the question. *We know that all costs will become incomes to factors or receipts of government agencies or of firms making replacement items.* To sum up again, factor costs become the incomes of workers, managements, owners of natural resources and of capital; and all these incomes together can be thought of as comprising the receipts of the household sector. Tax costs are paid to government agencies and become receipts

---

*We continue to forget about net exports until Chapter 13. We can think of them perfectly satisfactorily as a component of gross private investment.

of the government sector. Depreciation costs are initially accrued within business firms, and these accruals belong to the business sector. As long as worn-out capital is regularly replaced, these accruals will be matched by equivalent new receipts of firms that make capital goods.

What we have not yet established, however, is that these sector receipts will become sector *expenditures*. That is, we have not demonstrated that all households will now *spend* all their incomes on goods and services, or that government units will necessarily *spend* all their tax receipts on public goods and services, or that all firms will assuredly *spend* their depreciation accruals for new replacement equipment.

What happens if some receipts are not spent? The answer is of key importance in understanding the operation of the economy. A failure of the sectors to spend as much money as they have received means that some of the costs that have been laid out will *not* come back to the original entrepreneurs. As a result, they will suffer losses. If, for instance, our gross national product costs $900 billion to produce but the various sectors spend only $890 billion in all, then some entrepreneurs will find themselves failing to sell all their output. Inventories of unsold goods will begin piling up, and businessmen will soon be worried about "over-producing." The natural thing to do when you can't sell all your output is to stop making so much of it, so that businesses will begin cutting back on production. As they do so, they will also cut back on the number of people they employ. As a result, businessmen's costs will go down; but so will factor incomes, for we have seen that costs and incomes are but opposite sides of one coin. As incomes fall, the expenditures of the sectors might very well fall further, bringing about another twist in the spiral of recession.

This is not yet the place to go into the mechanics of such a downward spiral of business. But the point is clear. *A failure of the sectors to bring all their receipts back to the marketplace as demand can initiate profound economic problems.* In the contrast between an unshakable equality of costs and incomes on the one hand and the uncertain connection between receipts and expenditures on the other, we have come to grips with one of the most important problems in macroeconomics.

We shall have ample opportunity later to observe exactly what happens when receipts are not spent. Now let us be sure that we understand how the great circle of the economic flow is closed when the sectors *do* spend their receipts. Figure 10-3 shows how we can trace our "black, orange, and gray" dollars through the economy and how these flows suffice to buy back GNP for its total cost.

We can trace the flow from left to right. We begin on the left with the bar representing the total cost of our freshly produced GNP. As we know, this cost consists of all the factor costs of all the firms and government units in the nation, all the indirect tax costs incurred during production, and all the depreciation charges made during production.

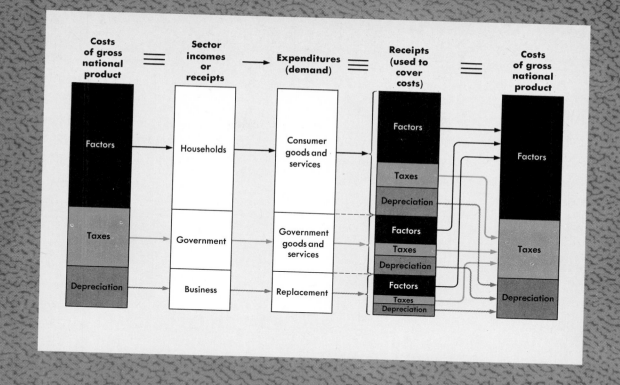

FIG. 10-3   **THE CIRCULAR FLOW, VIEW III**

The bar also shows us the amount of money demand our economy must generate in order to buy back its own output.

The next bars show us the transmutation of costs into sector receipts for householders, government units, and business firms (who retain their own depreciation accruals). This relationship between costs and sector receipts is one of *identity*—all costs *must* be receipts. Hence we use the sign ≡ to indicate that this is a relation of identities—of definitional differences only.

Thereafter we notice the crucial link. Each sector dutifully spends all its receipts, as it is supposed to. Our household sector buys the kinds of goods and services householders do in fact buy—consumption goods and services. Our government sector buys government goods and services, and our business sector buys replacement investment. This time we use an arrow (→) because this is emphatically *not* a relationship of identity.

Now note the next bar. Here we see what happens to these expenditures when they are received by the firms who make consumer goods, or by the firms or individuals who make goods and services bought by governments, or by the manufacturers of capital equipment. Each of these recipients will use the money he has received to cover factor payments, taxes, and depreciation for his own business. (What we show in our diagram are not these costs for each and every firm, but the aggregate costs for all firms selling to each sector.)

We are almost done. It remains only to aggregate the sector costs; that is, to add up all the factor costs, all the taxes, and all the depreciation accruals of *all* firms and government agencies—to reproduce a bar just like the one we started with. A circle of production has been completed. Firms and government units have received back on the marketplace a sum just large enough to cover their initial costs, including their profits for risk. The stage is set for another round of production, similar to the last.

GNP AS A SUM OF COSTS AND A SUM OF EXPENDITURES

Our bar graph also enables us to examine again the concept of gross national product, for now we can see that GNP can be looked at in one of two ways. We can think of measuring a year's gross national product as a sum of all the costs that have been paid out during that year: factor costs, indirect taxes, and depreciation. Or we can think of measuring the same GNP as the sum of the expenditures that bought this output; that is, consumption expenditure, government expenditure, and gross private investment expenditure. Since the final output is one and the same, we can see that the two methods of computing its value must also be the same.

An illustration may make it easier to grasp this identity of the two ways of measuring GNP. Suppose once again that we picture the economy as a gigantic factory from which the flow of production emerges onto a shipping platform, each item tagged with its selling price. There the items are examined by two clerks. One of them notes down in his book the selling price of each item and then proceeds to analyze that price into its cost components: factor cost (including profit), indirect taxes, and depreciation. The second clerk keeps a similar book in which each item's selling price is also entered, but his job is to note which sector—consumer, government, business investment, or export—is its buyer. Clearly, at the end of the year, the two clerks must show the same value of total output. But whereas the books of the first will show that total value broken down into various costs, the books of the second will show it broken down by its "customers"; that is, by the expenditures of the various sectors.

But wait! Suppose that an item comes onto the shipping platform without an order waiting for it! Would that not make the sum of costs larger than the sum of expenditures?

The answer will give us our final insight into the necessary equality of the two measures of GNP. For what happens to an item that is not bought by one of the sectors? It will be sent by the shipping clerk into inventory *where it will count as part of the business investment of the economy!* Do not forget that increases in inventory are treated as investment because they are a part of output that has not been consumed. To be sure, it is a very unwelcome kind of investment; and if it continues, it will shortly lead to changes in the production of the firm. Such dynamic changes will soon lie at the very center of our attention. In the meantime, however, the fact that unbought goods are counted as investment—as if they were "bought" by the firm that produced but cannot sell them—establishes the absolute identity of GNP measured as a sum of costs or as a sum of expenditures.

To express the equality with the conciseness and clarity of mathematics, we can write:

$$C + I + G + E \equiv F + T + D$$

Where *C, I, G,* and *E* are the familiar categories of expenditure, and *F, T,* and *D* stand for factor costs, indirect taxes, and depreciation.

It is now also very easy to understand the meaning of two other less frequently used measures of output. One of these is called *net national product* (NNP). As the name indicates, it is exactly equal to gross national product *minus depreciation.* The other measure, national income, we have already met. It is GNP *minus depreciation and indirect taxes.* This makes it equal to the sum of factor costs only. Figure 10-4 should make this relationship clear.

NNP AND
NATIONAL
INCOME

FIG. 10-4

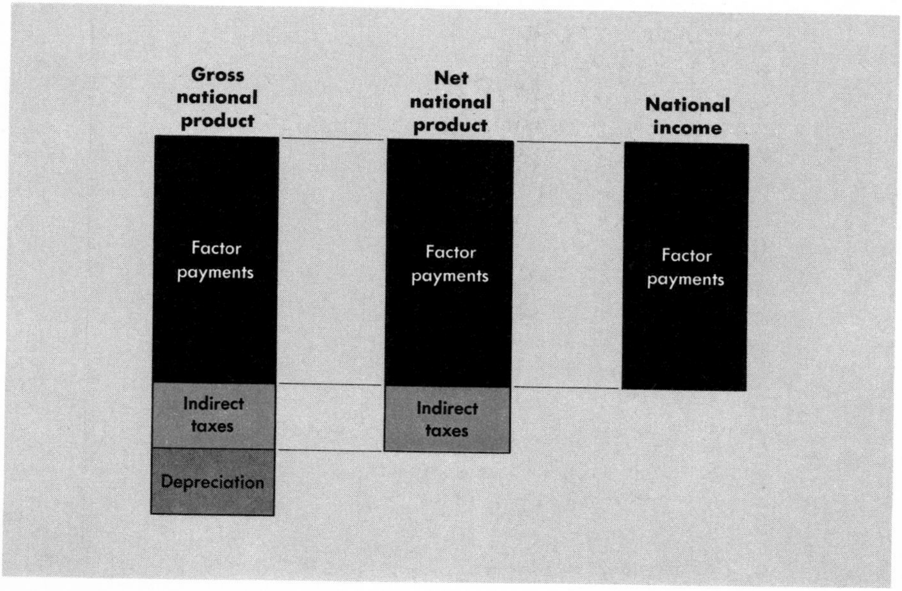

The "self-reproducing" model economy we have now sketched out is obviously still very far from reality. Nevertheless, the particular kind of unreality that we have deliberately constructed serves a highly useful purpose. An economy that regularly and dependably buys back everything it produces gives us a kind of bench mark from which to begin our subsequent investigations. We call such an economy, whose internal relationships we have outlined, an economy in *stationary equilibrium*, and we denote the changeless flow of costs into business receipts and receipts back into costs a *circular flow*.

We shall return many times to the model of a circular flow economy for insights into a more complex and dynamic system. Hence it is well that we summarize briefly two of the salient characteristics of such a system.

1. *A circular flow economy will never experience a "recession."*
Year in and year out, its total output will remain unchanged. Indeed, the very concept of a circular flow is useful in showing us that an economic system can maintain a given level of activity *indefinitely*, so long as all the sectors convert all their receipts into expenditure.

2. *A circular flow economy also will never know a "boom."*
That is, it will not grow, and its standard of living will remain unchanged. That standard of living may be high or low, for we could have a circular flow economy of poverty or of abundance. But in either state, changelessness will be of its essence.

In the chapters that follow, we must successively reintroduce the very elements that we have so carefully excluded. First, net saving and net investment, then technological change and population growth must one by one find their way back into our model. Thus, gradually it will approximate itself to the realities around us, allowing us to return from the abstract world of ideas to the concrete world of reality.

1. A great *circle of payments and receipts constantly renews the demand* that keeps the economy going. Income is pumped out to the participants in the production process, who then spend their incomes to buy the output they have helped to make, thereby returning money to the firms that again pump it out.

2. We seek to elucidate this circle by constructing a *model*—an economy stripped of everything that is not essential to the process we seek to understand. Our model simplifies and therefore highlights the relationships that underlie the macroeconomic process.

3. We use our model to show *how an economy can in fact buy back all of its own output*—how enough demand can be created to keep the economy going. To do so, we must show that *every item of cost to business firms can become demand* for them on the marketplace.

4. The first item of costs is *factor payments* (wages, rent, profits, interest). These payments for factor services are *the source of household income*. In turn, households can spend their incomes for *consumption goods*.

5. *Indirect taxes* are costs paid by firms to government agencies. In turn, these agencies spend their tax receipts for *government purchases*.

   (Note that direct taxes—income taxes—are not a cost of production, but a levy imposed on factors after they have been paid.)

6. *Depreciation* costs are costs incurred by *businesses* for the wear and tear of capital. They are accrued by business firms, who, in turn, are able to use them to purchase *replacement investment*.

7. *Materials* costs are payments to other firms. Ultimately, they can all be broken down into factor costs, indirect tax costs, and depreciation costs.

8. *The total value of output (GNP) can be seen not only as a sum of expenditures $(C + I + G + E)$, but as a sum of costs $(F + T + D)$.*

9. *All costs thus become sector receipts:* factor costs become household incomes; indirect tax costs become government receipts; depreciation costs become business receipts. In turn, *these sector receipts can be returned to the market as new expenditures* (demand).

10. This gives us *three streams of cost—income—expenditure* (demand):

    factor costs—household incomes—consumption expenditure

    indirect taxes—government receipts—government expenditure

    depreciation—business receipts—replacement expenditure

11. *The key linkage is that between receipts and expenditure. All costs must become receipts. But not all receipts need necessarily be spent.*

12. When all receipts are spent, then we have a perfect *circular flow*. In such a situation, the economy generates an unchanging flow of demand, and therefore experiences neither boom, recession, nor growth.

1. How can a model elucidate reality when it is deliberately stripped of the very things that make reality interesting?

2. Why do we need a model to show that an economy can buy back its own production?

3. What are factor costs? What kinds of factor costs are there? To what sector do factor costs go?

4. What are direct taxes? What are indirect taxes? Which are considered part of production costs? Why?

5. To whom are materials costs paid? Why are they not part of the sum total of costs in GNP?

6. What is depreciation? Why is it a part of costs? Who receives the payments or accruals made for depreciation purposes?

7. Show in a carefully drawn diagram how costs become income or receipts of the different sectors.

8. Show in a second diagram how the incomes of the various sectors can become expenditures.

9. Why is the link between expenditure and receipt different from that between receipt and expenditure?

10. What is meant by a circular flow economy? Why does such an economy have neither growth nor fluctuation?

11. Explain the two different ways of looking at GNP and write the simple formula for each.

12. Can we have demand without expenditure?

SAVING
AND INVESTMENT

11

Let us return for a moment to our original perspective, an aerial view of the economic flow. We will remember that we could see the workings of the economy as an interaction between the factors of production and their environment, culminating in a stream of production—some private, some public—that was used in part for consumption and in part for the replacement or the further building up of capital. In our model of a circular flow economy we saw how such an economy can be self-sustaining and self-renewing, as each round of disbursements by employers found its way into a stream of purchasing power just large enough to justify the continuation of the given scale of output.

Yet we all know that such a circular flow is a highly unreal depiction of the world. Indeed, it omits the most important dynamic factor of real economic life—the steady accumulation of new capital (and the qualitative change in the nature of the capital due to technology) that characterizes a *growing* economy. What we must now investigate is the process by which society adds each year to its stock of real wealth—and the effect of this process on the circuit of production and purchasing.

We begin by making sure that we understand a key word in this dynamic analysis—saving. We have come across saving many times by now in this book and so we should be ready for a final mastery of this centrally important economic term. In Chapter 9 (and previously in our discussion of the Great Depression in chapters 7 and 8) we spoke of saving in *real* terms as the act by which society relinquished resources that might have been used for consumption, thereby making them available for the capital-building stream of output. Now we must translate that underlying real meaning of saving into terms corresponding with the buying and selling, paying and receiving discussed in the preceding chapter.

What is saving in these terms? It is very simply *not spending all or part of income for consumption goods or services.* * It should be very clear then why saving is such a key term. In our discussion of the circular flow, it became apparent that expenditure was the critical link in the steady operation of the economy. If saving is not-spending, then it would seem that saving could be the cause for just that kind of downward spiral of which we caught a glimpse in our preceding chapter.

And yet this clearly is not the whole story. We also know that the act of investing—of spending money to direct factors into the production of capital goods—requires an act of saving; that is, of not using that same money to direct those factors instead into the production of consumers goods. *Hence, saving is clearly necessary for the process of investment.* Now, how can one and the same act be necessary for economic expansion and a threat to its stability? This is a problem that will occupy us during much of this book.

THE DEMAND GAP   It will help us understand the problem if we again have recourse to the now familiar diagram of the circular flow. But this time we must introduce into it the crucial new fact of net saving. Note *net* saving.

---

* Note "for consumption goods and services." Purchasing stocks or bonds or life insurance is also an act of saving, even though you must spend money to acquire these items. What you acquire, however, are assets, not consumption goods and services. Some acts of spending are difficult to classify. Is a college education, for instance, a consumption good or an investment? It is probably better thought of as an investment even though in the statistics of GNP it is treated as consumption.

Quite unnoticed, we have already encountered saving in our circular flow. In our model economy, when business made expenditures for the replacement of capital, it used money that *could* have been paid in dividends to stockholders or in additional compensation to employees. Before a replacement expenditure was made, someone had to decide not to allocate that money for dividends or bonuses. Thus, there is a flow of saving—that is, of nonconsumption—even in the circular flow.

But the saving is not *net* saving. Like the regular flow of replacement investment itself, the flow of saving that finances this replacement serves only to maintain the existing level of capital wealth, not to increase it. Hence, just as with investment, we reserve the term *net saving* for that saving which makes possible a rise in the total of our capital assets.

Gross and net saving are thus easy to define. *By gross saving we mean all saving, both for replacement and for expansion of our capital assets, exactly like gross investment. By net saving, we mean any saving that makes possible an increase in the stock of capital, again exactly as in the definition of net investment.*

We have already seen that an economy can maintain a circular flow when it saves only as much as is needed to maintain its capital. But now suppose that it saves more than that, as is shown in Fig. 11-1. Here householders save a portion of their incomes, over and above the amount saved by business to insure the maintenance of its assets.

What we see is precisely what we would expect. There is a gap in demand introduced by the deficiency of consumer spending. This means that the total receipts of employers who make consumer goods will be less than the total amounts they laid out. It begins to look as if we were approaching the cause of economic recession and unemployment.

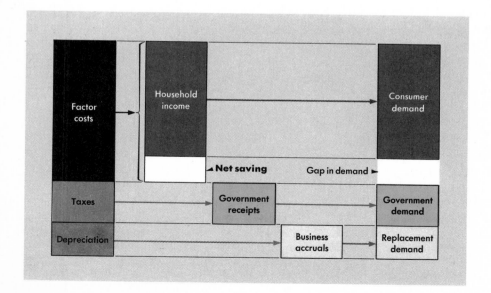

FIG. 11-1

THE DEMAND GAP

Yet, whereas we have introduced net saving, we have forgotten about its counterpart, net investment. Cannot the investment activity of a growing economy in some way close the demand gap?

This is indeed, as we shall soon see, the way out of the dilemma. But before we trace the way in which investment compensates for saving, let us draw some important conclusions from the analysis we have made up to this point.

1. *Any act of saving, in and by itself, creates a gap in demand, a shortage of spending. Unless this gap is closed, there will be trouble in the economic system, for employers will not be getting back as receipts all the sums they laid out.*

2. *If the gap is caused by saving that is implicit in depreciation, it can be closed by replacement expenditures. But if it is caused by net saving, over and above the flow needed to maintain the stock of capital, it will require net investment to be closed.*

3. *The presence of a demand gap forces us to make a choice. If we want a dynamic, investing economy, we will have to be prepared to cope with the problems that net saving raises. If we want to avoid these problems, we can close the gap by urging consumers not to save. Then we would have a dependable circular flow, but we would no longer enjoy economic growth.*

THE OFFSET TO SAVINGS

How, then, shall we manage to make our way out of the dilemma of saving? The previous diagram makes clear what must be done. If a gap in demand is due to the savings of households, then *that gap must be closed by the expanded spending of some other sector.* There are only two other such sectors: government or business. Thus in some fashion or other, the savings of one sector must be "offset" by the increased activity of another.

But how is this offset to take place? How are the resources that are relinquished by consumers to be made available to entrepreneurs in the business sector or to government officials? In a market economy there is only one way that resources or factors not being used in one place can be used in another. Someone must be willing and able to hire them.

Whether or not government and business *are* willing to employ the factors that are not needed in the consumer goods sector is a very critical matter, soon to command much of our attention. But suppose that they are willing. How will they be able to do so? How can they get the necessary funds to expand their activity?

There are four principal methods of accomplishing this essential increase in expenditure.

1. The business sector can increase its expenditures by *borrowing* the savings of the public through the sale of new corporate bonds.

2. The government sector can increase its expenditures by *borrowing* savings from the other sectors through the sale of new government bonds.

3. The business sector can increase its expenditures by attracting household savings into partnerships, new stock, or other *ownership or equity.*

4. Both business and government sectors can increase expenditures by *borrowing* additional funds from commercial banks.

There are other possibilities. Government has a very important means of increasing its command over resources, through taxing the household or business sectors. Business can also increase its expenditures by using its own accumulated past savings to finance new spending.

But the most important methods itemized above all have one attribute that calls them especially to our attention. Without exception they give rise to *claims* that reveal from whom the funds have been obtained and to whom they have been made available, as well as on what terms. Bonds, corporate or government, show that savings have been borrowed from individuals or banks by business and government units. Shares of stock reveal that savings have been obtained on an equity (ownership) basis, as do new partnership agreements. Borrowing from banks gives rise to loans that also represent the claims of one part of the community against another.

CLAIMS

We can note a few additional points about claims, now that we see how many of them arise in the economy. First, many household savings are first put into banks and insurance companies—so-called financial intermediaries—so that the transfer of funds from households to business or government may go through several stages; e.g., from household to insurance company and then from insurance company to corporation.

Second, not *all* claims involve the offsetting of savings of one sector by expenditures of another. Many claims, once they have arisen, are traded back and forth and bought and sold, as is the case with most stocks and bonds. These purchases and sales involve the *transfer of existing claims,* not the creation of new claims.

Finally, not every new claim necessarily involves the creation of an asset. If A borrows $5 from B, bets it on the races, and gives B his note, there has been an increase in claims, but no new asset has been brought into being to match it.

FIG. 11-2

**"TRANSFER"
OF SAVINGS**

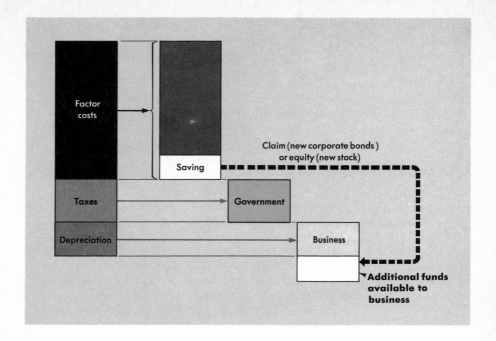

FIG. 11-3

**PUBLIC AND
PRIVATE
CLAIMS**

Now let us look at Fig. 11-2. This time we show what happens when savings are made available to the business sector by direct borrowing from households. Note the claim (or equity) that arises.

If the government were doing the borrowing, rather than the business sector, the diagram would look like Fig. 11-3. Notice that the claim is now a government bond.

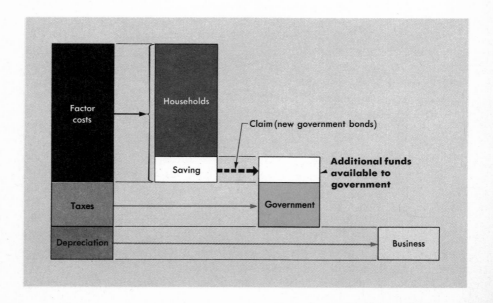

We have not looked at a diagram showing business or government borrowing its funds from the banking system. (This process will be better understood when we take up the problem of money and banking, in Chapter 16.) The basic concept, however, although more complex, is much the same as above.

There remains only a last step, which must by now be fully anticipated. We have seen how it is possible to offset the savings in one sector, where they were going to cause an expenditure gap, by increasing the funds available to another sector. It remains only to *spend* those additional funds in the form of additional investment or, in the case of the government, for additional public goods and services. The two completed expenditure circuits now appear in Fig. 11-4.

FIG. 11-4   **TWO WAYS OF CLOSING THE DEMAND GAP**

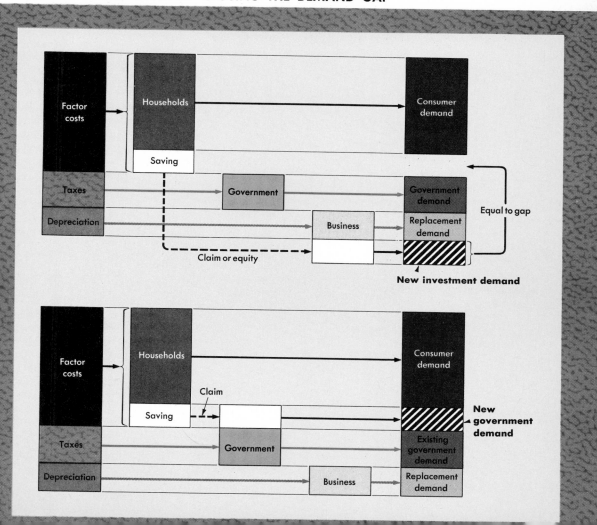

We shall not investigate further at this point the differences between increased public spending and increased business investment. What we must heed is the crucial point at issue: *if saving in any one sector is to be offset, some other sector (or sectors) must spend more than its income. A gap in demand due to insufficient expenditure in one sector can be compensated only by an increase in demand—that is, in expenditure—of another.*

Once this simple but fundamental point is clearly understood, much of the mystery of macroeconomics disappears, for we can then begin to see that an economy in movement, as contrasted with one in a stationary circular flow, is one in which sectors must *cooperate* to maintain the closed circuit of income and output. In a dynamic economy, we no longer enjoy the steady translation of incomes into expenditure which, as we have seen, is the key to an uninterrupted flow of output. Rather, we are faced with the presence of net saving and the possibility of a gap in final demand. Difficult though the ensuing problems are, let us not forget that saving is the necessary condition for the accumulation of capital. The price of economic growth, in other words, is the risk of economic decline.

REAL AND
MONEY
SAVING

This central importance of saving in a growing economy will become a familiar problem. At this juncture, where we have first encountered the difficulties it can pose, we must be certain that we understand two different aspects that saving assumes.

One aspect, noticed in our initial overview of the economy, is the decision to relinquish *resources* that can then be re-deployed into capital-building. This is the real significance of saving. But this "real" aspect of saving is not the way we encounter the act of saving in our ordinary lives. We think of saving as a monetary phenomenon, not a "real" one. When we save, we are conscious of not using all our incomes for consumption, but we scarcely, if ever, think of releasing resources for alternative employments.

There is a reason for this dichotomy of real and money saving. In our society, with its extraordinary degree of specialization, the individuals or institutions that do the actual saving are not ordinarily those that do the actual capital-building. In a simple society, this dichotomy between saving and investing need not, and usually does not, occur. A farmer who decides to build new capital—for example, to build a barn—is very much aware of giving up a consumption activity—the raising of food—in order to carry out his investment. So is an artisan who stops weaving clothing to repair his loom. Where the saver and the investor are one and the same person, there need be no "financial" saving, and the underlying real phenomenon of saving as the diversion of activity from consumption to investment is immediately apparent.

In the modern world, savers and investors are sometimes the same individual or group—as in the case of a business management that spends profits on new productive capacity rather than on higher executive salaries. More often, however, savers are not investors. Certainly householders, though very important savers, do not personally decide and direct the process of capital formation in the nation. Furthermore, the men and materials that households voluntarily relinquish by not using all their incomes to buy consumers goods have to be physically transferred to different industries, often to different occupations and locations, in order to carry out their investment tasks. This requires funds in the hands of the investors, so that they can tempt resources from one use to another.

Hence we need an elaborate system by which money saving can be "transferred" directly or indirectly into the hands of those who will be in a position to employ factors for capital construction purposes. Nevertheless, underlying this complex mechanism for transferring purchasing power remains the same simple purpose that we initially witnessed. Resources that have been relinquished from the production of consumption goods or services are now employed in the production of capital goods. Thus, *saving and investing are essentially real phenomena,* even though it may take a great deal of financial manipulation to bring them about.

A final important point. *The fact that the decisions to save and the decisions to invest are lodged in different individuals or groups alerts us to a basic reason why the savings-investment process may not always work smoothly.* Savers may choose to consume less than their total incomes at times when investors have no interest in expanding their capital assets. Alternatively, business firms may wish to form new capital when savers are interested in spending money only on themselves. This separation of decision-making can give rise to situations in which savings are not offset by investment, or in which investment plans race out ahead of savings capabilities. In our next chapters we will be investigating what happens in these cases.

TRANSFER PAYMENTS AND PROFITS

We have talked about the transfer of purchasing power from savers to investors, but we have not yet mentioned another kind of transfer, also of great importance in the over-all operation of the economy. This is the transfer of incomes from sector to sector (and sometimes within sectors).

Income transfers (called *transfer payments*) are a very useful and important means of reallocating purchasing power in society. Through transfer payments, members of the community who do not participate in production are given an opportunity to enjoy incomes that would otherwise not be available to them. Thus Social Security transfer payments make it possible for the old or the handicapped to be given an "income" of their own (not, to be sure, a currently *earned* income), or unemployment benefits give purchasing power to those who cannot get it through employment.

Not all transfers are in the nature of welfare payments, however. The distribution of money *within* a household is a transfer payment. So is the payment of interest on the national debt.* So is the grant of a subsidy to a private enterprise, such as an airline, or of a scholarship to a college student. Any income payment that is not earned by selling one's productive services on the market falls in the transfer category.

It may help to understand this process if we visualize it in our flow diagram. Figure 11-5 shows two kinds of transfers. The upper one, from the government to the household sector, shows a typical transfer of incomes, such as veterans' pensions or Social Security; the transfer below it reflects the flow of income that might be illustrated by a

FIG. 11-5

TRANSFER PAYMENTS

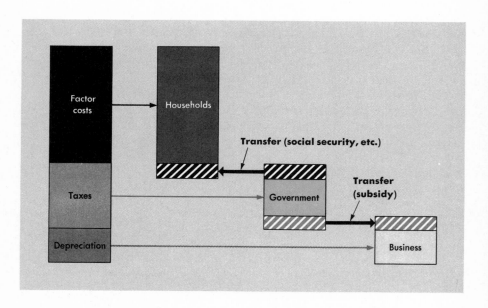

*Curiously, the payment of interest on corporate debt is not considered a transfer payment, but a payment to a factor of production. Actually, much government interest should also be thought of as a factor payment (for the loan of capital for purposes of public output); but by convention, all government interest is classified as a transfer payment.

payment to agriculture for crop support. Transfers *within* sectors, such as household allowances, are not shown in the diagram.

One thing we may well note about transfers is that they can only *rearrange* the incomes created in the production process; they cannot increase those incomes. Income, as we learned in the last chapter, is inextricably tied to output—indeed, income is only the financial counterpart of output.

Transfer payments, on the other hand, are a way of arranging individual claims to production in some fashion that strikes the community as fairer or more efficient or more decorous than the way the market process allocates them through the production process. As such, transfer payments are an indispensable and often invaluable agency of social policy. But it is important to understand that no amount of transfers can, in itself, increase the total that is to be shared. That can happen only by raising output itself.

We have mentioned, but only in passing, another means of transferring purchasing power from one sector to another: taxation. Heretofore, however, we have often spoken as though all government tax receipts were derived from indirect taxes that were added onto the cost of production.

In fact, this is not the only source of government revenue. Indirect taxes are an important part of state and local revenues, but they are only a minor part of federal tax receipts. Most federal taxes are levied on the incomes of the factors of production or on the profits of businesses after the other factors have been paid.

Once again it is worth remembering that the government taxes consumers (and businesses) because it is in the nature of much government output that it cannot be *sold*. Taxes are the way we are billed for our share—rightly or wrongly figured—of government production that has been collectively decided upon. As we can now see, taxes—both on business and on the household sector—also finance many transfer payments. That is, the government intervenes in the distribution process to make it conform to our politically expressed social purposes, taking away some incomes from certain individuals and groups, and providing incomes to others. Figure 11-6 shows what this looks like in the flow of GNP. (Note that the business sector is drawn with profits, as our next section will explain.)

As we can see, the exchanges of income between the household and the government sectors can be very complex. Income can flow from households to government units via taxation, and return to the household sector via transfer payments; and the same two-way flows can take place between government and business.

FIG. 11-6

TRANSFERS AND
INCOME TAXES

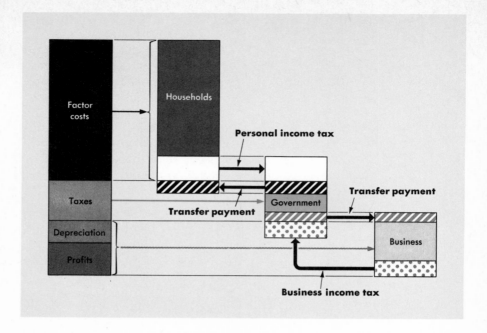

PROFITS
AND DEMAND

The last diagram has already introduced a new element of reality in our discussion. Taxes on business *income* presuppose that businesses make *profits.* Let us see how these profits fit into the savings-investment process.

During our discussion of the circular flow, we spoke of profits as a special kind of factor cost—a payment to the factor *capital,* in return for its contribution of risk-taking. But since we are no longer in a changeless circular flow economy, we can introduce a much more dynamic conception of profits. Now we can think of profits not merely as a factor cost (although there is always a certain element of risk-remuneration in profits), but as a return to especially efficient or forward-thinking firms who have used the investment process to introduce new products or processes ahead of the run of their industries. We can think of profits, too, as being in part the return accruing to powerful firms who exact a semimonopolistic return from their customers. In Part Three we will look much more carefully into the question of the origin of profits.

What matters in our analysis at this stage is not the precise explanation we give to the origin of profits, but a precise explanation of their role in maintaining a "closed-circuit" economy in which all costs are returned to the marketplace as demand. A commonly heard diagnosis for economic maladies is that profits are at the root of the matter, in that they cause a "withdrawal" of spending power or income from the community. If profits were "hoarded," or kept unspent, this might be true. In fact, however, profits can be spent in three ways. They may be

1. distributed as income to the household sector in the form of dividends or profit shares, to become part of household spending
2. spent by business firms for new plant and equipment
3. taxed by the government and spent in the public sector

All three methods of offsetting profits appear in Fig. 11-7.

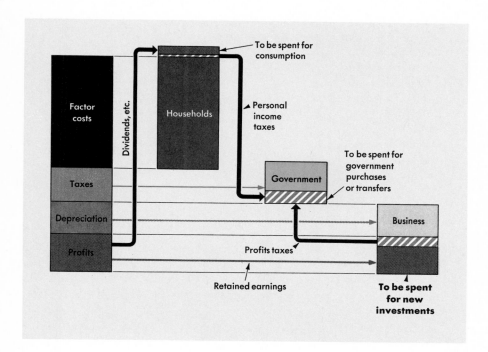

FIG. 11-7

PROFITS IN THE CIRCULAR FLOW

We can see that profits need not constitute a withdrawal from the income stream. Indeed, unless profits are adequate, businesses will very likely not invest enough to offset the savings of the household sector. They may, in fact, even fail to make normal replacement expenditures, aggravating the demand gap still further in this way.

Thus the existence of profits, far from being deflationary—that is, far from causing a fall in income—is, in fact, essential for the maintenance of a given level of income or for an advance to a higher level. Nonetheless, there is a germ of truth in the contentions of those who have maintained that profits can cause an insufficiency of purchasing power. *For unless profits are returned to the flow of purchasing power as dividends that are spent by their recipients, or as new capital expenditures made by business, or as taxes that lead to additional public spending, there will be a gap in the community's demand.* Thus we can think of profits just as we think of saving—an indispensable source of economic growth or a potential source of economic decline.

SAVING,
INVESTMENT,
AND GROWTH

We are almost ready to leave our analysis of the circle of production and income, and to proceed to a much closer study of the individual dynamic elements that create and close gaps. Before we do, however, it is well that we take note of one last fact of the greatest importance. In offsetting the savings of any sector by investment, we have closed the production and income circuit, much as in the stationary circular flow, but there is one crucial difference from the circular flow. Now we have closed the flow by diverting savings into the creation of *additional* capital. Unlike the stationary circular flow where the handing around of incomes did no more than to maintain unchanged the original configuration of the system, in our new dynamic saving-and-investing model *each closing of the circuit results in a quantitative change—the addition of a new "layer" of capital.* Hence, more and more wealth is being added to our system; and thinking back to our first impressions of the interaction of wealth and population, we would expect more and more productiveness from our human factors. Bringing with it complications with which we shall have to deal in due course, *growth* has entered our economic model.

SUMMARY

1. The critical element missing from the concept of the circular flow is *saving*. The key question is how an economy can buy back all its output when some of its receipts are saved rather than returned to the market through expenditure.

2. Saving poses a dilemma. On one hand, it breaks the circular flow and creates a *demand gap*. On the other hand, if there is *no saving*, there can be *no investment*.

3. The answer to the dilemma is that *saving*, which is essential for growth, *must be offset by additional expenditure.* This means that another sector must spend more than its income.

4. There are four main ways in which a sector can spend more than its income:
   - The *business sector can borrow* from the household sector.
   - The *government sector can borrow* from the household sector.
   - The *business sector* can attract household savings into *equities*.
   - Business and government can borrow from the *commercial banks*.

5. Although saving involves money, it is essentially a "real" process (as is investment). That is, its real meaning is that resources are released from consumption. The acts of releasing resources (saving) and the acts of employing them (investment) are usually performed by different groups in modern society.

6. *Transfer payments,* from one sector to another or within one sector, play an important part in *redistributing* income, but do not increase the total GNP.

7. Profits can be returned to the expenditure flow by being: (1) paid out as dividends, etc., to the household sector, where they can be used for consumption; (2) spent by business firms for new investment; or (3) taxed by the government and spent by it.

8. Saving thus requires investment to assure that all payments will be returned to the market as demand. Note, however, that the process of *investment adds to capital* and thereby increases productivity. Saving and investment are therefore an integral part of the *process of growth.*

1. What do we mean by a demand gap? Show diagrammatically.

2. How is a demand gap filled by business investment? Show diagrammatically.

3. Why is saving indispensable for growth?

4. Can we have planned business investment without saving? Saving without planned business investment?

5. Draw carefully a diagram that shows how savings can be offset by government spending.

6. How is it possible for a sector to spend more than its income? How does it get the additional money?

7. What is a transfer payment? Draw diagrams of transfers from government to consumers, from government to business. Is charity a transfer? Is a lottery?

8. Diagram the three ways in which profits can be returned to the expenditure flow. What happens if they are not?

9. Why is a problem presented by the fact that those who save and those who make the decision to invest are not the same people?

10. In what way is a circular flow economy different from an economy that saves and invests?

12 THE
CONSUMPTION SECTOR

With a basic understanding of the crucial role of expenditure and of the complex relationship of saving and investment behind us, we are in a position to look more deeply into the question of the determination of gross national product. For what we have discovered heretofore is only the *mechanism* by which a market economy can sustain or fail to sustain a given level of output through a circuit of expenditure and receipt. Now we must try to discover the *forces* that dynamize the system, creating or closing gaps between income and outgo. Hence, beginning with this chapter, we devote our attention to the actual behavior of the household, government, and business sectors and to their respective motivations for consumption, government purchases, and investment.

THE HOUSEHOLD SECTOR

Largest, most familiar, and in many respects more important of all the sectors in the economy is that of the nation's households—that is, its families and single-dwelling individuals (the two categories together called consumer units) considered as receivers of income and transfer payments, or as savers and spenders of money for consumption.

FIG. 12-1

CONSUMPTION
SECTOR, 1968

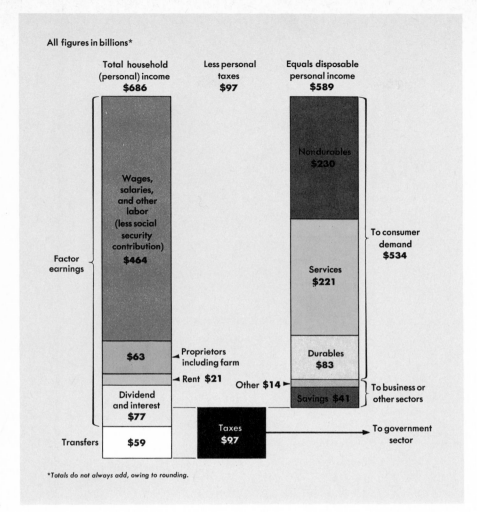

All figures in billions*

Total household (personal) income $686

Less personal taxes $97

Equals disposable personal income $589

Wages, salaries, and other labor (less social security contribution) $464

Factor earnings

$63

Proprietors including farm

◄ Rent $21

Dividend and interest $77

Transfers $59

Taxes $97

Nondurables $230

Services $221

Durables $83

Other $14 ►

Savings $41

To consumer demand $534

To business or other sectors

To government sector

*Totals do not always add, owing to rounding.

How big is this sector? In 1968 it comprised some fifty million families and some thirteen million independent individuals who collectively gathered in $686 billion in income and spent $548 billion.* As Fig. 12-1

*The Department of Commerce has recently redefined some categories of the national income accounts, and the word *consumption* today applies, strictly speaking, only to personal expenditures for goods and services. Included in total consumer spending, however, are sizeable amounts for interest (mainly on installment loans) and for remittances abroad, neither of which sums are included in the amount for goods and services. The proper nomenclature for the total of consumer spending (goods and services plus interest and remittances) is now *personal outlays*. We shall, however, continue to use the simpler term consumption, although our figures will be those for personal outlays.

Note, also, that the compilation of these figures is a time-consuming process in which earlier estimates are frequently subject to revision. Hence, figures for the components of consumption, or, for that matter, for almost all magnitudes in the economic process, are apt to vary slightly in successive printed statistics until, eventually, the "final" figures are arrived at.

shows, the great bulk of receipts was from factor earnings, and transfer payments played only a relatively small role. As we can also see, we must subtract personal tax payments from household income (or *personal income* as it is officially designated) before we get *disposable personal income*—income actually available for spending. It is from disposable personal income that the crucial choice is made to spend or save. Much of this chapter will focus on that choice.

SUBCOMPONENTS OF CONSUMPTION

Finally we note that consumer spending itself divides into three main streams. The largest of these is for *nondurable* goods, such as food and clothing or other items whose economic life is (or is assumed to be) short. Second largest is an assortment of expenditures we call consumer *services,* comprising such things as rent, doctors' or lawyers' or barbers' ministrations, theater or movie admissions, bus or taxi or plane transportation, etc., where we buy not a physical good but the work performed by someone or by some equipment. Last is a substream of expenditure for consumer *durable* goods which, as the name suggests, includes items such as cars or household appliances whose economic life is considerably greater than that of most nondurables. We can think of these goods as comprising consumers' capital.

There are complicated patterns and interrelations among these three major streams of consumer spending. As we would expect, consumer spending for durables is extremely volatile. In bad times, such as 1933, it has sunk to less than 8 per cent of all consumer outlays; in the peak of good times in the 1960's, it has risen to nearly double that. Meanwhile, outlays for services have been a steadily swelling area for consumer spending in the postwar economy. As a consequence of the growth of consumer buying of durables and of services, the relative share of the consumer dollar going to "soft goods" has been slowly declining. It is interesting to note, for example, that between 1950 and 1968, consumer spending for food fell from 23 per cent of all consumption to 19 per cent and that expenditures for apparel fell from 11 per cent to less than 9 per cent. Conversely, consumer spending on recreation and foreign travel and remittances climbed from 6.4 per cent to over 8 per cent.

CONSUMPTION AND GNP

These internal dynamics of consumption are of the greatest interest to someone who seeks to project consumer spending patterns into the future—perhaps as an aid to merchandising. But here we are interested in the larger phenomenon of the relationship of consumption as a whole to the flow of gross national product.

Figure 12-2 shows us this historic relationship since 1929. Certain things stand out.

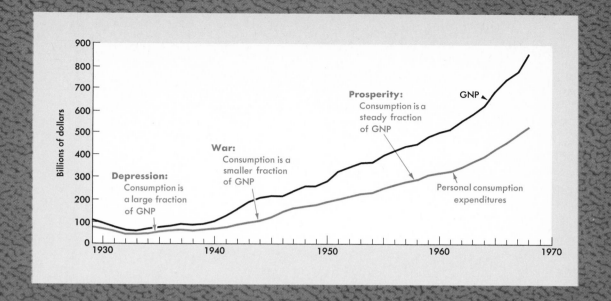

FIG. 12-2   CONSUMPTION AND GNP, CURRENT PRICES

1. *Consumption spending is by far the largest category of spending in GNP.*

Total consumer expenditures—for durable goods, such as automobiles or washing machines; nondurables, like food or clothing; and services, such as recreation or medical care—account for approximately two-thirds of all the final buying in the economy.

2. *Consumption is not only the biggest, it is also the most stable, of all the streams of expenditure.*

For consumption, as we have mentioned, is the essential economic activity. Unless there is a total breakdown in the social system, households will consume some bare minimum. Further, it is a fact of common experience that even in adverse circumstances, households seek to maintain their accustomed living standards. Thus consumption activities constitute a kind of floor for the level of over-all economic activity. Investment and government spending, as we shall see, are capable of sudden reversals; but the streams of consumer spending tend to display a measure of stability over time.

3. *Consumption is nonetheless capable of considerable fluctuation as a proportion of GNP.*

Remembering our previous diagrams, we can see that this proportionate fluctuation must reflect changes in the relative importance of investment and government spending. And indeed this is the case. As investment spending fell in the Depression, consumption bulked relatively larger in GNP; as government spending increased during the war, consumption bulked relatively smaller. The changing *relative* size of consumption, in other words, reflects broad changes in *other* sectors rather than sharp changes in consuming habits.

4. *Despite its importance, consumption alone will not "buy back" GNP.*

It is well to recall that consumption, although the largest component of GNP, is still *only* two-thirds of GNP. Government buying and business buying of investment goods are essential if the income-expenditure circuit is to be closed. During our subsequent analysis it will help to remember that consumption expenditure by itself does not provide the only impetus of demand.

SAVING IN HISTORIC PERSPECTIVE

This first view of consumption activity sets the stage for our inquiry into the dynamic causes of fluctuations in GNP. We already know that the saving-investment relationship lies at the center of this problem, and that much saving arises from the household sector. Hence, let us see what we can learn about the saving process in historic perspective.

We begin with Fig. 12-3, which shows us the relationship of household saving to disposable income—that is, to household sector incomes after the payment of taxes.

What we see here are two interesting facts. First, during the bottom of the Great Depression there were *no* savings in the household sector. In fact, under the duress of unemployment, millions of households were forced to *dissave*—to borrow or to draw on their old savings (hence the negative figure for the sector as a whole). By way of contrast, we notice the immense savings of the peak war years when consumers' goods were rationed and households were urged to save. Clearly, then, the *amount* of saving is capable of great fluctuation, falling to zero or to negative figures in periods of great economic distress and rising to as much as a quarter of income during periods of goods shortages.

In Fig. 12-4, however, we are struck by another fact. However variable the amounts, the savings *ratio* shows a considerable stability in "normal" years. This steadiness is particularly noteworthy in the postwar period. From 1950 to the present, consumption has ranged between roughly 92 to 95 per cent of disposable personal income—which is, of course, the same as saying that savings have ranged between 8 per cent and 5 per cent. If we take the postwar period as a whole, *we can see*

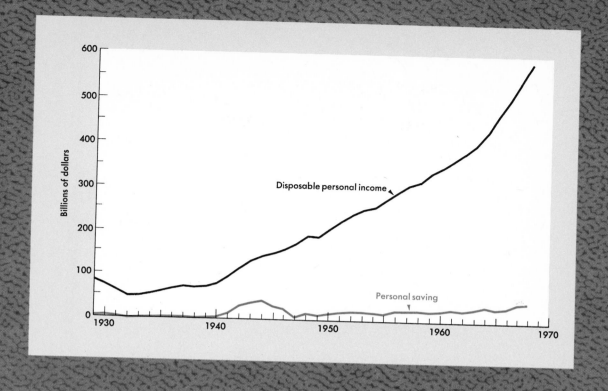

FIG. 12-3   SAVING AND DISPOSABLE INCOME

FIG. 12-4   SAVING AS PER CENT OF DISPOSABLE INCOME

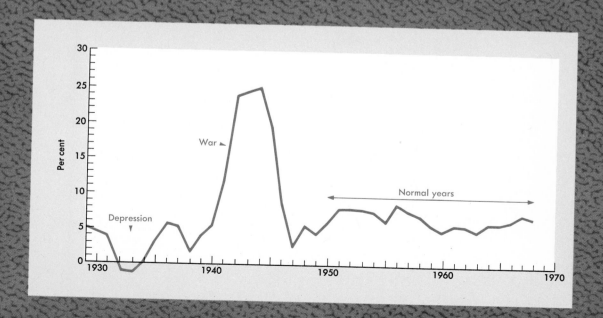

that in an average year we have consumed a little more than 94 cents of each dollar of income and that this ratio has remained fairly constant even though our incomes have increased markedly.

**LONG-RUN
SAVINGS
BEHAVIOR**

This stability of the long-run savings ratio is an interesting and important phenomenon, and something of a puzzling one, for we might easily imagine that the savings ratio would rise over time. Statistical investigations of cross sections of the nation show that rich families tend to save not only larger amounts, but larger *percentages* of their income, than poor families do. Thus as the entire nation has grown richer, and as families have moved from lower income brackets to higher ones, it would seem natural to suppose that they would also take on the higher savings characteristics that accompany upper incomes.

Were this so, the economy would face a very serious problem. In order to sustain its higher levels of aggregate income, it would then have to invest an ever larger *proportion* of its income to offset its growing ratio of savings to income. As we shall see in our next chapter, investment is always a source of potential trouble because it is so much riskier than any other business function. If we had to keep on making proportionally larger investments each year to keep pace with our proportionally growing savings, we should live in an exceedingly vulnerable economic environment.

Fortunately, we are rescued from this dangerous situation, because our long-run savings ratio, as we have seen, displays a reassuring steadiness. In fact, there has been no significant upward trend in the savings ratio for the nation's households since the mid-1800's, and there may have been a slight downward trend.*

**SHORT-RUN
VS. LONG-RUN
SAVINGS
BEHAVIOR**

How do we reconcile this long-run stability with the fact that statistical studies always reveal that rich families *do* save a larger percentage of their incomes than poor families? As the nation has moved, en masse, into higher income brackets, why has it not also saved proportionately more of its income?

The answer hinges on important differences between the savings behavior of typical families over a short period of time and over a longer period. In the short run, families in every income bracket do indeed increase their savings sharply as their incomes rise. Much of a salary raise or a windfall is likely to be used *at first* for savings purposes. Debts may be quickly paid off. Money may be allowed to pile up in the bank while plans are made to readjust living standards. Even when the

---

*Economists maintain a certain tentativeness about their assertions as to long-run trends, since the statistical foundation on which they are based is inevitably subject to some error and uncertainty.

increase in income is used for a splurge such as the purchase of a new car, income may be allowed to lie idle for a short period. Thus, in the short run, savings ratios for additions to income are typically higher than they were before the increase was received.

What is true for the short run, however, is not true for the long run. From decade to decade, and even from year to year, powerful pressures and pervasive changes in our environment seem to operate on families at all levels, giving rise to a slow, secular decline in the desire to save. The growth of Social Security and pension plans, the impingement of higher income taxes, the steady expansion of advertising and consumer credit, the temptations of affluence, and the spirit of keeping up with the Joneses—all these influences appear to have worked a gradual decline in the long-run desires of *all* income groups. In addition, despite the statistics that show a steady rise in savings-ratios from income class to income class, it is likely that families in different income groups save much more nearly equal proportions of their incomes than our "cross section" data show.*

As a result of these and still other motivations, savings behavior in the long run differs considerably from that in the short run. Over the years, American households have shown a remarkable stability in their rate of over-all savings. Its importance has already been mentioned. In a shorter period of time, however—over a few months or perhaps a year—households tend to save higher fractions of increases in their incomes than they do in the long run. The very great importance of this fact we shall subsequently note.

THE CONSUMPTION-INCOME RELATIONSHIP

What we have heretofore seen are some of the historical and empirical relationships of consumption and personal saving to income. We have taken the trouble to investigate these relationships in some detail, since they are among the most important causes of the gaps that have to be closed by investment. But the statistical facts in themselves are only

---

*For instance, Professor Milton Friedman has suggested that middle-class families who have suffered temporary reverses (and who are therefore counted in lower than their "regular" income brackets) will typically maintain their living standards and reduce their savings, thereby causing a lower savings ratio for these lower brackets than would be found if we included only "permanent" members of it. Conversely, families that have had a lucky year and are temporary residents of a higher bracket may save more than is customary for regular residents of that bracket, thereby exaggerating the saving propensities of the upper groups. The motivation to save, in order to provide future well-being, may well result in surprisingly similar savings ratios, at least in the broad spectrum of income brackets between the very low and the very high.

a halfway stage in our macroeconomic investigation. Now we want to go beyond the facts to a generalized understanding of what they mean. Thus our next task is to extract from the facts certain *relationships* that are sufficiently regular and dependable for us to build into a new dynamic model of the economy.

If we reflect back over the data we have examined, one primary conclusion comes to mind. This is the indisputable fact that the *amount* of saving generated by the household sector depends in the first instance upon the income enjoyed by the household sector. Despite the stability of the savings ratio, we have seen that the dollar volume of saving in the economy is susceptible to great variation, from negative amounts in the Great Depression to very large amounts in boom times. Now we must see if we can find a systematic connection between the changing size of income and the changing size of saving.

PROPENSITY
TO CONSUME

There is indeed such a relationship which lies at the heart of macroeconomic analysis. We call it the *consumption function* or, more formally, the *propensity to consume,* the name invented by John Maynard Keynes, who first formulated it.* What is this "propensity" to consume? It means that the relationship between consumption and income is sufficiently dependable so that we can actually *predict* how much consumption (or how much saving) will be associated with a given level of income.

TABLE 12 · 1

A PROPENSITY
TO CONSUME
SCHEDULE

BILLIONS OF DOLLARS		
Income	Consumption	Savings
$100	$80	$20
110	87	23
120	92	28
130	95	35
140	97	43

We base such predictions on a *schedule* that enables us to see the income-consumption relationship over a considerable range of variation. Table 12-1 is such a schedule, a purely hypothetical one, for us to examine.

One could imagine, of course, innumerable different consumption schedules; in one society a given income might be accompanied by a much higher propensity to consume (or propensity to save) than in

*The name, incidentally, is pronounced "Kanes," not "Keenes."

another. But the basic hypothesis of Keynes—a hypothesis amply confirmed by research—was that the consumption schedule in all modern industrial societies had a particular basic configuration, despite these variations. The propensity to consume, said Keynes, reflected the fact that on the average, men tended to increase their consumption as their incomes rose, but not by as much as their income. In other words, as the incomes of individuals rose, so did both their consumption *and their savings.*

Note that Keynes did not say that the proportion of saving rose. We have seen how involved is the dynamic determination of savings ratios. Keynes merely suggested that the *amount* of saving would rise as income rose—or to put it conversely again, that families would not use *all* their increases in income for consumption purposes alone. It is well to remember that these conclusions hold in going down the schedule as well as up. Keynes' basic "law" implies that when there is a decrease in income, there will be some decrease in the *amount of saving,* or that a family will not absorb a fall in its income entirely by contracting its consumption.

What does the consumption schedule look like in the United States? We will come to that shortly. First, however, let us fill in our understanding of the terms we will need for our generalized study.

The consumption schedule gives us two ways of measuring the fundamental economic relationship of income and saving. One way is simply to take any given level of income and to compute the percentage relation of consumption to that income. This gives us the *average propensity to consume.* In Table 12-2, using the same hypothetical schedule as before, we make this computation.

The average propensity to consume, in other words, tells us how a society at any given moment divides its total income between consumption and saving. It is thus a kind of measure of long-run savings behavior, for the ratios in which households divide their income between saving and consuming reflect established habits and, as we have seen, do not ordinarily change rapidly.

BILLIONS OF DOLLARS		
Income	Consumption	Consumption divided by income (Average propensity to consume)
$100	$80	.80
110	87	.79
120	92	.77
130	95	.73
140	97	.69

TABLE 12 · 2

**CALCULATION
OF THE
AVERAGE
PROPENSITY
TO CONSUME**

TABLE 12 · 3

CALCULATION OF THE MARGINAL PROPENSITY TO CONSUME

		BILLIONS OF DOLLARS		Marginal propensity to consume = Change in consumption ÷ change in income
Income	Consumption	Change in income	Change in consumption	
$100	$80	—	—	—
110	87	$10	$7	.70
120	92	10	5	.50
130	95	10	3	.30
140	97	10	2	.20

MARGINAL PROPENSITY TO CONSUME

But we can also use our schedule to measure another very important aspect of saving behavior: the way households divide *increases* (or decreases) in income between consumption and saving. This *marginal propensity to consume* is quite different from the average propensity to consume, as the figures in Table 12-3 (still from our original hypothetical schedule) demonstrate.

Note carefully that the last column in Table 12-3 is designed to show us something quite different from the last column of the previous table. Take a given income level—say $110 billion. In Table 12-2 the average propensity to consume for that income level is .79, meaning that we will actually spend on consumption 79 per cent of our income of $110 billion. But the corresponding figure opposite $110 billion in the marginal propensity to consume table (12-3) is .70. This does *not* mean that out of our $110 billion income we somehow spend only 70 per cent, instead of 79 per cent, on consumption. It *does* mean that we spend on consumption only 70 per cent *of the $10 billion increase* that lifted us from a previous income of $100 billion to the $110 billion level. The rest of that $10 billion increase we saved.

Much of economics, in micro- as well as macroanalysis, is concerned with studying the effects of *changes* in economic life. It is precisely here that marginal concepts take on their importance. When we speak of the average propensity to consume, we relate all consumption and all income from the bottom up, so to speak, and thus we call attention to behavior covering a great variety of situations and conditions. But when we speak of the marginal propensity to consume, we are focusing only on our behavior toward *changes* in our incomes. Thus the marginal approach is invaluable, as we shall see, in dealing with the effects of short-run fluctuations in GNP.

A DIAGRAM OF THE PROPENSITY TO CONSUME

The essentially simple idea of a systematic relationship between income and consumption will play an extremely important part in the model of the economy we shall soon construct. But the relationships we have thus far defined are too vague to be of much usefulness. We want to know if we can extract from the facts of experience not only a general dependence of consumption on income, but a *fairly precise method of determining exactly how much saving will be associated with a given amount of income.*

Here we reach a place where it will help us to use diagrams and simple equations rather than words alone. So let us begin by transferring our conception of a propensity to consume schedule to a new kind of diagram directly showing the interrelation of income and consumption.

FIG. 12-5   UNITED STATES' PROPENSITY TO CONSUME, 1929–1968

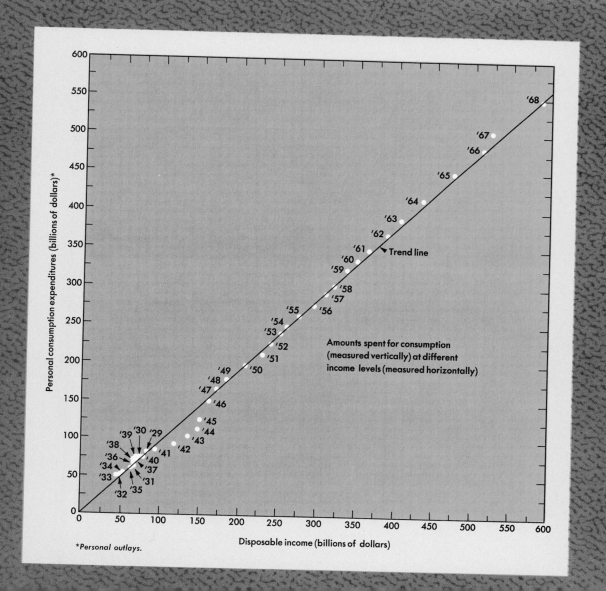

*Personal outlays.

The *scatter diagram* (Fig. 12-5) on page 233 shows precisely that. Along the vertical axis on the left we have marked off intervals to measure total consumer expenditure in billions of dollars; along the horizontal axis on the bottom we measure disposable personal income, also in billions of dollars. The dots tell us, for the year that the numerals indicate, how large consumption and income were. For instance, if we take the dot for 1966 and look directly below it to the horizontal axis, we can see that disposable personal income for that year was roughly $510 billion. The same dot measured against the vertical consumption axis tells us that consumption for 1966 was a little more than $475 billion. If we now divide the figure for consumption by that for income, we get a value of 93.1 per cent for our propensity to consume. If we subtract that from 100, our propensity to save must have been 6.9 per cent.*

Returning to the diagram itself, we notice that the black line which "fits" the trend of the dots does not go evenly from corner to corner. If it did, it would mean that each amount of income was matched by an *equal* amount of consumption—in other words, that there was no saving. Instead, the line leans slighly downward, indicating that as income goes higher, consumption also increases, but not by quite as much.

Does the chart also show us our marginal propensity to consume? Not really. As we know, our short-run savings propensities are higher than our long-run propensities. This chart shows our "settled" position, from year to year, after the long-run, upward drift of spending has washed out our marginal (short-run) savings behavior.

Nevertheless, if we look at the movement from one dot to the next, we get some notion of the short-run forces at work. During the war years, for instance, as the result of a shortage of many consumer goods and a general exhortation to save, the average propensity to consume was unusually low. That is why the dots during those years form a bulge below the main trend line. After the war, we can also see that the marginal propensity to consume must have been very high. As a matter of fact, for a few years, consumption actually rose faster than income, as people used their wartime savings to buy things that were unavailable during the war. Between 1946 and 1947, for example, disposable income rose by some $9.8 billion, but personal outlays rose by almost $18 billion! By 1950, however, the consumption-income relationship was back to virtually the same ratio as during the 1930's.

PROPENSITY
TO CONSUME,
IN SIMPLE
MATHEMATICS

There is another way of reducing to shorthand clarity the propensity to consume idea, particularly for those who find simple mathematics an expressive language. (Even those who do not should try to follow

---

*It is difficult to read figures accurately from a graph. The actual values are: disposable income, $512 billion; consumption, $478 billion; average propensity to consume, 93.4 per cent.

the very simple formulas below, if only because we shall often use the letters as abbreviations in our subsequent chapters.)

We begin by giving letters to the words we use again and again.

$$C = \text{consumption}$$
$$I = \text{investment}$$
$$S = \text{saving}$$
$$Y = \text{income}$$

Finally, we use the symbol $f(\ )$ to express the idea of *relationship*. Read it "function of (whatever is included in the parentheses)."

Now when we talk of $C = f(Y)$, we read it aloud as "consumption is a function of income." What this means is that consumption is related to income in some manner that can be described by a mathematical relationship.

What kind of relationship? Highly sophisticated and complex formulas have been tried to "fit" the values of C and Y. Their economics and their mathematics both are beyond the scope of this book. But we can at least get a clearer idea of what it means to devise a *consumption function* by trying to make a very simple one ourselves. If we look at Fig. 12-5 on p. 233, we can see that during the Depression years, at very low levels of income, around $50 billion, consumption was just as large as income itself. (In some years it was actually bigger; as we have seen, there was net dissaving in 1933.) Hence, we might hypothesize that a consumption function for the United States might have a fixed value representing this "bottom," plus some regular fraction designating the amount of income that would be saved for all income over that amount. Furthermore, recalling the stability of the savings ratio of about 6 per cent in the postwar years, we might hypothesize that we will consume 94 per cent of all income over the "bottom."

Such a formula would yield roughly accurate results. For 1968, for instance, it would predict that total consumption would equal $50 billion plus 94 per cent of all disposable income over $50 billion. This gives us a figure of $557 billion for consumption in 1966—less than 2 per cent off from the actual figure of $548 billion.*

---

*For those who are at home in simple algebra, we can generalize our results. We begin with a simple hypothetical formulation of the consumption function as follows:

$C = Y_0 + c\,(Y - Y_0)$, where
$C = \text{consumption}$
$Y_0 = $ the value of disposable income at the "bottom" (where $Y = C$)
$c = $ long-run ratio of C to Y, and
$Y = $ current value of disposable income
Substituting values for the United States in 1968, we get
$Y_0 = \$50$ billion
$c = .94$
$Y = \$589$ billion. Thus,
$C = \$50 + .94\,(589 - 50) = 556.6$

Let the reader be warned, however, that devising a reliable consumption function is much more difficult than this simple and uncritical test would indicate. In a model of the economy that is currently being studied at the University of Michigan, for example, it takes 13 equations to represent the various components of consumption. One equation, concerned solely with predicting the demand for automobiles, depends on only *part* of disposable personal income—the portion received as cash earnings and not as transfer payments, etc.—and on factors such as the number of cars on the road, the average age of the national fleet of cars, the size of consumers' assets, and still other variables.

Thus the process of translating economics into *econometrics*—that is, of finding ways to represent abstract theoretical relationships in terms of specific empirical relations—is a very difficult one. Nonetheless, even our simple example gives one an idea of what the economist and the econometrist hope to find: a precise way of expressing functional interrelations (like those between consumption and income), so that the relations will be useful in making predictions.

PASSIVITY OF
CONSUMPTION

Throughout this chapter we have talked of the dynamics of consuming and saving. Now it is important that we recall the main conclusion of our analysis, *the essential passivity of consumption as an economic process.* Consumption spending, we will recall, is a function of income. This means it is a *dependent* variable in the economic process, a factor that is acted *on,* but that does not itself generate spontaneous action.

To be sure, it is well to qualify this assertion. We have earlier paid special attention to the long-term stability of the savings ratio and pointed out that one cause of this stability was a general movement of all households toward consumption as their incomes grew. This dynamic, although slow-acting, behavioral trend has exerted a strong background force on the trend of the economy. Then, too, there have been occasions, the most famous being the years just following World War II, when consumption seemed to generate its own momentum and—as we have seen—raced out ahead of income. But this was a period when wants were intense, following wartime shortages, and when huge amounts of wartime savings were available to translate those wants into action. During the normal course of things, no matter how intense "wants" may be, consumers ordinarily lack the spendable cash to translate their desires into effective demand.

This highlights an extremely important point. Wants and appetites *alone* do not drive the economy upward; if they did, we should experience a more impelling demand in depressions, when people are hungry, than in booms, when they are well off. Hence the futility of those who urge the cure of depressions by suggesting that consumers should buy more! There is nothing consumers would rather do than buy more, if only they could. Let us not forget, furthermore, that consumers are at all times being cajoled and exhorted to increase their expenditures by the multibillion dollar pressures exerted by the advertising industry.

The trouble is, however, that consumers cannot buy more unless they have more incomes to buy with. It is true, of course, that for short periods they can borrow or they may temporarily sharply reduce their rate of savings; but each household's borrowing capacity or accumulated savings are limited, so that once these bursts are over, the steady habitual ways of saving and spending are apt to reassert themselves.

Thus it is clear that in considering the consumer sector we study a part of the economy that, however ultimately important, is not in itself the source of major changes in activity. Consumption mirrors and, as we shall see, can magnify disturbances elsewhere in the economy, but it does not initiate the greater part of our economic fortunes or misfortunes. For that, we must turn to the two remaining great sectors, where we shall find the driving elements of our economic mechanism.

SUMMARY

1. Consumption is the largest sector of economic activity, and accordingly the largest absolute source of demand within the economy. Nonetheless, *consumption alone will not create enough demand to buy all of the nation's output.*

2. Consumption in absolute amounts is capable of wide fluctuations, but *the relation of consumption to disposable income is relatively stable.*

3. Over the long run (since the mid-1800's), *the fraction of disposable income that has been saved seems to have been more or less unchanged.* This has prevented the economy from facing the problem of a growing proportion of saving. In the short run, the ratio of saving to increases in income is apt to be higher than over the long run.

4. We call the relation between saving and disposable income the *consumption function.* We can represent this function (relationship) in a *schedule* showing the division of disposable income, at different levels of income, between consumption and saving.

5. The consumption schedule shows that the *amount of consumption rises as income rises, but not by as much as income.* Therefore the amount of saving also rises as income rises.

6. From the consumption schedule we can derive two ratios. One shows us the relation between the *total income* and the *total consumption* of any period. We call this the *average propensity to consume.* The other shows us the relationship between the *change in income and the change in consumption* between two periods. This is called the *marginal propensity to consume.*

7. The average propensity to consume shows us how people behave with regard to consumption and saving over the *long run.* The marginal propensity to consume shows us how they behave over the *short run.*

8. The common abbreviations used in economics are: *C* for consumption, *I* for investment, *S* for saving and *Y* for income (note that *I* is used only for investment). We also use the symbol *f* followed by parentheses ( ) to express relationships. It is read "function of."

9. Consumption is generally regarded as a *passive economic force*, rather than an initiating active one. It is acted on by changes in income. Thus we generalize the force of consumption by saying that it is a *function of income:* $C = f(Y)$.

1. What are the main components of consumption? Why are some of these components more dynamic than others?

2. "The reason we have depressions is that consumption isn't big enough to buy the output of all our factories." What is wrong with this statement?

3. What do you think accounts for the relative stability of the savings ratio over the long run? Would you expect the savings ratio in the short run to be relatively stable? Why or why not?

4. What is meant by the consumption function? Could we also speak of a savings function? What would be the relation between the two?

5. Suppose that a given family had an income of $8,000 and saved $400. What would be its average propensity to consume? Could you tell from this information what its marginal propensity to consume was?

6. Suppose the same family now increased its income to $9,000 and its saving to $500. What is its new average propensity to consume? Can you figure out the family's marginal propensity to consume?

7. Draw a scatter diagram to show the following:

Family income	Savings
$4,000	$ 0
5,000	50
6,000	150
7,000	300
8,000	500

From the figures above, calculate the average propensity to consume at each level of income. Can you calculate the marginal propensity to consume for each jump in income?

8. How do you read $S = f(Y)$? From what you know of the propensity to consume, how would you describe the relation of S to Y?

9. Why can't we cure depressions by urging people to go out and spend?

THE INVESTMENT SECTOR

13

Consumption is activity everyone knows as an experienced economic actor in his own right; investing, on the other hand, is an economy activity foreign to most of us. For investing, in the context of macroeconomic analysis, has very little to do with the kind of "investing" familiar to us in the selection of stocks or bonds as personal assets. Investing, as the economist sees it, is an activity that uses the resources of the community to maintain or add to its stock of capital wealth.

Now this may or may not coincide with the purchase of a security. When we buy an ordinary stock or bond, we usually buy it from someone who has previously owned it, and therefore our personal act of "investment" becomes, in the economic view of things, merely a *transfer* of claims without any direct bearing on the creation of new wealth. A pays B cash and takes his General Manufacturing stock; B takes A's cash and doubtless uses it to buy stock from C; but the transactions between A and B and C in no way alter the actual amount of real capital in the economy. Only when we buy *newly issued* shares or bonds, and then only when their proceeds are directly allocated to new equipment or plant, does our act of personal financial investment result in the addition of wealth to the community. In that case, A buys his stock directly (or through an investment banker) from General Manufacturing itself, and not from B. A's cash can now be spent for new capital goods, as presumably it will be.

Thus investment, as economists see it, is a little-known form of activity for the great majority of us. This is true not only because real investment is not the same as personal financial investment, but because the real investors of the nation usually act on behalf of an institution other than the familiar one of the household. The unit of behavior in the world of investment is typically the business *firm,* just as in the world of consumption it is the household. Boards of directors, chief executives, or small-business proprietors are the persons who decide whether or not to devote business cash to the construction of new facilities or to the addition of inventory; and this decision, as we shall see, is very different in character and motivation from the decisions familiar to us as members of the household sector.

THE INVESTMENT SECTOR IN PROFILE

Before we begin an investigation into the dynamics of investment decisions, however, let us gain a quick acquaintance with the sector as a whole, much as we did with the consumption sector.

Figure 13-1 gives a first general impression of the investment sector in a recent year. Note that the main source of gross private domestic investment expenditure is the retained earnings of business; that is, the expenditures come from depreciation accruals or from profits that have been kept in the business. However, as the next bar shows, gross investment *expenditures* are considerably larger than retained earnings. The difference represents funds that business obtains in several ways.

1. It may draw on cash (or securities) accumulated out of retained earnings or depreciation accruals of *previous* years.

2. It may obtain savings from the household sector by direct borrowing or by sale of new issues of shares of stock or indirectly via insurance companies or savings banks or pension funds, and so on.

3. It may borrow from commercial banks.

The last of these sources of funds we will not fully understand until we reach Chapter 16, when we study the money mechanism. But our chart enables us to see that most gross investment is financed by business itself from its *internal* sources—retained earnings plus depreciation accruals—and that external sources play only a secondary role. In particular, this is true of new stock issues which, during the 1960's, raised only some 3 to 8 per cent of the funds spent by the business sector.

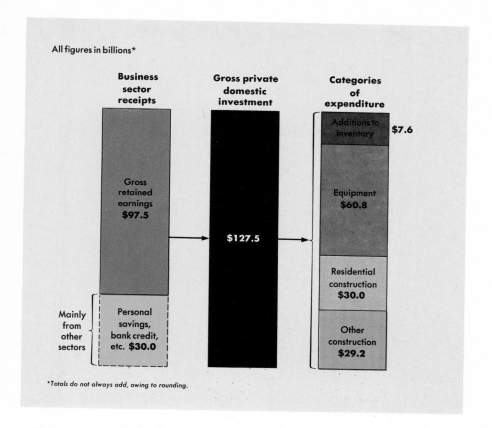

FIG. 13-1

**BUSINESS
SECTOR, 1968**

All figures in billions*

Business sector receipts

Gross private domestic investment

Categories of expenditure

Gross retained earnings **$97.5**

$127.5

Additions to inventory **$7.6**

Equipment **$60.8**

Residential construction **$30.0**

Other construction **$29.2**

Mainly from other sectors

Personal savings, bank credit, etc. **$30.0**

Totals do not always add, owing to rounding.

From the total funds at its disposal, the business sector now renews its worn-out capital and adds new capital. Let us say a word concerning some of the main categories of investment expenditure.

CATEGORIES OF INVESTMENT

1. *Inventories.*

At the top of our bar we note an item of $7.6 billion for *additions to inventory.* Note that this figure does not represent total inventories, but only *changes* in inventories, upwards or downwards. If there had been no change in inventory over the year, the item would have been zero, even if existing inventories were huge. Why? Because those huge inventories would have been included in the investment expenditure flow of *previous* years when they were built up.

Additions to inventories are capital, but they need not be additions to capital *goods.* Indeed, they are likely to include farm stocks, consumers goods, and other items of all kinds. Of course, these are goods held by business, and not by consumers. But that is the very point. We count inventory additions as net investment because they are output that has been produced but that has not been consumed. In another year, if these goods pass from the hands of business into consumers' hands, and inventories decline, we will have a negative figure for net inventory investment. This will mean, just as it appears, that we are consuming goods faster than we are producing them—that we are disinvesting.

Investments in inventory are particularly significant for one reason. Alone among the investment categories, inventories can be *rapidly* used up as well as increased. A positive figure for one year or even one calendar quarter can quickly turn into a negative figure the next. *This means that expenditures for inventory are usually the most volatile element of any in gross national product.* A glance at Fig. 13-2 shows how rapidly inventory spending can change. In the second quarter of 1960, we were *disinvesting* in inventories at an annual rate of almost $5 billion. Two

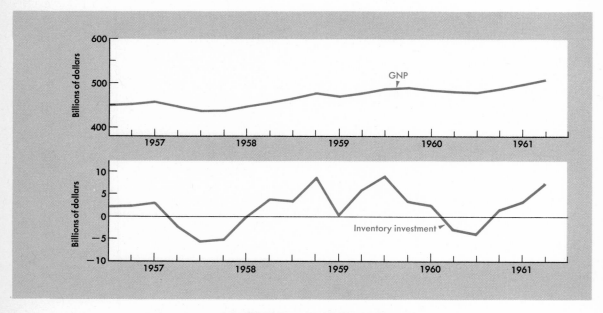

FIG. 13-2 **INVENTORY SWINGS AND GNP**

quarters later, we were building up inventories—*investing* in inventories—by roughly the same amount. Thus, within a span of six months, there was a swing of almost $10 billion in spending. And as the chart shows, this was by no means a unique occurrence.

As we shall see more clearly later, this volatility of investment has a great deal of significance for business conditions. Note that while inventories are being built up, they serve as an offset to saving—that is, some of the resources released from consumption are used by business firms to build up stocks of inventory capital. But when inventories are being "worked off," this avenue for closing the demand gap is no longer available. As we would expect, this can give rise to serious economic troubles.

2. Equipment.

The next item in our bar is more familiar: $60.8 billion for *equipment*. Here we find expenditures for goods of a varied sort—lathes, trucks, generators, computers, office typewriters.* The total includes both new equipment and replacement equipment, and we need a word of caution here. Exactly what does it mean to "replace" a given item of equipment? Suppose we have a textile loom that cost $100,000 and that is now on its last legs. Is the loom "replaced" by spending another $100,000, regardless of what kind of machine the money will buy? Suppose loom prices have gone up and $100,000 no longer buys a loom of the same capacity? Or suppose that prices have remained steady; but that owing to technological advance, $100,000 now buys a loom of double the old capacity. Such questions make the definition of "replacement" an accountant's headache and an economist's nightmare. We need not involve ourselves deeper in the question, but we should note the complexities introduced into a seemingly simple matter once we leave the changeless world of a stationary flow and enter the world of invention and innovation.

3. Construction.

Our next section on the diagrammatic bar is total *residential construction*. Why do we include this item of $30 billion in the investment sector when most of it is represented by new houses that householders buy for their own use?

The answer is that most houses are built by business firms (such as contractors and developers) who put up the houses *before* they are sold. Thus the original expenditures involved in building houses typically come from businessmen, not from households. Later, when the householder buys a house, he takes possession of an *existing* asset, and his expenditure does not pump new incomes out into the economy, but only repays the contractor who *did* pump new incomes out.

Actually this is a somewhat arbitrary definition, since, after all, businessmen own all output before consumers buy it. However, in macroeconomics, our goal is to understand growth and fluctuation in growth, and we define our terms to serve that purpose. Residential housing "behaves" very much like other items of construction, and it simplifies our understanding of the forces at work in the economy if we classify it as an investment expenditure rather than a consumer expenditure.

---

*But *not* typewriters bought by consumers. Thus the same good can be classified as a consumption item or an investment item depending on the use to which it is put.

The last item on the bar, $29.2 billion of *other construction,* is largely made up of the "plant" in "plant and equipment"—factories and stores and private office buildings and warehouses. (It does not, however, include public construction such as roads, dams, harbors, or public buildings, all of which are picked up under government purchases.) It is interesting to note that the building of structures, as represented by the total of residential construction plus other private construction, accounts for over half of all investment expenditure, and this total would be further swelled if public construction were included herein. This accords with the dominant role of structures in the panorama of national wealth we first encountered in Chapter 9. It tells us, too, that swings in construction expenditure can be a major lever for economic change.

INVESTMENT IN HISTORIC PERSPECTIVE

With this introduction behind us, let us take a look at the flow of investment, not over a single year, but over many years.

In Fig. 13-3, several things spring to our notice. Clearly, investment

FIG. 13-3   GROSS PRIVATE DOMESTIC INVESTMENT, 1929–1968

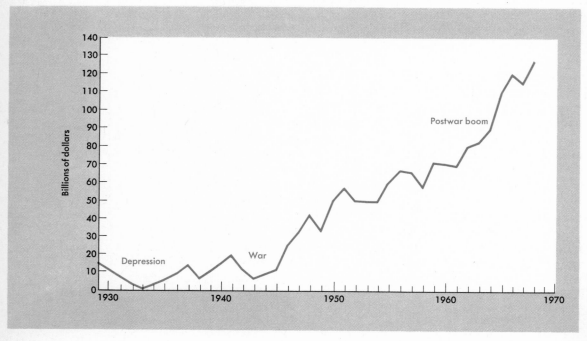

is not nearly so smooth an unperturbed flow of spending as consumption. Note that gross investment in the depths of the Depression virtually disappeared—that we almost failed to *maintain*, much less add to, our stock of wealth. (Net investment was, in fact, a negative figure for several years.) Note also how investment was reduced during the war years as private capital formation was deliberately limited through government allocations.

Two important conclusions emerge from this examination of investment spending:

First, as we have already seen, investment spending contains a component—net additions to inventory—that is capable of drastic, sudden shifts. This accounts for much of the wavelike movement of the total flow of investment expenditure.

Second, investment spending as a whole is capable of more or less total collapses, of a severity and degree that are never to be found in consumption.

The prime example of such a collapse was, of course, the Great Depression. From 1929 to 1933, while consumption fell by 41 per cent, investment fell by *91 per cent*, as we can see in Fig. 13-3. Similarly, whereas consumption rose by a little more than half from 1933 to 1940, investment in the same period rose by *nine times*.

This potential for collapse or spectacular boom always makes investment a source of special concern in the economic picture. But even the tendency toward inventory fluctuations, or toward milder declines in other capital expenditures, is sufficient to identify investment as a prime source of economic instability. As we have said before, there is often a tendency among noneconomists to equate all buying in the economy with consumer buying. Let us never lose sight of the fact that the maintenance of, and addition to, capital is also a part of GNP spending and that a considerable part of the labor force depends for its livelihood on the making of investment goods. Remember, from Chapter 7, that at the bottom of the Great Depression in 1933, it was estimated that one-third of total unemployment was directly associated with the shrinkage in the capital goods industry.

We shall want to look more closely into the reasons for the sensitivity of investment spending. But first a question must surely have occurred to the reader. For all its susceptibility to change, the investment sector is, after all, a fairly small sector. In 1968, total expenditures for gross private domestic investment came to less than $\frac{1}{6}$ of GNP, and the normal year-to-year variation in investment spending in the 1950's and 1960's was only about $5 billion to $10 billion, or 1 to 2 per cent of GNP. To devote so much time to such small fluctuations seems a disproportionate emphasis. How could so small a tail as investment wag so large a dog as GNP?

THE MULTIPLIER

The answer—as we may also recall from our historical survey of the Depression era—lies in a relationship of economic activities known as the *multiplier*. The multiplier describes the fact that *additions to spending (or diminutions in spending) have an impact on income that is greater than the original increase or decrease in spending itself.* In other words, even small increments in spending can *multiply* their effects (whence the name).

It is not difficult to understand the general idea of the multiplier. Suppose that we have an island community whose economy is in a perfect circular flow, unchanging from year to year. Next, let us introduce the stimulus of a new investment expenditure in the form of a stranger who arrives from another island (with a supply of acceptable money) and who proceeds to build a house. This immediately increases the islanders' incomes. In our case, we will assume that our stranger spends $1,000 on wages for construction workers, and we will ignore all other expenditures he may make. (We also make the assumption that these workers were previously unemployed, so that our stranger is not merely taking them from some other task.)

Now the construction workers, who have had their incomes increased by $1,000, are very unlikely to sit on this money. As we know from our study of the marginal propensity to consume, they are apt to save some of the increase (and they may have to pay some to the government as income taxes), but the rest they will spend on additional consumption goods. Let us suppose that they save 10 per cent and pay taxes of 20 per cent on the $1,000 they get. They will then have $700 left over to spend for additional consumer goods and services.

But this is not an end to it. The sellers of these goods and services will now have received $700 over and above their former incomes, and they, too, will be certain to spend a considerable amount of their new income. If we assume that their family spending patterns (and their tax brackets) are the same as the construction workers, they will also spend 70 per cent of their new incomes, or $490. And now the wheel takes another turn, as still *another* group receives new income and spends a fraction of it—in turn.

CONTINUING IMPACT OF RESPENDING

If our stranger now departed as mysteriously as he came, we would have to describe the economic impact of his investment as constituting a single "bulge" of income that gradually disappeared. The bulge would consist of the original $1,000, the secondary $700, the tertiary $490, and so on. If everyone continued to spend 70 per cent of his new income, after ten rounds all that would remain by way of new spending traceable to the original $1,000 would be about $38. Soon, the impact of the new investment on incomes would have virtually disappeared.

But now let us suppose that after our visitor builds his house and leaves, another visitor arrives to build another house. This time, in other words, we assume that the level of investment spending *continues* at the higher level to which it was raised by the first expenditure for a new house. We can see that the second house will set into motion precisely the same repercussive effects as did the first, and that the new series of respendings will be added to the dwindling echoes of the original injection of incomes.

FIG. 13-4

THE MULTIPLIER

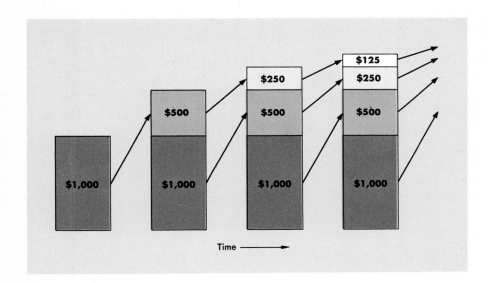

In Fig. 13-4, we can trace this effect. The succession of white bars at the bottom of the graph stands for the continuing injections of $1,000 as new houses are steadily built. (Note that this means the level of new investment is only being maintained, not that it is rising.) Each of these white bars now generates a series of secondary, tertiary, etc., bars that represent the respending of income after taxes and savings. In our example we have assumed that the respending fraction is 50 per cent.

Our diagram shows us two very important things.

1. *A steady flow of new investment generates an equally steady but larger flow of total incomes.*

It is very important to note that the incomes generated by respending are just as permanent as those due to the flow of investment itself.

2. *The rise in income due to a continuing flow of new investment gradually levels out.*

As the successive respending fractions become smaller, the rise in income approaches a plateau.

We can understand now that *the multiplier is the numerical relation between the initial new investment and the total increase in income.* If the initial investment is $1,000 and the total addition to income due to the respending of that $1,000 is $3,000, we have a multiplier of 3; if the total addition is $2,000, the multiplier is 2.

What determines how large the multiplier will be? The answer depends entirely on our marginal consumption (or, if you will, our marginal saving) habits—that is, on how much we consume (or save) out of each dollar of additional income that comes to us. Let us follow two cases below. In the first, we will assume that each recipient spends only one half of any new income that comes to him, saving the rest. In the second case, he spends three-quarters of it and saves one-quarter.

FIG. 13-5

COMPARISON OF TWO MULTIPLIERS

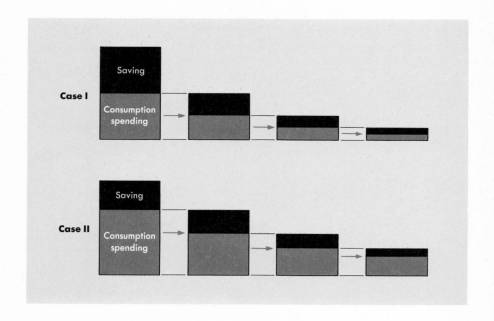

It is very clear that the amount of income that will be passed along from one receiver to the next will be much larger where the marginal propensity to consume is higher. In fact, we can see that the total amount of new incomes (the total amount of the boxes above) must be mathematically related to the proportion that is spent each time.

What is this relationship? The arithmetic is easier to figure if we use not the consumption fraction, but the *saving fraction* (the two are, of course, as intimately related as one slice of cake and the remaining cake). If we use the saving fraction, the *sum of new incomes is obtained by taking the reciprocal of* (i.e., inverting, or turning upside down) *the fraction we save.* Thus, if we save $\frac{1}{2}$ our income, the total amount of new incomes generated by respending will be $\frac{1}{2}$ inverted, or 2—twice the original increase in income. If we save $\frac{1}{4}$, it will be the reciprocal of $\frac{1}{4}$ or 4 times the original change.

We call the fraction of new income that is saved the *marginal propensity to save* (often abbreviated as mps). As we have just said, this fraction is the complement of an already familiar one, the marginal propensity to consume. If our marginal propensity to consume is 80 per cent, our marginal propensity to save must be 20 per cent; if our mpc is three-quarters, our mps must be one-quarter.

Understanding the relationship between the marginal propensity to save and the size of the resulting respending fractions allows us to state a very simple (but very important) formula for the multiplier:

change in income = multiplier × change in investment

Since we have just learned that the multiplier is determined by the reciprocal of the marginal propensity to save, we can write:

$$\text{multiplier} = \frac{1}{\text{mps}}$$

If we now use the symbols we are familiar with, plus a Greek letter Δ, delta, that means "increase in," we can write the important economic relationship above as follows:

$$\Delta Y = \frac{1}{\text{mps}} \times \Delta I$$

Thus, if our mps is $\frac{1}{4}$ (meaning, let us not forget, that we save a quarter of increases in income and respend the rest), then an increase in investment of $1 billion will lead to a total increase in incomes of $4 billion ($1 billion $\times \dfrac{1}{1/4} = $4 billion). Note that the mps is a complex or *double* fraction—it is $\dfrac{1}{1/4}$ and *not* $\frac{1}{4}$. If the mps is $\frac{1}{10}$, $1 billion gives rise to incomes of $10 billion; if the mps is 50 percent, the billion will multiply to $2 billion. And if mps is 1? This means that the entire increase in income is unspent, that our island construction workers tuck away (or find taxed away) their entire newly earned pay. In that case, the multiplier will be 1 also, and the impact of the new investment on the island economy will be no more than the $1,000 earned by the construction workers in the first place.

The importance of the size of the marginal savings ratio in determining the effect that additional investment will have on income is thus apparent. Now, however, we must pass from the simple example of our island economy to the more complex behavioral patterns and institutional arrangements of real life. The average propensity to save (the ratio of saving to disposable income) runs around 5 to 6 per cent. In recent years, the *marginal* propensity to save (the ratio of additional saving to increases in income) figured over the period of a year has not departed very much from this figure. If this is the case, then, following our analysis, the multiplier would be very high. If mps were even as much as 10 per cent of income, a change in investment of $1 billion would bring a $10 billion change in income. If mps were nearer 5 per cent—the approximate level of the average propensity to save—a change of $1 billion would bring a swing of $20 billion. Were this the case, the economy would be subject to the most violent disturbances whenever the level of spending shifted.

In fact, however, the impact of the multiplier is greatly reduced because the successive rounds of spending are damped by factors other than personal saving. One of them we have already introduced in our imaginary island economy. This is the tendency of *government taxation* to "mop up" a fraction of income as it passes from hand to hand. This mopping-up effect of taxation is in actuality much larger than that of saving. For every dollar of change in income, federal taxes will take up to 30 cents, and state and local taxes another 6 cents, compared with less than 5 cents that go into saving.

Another dampener is the tendency of respending to swell *business savings* as well as personal incomes. Of each dollar of new spending, perhaps 10 cents goes into business profits, and this sum is typically saved, at least for a time, rather than immediately respent.

Still another source of dampening is the tendency of consumers and businesses to increase purchases from abroad as their incomes rise. These rising *imports* divert 3 to 4 per cent of new spending to foreign nations and accordingly reduce the successive impact of each round of expenditure.

All these withdrawals from the respending cycle are called *leakages,* and the total effect of all leakages together (personal savings, business savings, taxes, and imports) is to reduce the over-all impact of the multiplier from an impossibly large figure to a very manageable one. The combined effect of all leakages brings the actual multiplier in the United States in the 1960's to around 2 for a period of about a year.*

To be sure—and this is very important—all these leakages *can* return to the income stream. Household saving can be turned into capital

---

*In dealing with the multiplier equation ($\Delta Y = \dfrac{1}{\text{mps}} \times \Delta I$), we can interpret mps to mean the total withdrawal from spending due to all leakages. This brings mps to around $\frac{1}{2}$, and gives us a multiplier of 2.

It is interesting to note that the leakages all tend to increase somewhat in boom times and to decline in recessions, which results in a slightly larger multiplier in bad times than in good.

formation; business profits can be invested; tax receipts can be disbursed in government spending programs; and purchases from foreign sellers can be returned as purchases *by* foreigners. What is at stake here is the regularity and reliability with which these circuits will be closed. In the case of ordinary income going to a household, we can count with considerable assurance on a "return expenditure" of consumption. In the case of the other recipients of funds, the assurance is much less; hence we count their receipts as money that has leaked out of the expenditure flow, for the time being.

The multiplier, with its important magnifying action, rests at the very center of our understanding of economic fluctuations. Not only does it explain how relatively small stimuli can exert considerable upward pushes, but it also makes much clearer than before how the failure to offset a small savings gap can snowball into a serious fall in income and employment.

For just as additional income is respent to create still further new income, a loss in income will not stop with the affected households. On the contrary, as families lose income, they cut down on their spending, although the behavior pattern of the propensity to consume schedule suggests that they will not cut their consumption by as much as their loss in income. Yet each reduction in consumption, large or small, lessens to that extent the income or receipts of some other household or firm.

We have already noted that personal savings alone do not determine the full impact of the multiplier. This is even more fortunate on the way down than on the way up. If the size of the multiplier were solely dependent on the marginal propensity to save, an original fall in spending would result in a catastrophic contraction of consumption through the economy. But the leakages that cushion the upward pressure of the multiplier also cushion its downward effect. As spending falls, business savings (profits) fall, tax receipts dwindle, and the flow of imports declines.

All of these leakages now work in the direction of mitigating the repercussions of the original fall in spending. The fall in business profits means that less will be saved by business and thus less withdrawn from respending; the decline in taxes means that more money will be left to consumers; and the drop in imports similarly releases additional spending power for the domestic market. Thus, just as the various leakages pulled money away from consumption on the way up, on the way down they lessen their siphoning effect and in this way restore purchasing power to consumers' hands. As a result, in the downward direction as in the upward, the actual impact of the multiplier is about 2, so that a fall in investment of, say, $5 billion will lower GNP by $10 billion.

Even with a reduced figure, we can now understand how a relatively small change in investment can magnify its impact on GNP. If the typical year-to-year change in investment is around $5 to $10 billion, a multiplier of 2 will produce a change in GNP of $10 to $20 billion, by no means a negligible figure. In addition, as we shall shortly see, the multiplier may set up repercussions that feed back onto investment. But more of that momentarily. First let us make two final points in regard to the multiplier.

1. *Other multipliers.*

We have talked of the multiplier in connection with changes in investment spending. *But we must also realize that any change in any spending has a multiplier effect.* An increase in foreigners' purchases of our exports has a multiplier effect, as does an increase in government spending or a decrease in taxes, or a spontaneous increase in consumption itself due to, say, a drop in the propensity to save. Any stimulus to the economy is thus not confined to its original impact, but gives a series of successive pushes to the system until it has finally been absorbed in leakages. We shall come back to this important fact in our next chapter.

2. *Idle resources.*

Finally, there is a very important proviso to recognize, although we will not study its full significance until Chapter 17. This is the important difference between an economy with idle resources—unemployed labor or unused machines or land—and one without them.

For *it is only when we have idle resources that the responding impetus of the multiplier is useful.* Then each round of new expenditure can bring idle resources into use, creating not only new money incomes but *new production and employment.* The situation is considerably different when there are no, or few, idle men or machines. Then the expenditure rounds of the multiplier bring higher money incomes, but these are not matched by the increased output.

In both cases, the multiplier exerts its leverage, bringing about an increase in total expenditure larger than the original injection of new spending. In the case without idle resources, however, the results are solely *inflationary,* as the increased spending results in higher incomes and higher prices, but not in higher output. In the case where idle resources exist, we can avoid this mere "money" multiplication and enjoy a rise in output as a result of our increased spending. Indeed, we can even speak of the *employment multiplier* in situations where there is considerable unemployment, meaning by this the total increase in employment brought about by a given increase in spending. We shall return in subsequent chapters to a fuller scrutiny of the difference between the case of idle and of fully employed resources, but we must bear the distinction in mind henceforth.

1. The investment sector is made up, not of households and their activities, but of *business firms adding to their capital assets.* By and large, these additions to business capital are financed out of *internal funds* (retained earnings and depreciation accruals) rather than from external sources (borrowing or new equities). The main categories of investment expenditure are additions to inventory, new equipment, residential housing, and other construction.

2. The main characteristic of all investment expenditure is its *potential instability.* In times of serious recession, net investment can virtually cease. Even in ordinary times, inventory investment is capable of drastic changes.

3. Changes in investment (or in any other kind of spending) are given larger economic impact because of the *multiplier effect.* This arises because incomes received from a new investment (or any other source) are *partly respent,* giving rise to additional new incomes which, in turn, are respent.

4. A single "burst" of investment creates a bulge in incomes which disappears over time; but a *continuing level of new investment creates a continuing higher level of new incomes.*

5. The size of the multiplier depends on the fraction of additional income spent for consumption by each new recipient. *The more the spending* (or the less the saving) *the greater will be the multiplier.*

6. *We calculate the multiplier by taking the reciprocal of the marginal propensity to save.* This gives us the important formula:

$$\Delta Y = \frac{1}{mps} \times \Delta I \ (\text{change in income} = \text{multiplier} \times \text{change in investment})$$

7. The *size of mps is determined by leakages.* There are four main leakages:
   - Saving
   - Taxation
   - Business profits
   - Imports

   Total leakages in the U.S. amount to about one-half of increases in income. Therefore the U.S. multiplier is about 2.

8. *Each of these leakages takes money out of the "automatic" respending circuit of consumption.* Money going into leakages *can* return to the economy via additional investment, but it does not do so as reliably as money that stays in the consumption flow.

9. Magnifying the effects on income of a fall in investment, the *multiplier works downward,* as well as upward.

10. The multiplier will have very different economic effects, depending on whether or not the economy is *fully employed.*

1. If you buy a share of stock on the New York Stock Exchange, does that always create new capital? Why, or why not?

2. Why are additions to inventory so much more liable to rapid fluctuation than other kinds of investment?

3. Why is investment capable of much more complete collapse than consumption?

4. Draw a diagram showing the multiplier effect of $1,000 expenditure when the marginal propensity to save is one-tenth. Draw a second diagram, showing the effect when the marginal propensity to consume is nine-tenths. Are the diagrams the same?

5. Compare two multiplier diagrams: one where the marginal propensity to save is one-quarter; the other where it is one-third. The *larger* the saving ratio, the larger or smaller the multiplier?

6. Calculate the impact on income if investment rises by $10 billion and the multiplier is 2. If the multiplier is 3. If it is 1.

7. Income is $500 billion; investment is $50 billion. The multiplier is 2. If inventories decline by $10 billion, what happens to income?

8. Draw a diagram showing what happens to $1 billion of new investment given the following leakages: mps 10 per cent; marginal taxation 20 per cent; marginal propensity to import 5 per cent; marginal addition to business saving 15 per cent. What will be the size of the second round of spending? the third? the final total?

9. If the marginal propensity to consume is three-quarters, what is the size of the marginal propensity to save? If it is five-sixths? If it is 70 per cent?

10. What is the formula for the multiplier?

INVESTMENT
AND EQUILIBRIUM

14

We have spent some time investigating how variations in investment spending can induce powerful repercussions in the national economy. But we have not yet asked the all-important question of why the flow of capital expenditure should be variable in the first place. Nor have we understood how GNP will settle down after it has been raised or lowered by more or less investment. In this chapter, we must look into these matters—into the motives behind the investment expenditure of the firm, and into the way that changes in investment can shift GNP from one level to another.

THE MOTIVATION OF INVESTMENT

Consumption spending, let us remember, is essentially directed at the satisfaction of the person. In an increasingly affluent society, we may not be able to say that consumer expenditure is any longer solely geared to necessity, but at least it obeys the fairly constant promptings of the

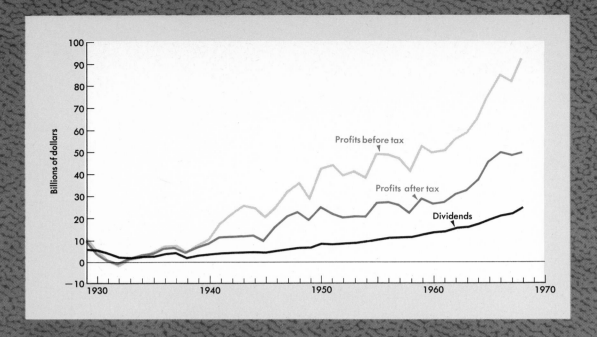

FIG. 14-1   **PROFITS, TAXES, AND DIVIDENDS**

cultural and social environment, with the result that consumer spending, in the aggregate, fluctuates relatively little, except as income fluctuates.

A quite different set of motivations drives the investment impulse. Whether the investment is for replacement of old capital or for the installation of new capital, the ruling consideration is virtually never the personal use or satisfaction that the investment yields to the owners of the firm. Instead, the touchstone of investment decisions is *profit*.

Figure 14-1 shows corporate profits since 1929, as well as their division into retained earnings, dividends, and taxes. What is strikingly apparent, of course, is the extreme fluctuation of profits between prosperity and recession. Note that corporations as a whole lost money in the depths of the Depression years, but that even in the lush postwar period, the swings from year to year have been considerable (compare 1958 and 1959).

Have corporate profits changed as a per cent of GNP? Surprisingly little. In 1929, corporate profits before tax amounted to about 10 per cent of GNP; from 1965 through 1968 about 11 per cent. Profits *after* taxes fell from some 8 per cent of GNP in 1929 to under 7 per cent over the same years. Profits after tax plus depreciation accruals remain unchanged at under 12 per cent. Corporate profits have, of course, increased sharply as a per cent of GNP from their level in the early 1900's, but this is because corporations themselves were not a dominant form of business organization until after World War I.

The chart shows us how corporate profits looked to businessmen when the books were tallied at the end of each year. But the results of his last year's operation, although very important, is not the main thing that motivates a businessman to invest. Primarily, he in interested in the profits he expects from *next year's* operations. His view is never backward, but always forward.

Note the important stress on *expectations*. One firm may be enjoying large profits on its existing plant and equipment at the moment; but if it anticipates no profits from the sale of goods that an *additional* investment would make possible, the firm will make no additions to capital. Another firm may be suffering current losses; but if it anticipates a large profit from the production of a new good, it may launch a considerable capital expenditure.

There is a sound reason for this anticipatory quality of investment decisions. Typically, the capital goods bought by investment expenditures are expected to last for years and to pay for themselves only slowly. In addition, they are often highly specialized. If capital expenditures could be recouped in a few weeks or months, or even in a matter of a year or two, or if capital goods were easily transferred from one use to another, they would not be so risky and their dependence on expectations not so great. But it is characteristic of most capital goods that they *are* durable, with life expectancies of ten or more years, and that they tend to be limited in their alternative uses, or to have no alternative uses at all. You cannot spin cloth in a steel mill or make steel in a cotton mill.

The decision to invest is thus always forward-looking. Even when the stimulus to build is felt in the present, the calculations that determine whether or not an investment will be made necessarily concern the flow of income to the firm in the future. These expectations are inherently much more volatile than the current drives and desires that guide the consumer. Expectations, whether based on guesses or forecasts, are capable of sudden and sharp reversals of a sort rare in consumption spending. Thus in its orientation to the future we find a main cause for the volatility of investment expenditures.

INDUCED AND AUTONOMOUS INVESTMENT

One kind of profit expectation, and the investment that stems from it, ties in closely with the analysis we have just made of the multiplier. This is an expectation of future profit derived from *an observed rise in current consumption spending*.

Many business firms decide to invest because they must expand their capacity to maintain a given share of a growing market. Real estate developers who build to accommodate an already visible suburban exodus, or supermarkets that build to serve a booming metropolis, or gas stations that must be built to serve a new highway, or additions to manufacturing capacity that must be made because existing facilities cannot keep up with demand—these are all examples of what we call *induced investment.*

<table>
<tr><td>

THE
ACCELERATION
PRINCIPLE

</td><td>

When rising consumption induces investment, we call the relationship the *acceleration principle* or the *accelerator.* In many ways it resembles the multiplier effect. The multiplier describes the effect that investment has on income via consumption spending; the acceleration principle describes the effect that consumption can have on income via investment spending. When consumption is rising and plant capacity is already tight, investment is likely to be induced, and this induced investment in turn will generate still *additional* incomes through the multiplier effect. Thus the multiplier effect and the acceleration principle can interact to yield even larger "secondary" impacts than either can alone. It is interesting to note that when the Council of Economic Advisers was arguing for the Kennedy tax cut before the Joint Economic Committee of the 88th Congress, it estimated that the pure multiplier effect on GNP was only a little over 2, but that the combined multiplier-accelerator effect was 3 to 4.

</td></tr>
<tr><td>

A MODEL
OF THE
ACCELERATION
PRINCIPLE

</td><td>

The acceleration principle thus helps us understand further how small increases in one sector can be magnified and spread throughout the economy. But beyond that, it enlightens us about a surprising thing. Let us discover it by imagining an industry with rising sales and fully utilized equipment and, therefore, induced investment. We will assume that our industry needs a capital equipment twice as large in dollar value as its annual volume of sales, in order to produce effectively. We also assume that 10 per cent of its capital equipment wears out and is replaced each year—that is, the average machine lasts ten years. Table 14-1 gives us a model of such an industry.

</td></tr>
</table>

In our first view of the industry, we find it in equilibrium with sales of, let us say, 100 units, capital equipment valued at 200 units, and regular replacement demand of twenty units. Now we assume that its sales rise to 120 units. To produce 120 units of goods, the firm will need (according to our assumptions) 240 units of capital. This is forty units more than it has, so it must order them. Note that its demand for capital goods now shoots from twenty units to sixty units: twenty units for replacement as before, and forty new ones. Thus investment expenditures *triple,* even though sales have risen but 20 per cent!

Now assume that in the next year sales rise further, to 130 units. How large will our firm's investment demand be? Its replacement demand

TABLE 14 · 1

Year	Sales	Existing capital	Needed capital (2 × sales)	Replacement	Induced new investment (2 × addition to sales)	Total investment
1	$100	$200	$200	$20	—	$20
2	120	200	240	20	$40	60
3	130	240	260	20	20	40
4	135	260	270	20	10	30
5	138	270	276	20	6	26
6	140	276	280	20	4	24
7	140	280	280	20	—	20
8	130	280	260	—	—	—
9	130	260	260	20	—	20

will not be larger, since its new capital will not wear out for ten years. And the amount of new capital needed to handle its new sales will be only twenty units, not forty as before. Its total investment demand has *fallen* from sixty units to forty.

What is the surprising fact here? It is that *we can have an actual fall in induced investment, though consumption is still rising!* In fact, as soon as the *rate of increase* of consumption begins to fall, *the absolute amount* of induced investment declines. Thus a slowdown in the rate of improvement in sales can cause an absolute decline in the orders sent to capital goods makers. This helps us to explain how weakness can appear in some branches of the economy while prosperity seems still to be reigning in the market at large.

Now look at what happens to our model in the eighth year, when we assume that sales slip back to 130. Our existing capital (280 units) will be greater by twenty units than our needed capital. That year the industry will have no new orders for capital goods and may not even make any replacements, since it can use its new machines in place of the discarded old ones. Its orders to capital goods makers will fall to zero, even though its level of sales is 30 per cent higher than at the beginning. The next year, however, if sales remain steady, it will again have to replace one of its old machines. Its replacement demand again jumps to 20. No wonder capital goods industries traditionally experience feast or famine years! *

There is, in addition, an extremely important point to bear in mind about the accelerator. *Its upward leverage usually takes effect only when an industry is operating at or near capacity.* When an industry is not near capacity, it is relatively simple for it to satisfy a larger demand for its goods by raising output on its underutilized equipment. Thus,

---

*Perhaps you have noticed a kind of wavelike movement in the orders for capital goods. We will return to this in Chap. 19 when we study business cycles.

unlike the multiplier, which yields its effects on output only when we have unemployed resources, the accelerator yields its effects only when we do *not* have unemployed capital. That is when induced investment is most likely to follow from increased consumption and when we are also most likely to suffer a decline in total investment, after an initial peak, once the rate of increase in consumption begins to taper off.

AUTONOMOUS INVESTMENT

Not all investment is induced by prior rises in consumption. In fact, perhaps the more significant category of investment is that undertaken in the expectation of a profit to be derived from a *new* good or a *new* way of making a good. This type of investment is usually called *autonomous* investment.

In autonomous investment decisions, prior trends in consumption have little or nothing to do with the decision to invest. This is particularly the case when new technologies provide the stimulus for investment. Then the question in the minds of the managers of the firm is whether the new product will create *new* demand for itself.

Technological advance is not, however, the only cause for autonomous investment, and therefore we cannot statistically separate autonomous from induced investment. With some economic stimuli, such as the opening of a new territory or shifts in population or population growth, the motivations of both autonomous and induced investment are undoubtedly present. Yet there is a meaningful distinction between the two, insofar as induced investment is sensitive and responsive to consumption, whereas autonomous investment is not. This means that induced investment, by its nature, is more foreseeable than autonomous investment.

At the same time, both spontaneous and induced investments are powerfully affected by the over-all investment "climate"—not alone the economic climate of confidence, the level and direction of the stock market, etc., but the political scene, international developments, and so on. Hence it is not surprising that investment becomes by far the most unpredictable of the components of GNP, and thus the key "independent" variable in any model of GNP.

THE DETERMINANTS OF INVESTMENT

The profit expectations that guide investment decisions are largely unpredictable. But there exists one guideline for investment decisions that works in a more determinable manner. This is the influence of the *rate of interest* on the investment decisions of business firms.

Typically, the rate of interest offers two guides to the investing firm. If the businessman must borrow capital, a higher rate of interest makes it more expensive to undertake an investment. For huge firms that target a return of 15 to 20 per cent on their investment projects, a change in the interest rate from 5 to 6 per cent may be negligible. But for certain kinds of investment—notably utilities and home construction—interest rates constitute an important component of the cost of investment funds. To these firms, the lower the cost of borrowed capital, the more the stimulus for investment.* The difference in *interest costs* for $1 million borrowed for twenty years at 3 per cent (instead of 4 per cent) is $200,000, by no means a negligible sum. Since construction is the largest single component of investment, the interest rate therefore becomes an important influence on the value of total capital formation.

A second guide is offered to those businessmen who are not directly seeking to borrow money for investment, but who are debating whether to invest the savings (retained earnings) of their firms. To them, the interest rate represents a standard of comparison for the returns expected from various investment projects. A businessman, looking ahead to the expected earnings of an investment, sees a series of probable returns (varying, perhaps, from year to year) stretching ahead for a more or less definite number of years into the future. He can reduce this series of expected returns to a single *rate* of return on the cost of the entire investment. This rate, which expresses the expected profitability of the investment, is called the *marginal efficiency of capital* (or the marginal efficiency of investment).

But what is the standard for an "adequate" marginal efficiency of capital? One standard is to compare this rate of expected profitability with the rate of interest.† If the marginal efficiency of capital is not higher than the rate of interest, it will hardly be worth the businessman's while to invest, since he could use his funds with less risk and at the same return by lending them out himself. The fact that his marginal efficiency of capital may be higher than the going rate of interest is no guarantee that he will invest; but if it is not higher, it is a virtual certainty that he will not invest.

*When interest rates are high, money is called "tight." This means not only that borrowers have to pay higher rates, but that banks are stricter and more selective in judging the credit worthiness of business applications for loans. Conversely, when interest rates decline, money is called "easy," meaning that it is not only cheaper, but literally easier to borrow.

† It should be noted that there is no one single thing called *the* rate of interest, but a whole complex of rates, depending on the risk differential among different loans. At any given moment, interest rates may range from 1 or 2 per cent for short-term government notes to 10 to 20 per cent for installment loans, etc. The businessman usually focuses on the range in this spectrum that represents the interest rate for bank loans to business enterprise. These, too, differ from bank to bank and from business to business, but the whole group of these rates tends to move up and down together.

We have been talking about the determining factors that ultimately affect the rate of investment, the background forces to which we must turn to account for any given level of investment spending (much as we turn to the habits of householders as the background force determining the level of consumption). We have found that these background forces for investment are not a single variable, like a propensity to consume income, but a mixture of variables: *increases in consumption that may induce investment; expected levels of profitability of new inventions, techniques, discoveries, etc.; and the marginal efficiency of capital compared with the rate of interest.*

Now we can go a step further. With a general understanding of the constellation of forces that determines investment, we can begin to understand how a particular level of output is set for the economy as a whole.

SAVING AND INVESTMENT

AN
INVESTMENT
MODEL

Let us begin as before, with a simple model; this time, a simple island economy having only two sectors: consumption and investment. We dispense with government and with the export sector for reasons of clarity in exposition. It will be easy enough to reintegrate them into the model, subsequently.

Next we establish schedules for consumption and saving at different levels of income. We have already worked with a hypothetical propensity to consume schedule, so let us merely repeat it here with a new column of figures that will represent the amount of investment spending at various levels of income.

TABLE 14 · 2

SCHEDULES OF
SAVING AND
INVESTMENT

FOR A HYPOTHETICAL ECONOMY (IN BILLIONS OF DOLLARS)			
Income	Consumption	Saving	Investment
$100	$80	$20	$28
110	87	23	28
120	92	28	28
130	95	35	28
140	97	43	28

From our previous discussion, we have seen that there is no simple functional relation between income and investment, but rather that many forces bear on the investment total. We could, for instance, imagine an investment schedule that rose with income (perhaps due to the accelerator) or one that fell because expectations turned sour. In our model, for the sake of simplicity, we have assumed a schedule of investment expenditures that remains constant at $28 billion. The subsequent analysis would be more difficult but not fundamentally different if we used a variable schedule.

If we now look at the last two columns, those for saving and investment, we can see a powerful cross play that will characterize our model economy at different levels of income, for the forces of investment and saving will not be in balance at all levels. At some levels, the propensity to save will outrun the act of purposeful investment; at others, the motivations to save will be less than the investment expenditures made by business firms. In fact, our island model shows that at only one level of income—120—will the savings and investment schedules coincide.

What does it mean when intended savings are greater than the flow of intended investment? It means that people are *trying* to save out of their given incomes a larger amount than businessmen are willing to invest. Now if we think back to the exposition of the economy in equilibrium, it will be clear what the result must be. The economy cannot maintain a closed circuit of income and expenditure if savings are larger than investment (or if investment is smaller than savings). This will simply give rise to a demand gap, the dangerous repercussions of which we have already explored.

But a similar lack of equilibrium results if intended savings are less than intended investment expenditure (or if investment spending is greater than the propensity to save). Now businessmen will be pumping out more than enough to offset the savings gap. The additional expenditures, over and above those that compensate for saving, will flow into the economy to create new incomes—and out of those new incomes, new savings.

Income will be stable, in other words, only when the flow of intended investment just compensates for the flow of intended saving. Investment and saving thus conduct a tug of war around this pivot point, driving the economy upward when intended investment exceeds the flow of intended saving; downward when it fails to offset saving.

The careful reader may have noticed that we speak of *intended* savings or of *intended* investments. This is because there is a formal balance between *all* saving and *all* investment in the economy at every instant. After all, saving and investment are only different names for the portion of economic output that is not consumed: from one point of view, this portion is "saved"; from another, it is "invested." But this strict balance between saving and investment is of no more analytic interest than the fact that both sides of a balance sheet always balance, whether a firm is making money or losing it. What matters in the determination of

GNP are the *actions* people are taking—actions leading them to try to save, or actions leading them to seek to invest. These are the activities that must be brought into balance and that will drive the economy upward or downward when they are out of balance. Meanwhile, a formal balance of saving and investment will be maintained because there will be temporary *unintended* saving (for instance, unexpected profits) or *unintended* investment (such as inventories that pile up or become depleted, not on purpose, but because business took an unexpected turn). These unintended items can provide our "balance sheet equality" of *S* and *I,* but they are important in dynamic analysis only insofar as they affect the powerful currents of our propensity to save and of our willingness to invest.

FIG. 14-2

THE 45°
INCOME LINE

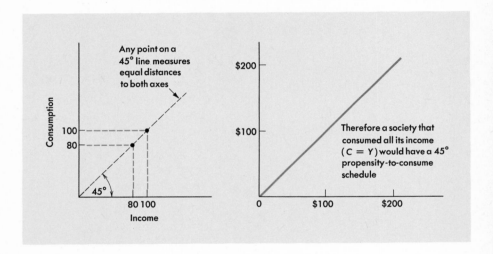

We can clarify the idea of equilibrium by reverting to a familiar figure, the propensity-to-consume diagram. Let us explore it more carefully than we have had a chance to, so far.

Suppose, for example, that a society consumed *all* its income at every level of income. In such a society, expenditures (consumption) would be exactly equal to income, and a line showing the relation of consumption to income would therefore lie exactly on the 45° "income line." The two diagrams in Fig. 14-2 should make this clear.

As we know, however, most societies do not consume an amount equal to their incomes, at least above the level of deep depression. For example, at a level of income represented on our chart by $100 billion, we could realistically imagine a society that consumed only $80 billion and saved the rest. How would we represent this on our graph?

The answer is shown in Fig. 14-3. Note that the dot measures $100 billion along the horizontal (income) axis, but only $80 billion on the vertical (expenditure) axis. Thus the dot represents the ratio of *C* to

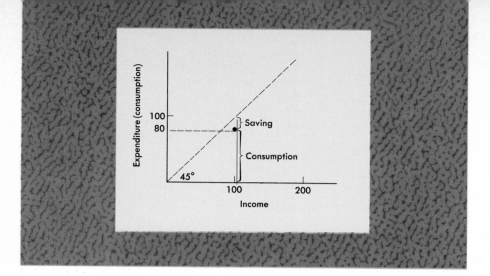

FIG. 14-3

**CONSUMPTION
AND SAVING
ON THE
EQUILIBRIUM
DIAGRAM**

Y, at an income of $100 billion, or the propensity to consume at that level.

But notice further that the vertical distance between the dot and the 45° income line measures the *difference* between our income and our expenditure. (If we spent all our income, the dot would be *on* the line; hence the distance between the line and dot shows us by how much our expenditure fell short of equaling our income.) This difference between income and expenditure on consumption is our saving. Thus Fig. 14-3 shows us our propensity to save at this given income, as well as our propensity to consume.

Now there remains only one additional complication. Most societies have positive saving at high income levels; but at very low levels of incomes, rich societies like the United States will *dissave;* that is, they will draw on accumulated savings and spend more than they currently earn. To represent such a state of affairs on our graph, we would have to show expenditure larger than saving. In Fig. 14-4, there is such a

FIG. 14-4

DISSAVING

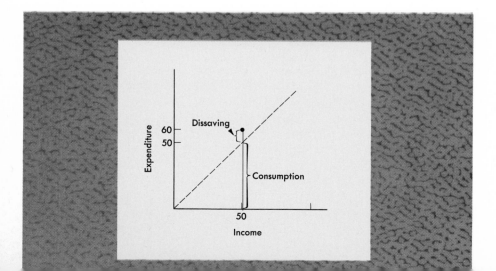

situation, in which income is only $50 billion and expenditure comes to $60 billion. Here dissaving is represented by the length of the line above the 45° income slope.

Perhaps the next step is already obvious. Our dots are in fact nothing but a depiction of the relation of C to Y at various levels of income. By drawing a line through them, we show the schedule of the propensity to consume at these levels of income. The slope of the line, which tells us by how much our consumption changes from one income level to the next, will be a geometric presentation of the marginal propensity to consume. The consumption schedule of our hypothetical economy would look like Fig. 14-5, where the varying amounts of saving and dissaving are clearly seen.

FIG. 14-5

**PROPENSITY
TO CONSUME
SCHEDULE**

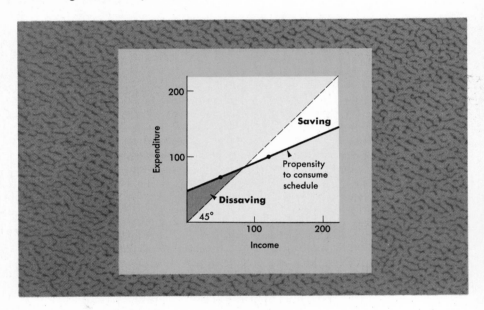

THE DETERMINATION OF EQUILIBRIUM

We are now ready to show how the equilibrium level of income can be determined from our diagram. That level, we remember, is where intended investment is equal to intended saving. But so far, our graph shows us only a schedule of consumption and saving at different income levels. Which is the actual amount of saving? And how shall we put investment into the picture?

Let us answer the second question first. In Table 14-2, we note that investment expenditures are scheduled to be $28 billion at *every* level of income. If we now add a second line 28 units higher than the consumption line, we will show the total amount of expenditure that

266

FIG. 14-6

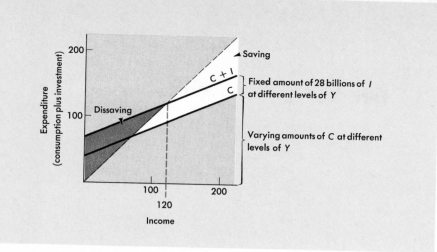

consumers and businessmen intend to make at all levels of income. Such a schedule is shown in Fig. 14-6.

We now have a schedule, represented by the $C + I$ line, that shows us how much total expenditure will be associated with *different* levels of income. Now we are ready for the first question. Given this schedule of investment desires and the slope of our propensity to consume, what will be the equilibrium level of expenditure and income? *We know the answer must be that the level of income at which investment equals saving.*

Our diagram now indicates exactly where this equilibrium level must be. It must lie at that level where the total amount of expenditure (as represented by the $C + I$ line) is just equal to the level of total income (as represented by the 45° income line). On the graph, equilibrium lies—just as in our table—at an income of $120 billion.

How do we know that some other point would not also represent an equilibrium? Suppose, for example, that we look at point X to the left of the equilibrium position in Fig. 14-7. Here investment is larger

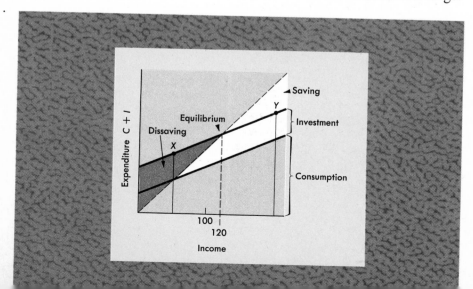

FIG. 14-7

than savings (which are negative to the left of the 45° line). Income would therefore be moving upwards, toward equilibrium. But similarly, a point such as *Y,* to the right of the equilibrium level, is also out of balance. Here investment can be seen to be less than savings, and income would therefore be falling toward the equilibrium point.

Thus what our diagram shows us is that *the point of equilibrium can be only where income equals expenditure.* And that point, we can now see, is precisely where investment and saving are also alike.

A CHANGE IN EQUILIBRIUM

Thus, given our investment schedule and our saving schedule, we see that there is one and only one equilibrium level at which income must settle. But this equilibrium need not be maintained. Suppose investment intentions now increase and that business firms spend *another* $28 billion for investment. Our line *C + I* changes to *C + I'*, as shown in Fig. 14-8. Now what happens?

By looking for the new intersection of the expenditure schedule (*C + I'*) and the 45° income line, we can see that the new equilibrium point lies at *X'*. If we now measure the amount of income represented by this new equilibrium point, we find it to be 175.

Here is a puzzle. We have increased our investment expenditure by 28. But our income has risen by 55. How can this be?

FIG. 14-8

SHIFTS IN EQUILIBRIUM

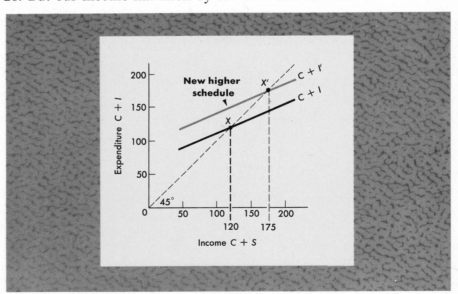

The answer lies in our now familiar multiplier. The increase of 28 in investment spending has brought about a *larger* increase in income because of the respending of the original additional income.

How much larger? That depends, of course, on the marginal propensity to save (or its complement, the marginal propensity to consume). The importance of this crucial pattern of behavior is demonstrated in our next diagram. In Fig. 14-9 we see the effect of the *same* increase in investment with two different marginal propensities to consume—which is to say, two different multipliers. We can imagine the diagram as showing the difference between two nations: both have the same national income, but one has a much higher marginal propensity to consume than the other.

FIG. 14-9

THE
MULTIPLIER
AND
EQUILIBRIUM

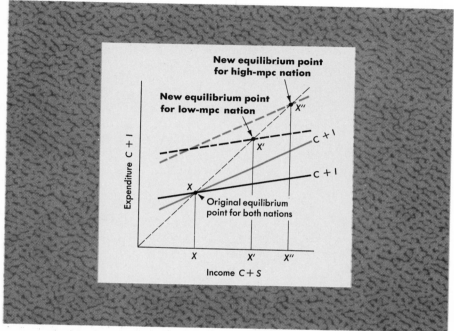

New equilibrium point
for high-mpc nation

New equilibrium point
for low-mpc nation

X''

X'

C + I

C + I

X

Original equilibrium
point for both nations

Expenditure C + I

X   *X'*   *X''*

Income C + S

We read the diagram by beginning at equilibrium point X. Through this point pass the combined consumption plus investment schedules of the two nations: the orange C + I schedule of a country with a high marginal propensity to consume, and the black C + I schedule of a country with a low mpc.

Now let us assume that investment in each country increases by the same amount, with the result that the schedules leap from their original position to the higher positions shown by the broken line parallel to each. Note how much further to the right is X'', the new equilibrium income of the high mpc nation, than X', the new equilibrium of the low mpc nation. This should not surprise us, for we already know that a high marginal consumption ratio exerts a stronger multiplier effect than a low ratio. What we see here is only the diagrammatic representation of how different marginal propensities influence the final equilibrium level of income.

ANOTHER APPROACH TO THE EQUILIBRIUM PROBLEM

The idea of equilibrium is never easy to grasp at first, but a second approach to the selfsame problem may clarify things. Suppose that we are back on our model island community and are asked by a group of businessmen to predict the island's income for the coming year. We know that income will be the sum of two expenditure streams—consumption and investment (we are still ignoring government)—so we send our two teams of researchers to discover people's intentions concerning their expenditures.

The first team goes to a sample of consumers' houses and asks, "How much will you be consuming next year?" The answer is a bit disconcerting: "It all depends on how large our incomes are," they tell us. What our poll-takers would find, in other words, is that consumption expenditures (or savings plans) could be predicted only in the form of a *schedule*, relating C to Y, or S to Y. In Fig. 14-10, we show this new (but quite obvious) saving/income relationship. Note that the vertical axis in this new diagram measures saving, not consumption.

FIG. 14-10

SAVINGS AND INCOME

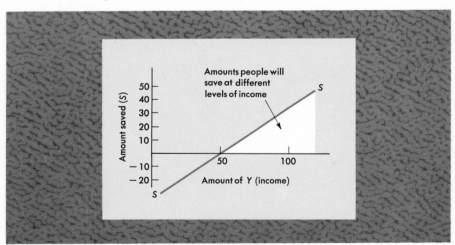

Now we turn to the poll of business intentions. Here, too, there is an element of "it depends," for some investment, as we know, will be induced by various consumption levels. Yet to a very large extent, businessmen *must* formulate their investment plans on a forward-looking basis, and we will assume that their capital budgets for the coming year are already set at a figure they divulge to us.

In Fig. 14-11 we show these budgets superimposed. It is obvious that

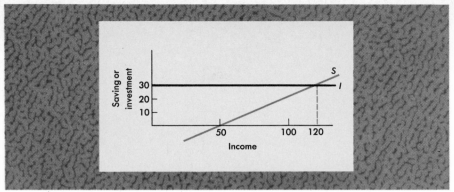

FIG. 14-11

**EQUILIBRIUM
ON THE
SAVING—
INVESTMENT
DIAGRAM**

the equilibrium level of income, measured along the horizontal axis, is determined by the point where the *S* and *I* curves intersect.

It is helpful to see the integral relation between our two different looking diagrams for equilibrium; in fact, the second diagram is taken right out of the first. In Fig. 14-12 we show the two ways of depicting

**TWO DIAGRAMS,
ONE SOLUTION**

FIG. 14-12

**TWO METHODS
OF SHOWING
EQUILIBRIUM**

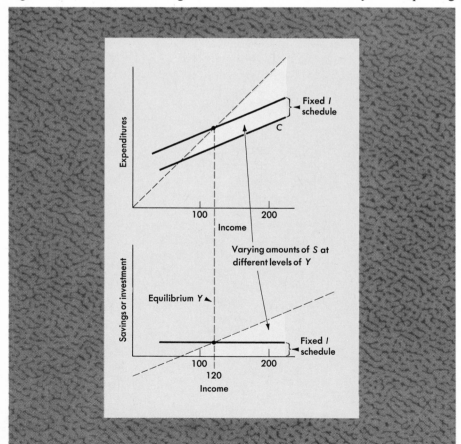

equilibrium, one above the other. Notice that the shaded triangle showing the propensity to save is transposed *unaltered* to the second diagram. It looks "flatter" only because we now ignore consumption and therefore put the savings triangle on a horizontal base instead of a sloping one. Our fixed investment schedule is also exactly the same in both diagrams, although once again, in the lower figure it is shown as a horizontal line, rather than as a line that is parallel to the sloping line *C*. Now it should be obvious why the equilibrium intersection point must be at the same figure on the income axis of both diagrams.

And what if investment expenditures change? We see the effect in Fig. 14-13, where the *I* curve jumps to *I'*. This too is only a different depiction of the process that we have already drawn in Fig. 14-8. A

FIG. 14-13

THE MULTIPLIER AND EQUILIBRIUM— ANOTHER VIEW

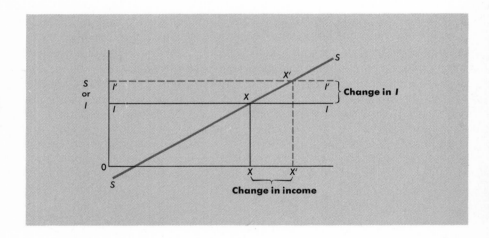

FIG. 14-14

MPS AND EQUILIBRIUM

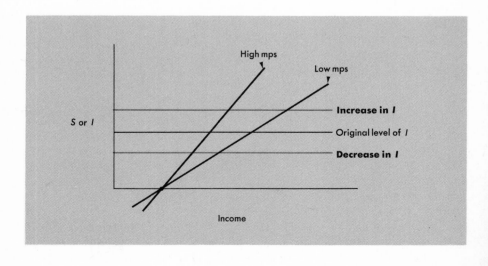

good exercise is to pencil in a higher I' line on both graphs in Fig. 14-12 and to prove to yourself that the new equilibrium point must be the same in both cases.

One last point before we move on. We know by now that the size of the multiplier depends on the marginal propensity to save. And we know further that the marginal propensity to save (like the marginal propensity to consume) determines the slope of the lines we draw on our diagrams. Fig. 14-14 has two propensity-to-save curves with different slopes. Indicate in pencil the original and new equilibrium points for each, and show that the lower the marginal propensity to save, the greater will be the multiplier effect, both for an increase or a decrease in investment spending.

THE IDEA OF EQUILIBRIUM

Thus we have begun to understand how GNP reaches an equilibrium position after a change in investment. Here it is well to remember, however, that the word "equilibrium" does not imply a static, motionless state. We use the word only to denote the fact that *given* certain behavior patterns of consumption and investment, there will be a determinate point to which their interaction will push the level of income; and *so long as the underlying patterns of consumption and investment remain unchanged, the forces they exert will keep income at this level.*

In fact, of course, the flows of consumption and investment are continually changing, so that the equilibrium level of the economy is constantly shifting, like a Ping-Pong ball suspended in a rising jet of water. Equilibrium can thus be regarded as a target toward which the economy is constantly propelled by the push-pull between saving and investment. The target may be attained but momentarily before the economy is again impelled to seek a new point of rest. What our diagrams and the underlying analysis explain for us, then, is not a single determinate point at which our economy will in fact settle down, but the *direction* in which it will go in quest of a resting place, as the dynamic forces of the system exert their pressures.

THE PARADOX OF THRIFT

The fact that income must always move toward the level where the flows of intended saving and investment are equal leads to one of the most startling—and important—paradoxes of economics. This is the so-called paradox of thrift, a paradox that tells us that the *attempt to increase saving* may, under certain circumstances, lead to a *fall in actual saving.*

The paradox is not difficult for us to understand at this stage. An attempt to save, *when it is not matched with an equal willingness to invest,* will cause a gap in demand. This means that businessmen will not be getting back enough money to cover their costs. Hence, production will be curtailed or costs will be slashed, with the result that incomes will fall. As incomes fall, savings will also fall, because the ability to save will be reduced. Thus, by a chain of activities working their influence on income and output, the effort to *increase* savings may end up with an actual *reduction* of savings.

This frustration of individual desires is perhaps the most striking instance of a common situation in economic life, the incompatibility between some kinds of individual behavior and some collective results. An individual farmer, for instance, may produce a larger crop in order to enjoy a bigger income; but if all farmers produce bigger crops, farm prices are apt to fall so heavily that farmers end up with less income. So too, a single family may wish to save a very large fraction of its income for reasons of financial prudence; but if all families seek to save a great deal of their incomes, the result—unless investment also rises—will be a fall in expenditure and a common failure to realize savings objectives. The paradox of thrift, in other words, teaches us that the freedom of behavior available to a few individuals cannot always be generalized to all individuals.*

A NOTE ON EXPORTS, INJECTIONS, AND LEAKAGES

With an initial understanding of the mechanism of equilibrium and disequilibrium behind us, we have reached a very important stage in our inquiry. The interactions of the macroeconomic variables now begin to come together and the causes and mechanics of prosperity and depression begin to reveal themselves to us.

Before we go on to complete our understanding, however, we must mention, if only in passing, a sector we have largely overlooked in this book. This is the foreign sector, or more properly the sector of net exports.

If we lived in a European, South American, or Asian country, we could not be so casual in our treatment of foreign trade, for this sector constitutes the very lifeline of many, perhaps even most, countries. Our own highly self-sustained economy in which foreign trade plays only

---

*The paradox of thrift is actually only a subtle instance of a type of faulty reasoning called the fallacy of composition. The fallacy consists of assuming that what is true of the individual case must also be true of all cases combined. The flaw in reasoning lies in our tendency to overlook "side effects" of individual actions (such as the decrease in spending associated with an individual's attempt to save more, or the increase in supply when a farmer markets his larger crop) which may be negligible in isolation but which are very important in the aggregate.

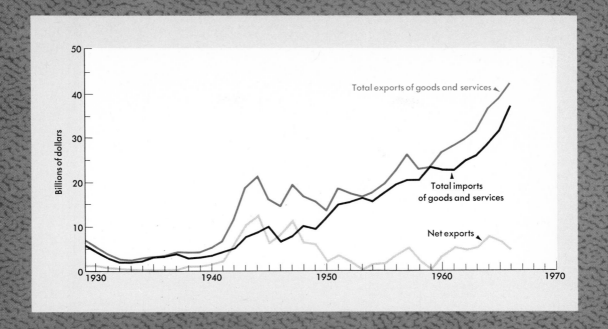

FIG. 14-15 EXPORTS, IMPORTS, AND NET EXPORTS

a small quantitative (although a much more important qualitative) role, is very much the exception rather than the rule.†

   In part, it is the relatively marginal role played by foreign trade in the American economy that allows us to treat it so cavalierly. But there is also another problem. The forces that enter into the flows of international trade are much more complex than any we have heretofore discussed. Not alone the reactions of American consumers and firms, but those of foreign consumers and firms must be taken into account. Thus comparisons between international price levels, the availability of foreign or domestic goods, credit and monetary controls, exchange rates—a whole host of "extraneous" considerations—lie at the very heart of foreign trade. To begin to unravel these interrelationships, one must study international trade as a subject in itself, and that we will defer until Part Four. Nevertheless, we should try to understand the main impact of foreign trade on the level of GNP, even if we cannot yet investigate the forces and institutions of foreign trade as thoroughly as we might like.

   We must begin by repeating that our initial overview of the economic system, with its twin streams of consumption and investment, was

IMPACT OF
FOREIGN
TRADE

†In Chapter 29 we shall see, however, that international currency problems can play a very important role in our economic affairs.

actually incomplete. It portrayed what we call a "closed" system, an economy with no flows of goods or services from within its borders to other nations, or from other nations to itself.

Yet such flows must, of course, be taken into account in computing our national output. Let us therefore look at a chart that shows us the main streams of goods and services that cross our borders, as well as a table of the magnitudes in our benchmark years.

First a word of explanation. Exports show the total value of all goods and services we sold to foreigners. Imports show the total value of all goods and services we bought from foreigners. Our bottom line shows the net difference between exports and imports, or the difference between the value of the goods we sold abroad and the value we bought from abroad. This difference is called *net exports,* and it constitutes the net contribution of foreign trade to GNP.

If we think of it in terms of expenditures, it is not difficult to see what the net contribution is. When exports are sold to foreigners, their expenditures add to American incomes. Imports, on the contrary, are expenditures that we make to other countries (and hence that we do not make at home). If we add the foreign expenditures made here and subtract the domestic expenditures made abroad, we will have left a net figure that will show the contribution (if any) made by foreigners to GNP.

What is the impact of this net expenditure on GNP? It is much the same as net private domestic investment. If we have a rising net foreign trade balance, we will have a net increase in spending in the economy. And this increase in spending, just like that arising from the addition of plant or equipment, will exert a magnified impact on GNP via the multiplier. Conversely, if our imports rise more rapidly than our exports, so that our net foreign trade balance declines or becomes negative, our GNP would decline—not only by the drop in net exports, but by the net fall in spending again magnified by the influence of the marginal propensity to consume.

LEAKAGES AND INJECTIONS

Thus we can consider the effects of the foreign trade sector as if it were a part of the investment sector, even though the underlying forces are extremely different. But as we broaden the model of our economy, from its original simple conception as a society that only consumes and invests, to one that now imports and exports, and in our next chapter to one that has, as well, an active government sector, it becomes convenient to widen our terminology somewhat when we speak of the determinants of GNP.

Now, instead of referring only to "saving" as the cause of a downward pressure on the level of expenditure, or to "investment" as the only cause of upward pressures, we can speak of *leakages in, or withdrawals from, the expenditure flow* or of *injections or additions to that flow.* The word *leakage* is, of course, already familiar to us from our analysis of the multiplier. Here we use it as a general term to describe any activity that diminishes the flow of spending—be it saving or increasing imports, or rising government taxes or growing business profits. Similarly, we speak of injections as any activity—investment, exports, government spending, or a spontaneous rise in consumption—that will increase the flow of spending.

The determination of output can then be generally described as the outcome of the balance between leakages or withdrawals of all kinds and injections or additions of all kinds. So long as injections are outpacing leakages, GNP will rise; when leakages overbalance injections, GNP will fall; and when the two are in a state of balance, GNP will be in stable equilibrium.

SUMMARY

1. The motivation for investment expenditure is not personal use or satisfaction, but *expected profit*. Note that investment is always geared to forward profit *expectations* rather than to past or present results.

2. We distinguish between two kinds of investment motivation. When investments are made to meet an expected demand arising from present or clearly indicated changes in consumption, we speak of *induced investment*. When investment is stimulated by developments (such as inventions) that have little relation to existing trends, we speak of *autonomous* investment.

3. Induced investment is subject to the *acceleration principle* which describes how a given increase in C can give rise to a proportionally larger increase in *I*. The acceleration principle also shows us that the absolute level of induced investment can fall, even though the level of C is still rising. Thus it helps explain the onset of recessions. Note that the acceleration principle "takes hold" only when an industry is at or near full utilization.

4. The *rate of interest* is, in two ways, an important determinant of investment. It directly affects the *cost of capital*. And it also provides a *standard of comparison* for the returns expected from investment. Unless the expected return from investment (called the marginal efficiency of investment) is higher than the rate of interest, it will not be reasonable to make the investment.

5. The level of income in the economy as a whole is moved upward or downward by the interplay of the schedules of intended saving and investment. *Only where intended S and intended I are equal will income be in equilibrium.*

6. We can show the idea of equilibrium in two kinds of diagrams. In one we ascertain what point on the C + I expenditure schedule lies on the 45° income line. In the other diagram, we find the point of intersection between the saving and the investment schedules on a graph that relates saving and investment (on the vertical axis) to income (on the horizontal axis). *Both graphs are only visual ways of showing the point of mutual compatibility between schedules of intended saving and investment behavior at different income levels.*

7. The graphs also show that changes in *I* lead to larger changes in *Y*. The reason for this is the slope of the *C + I* schedule (or in the saving-investment graph, of the *S* schedule). Since these slopes represent the marginal propensity to consume (or save), *the graphs merely present in visual form the familiar multiplier relationship.*

8. The new level of equilibrium of income, given a change in *I*, depends on two things: (1) *the size of the actual change in I*; and (2) *the multiplier.*

9. The fact that income must finally settle where the schedules of intended *S* and *I* converge leads to the famous *paradox of thrift.* This paradox tells us that the effort to save, unless matched by an equal effort to invest, will lead to an excess of *S* over *I*, and thereby drive income lower. At lower levels of income, there will be less *S*, rather than more. Thus the effort to save more has resulted in the economy's actually saving less! (Note that this occurs only if the effort to save is not matched by more investment.)

10. *Exports and imports* serve as stimuli for, or drags on, the expenditure flow. They act much as investment does in driving the level of income higher or lower. Therefore, we broaden our terminology to include exports and imports and similar stimuli by speaking of *injections* into, or *withdrawals* or *leakages* from, the expenditure flow.

QUESTIONS

1. Discuss the difference in the motivation of a consumer buying a car for pleasure and the same person buying a car for his business.

2. Which of the following are induced, and which autonomous, investment decisions: a developer builds homes in a growing community; a city enlarges its water supply after a period of water shortage; a firm builds a laboratory for basic research; an entrepreneur invests in a new gadget.

3. What is the basic idea of the acceleration principle? Describe carefully how the acceleration principle helps explain the instability of investment.

4. Assume that it costs 7 per cent to borrow from a bank. What is the minimum profit that must be expected from an investment before it becomes worthwhile? Could we write that $I = f(r)$ where *r* stands for the rate of interest? What would be the relation between a change in *r* and *I*? Would $I = f(r)$ be a complete description of the motivation for investment?

5. Suppose that an economy turns out to have the following consumption and saving schedule:

Income (billions)	Saving (billions)	Consumption (billions)
$400	$50	$350
450	55	395
500	60	440
550	70	480
600	85	515

Now suppose that firms intend to make investments of $60 billion during the year. What will be the level of income for the economy? If investment rises to $85 billion, then what will be its income? What would be the multiplier in this case?

6. Show the equilibrium income before and after the jump in investment on a C + I graph and on an S and I graph.

7. Exactly what is meant by "equilibrium"? Is a balloon floating in mid-air in equilibrium? Why? If gravity is saving, and the lift of hydrogen is investment, what economic magnitude is represented by the height of the balloon?

8. Is there an opposite to the paradox of thrift? Suppose everyone tried not to save but to spend all his income, and that businessmen did not alter their investment plans. What would happen? (Since there would be no more goods and a good deal more spending, wouldn't someone have to end up holding money and not being able to use it for consumption? Wouldn't the "paradox of spendthrift" lead to more saving, despite the effort not to save?) What does this tell us about the need to coordinate S and I plans to achieve a desired macroeconomic goal?

9. Explain how exports stimulate income and how imports depress it. Does this mean that imports are bad? Are savings bad?

15 THE GOVERNMENT SECTOR

We turn now to the last of the main sources of GNP—the government, and as before we shall begin by familiarizing ourselves with the sector in its long historical profile.

Figure 15-1 shows us the emergence of the government sector as a significant contributor to GNP, a process we have already discussed in Part One, and to which we will return later in this chapter.

GOVERNMENT IN THE EXPENDITURE FLOW

Now let us take a closer look at a recent year, to help us fit the government sector into the flow of national expenditure. Figure 15-2 shows us the familiar bars of our flow diagram. Note that indirect taxes, totaling some $75 billion in 1968, amounted to almost 9 per cent of

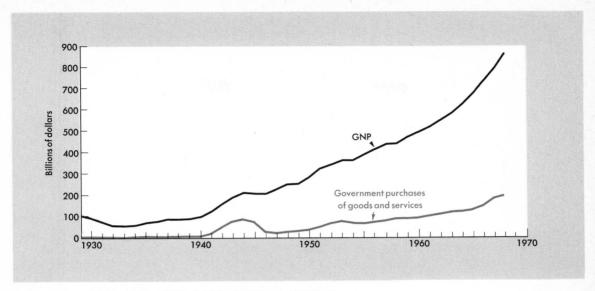

FIG. 15-1 GNP AND THE GOVERNMENT SECTOR

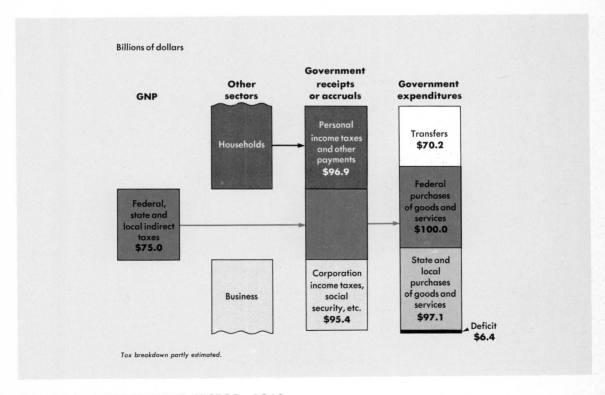

FIG. 15-2 GOVERNMENT SECTOR, 1968

the value of GNP. As can be seen, however, income taxes on households and businesses are much more important than indirect taxes in providing total government revenues. (What the diagram does not show is that about two-thirds of the indirect taxes are state and local in origin: property taxes, excise taxes, motor vehicle and gasoline taxes, and others. Income taxes and social security contributions constitute about nine-tenths of the income of the federal government.)

On the expenditure side, we see that state and local purchases of goods and services are as important as federal purchases in providing public demand. Since two-thirds of all transfer payments are federal in origin, however, total federal *expenditures* (as contrasted with purchases of goods and services) run about one-fifth higher than all state and local expenditures.

Finally, it is worth reminding ourselves of the different significance and impact of public purchases and transfers. Public purchases of goods and services, whether they originate with local or federal government, require the use of land, labor, and capital. They are thus *public production,* and constitute a net addition to GNP. Transfer payments, on the other hand, do not increase output. They are simply a reallocation of income, from factors to various groups of the community in the business sector or the household sector. Transfers, therefore, do not require new production and are not a part of GNP.

GOVERNMENT
SECTOR IN
HISTORICAL
PERSPECTIVE

How large does the public sector bulk in the total flow of GNP? Let us again try to put a perspective into our answer by observing the trend of government purchases over the years.

The striking change from prewar to postwar years is, of course, immediately visible. The government sector, taken as a whole, has changed from a very small sector to a very large one. In 1929, total government purchases of goods and services were only half of total private investment spending; in 1968, total government purchases were over 50 per cent *larger* than private investment. *In terms of its contributions to GNP, government is now second only to consumption.*

To make the point even more forcefully, it should be noted that Fig. 15-1 understates the full role of government spending, since it does not include transfer payments, but only purchases of goods and services. If we include the figure for transfer payments, the proportion of all government expenditure to GNP rises from approximately 20 per cent to 30 per cent. And since, as we have mentioned, two-thirds of these transfers are federal (Social Security, subsidies, and interest), the proportion of all *federal* spending to GNP rises from 11 per cent to about double that.

Thus, on the face of it, public expenditure is clearly an important source of economic activity. Nevertheless, to emphasize the rise in spending without stressing its causes would be misleading.

First, we should note that much of the growth in public expenditure has been contributed by the *rise of state and local, rather than federal, spending.* What has promoted this rise? The answer lies in the needs and capabilities of a highly urbanized and affluent society. The sheer administrative and housekeeping expenditures of our cities and states have grown enormously as huge populations have crowded into vast mega-cities. (The supervision of vehicular traffic alone requires the employment of one out of every ten state and local officials.) Equally important, the steadily rising educational reach of the population has vastly increased the need for public expenditure. In 1950 the states and localities spent less than $6 billion for elementary and secondary education; in 1968, they spent more than $29 billion. In 1950, institutions of higher education cost the states and localities just over $1 billion. In the late 1960's, the cost had risen beyond $10 billion.

Second, it is *important to separate the rise in federal defense spending from the rise in its nondefense expenditures.* As Table 15-1 shows, the rise of nondefense spending as a percentage of GNP is very small.*

TABLE 15 · 1

FEDERAL
NONDEFENSE
PURCHASES

Selected years	1929	1933	1940	1960	1961	1962	1963	1964	1965	1966	1967	1968
Per cent of GNP	1.0 (est)	3.0 (est)	4.0	1.7	1.8	2.1	2.3	2.4	2.5	2.2	2.3	2.5

*This raises the related question of how important armaments or defense spending is within the economy, and of how large a gap in our stream of expenditures would be created were peace to "break out."

In 1968, our total national defense expenditures (including overseas military aid and the expenses of the Atomic Energy Commission) came to approximately 9 per cent of GNP. Recently, a Cabinet Coordinating Committee reported on the probable reduction of expenditures for defense stemming from a cessation of hostilities in Vietnam. They projected a fall in spending of about $19 billion per year within 10 months following an end to the war. This did not, however, include an estimate of the amount by which private spending in defense industries would also contract. Without this secondary effect, the drop in spending would come to only 2 to 3 per cent of GNP; with it, it might be as high as 3 to 4 per cent.

We can look at such a prospective fall as both a danger and an opportunity. A fall of over $20 billion in expenditure, without any compensating offsets, would be a severe blow to the economy. But it is certain that there would be many offsets. Taxes could be reduced, increasing the ability of the private sector to spend. Or the reduction in war demands, plus the normal increase in federal revenues from a rising GNP, could be regarded as a peace-and-growth dividend available to finance the innumerable programs for public improvement that are now regarded as "too expensive." See *Economic Report of the President* (Washington, D.C., 1968), pp. 187–211.

We could also attempt to divide public expenditures into categories comparable to consumption and investment. The division is not a simple one to make, however. We could have no trouble tagging public construction for roads or airfields or dams as investment. But what are we to make of education expenditures? Economists believe that education is fully as important as capital goods for long-term growth. Shall we then count it as investment? Or what shall we make of spending on recreational facilities or on defense? The line between consumption and investment in the public sector is evidently much harder to draw than in the private sector. For reasons that we shall shortly discuss, it might be useful to list separately those items that are unquestionably additions to public capital. But since the distinction between capital and consumption in the public sphere is often unclear, economists take the line of least resistance and lump all kinds of public purchases, however varied, in one undifferentiated public sector.

But there is another reason why we differentiate between the private sectors and the public sector. This is the fact that the motivations of the public sector are different in a most important way from those of the private sectors.

We recall that the motivations for the household sector and the business sector are lodged in the free decisions of their respective units. Householders decide to spend or save their incomes as they wish, and we are able to construct a propensity to consume schedule only because there seem to be spending and saving patterns that emerge spontaneously from the householders themselves. Similarly, business firms exercise their own judgments on their capital expenditures, and as a result we have seen the indeterminacy and variability of investment decisions.

But when we turn to the expenditures of the public sector, we enter an entirely new area of motivation. It is no longer fixed habit or profit that determines the rate of spending, but *political decision*—that is, the collective will of the people as it is formulated and expressed through their local, state, and federal legislatures and executives.

As we shall soon see, this does not mean that government is therefore an entirely unpredictable economic force. There are regularities and patterns in the government's economic behavior, as there are in other sectors. Yet the presence of an explicit political will that can direct the income or outgo of the sector *as a whole* (especially its federal component) gives to the public sector a special significance. *This is the only sector whose expenditures and receipts are open to deliberate control.* We can exert (through public action) very important influences on the behavior of households and firms. But we cannot directly alter their economic activity in the manner that is open to us with the public sector.

FISCAL POLICY

The deliberate use of the government sector as an active economic force is a relatively new conception in economics. As we know from our historical survey, like so much of the apparatus of macroeconomic analysis, it stems essentially from the work of John Maynard Keynes during the Great Depression. At that time his proposals were regarded as extremely daring, but they have become increasingly accepted by economists.* Although the bold use of the economic powers of the public sector is far from commanding unanimous assent in the United States today, there is a steadily growing consensus in the use of fiscal policy—that is, the deliberate utilization of the government's taxing and spending powers—to help the stability and growth of the national economy.

The basic idea behind modern fiscal policy is simple enough. We have seen that economic recessions have their roots in a failure of the business sector to offset the savings of the economy through sufficient investment. If savings or leakages are larger than intended investment or injections, there will be a gap in the circuit of incomes and expenditures that can cumulate downward, at first by the effect of the multiplier, thereafter, and even more seriously, by further decreases in investment brought about by falling sales and gloomy expectations.

But if a falling GNP is caused by an inadequacy of expenditures in one sector, our analysis suggests an answer. Could not the insufficiency of spending in the business sector be offset by higher spending in another sector, the public sector? Could not the public sector serve as a supplementary avenue for the "transfer" of savings into investment?

As Fig. 15-3 shows, an expenditure gap can indeed be closed by "transferring" savings to the public sector and spending them.

The diagram shows savings in the household sector partly offset by business investment and partly by government spending. It makes clear that at least so far as the mechanics of the economic flow are concerned, the public sector can serve to offset savings or other leakages equally as well as the private sector.

How is the "transfer" accomplished? It is done much as business does it, by offering bonds that individuals or institutions can buy with their

---

*Reviewing a book in 1964 with the word "macroeconomics" in its title, Harold Somers wrote: "The name of Keynes is anathema in some circles. . . . As a result, courses bearing the name of Keynes are very scarce and one publisher . . . even boasts that his elementary economics book contains no mention of Keynes.

"All is not lost. There is available a very competent economist called Macro. This economist, Macro, is most versatile. He . . . encompasses everything that Keynes taught, might have taught, and would have denied teaching. . . ." (*American Economic Review*, March 1964, p. 138.)

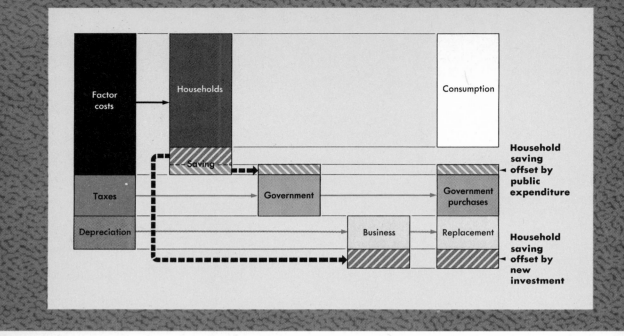

FIG. 15-3 PUBLIC EXPENDITURE AND THE DEMAND GAP

savings. Unlike business, the government cannot offer stock, for it is not run as a profit-making enterprise. However, we must note that the government can also tax incomes to finance its expenditures. This may have complicated results, for the taxes may not cause consumers to cut back their spending, but to curtail their saving—or more likely, to cut back some on both consumption and saving.

TAXES, EXPENDITURES, AND GNP

We will look more carefully into the question of how the government can serve as a kind of counterbalance for the private economy. But first we must discover something about the normal behavior of the public sector; for despite the importance of political decisions in determining the action of the public sector, and despite the multiplicity of government units and activities, we can nonetheless discern "propensities" in government spending and receiving—propensities that play their compensating role in the economy quite independently of any direct political intervention.

The reason for these propensities is that both government income and government outgo are closely tied to private activity. Government receipts are derived in the main from taxes, and taxes—direct or indirect—tend to reflect the trend of business and personal income. In fact, we can generalize about tax payments in much the same fashion as we can about consumption, describing them as a predictable function of GNP. To be sure, this assumes that tax *rates* do not change. But since rates change only infrequently, we can draw up a general schedule that relates tax receipts and the level of GNP. The schedule will show not only that taxes rise as GNP rises, but that they rise *faster* than GNP.

Why faster? Largely because of the progressive structure of the federal income tax. As household and business incomes rise to higher levels, the percentage "bite" of taxes increases, from around 20 per cent on the first dollar of taxable income to much higher percentages for high income brackets. Thus as incomes rise, tax liabilities rise even more. Conversely, the tax bite works downward in the opposite way.

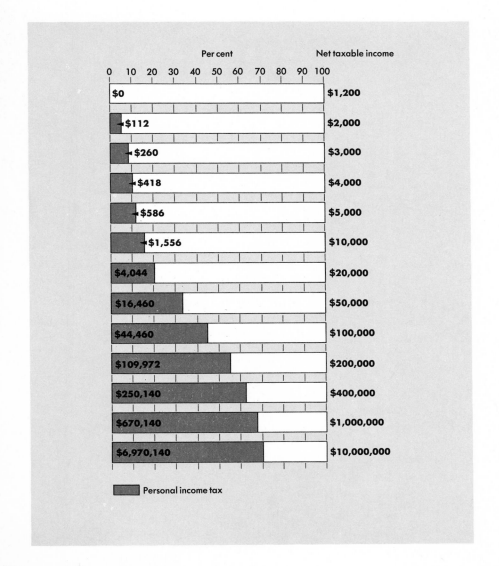

FIG. 15-4

PROGRESSIVE IMPACT OF THE FEDERAL INCOME TAX

As incomes fall, taxes fall even faster, since households or businesses with lowered incomes find themselves in less steep tax brackets. Figure 15-4 shows this changing tax bite on individual net taxable income.

Government expenditures also show certain "propensities," which is to say, *some government spending is also functionally related to the level of GNP.* A number of government programs are directly correlated to the level of economic activity in such a way that spending *decreases* as GNP *increases,* and vice versa. For instance, unemployment benefits are naturally higher when GNP is low or falling. So are many welfare payments at the state and local level. So, too, are disbursements to farmers under various agricultural programs.

<table>
<tr><td>

**AUTOMATIC
STABILIZERS**

</td><td>

All these automatic effects taken together are called the *automatic stabilizers* or the *built-in stabilizers* of the economy. What they add up to is an automatic government counterbalance to the private sector. As GNP falls because private spending is insufficient, taxes decline even faster and public expenditures grow, thereby automatically causing the government sector to offset the private sector to some extent. In similar fashion, as GNP rises, taxes tend to rise even faster and public expenditures decline, thereby causing the government sector to act as a brake.

</td></tr>
</table>

The public sector therefore acts as an automatic compensator, even without direct action to alter tax or expenditure levels, pumping out more public demand when private demand is slow and curbing public demand when private demand is brisk.

How effective are the built-in stabilizers? It is estimated that the increase in transfer payments plus the reduction in taxes offset about 35¢ of each dollar of original decline in spending. Here is how this works. Suppose that private investment were to fall by $10 billion. Because of the multiplier, household spending might well fall by another $10 billion, causing a total decline of $20 billion in incomes.

The action of the stabilizers, however, will prevent the full force of this fall. First, the reduction in incomes of both households and firms will lower their tax liabilities. Since taxes take about 35¢ from each dollar, the drop of $10 billion in incomes will reduce tax liabilities by about $3.5 billion. Most of this—let us say $3 billion—is likely to be spent. Meanwhile some public expenditures for unemployment insurance and farm payments will rise, pumping out perhaps $1 billion into the consumption sector, all of which we assume to be spent by its recipients.

Thus, the incomes of firms and households, having originally fallen by $10 billion, will be roughly offset by $4 billion in additional transfer incomes and in income made available by lessened tax obligations. As a result, the net decline in expenditure will be reduced from $10 billion to $6 billion (actually $6.5 billion, according to the calculations of the Council of Economic Advisers). The multiplier will then indeed effect this net reduction in spending, so that total incomes in the economy will fall by twice as much, or $13 billion in all. But this is considerably less than the fall of $20 billion that would otherwise have taken place.

This is certainly an improvement over a situation with no stabilizers. Yet if the drop in investment is not to bring about some fall in GNP, it will have to be *fully* compensated by an equivalent increase in government spending or by a fall in taxes large enough to induce an equivalent amount of private spending. This will require public action more vigorous than that brought about automatically. Indeed, it requires that the government take on a task very different from any we have heretofore studied, the task of acting as the *deliberate* balancing mechanism of the economy.

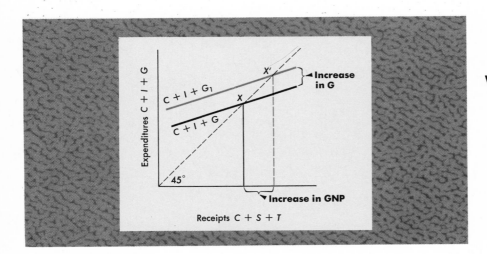

FIG. 15-5

NEW
EQUILIBRIUM
WITH INCREASED
GOVERNMENT
EXPENDITURE

A DIAGRAM OF
GOVERNMENT
SPENDING

There is nothing in our formal analysis to make us doubt that government can take on such a task. Government spending is just like private spending so far as its multiplier effects are concerned.* In the same fashion, government taxes serve to constrict private spending, much as additional saving would.

Hence we can draw a new diagram showing an equilibrium for an economy with various levels of public expenditure. In Fig. 15-5, we enlarge the familiar chart from the last chapter to include a new item on the expenditure axis—government purchases, or *G*—and a new item

---

*Although we should note that different kinds of private and public spending programs may have different multipliers if they go to different spending groups. A government public works program that uses unskilled labor is not apt to have the same initial repercussions on GNP as a private investment project in computers. Additional transfer expenditures may also have initial multiplier effects different from direct purchases of goods and services. And finally, different tax structures will cause changes in GNP to affect private spending differently.

on the receipts or income axis—taxes, or T. Once again we draw our 45° slanting line and our schedule of income possibilities, this time as consumption plus investment plus government purchases $(C + I + G)$.* Our new schedule shows an equilibrium point at X, where all expenditures, public or private, intersect the income line.

Now let us imagine that C and I remain unchanged but that the regular flow of government purchasing increases, raising total outlays from $C + I + G$ to $C + I + G'$, shown by the broken line. Our equilibrium point now shifts to X'. Once again we note that *the change in equilibrium income is greater than the change in initial expenditure.* The reason is, of course, the same as in the case with private investment. All additional injections of expenditure into the economy will exert a multiple income effect as they pass through successive (albeit diminishing) rounds of receipt and re-expenditure.

For clarity, let us go back again to our island community to predict the equilibrium level of GNP for the coming year. Again we send out our teams of pollsters, and as before, we take note of household consuming and saving intentions and of businessmen's investment plans. This time, however, we also study the community's tax schedules and inquire into the island's projected public expenditures.

As a result, our diagram of equilibrium includes more factors than it did formerly. In Fig. 15-6, we show the schedule of savings plans

FIG. 15-6

**EQUILIBRIUM
WITH PUBLIC
SECTOR ADDED**

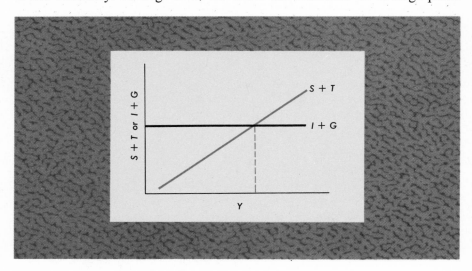

*Although we do not show it on the diagram, as we add government expenditures and taxation to our model, we must expect the slope of the previous propensity to consume schedule to change. We should picture the impact of taxes as reducing the slope of the curve, since rising income means even faster rising taxes. On the other hand, government expenditure may redistribute income away from savers toward spenders. Hence, one cannot generalize about the way in which the addition of G affects the slope of the propensity to consume schedule. The effect will vary according to the tax and expenditure programs. But it is well to bear this qualification in mind.

plus additional taxes at various levels of income. In the same diagram, the stream of investment is now increased to include projected public expenditures. As a result, the levels and the slopes of the two lines—one now representing leakages and one injections—are different from our former simple model. Yet the intersection of the two lines again tells us what we want to know; that is, given the commitments and propensities of private spending and saving, and public spending and taxing, where the income of our community will settle.

DEFICIT SPENDING

Thus from an analytic standpoint we can treat the contribution of government very much as if it were investment. Our diagrams of the sectoral flows and equilibrium relationships make it perfectly plain that the government sector can offset saving just as efficiently as the business sector can, from the point of view of maintaining a given level of spending.

Yet the suggestion that the government deliberately exercise compensatory powers opens a new question for us to consider. The use of the government budget as a stabilizing device means that the government must be prepared to spend more than its normal tax receipts. It must purposefully plan a budget in which outgo exceeds income, leaving a negative figure called a *deficit*.

Like a business, however, a government cannot spend money it does not have in a bank account. Therefore it must *borrow* from individuals, firms, or banks in order to cover its planned deficit. Deficit spending, in other words, means the spending of borrowed money, money derived from the sale of government bonds.

Can the government safely run up a deficit? Let us begin to unravel this important but perplexing question by asking another: can a private business afford to run up a deficit?

There is one kind of deficit that a private business *cannot* afford: a deficit that comes from spending more money on current production than it will realize from its sale. This kind of deficit is called a *business loss;* and if losses are severe enough, a business firm will be forced to discontinue its operations.

But there is another kind of deficit, although it is not called by that name, in the operations of a private firm. This is an excess of expenditures over receipts brought about by spending money on *capital assets.* When the American Telephone and Telegraph Company or the Consolidated Edison Company use their own savings or those of the public to build a new power plant, they do not show a "loss" on their annual statement to their stockholders, even though their total expenditures on current costs and on capital may have been greater than their sales. Instead, expenditures are divided into two kinds, one relating current costs to current income, and the other relegating expenditures on capital goods to an entirely separate "capital account." Instead of calling the excess of expenditures a "deficit," they call it "investment." *

DEBTS
AND ASSETS

Can A.T.&T. or Consolidated Edison afford to run deficits of the latter kind indefinitely? We can answer the question by imagining ourselves in an economic landscape with no disturbing changes in technology or in consumers' tastes, so that entrepreneurs can plan ahead with great safety. Now let us assume that in this comfortable economy, Consolidated Edison decides to build a new plant, perhaps to take care of the growing population. To finance the plant, it issues new bonds, so that its new asset is matched by a new debt.

Now what about this debt? How long can Consolidated Edison afford to have its bonds outstanding?

The answer is—forever!

Remember that we have assumed an economy remaining changeless in tastes and techniques, so that each year the new factory can turn out a quota of output, perfectly confident that it will be sold; and each year it can set aside a reserve for wear and tear, perfectly confident that the factory is being properly depreciated. As a result, each year the debt must be as good as the year before—no better and no worse. The bondholder is sure of getting his interest, steadily earned, and he knows that the underlying asset is being fully maintained.

Admittedly, after a certain number of years the new factory will be worn out. But if our imaginary economy remains unchanged and if depreciation accruals have been properly set aside, when the old plant gives out, an identical new one will be built from these depreciation reserves. Meanwhile, the old debt, like the old plant, will also come to an end, for debts usually run for a fixed term of years. Consolidated Edison must now pay back its debtholders in full. But how? The firm has accumulated a reserve to buy a new plant, but it has not accumulated a second reserve to repay its bondholders.

Nevertheless, the answer is simple enough. When the bonds come due in our imaginary situation, Consolidated Edison issues *new* bonds equal in value to the old ones. It then sells the new bonds and uses the new money it raises to pay off the old bondholders. When the

---

* Investment does not *require* a "deficit," since it can be financed out of current profits. But many expanding companies do spend more money on current and capital account than they take in through sales and thereby incur a "deficit" for at least a part of their investment.

292

transaction is done, a whole cycle is complete: both a new factory and a new issue of bonds exist in place of the old. Everything is exactly as it was in the first place. Furthermore, as long as this cycle can be repeated, such a debt could safely exist in perpetuity! And why not? Its underlying asset also exists, eternally renewed, in perpetuity.

To be sure, not many businesses are run this way, for the obvious reason that tastes and techniques in the real world are anything but changeless. Indeed, there is every reason to believe that when a factory wears out it will *not* be replaced by another costing exactly as much and producing just the same commodity. Yet, highly stable businesses such as Consolidated Edison or A.T.&T. do, in fact, continuously "refund" their bond issues, paying off old bonds with new ones, and never "paying back" their indebtedness as a whole. A.T.&T., for instance, actually did increase its total indebtedness from $1.1 billion in 1929 to $11.7 billion in 1968. Consolidated Edison Company actually did run up its debt from $240 million in 1929 to $1.9 billion in 1968. And the credit rating of both companies today is as good as, or better than, it was in 1929.

Thus some individual enterprises that face conditions of stability similar to our imaginary situations do actually issue bonds "in perpetuity," paying back each issue when it is due, only to replace it with another (and, as we have seen, *bigger*) issue.

Only a few very strong individual businesses can carry their debts indefinitely, but the business sector *as a whole* can easily do so. For although most individual businesses must prudently seek to retire their debts, as we look over the whole economy we can see that as one business extinguishes its debt, another is borrowing an even larger sum. Why larger? Because the *assets* of the total business sector are also steadily rising.

Table 15-2 shows this trend in the growth of corporate debt.*

Note that from 1929 through 1940, corporate debt *declined*. The shrinkage coincided with the years of depression and slow recovery,

Year	1929	1933	1940	1950	1965	1966	1967
Billions of dollars*	$47.3	47.9	43.7	60.1	210.3	229.7	253.9

*Maturity over one year.

TABLE 15 · 2

CORPORATE LONG-TERM DEBT

*We do not show the parallel rise in new equities (shares of stock), since changes in stock market prices play so large a role here. We might, however, add a mental note to the effect that business issues new stock each year, as well as new bonds. In the 1960's, net new stock issues have ranged from about $1 to $5 billion per annum.

when additions to capital plant were small. But beginning with the onset of the postwar period, we see a very rapid increase in business indebtedness, an increase that continues down to our present day.

If we think of this creation of debt (and equity) as part of the savings-investment process, the relationship between debts and assets should be clear. Debts are claims, and we remember how claims can arise as the financial counterpart of the process of real capital formation. Thus, rising debts on capital account are a sign that assets are also increasing. It is important to emphasize the *capital account.* Debts incurred to buy capital assets are very different from those incurred to pay current expenses. The latter have very little close connection with rising wealth, whereas when we see that debts on corporate capital account are rising, we can take for granted that assets are probably rising as well. The same is true, incidentally, for the ever-rising total of consumer debts that mirror a corresponding increase in consumers' assets. As our stock of houses grows, so does our total mortgage debt; as our personal inventories of cars, washing machines, and other appliances grow, so does our outstanding consumer indebtedness.

GOVERNMENT DEFICITS

Can government, like business, borrow "indefinitely"? The question is important enough to warrant a careful answer. Hence, let us begin by comparing government borrowing and business borrowing.

One difference that springs quickly to mind is that businesses borrow in order to acquire productive assets. That is, matching the new claims on the business sector is additional real wealth that will provide for larger output. From this additional wealth, business will also receive the income to pay interest on its debt or dividends on its stock. But what of the government? Where are its productive assets?

We have already noted that the government budget includes dams, roads, housing projects, and many other items that might be classified as assets. During the 1960's, federal expenditures for such civil construction projects averaged about $5 billion a year. Thus the total addition to the gross public debt during the 1960's (it rose from roughly $285 billion in 1959 to $358 billion in 1968) could be construed as merely the financial counterpart of the creation of public assets.*

Why is it not so considered? Mainly because, as we have seen, the peculiar character of public expenditures leads us to lump together all public spending, regardless of kind. In many European countries, however, public capital expenditures are sharply differentiated from public current expenditures. If we had such a system, the government's deficit on capital account could then be viewed as the public equivalent

---

*By the "gross" public debt we mean all federal obligations, including government bonds held by agencies of the federal government itself. The net debt is that portion of the total held by the public. In 1968 this was $229 billion.

of business's deficit on capital account. Such a change might considerably improve the rationality of much discussion concerning the government's deficit.

But there is still a difference. Private capital enhances the earning capacity of a private business, whereas most public capital, save for such assets as toll roads, does not "make money" for the public sector. Does this constitute a meaningful distinction?

We can understand, of course, why an individual business insists that its investment must be profitable. The actual money that the business will pay out in the course of making an investment will almost surely not return to the business that spent it. A shirt manufacturer, for instance, who invests in a new factory cannot hope that the men who build that factory will spend all their wages on his shirts. He knows that the money he spends through investment will soon be dissipated throughout the economy, and that it can be recaptured only through strenuous selling efforts.

Not quite so with a national government, however. Its income does not come from sales but from taxes, and those taxes reflect the general level of income of the country. Thus *any* investment money that government lays out, just because it enters the general stream of incomes, redounds to the taxing capacity or, we might say, the "earning capacity" of government.

How much will come back to the government in taxes? That depends on two main factors: the impact of government spending on income via the multiplier, and the incidence and progressivity of the tax structure. Under today's normal conditions, the government will recover about half or a little more of its expenditure.* But in any event, note that the government does not "lose" its money in the way that a business does. Whatever goes into the income stream is always *available* to the government as a source of taxes; but whatever goes into the income stream is not necessarily available to any single business as a source of sales.

This reasoning helps us understand why federal finance is different from state and local government finance. An expenditure made by New York City or New York State is apt to be respent in many other areas of the country. Thus taxable incomes in New York will not, in all probability, rise to match local spending. As a result, *state and local governments must look on their finances much as an individual business does.* The power of full fiscal recapture belongs solely to the federal government.

---

*We can make a rough estimate of the multiplier effect of additional public expenditure as 2 and of the share of an additional dollar of GNP going to federal taxes as 30 per cent (see page 250). Thus $1 of public spending will create $2 of GNP, of which 60¢ will go back to the federal government.

INTERNAL AND EXTERNAL DEBTS

This difference between the limited powers of recoupment of a single firm and the relatively limitless powers of a national government lies at the heart of the basic difference between business and government deficit spending. It helps us understand why the government has a capacity for financial operation that is inherently of a far higher order of magnitude than that of business. We can sum up this fundamental difference in the contrast between the *externality of business debts* and the *internality of national government debts.*

What do we mean by the externality of business debts? We simply mean that business firms owe their debts to someone distinct from themselves, whether this be bondholders or the bank from which they borrowed. Thus, to service or to pay back its debts, business must transfer funds from its own possession into the possession of outsiders. If this transfer cannot be made, if a business does not have the funds to pay its bondholders or its bank, it will go bankrupt.

The government is in a radically different position. Its bondholders, banks, and other people or institutions to whom it owes its debts belong to the same community as that whence it extracts its receipts. In other words, the government does not have to transfer its funds to an "outside" group to pay its bonds. It transfers them, instead, from some members of the national community (taxpayers) to other members of the *same* community (bondholders). The contrast is much the same as that between a family that owes a debt to another family, and a family in which the husband has borrowed money from his wife; or again between a firm that owes money to another, and a firm in which one branch has borrowed money from another. *Internal debts do not drain the resources of one community into another, but merely redistribute the claims among members of the same community.*

PROBLEMS OF A NATIONAL DEBT

A government cannot always borrow without trouble, however. Important and difficult problems of money management are inseparable from a large debt. More important, the people or institutions from whom taxes are collected are not always exactly the same people and institutions to whom interest is paid, so that servicing a government debt often poses problems of *redistribution of income.* For instance, if all government bonds were owned by rich people and if all government taxation were regressive (i.e., proportionately heavier on low incomes), then servicing a government debt would mean transferring income from the poor to the rich. Considerations of equity aside, this would also probably involve distributing income from spenders to savers, and would thereby intensify the problem of closing the savings gap.

In addition, a debt that a government owes to foreign citizens is *not* an internal debt. It is exactly like a debt that a corporation owes to an "outside" public, and it can involve payments that can cripple a firm.* Do not forget that the internality of debts applies only to *national* debts held as bonds by members of the same community of people whose incomes contribute to government revenues.

Finally, we must not overlook the practical difficulties of government spending. The problem is that there is usually a long lag between the time of recognition, when the need for more public spending is first admitted, and the actual expenditure of the money itself. The time lag may, in fact, be so long—eighteen to twenty-four months—that by the time the public expenditures take effect, the condition they were supposed to remedy may have disappeared or worsened. In either case, the original government program is no longer the proper one. To counteract this difficulty, many economists have urged that the government keep a "stockpile" of approved public works, to be rapidly put into effect when needed. Numerous political and technical difficulties surround this proposal, however.

Because of the time-lag problem, interest has recently focused on another method of achieving a government deficit: a deliberate tax cut (while holding expenditures steady). The purpose of such a tax cut is also to create a deficit in the government sector—but a deficit which is brought about not by increased government spending, but by encouraging increased *consumer* spending.

This is the method of stimulating the economy used in the now famous Kennedy tax cut of early 1964, and it is a method likely to be employed again when the need for government stimulus arises. It need hardly be said that cutting taxes is always politically popular and that tax cuts therefore have a somewhat easier time than increased spending programs have in getting through Congress. Yet even tax cuts take time to get through, and some economists have therefore suggested that we should have *flexible tax rates* that could be adjusted upward or downward, within limits, by presidential action to create quickly a budgetary deficit or surplus.†

Despite their speedy impact, tax cuts still present some problems.

---

* About 5 per cent of the U.S. debt is held by foreigners.

† An interesting problem in the offing is that of "fiscal drag." Because of its progressive tax schedules, the tax income of the federal government rises faster than GNP, as we have already seen. It is now estimated that a normally growing GNP will yield increased revenues of about $8 billion a year to the federal government. Unless these revenues are spent, they will cause a demand gap, just as any uncompensated savings would. Some economists, led by Walter Heller, Chairman of the Council of Economic Advisers under President Kennedy, are suggesting that the government should get rid of this "drag" by automatically distributing all or part of this surplus to the states where it would be used to bolster weak state finances and to help with their pressing expenditure needs. Thereafter, if there is still a surplus at the federal level, taxes can be trimmed or expenditures of various kinds increased. If the economy is in need of a brake, perhaps we can even pay back some of the national debt, that is, deliberately create a public demand gap. All this, needless to say, assumes the absence of armed conflict such as the Vietnam war.

One problem is that some of the tax cut will undoubtedly result in higher consumer saving, so that the net effect on demand of a tax cut of $1 billion will be less than the net effect of increased expenditures of $1 billion. The other difficulty is that tax cuts are not likely to stimulate demand among those portions of the population who are most in need of help during a recession, because their incomes are so low that they pay no income taxes. On the contrary, the increased flow of private purchasing activity may well bypass the most afflicted portion of the community.

There is no reason, however, why both tax cuts and increased expenditures cannot be used jointly, the one for speedy effect and the other for purposeful social action. We should recognize, nevertheless, that increasing demand by public action is not a simple matter, but one that poses very substantial problems of its own.

PERPETUAL PUBLIC DEBTS

These important caveats notwithstanding, can a national government have a perpetual debt even in a dynamic and changeful economy? We have seen that it can. To be sure, the debt must be constantly refunded, much as business refunds its debts, with new issues of bonds replacing the old. But like the business sector, we can expect the government debt in this way to be maintained indefinitely.

Will our public debt grow forever? That depends largely on what happens to our business debts and equities. If business debts and equities grow fast enough—that is, if we are creating enough assets through investment—there is no reason why government debts should grow. Government deficits, after all, are designed as *supplements* to private deficits. The rationale behind public borrowing is that it will be used only when the private sector is not providing enough expenditure to give us the GNP we need.

Nonetheless, the prospect of a rising national debt bothers many people. Some day, they say, it will have to be repaid. Is this true? It may aid us to think about the problem if we try to answer the following questions:

1. *Will public assets continue to increase?*

If so, we can understand why debts grow with them, just as is the case with private debts and private assets. Conversely, if we imagine that at some future date we will have enough public assets, then public debts should cease rising, just as one day when we have enough private capital, private debts and equities will cease growing. The reason will be simple enough: we will no longer need any more net saving or net investment. All our output will go for consumption and replacement.

2. *Can we afford to pay interest on a rising debt?*

The capacity to expand debts, both public and private, depends largely

TABLE 15 · 3

DEBT AND
INTEREST
COSTS

	Net interest $ billions	Interest as proportionate cost
All corporations (1962)	$18.4	2.0 per cent of receipts
Federal government (1968)	9.5	{ 6.2 per cent of receipts { 1.4 per cent of GNP

on the willingness of people to lend money, and this willingness in turn reflects their confidence that they will be paid interest regularly and will have their money returned to them when their bond is due.

We have seen how refunding can take care of the repayment problem. But what about interest? With a private firm, this requires that interest costs be kept to a modest fraction of sales, so that they can easily be covered. With government, similar financial prudence requires that interest costs stay well within the taxable capacity of government. The figures in Table 15-3 give us some perspective on this problem today.

It can be seen that interest is a much higher percentage of federal revenues than of corporate revenues. But there is a reason for this. Corporations are supposed to maximize their sales; the government is not supposed to maximize its tax income. Hence we must also judge the size of the federal interest cost in comparison with the size of GNP, the total tax base from which the government can draw. Finally, we should know that interest as a percentage of all federal expenditures has remained very steady in recent years, and it is actually much lower than in the 1920's, when interest costs amounted to about 20 to 30 per cent of all federal outlays.

3. *Can we afford the burden of a rising debt?*

What is the "burden" of a debt? For a firm, the question is easy to answer. It is the *interest cost* that must be borne by those who owe the debt. Here, of course, we are back to the externality of debts. *The burden of a debt is the obligation it imposes to pay funds from one firm or community to another.*

But we have seen that there is no such cost for an internal debt, such as that of a nation. The *cost* of the debt—that is, the taxes that must be levied to pay interest—becomes *income* to the very same community, as checks sent to bondholders for their interest income. Every penny that the debt costs our economy in taxes returns to our economy as income.

The same is also true of the principal of the debt. The debts we owe inside the nation we also *own* inside the nation—just as the I.O.U. a husband owes his wife is also an I.O.U. owned by the family; or, again, just as an amount borrowed by Branch A of a multibranch firm is owed to Branch B of the same firm.

There is a further point here. Internal debts are debts that are considered as financial *assets* within the "family." Nobody within A.T.&T. considers its debts to be part of the assets of the firm, but many thousands of people in the U.S. consider the country's debts to be their assets. Indeed, everyone who owns a government bond considers it an asset. Thus in contrast to external debts, paying back an internal debt does not "lift a burden" from a community, because no burden existed in the first place! When a corporation pays off a debt to a bank, it is rid of an obligation to an outside claimant on its property. But when a husband pays back a wife, the *family* is no richer, any more than the *firm* is better off if one branch reimburses another. So, too, with a nation. If a national debt is repaid, the national economy is not rid of an obligation to an outside claimant. We would be rid only of obligations owed to one another.

REAL BURDENS

This is not to say—and the point is important—that government spending is costless. Consider for a moment the main cause of government spending over the past fifty years: the prosecution of three wars. There was surely a terrific cost to these wars in lives, health, and (in economic terms) in the use of factors of production to produce guns instead of butter. But note also that all of this cost is irrevocably and unbudgeably situated in the past. The cost of all wars is borne during the years when the wars are fought and must be measured in the destruction that was then caused and the opportunities for making civilian goods that were then missed. The debt inherited from these wars is no longer a "cost." Today it is only an instrument for the transfer of incomes within the American community.

So, too, with debts incurred to fight unemployment. The cost of unemployment is also borne once and for all at the time it occurs, and the benefits of the government spending to combat unemployment will be enjoyed (or if the spending is ill-advised, the wastes of spending will be suffered) when that spending takes place. Afterward, the debt persists as a continuing means of transferring incomes, but the debt no longer has any connection to the "cost" for which it was made.

Costs, in other words, are *missed opportunities,* potential well-being not achieved. Debts, on the other hand (when they are held within a country) only transfer purchasing power and do not involve the nation in giving up its output to anyone else.

INDIRECT EFFECTS

Does this mean that there are no disadvantages whatsoever in a large national debt?

We have talked of one possible disadvantage, that of transferring incomes from spenders to savers, or possibly of transferring purchasing power from productive groups to unproductive groups. But we must pay heed to one other problem. This is the problem a rising debt may cause indirectly, but nonetheless painfully, *if it discourages private investment.*

If government spending serves to turn business expectations downward, then for each dollar of government spending, we may find that we must allow for a dollar *less* of private investment spending. Were such to be the case, the real burden of government deficits would be the new productive resources that might have been laid down in the country but were not.

This could be a very serious, real cost of government debts, were such a reaction to be widespread and long-lasting. It may well be (we are not sure) that the long drawn-out and never entirely successful recovery from the Great Depression was caused, to a considerable extent, by the adverse psychological impact of government deficit spending on business investment intentions. Business did not understand deficit spending and interpreted it either as the entering wedge of socialism (instead of a crash program to save capitalism), or as a wastrel and a hare-brained economic scheme. To make matters worse, the amount of the government deficit (at its peak $4 billion), while large enough to frighten the business community, was not big enough to begin to exert an effective leverage on total demand, particularly under conditions of widespread unemployment and financial catastrophe.

Today, however, it is much less likely that deficit spending would be attended by a drop in private spending. A great deal that was new and frightening in thought and practice in the 1930's is today well-understood and tested. The war itself was, after all, an immense laboratory demonstration of what public spending could do for GNP. The experience of 1954, 1958, and above all, of 1964 gives good reason to believe that deficit spending in the future will not cause a significant slowdown in private investment expenditure.

PERSONAL DEBTS AND PUBLIC DEBTS

In view of the fact that our national debt today figures out to approximately $1,700 for every man, woman, and child, it is not surprising that we frequently hear appeals to "common sense," telling us how much better we would be without this debt, and how our grandchildren will groan under its weight.

Is this true? We have already discussed the fact that internal debts are different from external debts, but let us press the point home from a different vantage point. Suppose we decided that we would "pay off" the debt. This would mean that our government bonds would be redeemed for cash. To get the cash, we would have to tax ourselves (unless we wanted to roll the printing presses), so that what we would really be doing would be transferring money from taxpayers to bondholders.

Would that be a net gain for the nation? Consider the typical holder of a government bond—a family, a bank, or a corporation. It now holds the world's safest and most readily sold paper asset from which a regular income is obtained. After our debt is redeemed, our families, banks, and corporations will have two choices: (1) they can hold cash and get *no* income, or (2) they can invest in other securities that are slightly *less* safe. Are these investors better off? As for our grandchildren, it is true that if we pay off the debt they will not have to "carry" its weight. But to offset that, neither will they be carried by the comfortable government bonds they would otherwise have inherited. They will also be relieved from paying taxes to meet the interest on the debt. Alas, they will be relieved as well of the pleasure of depositing the green Treasury checks for interest payments that used to arrive twice a year.

THE PUBLIC SECTOR AGAIN IN PERSPECTIVE

We have spent enough time on the question of the debt. Now we must ask what is it that close examination of the problems of government finance reveals, making them look so different from what we expect. The answer is largely that we think of the government as if it were a firm or a household, when it is actually something else. *The government is a sector;* and if we want to think clearly about it, we must compare it, not to the maxims and activities of a household or a firm, but to those of the entire consumer sector or the entire business sector.

Then we can see that the government sector plays a role not too dissimilar from that of the business sector. We have seen how businesses, through their individual decisions to add to plant and equipment, act in concert to offset the savings of consumers. The government, we now see, acts in precisely the same way, except that its decisions, rather than reflecting the behavior of innumerable entrepreneurs in a search for profit, reflect the deliberate political will of the community itself.

Persons who do not understand the intersectoral relationships of the economy like to say that business must "live within its income" and that government acts irresponsibly in failing to do so. These critics fail to see that business does *not* live within its income, but borrows the savings of other sectors, and thus typically and normally spends more than it takes in from its sales alone. By doing so, of course, it serves the invaluable function of providing an offset for saving that would otherwise create a demand gap and thereby precipitate a downward movement in economic activity.

Once this offsetting function is understood, it is not difficult to see that government, as well as business, can serve as a "spender" to offset savings, and that in the course of doing so, both government and business typically create new assets for the community.

Finally, we have seen something else that gives us a last insight into government spending. We have seen that the creation of earning assets is indispensable for business, because each asset constitutes the means by which an individual business seeks to recoup its own investment spending. But with the government, the definition of an "earning asset" can properly be much larger than with a business firm. The government does not need its assets to make money for itself directly, for the government's economic capability arises from its capacity to tax *all* incomes. So far as the government is concerned, then, all that matters is that savings be turned into expenditures, and thereby into taxable incomes.

As a result, government can and should be motivated—even in a self-interested way—by a much wider view of the economic process than would be possible or proper for a single firm. Whereas a firm's assets are largely its capital goods, the assets of a nation are not only capital wealth but the whole productive capacity of its people. Thus government expenditures that redound to the health or well-being or education of its citizens are just as properly considered asset-building expenditures as are its expenditures on dams and roads.

One last thought remains. We have seen that the government can undertake fiscal operations far beyond those of any single firm. What we have not considered are the *political dangers* that may result from such a course. Is the use of the public sector compatible with the freedom of action on which a market society is based?

Much ink has been spilled on the problem of the "mixed economy" —the economy in which the public sector undertakes some responsibilities formerly entrusted to the private sector. Unquestionably, a mixed economy produces problems of many kinds, and in our next chapters we shall have something to say about various criteria that bear on the use of the government's powers. Yet few economists today would advocate returning to an economy without a strong fiscal policy. We have come to understand that the operation of the economy depends on the interplay of the sectors, and that the public sector is the *only* one inherently and legitimately under our collective control.

We should understand as well that the idea of compensatory public finance is based on a *minimal interference* into the operations of the market economy. For what are the alternatives? One would be not to intervene at all and to allow the savings-investment balance to work itself out as the propensity to consume and the inducement to invest might dictate. The risk here is that an imbalance could well precipitate a severe and cumulative depression with unforeseeable social and political consequences. The other alternative is to penetrate directly into the decision-making activities of the economy, to enforce household or business spending in conformance with a central plan. Here the cost is plain: the severe infringement of personal economic freedom. As a means of correcting the gross mistakes of the economy without running the risks of these extremes, the compensatory use of the public spending power (together with the wise use of its monetary mechanism, about which we shall soon learn) has much to recommend it.

POLITICAL VS. ECONOMIC JUDGMENTS

In the end, an important distinction must be made between two kinds of judgments to be passed on government spending, one valid and one not. The valid judgments have to do with *how large the public sector should be, for what purposes it should be employed, or what techniques—such as tax cuts—are appropriate at a given time.* The public sector is rightfully subject to these judgments, where reasonable men may well differ.

The other kind of judgment concerns the "soundness" of fiscal policy itself, including in particular deficit spending, as a means of offsetting the savings gap. Here the issue is not the size of the public sector or the purpose for which it is used, for one can have a large deficit even with a small public sector. The issue in the second case concerns only the validity of the economic principles of sectoral analysis. Here political judgments must be laid aside, and the logic of government spending as a demand-creating device must be considered on its own merits, in the light of an understanding of the macroeconomic process as a whole. Reasonable men may still differ as to the relative worth of different government measures, but on the propriety of the basic economics of public finance there should be a large area of agreement.

SUMMARY

1. The *public sector* derives its income from three main sources: indirect taxes (mainly for state and local governments), personal income and other taxes, and corporate taxes. Expenditures for goods and services are roughly equally divided between federal government and state and local government, but the federal government is the larger source of transfer expenditures.

2. Comparing the 1960's with the 1920's, we find that the public sector has grown considerably as a proportion of GNP. During the 1960's, the level remains roughly unchanged. Federal purchases have grown largely for defense purposes.

3. The critical differentiating factor between the public and the private sectors is that the public sector can be deliberately employed as an instrument of *national economic policy.*

4. The use of government spending and taxing to achieve national growth or stability is called *fiscal policy.* There are two main instruments of fiscal policy: *expenditures* can be increased or decreased, and *taxes* can be raised or cut. The former acts much as an increase or decrease in private investment; the latter is mainly used to induce or to discourage consumer spending.

5. *Automatic stabilizers* help implement fiscal policy by lessening the momentum of booms and cushioning the impact of recessions. The stabilizers arise from the progressive incidence of income taxation, from expenditure programs geared to unemployment, and so on.

6. The use of the government budget as a deliberate antirecession instrument leads to *deficits.* These deficits are financed by *government borrowing* and hence lead to government debt.

7. The government debt can be thought of in the same way as much private debt: as the *financial counterpart of assets.*

8. *All debts, as long as their underlying assets are economically productive, can be maintained indefinitely* by being refunded when they come due.

9. In a *progressive and growing economy, debts increase* as assets rise. Debts are only a way of financing the growth in assets.

10. National governments have the power of fiscal recapture of any money spent by them—a power not available to state governments or even to the largest businesses. Hence national governments are in a fundamentally different position regarding the safety of their domestically-held debts. This difference is expressed in the concept of *internal debts* versus *external* ones.

11. Domestically-held national debts do not lead to bankruptcy. They do present important and difficult problems of *monetary management,* and they can also result in the *redistribution of income.* These are *real burdens* of the debt.

12. *Repaying the debt would not lift a burden from the economy.* Taxes would decrease (because the debt need no longer be serviced), but income would also decrease (because interest would no longer be paid). Former government bondholders would have to find another acceptable financial asset.

13. The confusion with which the public debt is often viewed arises from a failure to understand that *the government is not a "household" but a sector,* fully comparable to the business sector in its intersectoral operations.

14. Deficits can be incurred by *tax cuts* or by *increased expenditures.* Both present problems. *Tax cuts may not put income where it is needed.* Also, tax cuts will probably not be wholly spent, but will result in some additional saving. On the other hand, *increased expenditures may take much too long* to combat a turndown efficiently.

15. The true problem with regard to the public sector lies in the *uses to which its activities are put,* and *the skill with which its policies are managed.* These can be very important problems, but they do not involve the propriety of fiscal policy, as such.

1. What are the main differences between the public and the private sectors? Are these differences economic or political?

2. Show in a diagram how increased government expenditure can offset a demand gap. Show also how decreased government taxation can do the same.

3. Show diagrammatically how equilibrium is the result of the interplay of two sets of forces: on the one hand, investment and public spending; on the other hand, saving and taxation.

4. What is meant by the automatic stabilizers? Give an example of how they might work if we had an increase in investment of $20 billion and the multiplier were 2; and if the increase in taxes and the decrease in public expenditure associated with the boom in investment were $3 billion and $1 billion, respectively.

5. In what ways is a government deficit comparable to business spending for investment purposes? In what way is it not?

6. What is meant by the internality of debts? Is the debt of New York State internal? The debt of a country like Israel or Egypt?

7. What relation do debts generally have to assets? Can business debts increase indefinitely? Can a family's? Can the debt of all consumers?

8. What do you consider a better way of combating a mild recession—tax cuts or higher expenditures? Why? Suppose we had a deep recession, then what would you do?

9. In what sorts of economic conditions should the government run a surplus?

10. Suppose the government cuts taxes by $10 billion and also cuts its expenditures by the same amount. Will this stimulate the economy? Suppose it raises its expenditures and also raises taxes? Would this be a good antirecession policy?

11. What are the real burdens of a national debt?

12. Trace out carefully the consequences of paying back all the national debt.

13. How would you explain to someone who is adamantly opposed to all deficit financing that it is perfectly sound policy in certain circumstances?

14. What do you think are the principal dangers to be guarded against in public expenditure?

MONEY 16

We have almost completed our study of the determinants of gross national product, and soon we can combine the separate sectoral analyses into an over-all view of the economy. But first there is a matter that we must integrate into our discussion. This is the role that money plays in fixing or changing the level of GNP, along with the other forces that we have come to know.

Actually, we have been talking about money throughout our exposition. After all, one cannot discuss "expenditure" without assuming the existence of money. But now we must look behind this unexamined assumption and find out exactly what we mean when we speak of money. This will entail two tasks. In this chapter we shall investigate the perplexing question of what money *is*—for as we shall see, money is surely one of the most sophisticated and curious inventions of human society. Then in our next chapter, once we have come to understand what currency and gold and bank deposits are and how they come into being, we will look into the effect that money has on our economic operations.

THE SUPPLY OF MONEY

Let us begin, then, by asking—"What is money?" The question is by no means as simple to answer as it would appear. Coin and currency are certainly money. But are checks money? Are the deposits from which we draw checks money? Are savings accounts money? Stamps? Government bonds?

The answer is a somewhat arbitrary one. From the spectrum of possible candidates, we reserve the term *money* for those items used to make *payments.* This means that we include cash in the public's possession and checking accounts, because we pay for most things by cash or check. Surprisingly, it means that we do not count savings accounts, since we have to draw "money" *out* of our savings accounts, in the form of cash or a check, if we want to use our savings account to make an expenditure. So, too, we have to sell government bonds to get money. Stamps can sometimes be used to make small payments, but they are too insignificant to matter.

CURRENCY

Money, then, is mainly currency and checking accounts; and of these, currency is the form most familiar to us. Yet there is a considerable mystery even about currency. Who determines how much currency there is? How is the supply of coins or bills regulated?

We often assume that the supply of currency is "set" by the government that "issues" it. Yet when we think about it, we realize that the government does not just hand out money, and certainly not coin or bills. When the government pays people, it is nearly always by check.

Then who does fix the amount of currency in circulation? You can answer the question by asking how you yourself determine how much currency you will carry. If you think about it, the answer is that you "cash" a check when you need more currency than you have, and you put the currency back into your checking account when you have more than you need.

What you do, everyone does. The amount of cash that the public holds at any time is no more and no less than the amount that it *wants* to hold. When it needs more—at Christmas, for instance—the public draws currency by cashing checks on its own checking accounts; and when Christmas is past, shopkeepers (who have received the public's currency) return it to their checking accounts.

Thus the amount of currency we have bears an obvious, important relation to the size of our bank accounts, for we can't write checks for cash if our accounts will not cover them.

Does this mean, then, that the banks have as much currency in their vaults as the total of our checking accounts? No, it does not. But to understand that, let us follow the course of some currency that we deposit in our bank for credit to our account.

When you put money into a commercial bank,* the bank does not hold that money for you as a pile of specially earmarked bills or as a bundle of checks made out to you from some payer. The bank takes notice of your deposit simply by crediting your "account," a bookkeeping page recording your present "balance." After the amount of the currency or check has been credited to you, the currency is put away with the bank's general store of vault cash and the checks are sent to the banks from which they came, where, of course, they will be charged against the accounts of the people who wrote them.

There is probably no misconception in economics harder to dispel than the idea that banks are warehouses stuffed with money. In point of fact, however, you might search as hard as you pleased in your bank, but you would find no other kind of money that was yours but a bookkeeping account in your name. This seems like a very unreal form of money, and yet, the fact that you can present a check at the teller's window and convert your bookkeeping account into cash proves that your account must nonetheless be "real."

But suppose that you and all the other depositors tried to convert your accounts into cash on the same day. You would then find something shocking. There would not be nearly enough cash in the bank's till to cover your total withdrawals. In 1968, for instance, total demand deposits in the United States amounted to about $150 billion. But the total amount of coin and currency held by the banks was only $4.7 billion!

At first blush, this seems like a highly dangerous state of affairs. But second thoughts are more reassuring. After all, most of us put money into a bank because we do *not* need it immediately, or because making payments in cash is a nuisance compared with making them by check. Yet, there is always the chance—more than that, the certainty—that some depositors *will* want their money in currency. How much currency will the banks need then? What will be a proper "reserve" for them to hold?

For many years, the banks themselves decided what reserve ratio constituted a safe proportion of currency to hold against their demand deposits (the technical name for checking accounts). Today, however, most large banks are members of the Federal Reserve, a central banking system established in 1913 to strengthen the banking activities of the nation. Under the Federal Reserve System, the nation is divided into twelve districts, in each of which there is a Federal Reserve Bank owned (but not really controlled) by the member banks of its district. In turn,

---

*A commercial bank is a bank that is empowered by law to offer checking services. It may also have savings accounts. A savings bank has only savings accounts and may not offer checking services.

the twelve Reserve Banks are themselves coordinated by a seven-man Federal Reserve Board in Washington. Since the members of the board are appointed for fourteen-year terms, they constitute a body that has been purposely established as an independent, nonpolitical monetary authority.*

One of the most important functions of the Federal Reserve Board is to establish reserve ratios for different categories of banks, within limits set by Congress. Historically these reserve ratios have ranged between 13 and 26 per cent of demand deposits for city banks, with a somewhat smaller reserve ratio for country banks. Today, for larger banks the reserve city ratio is 17.5 per cent; the country ratio 13 per cent. The Federal Reserve Board also sets reserve requirements for "time" (similar to savings) deposits. These are 6 per cent. Do not forget, however, that time deposits do not count—or directly serve—as "money."

THE BANKS' BANK

Yet here is something odd! We noticed that in 1968 the total amount of deposits was $150 billion and that banks' holdings of coin and currency were only $4.7 billion. This is much less than the 17.5 per cent—or even 13 per cent—reserve against deposits established by the Federal Reserve Board. How can this be?

The answer is that cash is not the only reserve a bank holds against deposits. It also holds as its reserve *claims on other banks.*

What are these claims? Suppose you deposit a check from someone who has an account in Bank B into your account in Bank A. Bank A credits your account and then presents the check to Bank B for "payment." By "payment" Bank A does not mean coin and currency, however. Instead, Bank A and Bank B settle their transaction at still *another* bank where both Bank A and Bank B have their own accounts. These are the twelve Federal Reserve Banks of the country, where all banks who are members of the Federal Reserve System (and this accounts for banks holding most of the deposits in our banking system) *must* open accounts. Thus at the Federal Reserve Bank, Bank A's account will be credited and Bank B's account will be debited, in this way moving reserves from one bank to the other.†

In other words, *the Federal Reserve Banks serve their member banks in exactly the same way as the member banks serve the public.* Member

---

*This has resulted, on occasion, in sharp clashes of viewpoint with the Treasury Department or the Bureau of the Budget where fiscal and economic policy is formulated by each administration. There is some disagreement over whether the nation is better served by a Federal Reserve that can impede an economic policy it disagrees with or one that is bound to assist the economic aims of each incumbent administration. Generally speaking, however, there has been a harmony of views between the monetary and the fiscal authorities.

†When money is put into a bank account, the account is credited; when money is taken out, the account is debited.

banks automatically deposit in their Federal Reserve accounts all checks they get from other banks. As a result, banks are constantly "clearing" their checks with one another through the Federal Reserve System, because their depositors are constantly writing checks on their own banks payable to someone who banks elsewhere. Meanwhile, *the balance that each bank maintains at the Federal Reserve—that is, the claim it has on other banks—counts, equally as much as any currency, as part of its reserve against deposits.*

In 1968, therefore, when demand deposits were $150 billion and cash in the banks only $4.7 billion, we would expect the member banks to have had heavy accounts with the Federal Reserve banks. And so they did—$22.3 billions in all. Thus, total reserves of the banks were $27 billion ($4.7 billion in cash plus $22.3 billion in Federal Reserve accounts), enough for legal backing of all deposits.

FRACTIONAL RESERVES

Thus we see that our banks operate on what is called *a fractional reserve system.* The size of the minimum fraction is determined by the Federal Reserve, for reasons of control that we shall shortly learn about. It is *not* determined, as we might be tempted to think, to provide a "safe" backing for our bank deposits. For under *any* fractional system if *all* depositors decided to draw out their accounts in currency and coin from all banks at the same time, the banks would be unable to meet the demand for cash and would have to close. We call this a "run" on the banking system. Needless to say, runs can be terrifying and destructive economic phenomena.*

Why, then, do we court the risk of runs, however small this risk may be? What is the benefit of a fractional banking system? To answer that, let us look into our bank again.

LOANS AND INVESTMENTS

Suppose its customers have given our bank $1 million in deposits and that the Federal Reserve Board requirements are 20 per cent, a simpler figure to work with then the actual one. Then we know that our bank must at all times keep $200,000, either in currency in its own till or in its demand deposit at the Federal Reserve Bank.

But having taken care of that requirement, what does the bank do with the remaining deposits? If it simply lets them sit, either as vault cash or as a deposit at the Federal Reserve, our bank will be very "liquid," but it will have no way of making an income. Unless it charges a great deal for its checking services, it will have to go out of business.

---

*A run on a *single* bank can be met by other banks lending cash. But a run on all banks far exceeds the cash resources of the community. Do not forget, however, that nowadays most accounts are insured up to $15,000 by the Federal Deposit Insurance Corporation, an agency of the federal government. This makes a run highly improbable; and even if a run should occur, it assures most depositors that they will eventually get their money back.

And yet there is an obvious way for the bank to make an income, while performing a valuable service. The bank can use all the cash and check claims it does not need for its reserve to make *loans* to businessmen or families or to make financial *investments* in corporate or government bonds. It will thereby not only earn an income, but it will assist the process of business investment and government borrowing. Thus the mechanics of the banking system lead us back to the concerns at the very center of our previous analysis.

INSIDE THE BANKING SYSTEM

Fractional reserves allow banks to lend, or to invest in securities, part of the funds that have been deposited with them. But that is not the only usefulness of the fractional reserve system. It works as well to help enlarge or diminish the supply of investible or loanable funds, as the occasion demands. Let us follow how this process works. To make the mechanics of banking clear, we are going to look at the actual books of the bank—in simplified form, of course—so that we can see how the process of lending and investing appears to the banker himself.

ASSETS AND LIABILITIES

We begin by introducing two basic elements of business accounting: *assets* and *liabilities*. Every student at some time or another has seen the balance sheet of a firm, and many have wondered how total assets always equal total liabilities. The reason is very simple. Assets are all the things or claims a business owns. Liabilities are claims against those assets—some of them the claims of creditors, some the claims of owners (called the Net Worth of the business). Since assets show everything that a business owns, and since liabilities show how claims against these selfsame things are divided between creditors and owners, it is obvious that the two sides of the balance sheet must always come to exactly the same total.

T ACCOUNTS

Businesses show their financial condition on a *balance sheet* on which all items on the left side represent assets and all those on the right side represent liabilities. By using a simple two-column balance sheet (called a "T account" because it looks like a T), we can follow very clearly what happens to our bank as we deposit money in it or as it makes loans or investments.

We start off with the example we have just used, in which we open a brand new bank with $1 million in cash and checks on other banks. Accordingly our first entry in the T account shows the two sides of this transaction. Notice that our bank has gained an asset of $1 million, the cash and checks that it now owns, and that it has simultaneously gained $1 million in liabilities, the deposits that it *owes* to its depositors (who can, after all, take their money out any time).

Assets	Liabilities
$1,000,000 (cash and checks)	$1,000,000 (money owed to depositors)
Total $1,000,000	**Total $1,000,000**

As we know, however, our bank will not keep all its newly-gained cash and checks in the till. It may hang on to some of the cash, but it will send all the checks it has received, plus any currency that it feels it does not need, to the Fed for deposit in its account there. As a result, its T account will now look like this:

Assets		Liabilities	
Vault cash	$ 100,000	Deposits	$1,000,000
Deposit at Fed	900,000		
Total	**$1,000,000***	**Total**	**$1,000,000**

*If you will examine some bank balance sheets, you will see these items listed as "Cash and due from banks." This means, of course, cash in their own vaults plus their balance at the Fed.

EXCESS RESERVES

Now we recall from our previous discussion that our bank does not want to remain in this very liquid, but very unprofitable, position. According to the law, it must retain only a certain percentage of its deposits in cash or at the Federal Reserve—20 per cent in our hypothetical example. All the rest, it is free to lend or invest. As things now stand, however, it has $1 million in reserves—$800,000 more than it needs. Hence, let us suppose that it decides to put these *excess reserves* to work by lending that amount to a sound business risk. (Note that banks do not lend the excess reserves themselves. These reserves, cash and deposits at the Fed, remain right where they are. Their function is to tell the banks how much they may loan or invest.)

MAKING A LOAN

Assume now that the Smith Corporation, a well-known firm, comes in for a loan of $800,000. Our bank is happy to lend them that amount. But "making a loan" does not mean that the bank now pays the company in cash out of its vaults. Rather, *it makes a loan by opening a new checking account for the firm* and by crediting that account with $800,000. (Or if, as is likely, the Smith firm already has an account with the bank, it will simply credit the proceeds of the loan to that account.)

Assets		Liabilities	
Cash and at Fed	$1,000,000	Original deposits	$1,000,000
Loan (Smith Corp.)	800,000	New deposit (Smith Corp.)	800,000
Total	**$1,800,000**	**Total**	**$1,800,000**

Now our T account shows some interesting changes.

There are several things to note about this transaction. First, our bank's reserves (its cash and deposit at the Fed) have not yet changed. The $1 million in reserves are still there.

Second, notice that the Smith Corporation loan counts as a new asset for the bank because the bank now has a legal claim against the company for that amount. (The interest on the loan is not shown in the balance sheet; but when it is paid, it will show up as an addition to the bank's cash.)

Third, deposits have increased by $800,000. Note, however, that this $800,000 was not paid to the Smith firm out of anyone else's account in the bank. It is a new account, one that did not exist before.

THE LOAN IS SPENT

Was it safe to have opened this new account for the company? Well, we might see whether our reserves are now sufficient to cover the Smith Corporation's account as well as the original deposit accounts. A glance reveals that all is well. We still have $1 million in reserves against $1.8 million in deposits. Our reserve ratio is much higher than the 20 per cent required by law.

It is so much higher, in fact, that we might be tempted to make another loan to the next customer who requests one, and in that way further increase our earning capacity. But an experienced banker shakes his head. "The Smith Corporation did not take out a loan and agree to pay interest on it just for the pleasure of letting that money sit with you," he explains. "Very shortly, the company will be writing checks on its balance; and when it does, you will need every penny of the reserve you now have."

That, indeed, is the case. Within a few days we find that our bank's account at the Federal Reserve Bank has been charged with a check for $800,000 written by the Smith Corporation in favor of the Jones Corporation, which carries its account at another bank. Now we find that our T account has changed dramatically to look like this:

Assets		Liabilities	
Cash and at Fed	$ 200,000	Original deposits	$1,000,000
Loan (Smith Corp.)	800,000	Smith Corp. deposits	0
Total	**$1,000,000**	**Total**	**$1,000,000**

Let us see exactly what has happened. First, the Smith Corporation's check has been charged against our account at the Fed, and has reduced it from $900,000 to $100,000. Together with the $100,000 cash in our vault, this gives us $200,000 in reserves.

Second, the Smith Corporation's deposit is entirely gone, although its loan agreement remains with us as an asset.

Now if we refigure our reserves, we find that they are just right. We are required to have $200,000 in vault cash or in our Federal Reserve account against our $1 million in deposits. That is exactly the amount we have left. Our bank is now fully "loaned up."

But the banking *system* is not yet fully loaned up. So far, we have traced what happened to only our bank when the Smith Corporation spent the money in its deposit account. Now we must trace the effect of this action on the deposits and reserves of other banks.

We begin with the bank in which the Jones Corporation deposits the check it has just received from the Smith Corporation. As the following T account shows, the Jones Corporation's bank now finds itself in exactly the same position as our bank was when we opened it with $1 million in new deposits, except that the addition to this "second generation" bank is smaller than the addition to the "first generation" bank.

Assets		Liabilities	
Cash and at Fed	$800,000	Deposit (Jones Corp.)	$800,000
Total	**$800,000**	**Total**	**$800,000**

As we can see, our second generation bank has gained $800,000 in cash and in deposits. Since it needs only 20 per cent of this for required reserves, it finds itself with $640,000 excess reserves, which it is now free to use to make loans as investments. Suppose that it extends a loan to the Brown Company and that the Brown Company shortly thereafter spends the proceeds of that loan at the Black Company, which banks at yet a third bank. The following two T accounts show how the total deposits will now be affected.

SECOND GENERATION BANK
(after Brown Co. spends the proceeds of its loan)

Assets		Liabilities	
Cash and at Fed	$160,000	Deposits (Jones Corp.)	$800,000
Loan (to Brown Co.)	640,000	Deposits (Brown Co.)	0
Total	**$800,000**	**Total**	**$800,000**

THIRD GENERATION BANK
(after Black Co. gets the check of Brown Co.)

Assets		Liabilities	
Cash and at Fed	$640,000	Deposit (Black Co.)	$640,000
Total	**$640,000**	**Total**	**$640,000**

And as Fig. 16-1 makes clear, the process will not stop here, but can continue from one bank to the next as long as any lending power remains.

THE EXPANSION OF THE MONEY SUPPLY

If we now look at the bottom of Fig. 16-1, we will see something very important. Every time any bank in this chain of transactions has opened an account for a new borrower, *the supply of money has increased.* Remember that the supply of money is the sum of currency outside the banking system (i.e., in our own pockets) plus the total of demand

FIG. 16-1   EXPANSION OF THE MONEY SUPPLY

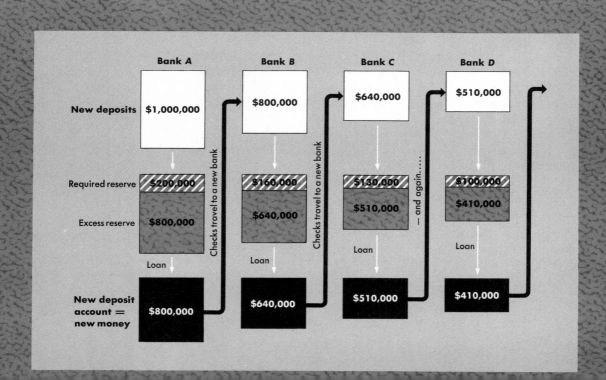

deposits.* As our chain of banks kept opening new accounts, it was simultaneously expanding the total check-writing capacity of the economy. Thus, money has materialized, seemingly out of thin air.

Now how can this be? If we tell any banker in the chain that he has "created" money, he will protest vehemently. The loans he made, he will insist, were backed at the time he made them by excess reserves as large as the loan itself. Just as we had $800,000 in excess reserves when we made our initial loan to the Smith Corporation, so every subsequent loan was always backed 100 per cent by unused reserves when it was made.

Our bankers are perfectly correct when they tell us that they never, never lend a penny more than they have. Money is not created in the lending process because a banker lends money he doesn't have. *It is created because you and I generally pay each other by checks that give us claims against each other's bank.* If we constantly cashed the checks we exchanged, no new money would be created. But we do not. We deposit each other's checks in our own bank accounts; and in doing so, we give our banks more reserves than they need against the deposits we have just made. These new excess reserves make it possible for our banks to lend or invest, and thereby to open still more deposit accounts, which in turn lead to new reserves.†

This all sounds a little frightening. Does it mean that the money supply can go on expanding indefinitely from a single loan? Wouldn't that be extremely dangerous?

It would of course be very dangerous, but there is no possibility that it can happen. For having understood how the supply of money can expand from an original increase in deposits, we may now understand equally well what keeps an expansion within bounds.

*We can now see why only currency *outside* the banks is counted as "money." Currency in a bank's vault or till counts as part of its reserves, and reserves are not money, because we cannot write checks against them.

†All this gives us a fresh insight into the question of what money is. We said before that it is whatever we use to make payments. But what do we use? The answer is a surprising one. We use *debts*—specifically, the debts of commercial banks. Deposits are, after all, nothing but the liabilities that banks owe their customers. Furthermore, we can see that one purpose of the banking system is to buy debts from other units in the economy, such as businesses or governments, in exchange for its own debts (which are money). For when a bank opens an account for a business to which it has granted a loan or when it buys a government bond, what else is it doing but accepting a debt that is *not* usable as money, in exchange for its deposit liabilities that *are* usable as money. And why is it that banks create money when they make loans, but you or I do not, when we lend money? Because we all accept bank liabilities (deposits) as money, but we do not accept personal or business I.O.U.'s to make payments with. Someone who would like to probe deeper into the curious (and very important) problem of money and how it affects our economy could do no better than to read the lucid and sparkling analysis by Peter L. Bernstein, *A Primer on Money, Banking and Gold,* 2nd ed. (New York: Random House, 1968, paperback).

1. *Not every loan generates an increase in bank deposits.*

If our bank had opened a loan account for the Smith Corporation at the same time that another firm had paid off a similar loan, there would have been no original expansion in bank deposits. In that case, the addition of $800,000 to the Smith account would have been exactly balanced by a decline of $800,000 in someone else's account. Even if that decline would have taken place in a different bank, it would still mean that the nation's total of bank deposits would not have risen, and therefore no new money would have been created. Thus, *only net additions to loans have an expansionary effect.* We will shortly see how such net additions arise in the first place.

2. *There is a limit to the rise in money supply from a single increase in loans.*

As Fig. 16-1 shows, in the chain of deposit expansion each successive bank has a smaller increase in deposits, because each bank has to keep some of its newly gained cash or checks as reserve. Hence the amount of *excess* reserve, against which loans can be made, steadily falls.

Further, we can see that the amount of the total monetary expansion from an original net increase in loans is governed by the size of the fraction that has to be kept aside each time as reserve. *In fact, we can see that just as with the multiplier, the cumulative effect of an increase in deposits will be determined by the reciprocal of the reserve fraction.* If each bank must keep one-fifth of its increased deposits as reserves, then the cumulative effect of an original increase in deposits, when it has expanded through the system, is five times the original increase. If reserves are one-fourth, the expansion is limited to four times the original increase, and so on.

3. *The monetary expansion process can work in reverse.*

Suppose that the banking system as a whole suffers a net loss of deposits. Instead of putting $1 million into a bank, the public takes it out in cash. The bank will now have too few reserves, and it will have to cut down its loans or sell its investments to gain the reserves it needs. In turn, as borrowers pay off their loans, or as bond buyers pay for their securities, cash will drain from other banks who will now find *their* reserves too small in relation to their deposits. In turn, they will therefore have to sell more investments or curtail still other loans, and this again will squeeze still other banks and reduce their reserves, with the same consequences.

Thus, just as an original expansion in deposits can lead to a multiple expansion, so an original contraction in deposits can lead to a multiple contraction. The size of this contraction is also limited by the reciprocal of the reserve fraction. If banks have to hold a 25 per cent reserve, then an original fall of $100,000 in deposits will lead to a total fall of $400,000, assuming that the system was fully "loaned up" to begin with.

If they had to hold a 20 per cent reserve, a fall of $100,000 could pyramid to $500,000.

4. *The expansion process may not be fully carried through.*
We have assumed that each bank in the chain always lends out an amount equal to its excess reserves, but this may not be the case. The third or fifth bank along the way may have trouble finding a credit-worthy customer and may decide—for the moment, anyway—to sit on its excess reserves. Or borrowers along the chain may take out cash from some of their new deposits and thereby reduce the banks' reserves and their lending powers. Thus the potential expansion may be only partially realized.

There is an interesting problem concealed behind this crisscrossing of deposits that leads to a slowly rising level of the money supply. Suppose that an imaginary island economy was served by a single bank (and let us forget about all complications of international trade, etc.), and suppose that this bank, which worked on a 20 per cent reserve ratio, was suddenly presented with an extra million dollars worth of reserves—let us say newly mined pure gold. Our bank could, of course, increase its loans to customers. By how much? *By five million dollars!*

In other words, our island bank, all by itself, could use an increase in its reserves to create a much larger increase in the money supply. It is not difficult to understand why. Any borrower of the new five million, no matter where he spent his money on the island, would only be giving his checks to someone who also banked at the single, solitary bank. The whole five million, in other words, would stay *within* the bank as its deposits, although the identity of those depositors would, of course, shift. Indeed, there is no reason why such a bank should limit its expansion of the money supply to five million. As long as the "soundness" of the currency was unquestioned, such a bank could create as much money as it wanted through new deposits, since all of those deposits would remain in its own keeping.

The imaginary bank makes it plain why ordinary commercial banks *cannot* expand deposits beyond their excess reserves. Unlike the monopoly bank, they must expect to *lose* their deposits to other banks when their borrowers write checks on their new accounts. As a result they will also lose their reserves, and this can lead to trouble.

This situation is important enough to warrant taking a moment to examine. Suppose that in our original example we had decided to lend the Smith Corporation not $800,000 but $900,000, and suppose as before that the Smith Corporation used the proceeds of that loan to pay the Jones Corporation. Now look at the condition of our bank after the Smith payment has cleared.

Assets		Liabilities	
Cash and at Fed	$ 100,000	Original deposits	$1,000,000
Loan (Smith Corp.)	900,000	Smith Corp. deposit	0
Total	**$1,000,000**	**Total**	**$1,000,000**

Our reserves would now have dropped to 10 per cent! Indeed, if we had loaned the company $1,000,000 we would be in danger of bankruptcy.

Banks are, in fact, very careful not to overlend. If they find that they have inadvertently exceeded their legal reserve requirements, they quickly take remedial action. One way that a bank may repair the situation is by borrowing reserves for a short period (paying interest for them, of course) from another bank that may have a temporary surplus at the Fed; this is called borrowing federal funds. Or a bank may quickly sell some of its government bonds and add the proceeds to its reserve account at the Fed. Or again, it may add to its reserves the proceeds of any loans that have come due and deliberately fail to replace these expired loans with new loans. Finally, a bank may borrow reserves directly from its Federal Reserve Bank, and pay interest for the loan. We shall shortly look into this method when we talk about the role of the Federal Reserve in regulating the quantity of money.

The main point is clear. A bank is safe in lending only an amount that it can afford to lose to another bank. But of course one bank's loss is another's gain. That is why, by the exchange of checks, the banking system can accomplish the same result as the island monopoly bank, whereas no individual bank can hope to do so.

INVESTMENTS AND INTEREST

If a bank uses its excess reserves to buy securities, does that lead to the same multiplication effect as a bank loan?

It can. When a bank buys government securities, it usually does so from a securities dealer, a professional trader in bonds. Its check (for $800,000 in our example) drawn on its account at the Federal Reserve will be made out to a dealer, who will deposit it in his bank. As a result, the dealer's bank suddenly finds itself with an $800,000 new deposit. It must keep 20 per cent of this as required reserve, but the remainder is excess reserve against which it can make loans or investments as it wishes.

Is there a new deposit, corresponding to that of the businessman borrower? There is: the new deposit of the securities dealer. Note that in this case, as in the case of the borrower, the new deposit on the books of the bank has not been put there by the transfer of money from some other commercial bank. The $800,000 deposit has come into being through the deposit of a check from the Federal Reserve Bank, which is not a commercial bank. Thus it represents a new addition to the deposits of the private banking system.

Let us see this in the T accounts. After our first bank has bought its $800,000 in bonds (paying for them with its Federal Reserve checking account), its T account looks like this.

Assets		Liabilities	
Cash at Fed	$ 200,000	Deposits	$1,000,000
Government bonds	800,000		
Total	$1,000,000	Total	$1,000,000

As we can see, there are no excess reserves here. But look at the bank in which the seller of the government bond has deposited the check he has just received from our bank:

Assets		Liabilities	
Cash	$800,000	New deposit of bond seller	$800,000
Total	$800,000	Total	$800,000

Here there are excess reserves of $640,000 with which additional investments can be made. It is possible for such new deposits, albeit diminishing each time, to remain in the financial circuit for some time, moving from bank to bank as an active business is done in buying government bonds. But the very activity in bidding for government bonds is likely to raise their price, and thereby lower their rate of interest.* A lower rate of interest on bonds makes higher yielding loans to business look more attractive. Thus, sooner or later, excess reserves are apt to be channeled to new loans as well as new investments. Thereafter the deposit-building process follows its familiar course.

CONTROLLING THE MONEY SUPPLY

We have now seen how a banking system can create money through the successive creation of excess reserves. But the key to the process is the creation of the *original* excess reserves, for without them the cumulative process will not be set in motion. We remember, for ex-

---

*A bond has a *fixed* rate of return and a stated face value. If it is a 4 per cent, $1000 bond, this means it will pay $40 of interest yearly. If the bond now sells on the marketplace for $1100, the $40 yearly interest will be less than a 4 per cent return. If the price should fall to $900 the $40 return will be more than 4 per cent. Thus the *yield* of a bond varies inversely—in the other direction—from its market price.

ample, that a loan will not result in an increase in the money supply if it is offset by a decline in lending somewhere else in the banking system; neither will the purchase of a bond by one commercial bank if it is only buying a security sold by another. *To get a net addition to loans or investments, however, a banking system—assuming that it is fully loaned up—needs an increase in its reserves.* Where do these extra reserves come from? That is the question we must turn to next.

THE ROLE OF THE FEDERAL RESERVE

In our example we have already met one source of changes in reserves. When the public needs less currency, and deposits its extra holdings in the banks, reserves rise, as we have seen. Contrariwise, when the public wants more currency, it depletes the banks' holdings of currency and thereby lowers their reserves. In the latter case, the banks may find that they have insufficient reserves behind their deposits. To get more currency or claims on other banks, they will have to sell securities or reduce their loans. This might put a very severe crimp in the economy. Hence, to allow bank reserves to be regulated by the public's fluctuating demand for cash would seem to be an impossible way to run our monetary system.

But we remember that bank reserves are not mainly currency; in fact, currency is a relatively minor item. Most reserves are the accounts that member banks hold at the Federal Reserve. Hence, if these accounts could somehow be increased or decreased, we could regulate the amount of reserves—and thus the permissible total of deposits—without regard to the public's changing need for cash.

This is precisely what the Federal Reserve System is designed to do. Essentially, the system is set up to regulate the supply of money by raising or lowering the reserves of its member banks. When these reserves are raised, member banks find themselves with excess reserves and are thus in a position to make loans and investments by which the supply of money will increase further. Conversely, when the Federal Reserve lowers the reserves of its member banks, they will no longer be able to make loans and investments, or may even have to reduce loans or get rid of investments, thereby extinguishing deposit accounts and contracting the supply of money.

MONETARY CONTROL MECHANISMS

How does the Federal Reserve operate? There are three ways.

1. *Changing reserve requirements.*

It was the Federal Reserve itself, we will remember, that originally determined how much in reserves its member banks should hold against their deposits. Hence by changing that reserve requirement for a given level of reserves, it can give its member banks excess reserves or can create a shortage of reserves.

In our imaginary bank we have assumed that reserves were set at 20 per cent of deposits. Suppose now that the Federal Reserve determined to lower reserve requirements to 15 per cent. It would thereby automatically create extra lending or investing power for our *existing* reserves. Our bank with $1 million in deposits and $200,000 in reserves could now lend or invest an additional $50,000 without any new funds coming in from depositors. On the other hand, if requirements were raised to, say, 30 per cent, we would find that our original $200,000 of reserves was $100,000 short of requirements, and we would have to curtail lending or investing until we were again in line with requirements.

Changing reserve ratios is a very effective way of freeing or contracting bank credit. But it is a massive instrument that sweeps across the entire banking system in an undiscriminating fashion. It is therefore used only rarely, when the Federal Reserve Board feels that the supply of money is seriously short or dangerously excessive and needs remedy on a countrywide basis. In early 1969, the board raised reserve requirements one-half per cent for all banks, partly to mop up excess reserves and partly to sound a general warning against what it considered to be a potentially dangerous inflationary state of affairs.

2. *Changing discount rates*

A second means of control uses interest rates as the money-controlling device. Recall that member banks that are short on reserves have a special privilege, if they wish to exercise it. They can *borrow* reserve balances from the Federal Reserve Bank itself, adding them of course, to their regular reserve account at the bank. The way member banks borrow is to take the government bonds they have bought and to use these as collateral, or to take the signed loan agreements they have received from their own customers and to "re-discount" these loans—that is, to borrow on them—from their Federal Reserve Bank.

The Federal Reserve Bank, of course, charges interest for lending reserves, and this interest is called the discount rate. By raising or lowering this rate, the Federal Reserve can make it attractive or unattractive for member banks to borrow to augment reserves. Thus in contrast with changing the reserve ratio itself, changing the discount rate is a mild device that allows each bank to decide for itself whether it wishes to increase its reserves or not. In addition, changes in the discount rate tend to influence the whole structure of interest rates—either tightening or loosening money in general.

3. *Open-market operations.*

Most frequently used, however, is a third technique called open-market operations. This technique permits the Federal Reserve Banks to change the supply of reserves by buying or selling U.S. government bonds on the open market.

How does this work? Let us suppose that the Federal Reserve authorities wish to increase the reserves of member banks. They will begin to buy government securities from dealers in the bond market; and to pay for these bonds, they will send Federal Reserve Bank checks in the amount of their purchases to dealers.

But notice something about these checks: *they are not drawn on any commercial bank!* They are drawn on the Federal Reserve Bank itself. The security dealer who sells the bond will, of course, deposit the Fed's check, as if it were any other check, in his own commercial bank; and his bank will send the Fed's check through for credit to its own account, as if it were any other check. *As a result, the dealer's bank will have gained reserves, although no other commercial bank has lost reserves.* On balance, then, the system has more lending and investing capacity than it had before. In fact, it now has *excess* reserves, and these, as we have seen, will spread out through the system. *Thus by buying bonds, the Federal Reserve has, in fact, deposited money in the accounts of its members, thereby giving them the extra reserves that it set out to create.*

Conversely, if the authorities decide that member banks' reserves are too large, they will sell securities. Now the process works in reverse. Security dealers or other buyers of bonds will send their own checks on their own regular commercial banks to the Federal Reserve in payment for these bonds. This time the Fed will take the checks of its member banks and charge their accounts, thereby reducing their reserves. *Since these checks will not find their way into another commercial bank, the system as a whole will have suffered a diminution of its reserves.* By selling securities, in other words, the Federal Reserve authorities lower the Federal Reserve accounts of member banks, thereby diminishing their reserves.*

PAPER MONEY AND GOLD

Here is a good place to clear up one last mystery of the monetary system—the mystery of where currency (coin and bills) actually comes from and where it goes. If we examine most of our paper currency, we will find that it has "Federal Reserve Note" on it; that is, it is paper

---

* Isn't this, some bright student will ask, really the same thing as raising or lowering the reserve ratio? If the Fed is really just putting money into member bank accounts when it buys bonds, and taking money out when it sells them, why does it bother to go through the open market? Why not just tell the member banks that their reserves are larger or smaller?

Analytically, our student is entirely right. There is however, cogent reason for working through the bond market. It is that the open-market technique allows banks to *compete* for their share of the excess reserves that are being made available or taken away. Banks that are good at attracting depositors will thereby get extra benefit from an increase in the money supply. Thus, rather than assigning excess reserves by executive fiat, the Fed uses the open market as an allocation device. Much more about this function of the market in Part Three.

money issued by the Federal Reserve System. We understand, by now, how the public gets these notes: it simply draws them from its checking accounts. When it does so, the commercial banks, finding their supplies of vault cash low, ask their Federal Reserve district banks to ship them as much new cash as they need.

And what does the Federal Reserve Bank do? It takes packets of $1's and $5's and $10's out of its vaults, *where these stacks of printed paper have no monetary significance at all,* charges the requisite amount against its member banks' balances, and ships the cash out by armored truck. So long as these new stacks of bills remain in the member banks' possession, they are still not money! But soon they will pass out to the public, where they will be money. Do not forget, of course, that as a result, the public will have that much *less* money left in its checking accounts.

Could this currency-issuing process go on forever? Could the Federal Reserve ship out as much money as it wanted to? Suppose that the authorities at the Fed decided to order a trillion dollars worth of bills from the Treasury mints. What would happen when those bills arrived at the Federal Reserve Banks? The answer is that they would simply gather dust in their vaults. *There would be no way for the Fed to "issue" its money unless the public wanted cash.* And the amount of cash the public could want is always limited by the amount of money it has in its checking accounts.*

Are there no limitations on this note-issuing or reserve-creating process?

Until 1967 there *were* limitations imposed by Congress, requiring the Federal Reserve to hold gold certificates equal in value to at least 25 per cent of all outstanding notes. (Gold certificates are a special kind of paper money issued by the U.S. Treasury and backed 100 per cent by gold bullion in Fort Knox.) Prior to 1964 there was a further requirement that the amount of gold certificates also be sufficient to give a 25 per cent backing as well to the total amount of member bank deposits held by the Fed. Thus the legal obligation not to go beyond this 25 per cent gold cover provided a strict ceiling on the amount of member bank reserves the Federal Reserve system could create or on the amount of notes it could ship at the request of its member banks.

All this presented no problem in, say, 1940, when the total of member bank reserves plus Federal Reserve notes came to only $20 billion, against which we held gold certificates worth almost $22 billion. Trouble began to develop, however, in the 1960's when a soaring GNP was

---

*What about wild inflations such as the German post-World War I or the Hungarian post-World War II debacles? Inflations such as these are not orderly price changes that can be discussed in terms of the supply of money, but reflect complete collapses of monetary systems where the public loses all faith in the monetary unit. There is no cure for such panics other than the constitution of a new monetary unit in which public faith will again reside.

accompanied by a steadily rising volume of both member bank reserves and Federal Reserve notes. By 1964, for example, member bank reserves had grown to $22 billion, and outstanding Reserve notes to nearly $35 billion. At the same time, for reasons that we shall learn more about in Part Four, our gold stock had declined to just over $15 billion. With $57 billion in liabilities ($22 billion in member bank reserves plus $35 billion in notes) and only $15 billion in gold certificates, the 25 per cent cover requirement was clearly imperiled.

Congress thereupon removed the cover requirement from member bank reserves, leaving all our gold certificates available as "backing" for our Federal Reserve notes. But even that did not solve the problem. Currency in circulation continued to rise with a record GNP until it exceeded $40 billion in 1967. Our gold stock meanwhile continued to decline to $12 billion in that year and threatened to fall further. The handwriting on the wall indicated that the 25 per cent cover could not long be maintained.

There were basically two ways out of the dilemma. One would have been to change the gold cover requirements from 25 per cent to, say, 10 per cent. That would have made our gold stock more than adequate to "back" our paper money (and our member bank deposits, too).*

The second way was much simpler. *It was simply to eliminate the gold cover entirely.* With very little fuss, this is what Congress did in 1967.

GOLD
AND MONEY

Does the presence or absence of a gold cover make any difference? From the economist's point of view it does not. Gold is a metal with a long and rich history of hypnotic influence, so there is undeniably a psychological usefulness in having gold "behind" a currency. But unless that currency is 100 per cent convertible into gold, *any* money demands an act of faith on the part of its users. If that faith is destroyed, the money becomes valueless; so long as it is unquestioned, the money is "as good as gold."

Thus the presence or absence of a gold backing for currency is purely a psychological problem, so far as the value of a domestic currency is concerned.† Gold is, however, the accepted medium of settling

---

*Actually—as we shall see in the note on the gold standard, following Chapter 29—the gold never really backed our currency, since no American was legally permitted to buy gold bullion.

†Some years ago a patriotic women's organization, alarmed lest the Communists had tunneled under the Atlantic, forced an inspection of the gold stock buried at Fort Knox. It proved to be all there. An interesting question arises as to the repercussions of having found the great vault to be bare. Perhaps we might have followed the famous anthropological example of the island of Yap in the South Seas, where heavy stone cartwheels are the symbol of wealth for the leading families. One such family was particularly remarkable insofar as its cartwheel lay at the bottom of a lagoon, where it had fallen from a canoe. Although it was absolutely irretrievable and even invisible, the family's wealth was considered unimpaired, since everyone knew the stone was there. A patriotic declaration by the ladies that the gold really *was* in Fort Knox might have saved the day for the United States.

accounts in international exchanges (where again, of course, its "value" is essentially psychological), so that the possession of a substantial gold stock has very real benefits in foreign relations, as we shall see in Part Four.

But the point is worth pursuing a little further. Suppose our currency *were* 100 per cent convertible into gold—suppose, in fact, that we used only gold coins as currency. Would that improve the operation of our economy?

A moment's reflection should reveal that it would not. We would still have to cope with a very difficult problem that our bank deposit money handles rather easily. This is the problem of how we could increase the supply of money or diminish it, as the needs of the economy changed. With gold coins as money we would either have a frozen stock of money (with consequences that we shall trace in the next chapter), or our supply of money would be at the mercy of our luck in gold-mining or the currents of international trade that funneled gold into our hands or took it away. And incidentally, a gold currency would not obviate inflation, as many countries have discovered when the vagaries of international trade or a fortuitous discovery of gold mines increased their holdings of gold faster than their actual output.

As we cautioned at the outset, money is a highly sophisticated and curious invention. At one time or another nearly everything imaginable has served as the magic symbol of money: whales' teeth, shells, feathers, bark, furs, blankets, butter, tobacco, leather, copper, silver, gold, and (in the most advanced nations) pieces of paper with pictures on them or simply numbers on a ledger page. In fact, anything is usable as money, provided that there is a natural or enforceable scarcity of it, so that men can usually come into its possession only through carefully designated ways. Behind all the symbols, however, rests the central requirement of faith. Money serves its indispensable purposes as long as we believe in it. It ceases to the moment we do not. Money has well been called "the promises men live by."

But the creation of money and the control over its supply is still only half the question. We have yet to trace how our money supply influences the flow of output itself—or to put it differently, how the elaborate institutions through which men promise to honor one another's work and property affect the amount of work they do and the amount of new wealth they accumulate. This is the subject to which our next chapter will be devoted.

SUMMARY

1. Money is defined as whatever we use to make *payments*. As such, in modern economies, the most important constituents of money are *currency outside the banking system* and *demand deposits* (checking accounts).

2. Currency flows into, and is drawn out of, checking accounts. There is, however, much less currency in banks than the total amount of checking accounts.

3. Banks are forced, by law, to hold *reserves* against stated fractions of their demand deposits. For most banks these reserves can be either in *vault cash* or in *accounts* at a *Federal Reserve Bank*.

4. There are *twelve Federal Reserve Banks* that service their member banks exactly as the member banks service the public. The Reserve Banks are coordinated by a policy-making Board of Governors (Federal Reserve Board) in Washington. The Board is empowered to change reserve ratios for city or country banks, within legally established limits, and to take other actions to control the supply of money.

5. The function of the reserves established by the Federal Reserve Board is not to ensure the "safety" of the currency, but to provide a means of *controlling the supply of money*.

6. Any reserves of a commercial bank over and above those imposed by the Federal Reserve are called *excess reserves*. Commercial banks earn profits by lending or investing amounts equal to their excess reserves.

7. When a bank makes a loan, it opens an account in the name of the borrower. This account is a *net addition to total deposits and is therefore new money*. Thus bank lending can increase the supply of money. Investing in government bonds is also likely to lead to new demand deposits.

8. New deposits created by loans are typically drawn on by checks that go into other banks. Here they also give rise to excess reserves and to the possibility of *further deposit creation through more loans or investments*.

9. The total amount of new money that the banking system can create depends on the *reserve ratio*. The size of credit expansion is determined by the reciprocal of the reserve ratio.

10. It is only the banking *system* that can expand the money supply up to the limit imposed by the reciprocal of the reserve ratio. A single bank can lend only up to the amount that it is prepared to "lose." *Hence each individual bank lends only an amount that is fully covered by its excess reserves.*

11. The Federal Reserve System controls the ability of the banking system to expand the supply of money by *controlling the amount of its reserves*. It can do so in three ways:
    - By changing *reserve ratios*
    - By changing the *discount rate*
    - By *open-market operations*

12. The most commonly used method is open-market operations. This is a means of controlling the size of reserves by *purchases and sales of government bonds on the open market*. When the Federal Reserve System buys bonds, it issues in payment its own checks, which enter the commercial banks and are added to their reserves. This gives the commercial banks excess reserves and enables them to make additional loans or investments. Selling bonds brings checks from

commercial bank accounts to the Federal Reserve Banks, and thereby lowers the reserve accounts of member banks. This reduces their ability to make loans or investments.

13. There is no longer any gold backing required behind member bank reserves, or behind Federal Reserve notes. The amount or percentage of gold cover is essentially arbitrary. *Gold plays only a symbolic role in a national monetary system. The true value of money ultimately reposes in the faith men have in it.*

1. Why do we not count cash in the tills of commercial banks in the money supply? Why don't we include savings accounts?

2. When you deposit currency in a commercial bank, what happens to it? Can you ask for your particular bills again? If you demanded to see "your" account, what would it be?

3. What determines how much vault cash a bank must hold against its deposits? Would you expect this proportion to change in some seasons, such as Christmas? Do you think it would be the same in worried times as in placid ones? In new countries as in old ones?

4. Is currency the main reserve of a bank? Do reserves ensure the safety of a currency? What function do they have?

5. What are excess reserves? Suppose a bank has $500,000 in deposits and that there is a reserve ratio of 30 per cent imposed by law. What is its required reserve? Suppose it happens to hold $200,000 in vault cash or at its account at the Fed. What, if any, is its excess reserve?

6. If the bank above wanted to make loans or investments, how much would it be entitled to lend or invest?

7. Suppose its deposits increased by another $50,000. Could it lend or invest this entire amount? Any of it? How much?

8. If a bank lends money, it opens an account in the name of the borrower. Now suppose the borrower draws down his new account. What happens to the reserves of the lending bank? Show this in a T account.

9. Suppose the borrower sends his check for $1,000 to someone who banks at another bank. Describe what happens to the deposits of the second bank. If the reserve ratio is 20 per cent, how much new lending or investing can it do?

10. If the reserve ratio is 20 per cent, and the original addition to reserves is $1,000, what will be the total potential amount of new money that can be created by the banking system? If the ratio is 25 per cent?

11. What is the difference between a banking system and a single competitive bank? Can a single bank create new money? Can it create more new money than an amount equal to its excess reserves? Can a banking system create more money than its excess reserves?

12. Suppose that a bank has $1 million in deposits and $100,000 in reserves, and is fully loaned up. Now suppose the Federal Reserve System lowers reserve requirements from 10 per cent to 8 per cent. What happens to the lending capacity of the bank?

13. If the discount rate rises from 5 per cent to 6 per cent, does that affect the willingness of banks to lend? How?

14. The Federal Reserve Banks buy $100 million in U.S. Treasury notes. How do they pay for these notes? What happens to the checks? Do they affect the reserves of member banks? Will buying bonds increase or decrease the money supply?

15. Now explain what happens when the Fed sells Treasury notes. Who buys them? How do they pay for them? Where do the checks go? How does payment affect the accounts of the member banks at the Federal Reserve Banks?

16. Why do you think gold has held such a place of prestige in the minds of men?

MONEY AND THE MACRO SYSTEM 17

In our preceding chapter, we found out something about what money is and how it comes into being. Now we must turn to the much more complicated question of how money works—of what effect changes in the supply of money have on the level of output. What happens when the banks create or destroy deposits? Can we directly raise or lower incomes by altering the quantity of money? Can we control inflation or recession by using the monetary management powers of the Federal Reserve System? These extremely important questions will be the focus of discussion in this chapter.

THE QUANTITY THEORY OF MONEY

One relation between money and economic activity must already have occurred to us. It is that the quantity of money must have something to do with *prices*. Does it not stand to reason that if we increase the

QUANTITY
EQUATION

supply of money, prices will go up, and that if we decrease the amount of money, prices will fall?

Something very much like this belief lies behind one of the most famous equations in economics. The equation looks like this:

$$MV = PT$$

where

M = *quantity of money* (currency outside banks plus demand deposits)
V = *velocity of circulation,* or the number of times per period or per year that an average dollar changes hands
P = *the general level of prices,* or a price index
T = *the number of transactions made in the economy* in a year, or a measure of *physical output*

If we think about this equation, its meaning is not hard to grasp. What the quantity equation says is that *the amount of expenditure* (*M* times *V,* or the quantity of money times the frequency of its use) *equals the amount of receipts* (*P* times *T,* or the price of an average sale times the number of sales). What the quantity equation *seems* to say, however, is that there is a direct *causal* connection between money and prices—that if you increase the amount of money, you will increase prices, or if you decrease the supply of money you will cause prices to fall.

QUANTITY THEORY

Is this causal relation true? Can we directly manipulate the price level by changing the size of our stock of money?

The original inventors of the quantity equation, over half a century ago, thought this was indeed the case. And of course it would be the

FIG. 17-1 **MONEY SUPPLY AND PRICES**

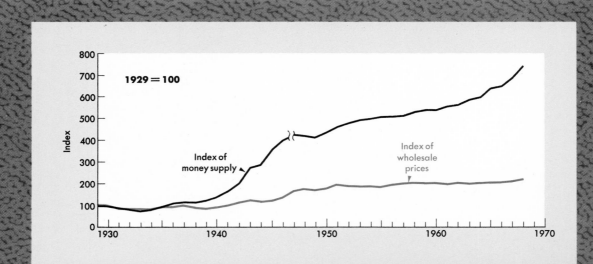

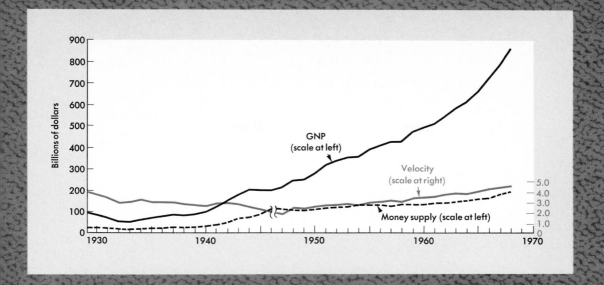

FIG. 17-2 **MONEY SUPPLY AND VELOCITY**

case, if everything else in the equation held steady while we moved the quantity of money up or down. In other words, if the velocity of circulation, *V*, and the number of transactions, *T*, were assumed to be fixed, changes in *M* would have to operate directly on *P*.

Can we test the validity of this assumption? There is an easy way to do so. Figure 17-1 shows us changes in the supply of money compared with changes in the level of prices.

A glance at Fig. 17-1 answers our question. Between 1929 and 1968, the supply of money in the United States increased over *sixfold*, while prices rose only *twofold*. Clearly, something *must* have happened to *V* or to *T* to prevent the sixfold increase in *M* from bringing about a similar increase in *P*. Let us see what those changes were.

Figure 17-2 gives us a first clue as to what is wrong with a purely mechanical interpretation of the quantity theory. In it we show how many times an average dollar was used to help pay for each year's output.* We derive this number by dividing the total expenditure for each year's output (which is, of course, the familiar figure for GNP) by the actual supply of money—currency plus checking accounts—for

CHANGES IN V

---

*Note that final output is not quite the same as *T*, which embraces *all* transactions, including those for intermediate goods. But if we define *T* so that it includes only *transactions that enter into final output*, *PT* becomes a measure of gross national product. In the same way, we can count only those expenditures that enter into GNP when we calculate *MV*. It does no violence to the idea of the quantity theory to apply it only to final output, and it makes statistical computation a good deal simpler.

each year. As the chart shows, the velocity of money fell by 50 per cent between 1929 and 1946, only to rise again to the 1929 level over the postwar years.

We shall return later to an inquiry into why people change their rate of spending, but it is clear beyond question that they do. This has two important implications for our study of money. First, it gives a very cogent reason why we cannot apply the quantity theory in a mechanical way, asserting that an increase in the supply of money will *always* raise prices. For if people choose to spend the increased quantity of money more slowly, its impact on the quantity of goods may not change at all: whereas if they spend the same quantity of money more rapidly, prices can rise without any change in M.

Second and more clearly than we have seen, the variability of V reveals that money itself can be a destabilizing force—destabilizing because it enables us to do two things that would be impossible in a pure barter economy. We can:

1. *delay between receiving and expending our rewards for economic effort*

2. *spend more or less than our receipts by drawing on, or adding to, our cash balances*

The Classical economists used to speak of money as a "veil," implying that it did not itself play an active role in influencing the behavior of the economic players. But we can see that the ability of those players to vary the rate of their expenditure—to hang onto their money longer or to get rid of it more rapidly than usual—makes money much more than a veil. Money (or rather, people's wish to hold or to spend money) becomes an independent source of change in a complex economic society. To put it differently, the use of money introduces an element of uncertainty into the circular flow.*

CHANGES
IN T

Now we must turn to a last and perhaps most important reason why we cannot relate the supply of money to the price level in a mechanical fashion. This reason lies in the role played by T; that is, by the volume of output.

Just as the early quantity theorists thought of V as essentially unvarying, so they thought of T as a relatively fixed term in the quantity equation. In the minds of nearly all economic theorists before the Depression, output was always assumed to be as large as the available resources and the willingness of the factors of production would permit. While everyone was aware that there might be minor variations from this state of full output, virtually no one thought they would be of

---

*Technically, the standard economic definition of money is that it is both a means of exchange and a store of value. It is the latter characteristic that makes money a potentially disturbing influence.

sufficient importance to matter. *Hence the quantity theory implicitly assumed full employment or full output as the normal condition of the economy.* With such an assumption, it was easy to picture T as an unimportant term in the equation and to focus the full effect of changes in money or in money spending (MV) on P.

The trauma of the Great Depression effectively removed the comfortable assumption that the economy "naturally" tended to full employment and output. At the bottom of the Depression, real output had fallen by 25 per cent in real terms—that is, after adjustment for changing price levels—and one-quarter of the labor force was unable to find work. Quite aside from what the Depression taught us in other ways, it made unmistakably clear that changes in the volume of output (and employment) were of crucial importance in the over-all economic picture.

How does our modern emphasis on the variability of output and employment fit into the over-all question of money and prices? The answer is very simple, but very important. We have come to see that *the effect of more money on prices cannot be determined unless we also take into account its effect on the value of transactions or output.*

It is not difficult to grasp the point. Let us picture an increase in spending, perhaps initiated by businessmen launching a new investment program, or by the government inaugurating a new public works project. These new expenditures will be received by many other entrepreneurs, as the multiplier mechanism spreads the new spending through the economy. But now we come to the key question. What will entrepreneurs do as their receipts increase?

It is at this point that the question of output enters. For if businessmen are operating factories or stores *at less than full capacity,* and if there is an *employable supply of labor available,* the result of their new receipts is almost certain to be an increase in output. That is, employers will take advantage of the rise in demand to produce and sell more goods and services. They may also try to raise prices and increase their profits further, but if their industries are reasonably competitive, it is doubtful that prices can be raised very much; other businessmen with idle plants will simply undercut them and take their business away. An example is provided by the period 1934 through 1940, when output increased by 50 per cent while prices rose by less than 5 per cent. The reason, of course, lay in the great amount of unemployed resources, making it easy to expand output without price increases.

Thus we reach a general conclusion of the greatest importance. *An increase in spending of any kind tends to result in more output and employment whenever there are considerable amounts of unemployed resources.* But this is no longer true when we reach a level of high employment or very full plant utilization. Now an increase in spending *cannot* quickly lead to an increase in output, simply because the resources for more production are lacking. The result, instead, will be a rise in prices, for no firm can lose business to competitors when competitors are unable to fill additional orders. Thus the corollary of our general conclusion is that *additional spending*—from any source—*is inflationary when it is difficult to raise output.*

INFLATION
AND PUBLIC
FINANCE

Notice that our discussion has shifted its ground. We began by trying to establish the relationship between the quantity of money and the price level. Thus there is still a missing link to be added, a link that will tie the quantity of money to the volume of expenditure.

We will return to that link shortly. But the implications of our discussion about expenditure and inflation are too important to leave at this point. For we can see that the conclusion we have reached puts a capstone on our previous analysis of deficit spending. It is now possible to add a major criterion to the question of whether or not to use the public sector as a supplement to the private sector. That criterion is whether or not substantially "full" employment has been reached.*

If the economy is operating at or near the point of full employment, additional net public spending will only add more MV to a situation in which T is already at capacity and where, therefore, P will rise. But note that this conclusion attaches to more than additional *public* spending. When full employment is reached, additional spending of any kind—public or private, consumption or investment—will increase MV and, given the ceiling on T, affect P.

A different conclusion is reached when there is large-scale unemployment. Now additional public (or private) spending will result not in higher prices, but in larger output and higher employment. Thus we cannot say that public spending in itself is "inflationary." Rather, we must see that *any kind of additional spending can be inflationary in a fully employed economy, and will not be inflationary in an underemployed one.*

FULL EMPLOYMENT VS. UNDEREMPLOYMENT

So we must distinguish between two fundamentally different situations in macroeconomics: the situation of full employment and that of under-employment. Policies that make sense when one situation obtains make no sense at all in the other. To spend more in the public or the private

*The definition of employment, as we shall see in Chapter 18, is far from simple, and "full" employment accordingly is a complex idea. Economists usually call employment "full" when about 96 per cent of all job seekers are at work.

sector is clearly a main objective for economic well-being in an under-employed economy, for more spending will lead to more output and employment. But to spend more in a fully employed economy is only to cause economic mischief, for now more spending will lead only to higher prices and not to more goods or jobs. Similarly, to balance budgets or to run a budget surplus in the public sector makes little sense when an economy is underutilized, but it is the course of wisdom when there are no idle resources to absorb additional expenditures.

It is impossible to overstress the importance of this major finding of macroeconomics. One of the main differences between contemporary economic thought and that of the past is precisely this sharp division between policies that make sense in full employment and those that make sense in conditions of underemployment. It was not that the economists of the past did not recognize the tragedy of unemployment or did not wish to remedy it. It was rather that they did not see how an economy could be in *equilibrium* even though there was heavy unemployment.

The dragging years of the Great Depression taught us not only that output could fall far below the levels of full utilization, but—and perhaps this was its most intellectually unsettling feature—that an economy could be plagued with unemployed men and machines for almost a decade and yet not spontaneously generate the momentum to reabsorb them. Today we understand this condition of unemployment equilibrium, and we have devised various remedial measures to raise the equilibrium point to a satisfactory level, including, not least, additional public expenditure. But this new understanding must be balanced with a keen appreciation of its relevance to the underlying situation of employment. Remedies for an underemployed economy can be ills for a fully employed one.

MONEY AND STICKY PRICES

There is only one last point to be made, but it is an important one. All along in our discussion we have taken for granted that we need a larger supply of money in order to expand output. But why should we? Why could we not grow just as well if the quantity of money were fixed?

Theoretically, of course, we could. If we cut prices as we increased output, a given amount of money (or a given amount of expenditure) could cover an indefinitely large real output. Furthermore, as prices fell, workers would be content not to ask for higher wages (or would even accept lower wages), since in real terms they would be just as well or better off.

It is not difficult to spot the flaw in this argument. In the real world, prices of many goods cannot be cut easily. If the price of steel rose and fell as quickly and easily as prices on the stock exchange, or if wages went down without a murmur of resistance, or if rents and other contractual items could be quickly adjusted, then prices would be flexible and we would not require any enlargement of our money supply to cover a growing real output.

In fact, as we know, prices are extremely "sticky" in the downward direction. Union leaders do not look with approval on wage cuts, even when living costs fall. Contractual prices cannot be quickly adjusted. Many big firms, as we saw in Chapter 6, administer their prices and carefully avoid price competition: note, for example, that the prices of many consumer items are printed on the package months before the item will be sold.

Thus we can see that a fixed supply of money would put the economy into something of a straitjacket. As output tended to increase, businessmen would need more money to finance production, and consumers would need more money to make their larger expenditures. If businessmen could get more money from the banks, all would be well. But suppose they could not. Then the only way a businessman could get his hands on a larger supply of cash would be to persuade someone to lend it to him, and his persuasion would be in the form of a higher rate of interest. But this rising interest rate would discourage other businessmen from going ahead with their plans. Hence the would-be boom would be stopped dead in its tracks by a sheer shortage of spending power.

A flexible money supply obviates this economic suffocation. The fact that banks can create money (provided that they have excess reserves) enables them to take care of businesses that wish to make additional expenditures. The expenditures themselves put additional money into the hands of consumers. And the spending of consumers in turn sends the enlarged volume of purchasing power back to business firms to complete the great flow of expenditure and receipt.

THE PROBLEM OF INFLATION

BOTTLENECKS AND WAGE PRESSURES

Our discussion of the effect of money on prices and output has brought us to the recognition of the critical distinction between spending more in a fully employed economy and in an underemployed economy. But this distinction, so important as a basic principle, must now be somewhat blurred. For in the real world, the economy does not move from unemployment to full employment across a clear line of demarcation. On the contrary, as spending increases, general unemployment gives way at first to "tight" labor areas or to shortages in plant capacity in a few areas. Thus bottlenecks are typically the first sign that we are crossing from a condition of general unemployment to one of only partial unemployment.

These bottlenecks, however, may begin to exert their constricting effect before the economy as a whole can be considered in a condition of healthy over-all employment. This is particularly the case if the bottleneck is a strategic industry, in which a price rise may lead to increases in the costs of many other industries. Bottlenecks may thus cause the beginnings of inflationary pressure *before* the economy as a whole has absorbed its unemployed.

Yet another cause of inflation, not necessarily connected with full employment, has been suggested by Professor William Baumol of Princeton. He has pointed to the fact that there is an inflationary consequence to the difference between productivity in the highly dynamic mass production industries and productivity in the much less technologically advanced service areas. Wage increases in the mass production industries tend to be more or less matched by increases in output per man. But high wages there also work to pull up wages in other sectors where higher pay is not matched by higher output: pay raises for teachers or firemen or office workers are not usually geared

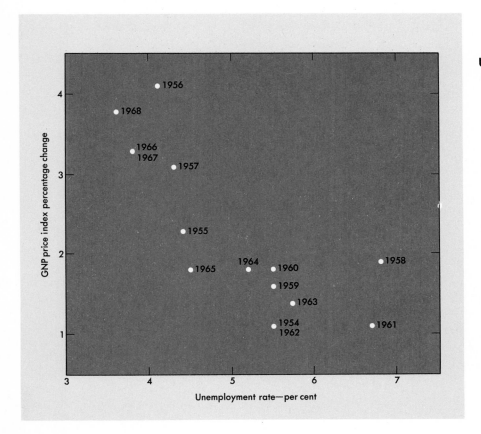

FIG. 17-3

THE UNEMPLOYMENT-INFLATION RELATION

to increases in their output. As a result, the volume of total wage payments tends to rise faster than the total output of all goods and services, with the result that prices, especially in the service areas, are pushed steadily upward. For example, from 1959 through 1968, the consumer price index rose 23 per cent. This mild inflationary trend, however, reflected a rise of only 7 per cent in the price of manufactured goods, combined with a rise of 38 per cent in the price of services.

INFLATION VS. UNEMPLOYMENT

The tendency of the economy to generate bottlenecks and wage increases that run ahead of increases in productivity creates a very serious problem—that of *choosing between a degree of inflation or a degree of unemployment.* For the experience of the 1950's and 1960's makes it appear that some rise in prices is probably unavoidable if we wish the economy to operate at high levels of output and employment.

The scatter diagram (Fig. 17-3) from the 1969 *Report of the Council of Economic Advisers,* shows the relationship between the unemployment rate in recent years and the degree of "price creep." Note that the lower the unemployment, generally speaking, the higher the degree of inflation.

THE PHILLIPS CURVE

This relation between unemployment and inflation can be generalized in Fig. 17-4, commonly called a *Phillips curve* after the English economist A. W. Phillips, who first plotted it.

In this generalized curve we do not show the exact per cent of

FIG. 17-4

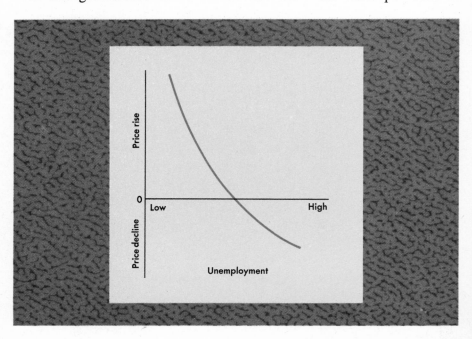

unemployment that is associated with any particular price rise or with price stability. This percentage may vary from one country or period to another, depending, for example, on how effective are its policies of combatting unemployment (a matter we will look into at the end of our next chapter) or on how competitive is its state of industry. Note in the previous scatter diagram for the United States (Fig. 17-3), for example, that we have had *different* rates of price rises associated with the *same* rate of unemployment in a number of years.

Nevertheless the basic problem of a "trade-off" between unemployment and inflation seems to be deeply built into the structure of all industrial systems, European as well as American. In Europe, for example, where the percentage of unemployment since World War II has been less than half of ours, the rate of inflation has been roughly double our own.

Does this mean that inflation has become a chronic fact of life, uncurable except at levels of unemployment that would be socially unacceptable?

There is certainly a great deal of evidence that high employment and *some* degree of rising prices go together. What economists hope is that a middle ground can be reached, where the damage done by both inflation and unemployment can be reduced to acceptable proportions.* A price rise of 1 or 2 per cent per year, for example, can be fairly easily tolerated, since there is usually an increase in the *quality* of goods from year to year. Thus a small rise in prices can be accepted as reflecting a gain in the real standard of living that those improved goods provide.

Similarly, a small amount of unemployment is also tolerable, although for different reasons. There is always a per cent or so of the labor force that is *voluntarily* unemployed because men have quit their jobs to look for something better. There is also a hard core of "unemployable" people whose physical disabilities or lack of education cannot be fitted into the job structure. This is a kind of unemployment that can and should be relieved through generous welfare policies. Thus, economists feel that a rate of unemployment of perhaps as much as 4 per cent can be reconciled with a high level of general well-being.

It is one thing to announce such a target, however, and another to

*The damage done by unemployment is self-evident. But what about inflation? Here the damage is more subtle. It consists, in the first place, of a forced *redistribution of income,* from those whose incomes are fixed—such as Social Security recipients—to those who happen to have fast rising wages or profits. Second, and perhaps more dangerous, inflation can have a self-generating momentum. A steady rise in prices of "only" 1 or 2 per cent a year can become built into businessmen's expectations, so that investment plans or, for that matter, consumers' expenditure plans anticipate higher prices as a way of life. This can lead to efforts to spend more money "now, while things are still cheap," than ordinary prudence would dictate. But the effect of *everyone's* following this course of action can lead to an acceleration in expenditures and a still faster pace of inflation. Inflation can breed more inflation, with the danger of an eventual speculative collapse.

achieve it. In every industrial nation the trade-off between unemployment and inflation has provided a problem that has so far defied a perfect solution; and in every industrial nation the claims of high employment have won over those of price stability. Thus in the United States a price creep of 2 to 3 per cent a year—more than we can explain by quality improvements—has troubled us for the past decade and seems likely to continue to bother us for the next.

MONEY AND EXPENDITURE

Our discussion has brought to a conclusion our first line of inquiry. Starting with the simple quantity theory, we have been led, step by step, into an investigation of the significant differences between a fully employed and an unemployed economy, and from there we have gone on to learn something of the causes of inflation.

But we have not yet supplied the missing link to which we referred earlier. We know now that an increase in expenditure will be inflationary only when we have a condition of reasonably full employment. What we do not know is whether an increase in the *supply of money*—say, as a result of Federal Reserve policy—will necessarily lead to a rise in the volume of expenditure. To put it differently, we have not yet asked whether in a more sophisticated version that focused on *expenditure* rather than on prices alone, the quantity theory might not be right.

THE CASE FOR THE QUANTITY THEORY

After many years of neglect, the importance of the quantity of money as a powerful economic force is again beginning to be recognized by many economists. At the base of the controversy, however, is the question, how powerful?

The most persuasive advocate of the predominant influence of money is Professor Milton Friedman of the University of Chicago, whom we have previously encountered in our chapter on consumption (p. 229 n.). Friedman insists that the quantity of money is *the* critical determinant of the volume of expenditure, and he gives some interesting and dramatic evidence in support of his views.

After the Russian Revolution of 1917, as you know, there was an enormous inflation in Russia when a new currency was introduced by the new Government and printed in large quantities. It depreciated until it became almost valueless. It was a hyper-inflation. All the time, there was some currency circulating which had been issued by the pre-revolutionary Government, by the Czarist Government. The Czarist Government was out of power; nobody expected it to return to power. Yet the value of the Czarist currency remained constant in terms of goods and rose very sharply in terms of the Bolshevik currency. Why? Because there was nobody to print any more of it. It was fixed in quantity and therefore it retained its value. Another story has to do with the American Civil War. The North overran the place in the South where the Southerners had been printing paper money to finance the war. The South had to move its headquarters. In the course of doing so, it could not print any money. As a result of this interruption, prices temporarily ceased rising. I conclude that if you want to analyse the process of inflation, "Cherchez la monnaie." [1]

Anecdotes even as striking as these do not make cases. What is the causal connection between the quantity of money and the volume of expenditure? Friedman believes it lies in a stubborn tendency of households and firms to keep their hands on cash balances that have a more or less constant real purchasing power. He believes that in the United States, for example, the public as a whole tends to hold cash balances equal to about $4\frac{1}{2}$ weeks of payrolls, household bills, and other normal expenditures. Thus, if the public finds itself, because of Federal Reserve actions, with larger balances than they feel they need, there will be a strong incentive to go out and spend them. But the result of everyone doing the same thing will only drive up prices, until these higher prices have reduced the real purchasing power of existing balances to their normal level.

By no means all economists are convinced of Friedman's hypothesis. They point out that the relationship between our cash balances, M, and our expenditure, MV, is really only another way of describing the velocity of circulation, V, and they stress that we *know* that velocity changes in response to changed economic conditions. Over the long run, as we have seen in Fig. 17-2, velocity can gradually decline—or rise. In the short run, people certainly sit on money when they *expect* prices to decline, and go on spending sprees when they expect them to rise. Although impressed by Friedman's data, the skeptics remain unpersuaded by his arguments.

We shall return to this controversy at the end of our chapter. Meanwhile, however, there remains another route by which changes in the quantity of money can affect expenditure, a route that is recognized by all economists. This is the influence exerted by changes in the quantity of money on the *rate of interest,* and thereby on the rate of investment spending.

How do changes in the quantity of money affect interest rates? The

MONEY AND
INTEREST
RATES

[1] Milton Friedman, *Inflation, Causes and Consequences* (New York: Asia Publishing House, 1963), p. 10.

easiest way to understand the connection is to trace the repercussions of an action of the Federal Reserve. Suppose the Fed wishes to encourage spending and therefore buys government bonds on the open market, or expands bank reserves by lowering the reserve ratio. As a result, banks will find themselves with extra funds that can be put to use. If they lend the funds to business, that takes care of the expenditure problem right there. But suppose banks use their excess reserves to buy bonds? The result will be a rise in bond prices, as banks bid for securities, and a *fall in bond yields*. The fall in yields is the same thing as a fall in interest rates. Money is now cheaper. As a result, we remember from our chapter on investment (p. 261), business will be encouraged to increase its rate of investment.

LIQUIDITY AND INTEREST RATES

FINANCIAL DEMAND FOR MONEY

Our analysis has forged an important link in the chain of our argument: more money leads to lower interest rates, which lead to more expenditure. But we are not yet quite ready to call the argument complete. Before we can claim to understand the full impact that money exerts on the economy, we have to broaden our view to take in one area of activity that has so far escaped our notice. This is the world of finance.

For not all the demand for cash balances comes from businessmen who must meet payrolls or who want to invest in capital goods or inventory or from consumers who want to make purchases of goods and services. There is also a powerful source of monetary demand from investors who want to hold larger or smaller amounts of cash as part of their *financial portfolios.*

Some of these investors will be individuals who have saved or inherited wealth and who regularly invest part of that wealth in stocks and bonds, keeping the rest in bank accounts. Other investors are institutions, such as life insurance companies or mutual funds, who are doing the same thing on a much larger scale. Still others are businesses who keep part of their liquid assets invested in short-term bonds, part in cash.

How much of our $190-odd billion in money supply belongs to this financial pool? We do not really know, *because the amount constantly varies.* Individuals and firms do not make absolutely hard and fast, unchanging decisions about how much of their wealth they will keep in cash. At certain times, for safety or to be in a position to make advantageous purchases on the securities markets, investors will want to be unusually "liquid," to hold large balances in cash. At other times, for different precautionary or speculative motives, people will be content with much smaller financial balances. So, too, when conditions in the economy demand a high rate of spending—when a boom is going on, for instance—many investors, particularly companies, will operate with as small idle bank balances as possible, because they will need their cash for transactions purposes—for payrolls and other expenditures. Again, when things are slacker, financial balances may tend to grow simply because there is less need for transactions balances.

The existence of a separate financial demand for money interests us for two reasons. As we shall shortly see, the financial demand for money complicates the task of monetary management. But in addition, the existence of financial balances plays a crucial role in determining the rate of interest itself.

Perhaps we have already intuitively sensed the connection that we are about to explore. If financial holders of cash can hold larger or smaller balances at different times, it stands to reason that one powerful inducement for them to vary the size of these balances will be the rate of interest. For when interest rates are low, the *opportunity cost* of holding cash is very slight; that is, when one can only get 2 per cent on a bond he passes up the opportunity to make only $20 if he does not put $1,000 cash into that bond. But when interest rates climb and the same bond is issued at 6 per cent, then it costs much more—$60—to remain liquid.

FIG. 17-5

LIQUIDITY PREFERENCE SCHEDULE

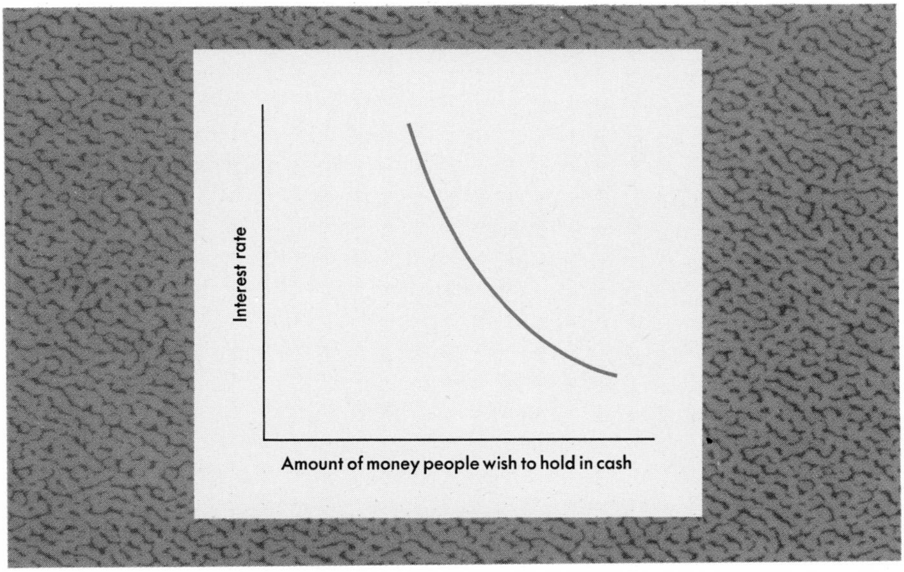

This general inverse relationship between the rate of interest and the willingness to be liquid is called *liquidity preference*. The phrase simply describes the observed fact that households and companies will generally seek to hold more cash when interest rates are low and less cash when they are high. Figure 17-5 gives us a diagrammatic view of this relationship.

Exactly how much cash will the public wish to hold if interest rates are, say, 4 per cent? We cannot predict unless we know what households and firms expect of the future, the amount of cash they need for transactions purposes, and many other things. In other words, on two different dates, at the same interest rate, the same public might very well wish to hold two *different* amounts of cash. But we are sure that at *all* dates the public will prefer to give up liquidity when rates go up and to gain liquidity when they go down.

LIQUIDITY PREFERENCE AND INTEREST RATES

Now we must take the final step. We have seen that interest rates determine whether we wish to hold larger or smaller cash balances, given our particular preferences for liquidity. But what determines the interest rate itself? The answer is the interplay of our liquidity preferences—that is, our different desires to hold cash—and the actual amount of money that exists. To anticipate a subject we shall study in Part Three, we can think of the rate of interest as a *price* determined by the supply of money and the demand for money. The supply of money is the quantity of money as determined by the Federal Reserve System. And the demand for money is nothing but the liquidity preference schedule with which we are now familiar.

FIG. 17-6

DETERMINATION OF THE INTEREST RATE

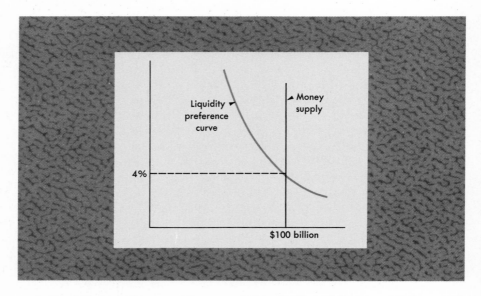

A liquidity preference diagram (Fig. 17-6) will help us understand this process more clearly. In the figure, a vertical line indicates the actual supply of money (which we will call $100 billion) set by the monetary authorities. Let us also assume that the going rate of interest is 4 per cent, which, as we can see, nicely balances the amount of money the people *want* to hold at that rate and the amount that is actually in existence.

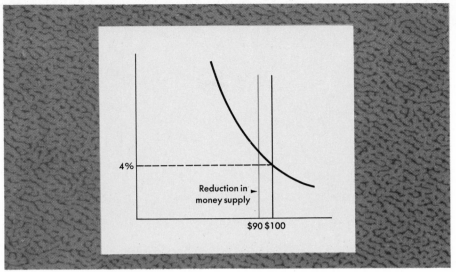

FIG. 17-7

**CHANGE IN
THE QUANTITY
OF MONEY**

4%

Reduction in ►
money supply

$90 $100

What we see here is a market in equilibrium, in which the quantity of money that is demanded is exactly equal to the amount that is supplied. But now let us suppose that the monetary authorities want to decrease the amount of money (perhaps to stop an inflation) and that they cut member bank reserves enough to bring about a fall from $100 billion to $90 billion in the total of demand deposits. Figure 17-7 shows us the new state of affairs.

Now we no longer have a nicely balanced market, as we had before. At the going rate of 4 per cent interest, people *want* to hold $100 billion in money, as our diagram shows. But there is actually only $90 billion available.

Thus households and firms want to hold more money than it is possible to hold! Of course, they do not know that. From the point of view of the public, all that has happened is that a great many investors or treasurers of firms feel that they aren't liquid enough, that their cash balances are too small. As a result, they will try to make their cash holdings bigger by selling stocks and bonds.

Now here is the important part. *Selling securities does not create a single additional dollar of money. It simply transfers money from one holder to another. But it does change the rate of interest. As the price of bonds falls, the yield on bonds rises.*

Now our next diagram (Fig. 17-8) shows what happens. As interest rates rise, the public is content to hold a smaller quantity of money. Hence a new interest rate, let us say 5 per cent, will emerge, at which the public is *willing* to hold the $90 billion that *they have to hold.* The attempt to get more liquid ceases, and a new equilibrium interest rate prevails.

FIG. 17-8

DETERMINATION
OF NEW
EQUILIBRIUM

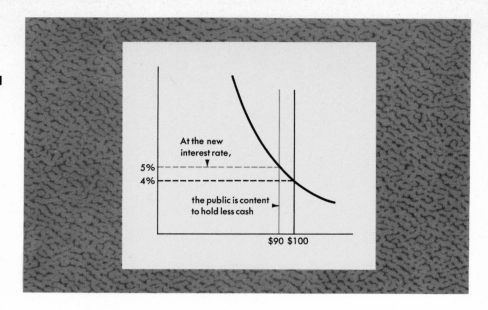

At the new
interest rate,

5%

4%

the public is content
to hold less cash

$90 $100

**THE ARGUMENT
IN REVIEW**

Now let us review once more the meaning of the process we have observed. The basic problem is to trace the way in which changes in the quantity of money can bring about changes in the rate of interest. The answer, we have seen, is that the rate of interest is determined by two elements: the position and "shape" of the liquidity preferences of the public and the quantity of money itself. By changing the quantity of money, the authorities can bring into being an amount of money larger or smaller than the public wishes to hold at the going rate of interest. Finding itself with more money (or less money) than it wishes to hold at that rate, the public will either buy bonds or other financial assets to get "out" of money, or sell bonds or other financial assets to get "into" money. In either event, the quantity of money will not change, but the price of bonds, and therefore interest rates, will.

THE ART OF MONETARY MANAGEMENT

We are finally ready to put together the many pieces of the puzzle. The concept of liquidity preference has provided us with the last necessary clue to the connection between changes in the quantity of money and changes in the expenditures of the public. It remains only to consider one aspect of the money problem: the art of managing the supply of money so that the *right* increases or decreases in the supply of money will be forthcoming at the right time.

Why "art"? Is not the task of the monetary authority very clear by now? By increasing the quantity of money, it pushes down interest rates.

By pushing down interest rates, it encourages investment expenditure. Hence, all it needs to do is to regulate the quantity of money so that investment expenditure proceeds at just the pace we need to keep a high, but not too high, level of employment.

Unfortunately, things are not quite that mechanical. Suppose, for example, that the Federal Reserve creates excess reserves, in the expectation that interest rates will go down and that new loans will be pumped into investment. But suppose that at the same time, the public's liquidity preferences are rising because investors feel nervous and want to be more liquid. Then the shift in the quantity of money, as shown in Fig. 17-9, will be offset by a shift in liquidity preferences, and the rate of interest will not change at all! The new money will simply wind up in larger financial cash holdings.

FIG. 17-9

**A SHIFT IN
LIQUIDITY
PREFERENCE**

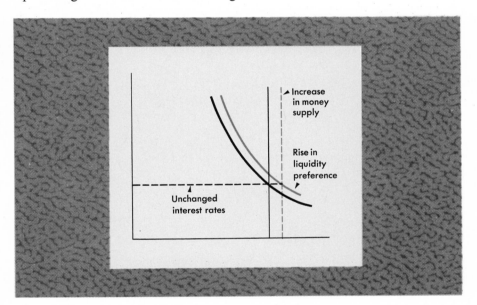

In other words, an attempt by the monetary authorities to drive down the rate of interest in order to encourage investment may be frustrated if the public uses all the additional funds for liquidity and not for expenditure. At the bottom of the Great Depression, for example, banks had huge excess reserves because businessmen would not risk expenditure for new capital projects. People had an insatiable desire for liquidity, and no attempted reductions of the rate of interest could persuade them to transfer money held for "security" into active expenditures.

In the same way, an attempt to raise interest rates and to halt price inflation by making credit tight may come to naught if the public reacts to higher interest rates by giving up its liquidity, thereby making funds available to others to finance increased transactions expenditure. Or take another instance: if the Fed tries to lower interest rates by increasing *M,* the effort may result in a general expectation of inflation and a movement out of bonds into stocks. In that case, interest rates, instead of falling, will go up! This actually happened in 1968.

We can see, then, that it is not always easy to bring about a desired change in *expenditure*—or even in interest rates—through a change in money supply. Policies of easy money may fail in their purpose of stimulating capital growth, and policies of tight money may not provide the check on inflation that is desired.

For these reasons, few economists today would rely on monetary measures as the *sole* remedy for either recession or inflation. At the same time, it is also clear from experience that changes in the quantity of money do exert powerful pressures in *ordinary* times. Then liquidity preference schedules are stable and the desire to hold "normal" cash balances in relation to income or expected expenditures may well provide the regulating force that Professor Friedman believes it does.

In unstable times, however, it seems equally clear that money's influence will not be so determinative. When expectations are pessimistic, trying to get business to increase its expenditures just by making bank credit easier may be, in the words of one economist, "like trying to push with a string." Dampening an inflationary spurt by credit measures alone may be more effective, but even this can be frustrated, as we have seen, if liquidity preferences are falling and the public is content to get along with smaller cash balances at the current rate of interest. Considerations such as these make monetary management an art, albeit an art that is built on a scientific foundation.

In practice, monetary policy cannot be separated from fiscal policy. When the economy is sluggish and capital expenditures lag, the appropriate remedy is a combination of a strong fiscal push through higher government expenditures or tax cuts and the monetary stimulant provided by Federal Reserve actions that raise excess reserves. Conversely, when the economy is "overheated," when prices are rising beyond the rate of a "normal" full-employment creep of 1 or 2 per cent a year, we need the restraint provided not only by tightening monetary supplies, but also by the braking action of a budget surplus brought about by tax increases or expenditure cuts or both.

Note, moreover, that fiscal policy will work much less effectively without a strong supporting monetary policy, just as monetary policy will be less effective without fiscal support. A deliberate government deficit, for example, will not cure a recession if the Federal Reserve has not loosened money supplies. In that case, the government would have to borrow its needed dollars from individuals and commercial banks that have no surplus investible funds. If the government is then to tempt money into its bond issues, it will have to make them more attractive than existing issues by offering a higher rate of interest. But this would serve to *discourage* private investment, which is exactly the opposite of what the government is seeking to do. So, too, a government surplus designed to slow down a boom will hardly prove effective if the banks are flush with unused reserves and in a position to expand their loans to business as fast as the government cuts back its own expenditures.*

All these difficulties make it clear that it is no easy task to adjust the supply of money to the flow of production, in order to encourage output and maintain stable prices. Mistakes in timing, premature alarms, and delayed rescues are virtually inescapable. For a monetary authority to act in such a way that subsequent economic historians will wholeheartedly approve of its decisions is to expect superhuman intelligence.

Yet it is well to reflect that some of the monetary problems we will undoubtedly encounter in the future should not necessarily be charged against the money mechanism as such. As long as there remain striking divergences in economic performance between region and region—say between Cumberland and California—or as long as there exist vast discrepancies in the ability of various parts of the economic world to gather funds or to withstand adversity—as the difference between huge and tiny businesses or between powerful unions and the ragged fringes of the labor force—or as long as the economic tides lift and drop such differently situated groups as corporate executives or farmers or industrial unions or Social Security retirees, then *any* turn of monetary events is bound to penalize some and reward others, often with cruel indifference. When these failures occur, however, they should remind us not only of the inadequacies of monetary or fiscal policies, but of the weaknesses of the environment that they reveal. It is the environment that then often needs to be strengthened or changed rather than the policy.

---

*There *are* times when fiscal and monetary policies are properly used in opposite directions. These instances usually have to do with balance of payments problems (that we will study in Part Four) or with situations in which economic growth and economic stability pose almost contrary requirements. Such problems are important for students of advanced monetary and fiscal policy, but they are better relegated to a footnote in this introduction to the subject.

SUMMARY

1. *The quantity equation, MV = PT,* is actually a truism, saying that expenditure (*MV*) equals receipts (*PT*). It was originally intended as a causal statement saying that an increase in the supply of money leads to higher prices.

2. This statement would be true only if *V* and *T* were fixed. In fact, *V is capable of considerable change* as businessmen and investors revise their attitudes about spending or holding cash balances.

3. Even more important, we find that *changes in the level of output are very marked over the long run.* This is contrary to the expectations of the early quantity theorists that the economy would always operate at full employment.

4. When a competitive economy is operating at less than full employment, an increase in the quantity of money (really in the volume of expenditure) leads to a rise in output rather than prices. *This distinction between the effects of additional expenditure, private or public, at full employment and underemployment, is one of the central conceptions of modern macroeconomics.*

5. The distinction is blurred in practice because *bottlenecks and differentials in productivity that bring rising prices before full employment is reached.* The choice between high employment and a rising price level, symbolized in a Phillips curve, is one of the most difficult that monetary and fiscal authorities must face.

6. We need a growing money supply to permit economic expansion in a world of *sticky prices.*

7. Increases or decreases in the supply of money exert their effect on *expenditures* in two different ways. One way may be through the desire of the public to hold cash balances that represent a more or less fixed amount of real purchasing power. The other way is through *the effect of changes in the quantity of money on interest rates.*

8. The quantity of money affects the rate of interest by its interaction with the *liquidity preferences* of the public. *Liquidity preference* means the willingness of firms and households to hold smaller cash balances when interest rates are high, and their desire to hold larger balances when rates are low. Thus, *the rate of interest is the price that balances the money holders' desire for liquidity with the opportunities for earning interest by surrendering their cash for securities.*

9. *Liquidity preferences* can complicate the job of monetary management by absorbing into financial balances cash that was intended to find its way into the transactions balances of the economy, or by supplying cash for transactions when the authorities wish to contact the availability of credit.

10. *Fiscal and monetary policy usually work side by side, each requiring the other.* Fiscal policy needs easy money to be effective in combating recessions, and tight monetary policies directed against inflation require fiscal stringency if they are to be effective.

1. Why is the quantity equation a truism? Why is the interpretation of the quantity equation that M affects P not a truism?

2. Suppose you are paid $140 a week and you put it in the bank. On each of the seven days of the week, you spend one-seventh of this sum. What is your average balance during the week? Now suppose that you spend the whole sum on the first day of the week. Will your average balance be the same? What is the relation between velocity of circulation and size of average balances?

3. What considerations might lead you, as a businessman, to carry higher cash balances? Could these considerations change rapidly?

4. The basic reason why the original quantity theorists thought that M affected P was their belief that V and T were fixed. Discuss the validity of this belief.

5. Why is the level of employment the critical determinant of fiscal policy?

6. If employment is "full," what will be the effects of an increase in private investment, supposing that everything else stays the same?

7. In what way can an increase in excess reserves affect V or T? Is there any certainty that an increase in reserves will lead to an increase in V or T?

8. Suppose that you had $1,000 in the bank. Would you be more willing to invest it if you could earn 2 per cent or 5 per cent? What factors could make you change your mind about investing all or any part at, say, 5 per cent? Could you imagine conditions that would make you unwilling to invest even at 7 per cent? Other conditions that would lead you to invest your whole cash balance at, say, 3 per cent?

9. Suppose that the going rate of interest is 4 per cent and that the monetary authorities want to curb expenditures and act to lower the quantity of money. What will the effect be in terms of the public's feeling of liquidity? What will the public do if it feels short of cash? Will it buy or sell securities? What would this do to their price? What would thereupon happen to the rate of interest? To investment expenditures?

10. Suppose that the monetary and fiscal authorities want to encourage economic expansion. What are the general measures that each should take? What problems might liquidity preference interpose?

11. If we have a price creep of 3 per cent a year at 5 per cent unemployment, what would you counsel as a proper economic policy?

18 EMPLOYMENT AND OUTPUT

We have reached a point in our investigations where we can now understand the forces that give rise to the flow of production. To that extent we have completed one long stage of our journey into macroeconomics. But our travel is not yet complete. We have concerned ourselves heretofore almost entirely with output in real or money terms, but we have somewhat thoroughly disregarded one crucial aspect of the real world: employment. In other words, we may now be able to give a general answer to the question of how GNP is determined, but we cannot as yet answer the equally important query: how is employment determined? How many people will be employed if GNP is of such-and-such a size? What are the forces that work for more or for less employment? Until we can come to grips with these problems, we have not fully answered the very questions that impelled us originally on our investigation.

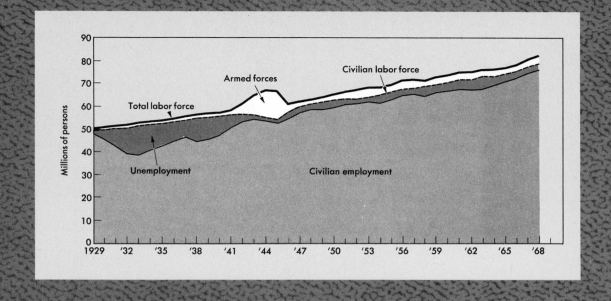

FIG. 18-1   UNITED STATES' LABOR FORCE, 1929–1968

EMPLOYMENT IN PERSPECTIVE

As before, let us begin by acquainting ourselves with the historical dimensions of the problem. In Figure 18-1, we see the main variables of the employment process—the total labor force and the total *civilian* labor force (members of the armed forces constituting the difference), total employment and its complement, unemployment.

Our attention is naturally drawn at first to the orange area that depicts the profile of unemployment. But we cannot discuss this aspect of the employment problem until we have looked into a more fundamental question: what determines the size of the total labor force itself, the size of the fraction of the population that is actively looking for work? For clearly, the volume of unemployment will depend, at least in part, on how many of a given population *want* to work.

What per cent of the American population does want to work? The answer, in round numbers, is about 60 out of every 100 persons over the age of 14. In itself, this fact does not mean very much. But suppose we now ask: is this fraction of the population growing or shrinking? Do more people or fewer people seek work today than, say, in 1890 or 1900? What is the outlook for the year 2000?

Here the answer is surprising. One would expect, perhaps, that as a society grows richer and more affluent, fewer people would seek

PARTICIPATION IN THE LABOR FORCE

355

employment. But that is not the case. Looking back to 1890 or 1900, we find that only 52 out of every 100 persons over 14 sought work. Looking forward is more uncertain; but if we can extrapolate (extend) the trend of the past several decades to the year 2000, we can expect perhaps as many as 65 persons out of 100 to be in the labor market by that date.

How can we explain this curious upward drift of the labor force itself? The answer is to be found in an examination of the different labor participation trends of different ages and different sexes. Figure 18-2 shows this very clearly.

FIG. 18-2

PARTICIPATION RATES

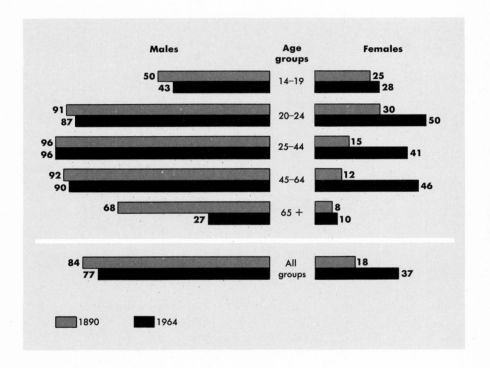

Note that the over-all trend toward a larger participation rate for the entire population masks a number of significant trends.

1. *Young males entering the labor force are older than those who entered in the past.*

A larger number of young men remain in high school now or go on to college, a trend that will certainly increase. Only a third of elementary school pupils now go on to college, but the ratio is steadily growing.

2. *Older males show a dramatic withdrawal from the labor force.*
The reason is the advent of Social Security and private pension plans. It is probable that the proportion of older males in the labor force will continue to fall as the retirement age is slowly reduced and as some still unprotected occupations come under Social Security or private pension arrangements.

3. *Counterbalancing this fall in male participation is a spectacular rise in total female participation. Indeed, the over-all trend toward an increasing search for work within the population at large is entirely the result of the mass entrance of women into the labor force.*

This surge of women into the labor market reflects several changing factors in the American scene (many of which, incidentally, can be found abroad as well). One of these is the growth of nonmanual, as contrasted with manual, jobs. Another is the widening cultural approval of working women and working wives—it is the amazing fact that the average American girl who marries today in her early twenties and goes on to raise a family will nevertheless spend twenty-five years of her life in paid employment after her children are grown. Yet another reason for the influx of women is that technology has released them from household work. And not least is the pressure to raise living standards by having two incomes within the household.

Actually, we must view the growing number of females in the labor force as part of a very old economic phenomenon whose roots we traced back to the Middle Ages—the monetization of work. For the upward trend of female participation does not imply an increasing amount of labor performed within society. Rather, it measures a larger amount of *paid* labor. In the 1890's, many persons worked long and hard hours on a family farm or in a family enterprise, and above all within a household, *without getting paid* and, therefore, were not counted as members of the "labor force." To a very considerable extent, the rising numbers of female participants in the labor force mirror the transfer of these unpaid jobs onto the marketplace where the same labor is now performed in an economically visible way. There is every likelihood this process will continue.

These are not, of course, the only factors that bear on the fundamental question of how many persons will seek work out of a given population. The drift from country to city, the decline in the number of hours of labor per day expected of a jobholder, the general lengthening of life, the growth of general well-being—all these changes bear on the decision to work or not. Over all, what the complex trends seem to show is that we are moving in the direction of a society where employment absorbs a larger fraction of the life (but not of the day) of an average woman, and a diminishing fraction of the life and of the day of an average man.

TABLE 18 · 1

LABOR FORCE
1962–1968

SHORT-RUN CHANGES (IN MILLIONS)							
	1962	1963	1964	1965	1966	1967	1968
Number in civilian labor force	70.6	71.8	73.1	74.5	75.8	77.3	78.7
Civilian employment	66.7	67.8	69.3	71.1	72.9	74.4	75.9
Unemployment	3.9	4.1	3.8	3.4	2.9	3.0	2.8

SHORT-RUN
CHANGES

These trends indicate the direction of persistent, albeit slow-moving, main currents within the total fraction of the population that seeks work. But when we concern ourselves with employment or unemployment on a year-to-year basis, we must also take heed of short-run shifts in and out of the active labor force. That is, while the decade-to-decade percentages reveal the gradual changes we have discussed, the proportion of the population actively seeking work from one year to the next, particularly the proportion of young people or women, may vary sharply. In Table 18-1, we can see how the labor force evidences these short-run expansions and contractions.

Notice that between 1962 and 1963, employment and unemployment *both* rose. One would think that as employment rose, unemployment would fall! Yet the same phenomenon appears between 1966 and 1967. How can this be?

FIG. 18-3

NET CHANGE IN
EMPLOYMENT
AND
LABOR FORCE
AUG. '65–
AUG. '66

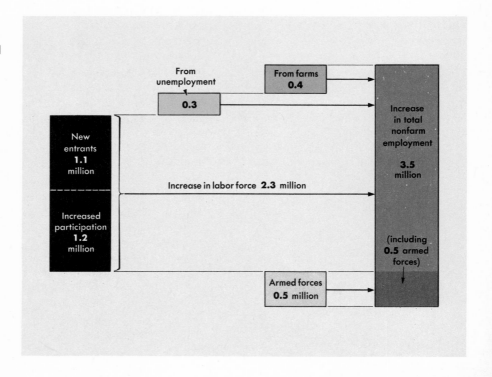

The answer to the apparent paradox lies in the short-run responsiveness or *income-elasticity,* of the labor supply. In good times when jobs are plentiful, more youths and women will seek work. The whole labor force will then temporarily expand; and since not all of it may find work, both employment and unemployment may show increases. The reverse is true in a year of recession. What happens then is that many will be discouraged by bad times and "withdraw" from the labor force, remaining in school or in the household. As a result, the number of unemployed will then be smaller than if the larger labor force of a boom year had continued actively looking for work.

In Fig. 18-3, we see how important increased participation can be in augmenting the work force in a recent year.

The concept of a variable participation rate (or an elastic supply) for labor in the short run helps to elucidate for us a term with which we shall be much involved in this chapter: unemployment.

Clearly, unemployment is not a static condition, but one that varies with the participation rate itself. Technically, the measure of unemployment is determined by a household-to-household survey conducted each month by the Bureau of the Census among a carefully selected sample. An "unemployed" person is thereupon defined not merely as a person without a job—for perhaps such a person does not *want* a job—but as someone who is "actively" seeking work but is "unable" to find it. Since, however, the number of people who will be seeking work will rise in good times and fall in bad times, figures for any given period must be viewed with caution. A relatively low unemployment rate *may* mean only that general discouragement has driven many job seekers from the search for work. Similarly, a tendency for the unemployment rate to remain relatively steady as employment rises may testify only to an increased number of persons who have been attracted into the labor force.

These cautions by no means invalidate the concept of unemployment; but they warn us against assuming that in measuring unemployment over time, we are measuring variations in a fixed quantity. An economist first looks at the labor participation figures and then at the unemployment rates before he judges the seriousness of the situation.

SHIFTING DEMANDS FOR LABOR

What we have studied thus far are the forces that determine the supply of labor—that is, the number of persons who will be looking for a job at any time. But the problem of employment and unemployment is not decided just from the supply side. Now we must add the demand side of the equation.

From the first circular flow diagram, nine chapters ago, up to the beginning of this one, we have constantly been concerned with demand, mainly *aggregate demand* or the total demand generated by the sum of all spending in the economy. Historically, most of the social ills of unemployment can be put on the doorstep of an inadequate aggregate demand—that is, of a level of expenditure not high enough to give jobs to all who want them.

Shortly, we will discuss the relation of aggregate demand to employment. But first we must put the force of "total spending" into perspective by viewing it in the context of an economy whose pursuits are constantly changing and which therefore constantly alters the structure within which spending is generated. This brings us back to the concerns of Chapter 5, where we have already seen how the industrialization of the economy gradually but profoundly altered the location and nature of work.

TABLE 18 · 2

DISTRIBUTION OF EMPLOYMENT

	PER CENT DISTRIBUTION OF ALL EMPLOYED WORKERS	
	1900	1968
Agriculture, forests, and fisheries	38.1	5.3
Manufacturing, mining, transportation, construction, utilities	37.7	38.9
Trade, government, finance, professional and personal services*	24.2	55.9

SOURCE: Calculated from *Historical Statistics*, p. 74; also from *Hearings*, Joint Economic Committee, 88th Congress; Part I, p. 193.

*It is customary to include transportation and utilities among the third, or service, area of activities. In this analysis, however, we group them with goods-producing or goods-handling activities, to highlight the drift into "purely" service occupations. Since domestic servants, proprietors, and the self-employed are omitted (owing to inadequate statistics), the table under-represents the labor force in the service and trade sector.

A glance at Table 18-2 gives added meaning to this shift in the job structure, for it is apparent that a pervasive transformation has occurred in the composition of the aggregate demand of society. An economy principally concerned with wresting goods from nature and then transforming them, or transporting them, has become increasingly a society concerned with selling or administering the activities of the relatively dwindling proportion who obtain, or fashion, or carry material wealth.

What accounts for this enormous change in the nature of the productive activity of society? Mainly, we can account for it by the interaction of two factors: technology and the changing demand for goods and services.

Underlying the great migration from "primary" occupations (farming, fishing, etc.) through "secondary" ones (manufacturing, etc.) into the "tertiary" service trades lies the impelling force of technology. Without the productive capacity given us by a technology that has developed in a certain sequence and form, this migration could not have taken place. In the agricultural and the manufacturing–mining–transporting–power fields we have experienced a startling increase in productivity, so that a dwindling manpower base can adequately provide the products required of them by society.

Agriculture presents, of course, the most extreme example of the power of technology to enhance productivity. Between 1880 and today, for instance, the time required to harvest one acre of wheat on the Great Plains has fallen from twenty hours to two. Meanwhile, the man-hours needed to raise 100 bushels of corn have dropped from 147 in 1910 to four or five. Not quite so dramatic but also far-reaching in their effect have been technological improvements in other areas. Table 18-3 shows the increase in productivity in various mining, transportation, and manufacturing activities over nearly two decades.

TABLE 18 · 3

INDEX OF
OUTPUT PER
MAN-HOUR
FOR
PRODUCTION
WORKERS

Industry	1950	1966
Coal mining	100	262
Railroad transportation	100	231
Basic steel	100	140
Paper and pulp	100	180
Petroleum refining	100	244 (1965)

SOURCE: Calculated from *Statistical Abstract*, 1968, p. 230.

Finally, by way of contrast to the very great degree of technological advance in the primary and secondary occupation sectors, we must note the laggard advance in productivity in the tertiary sector of activity. Output per man-hour in trade, for instance, or in education or in the service professions such as law or medicine or, again, in domestic or personal services such as barbering or repair work or in government has not increased nearly so much as in the primary and secondary sectors.*

In the previous chapter, we noticed the inflationary consequences of

---

*It is only proper to note that we cannot measure productivity of output in the service sector nearly so unambiguously as in the goods sector, and there is no doubt that the *quality* of many services has increased substantially. Compare, for example, the "productivity" of a surgeon operating for appendicitis in 1900, 1930, and 1960. On the other hand, insofar as we are interested in the effect of technology in increasing the saleable output of work, there seems little doubt of its considerable superiority in the goods-producing branches of the economy.

this lag. Now we note the *uneven entry* of technology to be one main cause behind the over-all migration of employment that we have discovered. Had we not enjoyed the enormous technical improvements in agriculture or mass production, but instead discovered vastly superior techniques of government services (in the sense of increasing the man-hour output of, say, policemen or firemen or teachers), the distribution of employment might look very different. We shall return to this point when we discuss the question of automation. At the moment, we need only accept the unequal efficiencies of technology in the various sectors of economic activity as constituting one main cause for the change in employment patterns.

INFLUENCE OF DEMAND

The differential rates of progress of technology are not, however, by themselves enough to explain the shift in employment. The fact that each farmer has become enormously more productive than his grandfather does not explain the decline of farm employment, nor does the enhancement of manufacturing and goods-handling productivity explain the stability of the employment ratios of these sectors. To account for the impact of technology on employment we must link the changes in productivity with the nature of the demand for the products emanating from these various industries and activities.

We can see this shift in demand in Table 18-4, showing the division

TABLE 18 · 4

DOMESTIC DEMAND FOR OUTPUT

PERCENTAGE DISTRIBUTION OF NATIONAL INCOME				
	1899–1908		1967	
Primary sector (agriculture)	16.7		3.5	
Secondary sector	36.7		44.3	
Mining		3.1		1.0
Manufacturing		18.4		30.2
Construction		4.5		5.1
Transportation, communication, and public utilities		10.7		8.0
Tertiary sector	46.5		52.1	
Trade		15.3		14.9
Miscellaneous services		9.6		11.9
Government		5.6		14.4
Finance and other		16.0		10.9

SOURCE: *Historical Statistics,* Series F34–43; *Survey of Current Business,* July, 1968, Table 1.12, p. 22. (GNP used net of foreign transactions.)

of national income among the three main sectors and their components.*

What we see here is a shift working in a direction different from the impetus of technology. Note that as productivity has increased in agriculture, demand for the products of agriculture has *fallen* as a per cent of total national expenditure. In technical language, the demand for food products was not "income-elastic"; that is, it did not rise proportionately with the rise in income. The result of this confrontation of a high-powered technology by a low-powered demand was a squeeze on employment. If the existing labor force in agriculture were equipped with the more productive techniques, the consequence would be a torrent of output that would far surpass the demand of the market. Instead, the new technology was utilized to permit a smaller labor force to fulfill demand, while the now redundant farm labor was forced to look elsewhere for employment.

Where did it go? In part, it was directed by the shift of both technology and demand to the secondary sector. Farmers, moving to factory towns, produced trucks and tractors, thereby transferring some agricultural tasks to manufacturing. Meanwhile, as incomes rose, purchasing power that was not required for food products turned to the purchase of manufactured goods, homes, power, communication, and other things. The result was that employment rose in this sector, as Table 18-2 shows. Equally important, however, by way of its employment-offering effects, was the rise of the "tertiary" occupations. Here an elastic demand for services of various kinds and an absence of revolutionary labor-saving techniques permitted employment to increase very rapidly.

What we seem to be witnessing, in these shifts, is a natural "evolution" of demand in an increasingly affluent and industrialized society. Demand appears to pass from an initial concentration on the products of the earth, to and through a focus on the products of manufacture, toward a "highest" stage, where it fastens on the enjoyment of the personal services made possible by a highly productive society and on the increased need to administer the internal affairs of a complex industrial mechanism. Thus we should note that the shift in employment visible in Table 18-2, already striking enough, would be made even more so, were we to transfer the growing "service" (i.e., administration and nonproduction) component in the secondary sector to the tertiary sector. In manufacturing alone, between 1950 and 1967, the nonproduction work force grew from 18 to 26 per cent of total employees.

EVOLUTION
OF DEMAND

*The figures actually show the *income originating in these sectors*. But we know from our macro-economic studies that this income must have been produced by the expenditures—the demand—of society as it was distributed among the sectors.

What light does this discussion of the demand for labor shed on our original inquiry into the problem of over-all employment? The conclusion points up the *importance of the shift in demand from less labor-requiring tasks to more labor-requiring tasks.* Had consumers not evinced a desire for the relatively more labor-using manufactures and highly labor-intensive services, the total labor time required to provision society would have been considerably less. We would then have become an economy that mainly produced agricultural goods very efficiently—that is, with relatively little labor input—and one that had but few "demands" for labor in other occupations.

Such a society would not necessarily suffer high unemployment. It could use its agricultural productivity, in the absence of other wants, to reduce the work week drastically; and by distributing the remaining quota of necessary work among its population, it could still give employment to all who sought it. Its standard of living, would of course, be no higher than the amount of agricultural produce it would then bring forth, but this would be a voluntarily chosen standard that accorded leisure a higher value than the nonagricultural goods and services that might have been produced.

It need hardly be said that the United States is not such a society. As our productivity in primary products has confronted the stone wall of our inelastic demand for primary products, we have shifted both our wants and our labor power into the secondary and tertiary sectors. Nonetheless, so great has been the rise in productivity in primary and secondary sectors that we have also been able to cut back our work week from sixty to forty hours. In other words, we have absorbed the employment-displacing effect of technology not only by shifting our demands, but *by substituting leisure for work.*

The conclusion, then, is that the demand for labor reflects the interplay of technology (which exerts differing leverages on different industries and occupations at different times) and of the changing demand for goods and services. Typically, the entrance of technology into industry has a twofold effect. The first is a raise the *potential* output of the industry, with its present labor force. The second is to enable the costs of the industry to decline, or its quality to improve, so that actual demand for the product will increase. But normally, the rise in demand is not great enough to enable the existing labor force to be retained along with the new techniques. Instead, some labor is displaced and must now find its employment elsewhere.

There are exceptions, of course. A great new industry, such as the automobile industry in the 1920's, will keep on expanding its labor force despite improved technology, for in such cases demand *is* sufficiently strong to absorb the output of the new technology, even with a growing labor force. Then too, there is the exception of capital-saving technology, making it possible for an industry to turn out the same product

TABLE 18 · 5

OUTPUT AND
EMPLOYMENT
INDICES

AGRICULTURE AND MANUFACTURING: 1950 = 100

	1950	1968
Manufacturing output	100	220
Manufacturing employment	100	129
Agricultural output	100	139
Agricultural employment	100	48

with a cheaper capital equipment, thereby making it attractive to expand production and to hire more labor.

But taking all industries and all technological changes together, the net result is unambiguous. As Table 18-5 reveals, technology has steadily increased our ability to create goods, both on the farm and on the factory floor, more rapidly than we have wished to consume them, with the result that employment in these areas has lagged behind output.

Note how agricultural output has increased by almost 40 per cent in this period, in part because of the needs of a rapidly growing population, while agricultural employment has shrunk by over 50 per cent; and notice that whereas manufacturing output has more than doubled, employment in manufacturing is up by only 29 per cent.

During this same period, however, our total civilian labor force increased by over 23 million. Where did these millions find employment? As we would expect, largely in the service sector.* Actual totals for employment in various parts of the economy appear in Table 18-6.

TABLE 18 · 6

NONFARM
EMPLOYMENT
1950, 1968

	1950	1968	Per cent increase 1950–1968
	(in millions)*		
Secondary sector			
Mining, manufacturing, construction, transportation, communication, and public utilities	22.4	27.9	25%
Tertiary sector			
Trade	9.4	14.1	50
Personal services	5.4	10.5	94
Government	6.0	12.2	103
Finance and other	1.9	3.6	89
Total tertiary sector	**22.7**	**46.5**	**105%**

*Omits household and self-employed workers.

* Note that the employment shift from agriculture "through" manufacturing is by no means limited to the United States. As Table 18-7 shows, it seems to be visible in all industrialized nations.

We have seen how the long-run employment trends reflect slow-moving changes in the supply and demand for labor, and we have had a glimpse of some of the problems these forces may create. Yet all this has seemed somehow at a considerable remove from the problems of saving and investment and credit creation that have absorbed us in the earlier chapters of this book. How can we now connect the supply and demand for labor with the fluctuations in aggregate expenditure and output that have served as our focus of attention heretofore?

Let us begin, as so often before, at the simplest possible starting point, an imaginary economy uncluttered by many of the complicating factors of real life, such as changing technology or tastes. Then it is easy to trace the cause of changes in employment. They must be the result of changes in GNP—that is, of changes in expenditure. In turn, we can trace these changes to our familiar basic motive forces: fluctuations in investment spending or in government spending (or on rare occasions to spontaneous changes in consumer spending).

In point of fact, even with technology and all other complexities added back in, the volume of spending is *still* the single most important determinant of employment. With the exception of only the war years, with their special demands on manpower, in every year from 1929 to the present, when GNP has risen, employment has also risen; and in every year that GNP has declined, employment has followed suit.

But the impact of spending on *unemployment* is not quite so simple as this over-all correlation of employment might suggest. We have already seen that short-run changes in GNP will bring about short-run changes in the labor participation rate, so that rising GNP can produce both more jobs *and* more unemployment. In the same way, a declining GNP will discourage participation and thereby "abolish" some unemployment by causing people to withdraw from the job market. During the 1960's, as we saw in Table 18-1, *unemployment and employment and GNP* all rose from 1962 to 1963 and again from 1966 to 1967.

TABLE 18 · 7

PERCENTAGE DISTRIBUTION OF EMPLOYMENT

	Farms	Manufacturing	Services
France, 1950	35%	45%	20%
France, 1966	17	40	43
West Germany, 1950	24	48	28
West Germany, 1966	11	49	39
Britain, 1950	6	56	39
Britain, 1962	3	47	49

Source: OECD. Figures may not total 100, owing to rounding.

Another reason why changes in spending may not be mirrored by changes in unemployment is that the age groupings of the population are not always the same. In some years there will be relatively more job seekers than in other years, with the result that a given increase in spending will leave more unemployed at some times than at others.

This has particular relevance for the years now ahead of us. If we compare the age distribution in 1960 with that for 1975, we can see a very marked increase in the number of young job seekers for whom additional spending will have to provide jobs.

TABLE 18 · 8

AGE GROUPS
IN THE
LABOR FORCE
1960, 1975

Age group	1960	1975	Per cent
	(millions)		increase
14–19	4.9	9.2	88
20–34	21.7	33.4	54
35–64	33.9	46.7	38
Over 65	3.1	3.7	19

Source: *Hearings,* Joint Economic Committee, 88th Congress, 1st Session 1, p. 203.

Note that the ranks of *youthful* job seekers will be disproportionately enlarged during the years ahead. Young people will, for a time, be coming onto the labor market faster than older workers are leaving it, with the result that the proportion of the entire population seeking work will temporarily rise. If the level of unemployment is also to be prevented from rising, there will have to be an unusually large increase in total national expenditure.

Our discussion of the supply side of employment allows us to understand why an increase in spending may not always be met by a proportional decrease in unemployment. But now we must consider an even more important reason on the demand side: technological change.

Why is technological change relevant to the demand for labor? One reason is that the introduction of new technology is usually achieved through the means of new capital investment. Hence, the steady process of investment, indispensable for the maintenance of an even flow of GNP, is a vehicle for the steady introduction of new technology into the economy. To be sure, not all investment incorporates technological change—some investment merely expands or duplicates existing facilities with very little, if any, changes in design or end use. Yet historically, investment and technology have gone hand in hand, the technology stimulating the new investment and the investment incorporating the new technology. In addition, much so-called replacement investment is actually the source of a steady upgrading of the quality of capital assets, as old and obsolete plants and parts are replaced by new and modern ones.

Thus technological change is closely allied with the ongoing flow of investment spending. But how does technological change affect the demand for labor? To answer the question, it will help us to differentiate between two kinds: demand-creating technology and cost-reducing technology.

NEW
DEMANDS

Let us suppose that an inventor patents a new product—let us say a stove that automatically cooks things to perfection. Will such an invention create employment?

We will suppose that our inventor assembles his original models himself and peddles them in local stores, and we will ignore the small increase in spending (and perhaps in employment) due to his orders for raw materials. Instead, let us fasten our attention on the consumer who first decides to buy the new product in a store, because it has stimulated his demand.

Will the consumer's purchase result in a *net* increase in consumer spending in the economy? If this is so—and if the new product is generally liked—it is easy to see how the new product could result in sizeable additional employment.

But will it be true? Our consumer has, to be sure, bought a new item. *But unless his income has increased, there is no reason to believe that this is a net addition to his consumption expenditures.* The chances are, rather, that this unforeseen expenditure will be balanced by lessened spending for some other item. Almost surely he will not buy a regular stove. (When consumers first began buying television sets, they stopped buying as many radios and going to the movies as often.) But even where there is no direct competition, where the product is quite "new," everything that we know about the stability of the propensity to consume schedule leads us to believe that *total* consumer spending will not rise.

Thus we reach the important conclusion that new products do not automatically create *additional* spending, even though they may mobilize consumer demand for themselves. Indeed, many new products emerge onto the market every year and merely shoulder old products off. Must we then conclude that demand-creating inventions do not affect employment?

EMPLOYMENT
AND
INVESTMENT

We are by no means ready to jump to that conclusion. Rather, what we have seen enables us to understand that if a new product is to create employment, it must give rise to new *investment* (and to the consumption it induces in turn). If the automatic stove is successful, it may induce the inventor to borrow money from a bank and to build a plant to mass-produce the item. If consumer demand for it continues to rise, a very large factory may have to be built to accommodate demand. As a result of the investment expenditures on the new plant, consumers' incomes *will* rise, and more employment will be created as they spend their incomes on various consumer items.*

When we think of a new product not in terms of a household gadget but in terms of the automobile, airplane, or perhaps the transistor, we can understand how large the employment-creating potential of certain kinds of inventions can be. Originally the automobile merely resulted in consumer spending being diverted from buggies; the airplane merely cut into railroad income; the transistor, into vacuum tubes. But each of these inventions became in time the source of enormous investment expenditures. The automobile not only gave us the huge auto plants in Detroit, but indirectly brought into being multibillion dollar investment in highways, gasoline refineries, service stations, and industries whose impact on employment has been gigantic. On a smaller, but still very large, scale, the airplane gave rise not alone to huge aircraft building plants, but to airfields, radio and beacon equipment industries, and others, whose employment totals are substantial. In turn, the transistor offered entirely new design possibilities for miniaturization and thus gave many businesses an impetus for expansion.

What sorts of inventions have this industry-building capacity? We can perhaps generalize by describing them as inventions that are of sufficient importance to become "indispensable" to the consumer or the manufacturer, and of sufficient mechanical or physical variance from the existing technical environment to necessitate the creation of a large amount of supporting capital equipment to integrate them into economic life.

Demand-creating inventions, then, can indeed create employment. *They do so indirectly, however—not by inducing new consumer spending, but by generating new investment spending.*†

Unfortunately, there is no guarantee that these highly employment-generative inventions will come along precisely when they are needed.

---

*To be sure, investment will decline in those areas that are now selling less to consumers. At most, however, this decline can affect only their replacement expenditures, which probably averaged 5 to 10 per cent of the value of their capital equipment. Meanwhile, in the new industry, an entire capital structure must be built from scratch. We can expect the total amount of investment spending to increase substantially, with its usual repercussive effects.

†We should mention one effect of demand-creating inventions on consumption. It is probable that without the steady emergence of new products, the long-run propensity to consume would decline instead of remaining constant, as we have seen in Chapter 12. In this way, demand-creating technology is directly responsible for the creation of employment, by helping to keep consumer spending higher than it would be without a flow of new products.

There have been long periods when the economy has not been adequately stimulated by this type of invention and when employment has lagged as a result. We shall return to these dynamic inventions when we discuss growth, in our last chapter. But first let us consider another kind of invention that affects employment.

By a cost-reducing invention, we generally mean an invention or an innovation that enables a manufacturer to turn out the *same* end product with less factor input. The factor that is saved may be, and often is, land or capital. But the type of cost-cutting invention that interests us here is probably the most common and surely the most important. These are *labor-saving* inventions or innovations, changes in technique or technology that enable an entrepreneur to turn out the same output as before, with less labor, or a larger output than before, with the same amount of labor.

Do such inventions "permanently" displace labor? Let us trace an imaginary instance and find out.

We assume in this case that an inventor has perfected a technique that makes it possible for a local shoe factory to reduce its production force from ten men to eight men, while still turning out the same number of shoes. Forgetting for the moment about the possible stimulatory effects of buying a new labor-saving machine,* let us see what happens to purchasing power and employment if the shoe manufacturer simply goes on selling the same number of shoes at the same prices as before, utilizing the new lower-cost process to increase his profits.

Suppose our manufacturer now spends his increased profits in increased consumption. Will that bring an equivalent increase in the total spending of the community? If we think twice we can see why not. For the increased spending of the manufacturer will be offset to a large extent by the decreased spending of the two displaced workers.

Exactly the same conclusion follows if our entrepreneur used his cost-cutting invention to lower the price of shoes, in the hope of snaring a larger market. Now it is *consumers* who are given an increase in purchasing power equivalent to the cut in prices. But again, their gain is exactly balanced by the lost purchasing power of the displaced workers.

Thus we can see that the introduction of labor-saving machinery does not necessarily imperil *incomes;* it merely shifts purchasing power from previously employed workers into the hands of consumers or into

---

*This is not an unfair assumption. The labor-saving technology might be no more than a more effective arrangement of labor within the existing plant, and thus require no new equipment; or the new equipment might be bought with regular capital replacement funds.

profits. But note also that *the unchanged volume of incomes is now associated with a smaller volume of employment. Thus the fact that there is no purchasing power "lost" when a labor-saving machine is introduced does not mean that there is no employment lost.*

Is this the end to our analysis of labor-displacing technology? It can be. It is possible that the introduction of labor-saving machinery will have no effect other than that of the example above: transferring consumer spending from previously employed labor to consumers or to entrepreneurs. But it is also possible that an employment-generating secondary effect may result. Our entrepreneur may be so encouraged at the higher profits from his new process that he uses his profits to invest in additional plant and equipment and thereby sets in motion, via the multiplier, a rise in total expenditure sufficient to re-employ his displaced workers. Or in our second instance, consumers may evidence such a brisk demand for shoes at lower prices that, once again, our employer is encouraged to invest in additional plant and equipment, with the same salutary results as above.*

The moral is clear. *Labor-displacing technology can offset the unemployment created by its immediate introduction only if it induces sufficient investment to increase the volume of total spending to a point where employment also rises.*

It is in connection with our foregoing discussion that the much talked-of threat of *automation* becomes most meaningful. By automation, we mean technological inventions that perform increasingly complex and often self-regulatory tasks, some on the factory floor and, more significantly, some previously associated with white-collar work. In the main, automation is clearly a cost-cutting and labor-saving kind of technology, although it has important applications for new products as well.

But one aspect of automation requires our special attention. It is the fact that automation represents the belated entry of technology into an area of economic activity that until now has been largely spared the impact of technical change. This is the area of service and administrative tasks that we have previously marked as an important source of growing employment. Thus the threat inherent in the new sensory, almost humanoid, equipment is not only that it may accelerate the employment-displacing effects in the secondary (manufacturing) sector. *More sobering is that it may put an end to the traditional employment-absorptive effects of the tertiary service and administrative sector.*

---

*Do not fall into the trap of thinking that the new higher demand for shoes, will, by itself, suffice to eradicate unemployment. To be sure, shoe purchases may now increase to previous levels or even higher. But unless their incomes rise, consumer spending on other items will suffer to the exact degree that spending on shoes gains.

What could be the implications of such a development? In simplest terms, it means that in the future, fewer people will be needed to produce the same quantity of services. The absorption of labor from agriculture and manufacturing into the ever-expanding service sector would now slow down or come to a halt, since the service sector could increase its output without hiring a proportionate increase in workers.

This *could*, of course, mean massive unemployment. But it need not. Just as our imaginary society limited its demand to agricultural goods and solved its labor problem by cutting the workweek, so a society that no longer needed to add labor as fast as its demands rose could easily solve the unemployment problem by more or less equitably sharing among its members the amount of labor it *did* require. To be sure, this raises many problems, not least among them the wage adjustments that must accompany such a reapportionment of hours.* But it makes clear that, essentially, the challenge of automation is one of finding a new balance in our attitudes toward work and leisure, and an equitable means of sharing work (and income, the reward for work) in a society where technology is beginning to invade the last precincts of human skills. The solution will assuredly not be an easy one, although it is by no means inherently impossible.

UNEMPLOYMENT IN THE U.S.

We have spoken of unemployment heretofore in a somewhat detached and analytic fashion. Now it is time to look at the actual figures in the United States and to consider how unemployment can be actively and effectively combatted.

Table 18-9 gives us the important statistics. The terrible percentages of the Great Depression need no comment. Rather, let us pay heed to the level of unemployment in the 1960's. Here the record is mixed. During the early years of the decade we were troubled with persistent levels of unemployment much too high to be healthy. In the later years, unemployment declined sharply, but there is the discomfort of tracing much of this decline to an increase in war spending.

---

*What society is trying to do in rolling back hours of work is to *share* work and incomes more equitably. This is good for those who would otherwise be unemployed, but it may not be so good for those who are lucky enough to have jobs at the time when unemployment becomes a problem. These workers will be glad to cut their workweek, but not so glad to cut their pay or to deprive themselves of increased pay in order to share incomes with their new workmates. In actuality, this source of potential conflict is softened because the process of shortening hours stretches out over fairly long periods and is often accompanied by rising productivity. As a result, hours may fall and weekly pay remain steady. But of course, if hours had not fallen, employed workers would have enjoyed a rise in pay.

TABLE 18 · 9

**UNEMPLOYMENT
IN THE U.S.**

Year	Unemployed (thousands)	Per cent of civilian labor force
1929	1,550	3.2
1933	12,830	24.9
1940	8,120	14.6
1944	670	1.2
1960	3,931	5.6
1961	4,806	6.7
1962	3,911	5.5
1963	4,070	5.7
1964	3,786	5.2
1965	3,366	4.5
1966	2,875	3.8
1967	2,975	3.8
1968	3,817	3.6

What is the cause of this unemployment? There is no single cause. All of the possible reasons for unemployment that we have studied in our text have a relevance to the current situation. In part, our labor participation rate has been high, especially among women, thereby swelling the job-seeking labor force. In part, our total GNP has not been large enough. In part, we have experienced a considerable amount of labor-displacing investment. In some industries, wages may have risen too fast. And other reasons that we have not specifically studied may be added as well, primary among them being discrimination against the Negro. For example, a larger percentage of white, male, high school *dropouts* secure employment than do Negro males who *graduate* from high school, and the average earnings of these Negro graduates are *lower* than the earnings of white dropouts.

Thus, unemployment strikes very unequally among groups of the population and areas of the country. For example, in 1968, when the average rate of unemployment for the labor force was 3.6 per cent, the rate among married men was only 1.6 per cent, whereas among young workers (16 to 19 years old) it was 12.7 per cent. For white workers as a whole it was 3.2 per cent; for Negro and Puerto Rican workers, 6.7 per cent. In New York City, the rate was 4 per cent; in East Harlem, 9 per cent; among teen-agers in Harlem, up to 30 per cent.

These facts suggest that combatting unemployment is a complex task that requires not one policy, but a variety of policies. Let us look into some of the major ones.

**COMBATTING
UNEMPLOYMENT**

1. *Increasing demand.*

We have learned that as a general rule, anything that increases the total demand of society is apt to increase employment. This is particularly true when unemployment tends to be widespread, both in geographic location and industrial distribution. Then the expansion of GNP, whether by the stimulation of private investment or consumer spending or government expenditure or net exports should prove the single most reliable means of creating more employment.

There is, however, a problem here. Doubtless, a vast amount of employment could be created if aggregate demand were enlarged; for instance, the systematic reconstruction of our cities, a task that is becoming an increasingly pressing necessity, could by itself provide millions of jobs for decades. So could the proper care of our rapidly-growing older population, or the provision of really first-class education for large segments of the population that lack it.

The problem is that these programs require the generation of large amounts of *public demand,* and this requires the prior political approval of the electorate. If this political approval is not forthcoming, the generation of additional demand will have to be entrusted to the private sector—that is, to individual entrepreneurs in search of a profit.

Can private enterprise, without a massive public investment program, generate sufficient demand to bring about full and lasting employment? One cannot be dogmatic about such questions, but there is at least some historical reason to be uncertain. Between 1950 and 1960, for example, private enterprise accounted for only one out of every ten new jobs created in the economy.[1] All the rest were created in the public or the private not-for-profit sector (universities, hospitals, etc). In the years since then, the private sector has been more labor-attracting; but by itself it is still far from capable of creating employment fast enough to absorb the increase in the labor force.

To this sobering trend in employment creation, we must also add the potentially serious, although as yet untested, effects of the new technology of automation, particularly as it may cut into job needs in the tertiary sector. Hence there seems to be good reason for caution in assuming that the private sector, unaided by public programs of investment, will be able to offer as much employment as the growing labor force demands. The likelihood is that a large enough aggregate demand will require the substantial use of public expenditure, whether for urban renewal and welfare services or for other ends.

2. *Wage policy.*

But suppose that a very high aggregate demand is maintained, through public or private spending. Will that in itself guarantee full employment?

The answer is that it will not if the spending creates only higher incomes for workers who are already employed, rather than new in-

[1] Eli Ginzberg, *The Pluralistic Economy* (New York: McGraw-Hill Book Company, 1965), p. 144.

comes for workers who are unemployed. Thus if we want to maximize the employment-creating effect of spending, whether private or public, we need to hold back wage raises at least until the unemployment has fallen to a socially acceptable level.

But if raising wages can impede the process of job creation, can cutting wages encourage it? The question is not a simple one, for lower wages set into motion contrary economic stimuli. On the one hand, lower wages cut costs and thereby tempt employers to add to their labor force. On the other hand, lower wages after a time will result in less consumption spending, and will thus adversely affect business sales. The net effect of a wage cut thus becomes highly unpredictable. If businessmen feel the positive gains of a cut in costs before they feel the adverse effects of a cut in sales, employment may rise—and thereby obviate the fall in consumption spending. On the other hand, employers may *expect* that the wage cut will lead to lower sales, and their pessimistic expectations may lead them to refrain from adding to their labor forces, despite lower costs. In that case, of course, employment will not rise. On balance, most economists today fear the adverse effects of wage-cutting more than they welcome the possible job-creating effects.

It seems, then, that maintaining wages in the face of an economic decline and restraining wage rises in the face of an economic advance is the best way of encouraging maximum employment. It is one thing, however, to spell out such a general guideline to action and another to achieve it. To maintain wages against an undertow of falling sales requires a strong union movement. But once times improve, this same union movement is hardly likely to exercise the self-restraint needed to forego wage raises, so that additional spending can go into the pockets of the previously unemployed. This poses another dilemma for a market society in search of a rational high employment policy, and there is at this moment no solution in sight.

3. *Remedying structural unemployment.*

Not all unemployment is due to insufficient demand. Some can be traced to "structural" causes—to a lack to "fit" between the existing labor force and the existing job opportunities. For instance, men may be unemployed because they do not know of job opportunities in another city, or because they do not have the requisite skills to get, or hold, jobs that are currently being offered. Indeed, it is perfectly possible to have structural unemployment side-by-side with a lack of manpower in certain fields.

A sharp debate has raged in the United States concerning the importance of structural reasons (as contrasted with a general deficiency of demand) in accounting for the present level of unemployment. Many observers have pointed out that the unemployed are typically grouped into certain disprivileged categories: race, age, lack of training, and unfortunate geographic location. The aged and the young, the Negro and the unskilled, the displaced West Virginian coal miner or Massachusetts textile worker are not quickly pulled into employment by a general expansion of demand. The broad stream of purchasing passes most of them by and does not reintegrate them into the mainstream of the economy. Hence stress is increasingly placed on measures to assist labor mobility, so that the unemployed can move from distressed to expansive areas, and on the retraining of men for those jobs offered by a technologically fast-moving society.

Retraining is, unfortunately, much easier when it is applied to relatively few persons than when it is proposed as a general public policy affecting large numbers of unemployed. Then the question arises: for what jobs shall the unemployed be trained? Unless we very clearly know the *shape* of future demand, the risk is that a retraining program will prepare workers only for jobs that may no longer exist when the workers are ready for them. And unless the *level* of future demand is high, even a foresighted program will not effectively solve the unemployment problem.

4. *Reducing the supply of labor.*

Finally, the possibility exists of attacking unemployment not from the demand side, but from the supply side, by cutting the workweek, lengthening vacations, and using similar measures. Essentially, the possibility held out by shortening the work-week is that a more or less fixed quantity of work will then be shared among a larger number of workers. This is entirely feasible and possible, provided that *the decrease in hours is not offset by an increase in hourly pay rates.* In other words, once again a rational wage policy holds the key between success and failure. Shorter hours, coupled with higher hourly wage rates, will merely raise unit costs (unless productivity rises quickly enough to compensate). This will certainly not contribute to increased employment. Shorter hours *without* increased hourly rates, on the other hand, may make it necessary for the employer to hire additional help in order to continue his established level of output.

Shortening hours of work can be a policy of despair. If people do not wish to change their working habits—the number of hours per week or the number of years in their lifetimes—then the cure for unemployment is surely to expand the demand for labor and not to diminish its supply. If private demand is inadequate to this task, then, as we have said, public demand may serve the purpose instead.

But an attack on unemployment that seeks to reduce the supply of labor, rather than to expand the demand for it, need not be a program of retreat. It can also become part of a deliberate and popularly endorsed effort to reshape the patterns and the duration of work as it now exists. Thus it may be possible to reduce the size of the labor force by measures such as subsidies that would induce younger people to remain longer in school or by raising Social Security to make it attractive for older people to retire earlier. Such policies can be useful not only in bringing down the participation rate and thus reducing "unemployment," but in affecting changes in the quality of life that would find general public approval.

We have done no more than cast an eye over the spectrum of possibilities before us. As we have said, the likelihood is that we shall have to cope with the employment program by using not one technique, but a variety. The large numbers of youths coming rapidly onto the labor market present a severe problem that must be met by extensive programs of training; and the belated entry of the Negro into full economic equality will require not only training but education—of whites as well as Negroes. So, too, the advent of an end to war spending would require the redeployment of skills and hands not only from one region to another, but from one industry to another. All this will require policy measures that are keyed to dealing with structural rather than aggregate unemployment.

But it is likely, particularly if we achieve a stable or even declining military budget, that we will also need to encourage aggregate demand if we are to absorb the full supply of job seekers coming onto the market. This will require fiscal and monetary measures aimed at helping private enterprise expand—policies that encourage entrepreneurs to borrow and invest and to take risks for the future.

At the same time, as we have indicated, there will very probably be a need for large programs of public expenditure. Here the question that seemed so academic at the end of the chapter on the government sector comes to life, for the issue is sharply posed in relation to not only the *ends* to which government expenditure should be aimed, but also the *means* by which fiscal policy can be given its greatest leverage.

Last and perhaps most distant is the possibility that we stand at the threshold of an age when technology will at last invade those areas of production that have heretofore escaped duplication by machine, and that the whole supply of human labor will require readjustment in the face of this radically changed environment. It is certainly likely that over the longer run, some further contraction will take place in the normal workday or workweek, and very likely in the worklife of the normal individual. This may be no more than a prospect for the future, but it is one to which we would be wise to direct our thoughts now.

SUMMARY

1. *Participation* in the working force has slowly increased over the long run. This is the net result of three forces: the *large-scale entry of women* into the labor force after child-bearing, partly offset by the *later entry and earlier retirement of males.*

2. Participation in the short run mirrors economic opportunity. *The labor force is elastic* and responds to increases in job openings. As a result, *it is possible for employment and unemployment* (meaning an active, although unsuccessful, search for work) *to increase at the same time.*

3. The demand for labor reflects not only the total spending of the economy, but also the structure of demand of that economy. In the United States, *this pattern of demand has slowly but substantially shifted* from products of the soil to products of manufacture, and even more strikingly to services of various kinds.

4. Along with this shift in demand has come an uneven impact of technology. Machines have very greatly boosted the productivity of the primary and secondary sectors, while relatively much less affecting the output per person of the tertiary sector.

5. As a consequence of these patterns of demand and of technology, *employment has been steadily shifted out of farming into manufacturing, and even more importantly into service and administration.* It is the prospective entry of new machinery into the tertiary sector that now poses the greatest problems for employment.

6. Large-scale unemployment is generally caused by *inadequate total demand.* This unemployment may be aggravated, or its cure made more difficult both by changes in technology, such as the trend to automation, and by irregularities in the *population age structure*—in particular by the prospect of large numbers of youths coming onto the labor market during the next decade.

7. Technology can both displace labor and create a demand for it. *Demand-creating technology increases employment through the creation of a substantial volume of new investment.* Labor-displacing technology does not diminish incomes but can shrink employment in particular industries.

8. Unemployment can be combatted in several ways, of which *increasing aggregate demand* is probably the single most important way. However, because of the labor-displacing properties of modern technology, it is uncertain that private demand alone can create and maintain full employment. Public expenditure will also probably be required.

9. The creation of additional employment requires a *wage policy* that prevents increased spending from swelling the incomes of the already employed, rather than giving new income to the unemployed. *Wage-cutting,* on the other hand, *is an uncertain and possibly dangerous mode of increasing employment,* since the adverse effects of lowered consumption may more than offset the positive effects of lowered costs.

10. *Structural unemployment* requires much more specific remedies than those provided by aggregate demand. Training and education programs are the main weapon against this kind of joblessness.

11. There is a long-term trend toward *leisure* in all advanced countries, and it is probable that this trend will continue. One way of alleviating unemployment is to convert it into leisure; i.e., by lengthening the period of schooling, advancing

the age of retirement, shortening the workday or week, and so on. This is probably a direction in which the economy will slowly move.

1. How do you account for the fact that there are more people per hundred who want to work today than there were 70 years ago, when the nation was so much poorer? How much does the monetization of labor have to do with this? How much is it a change in "life styles," especially for women? What do you expect for the very long run—say 100 years from now?

2. How can employment and unemployment *both* rise at the same time? What would you consider to be a useful definition of unemployment, one that could be easily used by interviewers in the field?

3. What do you think accounts for the shift in demand from primary to secondary and tertiary products? In particular, what do you think is the reason for the steady growth of services as a kind of output that society seems to want?

4. Suppose that technology in the 1890's had taken the following turn: a very complex development of machines and techniques for improving public and private supervisory and administrative techniques, very clever devices that performed salesmen's and clerks' services, but almost no improvement in agricultural techniques. What would the distribution of the labor force probably look like?

5. What is the relation between leisure and unemployment? Is a man who is retired before he wants to stop working "at leisure" or "unemployed"? Can one make a clear distinction between the two, or does it depend very largely on social customs, and other things?

6. Suppose that an inventor puts a wrist radio-telephone on the market. What would be the effects on consumer spending? What would ultimately determine whether the new invention were labor-attracting or labor-displacing?

7. Suppose that another new invention halved the cost of making cars. Would this create new purchasing power? What losses in income would have to be balanced against what gains in incomes? What would be the most likely way that such an invention could increase employment? Would employment increase if the demand for cars were inelastic, like the demand for farm products—that is, if people bought very few more cars despite the fall in prices?

8. Unemployment among the Negro population in many cities in the late 1960's was worse than it was during the Great Depression. What steps would you propose to remedy this situation?

9. Would raising wages, and thereby creating more consumption demand, be a good way to increase employment?

10. Do you believe that there exists general support for large public employment-generating programs? Why or why not? What sorts of programs would you propose?

11. How would you encourage private enterprise to create as many *jobs* as possible?

19 THE PROBLEM OF GROWTH

There remains for us to consider but one subject in our introduction to macroeconomics: the subject of growth. Actually, we have already been concerned for many pages with the main problem, if not the explicit theme, of growth. From the very beginning of our study, investment has been at the center of our focus. Up to this point, however, we have thought of investment mainly as the process by which savings were offset so that a given level of expenditure could be maintained, or in the preceding chapter, as the key to the dynamic process by which employment was sometimes created and sometimes destroyed. In all these considerations, *fluctuations* in the level of investment were all-important, a slowdown spelling recession and unemployment, an acceleration leading to the opposite.

Now we must see the process of investment in a somewhat different perspective. Whether it proceeds slowly or fast, investment consists in the addition of real wealth to the stock of wealth of the nation. Thus, so long as there is *any* net investment, our stock of capital is growing;

and with a growth in our capital, there should come a growth in our capacity to produce. In this way we can see that the process of investment leads inevitably to a consideration of economic growth, and it is to this subject that we now turn.

STRUCTURAL REQUIREMENTS OF GROWTH

How does growth take place? Through investment, we know. But how does investment take place? How does a society actually find the resources to devote to capital-building? In our rich, industrialized economy, such a question may seem pointless. We simply use our industrial equipment to make more industrial equipment. And for the necessary labor we simply employ the people who are already working in steel and other capital-goods industries.

But the matter-of-factness with which we answer the question hides from us the real structural significance of growth. For when we turn our gaze abroad or backward in time and ask how a poor society grows, the question is not so easy to answer. Such societies do not have steel mills waiting for orders, nor labor forces that are already deployed in capital-goods industries. How do they, then, create capital?

The process is by no means an obvious one. Suppose we have a very poor society (like an extremely underdeveloped nation) in which 80 per cent of the population tills the soil, equipped with so little by way of capital—mere spades and hoes—that it produces only enough to maintain itself and the remaining 20 per cent of society.

Who are the other 20 per cent? In reality, of course, they might be government officials, landlords, and others, but we will simplify our model by assuming that the whole 20 per cent is occupied in making the simple spades and hoes (the capital goods) with which the consumption-goods sector works. Like the farmers, the toolmakers labor from dawn to dusk; and again like the farmers, they are so unproductive that they can produce only enough capital to replace the spades and hoes that wear out each year.

Now how could such a society grow? If we look again at the capital-goods sector, we find a clue. For unlike the consumption-goods sector, we find here not one but two distinguishable kinds of economic activity going on. In the agricultural side, everyone is farming; but in the capital-goods side, not everyone is making the spades and hoes with which the agricultural laborers work. No matter how we simplify our model, we can see that *the capital-goods sector must carry out two different tasks.* It must turn out spades and hoes, to be sure. But part of the capital-goods labor force must also turn out a different kind of capital good—a very special kind that will produce not only spades and hoes, but also more of itself!

Is there such a kind of equipment? There is indeed, in a versatile group of implements known as *machine tools*. In our model economy, these may be only chisels and hammers that can be used to make spades, hoes, and more chisels and hammers. In a complex industrial system, machine tools consist of presses and borers and lathes which, when used ensemble, not only make all kinds of complicated machines but can also recreate themselves.

CAPITAL
FORMATION

Thus we encounter the unexpected fact that there is a strategic branch of capital creation that lies at the core of the whole sequence of economic growth.*

How does growth now ensue? Our model enables us to see that it is not simply a matter of bringing in peasants from the fields to make more spades and thereby to increase their productivity. For they will not be able to make spades until they have laid the ground by an increase in output of this strategic branch: before spades can be made, chisels and hammers must be made. Before textile or shoemaking or food-processing or transportation equipment can be made, machine tools must be made.

Thus at the core of the growth process—whether in a very backward nation or a highly industrialized one—we can see *two* great structural shifts that must take place:

1. *A shift of effort* within *the capital sector to increase its own productive capacity.*

2. *A shift of effort from the consumption sector to the capital sector, to man the growing volume of equipment which emerges from the enlarged capital sector.*

Can we actually trace this process in real life? The shifts *within* the capital sector are not always easy to see, because there is usually some excess capacity in the machine tool branch. By running overtime, for instance, it can produce *both* more machine tools *and* more hoes and spades. Yet if we examine a society in the process of rapid industrialization, such as the U.S.S.R. (or for that matter, the United States in its periods of rapid wartime industrial buildup) we can clearly see the

---

*This raises the perplexing question of how the machine-tool industry *began*, since it needs its own output to grow. The answer is that it evolved as a special branch of industrial production during the industrial revolution when, for the first time, machinery itself began to be made by machinery instead of by hand. A key figure in the evolution of the machine-tool industry was Maudslay, whose invention of the screw-cutting lathe was "one of the decisive pieces of standardization that made the modern machine possible." (Mumford, *Technics and Civilization*, p. 209.)

importance of this critical branch in setting a *ceiling* on the over-all pace of industrial expansion.

When we turn to the second shift, from the consumption sector into the capital sector, the movement in real life is very apparent. Table 19-1, for instance, shows us the proportion of the population engaged in agriculture for a number of industrialized nations at an early and a late stage of their transformations.

TABLE 19 • 1

LABOR FORCE IN AGRICULTURE

	PER CENT OF LABOR FORCE IN AGRICULTURE	
	Early 19th century	1966
France	63% (1827)	17%
Great Britain	31 (1811)	3
Sweden	63 (1840)	10
United States	72 (1820)	5

Sources: Colin Clark, *The Conditions of Economic Progress* (London: Macmillan & Co., Ltd., 1960), pp. 512, 514, 518; B. R. Mitchell, *Abstract of British Historical Statistics* (Cambridge: Cambridge University Press, 1962), pp. 60–61; and O.E.C.D.

Here we see in reality the wholesale emigration that takes place in the industrializing process (note that by 1811 Britain was already well on the road). Over the course of the nineteenth and twentieth centuries, these countries have lost two-thirds to four-fifths of their erstwhile farmers—not all to capital-building alone, of course, but to the whole industrial and commercial structure that capital-building makes possible. In this way, the process of economic growth can be seen in part as a great flow of human and material resources from simple consumption goods output to a hierarchy of industrial tasks—a flow that is even more dramatic in real life than we might have divined from our imaginary model.

THE HISTORICAL RECORD: STABILITY AND CYCLES

Thus, behind the phenomenon of growth we encounter a hidden structural shift of the greatest importance. Once the shift has taken place, however—once a large capital-building sector has been established—the process of adding to the stock of capital is greatly simplified. Indeed, we now get that long process of gradually increasing output that pro-

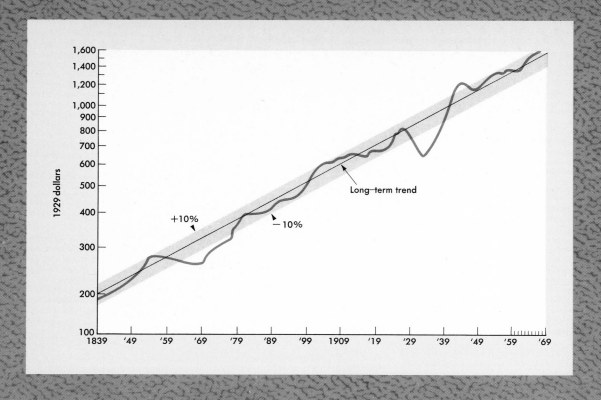

FIG. 19-1 TREND IN REAL GNP PER HEAD, 1839-1968

vides us with our ordinary starting point in the study of growth. In Fig. 19-1 we see the American experience from the middle of the nineteenth century.

How regular has been our average rate of growth? The answer is: astonishingly constant, whether we take an average over the past thirty-odd years since the Great Depression, or whether we go back to the earliest reliable statistics and calculate our growth rate since the 1870's (or even 1830's). As the chart shows, the swings are almost all contained within a range of 10 per cent above or below the trend. The trend itself comes to about 3.5 per cent a year in real terms, or a little over 1.5 per cent a year per capita.*

*This is a very good time to stress the dangers of intertemporal comparisons of GNP voiced in Chapter 9. In case you have forgotten, they are: (1) the *quality* of output varies greatly over a long span of time, favorably and otherwise; (2) part of GNP is *imputed* and this portion varies over time; (3) there is a long-term *monetization of household tasks* that adds a deceptive component of growth; and (4) *not all of GNP*—and different amounts in different periods—*adds to well-being*. All in all, growth statistics should be used with caution in making comparative statements about output and welfare in two widely separated periods.

TABLE 19 · 2

**U.S. RATES
OF GROWTH
1895–1905**

1895–1896	− 2.5%	1900–1901	+11.5%
1896–1897	+ 9.4	1901–1902	+ 1.0
1897–1898	+ 2.3	1902–1903	+ 4.9
1898–1899	+ 9.1	1903–1904	− 1.2
1899–1900	+ 2.7	1904–1905	+ 7.4

Source: *Long Term Economic Growth* (U.S. Dept. of Commerce, 1966), p. 107.

How do we account for this long, steady ascent? In part, the answer cites the underlying forces of propulsion that we have already discussed in our historic survey on American economic development. We will not review that chapter of history now, although we will return to the forces of growth in a somewhat more analytical focus at the conclusion of this chapter.

But the second part of the answer is equally important. It is that year-by-year growth was *not* so smooth and steady as the long-term growth rates suggest. Take the years 1895 to 1905, very smooth-looking in Fig. 19-1. As Table 19-2 reveals, the advance was anything but steady.

Or examine a more recent period, not year by year, but in groups of years. Here is the record of the U.S. economy—or rather, the records of the U.S. economy—between 1922 and 1967. As we can see, the rate of growth has varied greatly in different periods.

FIG. 19-2   SHORT-TERM VARIATIONS IN THE RATE OF GROWTH

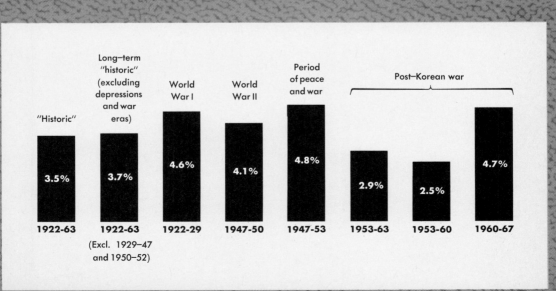

This extraordinary sequence of ups and downs, rushes of growth followed by doldrums, introduces us to a fascinating aspect of the subject of growth—*business cycles*. For if we inspect the profile of the long ascent carefully, we can see that its entire length is marked with irregular tremors or peaks and valleys. Indeed, the more powerful the magnifying glass we apply—which is to say, the more closely we examine year-to-year figures—the more of these tremors and deviations we discover, until the problem begins to be which of these many vibrations to consider significant and which to discard as uninteresting.

The problem of sorting out the important fluctuations in output (or in statistics of prices or employment) is a difficult one. Economists have actually detected dozens of cycles of different lengths and amplitudes, from very short rhythms of expansion and contraction that can be found, for example, in patterns of inventory accumulation and decumulation, to large background pulsations of seventeen or eighteen years in the housing industry, and possibly (the evidence is unclear) swings of forty to fifty years in the path of capitalist development as a whole.

Generally, however, when we speak of "the" business cycle we refer to a wavelike movement that lasts, on the average, about eight to ten years. In Fig. 19-3 this major oscillation of the American economy stands forth very clearly, for the chartist has eliminated the underlying tilt of growth so that the profile of economic performance looks like a cross section at sea level rather than a cut through a long incline.

FIG. 19-3

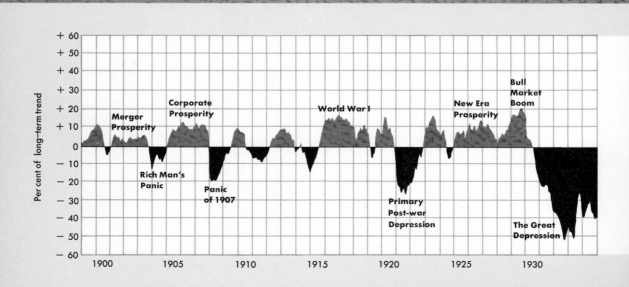

FIG. 19-4

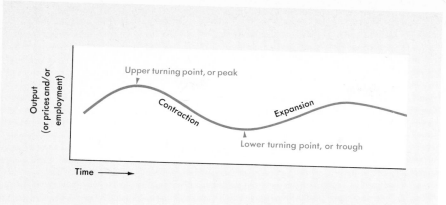

Upper turning point, or peak

Contraction

Expansion

Output
(or prices and/or
employment)

Lower turning point, or trough

Time ——▶

In a general way we are all familiar with the meaning of business cycles, for the alternation of "boom and bust" or prosperity and recession (a polite name for a mild depression) is part of everyday parlance. It will help us study cycles, however, if we learn to speak of them with a standard terminology. We can do this by taking the cycles from actual history, "superimposing" them, and drawing the general profile of the so-called *reference* cycle that emerges. It looks like Fig. 19-4.

This model of a typical cycle enables us to speak of the "length"

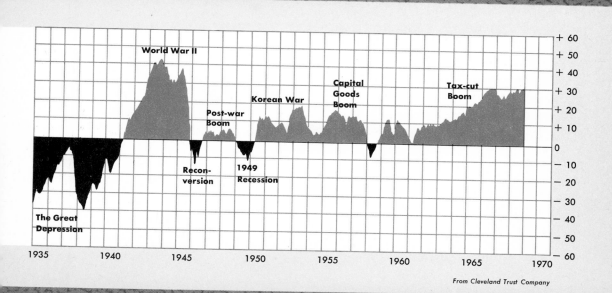

World War II

Korean War

Capital
Goods
Boom

Tax-cut
Boom

Post-war
Boom

Recon-
version

1949
Recession

The Great
Depression

1935   1940   1945   1950   1955   1960   1965   1970

+60 +50 +40 +30 +20 +10 0 −10 −20 −30 −40 −50 −60

From Cleveland Trust Company

of a business cycle as the period from one peak to the next or from trough to trough. If we fail to measure from *similar* points on two or more cycles, we can easily get a distorted picture of short-term growth—for instance, one that begins at the upper turning point of one cycle and measures to the trough of the next. Much of the political charge and countercharge about growth rates can be clarified if we examine the starting and terminating dates used by each side.

CAUSES
OF CYCLES

What lies behind this more or less regular alternation of good and bad times?

Innumerable theories, none of them entirely satisfactory, have been advanced to explain the business cycle. A common business explanation is that waves of optimism in the world of affairs alternate with waves of pessimism—a statement that may be true enough, but that seems to describe the sequence of events rather than to explain it. Hence economists have tried to find the underlying cyclical mechanism in firmer stuff than an alternation of moods. One famous late-nineteenth-century economist, W. S. Jevons, for example, explained business cycles as the consequence of sunspots—perhaps not as occult a theory as it might seem, since Jevons believed that the sunspots caused weather cycles that caused crop cycles that caused business cycles. The trouble was that subsequent investigation shows that the periodicity of sunspots was sufficiently different from that of rainfall cycles to make the connection impossible.

Other economists have turned to causes closer to home: to variations in the rate of gold mining (with its effects on the money supply); to fluctuations in the rate of invention; to the regular recurrence of war; and to yet many other factors. There is no doubt that many of these events can induce a business expansion or contraction. The persistent problem, however, is that none of the so-called underlying causes itself displays an inherent cyclicality—much less one with a periodicity of eight to ten years.

Then how do we explain cycles? Economists today no longer seek a single explanation of the phenomenon in an exogenous (external) cyclical force. Rather, they tend to see cycles as our own eye first saw them on the growth curve, as *variations in the rate of growth that tend to be induced by the dynamics of the growth process itself.* As we shall see, our knowledge of macroeconomics will quickly give us the clue to the mechanism at work.

MECHANISM
OF BUSINESS
FLUCTUATION

Let us assume that some stimulus, such as an important industry-building invention, has begun to increase investment expenditures. We can easily see how such an initial impetus can generate a cumulative and self-feeding boom. As the multiplier and accelerator interact, the first burst of investment stimulates additional consumption, the additional consumption induces more investment, and this in turn re-invigorates consumption. Meanwhile, this process of mutual stimulation serves to lift business expectations and to encourage still further expansionary spending. Inventories are built up in anticipation of larger sales. Prices "firm up" and the stock market rises. Optimism reigns. A boom is on.

What happens to end such a boom? There are many possible reasons why it may peter out or come to an abrupt halt. It may simply be that the new industry will get built, and thereafter an important stimulus to investment will be lacking. Or even before it is completed, wages and prices may have begun to rise as full employment is neared, and the climate of expectations may thereupon become wary rather than hopeful. (Businessmen have an old adage that "what goes up must come down.") Meanwhile, perhaps tight money will choke off spending plans or make new projects appear unprofitable.

Or investment may begin to decline because consumption, although still rising, is no longer rising at the earlier *rate* (the acceleration principle in action). Previously (p. 259n.) we noticed that the action of the accelerator, all by itself, could give rise to wavelike movements in total expenditure. The accelerator, of course, never works "all by itself," but it can exert its upward and downward pressures within the flux of economic forces and in this way give rise to an underlying cyclical impetus.

It is impossible to know in advance what particular cause will retard spending, but it is all too easy to see how a hesitation in spending can turn into a general contraction. Perhaps warned by a falling stock market, perhaps by a slowdown in their sales or an end to rising profits, businessmen begin to cut back. Whatever their initial motivation, what follows thereafter is much like the preceding expansion, only in reverse. The multiplier mechanism now breeds smaller rather than larger incomes. Downward revisions of expectations reduce rather than enhance the attractiveness of investment projects. As consumption decreases, prices fall and unemployment begins to show up. Inventories are worked off. Bankruptcies become more common. We experience all the economic and social problems of a recession.

But just as there is a "natural" ceiling to a boom, so there is a more or less "natural" floor to recessions.* The fall in inventories, for example, will eventually come to an end: for even in the severest recessions, merchants and manufacturers must have *some* goods on their shelves and so must eventually begin stocking up. The decline in expenditures will lead to easy money, and the slack in output will tend to a lower level of costs; and both of these factors will encourage new investment

---

*In retrospect, the tremendous and long-lasting collapse of 1929 seems to have been caused by special circumstances having to do mainly with speculation and monetary mismanagement.

projects. Meanwhile, the automatic stabilizers of government fiscal policy will slowly make their effects known. Sooner or later, in other words, expenditures will cease falling, and the economy will tend to "bottom out."

THE ANATOMY OF GROWTH

Thus, business cycles appear as accelerations and decelerations to the underlying momentum of growth. But why growth? How do we know that the peak of one cycle will be higher than the peak of the previous one? What accounts for the underlying tilt to the whole cycle chart?

The essential reason is one that we are very familiar with. Even in the doldrums of recession (except for a very few severely depressed years) the economy manages to lay down a net increment of wealth in the form of investment, and this investment then adds its leverage to that of the entire stock of capital with which society works. So, too, every year, the labor force tends to grow as population increases, adding another component of potential input to the economic mechanism.

This does not mean, as we well know, that the economy will therefore *automatically* utilize its full resources. Unused men and unused machines are very well known to us in macroeconomic analysis. But the steady addition to the factors of production does mean that the *potential* of the economy will be steadily rising. *Growth is thus introduced into the system by the steady addition to its basic instruments of production, both human and material.* If we multiply the slowly rising hours of total labor input by a "productivity coefficient" that reflects, among other things, our slowly rising stock of capital, we can derive a trend line of *potential GNP.* The question we then face is to see how much of this potential volume of output we will actually produce.

ACTUAL VS. POTENTIAL GNP

As Fig. 19-5 shows, all through much of the 1950's and 1960's potential output ran well ahead of the output we actually achieved. Indeed, between 1958 and 1962 the amount of lost output represented by this gap came to the staggering sum of $170 billion, or nearly $1,000 per person. Even in 1964, a very prosperous year, the President's Council of Economic Advisers reported that we could have added another $25 billion to $30 billion to GNP—more than $300 per family—if we had brought unemployment down from 5 to 4 per cent and had also found jobs for the larger labor force that would have sought work in a climate of full employment.

FIG. 19-5

**ACTUAL AND
POTENTIAL GNP**

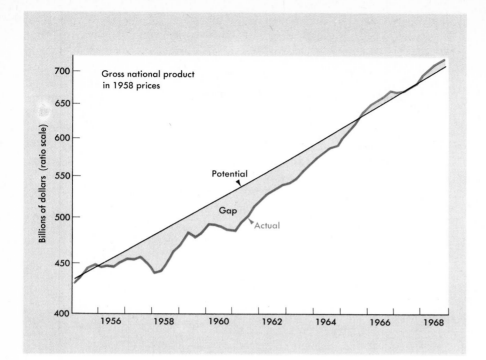

The problem of a potential growth rate opens an aspect of the investment process that we have not yet considered. Heretofore, we have always throught of investment primarily as an income-generating force, working through the multiplier to increase the level of expenditure. Now we begin to consider investment also as a *capacity-generating* force, working through the actual addition to our plant and equipment to increase the productive potential of the system.

No sooner do we introduce the idea of capacity, however, than a new problem arises for our consideration. If investment increases potential output as well as income, the obvious question is: will income rise fast enough to buy all this potential output? Thus at the end of our analysis of macroeconomics we revert to the question we posed at the beginning, but in a more dynamic context. At first, we asked whether an economy that saved could buy back its own output. Now we must ask whether an economy that grows can do the same.

The question brings us to consider a new relationship, unlike any we have considered before. The *marginal capital-output ratio,* as the formidable name suggests, is not a relationship that describes behavior, as the multiplier does. It describes a strictly technical or engineering or organizational relationship between an *increase in the stock of capital and the increase in output that this new capital will yield.*

Note that we are not interested in the ratio between our entire existing stock of capital (most of which is old) and the flow of total output, but only in the ratio between the *new* capital added during the period and the *new* output associated with that new capital. Thus the marginal capital-output ratio directs our attention to the *net investment* of the period and to the *change in output* of the period. If net investment was $60 billion and the change in output yielded by that investment was $20 billion, then the marginal capital-output ratio was 3.

INCOME
VS. OUTPUT

The marginal capital-output ratio gives us a powerful new concept to bring to bear on the problem of attaining and maintaining a high, steady rate of growth, for we can now see that the problem of steady growth requires the balancing out of two different economic processes. Investment raises productive capacity. *Increases* in investment raise income and demand. What we must now do is investigate the relationship between these two different, albeit related, economic variables.

Let us begin with a familiar formula that shows how a change in investment affects a change in income. This is, of course

$$\Delta Y = \frac{1}{s} \Delta I$$

which is nothing but the multiplier.

Now we need a new formula to relate I, the rate of net investment (*not* ΔI, the change in net investment) and ΔO, the change in dollar output. This will require using a symbol for the marginal capital-output ratio, a symbol that expresses how many dollars' worth of new output we will get for each dollar of investment. If we use the symbol σ (sigma) we can write this formula as follows:

$$\Delta O = \frac{I}{\sigma}$$

Obviously, if sigma is one-third, we will get $1 of additional output for every $3 of net investment; if it is one-half, we will get $1.50 of additional output for the same new investment.

We now have two formulas, the first telling us by how much *income* will rise as investment grows, the second telling us by how much the value of *output* will rise as the consequence of the flow of investment. Can we put the formulas together to ascertain by how much investment must rise each year to give us the added income we will need to buy the addition to output?

Our formulas enable us to answer that question very precisely. Increased income is ΔY. Increased output is ΔO. Since $\Delta Y = \dfrac{1}{s}\Delta I$ and $\Delta O = \dfrac{1}{\sigma}$, then ΔY will equal ΔO if $\dfrac{1}{s}\Delta I$ equals $\dfrac{1}{\sigma}$. *Thus the formula for balanced growth must be:*

$$\frac{1}{s}\Delta I = \frac{I}{\sigma}$$

If we now multiply both sides of the equation by s, and then divide both sides by I, we get

$$\frac{\Delta I}{I} = \frac{s}{\sigma}$$

What does this equation mean? It tells us what *rate of growth of investment* ($\Delta I/I$) is needed to make $\Delta O = \Delta Y$. In words, it tells us by what percentage investment spending must rise to make income payments keep pace with dollar output. That rate of growth is equal to the marginal savings ratio divided by the marginal capital-output ratio. Suppose, for instance, that the marginal savings ratio (including leakages) is $\tfrac{1}{3}$ and that the marginal capital-output ratio is $\tfrac{1}{3}$. Then investment would have to grow year by $\tfrac{1}{9}$ ($\tfrac{1}{3} \times \tfrac{1}{3}$) to create just enough income to match the growing flow of output. If the rate of investment grew faster than that, income would move out ahead of output and we would be pushing beyond the path of balanced growth into inflation. If the rate of growth of investment were smaller than that, we would be experiencing chronic overproduction with falling prices and sagging employment.

What is the rate at which investment should rise for balanced growth in the United States? The question is difficult to answer for many reasons: capital-output ratios present tricky statistical problems; *net* investment is not simple to calculate; and our marginal leakages do not always behave as tamely as they do in textbooks. Hence we shall sidestep the difficult *empirical* problem posed by the requirements for balanced growth and concentrate on the general insight the concept gives us. For the purpose of our analysis is not to allow us to prescribe the proper growth for investment, but to make clear the critical *relationship* between growth in income and growth in output. Our analysis shows us that we can have a "growth gap" if our leakages are too high, so that increases in investment (or for that matter, any increase in injections) do not generate enough new purchasing power; or if our marginal capital-output ratio changes, so that a given amount of investment increases our potential output (our capacity) too fast.

Suppose that we are not generating income fast enough to absorb our potential output. Suppose, to go back to Fig. 19-5, that we have a persistent growth gap similar to that of the late 1950's. How can we bring the economy up to its potential?

Our formula for balanced growth gives us the answer. The relationship between the growth of incomes and the growth of output depends above all on the rate at which investment *increases*. Thus, if expenditures fall short of the amount needed to absorb potential output, the answer is to raise the rate of investment or, perhaps more realistically, to raise the rate of growth of all expenditures, public and private. Conversely, of course, if we find ourselves pushing over the trend line of potential growth into inflation, as in the late 1960's, the indicated policy is to lower the rate of growth of investment (or of investment and government and consumption) to bring the flow of rising incomes back into balance with the rise of output.

Thus the critical element in balancing a growing economy is not the *amount* of investment needed to fill a given demand gap, but the *increase* in investment (or other injection–expenditure) needed to match a growing output capacity with a large enough demand.

Yet, in the long run, the problem of unemployed resources may not be the most important problem we face. For when we look a few decades ahead, we begin to see that even the trajectory of full employment growth sets limits to our economic grasp. For instance, in 1960 a rather conservative Commission on National Goals established by President Eisenhower laid down a set of "goals"—from enhanced consumption through a variety of improved public and private pro-

FIG. 19-6

THE DIFFERENCE THAT GROWTH RATES MAKE

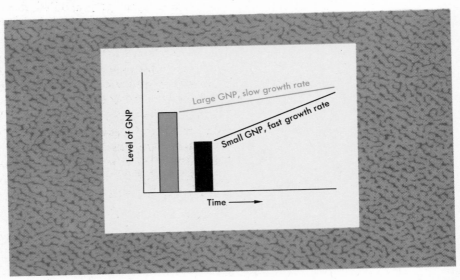

grams—to be achieved by 1975 in some fifteen areas of national economic activity. Recently, the National Planning Association "costed out" these goals to see how many of them we were likely to reach. Its conclusion was *that even if output grew at 4 per cent a year (14 per cent faster than the traditional 3.5 per cent rate), our GNP in 1975 would fall short by $150 billion of achieving the aspirations of the Eisenhower Commission!* GNP would then amount to $981 billion (in 1962 prices), whereas the cost of the desired goals would come to $1,127 billion. Only by raising the national growth rate to 5.5 per cent (which would mean working the economy under a wartime-like forced draft) could we fulfill the program envisioned by the commission.

As this example makes clear, changes in growth rates of "only" a percentage point make very large differences in the absolute amount of output after a few years.* Indeed, if GNP grew at a 3 per cent rate instead of a 4 per cent rate, the shortfall to the commission's goal would increase from $150 billion to $375 billion. When we look to the future, in other words, it is not the present level of GNP that determines the outlook nearly so much as the rate at which that GNP will grow, as Fig. 19-6 illustrates.

THE CAUSES OF GROWTH

EXTENSIVE
INVESTMENT

Thus we must think of growth not only as a means of remedying the underuse of resources, but as setting the trajectory that will define for us the scope of our realizable potential. But this changes our focus from one of merely increasing expenditures to one that asks the more fundamental question of how our capacity to produce can be increased.

One answer to that fundamental question is obvious enough. The simplest way for an economy to raise its output is to increase its use of human and material resources—in more technical terms, *to increase factor inputs.* Indeed, total inputs *must* grow if the new members of the community are to get at least as large a share of output as the older members.

We cannot grow very successfully, however, if we try to use only the

---

* Recently, Professor Kenneth Boulding pointed out that before World War II no country sustained a growth of GNP per capita of more than 2.3 per cent, whereas since World War II at least one country—Japan—has achieved and held a rate of growth of per capita GNP of 8 per cent. Writes Boulding: "The difference between 2.3 per cent and 8 per cent may be dramatically illustrated by pointing out that [at 2.3 per cent] children are twice as rich as their parents—i.e., per capita income approximately doubles every generation—while at 8 per cent per annum, children are six times as rich as their parents." However, Boulding doubts that such rates of increase can be long maintained, for they would soon bring us up against absolute barriers of resources that would throttle growth back to a much slower pace. (*The Public Interest,* Fall 1966, p. 38.)

existing capital equipment for employing new members of the work force. The peasants who are born into our model underdeveloped economy, must be given spades—and this means, as we know, that there must be a prior increase in the output of hammers and chisels. In a highly developed industrial economy, an expanding labor force must be matched with new capital of all kinds (which requires additional machine-tool output). Failure to keep the capital-labor ratio constant will result in a steady falling-behind of the newer members of the labor force and a consequent diminution of growth.

PRODUCTIVITY

Yet it is apparent that merely to match each new worker with as much equipment as his predecessors' is something like running to stay in place. This kind of *extensive* investment which "widens" the amount of capital wealth is essential if we are not to fall behind, but it does not result in our forging ahead. For that, we must *gain* output per capita—we must achieve more output for each unit of input, rather than maintain the previous level. The efficiency or *productivity* of our factors must be enhanced.

TABLE 19 · 3

REAL OUTPUT PER MAN-HOUR

	1947	1968 (prelim.)
Agriculture	100	346
Manufacturing	100	188

As we learned in the preceding chapter and as Table 19-3 reiterates, our inputs *have* been getting steadily more productive, both in industry and agriculture. On the average, during the 1950's and the mid-1960's, our labor productivity (our rate of output per man-hour of input) increased by some 2.9 per cent a year, averaging industry, where it has been slower, and agriculture, where the rate has been very high. How important this increase in productivity has been in making possible our national growth is apparent in Fig. 19-7.

The chart shows that increases in productivity account for by far the larger part of our aggregate economic growth since World War II. The low labor input figure is, of course, partly the result of a rising rate of unemployment during many of these years, when we were not putting to work as many of our increased numbers of workers as we might have. But even if 1947 rates of employment had been maintained, the role of productivity-increases would still have been predominant.

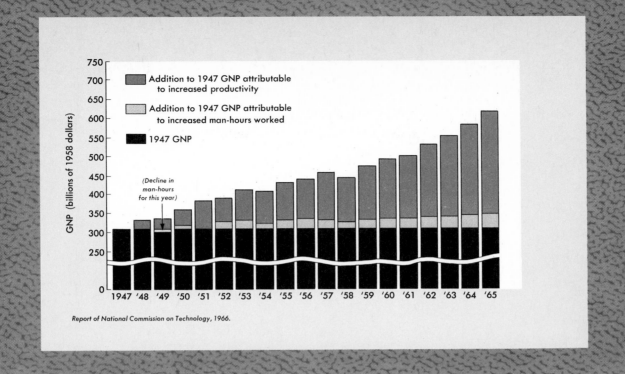

FIG. 19-7   **SOURCE OF GNP INCREASES, 1947–1965**

What accounts for the increase in labor productivity? Generally, we can distinguish four principal sources.

1. *Increased skills and education.*

In the short run, the dexterity, skills, and adaptability of the labor force make a tremendous difference in the amount of output obtainable from a given capital apparatus. Fiascoes of production testify to the absence of these determining influences in underdeveloped areas where modern plants must often be opened without a trained work force. In the longer run, it is not so much skills as general education that determines the output per individual worker. Contemporary studies place more and more stress on the productivity gains to be had from education, and attribute as much as one-fifth of the total U.S. growth rate to the steadily rising "stock" of education incorporated in the average worker.

2. *Economies of large-scale production.*

A second source of increased productivity per unit of input is the magnifying effect of mass production on output. Typically, when the organization of production reaches a certain critical size, especially in manufacturing, so-called "economies of scale" become possible. Many of these are based on the possibility of dividing complex operations into a series of simpler ones, each performed at high speed by a worker aided by specially designed equipment. It is difficult to estimate the degree of growth attributable to these economies of size. Certainly during the era of railroad-building and of the introduction of mass production, they contributed heavily to growth rate. In a careful study of the contemporary sources of U.S. growth, Edward F. Denison estimates that new economies of large-scale production add only about 10 per cent to our annual rate of productivity increase.*

3. *Deepening of capital.*

We have talked of the "widening" of capital, as each new worker was given the necessary equipment to put him on a productive par with his fellows. Now we must add the concept of the "deepening" of capital, or increasing amount of capital with which each worker is equipped. Clearly, if we give each worker more machinery and other types of capital goods to work with, we should expect him to be able to increase his output for each hour's work. Over the long course of economic growth, increased productivity has required the slow accumulation of very large capital stocks per working individual. Thus investment that increases capital per worker is, and will probably continue to be, one of the most effective levers for steadily raising output per worker. But unlike the steady widening of capital, the deepening of capital is not a regular process. Between 1929 and 1947 there was no additional capital added per worker! This was, of course, a time of severe depression and thereafter of enforced wartime stringencies. Since 1947, the value of our stock of capital per worker has been growing at about 2.7 per cent a year. As we shall see, immediately following, however, the *size* of this additional stock of capital is of less crucial importance than the *productivity* of that capital—that is, its technological character.

4. *Technology.*

We have just mentioned the fourth and last main source of increases in productivity—technology. During the past half century, GNP has consistently grown faster than can be accounted for by increases in the work force or the size of the capital stock. (Even during the 1929–1947 era, for instance, when capital stock per worker remained fixed, the output of GNP per worker grew by 1.5 per cent a year.) Part of this "unexplained" increase can be attributed to some of the sources of growth we have itemized above—mainly education and training, and economies of scale. But contemporary economic investigation increasingly attributes the bulk of the "bonus" rate of growth to the impact of new technology.

The Sources of Economic Growth in the United States (New York: Committee for Economic Development, 1962).

The term is, admittedly, somewhat vague. By "new technology" we mean new inventions of the demand-creating kind we have talked about, innovations of a labor-displacing (but productivity-enhancing) kind, the growth of knowledge in the form of research and development, changes in business organization or in techniques of management, and many other activities. What is increasingly apparent, however, is that the search for new products and processes is the main force behind much productivity-enhancing investment. Thus while investment has become less important for growth simply as a means of adding sheer quantities of capital to the labor force (although that is still a very important function, particularly in construction), it remains the strategic variable as the carrier of technological change.

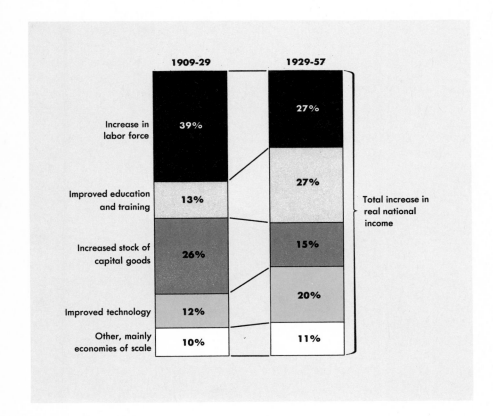

FIG. 19-8

SOURCES OF U.S. ECONOMIC GROWTH

It is time to sum up what we have covered. We have seen that long-term growth proceeds from two sources: *more* input and more *productive* input, and we have been concerned with studying some of the main facets of both kinds of growth. Perhaps we can summarize our findings in Fig. 19-8, comparing the sources of growth in two eras of our past.

Note the declining importance played by increases in numbers of workers or sheer dollar value of capital, and the increasing importance of the "intangibles" of education and technology. To a number of observers, this shift implies that we have been slowly moving into a new phase of industrial organization in which productivity will more and more reflect the application of scientific knowledge, rather than the brute leverage of mechanical strength and power. Whether this "post-industrial" society will grow at a faster or slower rate than in the past is a question that we will not be able to answer for many years.

VALUE OF GROWTH

Will we want to grow as fast as possible in the future? It is tempting to assume that growth is in itself an economic goal of the highest priority, but the matter is not quite that simple. Insofar as it brings material benefits to millions who still experience the meanness of poor food and tawdry surroundings, economic growth surely comes as an unalloyed gain. The question is, however, whether the increases in output in an affluent society will go to those whose need is greatest, or whether they will be dissipated for other purposes. Spending for arms and rockets to the moon, for Cadillacs that cruise the streets above crowded subway systems, for luxury apartment houses that look out over the slums—this also counts in the national books as "growth." It is all too possible to make a fetish of growth and to fail to inquire into the quality of the life that growth brings or the social shortcomings it conceals.

These reflections on the purpose and application of growth bid fair to assume greater and greater relevance in the years ahead. Already we have reached a stage in our national economic development when the poorer families in the nation are no longer immediately helped by the normal process of growth. As we have seen, the majority of the poor in America are not the employed, who *will* benefit from the growth they help create. The poor today are the aged, the sick, the racially disprivileged, the inhabitants of rural backwaters, whose link to the productive mechanism is insubstantial or lacking entirely. If they are to share in the proceeds of an expanding economy, measures must be taken to direct a portion of our annual increments of output into their hands. Otherwise, growth is likely to increase the disparity between the affluent and the disfavored, bringing not a sense of greater national well-being, but a heightening of social tensions and unrest.

Yet, with all these caveats, it is well that we conclude our study of macroeconomics with a sense of the great possibilities hinging on the trajectory of growth. Enormous opportunities for self-realization reside in the vast productive potential toward which we are moving; and however much it may test us to put that potential to good use, the irrefutable fact is that we must gain it before we can put ourselves to the test. Perhaps in the end, the purpose of the study of macroeconomics is to help create an economically literate and concerned citizenry who will urge and support the policies that will give us high growth and the wise use of the affluence that will result from it.

1. Growth in output derives from *investment that adds to our stock of capital wealth*. In an industrialized society, this investment is achieved by utilizing an existing capital-goods sector. But in a poor society, the process is much more difficult.

2. In such a poor society, we can see that the *capital-goods sector consists of two subsectors:* one producing capital goods that, in turn, make the equipment used in the consumption-goods sector; and the other making machine tools, capital goods that can create more capital goods.

3. *Thus growth requires two shifts:* (1) the machine-tool capacity of the capital-goods sector must be enlarged and (2) resources must be shifted from the consumption sector to the capital goods sector.

4. United States growth has been shown a *persistently steady rate* of 3.5 per cent—1.5 per cent per capita—for well over a century. From *year to year,* however, the *rate of growth is very uneven.*

5. We can discern *many cyclical patterns* in the year-to-year variations. The most important is "the" *8 to 10 year business cycle.* We designate its main features as upper and lower turning points (or peak and trough), expansion and contraction.

6. Many causes have been suggested to explain the business cycle, but none has been wholly satisfactory in accounting for its *cyclicality* or in explaining why its *periodicity* is 8 to 10 years.

7. Economists today explain the cycle as *variations in the rate of expansion.* The interaction of the multiplier and the accelerator explain the expansive and contractive phases. Upper turning points are usually caused by one or more of the many economic strains induced by the expansion itself; lower turning points tend to come about from the "bottoming out" of the contractive spiral.

8. Actual growth often falls behind *potential growth* or full employment growth. The wastage in output is best avoided by maintaining a high rate of aggregate demand.

9. The goal of a high steady rate of growth leads us to investigate the problem of matching our increase in capacity, or potential output, with a sufficient increase in purchasing power, or income. Increases in capacity depend on the *marginal capital-output ratio,* which describes the relationship between an increase in capital stock and the increased flow of output from that new stock. Increases in demand result from the multiplier, which magnifies the income-effect of a *rise* in investment (or of any injection). Balanced growth will occur when the income effect is just equal to the capacity effect.

10. If growth falls below the potential of the economy, the remedy lies in increasing the rate of growth of expenditures in the economy, both private and public. If we exceed our potential, the remedy is to cut the rate of growth of these expenditures.

Potential growth depends on deeper causes. One of these is the *amount of labor input and the extensive investment* needed to maintain labor/capital ratios. A second and more important cause is *improved productivity.*

12. Productivity, in turn, results from many sources. Among the most important are: *increased skills and education, economies of large-scale production, deepening of capital equipment,* and *technological advance.* Increasingly, growth has resulted from enhanced education and technology rather than from more inputs of labor or capital.

13. Growth is not an end in itself, but only a *means to an end.*

QUESTIONS

1. Describe carefully the shifts in labor needed to begin the process of growth in a very simple economy. Are such shifts visible in an advanced economy?

2. What is the special property of machine tools? Is there a very simple article of output that is also capable of the dual uses of machine tools? How about the seed corn held back by a farmer?

3. How do you explain the fact that the year-to-year growth of the United States is so much more irregular than the long-term growth?

4. Describe the course of events in a "typical" business cycle. How does such a cycle get started? How does it build up? What is likely to bring it to an end? How does the decline come about? What stops it?

5. Do you think that the policies needed to minimize the fluctuations of the business cycle are the same as those needed to accelerate long-term growth? Discuss what you would do to improve stability and to augment potential output.

6. What is meant by the marginal capital-output ratio? How is it different from the multiplier?

7. Write the formula for changes in *capacity* and for changes in *income.* Show algebraically how an increase in income can match an increase in output. *Explain* what the formula of balanced growth means.

8. What is different between a demand gap, in our original analysis, and a growth gap? Explain how the remedy in one case is a given amount of investment, and in the other, a rate of growth of investment.

9. What is extensive investment? What is intensive investment? Which is more conducive to growth?

10. Why is productivity so important in achieving growth? What are its main sources? What would you recommend as a long-term program to raise American productivity?

11. What do you think are the main purposes to which growth should be directed? How would you arrange for growth to be directed to these ends?

three

MICROECONOMICS

ANATOMY OF A MARKET SYSTEM

INTRODUCTION TO THE MICROECONOMY 20

Thus far we have looked at the economic panorama from two very different perspectives. In the first part of our text we surveyed the scene from an historical vantage point that gave us a sense of the evolution of things, a feeling for the direction in which our own world was drifting. Then, in the second part, we took another look at the economy, this time not from a position that highlighted long-term currents of change, but from one that illumined the problems of its day-to-day operation as a vast mechanism for producing an aggregate flow of goods and services.

Now we pass to a third, and in some ways most basic, view of economic society—one that brings us *within* the economy to a degree that we have not as yet experienced. Put differently, we know a good deal about the operation of "the system" as a whole, but very little about the activities of the individuals who, in their various roles, make the system behave as it does. The study of microeconomics will introduce us to this essential aspect of the economic process.

How is it that we have been able to study so much about the workings of the system without learning about the basic role of the individual? The answer is that we already *have* touched on microeconomic problems, without, however, stopping to examine them in detail. Throughout macroeconomies, for example, we have referred to supply and demand, but until now we have neither looked very carefully into the meaning of those words nor sought to make clear how these "forces" in the market system originated in the specific behavior of buyers and sellers. So, too, we have talked of investment or employment or consumption without pausing to examine these economic processes in terms of their behavioral roots—that is, without looking into the *individual decisions* to expand production or to hire or fire a worker or to buy a commodity, out of which the aggregate phenomena themselves arose.

Yet all these large-scale economic processes necessarily have their origins in the behavior patterns of individuals or firms. Inflation and deflation, the operations of the multiplier or the workings of the credit system, all take place through changes in the market actions of households or businesses.

The point leads to a conclusion of importance: *Every macroeconomic process has its microeconomic base.* All the problems we have studied as aggregative economic movements can be resolved under the microscope of economic inquiry into the motions of large numbers of individual market participants. Macro- and microeconomics are thus not two separate fields of economics, but only two approaches to the selfsame processes and problems.

Why the two perspectives? The answer is that one approach by itself fails to illumine the whole range of economic concerns. Macroeconomics is not very pertinent, for instance, if we are interested in the effect of monopoly on prices—a problem that microtheory lights up brilliantly. Microtheory, on the other hand, is of relatively little use when we investigate the level of output as a whole, a problem that lies at the very center of macroeconomics. Perhaps some day a new approach to economics will combine the broad scope of macrotheory with the finer scrutiny of microtheory, but until that time, someone who wants to understand how a market system works has no choice but to supplement his macro perspective with a view of economics at the micro level.

What do we see when we approach the economy from this new angle of vision? Our first impression is totally unlike that of macroeconomics. Perhaps we remember looking down from our initial flight over the economy on the broad and impressive landscape of our national wealth.

Nothing so orderly greets our eye as the aircraft alights and we take our first glimpse of the economy at close range.

We seem to have landed in a scene of considerable confusion. The patterns so clearly distinguishable from above have disappeared; where there was order there is now a seeming chaos. Land, labor, and capital, for instance—those factors of production whose interaction we followed so easily from the air—turn out at ground level to be nothing but thousands of men and women bustling around in search of someone to hire their services: it is hard to see a man as a "factor of production" when he is sitting in an employment office or in a brokerage office, and still more difficult to think of his actions—taking a job or not, buying a stock or selling it—as part of a large-scale social process. So, too, consumption and investment—those majestic rivers of expenditure on which depend the aggregate flow of output—now appear as nothing more than the activities of housewives in supermarkets, or the decisions of the supermarket operator as to whether or not to add another checkout counter. Even the price level disappears; there is no "level" at close quarters, but only a thousand different prices, some in motion, some not.

Our overriding first impression of the microeconomy is no longer one of orderly and clearly distinguishable patterns of behavior, but of the most highly individualistic, uncoordinated, perhaps even disorderly behavior. We seem no longer to be observing an economy, but to be watching a bazaar. And our first impression is entirely correct. We have landed in the market.

THE MARKET AS A SYSTEM

The market is not, of course, a bazaar; it is a system. The confusion of shoppers, job seekers, prices is not confined to a single locale but is diffused throughout every part of the society to which our eyes now turn. The buying and selling that we see are not merely casual activities, but somehow bind the whole system together, providing not alone the dynamic impulse but the guiding hand to a process that, when viewed from above, seemed to take place without any individual motivation at all.

How does the market system exert its controlling as well as its impelling force? The question reminds us again of the consternation expressed by the delegation from an underdeveloped country to whom we talked in Chapter 1. The representatives of a traditional society found it hard to believe that a community of unrestrained buyers and sellers could hang together and solve its economic problems. Now that we are face to face with the market in reality it is not so easy for us, either, to be certain that it can.

Perhaps it will help if we refresh our memory of what the market system is supposed to do. We remember from our early introduction to the market society that all economic systems had to solve the twin tasks of production and distribution—of determining *what* goods to produce and *how* to produce them, and of deciding *to whom* to give them. In our first approach we stressed the social aspect of these questions—that is, the problem of devising social institutions that would be capable of mobilizing men and securing their assent to some division of their output. But whereas that emphasis was necessary as a prelude to learning how the market society itself evolved, it is less useful when we can now take such a society for granted and inquire into its economic mechanism.

Let us therefore look at the tasks of the market once again, in a somewhat different light. Suppose we have an island where we can make only two kinds of output. We can use our land, labor, and capital to grow grain or we can use them to raise cattle for milk. Now suppose that we used all of our resources for grain production for one year and found that we could grow 1,000 tons of grain. The following year, we put our whole effort into dairy farming and discovered that we netted 500 gallons of milk. We would now have discovered two extreme production possibilities for the allocation of our social effort.

But the chances are that we would prefer to have a mixture of grain and milk, rather than all of one and none of the other. Hence we would have to find out, by experimenting, what combinations of grain and milk we could enjoy by using some of our resources for each occupation. Fig. 20-1 shows us what kind of *production-possibility curve* we might in fact have.

FIG. 20-1

PRODUCTION-POSSIBILITY CURVE

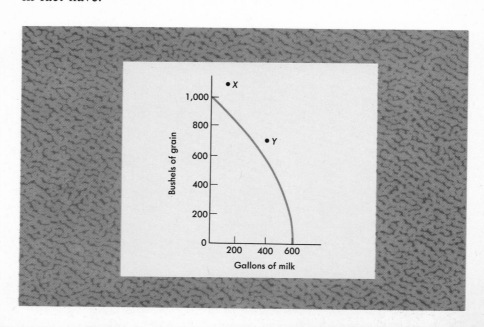

The production possibility curve shows us a number of things. First it makes vivid the material meaning of the word *scarcity*. Any point outside the frontier of the curve is unattainable for our island community, given its present resources. This is obviously true of point *X*. But look at point *Y*. This is an output that represents roughly 700 bushels of grain and 400 gallons of milk. Either one of these goals, taken separately, lies well within the production possibilities of the island. What the curve shows us is that *we cannot have both at the same time*. If we want 700 bushels of grain, we must be content with less than 400 gallons of milk: and if we want 400 gallons of milk we will have to settle for about 600 bushels of grain. Thus we see that *at the core of the production problem lies the necessity for choice.* This unavoidable choice is imposed, of course, by the existing resources and our technical knowledge. But the frontier of possibilities is not static. As capital and knowledge grow, the frontier can advance, so that what was impossible in the past becomes attainable in the future. For instance, the invention of a new cattle fodder might raise the production-possibility of milk on our island. Then our production-possibility curve would look like Fig. 20-2.

FIG. 20-2

EXPANDING
THE FRONTIER

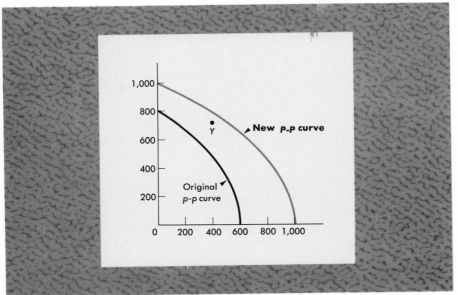

We could now easily produce 700 bushels of grain and 400 gallons of milk—in fact, more of either or more of both. But the location of point *Y* in Fig. 20-2 makes clear another meaning of the *p-p* curve. The curve shows our production possibilities *when we use our resources fully.* If we fail to employ all our land, labor, and capital (or if we use them ineffectively) we will end up with a collection of goods, such as *Y*, that falls short of our potential. From our study of macroeconomics, we know that this is all too often the case.

The production possibility curve illumines for us more than the choice we may have to make between alternative goods such as grain and milk. We can use the concept to illustrate as well the choice between consumption and investment for a fully employed society, or between the division of output into public or private use. In fact, with a little imagination we can construct a three-dimensional production-possibility *surface* that will show us the limits imposed by scarcity on a society that divides its output among three uses, such as consumption, investment, and government. Figure 20-3 shows what such a diagram looks like.

FIG. 20-3

A PRODUCTION-
POSSIBILITY
SURFACE

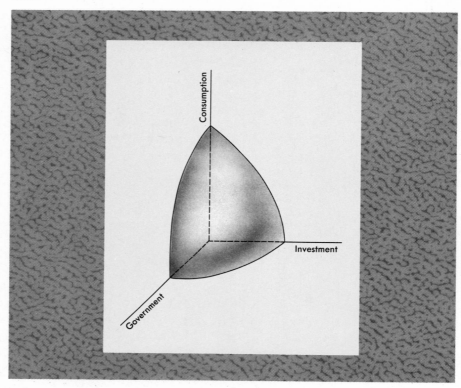

Note how the production-possibility surface swells out from the origin like a wind-filled spinnaker sail. Any place on the sail represents some combination of consumption, investment, and government spending that is within the reach of the community. Any place "behind" the surface represents a failure of the economy to employ all its resources. It is a graphic depiction of unemployment of men or materials.

One last point deserves clarification before we move on. The alert student may have noticed that all the production-possibility curves have bowed shapes. The reason for this lies in the *changing efficiency* of our resources as we shift them from one use to another. When we are concentrating all our resources on grain, for example, we have to use some land, labor, and capital that would be much better suited to producing milk. Hence the initial transfer of some resources out of grain and into milk gives us a relatively larger gain in milk than our loss in grain—which is why the curve at this end of the graph slopes "milkward" rather than "grainward." At the other end of the curve, just the opposite considerations prevail. Now we have to cram into milk production the last units of resources that must be withdrawn from the grain production to which they are better suited. Hence, here the gain in milk output is proportionately much less than at the other end of the scale, and the loss in grain output proportionately much more. Therefore the curve now slopes more sharply in the direction of grain than milk.

We call this changing efficiency, represented by the bowed curve, the *law of increasing costs*. Note that it is a law imposed by nature, rather than behavior. For what would it mean if the curve connecting the two points of all-out grain or milk production were a straight line? It would mean that as we shifted resources from one use to the other, we would always get exactly the same results: the last man and the last acre put into milk would give us exactly as much milk, at the loss of exactly as much grain, as the first man and the first acre.

This *could* be the case, of course, but it implies that there is absolutely no difference from one man, or acre, to another, or that it made no difference as to the *proportions* in which factors, even if they were homogenous, were combined. That is a very unrealistic assumption. Men and land (and any other resource) *are* different and different products *do* utilize them in different proportions. Hence, as we shift them from one use to another, assuming that we always choose the resources best suited for the job, society's efficiency changes. At first we enjoy a very low cost in terms of what we must give up for what we get; thereafter, an increasing cost. Although the shapes of production-possibility curves may have considerably different contours, the unevenness of nature's gifts make most of them bowed, or concave from below. We will study more about the limitations imposed by nature when we come to the law of diminishing returns in Chapter 24.

The production-possibility curve gives a fresh meaning to the tasks of the market, in particular to the questions of what goods to produce and how to produce them. It makes us see that economics is basically concerned with choices and decisions that result in different levels and assortments of output.

But there is something of a puzzle in the contrast between the production-possibility diagram with its clear-cut outline of economic choice and the milling confusion of the marketplace. We turned to the production-possibility curve to clarify the tasks that the market as a system was to perform. But we have yet to understand how a particular point X or Y on the diagram is brought into being. Who decides whether society will use its resources for milk or grain, or public or private use or what combination of them? Who determines whether society operates on the frontier of its potential or suffers the consequences of a less-than-full use of resources?

The answer, of course, is the interaction of individuals and firms we call the market system. Thus we study the market mechanism to learn about not only the potentialities of a system, but about its actualities, for microeconomics will teach us how the financial exchanges of buyers and sellers bring about the actual level and composition and disposition of output in our society.

FIG. 20-4

**CIRCULAR FLOW
IN MICROVIEW**

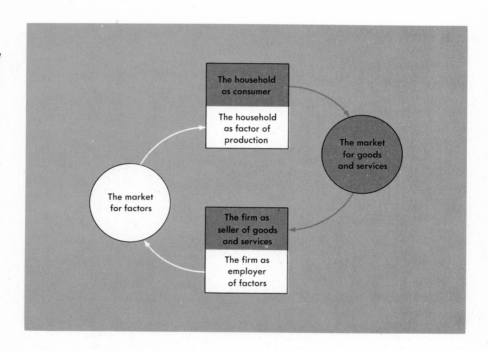

**CIRCULAR
FLOW
AGAIN**

How does the market, with its immense confusion of individuals and firms, determine the allocation of society's resources? If we are to answer this question we will have to disentangle the market's activities and discover in its flux some pattern that will allow us to grasp how it works.

Is there such a pattern? Indeed, there is—and what is more, exactly the same pattern that originally illumined the economy from the perspective of macroeconomics. There, we recall, we first understood the structure of the macro system as a great circular flow that linked together the expenditures of the sectors and the receipts of the various firms, and then the expenditures of firms and the receipts of the sectors. Now if we look carefully into the market we can find the selfsame circular flow, only reduced from its vast national dimensions to the tiny circuits that bind together individual households and individual firms. We can see the circular flow in Fig. 20-4. Note that the units of the microeconomic world, households (or individuals) and firms, interact in two ways, just as they do in the macro process. Each household, acting as a consumer, buys goods from individual firms who act as sellers. And each household, now acting as a factor of production, sells its services to firms who now become buyers. Thus, as before, a flow of spending from households to firms, and a return flow from firms to households, binds the system together.

But why bother to retrace a circular flow that is already familiar to us? The answer is that an examination of the flow gives us a clue to *where* the transactions of the marketplace exert their pushes and pulls on the allocation of goods and resources that we examined in the production-possibility curve. For looking at the circular flow, we notice that it passes through two markets. One of these, the *market for goods and services,* is certainly a key location for the allocation of goods to various uses. Equally important, we can see, is the *market for factors* through which the flow of expenditure returns to the household where it originated: here is certainly where the distribution of incomes (and therefore of shares in the total output) must be determined. Last, there is the firm itself, where the services of the factors are combined to yield a flow of output. This must be where the system determines in what way output shall be produced.

Hence we begin to see how the complicated flux of the market system can be untangled. One by one we must study the market for goods and then that for factors and then the internal operations of the firm, to find out how the system decides *what goods* to produce and *to whom* to give them and *how to produce them.* It will take us several chapters before the links can be joined and the system as a whole set into motion. But by then we will have learned a good deal about what the economy looks like at the micro level.

SUMMARY

1. Microeconomics *is an approach* to economics that begins with the actions of *individuals and firms* in the market process.

2. *Every macroeconomic process has its roots in microeconomic behavior.*

3. The market is a system for the solution of the basic economic problems of *production* and *distribution*. We can visualize the basic production tasks of the market by means of a *production-possibility diagram*.

4. The production-possibility curve makes clear the limiting fact of scarcity and the consequent need for *choice*. It also indicates clearly the difference between the full use of resources and their inefficient or partial use.

5. The bowed shape of production-possibility curves reflects the *law of increasing costs*. This basic economic relationship describes the fact that our efficiency changes as we shift resources from one use to another, and that typically we experience a decreasing efficiency (with the consequence of increasing costs) as we move more and more resources into the production of any given item.

6. The market brings about the dispositions of the real economy through a *network of transactions*. We can simplify this network into a *circular flow*, similar to that in the macroeconomy.

7. The circular flow reveals the critical points at which the market performs its tasks—*the market for goods and services, the market for factors, and the internal workings of the firm*. Here is where society faces the three critical questions: what to produce, how to produce it, and to whom to distribute it.

QUESTIONS

1. What is meant by the microeconomic roots of behavior? What is the microeconomic base of the following macrophenomena: inflation, depression, economic growth, the demand gap? Is there such a thing as macroeconomic *behavior*?

2. What is meant by the market as a *system*?

3. Describe the circular flow as it appears from the micro viewpoint. What relation does it bear to the circular flow from the macro viewpoint?

4. What is the difference between the market for goods and that for factor services? On which market is the household a seller? The firm a seller? Can household and firm both be on the same side of the same market?

5. What would a production possibility curve look like for a society that could produce either a million cars per year or 100,000 buildings? Now suppose that technical advances made it possible to build 200,000 buildings, but only the same number of cars. In what way would the curve shift? Mark a point x to show where a fully employed society might locate its production, to yield both cars and buildings (in whatever proportions you wish). Mark another point y to show the consequence of unemployment for such a society. Mark still another point z to show a point that is beyond the production capacity of the society, even though it represents fewer cars and fewer buildings than the economy could produce if it concentrated on either one of those alone.

THE MARKET
FOR GOODS

21

The market for goods is the part of the market system with which we are all most familiar, for we constantly enter it as purchasers of commodities.* Now we must scrutinize this market to learn how it actually works—to discover not only how prices are formed by trans-

*For many years, the late E. H. Chamberlain used to enliven his famous course at Harvard on the workings of the market by dividing his students into "sellers" and "buyers," giving to each person secret instructions about the price range he was allowed to operate within. Thereafter the students were loosed into a free-for-all, each to make bargains with the other side as best he could. As each buyer and seller reached accord, their agreed-upon price was shown to Professor Chamberlain. At the end of the session, the average of the prices reached in the classroom was compared with the average of the price options given out. Chamberlain noted that the class result was regularly *under* the true average of buying and selling options, and he hypothesized that this was due to the superior skill his students had already accumulated as buyers, and their relative unfamiliarity with the role of seller.

actions of individuals and firms, but also how these prices, once formed, help carry out the allocatory tasks of the market system as a whole.

Everyone knows, whether or not he has taken a course in economics, that prices in the market reflect "supply and demand." When the price of milk goes up, we all say that the demand for milk must have risen for some reason or other, or that the supply of milk must have been cut. But this very general appreciation of the "forces" at work only begins to explain how prices are actually determined, and tells us nothing about how these prices in turn affect our own behavior.

BEHAVIOR AND PRICES

What is the meaning of supply and demand? Our acquaintance with the rise of market society tells us a good deal about the kind of behavior the terms describe. We remember that the emergence of the market system forced individuals to shift for themselves in a harsh world where private transactions determined both their incomes and their expenses. In such a world, sheer self-preservation dictated that buyers and sellers had to follow the arrow of price advantage if they were going to survive, much less prosper. Hence buying as cheaply as possible and selling as dearly as possible became the cardinal rule of behavior for both individuals and firms in a market setting. Added to this was the growing acceptance of economic gain as a primary goal of economic life, and the rule of Buy Cheap and Sell Dear was given a second social sanction.

These historic motives of self-preservation and economic gain have changed considerably as the extreme pressures of early capitalism have given way to the far more sheltered setting of contemporary capitalism. Yet, albeit in the pursuit of somewhat altered objectives, we still usually behave as buyers by trying to spend as little as possible for the goods we want, and as sellers by trying to get as much as we can for the goods and services we have to offer.

This clearly makes *the prices of goods* very important as stimuli that guide our behavior. Comparative prices enable us to make choices that will improve our economic position. But prices do more than this. *Prices also become signals that direct our behavior.* In fact, it is through our reaction to prices that self-interest becomes a "force" on the marketplace.

But since buyers and sellers have conflicting self-interests, how can this be? The answer is that the same price signal gives rise to *different* behavior, depending on which side of the market we are. A rising price will usually look bad for buyers but good for sellers. Falling prices will generally be in the self-interest of buyers (who can now satisfy their wants for less money), but against the self-interest of sellers (who will now get less return for their efforts). Thus we begin to see that the price mechanism may be the way of satisfying divergent interests, of bringing together parties whose economic gains lie in opposing directions. That is why microeconomics is sometimes called *price theory*.

CONDITIONS OF SUPPLY AND DEMAND

Let us explore this idea by looking more carefully into the actual considerations that guide me as a buyer or seller.

When I enter the market for goods, which I do virtually every time I walk along a street, two factors determine whether or not I will actually become a buyer and not just a window-shopper. The first factor is the *tastes and desires* that decide whether I am willing to spend my money on the things I see. The windows of shops are crammed with many things that I could afford to buy if I wanted to, but which I simply do not wish to own. Perhaps if they were very cheap, I might wish to buy them; or possibly I would not even want them if they were free. For such goods, for which my desires are too weak to motivate me, my demand is zero.

On the other hand, my tastes and desires alone by no means suffice to make me a buyer. The shop windows are also full of goods that I would very much like to own but that I cannot afford to buy because they are too expensive: my demand for Rolls Royces is also zero. Thus demand hinges on the *ability*—the possession of sufficient wealth or income—as well as on the *willingness* of the buyer. If it did not, the poor, whose wants are always very large, would constitute the greatest source of demand.

Note that my demand for goods depends on both my willingness and my ability to buy them *at their going price.* From this it follows that the amount of goods I will demand will change as their prices change. If I see a sports car for $10,000 I am likely to be neither willing nor able to make the purchase, whereas the same car at $5,000 would find me both a great deal more willing and much more able; and at $2,000, it might set me to wondering if perhaps I should not buy two.

In the same way, willingness and ability both enter the market force of supply. Many suppliers of goods would be *willing* to offer certain commodities or services at certain prices, but are unable to do so because they lack the skills or the access to certain materials. Other suppliers may be perfectly *able* to offer the commodity at that price but may be unwilling to do so because they would incur a loss by doing so, or because of some other disinclination. Once again, price enters into the middle of this decision. At $10,000 many enterprisers would be willing (although not all might be able) to produce sports cars; at $5,000 the willingness and ability would be much reduced; and at $2,000 no one might be prepared to supply a single car.

This simple dissection of the considerations behind buying and selling tells us a good deal: supply and demand are terms that indicate our willingness and ability to sell or buy certain quantities of goods at certain prices. *Supply and demand are thus concepts that link our market behavior with price.*

There is a point to be cleared up here before we go on. We have no difficulty in understanding why our ability to buy a commodity should decline as the price rises or increase as the price falls—our wealth simply stretches further or less far. But why should our willingness be related to price?

Economists answer this question by postulating that as we increase the quantities that we own of any good (within a given time period), the pleasures and benefits derived from successive units of that good will decline. Hence we will be less and less willing to go on buying more and more of the same good, because its *marginal utility*—the increment of satisfaction we derive from each additional unit—will diminish.

Suppose for example that a man were dying of thirst on the Sahara. The marginal utility to him of a pint of water per day would be immense, and he would pay a vast sum for just one pint. So too, perhaps, for the second or third pint. But after a certain number of pints per day, the utility of the next pint begins to fall. If such a man has 40 or 50 pints of drinking water a day, the marginal utility of the 41st or the 51st may be next to nothing. This does not mean that the *total* utility he enjoys is less than that of a man who is desperately short of water; just the opposite. But the *addition* to his utility of still another pint will have fallen so low that he will be willing to pay only very little for it.

The notion of diminishing marginal utility also clears up another puzzle of economic life. This is why we are willing to pay so little for bread, which is a necessity for life, and so much for diamonds, which are not. The answer is that we have so much bread that the marginal utility of any loaf we are thinking of buying is very little, whereas we have so few diamonds that each carat has a very high marginal utility. If we were locked inside Tiffany's over a long holiday, the prices we would pay for bread and diamonds, after a few days, would be very different from those we would have paid when we entered.

This relationship between price and quantity yields a conception of demand and supply that is different from the one that we ordinarily carry about in our heads. We are used to thinking about demand, for instance, as denoting a single purchase at a single price, or supply as referring to the readiness of a storekeeper to sell a certain good at a given price.

But that is not the idea of supply and demand as these words describe the behavior that drives the market system. *Demand and supply in their proper economic sense refer to various quantities of goods or services that we are willing and able to buy (or sell) at various prices at a given time.*

In other words, demand and supply both refer to *functional* relationships, or to the interdependence of price and quantity. This is a condition of which we do not often become conscious, but an imaginary situation may bring out the essential point. Suppose that you went into a clothing store to buy shirts and were waited on by an inexperienced clerk. Having found some shirts you liked, you asked the price and were told they were five dollars. "Very well," you say, having consulted your state of mind and your pocketbook, "I'll take three of them."

The salesman is about to write up the order when he stops in embarrassment. "I'm sorry, sir," he says, "I'm afraid I got the price wrong. It should be six dollars."

At six dollars you may be able to buy the shirts, but we will assume that you are no longer willing to—they are "too expensive." But just as you are about to leave the clerk reappears. "I'm wrong about the price again," he admits. "These are six dollar shirts, all right, but they're on sale, reduced to $4.50."

At the new price, you make another mental calculation. "Very well," you say, "I'll take four."

Our example is meant to illustrate an aspect of demand that we do not ordinarily encounter in real life, when prices rarely change so rapidly. This is the fact that our "demand" covers a whole range of different quantities that we are willing and able to buy at different prices at a given time, and not just one quantity that we do buy (or do not buy) at a given price.*

The same functional relationship is of course visible between price and the quantity we are willing and able to sell, but now the relationship goes the other way. A tailor, for example, might be willing to make ten shirts a day if he could sell them for $6 each, whereas if the price dropped to $5 he would make only 3, using his time to make other garments; and at $4.50 he would make none.

If we make a tabulation of the amounts of a commodity that will be bid for and offered at different prices, we present a *schedule* of demand and supply. For the example of shirts, it would look like Table 21-1.

TABLE 21 · 1

Price	Quantity demanded	Quantity supplied
$6.00	0	10
5.00	3	3
4.50	4	0

* Just for the sake of completeness, we ought to note that there is a class of so-called *luxury goods* for which the quantity demanded rises as their prices go up. The reason is that part of the utility of these goods is their price. It is not for nothing that Joy perfume advertises itself as "the most expensive perfume in the world." Its sales would probably fall sharply if it dropped its price and announced itself as "the second most expensive perfume in the world."

FIG. 21-1

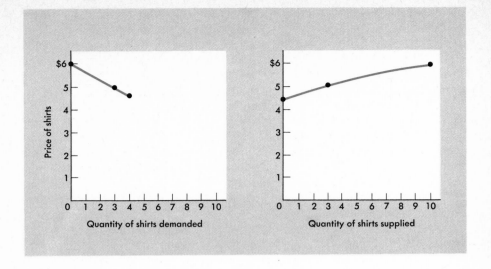

From here it is only a step to graphs representing these schedules in the very convenient form of *demand and supply curves.* The schedules for shirts are plotted in Fig. 21-1.

Perhaps we have already grasped the next step of our analysis. The fact that supply and demand schedules (or curves) show *contrary functional relationships* between prices and quantities suggests that from the interplay of these different market forces an equilibrium might be reached—a point at which price will balance the force of demand against that of supply. In the case below, this equilibrium price is obviously $5, since I will be willing and able to buy three shirts at that price and the tailor is willing and able to make them for me.

INDIVIDUAL AND COLLECTIVE DEMAND

Now we must add one last word before we continue our study of supply and demand. Thus far we have considered only the factors that make a single individual more willing and able to buy as prices fall, or less willing and able to sell. But generally when we speak of supply and demand we mean markets in which each side is composed of many suppliers and demanders. That gives us an additional reason for the slope of each curve. If we assume that most individuals have somewhat different willingnesses and abilities to buy, because their incomes and their marginal utilities are different; or that they have unequal willingnesses or abilities to sell, then we can see that *a change in price will bring into the market new buyers or sellers.* As price falls, for instance, it will trigger off the willingness or ability to buy of one person after another, thereby adding to the quantity of the good that will be purchased at that price; and conversely, as prices rise, the entry of sellers into the market will increase, and the quantity of goods they offer will rise accordingly.

TABLE 21 · 2

Price	$50	$45	$40	$35	$30	$25	$20	$15	$10	$5
Quantity (thousand prs.)										
Demanded	1	5	10	20	25	30	40	50	75	100
Supplied	125	90	70	50	35	30	20	10	5	0

Let us investigate a case of collective demand and collective supply by examining the supply and demand schedules for shoes for a small city over a period of a year. Suppose we discover that the price-quantity relationships look like Table 21-2.*

As before, the schedules tell us that buyers and sellers react differently to prices. At high prices, buyers are either not willing or unable to purchase more than small quantities of shoes, whereas sellers would be only too willing and able to flood the city with them; at very low prices, the quantity of shoes demanded would be very great, but few shoe manufacturers would be willing or able to gratify buyers at such low prices.

But if we now look at *both* schedules at *each* price level, we discover an interesting thing. *There is one price—$25 in our example—at which the quantity demanded is exactly the same as the quantity supplied.* At every other price, either one schedule or the other is larger, but at $25 the amounts in both columns are the same—30,000 pairs of shoes. We call this balancing price the *equilibrium price,* and we shall soon see that it *is* the price that emerges spontaneously in an actual market where supply and demand contend.†

EMERGENCE OF THE EQUILIBRIUM PRICE

How do we know that an equilibrium price will be brought about by the interaction of supply and demand? The process is one of the most important and fundamental in all of economics, so we should understand it very clearly.

*Do these price-quantity relations have to be orderly and logical—that is, as the price falls by $5 increments, should demand or supply change in some regular fashion? The answer could be yes or no. In some markets, the relationship of demand or supply to price may be a very regular one; in others it is possible that reactions will be irregular and "illogical." This is a complicated subject, but it is well to be aware that demand and supply curves do not have to be as straight or smooth as they always appear in textbooks.

†Of course we have made up our schedules so that the quantities demanded and supplied would be equal at $25. The price that actually brought about such a balancing of supply and demand might be some odd number such as $25.01.

Suppose in our example above that for some reason or other the shoe retailers in our city put a price tag on their shoes not of $25 but of $45. What would happen? Our schedules show us that at this price shoe manufacturers will be pouring out shoes at the rate of 90,000 pairs a year, whereas customers would be buying them at the rate of only 5,000 pairs a year. Shortly, the shoe factories would be clogged with unsold merchandise. It is plain what the outcome of this situation must be. In order to realize some revenue, shoe manufacturers will begin to unload their unsold stocks of shoes at lower prices.

As they do so, the situation will begin to improve. At a price of $40, demand picks up from 5,000 pairs to 10,000, while at the same time the slightly lower price discourages producers enough so that output falls from 90,000 pairs to 70,000. Shoe manufacturers are still turning out more shoes than the market can absorb at the going price, but the difference between the quantities supplied and the quantities demanded is now smaller than it was before.

Let us suppose that the competitive pressure continues to reduce prices so that shoes soon sell at $30. Now a much more satisfactory state of affairs exists. Producers will be turning out 35,000 pairs of shoes, and consumers will be buying them at a rate of 25,000 a year. But still there is an imbalance, and some shoes will still be piling up, unsold, at the factory. Prices will therefore continue to fall. Eventually they reach $25. At this point, the quantity of shoes supplied by the manufacturers—30,000 pairs—is exactly that demanded by customers. There is no longer a surplus of unsold shoes hanging over the market and acting to press prices down. *The market clears.*

Now let us quickly trace the interplay of supply and demand from the other direction. Suppose that prices were originally $5. Our schedules tell us that customers would be standing in line at the shoe stores, but that producers would be largely shut down, unwilling or unable to make shoes at those prices. We can easily imagine that customers, many of whom would gladly pay more than $5, let it be known that they would welcome a supply of shoes at $10 or even more. If enough customers bid $10, a trickle of shoe output begins. But the quantity of shoes demanded at $10 far exceeds the available supply. Customers snap up the few pairs around, and shoe stores tell suppliers they could easily get $20 a pair. Prices rise accordingly. Now we are getting closer to a balance of quantities offered and bid for. At $20 there will be a demand for 40,000 pairs of shoes and output will have risen to 20,000 pairs. But still the pressure of unsatisfied demand raises prices further. Finally a price of $25 is tried. Now, once again, the quantities supplied and demanded are exactly in balance. There is no further pressure from unsatisfied customers to force the price up further, because at $25 no customer who can afford the price will remain unsatisfied.

Thus we can see how *the interaction of supply and demand brings about the establishment of a price at which both suppliers and demanders are willing and able to sell or buy the same quantity of goods.* We can visualize the equilibrating process more easily if we now transfer our supply and demand schedules to graph paper. Figure 21-2 is the representation of the shoe market we have been dealing with.

FIG. 21-2

DETERMINATION
OF AN
EQUILIBRIUM
PRICE

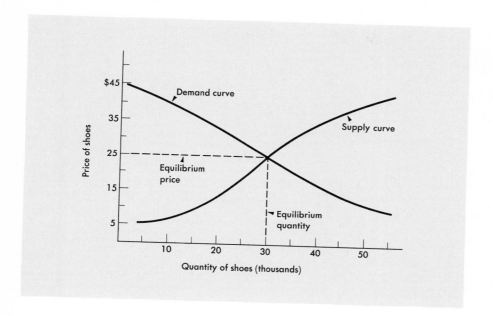

The graph shows us at a glance the situation we have analyzed in detail. At the price of $25, the quantities demanded and supplied are equal—30,000 pairs of shoes. But the graph also shows more vividly than the schedules why this is an *equilibrium* price.

Suppose that the price were temporarily lifted above $25. If you will draw a horizontal pencil line from any point on the vertical axis above the $25 mark to represent this price, you will find that it intersects the demand curve before it reaches the supply curve. In other words, *the quantity demanded is less than the quantity supplied at any price above the equilibrium price, and the excess of the quantity supplied means that there will be a downward pressure on prices, back toward the equilibrium point.*

The situation is exactly reversed if prices should fall below the equilibrium point. Now the quantity demanded is greater than that supplied, and the pressure of buyers will push the price up to the equilibrium point.

Thus equilibrium prices have two important characteristics:

1. *They are the prices that will spontaneously establish themselves through the free play of the forces of supply and demand.*
2. *Once established, they will persist unless the forces of supply and demand themselves change.*

There is one last thing carefully to be noted about equilibrium prices. *They are the prices that bring about an equality in the quantities demanded and the quantities supplied.* They are not the prices that bring about an equality of "supply and demand." Probably the commonest beginning mistake in economics is to say that supply and demand are equal when prices are in equilibrium. But if we remember that both supply and demand mean the *relationships* between quantities and prices, we can see that this would mean that the demand schedule and the supply schedule for a commodity were alike, so that the curves would lie one on top of the other. In turn, this would mean that at a price of $50, buyers of shoes would be willing and able to buy the same number of shoes that suppliers would be willing to offer at that price, and the same for buyers at $5. If such were the case, prices would be wholly indeterminate and could race high and low with no tension of opposing interests to bring them to a stable resting place.

Hence we must take care to use the words *supply* or *demand* to refer only to relationships or schedules, and to use the longer phrase *quantity demanded* or *quantity supplied* when we want to speak of the effect of a particular price on our willingness or ability either to buy or sell.

THE ROLE OF
COMPETITION

We have seen how stable, lasting prices spontaneously emerge from the flux of the marketplace. But we have silently passed over a basic condition for the formation of these prices. This is the role played by competition in the operation of the market mechanism.

How does competition fit into the process of establishing equilibrium prices? The answer is that it provides the regulator that "supervises" the orderly working of the market. It does so because economic competition, unlike the competition for prizes outside economic life, is not a single contest, but a *continuing process*—a race in which the runners never win but must go on endlessly trying to stay in front to avoid the penalties of falling behind.

Second, unlike the contests of ordinary life, economic *competition involves not just a single struggle among rivals, but two struggles,* one of them between the two sides of the markets and the other among the marketers on each side. For the competitive marketplace is not only where the clash of interest between buyer and seller is worked out by the opposition of supply and demand, but also where buyers contend against buyers and sellers against sellers.

It is this double aspect of the competitive process that accounts for its usefulness. A market in which buyers and sellers had no conflict of interest would not be competitive, for prices could then be arranged at some level convenient for both sides, instead of representing a compromise between the divergent interests of the two. And a market that was no more than a place where opposing forces contended would be only a tug of war, a bargaining contest with an outcome about which we could say nothing unless we knew the respective strengths and cunning of the two sides.

It is the fact that each side of the price contest is also contesting against itself—the fact that vying takes place not merely *between* those who want high prices and those who want low ones, but on each side of this divide *among* marketers whose self-interest urges them to meet the demands of the other side—that makes a competition a process that drives buyers and sellers to a meeting point. If some of our unsatisfied shoe buyers, for example—although preferring low prices to high ones —were not pushed into offering a little higher price than the prevailing one by their desire to get shoes, and if some unsatisfied sellers, although hoping for high prices, were not driven by self-interest to offer a price a little below that of their rivals, the price would not move to that balancing point where the two sides arrived at the best possible settlement.

Thus competition is a key condition for the operation of a market system. What are we to make, then, of the fact that we know that monopolistic and oligopolistic elements are to be found in many markets in the real economy? We shall have to wait until Chapter 26 before we can fully analyze the effect that these market imperfections have on the solutions to market problems; but suffice it to say now that for all the departures they will introduce from the competitive model, the basic relevance of that model will still apply. Moreover, until we have understood how a competitive market works, we will not be able to understand the differences that monopoly or oligopoly introduce.

Hence, during the next several chapters we will be proceeding under the assumption of "pure" competition. In due course we will examine very carefully exactly what we mean by this kind of competition and the extent to which economic reasoning built on it is applicable to the real world. But there is a good deal to learn before we add these finishing touches to our microeconomic knowledge.

PRICES AND ALLOCATION

We have already cleared up a good deal of the mystery about how prices are formed in a market system. Although we have not really looked into supply curves (and we cannot until we probe the operations of the firm) we understand in general that prices for most goods on the marketplace reflect the interplay of the demand schedules of consumers and the supply schedules of producers. In our next chapter we will see how changes in demand affect prices and how various characteristics of demand exert different influences on the price structure.

But before we turn to the dynamics of supply and demand, there is a further illumination that our understanding of the price mechanism can shed on the problems of microeconomics. It begins to explain to us how the market system solves the problems of allocation with which it is entrusted. In particular it clears up the puzzle of how the market system *rations* goods among claimants.

In one form or another, rationing—or the allocation of goods among claimants—is a disagreeable but inescapable task that every economic system must carry out; for in all societies, the prevailing reality of life has been the inadequacy of output to fill the needs of the people. In traditional economies, we will remember, rationing is performed by a general adherence to rigidly established rules that determine the rights of various individuals to share in the social product, whether by caste or class or family position or whatever. In command societies, the division of the social product is carried out in a more explicitly directed fashion, as the authorities—lords, priests, kings, commissars—determine the rights of various groups or persons to share in the fruits of society.

A market society, as we know, dispenses with the heavy hand of tradition or the arbitrary one of command, but it too must impose some system of rationing to prevent what would otherwise be an impossibly destructive struggle among its citizens. This critical allocative task is also accomplished by the price mechanism. *For one of the prime functions of a market is to determine who shall be allowed to acquire goods and who shall not.*

TABLE 21 · 3

Price	$11	$10	$9	$8	$7	$6	$5	$4	$3	$2	$1
Number willing and able, at above price, to											
buy one unit	0	1	2	3	4	5	6	7	8	9	10
sell one unit	10	9	8	7	6	5	4	3	2	1	0

Imagine a market in which we have ten buyers, each willing and able to buy one unit of a commodity, but each having a different price that is agreeable to him, and ten suppliers, each also willing and able to put one unit of supply on the market, again each at a different price. Such a market might look like Table 21-3.

As we can see, the equilibrium price will lie at $6, for at this price there will be five suppliers of one unit each and five purchasers of one each. Now let us make a graph in which each bar stands for a single individual, and where the height of the bar tells us how much that individual will be willing to pay for the unit of the commodity or how much he would sell it for. If we line up our marketers in order of their demand and supply capabilities, our market will look like Fig. 21-3.

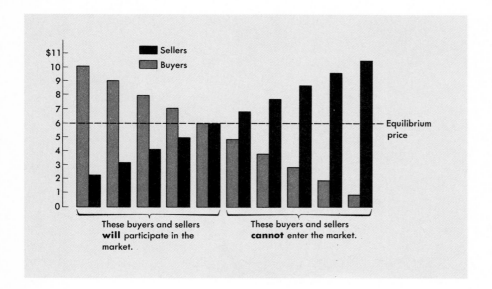

FIG. 21-3

HOW THE MARKET RATIONS

What we have drawn is in fact nothing but a standard supply and demand diagram. But look what it shows us. All the buyers who can afford and are willing to pay the equilibrium price (or more) will get the good they want. All those who cannot, will not. So, too, all the sellers who are willing and able to supply the commodity at its equilibrium price or less will be able to consummate sales. All those who cannot, will not.

Thus the market, in establishing an equilibrium price, has in effect allocated the goods among some buyers and withheld it from others, and permitted some sellers to do business and denied that privilege to others. In our previous case, anyone who could pay $25 or more got a pair of shoes, and all those who could not were unable to get shoes; while all producers who could turn out shoes for $25 or less were able to do business, and those who could not meet that price were unable to make any sales at all.

Note that the market is in this way a means of excluding certain people from economic activity—namely, customers with too little money or with too weak desires, or suppliers unwilling or unable to operate at a certain price.

The rationing system of the market is both its triumph and its trouble. At the outset of our book we briefly surveyed the problems of non-market control mechanisms. In the case of tradition, we remember, the problem is the profound inertia that comes from a static arrangement of economic duties and rewards. In the case of command economies, the problem lies in the difficulty of administering a system without resort to bureaucratic inefficiency on the one hand or dictatorial intervention on the other.

Against these very grave difficulties of other systems, the price system has two great advantages: (1) *it is highly dynamic,* and (2) *it is self-enforcing.* That is, on the one hand it provides an easy avenue for change to enter the system, while on the other, it permits economic activity to take place without anyone "overseeing" the system.

The second (self-regulating) attribute of the market is especially useful with regard to the rationing function. In place of ration tickets with their almost inevitable black markets or cumbersome inspectorates or queues of customers trying to be first in line, *the price system operates without any kind of visible administrative apparatus or side effect.* The energies that must go into planning, or the frictions that come out of it, are alike rendered unnecessary by the self-policing market mechanism.

On the other hand, the system has the defects of its virtues. If it is efficient and dynamic, it is also devoid of values: it recognizes no priorities of claim to the goods and services of society except those of wealth and income. In a society in which all shared alike, or in which incomes were distributed in accordance with some universally approved principle, this neutrality of the market would be perfectly acceptable, for then each would enter the market on equal terms or at least with advantages and disadvantages that bore the stamp of social approval.* But in a society in which inheritance still perpetuates large fortunes made in the past, and where unemployment or old age can bring extreme deprivation, the rationing results of the market often affront our sense of dignity.

Therefore every market society interferes to some extent with the "natural" outcome of the price rationing system. In times of emergency, such as war, it issues special permits that take precedence over money and thereby prevent the richer members of society from buying up all the supplies of scarce and valuable items, such as gasoline. In depressed areas, it may distribute basic food or clothing to those who have no

---

*Suppose incomes were distributed absolutely evenly among all families. What would happen to prices? Since tastes are different among different individuals, there would no doubt be a rush to buy some commodities, the prices of which would soar, and a disinclination to buy others, the prices of which would sink. In the end (forgetting about costs for the moment), relative prices would reflect the relative marginal utilities of different goods to the population, and the people who would consume the more expensive goods would be those whose tastes made them willing to spend their money on them.

money to buy them. And to an ever-increasing extent it uses its taxes and transfer payments to redistribute the ration tickets of money in accordance with the prevailing sense of justice and right.

Our view of the price system as a rationing mechanism helps to clarify the meaning of two words we often hear as a result of intervention into the market-rationing process: *shortage* and *surplus*.

What do we mean when we say there is a *shortage* of housing for low income groups? The everyday meaning is that people with low incomes cannot find enough housing. Yet in every market there are always some buyers who are unsatisfied. We have just noted, for instance, that in our shoe market, all buyers who could not or would not pay $25 had to go without shoes. Does this mean there was a shoe "shortage"?

Certainly no one uses that word to describe the outcome of a normal market, even though there are always buyers and sellers who are excluded from that market because they cannot meet the going price. Then what does a "shortage" mean? *We can see now that it usually refers to a situation in which the price has been fixed by some nonmarket agency, such as the government, below the equilibrium price.*

FIG. 21-4

SHORTAGES

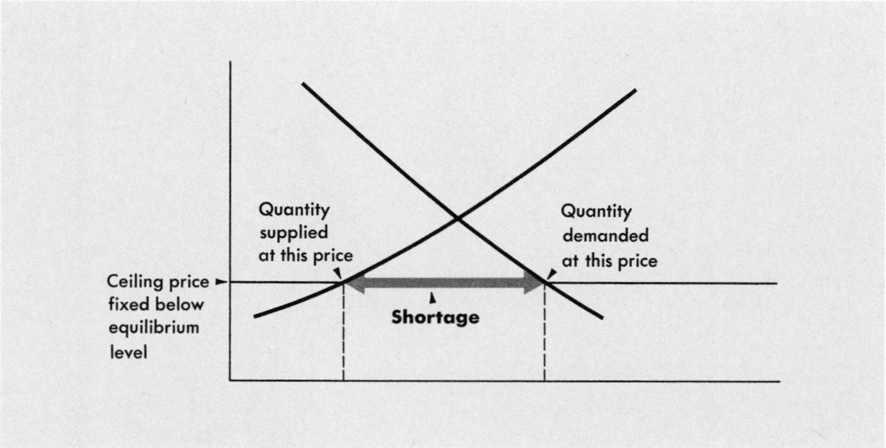

Figure 21-4 shows us such a situation. Note that at the price established by the government, the quantity demanded is much greater than the quantity supplied. If this were a free market, the price would soon rise to the equilibrium point, and we would hear no more about a shortage. But so long as the price is fixed at ceiling level, this equilibrating process cannot take place. Thus the quantity demanded will

FIG. 21-5

SURPLUSES

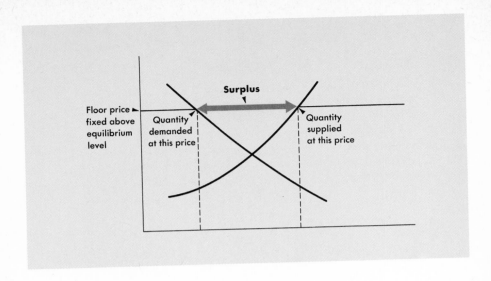

remain larger than the quantity supplied, and some buyers will go unsatisfied *even though they are willing and able to pay the going price.*

The opposite takes place with a surplus. Here, in Fig. 21-5, we see a price floor fixed above the equilibrium price, as when the government supports crops above their free market price.

Now we have a situation in which the quantity supplied is greater than that demanded (note that we do not say that "supply" is greater than "demand"). In a free market the price would fall until the two quantities were equal. But if the government continues to support the commodity, then more will be produced than the amount for which there will be private buyers. The unsold amounts will be a "surplus."

Thus the words shortage *and* surplus *mean situations in which there are sellers and buyers who are willing and able to enter the market at the going price but who remain active and unsatisfied because the price mechanism has not eliminated them.* This is very different from a free market where there are unsatisfied buyers and sellers *who cannot meet the going price* and who are therefore not taken into account. Poor people have no demand for fresh caviar at $40 per pound and therefore do not complain of a caviar shortage, but if the price of fresh caviar were set by government decree at $1 a pound, there would soon be a colossal "shortage."

What about the situation with low cost housing? Essentially what we mean when we talk of a shortage of inexpensive housing is that we view the outcome of this particular market situation with noneconomic eyes and pronounce the result distasteful. By the standards of the market, the poor who cannot afford to buy housing are simply buyers at the extreme lower right end of the demand curve, and their elimination from the market for housing is only one more example of the rationing process that takes place in *every* market. When we single out certain goods or services (such as doctor's care or higher education) as being in "short supply," we imply that we do not approve of the price mechanism as the appropriate means of allocating scarce resources in these particular instances. This is not because the market is not as efficient a distributor as ever. It is because in these instances we feel that the underlying distribution (or maldistribution) of income causes the outcome of the market rationing process to clash with other standards of the public interest that we value even more highly than the standard of efficiency.

SUMMARY

1. In the market system, prices give *stimuli* or *signals* telling us how to act to *increase our pecuniary advantage*. Microeconomics is therefore often called *price theory.*

2. *Price stimuli give rise to different economic reactions depending on what side of the market we are located*—that is, whether we are buyers or sellers.

3. The actions of both buyers and sellers reflect both their *willingness* and their *ability* to purchase or sell. Thus the words *demand* and *supply* tell us what *quantities* will be bought and sold *at different prices.*

4. Our willingness to buy larger quantities at lower prices is explained by the hypothesis that the *marginal utility of goods diminishes* as we possess more and more of them (within a fixed period of time). Note that this is not the same as saying that *total* utility declines.

5. *Demand and supply are both functional relationships* that describe our behavior at different prices.

6. In a competitive market, prices will be determined by the interaction of buyers and sellers. *At low prices the quantities demanded will exceed the quantities supplied, and vice versa at high prices. The prices at which the quantities demanded and supplied are equal is called the equilibrium price.* (Note that "demand" and "supply" are *not* equal at this price.)

7. *At equilibrium prices the market clears.* Because quantities demanded and supplied are identical, there are no unsatisfied buyers or sellers able and willing to enter the market and therefore to alter its quantities offered or sought.

8. Equilibrium prices will *spontaneously establish themselves* in competitive markets and will *persist* until the forces of supply or demand change.

9. Markets depend not only on *self-interest,* but on the force of *competition.* This is the outcome of *two struggles*—one across the market and another on either side of the market.

10. Prices perform an *allocatory function, rationing goods* among those buyers and sellers who are willing and able to enter the market at the going price. This rationing system is *highly dynamic* and is *self-enforcing.* At the same time, it recognizes no distributive principles or values except those of wealth.

11. *Shortages and surpluses* refer to situations in which prices have been imposed on a market and are below or above the equilibrium price. We do not count as victims of shortage or surplus the unsatisfied buyers or sellers we encounter in an equilibrium market. When we do label a situation as "shortage" or "surplus," it means that we do not approve of the market system as an appropriate rationing device for that good or service.

QUESTIONS

1. Why is microeconomics called price theory? What different things does the same price signal mean to buyers and sellers? Do sellers and buyers, for example, both like falling prices?

2. What is meant by saying that demand is a function of price? Does this mean that we will buy more of a good when its price goes up? What are the motivational roots of "demand"? Why is not our ability to buy—our income—enough to give us a demand schedule?

3. Why would the marginal utility of bread and diamonds change if you were locked in Tiffany's over the weekend? Why are so many necessities of life so inexpensive, when they are indispensable?

4. Draw up a hypothetical demand schedule for yourself for one year's purchases of books, assuming that the average price of books changed from $10 through $1.

5. Draw up a supply schedule for your local bookstore, assuming that book prices ranged from $1 to $10.

6. What is the equilibrium price of books in your examples above? Exactly what do you mean by equilibrium price? What is special about the quantities demanded and supplied at this price?

7. What is the difference between "supply and demand" and "quantity supplied" and "quantity demanded"?

8. What do we mean when we say that there are two aspects to competition? What are they? Why is any one not enough?

9. What is meant by allocation? How do prices allocate goods among buyers?

10. What is meant by a surplus? A shortage? Draw diagrams to illustrate each.

11. A British critic of their National Health Service has written: "If taxi fares and meters were abolished and a free National Taxi service were financed by taxation, who would go by car or bus, or walk? . . . The shortage of taxis would be endemic, rationing by rushing would go to the physically strong, and be more arbitrary than price, and the 'taxi crisis' a subject of periodic agitation and political debate." Discuss this statement in view of what you know about the rationing mechanism. What light does it throw on the "shortage" of doctors in England today? Assuming that the argument is valid in its charge that taxi rationing by rushing would be more arbitrary than by price, does it follow that medical rationing by price is the least arbitrary system?

THE MARKET
IN MOVEMENT 22

We have learned how equilibrium prices emerge "mysteriously and marvellously" from the wholly unsupervised interaction of competing buyers and sellers; and we have seen how those prices, once formed, silently and efficiently perform the necessary social task of allocating goods among buyers and sellers. Yet our analysis is still too static to resemble the actual play of the marketplace. For one of the attributes of an equilibrium price, we remember, is its lasting quality, its persistence. But the prices around us in the real world are often in movement. How can we introduce this element of change into our analysis of microeconomic relations?

The answer is that the word *equilibrium* in micro analysis no more implies changelessness than it did in macro analysis. Equilibrium prices are indeed lasting—so long as the forces that produce them do not change, but just as shifts in saving and investment continuously reset the point of equilibrium for GNP, so changes in supply and demand constantly alter the resting point of individual prices.

SHIFTS IN DEMAND AND SUPPLY

But what makes supply and demand change? If we recall the definition of those words, we are asking *what might change our willingness or ability to buy or sell something at any given price?* The basic reasons are not difficult to discover. Suppose, for instance, that in the course of our previous adventure in shirt buying, we had taken out our wallet and found that we had less money in it than we imagined. Such a change in our financial circumstances would be very likely to alter the quantity of merchandise we were willing and able to acquire. The discovery of more money would affect our demand in the opposite direction.

A similar change in financial circumstances would also alter the willingness and ability of the supplier to make various quantities of shirts at various prices. If the cost of shirt material fell sharply, our tailor might be perfectly willing and able to make shirts at $4.50 (whereas formerly he could not afford to); and might find it profitable to make more shirts than he did previously, at higher prices.

Psychological changes in our condition as buyers or sellers can alter our willingness and ability to buy or sell equally as much as financial changes. A change in our tastes, induced by advertising or whatever, can make us more or less willing to spend our money for a given commodity, even though its price remains the same. A change in our attitudes toward work may make us more or less willing to undertake a given job at a given price: our tailor may decide to give up tailoring altogether or to make his fame as a designer of shirts. Either would change the quantity of shirts he would produce at various prices.

Thus changes in taste or attitudes, or in income or wealth will shift our whole demand schedule, and the same changes, plus any change in costs, will shift our whole supply schedule. Note that this is very different from a change in the quantity we buy or sell when *prices* change. In the first case, as our willingness and ability to buy or sell is increased or diminished, *the whole demand and supply schedule (or curve) shifts bodily.* In the second place, when our basic willingness and ability is unchanged, but prices change, our schedule (or curve) is unchanged, but *we move back or forth along it.*

Here are the two cases to be studied carefully in Fig. 22-1. Note that when our demand schedule shifts, we will buy a *different amount at the same price.* If our willingness and ability to buy is enhanced, we will buy a larger amount; if they are diminished, a smaller amount. Similarly, the quantity a seller will offer will vary as his willingness and ability are altered. Thus demand and supply curves can shift about, rightward and leftward, up and down, as the economic circumstances they represent change. In reality, these schedules are continuously in change, since tastes and incomes and attitudes and technical capabilities (which affect costs and therefore sellers' actions) are also continuously in flux.

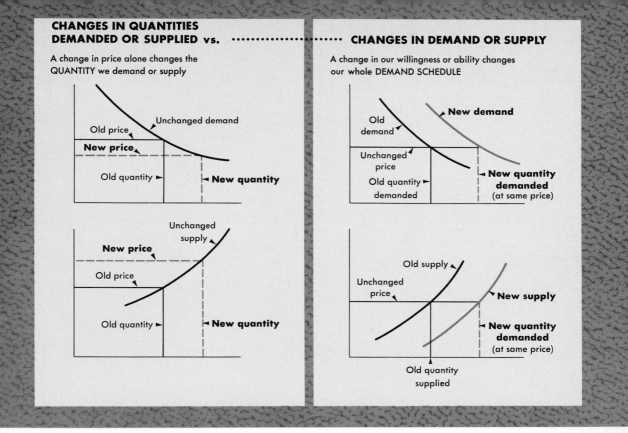

FIG. 22-1 CHANGES IN QUANTITIES DEMANDED OR SUPPLIED VS. CHANGES IN DEMAND OR SUPPLY

How do changes in supply and demand affect prices? We have already seen the underlying process at work in the case of shoes. Changes in supply or demand will alter the *quantities* that will be sought or offered on the market at a given price—an increase in demand, for instance, will raise the quantity sought. Since there are not enough goods offered to match this quantity, price will be bid up by unsatisfied buyers to a new level at which quantities offered and sought again balance. Similarly, if supply shifts, there will be too much or too little put on the market in relation to the existing quantity of demand, and competition among sellers will push prices up or down to a new level at which quantities sought and offered again clear.

In Fig. 22-2, we show what happens to the equilibrium price in two cases—first, when demand increases (perhaps due to a sudden craze for the good in question); second, when demand decreases (when the craze is over). Quite obviously, a rise in demand—other things being equal—will cause prices to rise; a fall will cause them to fall.

We can depict the same process from the supply side. In Fig. 22-3, we show the impact on price of a sudden rise in supply and of a fall. Again the diagram makes clear what is intuitively obvious: an increased

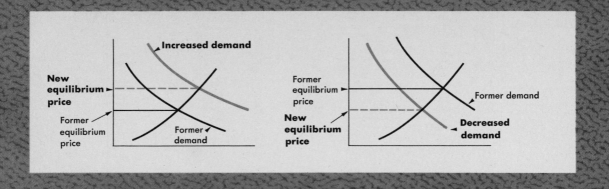

FIG. 22-2   SHIFTS IN DEMAND CHANGE EQUILIBRIUM PRICES

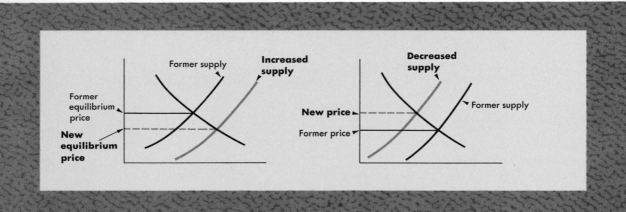

FIG. 22-3   SHIFTS IN SUPPLY CHANGE EQUILIBRIUM PRICES

FIG. 22-4

HOW SHIFTS
IN BOTH
SUPPLY AND
DEMAND
AFFECT
PRICES

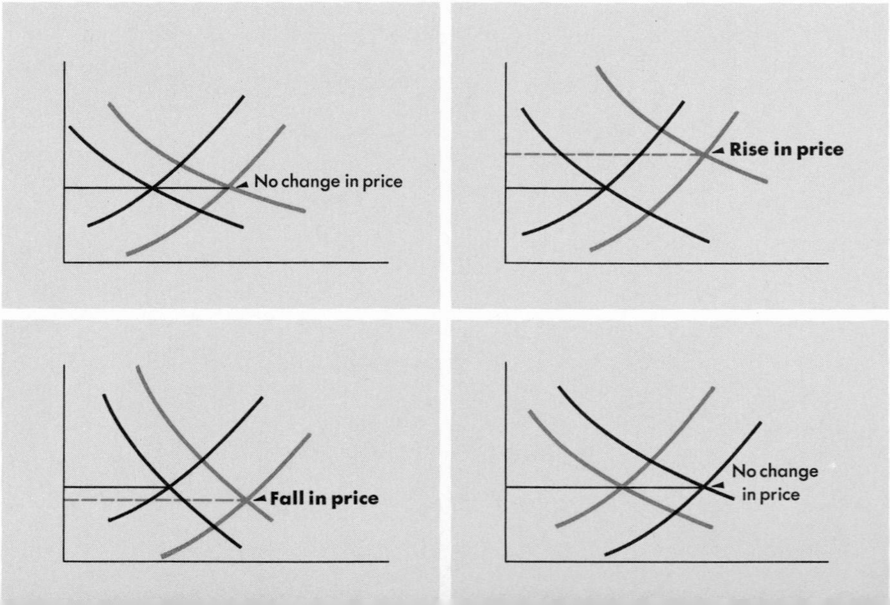

436

supply (given an unchanging demand) leads to lower prices; a decreased supply to higher prices.

And if supply and demand *both* change? Then the result will be higher or lower prices, depending on the shapes and new positions of the two curves—that is, depending on the relative changes in the willingness and ability of both sides. Figure 22-4 shows a few possibilities.

ELASTICITY

We have seen how shifts in demand or supply affect price. But *how much* do they affect price? Suppose, for example, that demand schedules have increased by 10 per cent. Do we know how large an effect this change will have on price?

These questions lead us to a still deeper scrutiny of the nature of supply and demand, by way of a new concept called *elasticity* or, more properly, *price elasticity*. Elasticities describe the shapes of supply and demand curves, and thereby tell us a good deal as to whether a given change in demand or supply will have a small or large effect on price.

Figure 22-5 illustrates the case with two supply curves. Our diagrams show two commodities selling at the same equilibrium prices and facing identical demand schedules. Note, however, that the two commodities have very different supply curves. In both cases demand now increases by the same amount. Notice how much greater is the price increase in the case of the good with the inelastic supply curve.

Similarly, the price change that would be associated with a change in supply will be greater for a commodity with an inelastic demand curve than for one with an elastic demand curve. Figure 22-6 shows two identical supply curves matched against very different demand curves. Note how much greater is the fall in price of the commodity for which demand is inelastic.

Clearly, elasticities are powerful factors in explaining price movements.* This is because the word "elasticity" refers to our sensitivity of response to price changes. What we mean by an elastic demand (or supply) is that, as buyers or sellers, our willingness or ability to buy or sell is strongly affected by changes in price, whereas when our schedules are inelastic, the effect is small. In more precise terms, *an elastic demand (or supply) is one in which a given percentage change in*

---

*We should notice that we can use another term—*income elasticity*—to describe the response of our willingness and ability to buy and sell, not to a change in price, but to a change in our incomes. There are some goods—cigarettes are evidently one—in which the quantities we buy seem to be more influenced by changes in income than by normal fluctuations in price. For other goods, such as coffee, it has been estimated that housewives' purchases are more influenced by changes in price than by fluctuations in income. In the real world, price and income elasticities are inextricably mixed, but we will confine our attention here to the simpler case of price elasticity alone.

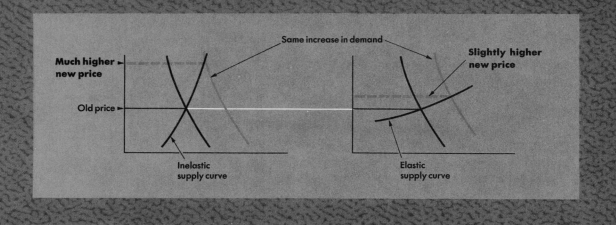

HOW ELASTICITY OF SUPPLY CURVE AFFECTS PRICE

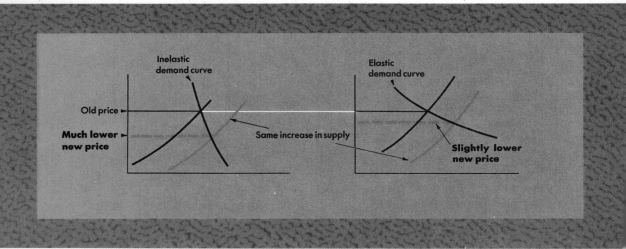

FIG. 22-6 HOW ELASTICITY OF DEMAND CURVE AFFECTS PRICE

prices brings about a larger percentage change in the quantity demanded (or supplied). An inelastic schedule or curve is one in which the response in the quantities we are willing and able to buy or sell is proportionally less than the change in price.†

It helps if we see what elasticities of different kinds look like. Figure 22-7 is a family of supply and demand curves that illustrates the range of buying and selling responses associated with a change in prices.

---

†Notice that elasticity is a *quantitative* notion—that it is measured by changes in quantities bought or sold compared with changes in price. This caution is needed because it is possible to make demand or supply curves "look" elastic or inelastic by changing the calibration of the horizontal or vertical axes on a diagram. For simplicity's sake we will continue to rely on the visual "look" of elasticity and inelasticity, but the student should remember that the real test is provided by the proportional changes in quantities, not by the possibly misleading shapes he sees. There is more about elasticity in Professor Hannaford's *Student's Guide,* Chapter 22.

FIG. 22-7

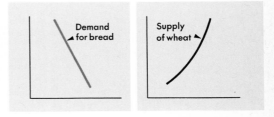

TOTALLY INELASTIC DEMAND OR SUPPLY. The quantity offered or sought is unchanged despite a change in price. Examples: Within normal price ranges there is probably no change at all in the quantity of table salt bought. Similarly, a fisherman landing a catch of fish will have to sell it all at any price within reason.

INELASTIC DEMAND OR SUPPLY. Quantity offered or sought changes proportionately less than price. Examples: We probably do not double bread purchases if the price of bread halves. On the supply side, the price of wheat may double, but farmers are unable (at least for a long time) to offer twice as much wheat for sale.

UNIT ELASTICITY. This is a special case in which quantities demanded or supplied respond in exact proportion to price changes. (Note the shape of the demand curve.) Examples: Many goods may fit this description, but it is impossible flatly to state that any one good does so.

ELASTIC DEMAND OR SUPPLY. Price changes induce proportionally larger changes in quantity. Examples: Many luxury goods increase dramatically in sales volume when their price is lowered. On the supply side, elastic demand usually affects items that are easy to produce, so that a small price rise induces a rush for expanded output.

TOTALLY ELASTIC DEMAND OR SUPPLY. The quantity supplied or demanded at the going price is "infinite." Examples: This seemingly odd case turns out to be of great importance in describing the market outlook of the typical small competitive firm. Merely as a hint: For an individual farmer, the demand curve for his output at the going price looks horizontal because he can sell all the grain he can possibly raise at that price. A grain dealer can also buy all he wants at that price.

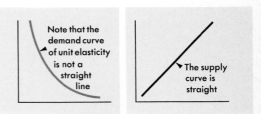

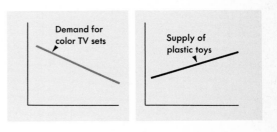

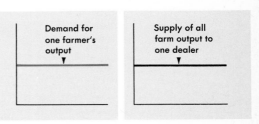

Elasticities not only affect the determination of market prices, they also have a very great effect on the fortunes of buyers and sellers in the marketplace. That is, it makes a great deal of difference to a buyer whether the supply curve of a commodity he wants is elastic or not, for that will affect very drastically the amount he will have to spend on that particular commodity if its price changes; and it makes an equal amount of difference to a seller whether the demand curve for his output is elastic or not, for that will determine what happens to his total revenues as prices change.

Here is an instance in point. Table 22-1 shows three demand schedules: elastic, inelastic, and of unit elasticity. Let us see how these three differently constituted schedules would affect the fortunes of a seller who had to cater to the demand represented by each.

Now a very interesting result follows from these different schedules. *The total amount spent for each commodity (and thus the total amount*

TABLE 22 · 1

DEMAND SCHEDULES FOR THREE GOODS

	QUANTITIES DEMANDED		
Price	Inelastic demand	Unit elasticity	Elastic demand
$10	100	100	100
9	101	111 1/9	120
8	102	125	150
7	103	143	200
6	104	166 2/5	300
5	105	200	450
4	106	250	650
3	107	333 1/3	900
2	108	500	1,400
1	109	1,000	3,000

TABLE 22 · 2

TOTAL EXPENDITURES (or receipts)

Price	Good with inelastic demand	Good with unit elasticity demand	Good with elastic demand
$10	1,000	1,000	1,000
9	909	1,000	1,080
8	816	1,000	1,200
7	717	1,000	1,400
6	612	1,000	1,800
5	525	1,000	2,250
4	424	1,000	2,600
3	321	1,000	2,700
2	216	1,000	2,800
1	109	1,000	3,000

received by a firm) will be very different over the indicated range of prices. In Table 22-2 are the amounts spent (price times quantity).

We can see that it makes a lot of difference to a seller whether he is supplying goods for which the demand is elastic or not. *If demand is elastic and he cuts his price, he will take in more revenue.* If his demand is inelastic and he cuts his price, he will take in *less* revenue. (This has typically been the case with farm products, as we recall from our history.)

Conversely, a businessman who raises his price will be lucky if the demand for his product is inelastic, for then his receipts will actually increase. Compare the fortunes of the two businessmen depicted in Fig. 22-8. Note that by blocking in the change in price times the change in quantity, we can show the change in receipts. (Because we have ignored changes in costs, we cannot show changes in profits.)

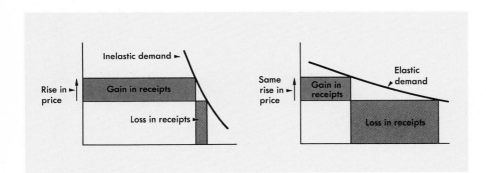

FIG. 22-8

HOW ELASTICITIES AFFECT RECEIPTS WHEN PRICES CHANGE

Our figure shows something else. Notice that if we reverse the direction of the price change, our businessmen's fortunes take a sharp change. A demand curve that is elastic spells bad news for a businessman who seeks to raise his price, but the same demand curve brings good fortune to a businessman who intends to cut prices. Just the opposite is the case with an inelastic demand curve: now the condition of demand is favorable for a price rise, since the seller will hold most of his sales even at the higher price, but inelastic demand is bad for someone who cuts prices, since he will gain few additional customers (or his old ones will increase their purchases only slightly) when prices fall.

Obviously, what every businessman would like to have is a demand for his product that was inelastic in an upward direction and elastic at lower than existing prices, so that he stood to gain whether he raised or lowered prices. As we shall see when we study pricing under oligopoly, just the opposite is apt to be the case.

Because elasticities are so important in accounting for the behavior of prices, we must press our investigation further. However, we must leave the supply side of elasticity to be studied in our next chapter when we look into the behavior of factors and for later chapters when we will study the operation of firms. Here we will ask why are demand curves shaped the way they are? Why is our price (or income) sensitivity for some commodities so great and for others so slight?

If we think of a good or service for which our demand might be very inelastic—say eyeglasses (assuming we need them)—and compare it with another for which our demand is apt to be highly elastic—say, a trip to Europe—the difference is not difficult to grasp. One thing is a necessity; the other is a luxury. But what do we mean by *necessity* and *luxury?* If we think more carefully about the terms, we can define them still more clearly in terms of the ease with which we can *substitute* other goods or services in their place.

A necessity is a good for which it is hard to find substitutes. If we need eyeglasses, we will spend a great deal of money, if need be, to acquire a pair. Hence such a necessity has a very inelastic demand curve.

Necessities are never absolute in the sense that nothing can be substituted for the commodity in question. High enough prices will drive buyers to *some* substitute, however imperfect.* Just when will the buyer be driven to the "next-best thing"? Traditionally, economists describe the decision as determined by a comparison of the marginal utility derived from a dollar's worth of the high-priced item with that derived from the lower-priced substitute. As the price of champagne goes up and up, there comes a point when we would rather spend our next dollar for a substantial amount of beer, rather than for a sip of champagne.

We can describe *all* consumer purchasing as following this pattern of maximizing marginal satisfactions. Presumably we always buy the thing that gives us the highest marginal utility for the dollar we are spending at any particular moment. As we buy more of the "best" thing, its marginal utility to us diminishes. When the marginal utility of another unit of the "best thing" has finally fallen below the marginal utility of the "next-best thing," we switch over. That is, when we have drunk so much champagne that the marginal utility of another dollar's worth is now less than the marginal utility of a dollar's worth of beer, we spend our next dollar on beer, since our enjoyment will be maximized by doing so.

*What *would* be the substitute for eyeglasses? For a very nearsighted person, the demand for one pair of glasses would be absolutely inelastic over a considerable price range. But when glasses got to be, say, $500 a pair, substitutes would begin to appear. At those prices, one could hire someone to guide him around or to read aloud. Admittedly this is less satisfactory than having glasses; but if the choice is between spending a very large amount on glasses and on personal help, the latter might seem preferable.

In fact, we always face an immense choice of goods on which we could spend our next dollar. As a result, we end up with a situation in which the marginal utility of a dollar spent by us for *any* good brings in the same amount of satisfaction. We say "presumably," since marginal utility cannot actually be measured. A number of economists have correctly pointed out that there can be no *proof* that we equalize marginal utilities by our actions. Nonetheless, the concept of maximizing our marginal utilities by "comparison shopping" seems to offer a plausible description of the motives that guide us as buyers.

We have seen that necessities have inelastic demand curves, so that we stick to them as prices rise. But what about when they fall? Won't we rush to buy necessities, just because they *are* necessities? Won't that make their demand curves elastic?

Surprisingly, the answer is that we do not rush to buy necessities when their prices fall. Why? The answer is that necessities are the things we buy *first,* just because they are necessities. Having bought what we needed before the fall in price, we are not tempted to buy much more, if any more, after the fall. Bread, as we commented before, is a great deal more valuable for life than diamonds are, but we ordinarily have enough bread, so that the marginal utility of another loaf is no greater than that of an equivalent expenditure on any other good. Thus, as the price of bread drops, the quantity we seek expands only slightly. So, too, with eyeglasses.

Compare the case with a luxury, such as a trip to Europe. There are many substitutes for such a trip—trips out West, trips South, or some other kind of vacation. As a result, if the price of a European trip goes up, we are easily persuaded to switch to some alternative plan. Conversely, when the price of a European trip gets cheaper, we are quick to substitute *it* for other possible vacation alternatives and our demand accordingly displays its elastic properties.

Do not make the mistake, however, of thinking that elasticity is purely a function of whether items are "expensive" or not. Studies have shown that the demand for subway transportation in New York City is price-elastic, which hardly means that riding in the subway is the prerogative of millionaires. The point, rather, is that the demand for subway rides is closely affected by the comparative prices of substitutes—bus fares and taxis. Thus *it is the ease or difficulty of substitution that always lies behind the various elasticities of demand schedules.*

OTHER INFLUENCES ON DEMAND

Time also plays an important role in shaping our demand curves. Suppose, for example, that the price of orange juice suddenly soared, owing to a crop failure. Would the demand for orange juice be elastic or inelastic?

In the short run, it would certainly be more inelastic than in the longer run. Lovers of orange juice would likely be willing to pay a higher price for their favorite juice because (they would believe) there was really no other juice quite as good. But as the weeks went by they might be tempted to try other breakfast juices, and no doubt some of these experiments would "take." Substitutes would be found, after all.

The point is that it takes time and information for patterns of demand to change. Thus demand curves become more elastic as time goes on, and the range of discovered substitutes becomes larger.

SUBSTITUTION AND DEMAND

There is a last point we should make before we leave the subject of substitution. We have seen that the substitutability of one product for another is the underlying cause of elasticity. Indeed, more and more we are led to see "products" themselves as bundles of utilities surrounded with other competing bundles that offer a whole range of alternatives for a buyer's satisfaction.

What is it that ultimately determines how close the substitutes come to the commodity in question? As with all questions in economics that are pursued to the end, the answer lies in two aspects of reality before which economic inquiry comes to a halt. One of these is the human being himself, with his tastes and drives and wants. One man's substitute will not be another's.

The other ultimate basing point for economics is the technical and physical nature of the world that forces certain relationships of ends and means upon us. Cotton may be a substitute for wool because they both have the properties of fibers, but diamonds are not a substitute for the same end-use because they lack the requisite physical properties. Diamonds, as finery, may be a substitute for clothes made out of cotton, but until we learn how to spin diamonds, they will not be a substitute for the cloth itself.

Because substitutes form a vast chain of alternatives for buyers, changes in the prices of substitutes change the positions of demand curves. Here is a new idea to be thought about carefully. Our existing demand curve for bread or diamonds has the shape (elasticity) it does because substitutes exist at various prices. But when the prices of those substitutes *change,* the original commodity suddenly looks "cheaper" or "more expensive." If the price of subway rides rises from 20 cents to 25 cents, while the price of taxi rides remains the same, we will be tempted to switch part of our transportation from subways to taxis. If subway rides went to 50 cents, there would be a mass exodus to taxis. Thus we should add changes in the prices of substitutes to changes in taste and in income when we consider the possible causes of a shift in demand. If the price of a substitute commodity rises, the demand for the original commodity will rise; and as the price of substitutes falls, demand for the original commodity will fall. This may, of course, bring changes in the price of the original commodity.

There is another connection between commodities besides that of substitution—the relationship of *complementarity*. Complementarity means that some commodities are technically linked, so that you cannot very well use one without using the other, even though they are sold separately. Automobiles and gasoline are examples of such complementary goods, as are cameras and film.

Here is another instance in which changes in the price of one good actually affects the position of the demand curve for the other. If the price of film goes up, it becomes more expensive to operate cameras. Hence the demand for cameras is apt to drop. Note that the price of cameras has not changed in the first instance. Rather, when the price of the complementary good—the film—goes up, the whole demand curve for cameras shifts to the left. Thereafter, the price of cameras is apt to fall as well.

We are almost ready to take our first overview of the whole market system, but there is still a missing link in our analysis chain. We have dealt thus far largely in terms of individual demand and supply schedules and curves—that is, in terms of the motivation between one person's willingness and ability to buy or sell. All through our macroeconomic studies, however, we spoke of demand and supply in collective or sectoral or national terms. How do we connect the two?

When we speak of the national demand for, or supply of, a good or service, we are really doing no more than adding up all the demand schedules of the individuals concerned. Thus the national demand for automobiles is a schedule whose shape and position reflects the sum of the tastes, incomes, preferences, etc., of all persons willing and able to buy cars.

The situation is more complicated, however, when we speak of demand on a still larger scale—for instance, the demand for all consumption goods, or the demand for GNP itself. Some of the relationships we have discovered in this chapter continue to hold. We have already spoken of the effect of a change in income on total consumption demand when we discussed the propensity to consume schedule. We can now see this schedule as a demand curve that relates our willingness and ability to buy all consumption goods at different levels of aggregate income. On the other hand, some attributes of demand at the micro level disappear when we magnify them to macro size. For example, problems of changing tastes, or of substitutes and complements, are usually unimportant in analyzing macroeconomic phenomena, for they represent shifts *within* the sphere of consumption and do not affect the *total* of consumption spending.

More complex is the matter of price and total spending. Can we speak of a price elasticity of total consumption demand? Will consumption spending fall, as a percentage of disposable personal income, if all prices rise? The trouble in answering this question from the perspective of microeconomics is that we have to balance two contradictory effects. Higher prices throughout the economy will mean higher incomes for some people and therefore increased consumer demand. For others however, higher prices will bear against fixed incomes and may well cause a contraction in total expenditures. (Then, just to complicate matters further, higher prices will mean both higher revenues and higher costs to producers, thereby involving us in the supply side of the situation.)

It is easier to deal with questions such as this by going over to the macroeconomic perspective and coping directly with statistical aggregates, such as the marginal propensity to consume, than by trying to calculate the positive income elasticities of millions of consumers against the negative price elasticities of others. Nonetheless, the illustration reminds us that the macro effects we deal with are made up, in fact, of innumerable small micro reactions which constitute the fundamental source of all private economic activity.

THE MARKET AS A
SELF-CORRECTING MECHANISM

We have begun to see how the market for goods and services operates as a dynamic, constantly altering—and yet self-adjusting—mechanism. From the interplay of supply and demand schedules for goods emerge equilibrium prices of those goods. Yet these prices are rarely at rest. As the incomes and tastes of the throngs of goods-seekers change—or as the conditions of supply change—the prices of goods are continuously seeking new levels that will equate, if only for a moment, the quantities offered and sought. Moreover, as the prices of goods change, new ripples of disturbance are set into motion, for each good is a substitute for (or perhaps a complement of) others, and thus as each price changes, it will induce shifts in the demand curves that affect other prices. Meanwhile, the ever-shifting pattern of prices is silently carrying out its task of allocating the products on the market among the throng seeking them, distributing goods and permitting sales to those who meet the test of going prices, and quietly but uncompromisingly refusing them to those who do not.

How is order maintained in this extraordinary flux of activity? We have learned a good deal about some of the basic principles that keep the process smoothly and continuously working. One of these, we have seen, is the pressure of self-interest that drives buyer and seller to seek their respective economic advantages—the buyer searching for the cheapest market for the good or service he wants, the seller looking for the highest price for the commodity he wants to sell. The other is the continuous pressure of competition that serves to bring buyer and seller together at a point acceptable to both.

Do self-interest and competition alone guarantee the orderly working of the market? As we shall see, they do not. But to understand why not, we must investigate what we mean by an "orderly" market, in the first place.

We have already seen one meaning for the word *orderly* in the extraordinary ability of a market situation to produce equilibrium prices that serve to bring together buyers and sellers in a stable situation of exchange, despite the different directions in which their self-interests propel them.

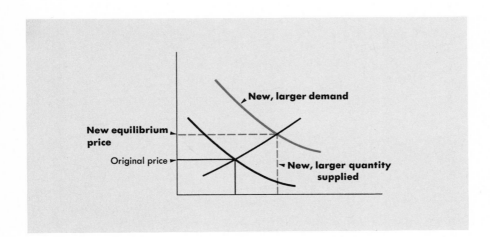

FIG. 22-9

SHORT-RUN
CHANGE IN
EQUILIBRIUM
PRICE

But we cannot confine orderliness to such a static solution. What happens when things change? Suppose, for example, that the demand curve for shoes shifts because the number of people in town has increased. The first effect of this, we know, will be a new, higher equilibrium price for shoes, as Fig. 22-9 shows. Notice also that at the new higher price, the quantity of shoes supplied will also be larger than it was before.

For the short run, this provides an orderly solution to the problem of change. There is now a new level of prices as stable as before, and a new equally stable level of output. (To be sure, there have been shifts in patterns of spending and in incomes that may exert pressures elsewhere on the economy, but we will ignore that for the moment. As far as the market for shoes is concerned, the problem of change has been met in an orderly way.)

In the long run, however, the process of adjustment is apt to be more complicated.* At higher shoe prices, entrepreneurs in other lines are apt to move into the industry, with the result that the whole supply curve of shoes shifts to the right. As a result, shoe prices will again fall (although we cannot tell by how much unless we know more about the costs of the industry). This solution would look like Fig. 22-10.

FIG. 22-10

POSSIBLE
LONG-RUN
CHANGE IN
EQUILIBRIUM
PRICE

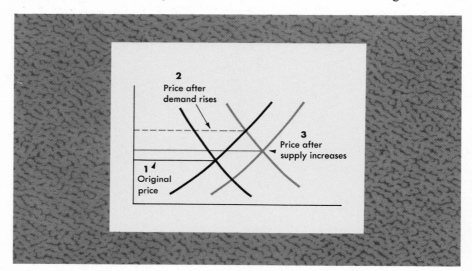

Here are two orderly outcomes to a disturbing change. What would be workable outcomes for a *fall* in demand? In the simplest short-run case, a new lower price and a smaller output. A longer-run solution might entail an exodus of suppliers and of capital equipment from the industry, so that the supply curve moved leftward and prices again recovered from their initial drop. Whichever the solution, *in the end we would again have stable prices and outputs.*

UNSTABLE
SITUATIONS

Now look at a less reassuring case. This time let us suppose that it takes a considerable time before a larger or smaller demand for a product can be met by a larger or smaller output. Since it takes many

---

*The "long run" is not just a vague figure of speech. It means, in cases like this, the time necessary for producers to build new plant and equipment. Conversely, in the "short run," producers are limited to adjusting their supplies as best as they can from their given plant and equipment.

FIG. 22-11

THE COBWEB

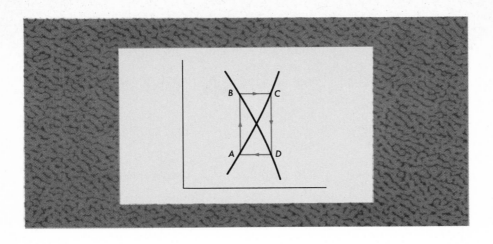

months between planting and harvesting, we will choose Christmas trees as the commodity to illustrate this situation for us.

In Fig. 22-11, we show the supply and demand curves for Christmas trees and imagine that the quantity supplied is initially indicated by point *A* on the supply schedule.

We can see that quantity *A* will sell at price *B*. Figuring that this will be next year's price, tree growers now plant the amount they are willing and able to offer at price *B*—quantity *C*. Alas, when the harvest comes, it is found that quantity *C* will fetch only price *D*. Now the process goes into reverse. Growers will figure that next year's price will be *D*, and they plant amount *A*, since at price *D* the quantity they wish to supply is no more than that. Thereupon, next harvest time, the price goes back to *B*—and around we go. If the supply and demand schedules were differently sloped, we *could* have a so-called cobweb that converged toward equilibrium as we show on the left of Fig. 22-12; and we could also have one that "exploded"—as we can see on the right.

FIG. 22-12

STABILIZING
AND EXPLOSIVE
COBWEBS

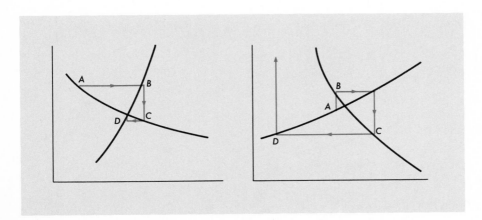

Cobwebs show us that markets need not necessarily produce equilibrium prices. Why, then, do most markets tend toward a resting point and not gyrate or explode like our examples? The answer is that, unlike the cobweb assumptions, most changes in supply are *gradual* and *continuous,* so that prices steadily fall as supplies augment, or rise as they dwindle, thus guiding buyer and seller to the appropriate adjustments.

DESTABILIZING EXPECTATIONS

Cobwebs are something of an anomaly in the market, although they illustrate an important point. But there is another cause of instability that is far from a rarity in the market process. This is the potentially disturbing effect of changes in *expectations* on prices and outputs.

We have already encountered expectations as a central agency of economic change when we looked into the motives behind business investment. But investment, for an ordinary business firm, is not an activity undertaken daily. Hence expectations play their role only when a decision must be made whether to expand operations or not.

Not so, in the marketplace. There expectations affect the decisions of marketers virtually every time a purchase or sale is contemplated. More than that, *as expectations change, the motive of self-interest will drive buyers and sellers in directions that imperil the orderly adjustment of the market process.*

To understand this very important point, you must put yourself in the shoes of a buyer or seller who suddenly faces a change—let us say a fall—in prices. What must *you* do to make the market react to that fall in an orderly way, by reaching a new stable equilibrium price?

The answer is that you must behave as our now familiar diagrams say you will behave. As a buyer, you must respond to the fall in price, by buying a larger quantity. As a seller, you must respond by offering somewhat less to the market. In this way, a new stable point of rest will be reached, either further down the demand curve, or—if some suppliers leave the field after a time—perhaps at a higher price along a new supply curve.

But what will make you behave this way? The answer is that your self-interest will, *if you expect that the price fall will go no further or eventually turn around.* Then as a buyer, it will pay you to take advantage of lower prices, and as a seller it will cut your losses if you now offer less for sale.

Now suppose, however—and here is the case to be thought about carefully—*that you expect prices to keep on falling.* Then what will your self-interest guide you to do? As a buyer, you will *not* buy more, because you figure, quite correctly, that if you hold off, you will get things still cheaper tomorrow. So too, as a seller, you will *not* offer less, because you fear that if you do not sell as much as you can immediately, you will get even worse prices tomorrow. Thus, in place of the stabilizing reactions that bring a halt to price changes or that may even initiate price reversals, *when expectations themselves are based on runaway price changes, they bring about behavior that creates the very situation they fear.* For in these cases, as buyers hold back and sellers rush forward, the imbalance between quantities supplied and demanded will worsen, and prices will fall further.

The same expectational problem can upset a situation with rising prices. Again, an orderly market requires that the price rise be limited or in time turned around. This requires buyers to demand smaller quantities and sellers to offer larger ones. Both will do exactly that if they anticipate that prices will not rise further. But if expectations become "destabilizing," buyers will react to rising prices by *increasing* the quantities they demand, in order to get them at a better price today than tomorrow; and sellers will hold *back their* supplies, hoping to sell them at higher levels tomorrow. As a result, quantities demanded will increase and supplies offered will fall, and the price rise will accelerate rather than come to a halt.

How are such instabilities handled? What effect do they have on the market? In the nature of things, usually they are short-lived affairs that result in wild splurges and busts that disrupt particular markets but do not derange the system as a whole. Sometimes, though, destabilizing reactions can become generalized throughout the whole goods market, as they do when buyers and sellers generally expect an inflation or a depression, and proceed to rush in or hold back in a way that aggravates the very thing they dread. In these cases, destabilizing reactions can be of the gravest importance and must be countered by public policies or public pronouncements aimed at changing peoples' anticipations of the future, so that self-interest will again move them in the direction that brings order rather than disorder.

The narrow line that separates order from disorder, and stability from instability, brings us at the end of this chapter to a final perspective on the subject we are studying. This is the relation of microtheory to the reality of the markets and market behavior in the real world.

Most of us study microtheory in the expectation that it will describe the way markets really are, and therefore serve us in a *predictive* way. And so it will, in a great many cases. When Macy's wants to increase its sales, it lowers its prices in the confident expectation that microeconomics is right when it says that the quantity demanded at lower prices is greater than that at higher ones. Microtheory does describe actual behavior in all "ordinary" cases, and we can and do predict successfully according to its logic.

But sometimes—and these times may be very important—the market does not behave in the way that microtheory describes as the normal case. As we have just seen, this is when expectations turn the normal price-quantity relationships upside down. Yet even in these cases, microeconomics has a special relevance. For it then tells us what behavior would restore normality, and therefore serves as our guidebook when we seek to bring that behavior about. When it is used in this way, price theory is *normative* rather than predictive; that is, it tells us how to achieve a desired state of affairs, rather than what will be the outcome of the existing state, left to itself. Both uses are important, one for understanding how the market system is ordinarily capable of producing an orderly solution to the tasks it performs despite the incredibly complicated stimuli that beat upon it; the other for giving us the necessary knowledge to reintroduce order into the system when, under the influence of wild expectations, it threatens to break down.*

* For the fullest discussion of these problems, see Adolph Lowe, *On Economic Knowledge* (Harper & Row, 1965).

1. Equilibrium prices change when *supply or demand schedules change*. In turn these schedules change when our willingness or ability to buy or sell is altered.

2. *Changes in taste or income* lie behind shifts in demand schedules; behind changes in supply lie *changes in attitudes or costs*.

3. A change in demand (or supply) means a shift of the whole *schedule*. This must be contrasted with changes in the *quantity demanded* (or supplied) which refers to movements *along given curves*.

4. Shifts in demand or supply mean that *different quantities* will be sought or offered *at the same price*.

5. Price elasticities measure the proportionate change in quantities offered or sought when prices change. *Elastic demand* (or supply) means that the *percentage change in quantities demanded* (or supplied) *will be larger than the percentage change in price;* inelastic demand (or supply) means that the percentage quantity change is smaller than the percentage price change.

6. Price elasticities very greatly affect price changes. Price changes will be larger when demand and supply curves are inelastic than when they are elastic. *Elasticities also affect the receipts of the seller or the expenditures of the buyer.*

7. Elasticities reflect the ease or difficulty of *substitution*. Hence, elasticities typically increase over time, as new substitutes are found or as information about them spreads. The *ease of substitution* is an important concept that helps us define what a ''commodity'' is.

8. Substitutes are commodities for which the demand rises when the price of the original commodity rises, and for which demand falls when the price of the original commodity falls.

9. *Complements* are commodities that are technically linked to one another. The demand for one of them therefore falls when the price of the linked commodity rises and rises when the price of the linked commodity falls. This case is just the opposite from that of substitutes.

10. The market is ordinarily a self-correcting and orderly mechanism. By ''orderly'' *we mean that changes in supply or demand produce new, stable prices and outputs*.

11. In some instances, the outcome of the market is not orderly. One of these is the cobweb situation, where the reaction of supply to demand is not continuous. More important is the case *when expectations are not ''stabilizing.''*

12. Orderly markets depend on buyers responding to price falls by buying more, and on sellers responding to price falls by offering less. *When either side expects the price fall to continue, these orderly reactions will not be forthcoming.* The result can be a runaway price situation. (The same effect can occur when price rises are not met by the orderly behavior of decreased buying and increased offering.)

13. Microtheory has two uses. It *predicts* the outcome of market situations when behavior is orderly and normal. When behavior is not orderly, it informs us as to *what kind of behavior is needed to restore stability and order to the market.*

1. What changes in your economic condition would increase your demand for clothes? Draw a diagram to illustrate such a change. Show on it whether you would buy more or less clothes at the prices you formerly paid. If you wanted to buy the same quantity as before, would you be willing and able to pay prices different from those you paid earlier?

2. Suppose that you are a seller of costume jewelry. What changes in your economic condition would decrease your supply curve? Suppose that costs dropped. If demand were unchanged, what would happen to the price in a competitive market?

3. Draw the following: an elastic demand curve and an inelastic supply curve; an inelastic demand curve and an elastic supply curve; a demand curve of infinite elasticity and a totally inelastic supply curve. Now give examples of commodities that each one of these curves might represent.

4. Show on a diagram why elasticity is so important in determining price changes. (Refer back to the diagrams on p. 438 to be sure that you are right.)

5. Draw a diagram that shows what we mean by an increase in the quantity supplied; another diagram to show what is meant by an increase in supply. Now do the same for a decrease in quantity supplied and in supply. (Warning: it is very easy to get these wrong. Check yourself by seeing if the decreased supply curve shows the seller offering less goods at the same prices.) Now do the same exercise for demand.

6. How does substitution affect elasticity? If there are many substitutes for a product, is demand for it elastic or inelastic? Why?

7. Show on a diagram (or with figures) why you would rather be the seller of a good for which demand was elastic, if you were in a market with falling prices. Suppose prices were rising—would you still be glad about the elasticity of demand?

8. By and large, are luxuries apt to enjoy elastic or inelastic demands? Has this anything to do with their price? Can high-priced goods have inelastic demands?

9. Why is demand more apt to become elastic over time?

10. The price of pipe tobacco rises. What is apt to be the effect on the demand for pipes? On the demand for cigars?

11. What is meant by an orderly market? If prices fall, how should you behave as a buyer to insure an orderly market? As a seller? What might make you behave differently?

12. If we faced the prospect of a runaway inflation, what public statement would you advise the President to make?

THE MARKET
FOR FACTORS 23

When we now look around at the hum of transactions on the marketplace, a great deal has become clear to us. We understand how prices are formed for the goods and services that are traded there, why and how those prices change, and the way in which changes are normally kept within bounds so that the system can maintain an orderly flow of output. We understand, as well, how those very same prices serve as rationing agencies for the society, distributing the output of the economy among those who are capable of paying for it.

But who *is* capable of paying for it? Through the market pass men and women in all walks of life, in all occupations, in all degrees of property ownership. Some are rich, some poor; some are very well treated by the market, some pushed aside by its operation. Does micro-economics shed light on this side of the market mechanism? Does it explain the causes of individual riches and poverty?

Anyone who first looks at the realities of income distribution recognizes that there are some aspects of it that microeconomics has little to say about. At one end of the scale of income distribution are the 20 million to 25 million individuals who, as families, have less than $60 a week; or as single individuals, less than $30; at the other end are the few hundred individuals whose incomes from property alone are over a million dollars each. Microeconomics does not enlighten us much concerning the root causes of these extremes of income. As we have already seen at the conclusion of Chapter 8, if we want to understand the reasons for poverty (particularly the poverty of the slums and of racially disprivileged groups), it is sociology and psychology and political science to which we must turn rather than to price theory, while the presence of vast private fortunes requires us to learn about economic history and the workings of the tax laws quite as much as about the operations of the market for factors.

Microeconomics, in other words, will not help us understand the origin or nature of incomes that have relatively little to do with the operation of the market mechanism. Those who are outside the market framework in the enclaves of the slums, or those whose incomes represent the inheritance of great sums won in the past do not fall mainly within the microeconomic examination of the factor market. Yet, about 85 per cent of the population that lies above the poverty line and that enters the market regularly to earn its income, microtheory will tell us a good deal. If it cannot explain for any single individual exactly why his income is what it is, it will at least tell us what kinds of forces bear on his earning capacity, and therefore how changes in the market are likely to affect his economic future.

LAND, LABOR, AND CAPITAL

In a very general way we already know the answer to the problem of individual earnings. Men make what they make because they sell their services in the market for the factors of production and receive as their reward whatever price the market puts on their contribution.

This general explanation serves only to orient us to the more interesting and difficult aspects of the problem, but even the first view makes one important thing clear. It is that the market for factors is essentially one in which *productive services* are bought and sold. When a firm buys Labor, it does not (except in a slave economy) buy an actual human being. It hires him, which is a very different thing, for it means that it buys his labor only, and not the physical asset (his body) in which it is contained.

The same differentiation between productive services and assets must be noticed in the markets for Land and Capital. When a farmer buys land, what he is willing to pay for are the powers of fertility contained in the soil. True, in order to get the use of those powers, he may want to, or have to, buy the real estate itself. In that case, however, the price

of the asset will depend entirely on the *yield* that the land is expected
to produce. Suppose our farmer is hoping that land values themselves
will rise. Then he is acting as a speculator rather than as a farmer and
is betting that the value of the *future services* of that land (where perhaps
he hopes one day a factory will stand) will be so much higher than
the value of its present services, that values will increase. (If he is wrong
in his guess, he will be saddled with very high-priced land for farming—a thought that explains a good deal of the ill-fortunes that have
beset the American farmer from time to time.)

Does a manufacturer also buy the services of capital? Indeed he does.
When he buys a machine, his demand for it will depend on his estimate
of the present and future returns the machine will bring, so that the
price he will offer derives directly from the value of the machine's
services. Suppose he acquires money—that is, suppose he borrows funds
from someone else? In that case the price he will pay for the temporary
use of these funds—the *interest* cost—will certainly be governed by the
present and prospective profits he expects to derive from using the
money he has borrowed.*

Thus, when we speak of the market for factors we are actually talking
about the value of their *services*. Clearly, there is a relation between
the value of those services and the so-called capitalized value at which
the asset itself sells for, but that is a complicated problem into which
we need not go.

THE SUPPLY CURVES OF FACTORS

What do we know about the willingness and ability of the owners of
land, labor, and capital to offer their services on the marketplace at
varying prices for these services?

Except for the important case of labor (about which more in a
moment), we really do not know too much about the shapes of the
individual supply curves of land and capital. Will a man with a certain
capital sum be willing to lend more of it when interest goes up—or
will he lend more when interest declines, so that he can get as much
income as before? In the same way, will a typical landowner increase
or decrease the amount he rents out as rentals rise and fall?

These questions are difficult to answer for the individual. For the
community, however, they are simpler to deal with. A rising price of
land tempts many owners of real estate who were not previously "in

---

* Is money itself a factor of production? Not in the technical sense of the term. Money can buy
factors of production—land, labor, or capital goods—but it does not in itself contribute to output.

the market" to rent out their land or their rooms or their houses. So, too, a rising price of interest attracts savings from people who were formerly not interested in saving, or brings about switches of money from checking accounts into interest-bearing accounts or securities.

THE SUPPLY CURVE OF LABOR

Hence we assume that aggregate supply curves of land and capital have the normal upward rising and rightward sloping shapes. The individual *labor supply curve* is an interesting exception, however. As Fig. 23-1 shows us, it has a curious shape. Up to wage level *OA,* we have no trouble explaining things. The curve simply tells us that normally we will not be willing and able to work longer hours (i.e., to offer more of our labor services within a given time period) unless we are paid more per hour. Economists speak of the *increasing marginal disutility* of labor, meaning by this that the bother and toil of work mounts after a time, so that we will not labor long hours unless the reward per hour rises enough to compensate us for our added pains.

FIG. 23-1

THE BACKWARD-BENDING SUPPLY CURVE OF LABOR

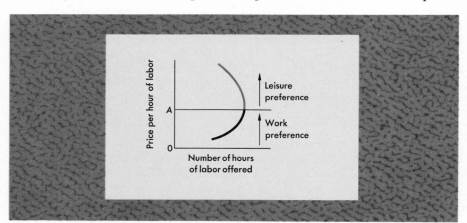

How then do we explain the "backward-bending" portion of the rising curve above wage level *OA?* The answer lies in adding to the rising marginal disutility of labor the falling marginal utility of *income* itself, on the assumption that an extra dollar of income to a man who is making $10,000 is worth less than the utility of an additional dollar when he was making only $5,000.

Together, these two forces explain very clearly why the supply curve of labor bends backward above a certain level. Take a man who has been tempted to work 70 hours a week by wage raises that have finally reached $5 an hour. Now suppose that wages go up another 10 per cent. It is possible of course, that the marginal utility of the additional income may outweigh the marginal disutility of these long hours, so that our man stays on the job or even works longer hours. If, however, his marginal utility of income has reached a low enough point and his marginal disutility of work a high enough point, the raise may bring a new possibility: he may work *fewer* hours and enjoy the same (or a somewhat higher) income as well as additional leisure. For example, as his pay goes up 10 per cent, he may reduce his workweek by 5 per cent.

Backward bending supply curves help explain the long secular trend toward reducing the workweek. Over the last century, weekly hours have decreased by about 40 per cent. Although many factors have converged to bring about this result, one of them has certainly been the desire of individual men and women to exchange the marginal utility of potential income for that of increased leisure.

These psychological considerations behind supply curves are the counterpart of the tastes and desires behind our demand curves. Yet, when we discussed demand, we found technical reasons, such as substitution and complementarity, as well as psychological ones, for the differing positions and shapes of demand curves. Are there technical reasons to be looked for also in explaining the nature of the supply curve of factors?

One such comes immediately to mind: the potential *geographic mobility* of factors. Suppose there is a sudden rise in the demand for labor in a particular locality. We would expect to witness a rise in the price of labor, at least for a while. But then the higher price of labor should serve to attract this factor of production from other areas, and in this way bring about a compensating increase in supply to mitigate or reverse the price rise.

Mobility is thus an enormously important technical condition affecting the shape and position of the labor supply curve. More than a million American families change addresses in a typical year, so that over a decade the normal mobility of the labor force may transport 15 to 20 million people (including wives and children) from one part of the country to another. Without this potential influx of labor, we would expect wages to shoot up steeply whenever an industry in a particular locality expanded, with the result that further profitable expansion might then become impossible.

We also speak of mobility of labor in a vertical sense, referring to the movement from occupation to occupation. Here the barriers to mobility are not usually geographical but institutional (for instance, trade union restrictions on membership) or social (discrimination against the upward mobility of Negroes) or economic (the lack of sufficient income to gain a needed amount of education). Despite these obstacles, occupational mobility is also very impressive from generation to generation, as the astounding changes in the structure of the U.S. labor force (see p. 101) have demonstrated.

Here again the upward streaming of the population in response to the inducement of better incomes makes the long-run elasticities of supply of favored professions much more elastic than they are in the short run. This is a force tending to reduce the differences between income extremes, since the mobility of labor will not only shift the supply curve to the right in the favored places to which it moves (thereby exerting a downward pressure on incomes), but will move the supply curve to the left in those industries it leaves, bringing an upward impetus to incomes. Figure 23-2 shows how this process works.

FIG. 23-2

EFFECT OF LABOR MOBILITY ON RELATIVE WAGES

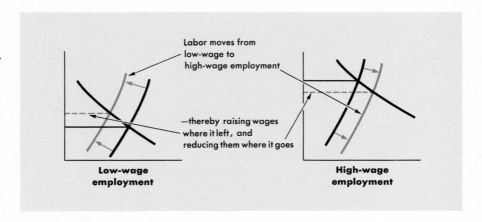

Labor moves from low-wage to high-wage employment

—thereby raising wages where it left, and reducing them where it goes

Low-wage employment

High-wage employment

TIME AND TECHNICAL SPECIFICITY

Mobility is by no means an attribute of labor alone. Take that seemingly least mobile of factors, land. In the very short run, the supply curve of land to any one industry is likely to be very inelastic. For example, if the orangegrowers of Florida want to increase their crop acreage within a year, they may find that it is very difficult to do so. But over a stretch of years, it is surprising how "mobile" the supply of land can become. Acres formerly devoted to other crops can be put into oranges. If the price of oranges goes high enough, it may even pay to reclaim land from urban or industrial use. To be sure, in the long run, the amount of land suitable for orangegrowing is limited, so that at some point the supply curve becomes totally inelastic. But over a very long intermediate range, land is in elastic supply. A graph of the short- and long-run supply curve of land for a given purpose would look like Fig. 23-3.

The example of land makes clear that it is not only geographic mobility but *technical specificity* that determines the responsiveness of a factor to changes in price. This helps explain why *time* plays such an important role in the elasticity of factor supply. Supply curves, like demand curves, are much more elastic over time because the process of redeploying factors from one use to another typically requires efforts that cannot be quickly brought to bear.

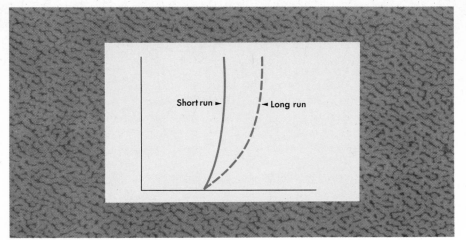

FIG. 23-3

**SHORT-RUN
AND LONG-RUN
SUPPLY OF LAND**

Short run ►   ◄ Long run

Suppose, for instance, that there is a sudden increase in the demand for steel products in the South and a simultaneous fall in the demand for lumber. In the short run there is not very much mobility that can be expected of the capital in these two industries. Lumber mills cannot be used to make steel. Hence the supply of steel mill services would be steeply inelastic. Over a period of time, however, the supply of capital, like land and labor, gains mobility. The lumber mills will eventually become depreciated or will be sold, and funds may thereupon be directed into steel. Or new mills will be built by funds supplied by other parts of the country. In other words, capital goods are usually limited in their flexibility of use, but money capital is tremendously mobile. In this way, the flow of money capital from one industry to another serves the same purpose as the flow of labor between employments, increasing the quantities of the factor where its price is rising, and diminishing it where it is not, in this way acting to keep the discrepancies between industries at a minimum.

RENTS AND INCOMES

The importance of time in bringing about increases in factor supplies alerts us to a very important reason for the existence of very large incomes (and very large disparities of incomes) in the short run. This is the phenomenon of *quasi rent* (sometimes also called *economic rent*).

Quasi rents, or economic rents, are not the same as the rent on land, and the unfortunate fact that the terminology is so close has justifiably aggravated a good many generations of students. Hence let us begin by making a clear distinction between the two. *Rent is the payment we make to induce the owner of land to offer the services on the market.* If we cease to pay rent or pay less rent, the amount of land offered on the market will fall. If we pay more, it will rise. Thus rent is both a payment made to a factor of production to compensate its owner for its services, and an element of cost that must enter into the calculation of selling prices. If a farmer must pay $100 rent to get an additional field he needs, that $100 will clearly be part of the cost of producing his new crop.

Quasi rents or economic rents are different from this. *First, the term applies to all resources—land, labor, or capital goods. Second, it is not a return earned by the factor, in that the payment has nothing to do with inducing the factor to enter the market. Third, quasi rents are not a cost that helps to determine selling price, but they are earnings that are determined by selling price.* Let us see what these differences mean.

An illustration may help clarify the problem. Figure 23-4 shows the supply curve for first-class office space in New York City. Note that over a considerable range there is an unchanging price for space— evidently there is all the space anyone can want up to quantity OX at a price (determined, let us say, by given costs) OA. The receipts of landlords—OA times OX—are real rent in the sense of being a necessary payment for the resources used. If no rent were paid, no space would be offered; as more is paid, more is forthcoming.

FIG. 23-4

QUASI RENT
AND REAL RENT

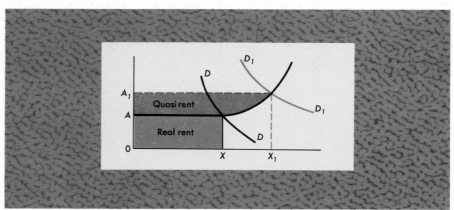

But now suppose that the demand for office space increases from DD to $D_1 D_1$. The supply of space is now stretching thin, and additional first-class offices are hard to get, or expenditures are required to upgrade "second-class" space. The price rises accordingly from OA to OA_1.

Now we must differentiate carefully between rent and quasi rent. As the price rises, the quantity of space increases from OX to OX_1. Hence, for each unit of *additional* space the higher price was needed in order to bring that particular unit onto the market. But the higher price A_1

of space will not just apply to these new units. All "first-class office space" will go up in price. As a result, all the space represented by OX_1 will now receive a rental of OA_1, instead of OA. *But this increase in rental served no purpose in bringing these original units (OX) into the market. The additional revenue comes to them solely because the supply curve of which they are a part has become upward sloping. Thus economic rent or quasi rent is a return that accrues to factors by virtue of their scarcity, not by virtue of their contribution to output.*

Note also that the amount of quasi rent is determined by the selling price. At the margin of the supply curve, where supply and demand meet, the last unit of supply earns its full return (for it would not appear on the market for less). Therefore we call rent, which induces this last unit to come onto the market, *price-determining*. Note, however, that all the previous intramarginal units are the beneficiaries of a situation in which they play no active role at all. The quasi rents they receive are thus *price-determined.* Finally, if the supply curve becomes totally inelastic—if we simply run out of first-class office space—then quasi rents will be received by all units, including the marginal ones, as Fig. 23-5 makes clear.

FIG. 23-5

QUASI RENTS
AND EARNINGS

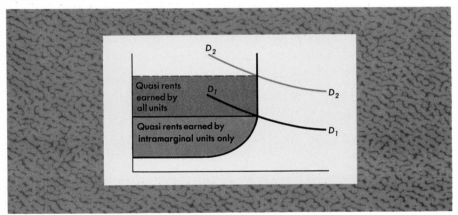

Note carefully that the concept of quasi rent or economic rent is not limited to land. Take car rentals, for instance. Let us suppose that there is a going rate for cars, and that we can rent all the car transportation we need at that price. Suddenly there is a jump in demand, and the rentable car fleet is too small. Rentals will rise. If no additional cars come into the market, the fleet owners will simply enjoy economic rents on all their cars. But quite possibly the rising rental will bring new cars into the supply curve: fleet owners will expand their fleets; or private owners may rent cars on their own. These marginal cars will be earning no more than the return required for their addition to the supply curve, so that we cannot call their earnings an economic rent. But the previous cars, all of which will enjoy the rise in rates, are the sources of quasi rents for their owners.

In the same way the earnings of actors or authors or of the owners of any scarce talent or skill are likely to be partly economic rents. An actress might be perfectly content to offer her services for a fine movie role of $50,000, but she may be able to get $100,000 for the part because of her "name." The first $50,000, without which she would not work, is her wage; the rest is an economic rent. So, too, a plumber who would be willing to work for standard wages, but who gets double because he is the only plumber in town, earns economic rents. And as we shall see in our next chapter, economic rent also helps to explain part of business profits.*

The concept of economic rent gives us a much-needed insight into the cause of income differentials. Anything that inhibits the mobility of factors—anything that impedes their pursuit of self-interest by moving from lower to higher-paid occupations or localities—creates or perpetuates economic rents. Barriers of race and wealth, of patents and initiation fees, of geography and social custom—all give rise to shelters behind which economic rents flourish. Some of these barriers cannot be helped in the short run, and others may simply reflect the occasional virtuosity of a few performers: baseball stars and great painters both earn rents, not because they are the beneficiaries of factor immobility, but simply because they are unique performers whose output (supply curve) is fixed, and who therefore enjoy the rewards of a high demand. Many other rents, however, are the creations of artificial scarcity and can be remedied by removing these man-made barriers.

Economic rents are clearly a source of waste for society, for they reward factors more generously than is necessary for their services. Why do we not remove them, therefore, by price controls? The answer is that price controls would create a situation of "shortage" such as we discussed on p. 429. For instance, a price ceiling to prevent rented cars from earning quasi rents would force us to adopt some rationing system other than price, to determine who would get the available cars. Thus economic rents still serve a purpose in aiding the allocation tasks of the market.

Can we not remove economic rents by taxation? We can indeed, insofar as we are able to tax the *original* receiver of such a rent—for

---

*A good deal of the very high incomes of corporate managers is also probably economic rent. In 1962, according to Robert Averitt (*The Dual Economy*, W. W. Norton, 1968, p. 178) the salaries and bonuses paid to the fifty-six officers and directors of General Motors exceeded the combined remuneration received by the President of the United States, the Vice-President, 100 senators and 435 representatives, 9 Supreme Court Justices, 10 cabinet members, and the governors of 50 states. How could we ascertain whether the incomes of the General Motors executives (or for that matter, of the officials of government) contained economic rent? The answer is simple: we would have to reduce their incomes and observe whether they reduced their output of work. Presumably that is what the income tax tries to do, and as far as we can see, the payment of a portion of income to the government does not seem to affect the supply curve of labor for executive skill. The presumption, then, is that a good part of their income *is* an economic rent, which the income tax siphons off in part.

example, the movie actress or the original fleet owner. In the case of the car owner, however, his fleet may be sold to a second owner. In that case, the price of the cars when sold, will reflect their higher earnings, and the second owner, although presumably making normal profits, will no longer make a quasi rent. Hence economic rents are capturable by taxation only when the taxes affect the original beneficiary.

Inelasticities of supply (and economic rents) help us to explain how some of the price adjustments we studied in the last chapter actually take place on the market.

Take the case of the increase in the demand for eggs. Suppose that housewives, for whatever reason, begin to buy larger quantities of eggs from their grocers. Most grocers will not raise prices, the way we have assumed that they will. Many small businesses price on a "mark-up" basis—adding a fixed percentage to the price charged them by their own suppliers. Hence when the demand for eggs rises, grocers will notice it only because their egg stocks run out, and their response will be only to order more eggs from their wholesale suppliers. Since wholesalers are prepared for such emergencies and have extra stock on hand, the higher demand of housewives can be accommodated without any increase in price, as Fig. 23-6 shows.

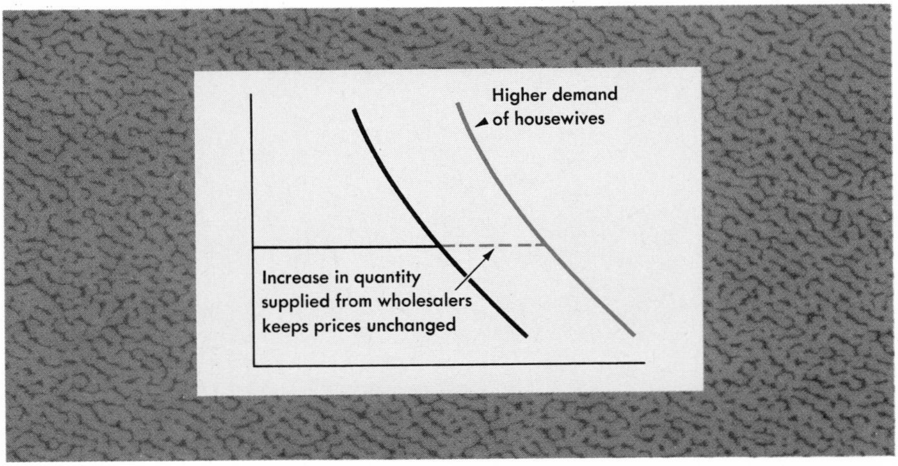

FIG. 23-6

CHANGE IN
DEMAND
AND PRICE:
STAGE I

Higher demand of housewives

Increase in quantity supplied from wholesalers keeps prices unchanged

But now suppose that the higher demand of housewives persists for a week. Grocers keep renewing their larger egg orders, and wholesalers soon find themselves out of stock. They begin to place larger orders with the egg farmers who supply them. Here we encounter a situation with an *inelastic* supply. Presumably the egg farms are already shipping all their eggs, so that orders for additional quantities have no (or very little) effect on production, at least in the short run. Instead, egg prices

FIG. 23-7

**CHANGE IN
DEMAND
AND PRICE:
STAGE II**

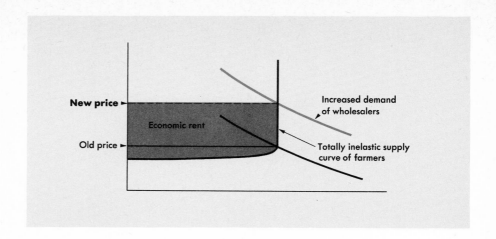

on the farm will now go up, and egg farmers will earn economic rents on their chickens. We can see this in Fig. 23-7.

Note further that once egg prices have been raised by the farmer, costs go up to wholesalers, who must now raise the price of eggs to grocers, who in turn will pass along the boost to consumers. If the housewife then asks the grocer why egg prices are higher, the grocer will answer perfectly correctly that "costs are up." And so they are— because demand is up. The cause of the whole change in prices has been the increased demand of the housewife, but the mechanism for raising prices has involved a series of markets, with the kingpin market that in which supplies were inelastic.*

INCOME DIFFERENCES

**DIRECT
DEMAND
FOR FACTORS**

We have come to understand something of the complex forces at work in the factor market, where the incomes are generated that will buy the wares in the goods market. But our explanation is obviously incomplete until we have looked into the demand for factors as well as their supply.

In part, we already understand the demand for factors from our previous chapters. A portion of the labor force, or of land, or capital

---

* I have adapted this example from Armen A. Alchian and William R. Allen, *University Economics,* 2nd. ed. (Belmont, Calif.: Wadsworth Publishing Co., Inc., 1967), p. 105f., one of the best expositions of the market mechanism I have ever seen.

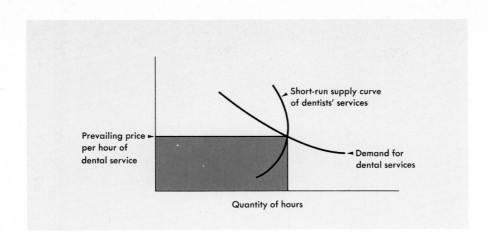

FIG. 23-8

DEMAND AND
SUPPLY FOR
LABOR
CONSUMED
AS A SERVICE

Prevailing price ►
per hour of
dental service

Short-run supply curve
of dentists' services

◄ Demand for
dental services

Quantity of hours

is demanded directly by consumers for their own personal enjoyment, exactly the same as a good or service. This kind of demand for factors of production takes the guise of the demand for lawyers and barbers and servants, or the demand for plots of land for personal dwellings, or the demand for cars and washing machines and the like that consumers hold as personal capital goods. To the extent that factors are demanded directly for such consumer purposes, there is nothing that differs in analyzing the price they receive from the price of any good.

Take the price of dental services, for example, which obviously determines much of the income of dentists. We can draw a demand curve for dentists' services which will certainly slope downward (and will probably be highly income- and price-elastic), and we can draw a supply curve of dentists' services which, in the short run anyway, will probably be fairly inelastic and perhaps backward sloping. Figure 23-8 then shows us how much a typical dentist makes.

Now suppose that we compare the prices per hour of a number of occupations in which demand stems directly from the consumer, and that we find the result to look like Table 23-1.

How can we explain the differentials we find? Part of the answer lies in the differently shaped and located demand curves for these different services. What we must know, in other words, is the amount of money a consumer of a given income level is willing to spend for different quantities of the services of lawyers, dentists, barbers, and

TABLE 23 · 1

	Lawyers	Dentists	Barbers	Baby-sitters
Prices per hour	$10	$8	$4	$1

baby-sitters, and also the elasticities of his demand curves for these various services.

But a knowledge of the pattern of demand only sets the stage. We also need to know why the supply curve of different occupations is differently located and why each has the shape it does. And here we must look in particular for reasons that make some supply curves more inelastic than others over the long run—that is, reasons that prevent labor from moving out of low-paid occupations such as baby-sitting or barbering into high paid ones like dentistry and the legal profession.

We are already alerted to the role that institutional and social barriers to mobility can play here, so that we recognize some of the income differential we see as an *economic rent.* But that is not the whole story. Part of the difference in the pay of two occupations may also reflect *different estimates of its marginal disutility.* Thus dangerous work typically pays a premium over safe work, because the higher disutility of dangerous work requires an additional incentive to attract labor to it. It is interesting to reflect that in a world without any barriers to occupational mobility at all, dangerous and dirty work would command the highest remuneration in the society, and easy and pleasant work the lowest. In such a world coal miners would make much more than lawyers, for there would be a flood of labor into law and a general exodus of labor from coal mining, with the expected effects on the market price of each. That is why one effect of prosperity is to raise the relative wages of "dirty work," since good times tend to improve mobility and thereby enable workers in low-grade occupations to move laterally or vertically to better ones.

But there is still another ingredient in determining the differential of incomes. This is the *investment that different occupations require.* It takes very little training to be a baby-sitter; a fair amount to be a barber; a lot to be a dentist or lawyer. The investment expenditures for these different occupations take the form, mainly, of education—which is one reason why it seems odd to classify education as a consumers' good in the national income accounts (see p. 208n.). The point is that the money that has been poured into a long education must be expected to earn a return: therefore, part of the higher incomes of trained people consists really of interest on the capital sums invested in their careers. Here, of course, is where the underlying distribution of wealth affects the distribution of income, for the sons of the rich have better chances than those of the poor in investing in their own futures.

Finally there is the plain fact of *the differences in human abilities.* Here there is an interesting bit of corroborative evidence. We believe that the distribution of abilities for nearly all skills follows the well-known "bell curve," with a few people at the very low and the very talented ends of the scale and with most people grouped evenly around a middle point, as Fig. 23-9 shows.

Yet when we study the distribution of incomes within a given trade,

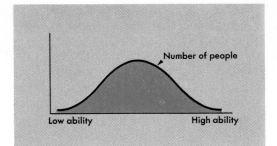

FIG. 23-9

**NORMAL
BELL CURVE**

FIG. 23-10

**"SKEWED" CURVE
OF WAGE
DISTRIBUTION**

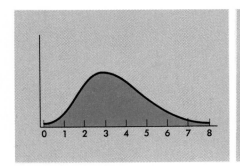

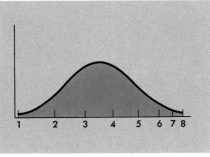

FIG. 23-11

**ARITHMETIC
SCALE (LEFT);
LOGARITHMIC
SCALE (RIGHT)**

we usually find that the distribution is "skewed," with most of the individuals clustered at the low end of the scale (Fig. 23-10).

This would seem to deny the validity of the effect of ability on earnings—until we make an adjustment in the scale on which we plot earnings. Instead of measuring them on a regular arithmetic scale, we must plot them on a *proportional* (logarithmic) scale which gives equal emphasis to equal percentages of changes, as shown in Fig. 23-11. Then we discover that the distribution of earnings does indeed show a bell configuration that reflects the distribution of underlying abilities.*

---

*See E. H. Phelps Brown, *The Economics of Labor* (New Haven: Yale University Press, 1962), pp. 154, 156.

What conclusion can we then reach about the reasons for disparities of incomes, at least in those occupations in which demand stems directly from the consumer? We have seen that these disparities stem from two sets of causes, one transient and one not.

The transient—but very powerful—reasons involve all those social barriers that hinder the movement of factors from low-paid to high-paid employments and uses. Wealth on the one hand, prejudice and discrimination on the other are probably the main roots of differences in the capacity to move vertically or geographically or occupationally. Insofar as these impediments are social, however, they are capable of being by-passed or leveled, and indeed, the history of Western society is marked by a slow but gradual demolition of traditional or hereditary barriers and of a gradual opening of achievement to all talents.

There are, however, still more deep-seated reasons for variations in earnings in the differing marginal disutilities in which the spectrum of occupations is held, and in the differing "innate" abilities of men. We must conclude that in a world where the social barriers of privilege had been finally dismantled, differences would still be observed in the levels of reward, although they would probably be very unlike those we see today.

PROPERTY
INCOME

Note that these explanations involve only labor (in all its range of skills) and do not compare incomes earned by labor and those earned by capital or land. Microtheory can tell us why capital in one industry is more profitable than in another (there may be difficulties in mobility, for instance, that impede the flow of capital into the high-earnings industry), or why land brings different prices in different localities or times. But it cannot compare the income of a landowner or that of a capitalist with an income earned purely from work. This is because the ownership of assets in a market system is not realistically to be pictured as the result of a race for wealth that each generation conducts anew from an impartial starting line, but reflects to a large degree inequalities of private property formed in the past and perpetuated by inheritance.

TABLE 23 · 2

DISTRIBUTION
OF WEALTH
AMONG
HOUSEHOLD
UNITS, 1962

Size of asset holdings	Per cent of households
$ 0 to $ 999	25.8%
1,000 to 4,900	18.0
5,000 to 9,999	16.0
10,000 to 24,999	23.0
25,000 to 49,999	11.0
50,000 to 99,999	5.0
100,000 and over	1.2

For example, the Board of Governors of the Federal Reserve System studied 57.9 million household units and reported on the distribution of wealth among them in 1962 (Table 23-2).

Effectively, one-quarter of the population owned no assets (other than its household goods, the depreciated value of its automobile, and its small bank balance, if any), and another 18 per cent owned little more than the value of its house. At the other end of the scale, however, are the 1 per cent of the most favorably situated households who, according to a study by National Bureau of Economic Research, own at least one-third of all privately owned wealth and up to three-quarters of all corporation stock.[1]

Such figures make it impossible to consider the distribution of the ownership of capital assets as a process for the outcome of which current market activity is to be held responsible. Instead, we are forced to return to the perspective of economic history to evaluate the sources of this wealth and its probable distribution in the future.

One reflection in this regard is interesting and germane, however. When we trace the over-all division of the social product between the share going to property and that going to labor (of all skills), we find the property share to have fallen slightly since the beginning of the twentieth century. In the decade 1900–1909, corporate profits and all interest and rent took 21.4 per cent of national income; in the 1960's, this has slipped to under 19 per cent. These measures are far from exact, but they suggest that the rewards to property are certainly not growing.

DERIVED DEMAND

There remains only the last, but most important aspect of factor pricing—the case in which demand arises not from a consumer but from a firm. What is the difference? It is that when a consumer hires a factor, he does so because of the personal enjoyments—the utilities—he will gain from doing so. No such consideration affects the entrepreneur's decision to buy factor services. When a businessman enters the factor markets, he does so not because land, labor, or capital will afford him increased utilities, but because using those factors will bring profits to his firm. Thus, unlike the direct demand of a consumer, the firm's demand for factors is a *derived demand.*

How much will a businessman pay for a factor's services? We can see that the answer must have something to do with how much the factor is worth to him and that, in turn, this will involve the productivity of the factor—its contribution to output. But these questions bring us to the last of the processes by which the market system is knit together. We are finally ready to invade the precincts of the firm.

[1] See *Survey of Financial Characteristics of Consumers,* Board of Governors of the Federal Reserve System, Washington D.C., 1963, p. 151; and Robert Lampman, *Changes in the Share of Wealth Held by Top Wealth Holders, 1922–1956, op. cit.*

SUMMARY

1. The rewards to land, labor, and capital are paid for the *services* that each offers on the market.

2. The supply curves of individual landowners and capitalists are indeterminate. But the supply curve for land or for capital in the aggregate is probably upward sloping, since a rise in price attracts new land and capital into the market.

3. The labor supply curve is typically *backward bending* above a certain price. This reflects the *increasing marginal disutility of work* and the *diminishing marginal utility of income*.

4. The elasticity of factor supply curves depends in large part on the *mobility of factors*. This is affected by geographical considerations, although more importantly by social and technical barriers and by the unequal distribution of wealth.

5. *Quasi rents* are an important constituent of earnings in all cases in which mobility is impaired. Quasi rents must be differentiated from *rents* in that they have nothing to do with increasing the supply of a factor on the market. Quasi rents can be found in many labor, land, and capital earnings. *Quasi rents are determined by price*, rather than helping to determine the price, as is the case with true rent.

6. Insofar as the demand for factors issues directly from consumers, we can explain factor earnings (incomes) by simple supply and demand analysis. In this case, however, we must note the following causes for differentials in incomes:
   - *Different marginal disutilities* of different employments
   - The different *amounts of investment* required for different occupations
   - Underlying differences in *abilities*

7. *Property incomes* cannot be compared directly with factor incomes. There is some evidence that property incomes are slowly declining as a claimant on national income.

8. Entrepreneurial demand for labor, unlike that of consumers, is *derived demand*. It depends on the expected profitability of hiring labor, not on the utilities to be enjoyed from it.

1. When a suburban homeowner buys "land," what services is he actually buying? When he hires domestic help, what services is he buying? When he borrows money from a bank?

2. Suppose you had $10,000 and that you had invested half of it at 6 per cent. If the rate of interest went up to 7 per cent would you be tempted to invest more? Or the same? Or might you think that it would be wise to invest a little less, since your income was now higher? Are there reasonable arguments for all three?

3. What do you think the supply curve of executive labor looks like? Is it backward bending? Would you expect it to be more or less backward bending than the supply curve of common labor? Why?

4. What do you think are the main impediments to factor mobility in the labor market? Location? Education? Discrimination? Wealth? How would you lessen these barriers?

5. How technically "specific" is a printing press? A lathe? In the long run, how can the capital in a printing press be moved from one use to another?

6. Exactly what is meant by rent? Does rent have something to do with the quantity of land offered on the market? What is quasi rent? If quasi rents go up, does this mean that more of a good is being offered?

7. What is meant by saying that rent is price-determining and that quasi rent is price-determined? Show the answer in a diagram.

8. Trace the consequences of a rise in the demand for beef on the price of beef. What have the various elasticities of supply of different stages in beef production to do with the eventual effect of a rise in demand on price?

9. Draw a supply and demand diagram for domestic help. What changes in demand or supply might affect domestics' wages? To what extent would you explain the relatively low level of domestics' wages in terms of marginal disutility? Lack of wealth? Investment?

10. In a world without any disparities in inherited wealth, what trends would you expect to find in the occupational differences in income? Would any income differences remain among occupations? Within occupations? What would each be traceable to?

24 THE FIRM IN THE FACTOR MARKET

From our survey of economic history we already know something of the variety of businesses that make up the American economic scene, and in particular of the predominating importance of the great corporation. But in this first look into the workings of the firm we shall be dealing with a kind of enterprise very different from that giant corporation whose powers and whose relative exemption from price competition interested us so much in Part One. Here we shall concern ourselves with the other end of the business scale, learning how very small businesses with little or no power manage to survive, exposed to the full blast of competition.

There are good reasons for this initial limitation of our investigation. First, the kind of small, highly competitive firm we will describe exists as an important reality on the business scene, and we must understand how such firms do in fact survive and what role they play. Second, even the biggest and most monopolistic firms bear certain family resemblances to small competitive ones, so that our study will lay the groundwork for a later analysis of very big business. And last, until we have grasped how the market mechanism works with small competitive firms, we will not be in a position to understand and to measure the difference that large firms and imperfect competition add to the system.

In addition to limiting our scrutiny to markets made up of small, competitive firms, we will add two assumptions about the behavior of these firms—one of them realistic and one perhaps not. The unrealistic assumption is that our firm acts *intelligently and rationally* in the pursuit of its goals. Since the world is littered with the bankruptcies that result from mistaken calculations and foolish decisions, this assumption may strain our credulity, but at least it will do no violence to understanding the *principles* of the market system.

Second, we will assume that our firm is motivated by a desire to *maximize its profits in the short run*—that is, day by day. Later, when we study the operations of very large firms we shall have to ask whether this maximizing assumption makes much sense in their case. But when we deal with the "atomistic" competition of small firms, the assumption stands up very well *because as we shall see, it is only by trying to maximize short-term profits that small firms manage to survive at all.* This gives to microtheory the same two-sided relevance that we noted in the case of its description of the competitive market. Microtheory tells us how small firms actually do behave—and thereby enables us to make predictions about the way the market system works—and it also serves as a goal-oriented description of how small business firms *should* conduct their affairs if they hope to survive.

ECONOMICS OF THE FIRM

What are the problems and pressures that beset the small firm in its fight for survival? They will become gradually clear to us as we move along. But at the outset one problem attracts our attention not only because it is unresolved from our last chapter, but because it bears directly on the ability of the firm to make profits. This is how a firm decides how many factors to hire and in what proportions to combine them.

Suppose, for example, that we are considering opening a bookstore. The first question that we will have to answer is how much land, labor, and capital we will need in the form of space that we rent, help that we hire (including ourselves), and equipment or inventories of books that we must have. No matter what business we are in, there will be

THE PROBLEM
OF SCALE

some minimum size below which we know we cannot operate profitably. A bookstore may be very small, but it has to have *some* reasonable number of books on the premises, and it must have at least one person around to sell them. If we were in a somewhat more technical line of work—say, manufacturing plastic parts—we would base the minimum size of our plant on the machinery that would be essential for our operation. If we were in a highly complex mass assembly business, such as typewriters, the *smallest* efficient plant might run into an investment of millions of dollars and would require a work force of thousands of people. But that would take us well out of the world of atomistic competition to which we are still devoting our attention.

In other words, the first decision about the hiring of factors involves the choice of *scale,* and that choice, it can be seen, is basically determined by the prevailing technology. In every kind of business there is usually a minimum size of establishment below which it is impossible to operate competitively because one of the factors would not be present in large enough quantity to allow certain technical efficiencies to be realized. This fact, in turn, arises because factors are not infinitely divisible for all uses—there is always a minimum amount of one factor that must be applied if a certain output is to be secured. In agriculture, for example, this minimum may be established by requirements of acreage; in manufacturing it is likely to be set by the irreducible requirements of the needed capital equipment. It is simply not possible to build an efficient automobile plant that will fit into a cigar store or to raise cattle profitably in a suburban back yard.

FACTOR MIX

But once the minimum size of our enterprise has been established, we know the amount of only *one* factor we will have to hire if we are to open shop. Suppose that the limiting factor is land and that we decide that the smallest profitable bookstore would have to have at least 500 square feet of space. There is still the question of how much of the other factors we are to add to the predetermined factor of land. Assuming that we had $10,000 to spend, where should we put our money—into a large inventory of books and a small sales and office force (perhaps only ourselves), or into two or more salespeople working with a smaller inventory of books?

This question involves us not in a determination of the scale of the enterprise, but of the *mix of factors* that will be most profitable within a given scale. To go back to our plastics manufacturer for a moment, assume that he decides what the minimum investment in machinery will be for a profitable operation. He will then have to decide whether to spend relatively more money on land or on labor. Perhaps he has a choice of building his plant in two areas—one in which land is expensive but labor abundant, another where land is very cheap but labor is dearer. Which should he choose?

The answer to these problems takes us back to consider an attribute of the factors of production that we have been able to overlook until now, because we were considering their output as if it were a consumers' good to be directly enjoyed. *When a factor is being hired by a firm, the firm considers the usefulness of that factor as a means to an end*—the end being the output of its own product, be that the sale of books or plastics. Therefore it is the *profitability of the factor* that interests the businessman who is considering which factor to hire. If land will produce more business for him than labor, he will hire land. If a sales clerk will sell more books for us than having a larger inventory of books, we will hire a sales clerk. The question is, how do we know which factor will be the better buy?

LAW OF VARIABLE PROPORTIONS

As we shall see, this is by no means a simple question to answer, for many considerations bear on the decision to hire a factor or not, or on the choice of one factor over another. But in the center of any businessman's calculations lies one extremely important fact to which we must now pay close attention. This is the physical productivity of different factors—their capacity to increase his output—and more than that, *the changing physical productivity that results from combining different amounts of one factor with fixed amounts of the others.*

Let us begin with a case that is very simple to imagine. Suppose we have a farmer who has a farm of 100 acres and a certain amount of equipment, and no labor at all. Now let us picture our farmer first hiring one man, then a second man of the same abilities, then a third, and so on. Obviously, the output of the farm would grow. What we want to find out, however, is whether it will grow in some clearly defined pattern that we can attribute to the changing amounts of the factor that is being added.

What would such a curve of productivity look like? Assume that one man, working the 100 acres alone as best he can, produces 1,000 bushels of grain. A second man, helping the first, should be enormously valuable, because two men can begin to specialize and divide the work, each doing the jobs he is better at and saving the time formerly wasted by moving from one job to the next. As a consequence, output may jump to 3,000 bushels. Since the *difference* in output is 2,000 bushels, we speak of the *marginal productivity* of labor, when two men are working, as 2,000 bushels. Note that we should not (although in carelessness we sometimes do) speak of the marginal productivity of the second *man.* Alone, his efforts are no more productive than those of the first man: if we fired the first man, worker number 2 would only produce 1,000 bushels. What makes the difference is the jump in the combined productivity of the *two* men, once specialization can be introduced. Hence we should speak of the changing marginal productivity of *labor,* not of the individual.

It is not difficult to imagine an increasing specialization taking place with the third, fourth, and fifth man, so that the addition of another unit of labor input in each case brings about an output larger than was realized by the average of all the previous men. Remember that this does not mean the individual factor units themselves are more productive. *It means that as we add units of one factor, the total mix of these units plus the fixed amounts of other factors, forms an increasingly efficient technical combination.* *

We call the range of factor inputs, over which average productivity rises, a range of *increasing average returns.* It is, of course, a stage of production that is highly favorable for the producer. Every time he adds a factor, efficiency rises. (As a result, as we shall see in our next chapter, costs per unit of output fall). The rate of increase will not be the same, for the initial large marginal leaps in productivity will give way to smaller ones—that is, *marginal* output is actually falling. But the over-all trend of productivity, whether we measure it by looking at *total* output or at *average* output per man, will still be up. And all this keeps on happening, of course, because the factor we are adding has not yet reached its point of maximum technical efficiency with the given amount of the other factors.

<table>
<tr><td>DIMINISHING
RETURNS</td><td>Then our farmer notices a disconcerting phenomenon. At a certain point, average productivity no longer rises when he adds another man. Total output will still be rising with the addition of more men, but a quick calculation reveals that the last man on the team has added so little to the productivity of the farm that *average* output per man has actually fallen.†</td></tr>
</table>

What has happened has been that we have overshot the point of

---

*With each additional man, the proportions of land, labor, and capital are altered, so that the change in the level of output should rightfully be ascribed to new levels of efficiency resulting from the interaction of *all three factors*. But since labor is the factor whose input we are varying, it has become customary to call the change in output the result of a change in "labor productivity." If we were altering land or capital alone, we would call the change the result of changes in their productivities, even though, as with labor, the real cause is the changing efficiency of *all* factors in different mixes.

†It is also possible to speak of the onset of diminishing returns as soon as *marginal* product begins to fall, even though average productivity is rising. Usage varies; the underlying relationships do not.

maximum technical efficiency, and that labor is now beginning to "crowd" the land or the equipment. Opportunities for further specialization have become nonexistent—worse yet, additional labor is forced to perform so inefficiently that the *average* output of the whole labor force is pulled down. We *call this state of falling average performance a condition of decreasing average returns.* As the words suggest, we are getting back less and less as we add the critical factor—not only from the "marginal" man, but from the average efforts of all the men. (Now, of course, costs will be rising per unit.) If we went on foolishly adding men, eventually the addition of another worker would add nothing to total output. In fact, the next worker might then so disrupt the factor mix that *total* output would actually fall and we would be in a condition of negative returns.

This changing profile of physical productivity is one of the most important generalizations that economics makes about the real world. It will help us to think it through if we now study the relationships of marginal and average productivity and of total output in Table 24-1.

TABLE 24 · 1

Number of men	Total output	Marginal productivity (change in output)	Average productivity (total output ÷ no. of men)
1	1,000	1,000	1,000
2	3,000	2,000	1,500
3	5,500	2,500	1,833
4	7,800	2,300	1,950
5	9,800	2,000	1,960
6	11,600	1,800	1,930
7	13,100	1,500	1,871
8	14,300	1,200	1,790

All three columns are integrally related to one another, and it is important to understand the exact nature of their relationships. The column for marginal productivity shows the *change* in output as we add each man; it is therefore derived by subtracting the total output at one level of employment (say the 7,800 bushels reaped by 4 men) from the output of the previous level of 5,500 bushels. Or if we wish, we can think of the total output column being obtained by adding up the successive marginal increments that come with additional personnel. The average productivity column is, of course, simply the total output divided by the number of men.

One thing must be carefully studied in this example. Note that marginal productivity begins to diminish with the fourth man, who adds only 2,300 bushels to output, and not 2,500 as did his predecessor. Average productivity, however, rises until we hire the sixth man, because the fifth man, although producing less than the fourth, is still more productive than the average output of all four men. *Thus marginal productivity can be falling while average productivity is still rising.*

The three curves in Fig. 24-1 actually all show the same thing, only in different ways. The top curve shows us that as we add men to our farm, output at first rises very rapidly, then slowly, then actually declines. The marginal productivity curve shows us *why* this is happening to total output: as we add men, the contribution they can make to output changes markedly, at first each man adding so much that average output grows rapidly; thereafter marginal output falling but average output still rising; finally each man adding so little that he actually pulls down the average that obtained before his hiring. And the average curve, as we have just indicated, merely sums up the over-all output in an arithmetical way by showing us what the average person contributes to it.

FIG. 24-1

**THE LAW OF
VARIABLE
PROPORTIONS**

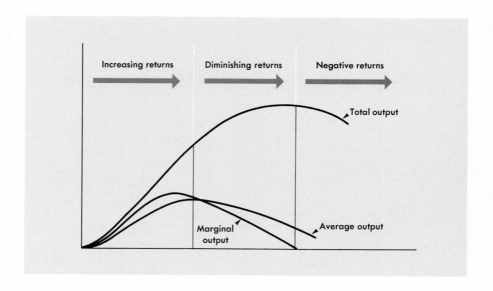

Put into the form of a generalization, we can say that *as we add successive units of one factor to fixed amounts of others, the average output of the units of the variable factor will at first rise and then decline. We call this the law of variable proportions or the law of diminishing returns, or we can simply talk about it as the physical productivity curve.*

**THE LAW
REVIEWED**

The generalizations of the law of variable proportions constitute one of the key insights that a study of microeconomics gives us into the workings of the real world. Hence let us be certain that we understand exactly what the law says and implies.

1. The law of variable proportions describes what happens to physical productivity when we add units of one factor and *hold the others constant.* As we added labor in the example above, we did not also add land or capital. Had we done so, there would have been no way of ascribing changes in output to the addition of one factor rather than the other.

2. The law applies to the additions of *any* factor to fixed quantities of the others. Suppose that we had started with a fixed amount of labor and capital and had added successive acres of land. The first acre would not have been very productive, for we would have had to squeeze too much labor and capital into its area. The second acre would have permitted a better utilization of all three factors, and so "its" marginal productivity would have been much higher. But in time the addition of successive units of land would pass the point of optimum mix, until another acre would add so little yield that the average production of all acres would be pulled down. And the same pattern of increase, diminution, and final decrease would of course attend the addition of doses of capital—say successive bags of fertilizer or additional tractors—to a fixed amount of land and labor.

3. Unlike many other "laws" in economics, the law of variable proportions has nothing to do with behavior. The actions of men on the marketplace, or the impulses or restraints of utility and disutility, play no role in diminishing returns. *Essentially, the law expresses a constraint imposed by the laws of nature.* If there were no such constraint, we could grow all the food required by the world in a single acre, or even in a flowerpot, simply by adding more and more labor and capital.

Economics, as we have said before, is the study of how men seek to provision themselves, of how society solves the universal problem of production and distribution. Through most of this book we have been concerned with the *social* aspects of this problem—with the difficulties in arranging the institutional and behavioral requirements for survival and growth. It is well to bear in mind that nature also imposes its conditions on man, and nowhere more visibly than in the diminishing returns that ultimately hamper all his efforts.

This technological or physical reason behind the law of diminishing returns is related to that behind the law of increasing costs that we met on p. 411. Here we are interested in learning why the marginal output of a given good decreases as a single factor is added to given quantities of other factors; previously, we wanted to know why the marginal output of a given good decreased as we shifted *all factors* from other uses to produce that good. In both cases the critical element lies in the fact that technology or nature decrees a certain "mix" as the optimal resource combination for making any good. When we move factors from one use to another, sooner or later we encounter one factor that will become scarce relative to the others. From that point on, additional units of the other factors cannot be employed at maximal efficiency, and marginal output must fall.

MARGINAL REVENUE AND MARGINAL COST

But now we must get back to our point of interest—the firm seeking to hire factors to its own best advantage. Is a knowledge of factor productivity all a businessman needs? To revert to our first illustration, suppose we knew that a single salesperson in our bookstore had a productivity of (i.e., could sell) 5 books a day. Would that alone tell us if we should hire him?

The question answers itself. Before we can hire the clerk or any other factor, we have to know two other things: (1) *we have to know what the unit of the factor will cost,* and (2) *we have to know how much revenue our firm will get as a result of hiring that unit of the factor.*

For instance, if the price of a salesperson is $6,000 and if we think his activity as a salesperson will add 5 books a day to our sales, at an average price per book of $5, then if he works for 250 days, he will bring in revenues of $6,250 (5 × $5 × 250). Obviously it will pay to hire him.* On the other hand, if his productivity were less—if he sold only 4 books per day—then the revenues from hiring him would be only $5,000 (4 × $5 × 250), or $1,000 less than his wage. He would be a dead loss.

Our illustration enables us to see the general process by which entrepreneurs make their hiring decisions, and also enables us to see how productivity fits into those decisions. Whenever we are considering hiring any factor, we compare in our minds two sums. On the one hand, any increase in the units of the factor we hire will raise our cost. On the other hand, that same increased use of one factor should increase our output, and therefore our revenue. The conclusion is very simple. *If the marginal revenue expected from the addition of a unit of a factor is greater than the marginal cost of a unit of the factor, it pays to hire it. If the marginal cost is greater than the marginal revenue, it does not.* (Furthermore, it may even raise our profits if we fire factors, provided

---

*For simplicity's sake, we assume that the bookstore gets its books free. We will take up the problem of business costs in our next chapter.

that in each case we reduce our costs by more than we reduce our revenues.)

Just where does productivity fit into this picture? The answer is that productivity tells us how much additional physical output we can get from hiring additional units of a factor. Thus, if we know what the unit of the factor will cost and what the sales price of our output will be, it is productivity that determines whether a factor will be worth its hire or not.

Let us see how this actually works in practice. In the schedules below we go back to our farm, this time armed with two new pieces of information. We know that labor costs $4500 per man and that a bushel of wheat sells for $2.50. (Later we will look into *how* we know these things, but now we can take them for granted.) Our farm schedule of marginal cost and marginal revenue therefore looks like Table 24-2.

TABLE 24 · 2

Number of men	Marginal cost per man @ $4,500	Marginal output per man (from Table 24-1)	Marginal revenue per man (output × $2.50)	Marginal profit or loss per man
1	$4,500	1,000	$2,500	− 2,000
2	4,500	2,000	5,000	500
3	4,500	2,500	6,250	1,750
4	4,500	2,300	5,750	1,250
5	4,500	2,000	5,000	500
6	4,500	1,800	4,500	0
7	4,500	1,500	3,750	− 750
8	4,500	1,200	3,000	− 1,500

What does our table tell us? Our first man seems to be very unprofitable, for he costs us $4,500 and brings in only $2,500. We suspect, however, that he is so inefficient because he is trying to spread his one unit of labor over the whole farm. The addition of a second man confirms our suspicions. He also costs us $4,500, but brings in $5,000. (Remember it is not the second man himself who does so, but the two men working together who give rise to an increase in revenues of that amount.) The third and fourth and fifth men also show profits, but when we reach the sixth man, the law of diminishing returns brings its decisive force to bear. The sixth man is unable to increase the productivity of the team by more than $4,500, which is just his hire. It is not worthwhile to engage him.

Are we certain that hiring five men will really maximize the profits of the farm? We can find out by adding up our *total* costs and our *total* revenues and figuring our profit at each level of operation.* (We get the totals by adding each marginal increment to the preceding sum of costs or revenues.)

TABLE 24 · 3

Number of men	Total cost of men	Total revenue	Profit (total revenue less cost)
1	$ 4,500	$ 2,500	− $2,000
2	9,000	7,500	− 1,500
3	13,500	13,750	250
4	18,000	19,500	1,500
5	22,500	24,500	2,000
6	27,000	29,000	2,000
7	31,500	32,750	1,250
8	35,000	35,750	750

As we can see, our best profit comes with the hire of 5 men. The addition of a sixth does us no good. A seventh lowers our net income —not for any lack of skill or effort on his part, but because with seven men the mix of labor and the fixed amounts of other factors is no longer so efficient as before.

We can also see now how neatly the physical productivity curve ties together marginal cost and marginal revenue. For three things would entice us to hire the sixth or even the seventh man.

1. *A fall in cost.* If wages dropped to any figure under $4,500, our sixth man will immediately pay his way. By how much would they have to drop to make it worthwhile to hire the seventh man? Marginal revenue when seven men are working is only $3,750. The wage level would have to drop below that point to bring a profit from seven men.

2. *A rise in the price of output.* If the demand for grain increased, and the price of grain went to $3, our calculations would change again. Now the sixth man is certainly profitable: adding him now brings a marginal revenue of 1,800 bushels × $3 or $5,400, far above his wage. Is the seventh man profitable? His physical productivity is 1,500 bushels. At $3 per bushel he is not quite worth hiring. At $3.01 he would be.

3. *An increase in productivity.* If a change in skills or techniques raises the physical output of each man, this will also change the margin of profitable

*We are really fooling ourselves when we "check" on our former calculations about marginal changes by looking at the totals. For the totals are themselves nothing but the sum of the marginal changes! As long as each man brings *some* addition to revenue, large or small (that is, so long as marginal revenue is larger than marginal cost when that man is hired), then the total of all revenues must be growing larger too. When we add up the marginal contributions, we measure each different-sized contribution. We should not consider it surprising that the whole contains the sum of what we put into it.

factor use. Any small increase will lead to the employment of the sixth man.*

We have talked, so far, as if an entrepreneur had only one "scarce" factor, and as if his only task were to decide how much of that factor to add. But that is not quite the problem faced by the businessman. He has to make up his mind not only *whether* to add to his output at all, but *which* factor to hire in order to do so.

How does a businessman make such a choice? How would we choose between adding a salesclerk to our bookstore or adding inventory, or how would our farmer decide between hiring labor or spending the same sum on capital or land? Suppose that our farmer has already hired four men to work for him and has also rented a certain amount of land and used a certain amount of capital. Now when he thinks about expanding output he needs to know not only how much the addition of another man will yield him, but *what the alternatives are.*

They might look like this:

1. He can hire a fifth worker for $4,500 who will, as we know, bring about an increase of $5,000 in revenues.

2. He could spend the same amount on land, renting, let us say, 10 acres that would increase his output by 2,100 bushels, worth (@ $2.50) $5,250.

3. For the same outlay he could engage the services of a tractor that would add 2,200 bushels a year to his output, worth $5,500.

The problem is not difficult. If the farmer compares marginal costs and marginal revenues of his three alternatives, he will find his course.

Factor	Marginal cost	Marginal revenue	Profit
Additional man	$4,500	$5,000	$ 500
Additional land	4,500	5,250	750
Additional capital	4,500	5,500	1,000

Obviously, the tractor is the best buy, and he should spend his money on tractors, not on land or labor, as long as the relative prices and productivities of the three factors remain unchanged.†

---

*We can see that an increase in productivity leads to an increase in employment in the case of an individual firm. But we cannot generalize that an increase in the productivity of *all* workers will lead to increase in total employment. That depends on what happens to aggregate demand or to the structure of employment. This is a problem we studied in macroeconomics (see p. 359f.).

†Ideally, an economist would wish to compare the marginal productivities of much smaller amounts of these three factors; i.e., an hour's worth of labor or a very small parcel of land or a day's use of a tractor. We have dealt in big chunks because factors often do come in indivisible units, and because this is the way the problem usually looks in the business world.

But will factor prices remain unchanged? The question brings us back to the answered query of our last chapter: how are factor prices determined when firms, rather than consumers, provide the demand? We have taken a long detour into productivity because we could see that productivity was inextricably entangled in the firm's calculations as it bid for factors. But it was just this, the outcome of this bidding process, that we wanted to track down in the first place. Now we should be in a position to do so. We must begin by examining a critical supposition about factor pricing that we have already introduced very quietly. You will remember we assumed that the farmer was able to bid for additional land, or for any other factor, *without thereby affecting its price.*

Why were we able to make this assumption? The answer follows from the premise of atomistic firms from which we started. The amount of land or labor or capital that such a small firm can add to its operations is so insignificant a portion of the total supply of that factor that the individual firm's demand does not affect the price of the factor at all. If there are 100,000 young women looking for sales work in New York City, the addition of a few salespeople in any single business will not change the going price for salespeople at all. Neither will a small farmer's demand, by itself, alter the rent of land, nor will one firm's demand for capital change the rate of interest.

For one small firm, the supply curve of any factor looks like a horizontal line. It is infinitely elastic, because a firm can engage all of the factor it requires at the going price without affecting the price of that factor at all.

FIG. 24-2

**SUPPLY CURVE
TO ALL FIRMS VS.
SUPPLY CURVE
TO ONE FIRM**

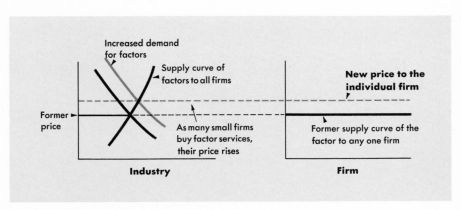

But this is not the case when many small firms all begin to demand the same factor. If all stores are looking for sales help, the salaries of salespeople will rise. If many farmers seek land or capital, rentals or interest rates (or the prices of capital goods) will go up. As a result, each individual firm will find that the going price for the factor in general demand has a mysterious tendency to rise, as Fig. 24-2 shows.*

Supply and demand sets the prices of factors, just as it does when consumers buy them, but now the demand is exercised by a whole cluster of firms or by an industry. The individual firm has no impact on the market and no choice but to accept its price as given.

We can now finish our whole analysis of the pricing of factors. We remember that in our last example it was profitable for farmers to buy tractors, rather than land or labor. Now we must suppose that many farmers, finding themselves in the same situation, all bid for tractors. The result, of course, is that tractor prices will rise. The consequence of this, plainly, is that tractors become less profitable to the farmer, compared with land or labor, than they were originally. Suppose, for example, that the price of tractor hire goes up to $5,000; so that for an outlay of $4,500 a farmer can now afford to get a tractor on his place only four days out of the week instead of five (or if he buys a tractor, he has to get a smaller model). Since the expenditure of $4,500 will now buy fewer tractor inputs, the tractor's addition to output will also decrease. Let us imagine that tractor output falls by almost one-fifth with the cut in tractor hours. Then $4,500 of expenditure will bring an increase in output of 1,800 bushels instead of 2,200. At $2.50 per bushel, the marginal revenue from using a tractor now amounts to only $4,500. There is no net profit in using tractors at all!

Actually things will work out in less dramatic fashion than this. As tractor prices rise (and as the marginal productivity of tractors falls, owing to their more intensive use), the profit advantage between tractors and land will narrow. At a certain point land will be just as attractive to farmers as tractors. Thereafter, since both land and tractors are still better buys than labor, the price of *both* land and tractors will continue to rise. Again as a result, the profit difference between them and labor will narrow until the same profit will be derived from an equal expenditure on any of the three factors. Now, finally, the prices of *all three* factors may rise if there is still a profit obtainable from using them. Only when rising prices and falling marginal productivities make it no longer profitable to seek any more factors at all will the bidding stop and factor prices stabilize.

Now perhaps we can stand back and review the process.

1. *An entrepreneur who makes a profit in a competitive market will seek to expand his output to increase that profit. This will require hiring additional factors.*

*The diagram does not emphasize a very important difference in *scale*. One inch along the horizontal axis of the industry diagram on the left may represent 100,000 units. The same inch along the firm's horizontal axis would then stand for only a few hundred units.

2. *When deciding which factor to hire, an entrepreneur will compare the dollar return he will get from an equal dollar outlay on different factors. The size of these relative returns will depend on the relative costs of the various factors and on their different physical productivities.*

3. *All entrepreneurs in a given industry will normally discover that one factor is more profitable than any other, at a given time, and all will concentrate their demand on that factor. As a result, the price of that factor will rise; and as more of it is used, its marginal productivity will decline. Hence its profit advantage over the other factors declines.*

4. *As the result of continuously bidding for the most profitable factor, the profitability of all factors will be equalized. There will then be no advantage to spending a given sum on land instead of labor, or on capital instead of land, and so on. Instead, all factors will now be equally sought.*

5. *Finally, all factors will be bid up in price until there is no longer any profit to be had from using any more of any of them. At that point the expansion of the industry stops, and the prices of factors remain steady.*

THE MARKET SOLUTION TO DISTRIBUTION

Perhaps we can already see, from this brief capsule of the factor-hiring process, the remarkable nature of the market solution to the problem of distribution. For our bidding process has not only eliminated any advantages of profit enjoyed by one factor over another, but it also has led to three striking results.

1. *It has eliminated exploitation.*

We have seen that as long as the marginal revenue from the employment of any factor exceeds its marginal cost, firms will bid for that factor. As a result, its price will rise (and its productivity may fall) until marginal revenue and marginal cost are equal. Suppose, for example, that the value of labor's marginal product was $6,000 but that labor was paid only $5,000. The possibility of making $1,000 profit per worker would lead to a general demand for labor, and the increased use of labor would lead to a fall in its marginal product. Together, competitive bidding and falling marginal productivity would bring a new price for labor—let us say $5,800—at which *MC* and *MR* would be equal. Labor would thereupon be paid a wage equal to the value of its marginal product.

Two observations must be made about this result. First, it is important to stress that the elimination of exploitation depends on the existence of a perfect market. Prejudice, ignorance, inequalities of starting point, or other barriers will prevent the auction for factors from taking its full effect. Hence, in the real world, pockets of exploitation certainly exist despite the existence of the market. Second, a world in which labor is paid the full value of its marginal product may not necessarily be a world that accords with our sense of moral equity. At the end of this chapter, we shall look more carefully into the question of whether the outcome of the market process is to be judged as "just."

2. *At the end of the bidding process, all factors will be priced so that their relative rewards will mirror their relative marginal productivities.*

This is easiest to see by means of an illustration. Let us suppose that we have two grades of labor—skilled and unskilled—and that skilled labor produces twice as much per hour as unskilled labor in a given industry. Further, we will suppose that unskilled labor is paid $1 per hour, whereas skilled labor is paid $3 per hour.

Which would an entrepreneur hire, assuming that he could freely substitute one kind of labor for the other in his plant? For $1 outlay on unskilled labor he gets, let us say, 10 units of output. For $3 outlay on skilled labor he gets twice that, or twenty units. Thus a unit of output produced by unskilled labor costs 10¢ and a unit produced by skilled labor costs 15¢.

Of course our employer will use unskilled labor. So will all employers. The price of unskilled labor will accordingly rise. At $1.50 an hour, its ten units of output will now cost 15¢ each, the same as skilled labor. At this point, employers no longer prefer unskilled labor. Its price will now settle down. Notice, however, that the price of the two grades of labor is now exactly proportional to their marginal productivities:

$$\frac{\text{Unskilled labor}}{\$1.50} \quad = \quad \frac{\text{Skilled labor}}{\$3.00}$$
$$\frac{\$1.50}{10 \text{ units}} \quad = \quad \frac{\$3.00}{20 \text{ units}}$$

As we have seen, precisely the same bidding process, with precisely the same result, has taken place between land and labor, or labor and capital, and so on. Thus we can generalize the outcome of the competitive auction as follows:

$$\frac{\text{Price of Factor A}}{\text{Marginal productivity of Factor A}} = \frac{\text{Price of Factor B}}{\text{Marginal productivity of Factor B}}$$

Thus, in a settled competitive market, if one unit (say an acre) of land rents for $500 and a unit of capital (say a machine) can be hired for $1,000, and a unit of labor (say a man-year) costs $5,000, then we know that the marginal productivity of an acre of land is only half that of a machine, and one-tenth that of a man. Once again, let us caution that these results assume that the market will be perfectly competitive.

3. *As firms seek to equalize factor yields, they will also be maximizing efficiency.*

We have left until last what is perhaps the most important effect of the competitive bidding process we have been investigating. It is that the search for the most profitable factor requires that an entrepreneur always hires the factor that makes the *largest physical contribution to output for a given expenditure.* In our previous example, as long as tractors were the best buy for farmers, it meant that a dollar's expenditure on tractor services yielded more output than a dollar's expenditure on any other factor; and when all factors were ultimately sought for equally, it was because the physical contribution of a dollar's worth of each was the same.

Thus the process of competitive bidding for factors steers the system in the direction of maximizing efficiency; that is, toward getting the largest possible physical return from any given expenditure on factors. As we shall have reason to see when we turn to the study of planned economies in Chapter 30, this built-in impetus toward the efficient utilization of resources is one of the most powerful sources of economic advantage for market economies.

MINIMUM
WAGES

Our analysis has begun to reveal the extraordinary attributes of the market system as a distributive mechanism. But it also reveals this disturbing fact: attempts to interfere with the market mechanism for pricing factors may bring unexpected and unwanted effects. Take for example the problem of low-priced labor. Suppose the government decided tomorrow to eliminate all low-paid work by legislating a minimum wage of $100 a week (or suppose that trade unions accomplished the same thing through bargaining).

What would be the result? As the price of low-paid labor rises, the differential in pay that compensated for its lower productivity is removed. The unavoidable consequence is that entrepreneurs will swing their factor demand toward other factors—land, capital, or high-priced labor—because a dollar of expenditure will now bring them a larger return from these factors. Hence the result of the minimum wage is very likely to bring unemployment to the very persons it was designed to help!

How *much* unemployment depends on how "substitutable" is the factor in question. Suppose the new minimum wage affects the pay of grocery boys. Grocers will try to use trucks to make deliveries wherever possible instead of sending boys on bicycles, or they will simply eliminate some deliveries. If it is possible to persuade customers to carry their own groceries, or if it is not too expensive to deliver groceries by truck, many delivery boys will be let go. In the latter case, in more technical terms, if capital can be substituted for labor, a slight rise in the price of labor will mean a considerable swing from labor-using to relatively capital-using techniques. In that case, delivery boys' aggregate incomes are likely to suffer.

If, on the other hand, grocers find that they can't replace the delivery boy system, they will be forced to retain most of the boys and to pay them higher wages. As a result, grocery prices will rise somewhat, and the quantity of groceries demanded will decrease—how much or little depending on the price-elasticity of demand for groceries. If demand is very elastic, sales will fall off sharply, and many delivery boys will be fired because there is no need for them. If enough are fired, the income of the whole group may even fall. On the other hand, if demand is inelastic, grocery sales will remain relatively unchanged, few delivery boys will be let go, and their incomes as a whole will rise.

Thus the effect of setting floors under factor prices is difficult to predict insofar as its effect on *incomes* is concerned. Here everything depends on the technical ease of substituting other factors in place of the one whose price has been pushed up, and on the elasticities of demand for the final good or service itself. But the effect on *employment* must always be adverse, although again its extent will hinge on substitutability and elasticities of demand for final products.

Hence the efforts of government authorities or of trade unions to raise wages can backfire and actually reduce the incomes as well as the employment of those affected. To point this out is not to preach against such efforts. There are powerful arguments of social justice that favor some interventions into the market process. But one must not overlook the fact that interventions to "remedy" the rewards of the market will invariably bring their side effects. A thoughtful social policy will anticipate these effects and will not intervene into the market without plans for coping with the repercussions that are apt to ensue.

But why interfere in the market process at all? Is not the market's solution to the problem of distribution a just and equitable one? If A is twice as productive as B, should he not be paid twice as much?

There are two important caveats before we accept this deceptively attractive proposition. First, as we have repeatedly warned, the market will not price factors according to their marginal productivities if there are impediments to the free movement of factors within society. The same barriers that we discovered in our last chapter, where demand originated with consumers rather than with business firms, distort the entrepreneurial determination of income as they do the direct pricing factors. Tariffs or union barriers or patent restrictions, immobilities due to geographical location or lack of education—all impair the achievement of the solution that microtheory promises. In addition, in the real world, where firms are by no means always the small competitive units we have dealt with, the buyer of factors may be able to pay them less than their marginal productivity warrants, because there are no competitive firms to bid factors away. Hence, as was the case previously, we must not make the serious error of confusing the distribution of incomes in the real world with that of an ideal market, or commit the error of defending those incomes on the basis of theoretical premises that may not fit the case.

Second, even if all factors were remunerated in proportion to their productivities, it does not follow that the resulting levels of compensation would be "just." Even if one man is twice as productive as another, there is no inherent reason why he "should" be compensated twice as highly. Should a young worker, who is unmarried, make more money than an older one with a large family? Nor is there any inherent reason that, because a dollar's worth of land or capital makes a larger contribution to output than a dollar's worth of labor, the *owners* of those resources should therefore receive a compensation as large as the marginal revenue product of "their" resources. As John Stuart Mill wrote in a famous passage in his *Principles of Economics* in 1848:

The things are there; mankind individually or collectively can do with them as they please. They can place them at the disposal of whomsoever they please, and on whatever terms. The distribution of wealth . . . depends on the laws and customs of society. The rules by which it is determined are what the opinions and feelings of the ruling portion of the community make them, and are very different in different ages and countries, and might be still more different, if mankind so chose.

Thus the market solution must be judged on its *efficacy,* not on its "intrinsic" merits. The rewards meted out by the market serve a purpose—to maintain the efficiency of the market system—but we should not confuse their functional merits with their moral worth. This is particularly pertinent to a society of considerable affluence in which the sheer necessity for efficiency of output becomes a matter of less pressing moment and in which, accordingly, other noneconomic standards can be allowed to play a more prominent role in the establishment of the community's goals.

1. The study of the firm concentrates initially on the small enterprise. It assumes that such enterprises act intelligently and rationally and that they *try to maximize their profits in the short run.*

2. In all enterprises there is a *minimum size* or scale necessary for effective competition. This size is essentially determined by technology.

3. The choice of the amounts of the remaining factors to be added will be determined by their *profitability.*

4. Their profitability in turn will depend to an important degree on their *productivity.* This leads to the discovery that as we add any factor to a fixed supply of other factors *its marginal productivity changes.* Initially it rises, and we enjoy increasing average returns. Subsequently it begins to decline, and the average drops. At this point we enter the stage of diminishing average returns.

5. The *law of diminishing returns* (or *variable proportions*) applies to any factor, provided that we hold the amounts of the other factors fixed. It is entirely a natural phenomenon, not a behavioral one.

6. Marginal productivity is a critical element in determining the *marginal revenue* we can expect from hiring a factor. This marginal revenue will then be compared with marginal cost, to determine whether the unit of the factor is profitable.

7. The addition of factors is made by *comparing the returns from alternative factor mixes.* The factor yielding the highest return per dollar will be the factor that is hired.

8. *The process of many entrepreneurs bidding for the most profitable factor will raise its price.* Any single entrepreneur can bid for a factor without affecting its price; but when all firms bid for the same factor, its price rises.

9. This bidding process will eventually *equalize the return* to be had among all factors. The result is threefold:
   * *All factors will be sought as long as their marginal cost is less than their marginal revenue:* i.e., there will be no exploitation.
   * *All factors will be priced relative to one another in proportion to their marginal productivities.*
   * *Factors will be combined in the most efficient possible way.*

10. *If any factor price is "artificially" raised, its employment must be reduced* because other factors will now be relatively cheaper. Whether or not the more expensive factor suffers a fall in income depends on the technical possibilities of substitution and on the elasticity of demand for the end product.

11. The pricing of factors according to their respective marginal productivities is an *efficient but not necessarily "just" solution* to the problem of distribution.

1. Suppose that you were about to open a small business—say a drugstore. What do you think would be the factor that was critical in determining the scale of your operation? Name businesses in which land, labor, and capital, respectively, would play this limiting role.

2. Once you had decided on your scale, what consideration would be uppermost in your mind when you were deciding how much of the other two factors to hire? What is the cardinal rule you would have to bear in mind in deciding if a unit of a factor would or would not pay its way?

3. One thing that would affect your decision to hire or not to hire a factor would be the amount of physical increase in output it would yield. What is the generalization we make about the change in output associated with combining more and more of one factor to a fixed combination of others? Is this generalization based on behavior? State the law of variable proportions as carefully as you can.

4. What is meant by marginal productivity? What is its relation to average productivity? Suppose that you were considering the increase in your drug sales that would result from adding square feet of space. Draw up a schedule showing that the addition of square footage (in units of 100 sq ft) would at first yield increasing returns (dollars of sales) and then diminishing returns.

5. Suppose that a manufacturer had the following information for a given plant and number of men:

Number of machines	1	2	3	4	5	6	7	8
Total output (units)	100	250	450	600	710	750	775	780

What would be the marginal productivity of each successive machine? The average productivity from using additional machines? When would diminishing *marginal* productivity set in? Diminishing *average* productivity?

6. Why must we hold the other factors constant to derive the law of variable proportions?

7. Suppose that each machine in our example above cost $1,000 and that each unit of output sold for $10. How many machines would it be most profitable to hire? (Figure out the marginal revenue and marginal cost for each machine added.)

8. What would be the most profitable number to have if the cost of the machine rose to $1,500? If the price per unit of sales fell to $9?

9. Suppose that our manufacturer found he had the following alternatives:
   - He could spend $1,000 on a machine that would add 115 units to sales (each unit selling at $10).
   - He could spend $5,000 to hire a new man who would increase output by 510 units.
   - He could rent new space for $10,000 that would make possible an increase in output of 1,100 units.

   How would he know which was the best factor to hire? Would he have to begin by asking what is his dollar return per dollar of cost in each case?

What is this in the case of the machine? The new man? The land? Which is the best buy?

10. If one manufacturer in a competitive market adds to his factor inputs, will that affect their price? What happens when all manufacturers bid for the same factor? In the example above, which factor will be bid for? What will happen to its price? What will then be the "best buy"? What will happen to *its* price? What will be the final output of the bidding?

11. In the end, what will be the relation between the prices of factors? Will it be proportional to their costs? To their average outputs? To their marginal productivities? Explain carefully which is correct.

12. How do we know that there will be no "exploitation" of factors in a competitive market?

13. Suppose that the manufacturers of a certain kind of machinery got together (illegally) and agreed to keep its price above the level that would be set in a competitive market. What would happen to the number of machines they sold? What would we have to know before we could predict the effect on their total incomes?

14. By and large, do you think the market is a just allocator of incomes? If not, why not; and what would you suggest to improve it?

25 EQUILIBRIUM OF THE FIRM

We have reached the last step in our analysis of the circular flow in the marketplace. We have learned how households create a demand for goods and services by spending their incomes in the market, and we have had a glimpse of the supply of goods and services coming to meet their demand. Then we have followed those selfsame householders in their role as factors of production, and we have discovered how the incomes they had spent were earned by selling their services to other individuals and to firms.

Now it remains only to close the circuit. We must complete the circular flow inside the firm itself: watch the enterprise receive revenues from the market and transfer them to the pockets of its factors of production. At the same time, we can complete our picture of how the firm, which is the active pump of the circular flow, serves both as an agency of the market system and as an organization in search of its own private ends.

INSIDE THE FIRM:
FIXED AND VARIABLE COST

This will require us once again to put ourselves in the shoes of an imaginary entrepreneur. Since we have already become familiar with the firm's calculations in regard to buying factor services, let us begin our inquiry into the firm by extending our knowledge into a full appreciation of what the cost problem looks like to the entrepreneur.

We know that a firm's total costs must rise as it hires additional factors. Yet if we put ourselves in a businessman's position, we can see that our total costs are unlikely to rise as fast as our additional factor costs, because there are some costs of production that will not be affected by an increase in factor input. Real estate taxes, for example, will remain unchanged if we hire one man or 100—so long as we do not acquire additional land. The depreciation cost of machinery will not be affected by additions to land or labor. Rent will be unchanged, unless the premises are expanded. The cost of electric light will not vary appreciably despite additions to labor or machinery. Neither will the salary of the president. *Thus some costs, determined by legal contract or by usage or by the unchanging use of one factor, do not vary with output. We call these fixed costs.*

In sharp contrast with fixed costs is another kind of cost that does vary directly with output. Here are most factor costs, for generally we vary inputs of labor and capital (and sometimes land) every time we seek a new level of production. To increase output almost always requires the payment of more wages and the employment of more capital (if only in the form of inventories) and sometimes the rental of more space. *We call all costs that vary with output variable costs.*

PER UNIT COST

This important dichotomy between fixed and variable costs also requires us to shift our view a little within the business enterprise. We have been mainly concerned with calculating the costs of *inputs* in relation to their marginal productivities, but fixed costs do not lend themselves to this kind of treatment. Hence we must now turn around and begin to think about costs in relation to *output*.

In particular, we have to learn to think in terms of *cost per unit of output*. As we have seen, when a manufacturer (or a farmer or a storekeeper) expands his output, his total costs usually rise because his variable costs are going up, but total costs do not rise as fast as variable costs, because his fixed costs are set. But it is not easy to work with this upward rising curve of total costs. Hence businessmen and economists usually convert the figures for total cost into *unit costs* by dividing the total cost by the number of units of goods produced. This results, of course, in a figure for the *average cost per unit of output*. We shall see that this gives us a very useful way of figuring what happens to costs as output expands.

There is certainly no difficulty in picturing what happens to fixed costs per unit of output as output rises. By definition, they must fall. Suppose a manufacturer has fixed costs (rent, certain indirect taxes, depreciation, and overhead) of $10,000 a year. If he produces 5,000 units of his product per year, each unit will have to bear $2 of fixed costs as its share. If output rises to 10,000 units, the unit share of fixed costs will shrink to $1. At 100,000 units it would be a dime. Thus a curve of fixed costs per unit of output would look like Fig. 25-1.

FIG. 25-1

**PROFILE OF
FIXED COSTS
PER UNIT**

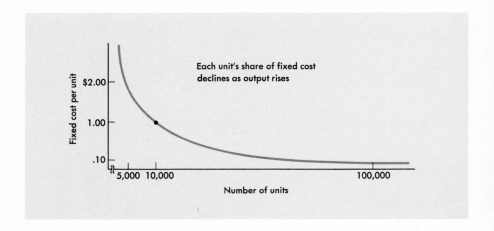

TABLE 25 · 1

Number of men	Total output	Marginal product
		(units)
1	5,000	5,000
2	13,000	8,000
3	23,000	10,000
4	32,000	9,000
5	39,000	7,000
6	42,000	5,000
7	44,000	2,000

What about variable costs per unit? Here the situation is more complex, for it depends directly on the analysis of the productivity curve we discussed in our last chapter. Hence, let us first set up a schedule of output for our manufacturer (Table 25-1), showing how the total numbers of units he produces will rise at first rapidly, then more slowly, as he adds labor input to his plant.

To convert this schedule of physical productivity into a unit cost figure, we must do two things: (1) we must know the cost of the factor in question, so that we can calculate total variable cost for each level of output, and (2) we must then divide the total variable cost by the number of units to get average variable cost per unit of output. Here are the figures (assuming that the going wage is $5,000).

TABLE 25 · 2

Number of men	Total variable cost @ $5,000 per man	Total output (units)	Average variable cost per unit of output
1	$ 5,000	5,000	$1.00
2	10,000	13,000	.77
3	15,000	23,000	.65
4	20,000	32,000	.63
5	25,000	39,000	.64
6	30,000	42,000	.71
7	35,000	44,000	.80

Notice that average variable costs per unit decline at first and thereafter rise. The reason is by now clear enough. Variable cost increases by a set amount—$5,000 per man—as factors are added. Output, however, obeys the law of variable proportions, increasing rapidly at first and then displaying diminishing returns. It stands to reason, then, that the variable cost *per unit* of output will be falling as long as output is growing faster than costs, and that it will begin to rise as soon as additions to output start to get smaller.

If we graph the typical variable cost curve per unit of output, it will be the dish-shaped or U-shaped profile that Fig. 25-2 shows.

FIG. 25-2

PROFILE OF
CHANGING
VARIABLE
COSTS
PER UNIT

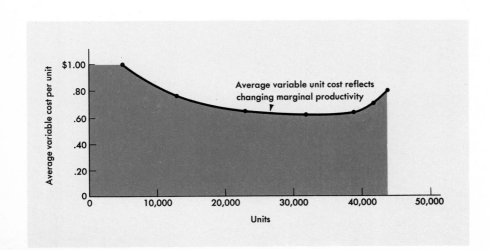

Average variable unit cost reflects changing marginal productivity

We can now set up a complete cost schedule for our enterprise by combining fixed and variable costs, as in Table 25-3. Notice how marginal costs begin to turn up *before* average costs.

TABLE 25 · 3

Number of men	Total cost ($10,000 fixed cost + $5,000 per man)	Output (units)	COST PER UNIT OF OUTPUT	
			Average (total cost ÷ output)	Marginal*
1	$15,000	5,000	$3.00	$ —
2	20,000	13,000	1.54	.63
3	25,000	23,000	1.09	.50
4	30,000	32,000	.94	.55
5	35,000	39,000	.90	.71
6	40,000	42,000	.95	1.67
7	45,000	44,000	1.02	2.50

*Ideally, we should like to show how marginal cost changes with *each* additional unit of output. Here our data show the change in costs associated with considerable jumps in output as we add each man. Hence we estimate the marginal cost per unit by taking the *change in total costs* and dividing this by the *change in total output*. The result is really an "average" marginal cost, since each individual item costs actually a tiny fraction less than, or more than, its predecessor. We have shown the data this way since it is much closer to the way businessmen figure.

FIG. 25-3

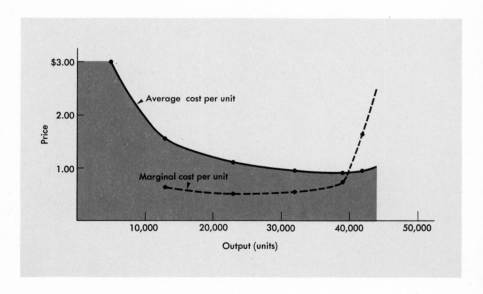

If we graph the last two columns of figures—average and marginal cost per unit—we get the very important diagram in Fig. 25-3.

We have reached the end of our cost calculations, and it will help to take stock of what we have done. Actually, despite all the figures and diagrams, the procedure has been quite simple.

1. We began by seeing what would happen to our *fixed costs* per unit as we expanded output. Since fixed costs, by their nature, do not increase as production increases, the amount of fixed cost that had to be charged to each unit of output fell sharply as output rose.

2. Next we calculated the *variable costs* that would have to be borne by each unit as output increased. Here the critical process at work was the law of variable proportions. As the marginal productivity of factors increased, variable cost per unit fell. But when the inevitable stage of diminishing returns set in, variable costs per unit had to rise.

3. Adding together fixed and variable costs, we obtained the *total unit cost* of output. Like the variable cost curve, average total unit costs are dish-shaped, reflecting the diminishing marginal productivity of factors as output grows.

4. Finally, we show the changing *marginal cost per unit*—the increase in total costs divided by the increase in output. As before, it is the changing marginal costs that the entrepreneur actually experiences when he alters output. It is the increase at the margin that changes his total cost, and which therefore determines his average cost.

Actually, the cost profile that we have worked out would be known by any businessman whether he had ever studied microeconomics or not. Whenever a firm starts producing, its average cost per unit of output is very high. A General Motors plant turning out only a few hundred cars a year would have astronomical costs per automobile.

But as output increases, unit costs come down steadily, partly because overhead (fixed costs) is now spread over more units, partly because the factors are used at much greater efficiency. Finally, after some point of maximum factor efficiency, average unit costs begin to mount. Even though overhead continues to decline, it is now so small a fraction of cost per unit that its further decline does not count for much, while the rising inefficiency of factors pushes up variable cost per unit steadily. If General Motors tries to jam more cars through a plant than it is designed to take, the cost per auto will again begin to soar.

So much for the average cost per unit. By directing our attention to the *changes* that occur in total cost and total output every time we alter the number of factors we engage, the marginal cost curve per unit simply tells us why all this is happening. In other words, as our plant first moves into high gear, the cars we add to the line (the marginal output) will cost considerably less than the average of all cars processed previously; later, when diminishing returns begin to work against us, we would expect the added (marginal) cars to be high-cost cars, higher in cost than the average of all cars built so far.

Since the cost of marginal output always "leads" the cost of average output in this way, we can understand an important relationship that the marginal and average curves always bear to one another. *The marginal cost curve always cuts the average cost curve at the lowest point of the latter.*

Why? Because as long as the additional cars are cheaper than the average of all cars, their production must be *reducing* average cost—that is, as long as the marginal cost curve is lower than the average cost curve, the average cost curve must be falling. Conversely, as soon as additional output is more expensive than the average for all previous output, that additional production must *raise* average costs—again, (look at the previous diagram) as soon as marginal cost is above average cost, average cost must begin to rise. Hence it follows that the *MC* (marginal cost) curve must cross the *AC* (average cost) curve at the minimum point of the latter. This relationship has nothing to do with economics, as such, but with simple logic, as Fig. 25-4 may elucidate.

FIG. 25-4

RELATION OF MARGINAL AND AVERAGE COST PER UNIT

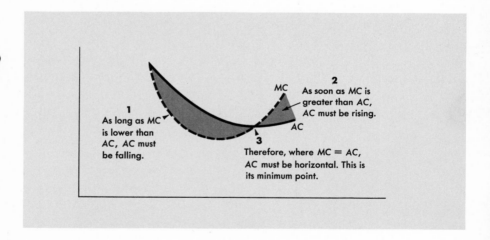

1 As long as MC is lower than AC, AC must be falling.

MC

2 As soon as MC is greater than AC, AC must be rising.

AC

3 Therefore, where MC = AC, AC must be horizontal. This is its minimum point.

FROM COST TO REVENUE

The cost profile gives us a clear picture of what happens to unit costs as our firm hires additional factors. But that is only half the information we need to understand how a firm operates with one foot in the factor market and the other in the market for goods. Now we need a comparable profile of what happens to revenues as the firm sells the output its factors have made for it.

This brings us over from supply to demand—from dealing with factors who are selling their services, back to householders who are buying goods. What the entrepreneur wants to know is whether "the market" will buy his goods and if so, at just what price it will buy them. In other words, he wants to know the demand curve for his particular output. If he knows that, he can easily figure what his revenues will be.

What does the demand curve look like for a small competitive firm? Let us take the case of our manufacturer, with whose costs we are now familiar, and assume that the "units" he is making are simple metal stampings of which several million are sold each year. Our manufacturer knows two things about the market for those stampings. First, he knows that there is a "going" price for stampings (which we will say is $1.50) that is established by "the market." Second, he knows that he can personally sell all the stampings he can make at the going price without altering that price by so much as a penny—that "the market" will not be affected whether he closes down his shop entirely or whether he sells every last stamping he can afford to make at the price the market offers.

What our manufacturer knows in his bones, we can translate into economics. The price of any commodity is set in the goods market by the interplay of supply and demand. Our firm is one of the many suppliers whose willingness and ability to sell at different prices (which are, of course, largely determined by their costs) makes up the supply curve. The demand curve for the commodity is familiar to us as the expression of the consumers' willingness and ability to buy.

But now we can also see that as far as the output of any *one* small firm is concerned, the demand for *its* output is a horizontal line—that there is an "infinite" willingness to buy its product, provided it can be supplied at the going price. The output of any one seller, in other words, is too small to affect the equilibrium price for the market as a whole. Why, then, cannot an ambitious firm make an "infinite" profit by expanding its sales to match demand? The shape of its cost curve gives the answer. As factor productivity declines, marginal costs soon rise above selling price.

Thus the competitive firm operates between two horizontal curves. On the supply side it faces a perfectly elastic supply of factors, meaning that it can hire all the factors it wishes without changing prices an iota in the factor market. On the demand side it also faces a perfectly elastic curve, meaning that it can sell as much as it can produce without any perceptible price effect here, either. The firm is thus squeezed between two forces that it is powerless to change. As a result, it must devote all its energies to those parts of the market process that are in its control—the efficient combining of factors to minimize its costs, and the selection of the most profitable scale and line of output.

AVERAGE AND MARGINAL REVENUE

Facing a known demand curve, our manufacturer can now calculate his revenues. He will take in an amount determined by his total unit output multiplied by the price of each unit. And since, with a horizontal demand curve, the price of each unit will be exactly the same price as the previous one, the marginal revenue of each unit sold—that is the additional amount it will bring in—will be unchanged no matter how much is sold by the firm. If the selling price is $1.50, then the marginal revenue per unit will be $1.50. As a result, average revenue per unit will also be $1.50. The schedules of revenue will look like Table 25-4. We can see that a graph of the average and marginal costs curves for this (or any) small, highly competitive firm would be horizontal as in Fig. 25-5.

TABLE 25 · 4

Output (units)	Price per unit	Marginal revenue per unit	Total revenue	Average revenue per unit
5,000	$1.50	$1.50	$ 7,500	$1.50
10,000	1.50	1.50	15,000	1.50
20,000	1.50	1.50	30,000	1.50
40,000	1.50	1.50	60,000	1.50

FIG. 25-5

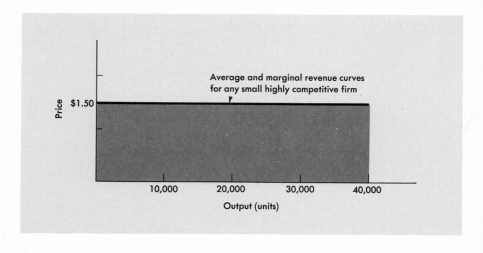

Average and marginal revenue curves for any small highly competitive firm

MARGINAL REVENUE AND MARGINAL COST

Now we have all the information we want. We have a cost profile that tells us what happens to unit costs as we hire or fire factors. We have a revenue profile that tells us what happens to unit revenues as

504

we do the same. It remains only to put the two together to discover just how much output the firm should make to maximize its profits.

We can do this very simply by superimposing the revenue diagram on top of the cost diagram. The point where the marginal revenue and the marginal cost curves meet should indicate exactly what the most profitable output will be. As we can see in Fig. 25-6, it is just about at 43,000 units.

FIG. 25-6

THE POINT OF OPTIMUM OUTPUT

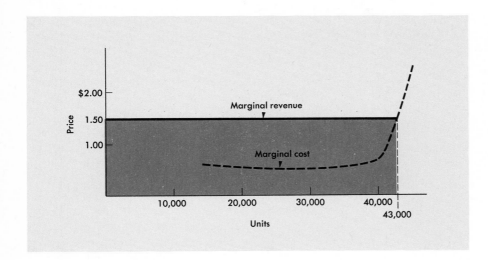

Why is this the point of best possible output? Because another unit of output—as we can see by looking at the two curves—will cost more than it brings in, while a unit less of output would deprive us of the additional net revenue that another unit of output could bring.

What is the total amount of profit our firm makes at this level of output? That is very difficult to tell from the diagram above, since it is hard to figure out what total cost is. But with the addition of our familiar curve of average costs per unit, we can tell at a glance. Average costs, as we know, are nothing but total costs reduced to a per-unit basis. Average revenues are also on a per-unit basis. Hence, *if we compare the average unit revenue and cost curves at any point, they will tell us at a glance what total revenues and costs look like at that point.*

Figure 25-7 reveals what our situation is at the point of optimum output. (This time we generalize the diagram rather than putting it into the specific terms of our illustrative firm.)

The diagram shows several things. First, as before, it indicates our most profitable output as the amount *OA* — the output indicated by the point *X,* where the marginal revenue and marginal cost curves meet. Second, it shows us that at output *OA,* our *average cost* is *OC* (= *AB*)

FIG. 25-7

**THE FIRM IN
EQUILIBRIUM
WITH PROFITS**

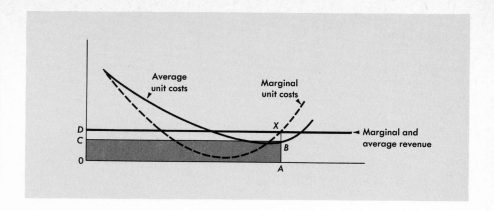

and our *average revenue* is *OD* (= *AX*), the same as our marginal revenue, since the demand curve for the firm is horizontal. Our profit on the *average* unit of output must therefore be *CD* (= *BX*), the difference between average costs and average revenues at this point. The *total* profit is therefore the rectangle *CDXB*, which is the average profit per unit (*CD*) times the number of units.

We can translate this result in terms of our firm. At the point where *MC = MR,* it is making about 43,000 stampings, as Fig. 25-6 shows, at an average cost that we will estimate at $1.00 per unit. (Table 25-3 does not show us the exact cost at 43,000 units, but it does show that it lies between 95¢ and $1.02.) Since selling price is $1.50, we are making 50¢ per unit on 43,000 units, or a total of $21,500. This is as much money as our firm can make, given the price for its product and the going prices of factors.*

However satisfactory from the point of view of the firm, this is not yet a satisfactory stopping point from the point of view of the system as a whole. If our firm is typical of the metal stamping industry, then small firms throughout this line of business are making profits comparable to ours. Unhappily for them, there are numerous businesses in other lines of endeavor that do not make $21,500 of clear profit. *Hence entrepreneurs in these lines will now begin to move into our profitable industry.*

**ENTRY
AND
EXIT**

Perhaps we can anticipate what will now happen. Our firm is now going to experience the same "mysterious" change in prices that we have already witnessed in the factor market, when many firms altered their demands for land or labor or capital and the prices of these factor

---

*We will have more to say about profit later. At this juncture, it should be said only that profit is what is left *after* all factors have been paid, including management's salaries.

services changed accordingly. Only this time, it is the price of goods that will change, not that of factors. For the influx of entrepreneurs from other areas will move the industry supply curve to the right and thereby reduce the going price. As it falls, our own business will experience a disconcerting fall in the price for its goods which it is powerless to stop. We can see the process in Fig. 25-8.

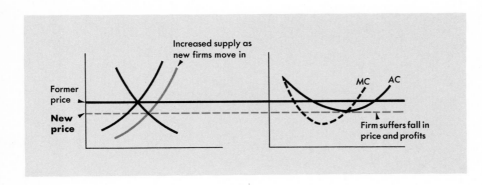

FIG. 25-8

THE INDUSTRY
IN ADJUSTMENT
TO PROFITS

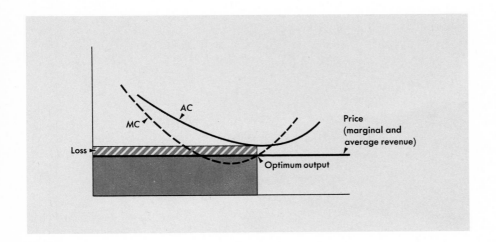

FIG. 25-9

THE FIRM
SUFFERING
A LOSS

How long will this influx of firms continue? Suppose that it continues until price falls *below* the average cost curve of our representative firm. Now its position looks like Fig. 25-9. Output will still be set where $MC = MR$, but now the average cost curve is above the average revenue curve at this point. The unavoidable result is a loss for the firm, as the diagram shows.

What will happen? Clearly, we need a reverse adjustment process—an exodus of firms into greener pastures, so that the supply curve for our industry can move to the left, bringing higher prices for all producers.

FIG. 25-10

**INDUSTRY
ADJUSTMENT
TO LOSSES**

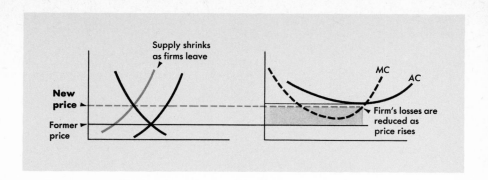

This may not be a rapid process, but eventually depreciation and the withdrawal of producers should bring about the necessary adjustment, shown in Fig. 25-10.*

**LONG-RUN
EQUILIBRIUM**

Finally we reach a point of equilibrium both for the firm and the industry (or the system as a whole). It looks, of course, like Fig. 25-11. Note that this position of equilibrium has two characteristics.

FIG. 25-11

**THE MARGINAL
FIRM IN
EQUILIBRIUM
WITH NO PROFIT**

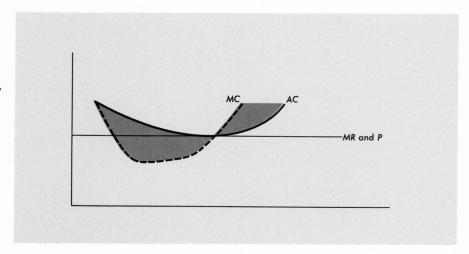

*There is an interesting reason for this slowness. A firm can suffer losses for quite a while, as long as its revenues are high enough to pay its variable costs and a little more. In that case, it can meet some of its fixed costs from its operating income. If it shut down entirely, *its fixed costs would continue.* Thus it will lose less money if it continues to produce—provided always that its revenues meet its variable costs in full and cover part, if not all, of its fixed expenses. Eventually, of course, such a firm will go bankrupt, for it will be spending more than it is taking in. But it will go bankrupt more quickly if it stops producing altogether, for then it could pay none of its fixed costs! Hence it will go on producing, thereby delaying the needed market adjustment.

1. *Marginal cost equals marginal revenue,* so there is no incentive for the individual entrepreneur to alter his own output.

2. *Average cost equals average revenue* (or price), so there is no incentive for firms to enter or leave the industry.

Thus we can state the conditions for the equilibrium resting point of our firm and industry as being a four-way equality:

$$P = MR = MC = AC$$

We have reached an equilibrium both for the firm and for the industry, but it is certainly an uncomfortable one for ourselves as typical manufacturers. For in the final resting point of the firm, it is clear that *profits have been totally eliminated.* Is this a realistic assumption?

The question forces us to confront the slippery question of what "profits" are. By definition, they are not returns to factors, for these payments have already been made by the firm—including all payments made to entrepreneurs for the full value of their contribution to output.

To put it differently, we do not include in the term *profit* any revenues the firm *must* have to stay in business. An accountant, examining the books of a marginal firm in an industry, might find that there was a small bookkeeping profit. But an economist, looking at these revenues, would not call this sum a true economic profit if it were necessary to maintain the firm (or its entrepreneur) in operation. We should note as well that profits are usually figured as a return on the capital invested in a firm, not as a return on each unit sold. It is simpler for our purposes, however (and it does no violence to the argument) to talk of profits in relation to output (= sales) rather than as a return on investment.

What are profits, then? There have been numerous attempts to define them as the return for risk, or for innovation, and so on. But however we describe them, we are driven to the conclusion that in a "perfect" competitive market, the forces of competition would indeed press toward zero the returns of the *marginal* firms in all industries, so that the cost and revenue profile of the last firms able to remain alive in each industry would look like our diagram.

Note, however, that these are marginal firms. Here is a clue to how profits can exist even in a highly competitive situation. In Fig. 25-12, we show the supply curve of an industry, broken down into the individual supply curves of its constituent firms. Some of these firms, by virtue of superior location, or access to supplies, or managerial skills will be lower-cost producers than others. When the industry price is finally established, they will be the beneficiaries of the difference between the going price (which reduces the profits of the marginal firm to zero) and the lower unit costs attributable to their superior efficiency.

FIG. 25-12

**INTRAMARGINAL
PROFITS**

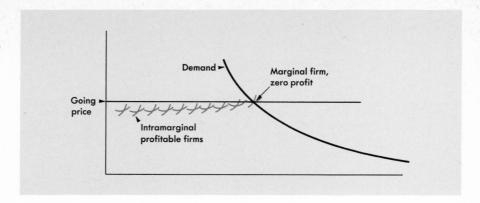

Really, these intramarginal profits are *quasi rents.* That is, they result from scarcities—of location, or managerial talents, or whatever—that earn a high return. If, through a fall in price, any one of these firms were suddenly put at the margin of production, it would continue to produce, fully covering its costs, but earning no profits. Even without a fall in price, we would expect intramarginal rents to diminish over time, owing to factor mobility. Badly located firms will pick up and move, or newcomers will locate favorably and thereby displace a firm at the margin. Managerial skills will be learned elsewhere or hired. Thus in the long run, we must expect the *tendency* in a fully competitive market to be a constant pressure toward lower prices, and thus toward the elimination of quasi rents.

LONG RUN AND SHORT RUN

We have seen how the market makes it necessary for firms to produce goods at the lowest points along their average unit cost curves and to sell those goods at prices that will yield no profit to the least efficient firm in the industry. Yet there is one last adjustment process to consider. In all our investigations into the firm's operations, we have hitherto taken for granted that the *scale of output* would remain unchanged. As a result, all of our adjustments have involved us in moving back and forth along a cost curve that was basically set in place by one or more limiting factors.

This may be accurate enough in the short run, when most firms are circumscribed by a given size of plant, but it certainly does not describe the long run. *For in the long run, all costs are variable.* A firm can usually enlarge its scale of plant; and as the scale increases, it is often possible to realize additional savings in cost, as a result of still finer specialization of the production process. If our expanding firm confines its growth to a single plant, the cost curves of these successive scales of output are apt to look like Fig. 25-13.

FIG. 25-13

LONG-RUN COST CURVE

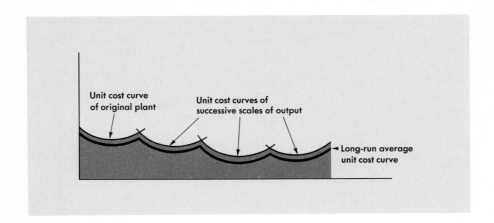

Unit cost curve of original plant

Unit cost curves of successive scales of output

Long-run average unit cost curve

If we connect the successive short-run cost curves attributable to various scales of output, we get a *long-run average unit cost curve* shown in the heavy line below. We have already explained that its initial downward slope is due to savings that size continues to bring in the utilization of factors. The extent to which a firm will be able to realize these so-called *economies of scale* depends mainly on the technological possibilities in its industry. In Chapter 5 we saw how the development of mass production in the late nineteenth century brought about a change in many industries from atomistic competition to the domination of a few, very large-scale producers.

Our diagram shows, however, that economies of scale do not go on forever. At some point—again determined by technology—the limits of efficient plant operation are reached. A sprawling enterprise begins to stretch too thin the coordinating powers of management. *Diseconomies of scale* enter, and the long-run unit cost curve again begins to mount.

Note, however, that these long-run cost curves apply to individual *plants*. What about a firm that pushes each plant to its optimum size and then adds a new plant, or a firm that diversifies its efforts among many different kinds of businesses, like the conglomerates? Does it also face a long-run, upward sloping cost curve, owing perhaps to eventual diseconomies of management? We really do not know the answer. To hazard an unsubstantiated guess, it may well be that the new technology of information retrieval has so increased the efficiency of management that the economically effective size of multiplants or diversified plants is today extremely large. For all practical purposes, the long-run cost curve is probably horizontal or perhaps even falling.*

INCREASING OR DECREASING LONG-RUN COSTS

There is still, however, another way in which our firm's long-run costs can be altered. Together with all of its competitors it may be subject to *increasing or decreasing costs for the industry as a whole.*

The source of these changes in cost do not lie within the firm, in the relative efficiency of various factor mixes. Rather, they are changes thrust upon the firm—for better or worse—by the interaction of the growing industry of which it is a part and the economy as a whole. A new industry, for example by its very expansion may bring into being satellite firms that provide some of its necessary inputs; and as the main new industry grows, the satellites also expand and thereby realize economies of scale that will benefit the main industry itself. The automobile industry was surely an instance of such long-run falling costs (for a long period, at least) resulting from the economies of scale enjoyed by makers of tires, makers of batteries, and other equipment. In turn, the rise of low-cost trucking brought "external economies" to many other industries.

Industries may also experience long-run rising costs if their expansion pushes them up against factor scarcity of a stubbornly inelastic kind. Extractive industries, for example, may be forced to use progressively less-accessible mineral deposits; or agricultural industries may be forced to use progressively less-fertile or less-conveniently-located land. Such industries would experience a gradual rise in unit costs as their output increased.

Are most industries the beneficiaries of decreasing cost or the victims of increasing cost? Empirical studies seem to suggest that save for youthful, growing industries, and for the special case of extractive ones, most industries enjoy a middle position of roughly constant long-run unit costs, at least over a considerable period of time. That is, for most industries it is probably accurate to state that the so-called *external economies* or *diseconomies* are much less important than internal economies or diseconomies.

THE COMPETITIVE ENVIRONMENT

Our consideration of the forces bearing on long-run costs brings our discussion of the firm to an end. We have seen how the firm has closed

---

*For an interesting discussion of this point, see Robert T. Averitt, *The Dual Economy, op. cit.,* pp. 105–9.

the circular flow by transforming its receipts from householders into payments to its factors, and we have simultaneously watched as it performed its social function of combining factors as efficiently as possible in the course of pursuing its short-run profits.

Now we must ask a question that has surely occurred to the reader. Does the world really behave as microtheory has portrayed it? Do firms really equate marginal costs and revenues or balance the advantages of one factor versus another with the fine precision that our model has indicated? That is not a question we can fully answer until our next chapter. But we already know one condition that must be fulfilled if firms are to behave as we have pictured them. This is the condition of "pure" competition to which we have already referred as the environment we would take for granted during our initial microeconomic investigations. Now is the time to look carefully into exactly what the term means.

In general, when economists use the term *pure competition,* they imply three necessary attributes of the market situation:

PURE COMPETITION DEFINED

1. *Large numbers of marketers.*

Unless there are numerous buyers and sellers facing one another across the market and jostling one another on each side of it, the competitive process will not fully work itself out. When the number of marketers is few (whether as buyers or sellers) the vying among them that gives competition its resistless force is apt to be muted or even lacking entirely. As the extreme case of this we have outright *collusion,* in which a few buyers or sellers agree to bid only at one low price or to offer only at one high price. But even when collusion is absent, fewness of buyers or sellers will lead, as we shall see in our next chapter, to results that are considerably at variance with those of the competitive process we have assumed.

How many buyers or sellers does it take to make a fully competitive market? There is no clear-cut answer. The critical number is reached when no firm, by varying its scale of output, is able to affect the price of the factors it buys or the product it sells. We have pictured this condition in terms of the horizontal factor supply and market demand curves that present the purely competitive firm with the unalterable data of factor and goods prices to which it must accommodate itself. *Thus under conditions of pure competition, the only thing the firm can control is its scale of output and the mix of factors it uses; all prices are beyond its power to influence.*

2. *Ease of entry into, and exit out of, industries.*

A second prerequisite for so-called pure competition is a condition that we have already relied upon frequently in discussing the operation of the market. *This is the ability of firms and factors to move freely and easily from one industry to another in search of the highest possible return.* Only in this way can supply and demand schedules move rightwards and leftwards, bringing about the needed adjustments of quantities and prices.

We have seen as well that this is by no means an easy set of conditions to achieve. With firms, as previously with factors, it rules out all legal barriers to interindustry movement, such as restrictive patents. But beyond this it implies that industries in which the initial scale of manufacture is very large cannot be considered as meeting the requirements for pure competition. In automobile or steel manufacturing, for example, in which the minimum size of plant entails an investment of millions of dollars, the degree of competitive pressure from "outside" entrepreneurs is obviously much less than in the stationery store business, where a newcomer can enter for an investment of a few thousand dollars.

Ease of exit is a no less necessary and equally demanding requirement. The competitive process will not shift about supply curves if some producers cannot withdraw their investments in land or capital and move them to alternative uses. Yet, as we have seen, this inability to move out can indeed retard adjustments of supply, particularly in industries with large fixed investments that are highly "specific" in their use. Such industries may go on producing even if they cannot cover their full costs, as long as their revenues bring in enough to nibble away at fixed expenses (see p. 508 n). Thus the problems of securing easy entry and exit further restrict the environment of pure competition to industries in which no large or technically specific investments are required.

3. *Nondifferentiated goods.*

But even these strict conditions still do not define the state of competition we have implicitly assumed. It is possible for a market to consist of many small buyers and sellers, each operating with relatively simple equipment, and yet these firms may not compete fully against one another. This is the case when each firm sells a product that is *differentiated* (or distinguishable) from that of its competitors. For if there is a difference, however slight, between one man's product and another's, the demand curve for the product of each will be sloping rather than horizontal, even if the slope is very small. As a result, product differentiation will enable a seller to hold onto *some* of his trade even if his price is a trifle higher than his competitor's, whereas in a purely competitive market where goods and services are indistinguishable from one another, no marketer can depart in the slightest degree from the prevailing price.

There are markets in which perfectly anonymous undifferentiated commodities are sold—for example, the market for grain or for coal or for common labor, in which no seller can ask even a penny more for his product or services than the going price. In the great bulk of retail and wholesale markets, however, such totally undifferentiated products are the exception rather than the rule.

Why must commodities be exactly alike for a state of pure competition to exist? The answer is that *only identical commodities compete solely on the basis of price.* Much of what we call "competition" in the impure markets of the real world consists in differentiating products through style, design, services, etc., so that they will *not* have to compete just on price. We shall look into this very common case of "imperfect competition" in our next chapter. But we must rule it out as a permissible form of competition to bring about the exact results of our market analysis thus far. The essential rule for a purely competitive market is that the word "competition" must mean *price competition only.*

Obviously, pure competition is an extremely demanding state of affairs. It requires small and numerous firms selling identical products in a highly mobile and fluid environment. Does such a market in fact exist?

It has been customary to claim that farming constitutes a perfect example of pure competition, since its units are very numerous and its main products undifferentiated. But farming lacks one qualification. It has proved to be a very difficult occupation to move out of when prices fall. Of the roughly 3.5 million farms in the United States, about one million sell less than $5,000 worth of farm products a year and are, by any definition, uneconomical operations. Yet submarginal farmers are reluctant to leave an occupation that gives them at least a minimal security, for the frightening insecurity (and perhaps even worse economic luck) of the city.

The world of retailing qualifies much more readily in terms of easy entry and exit, and it is characterized by many small firms. But retailing loses out on the question of differentiation. The very essence of most retail establishments, even if they sell exactly the same wares as the competitor down the street (in fact, especially if they do), is to try to be "different."

Hence the search for perfect examples of pure competition is apt to end with very few cases. Why, then, do we spend so much time analyzing it?

The answer is twofold. In part it lies in the fact that as much as 40 or 50 per cent of the output of the nation comes from sectors that *resemble*—even though they do not exactly qualify for—pure competition. The service trades, the wholesale markets, much retailing, some raw material production are near enough to being "pure" in their competitive structures, so that we can apply the reasoning of price theory very closely in understanding the market results we see in those industries.

But there is a second reason as well. Even in those sectors or industries where pure competition obviously does not apply—in the monopolistic or oligopolistic situations with which our next chapter will be concerned—the mechanism of the market will still be clearly discernible. Supply and demand, factor productivities, marginal revenue and marginal cost will continue to be the prevailing guidelines. Hence we must understand the basic elements of microeconomics because most of them will still apply. And unless we know to what results these elements lead us in the ideal environment of pure competition, we will hardly be in a position to know what a difference monopoly or oligopoly make to the workings of the market system.

SUMMARY

1. We divide costs within the firm into *fixed and variable costs*. Variable costs change with the addition or discharge of factors. Fixed costs are contractual costs or costs that are associated with the unchanged use of one factor. They do not vary with output.

2. Both fixed and variable (and total) costs are usually calculated *per unit of output*. *Fixed costs decline per unit of output as total output increases.*

3. *Variable costs first decline and then rise*, reflecting the increasing and then diminishing marginal productivity of the factors. The typical shape of the variable unit cost curve is *U-shaped* or *dish-shaped*.

4. Adding together fixed and variable costs, we get a *dish-shaped unit cost curve for the firm.*

5. The marginal cost curve shows us the actual operative factor at work. The relation of marginal and average figures to one another is such that the *marginal unit cost curve always cuts the average unit cost curve at the lowest point of the latter.*

6. *The competitive firm operates between two horizontal curves: The demand curve for its product is infinitely elastic. The supply curve of factors to itself is also infinitely elastic.* That is, it can sell all it can profitably make without disturbing the market price, and it can hire or fire all the factors it wishes without disturbing their price. The only process under its control is the combination of factors to secure maximum efficiency.

7. *The point of maximum profit is that output where marginal revenue just equals marginal cost.* In a competitive market for a single firm, marginal revenue and average revenue are both equal to price. Therefore it pushes its output until the marginal cost of the last unit just equals price. Any output more than this would incur losses, and any output less than this would fail to gain all potential profit.

8. If a competitive firm enjoys profits in this position of $MC = MR$, it will experience *an influx of firms from other areas.* This will cause industry supply to increase and prices to fall. Conversely, if it experiences a loss, there will be a gradual *exodus of firms* until supply for the industry falls and prices rise.

9. *The equilibrium point for the competitive firm is reached when marginal revenue equals marginal cost, and average cost equals price.* At this point there is no

incentive for the entrepreneur to alter his scale of output or for firms to leave or enter the industry.

10. In a competitive market, the *marginal* firm enjoys no profit. Intramarginal firms may have quasi rents.

11. In addition to changes in cost from moving along a fixed unit cost curve, firms can enjoy *economies of scale,* provided that the technology of the industry leads to these. At some point, economies of scale cease and the long-run cost curve again turns up.

12. In addition, *external economies or diseconomies* can affect the cost curves of all firms within an industry. For most industries a condition of roughly *constant* long-term costs seems to prevail.

13. The environment of the firm is assumed at first to be that of pure competition. By this we mean a market in which there are:

- *Large numbers of marketers.* As a result, each faces a market situation, both with regard to factors and goods, in which his own actions are powerless to affect prices. Only the factor mix is under the control of the competitive entrepreneur.
- *Ease of exit and entry.* This requires the absence of all barriers to mobility, including that of size and technical specificity.
- *Nondifferentiated products.* This insures the restriction of competition to price alone.

14. Pure competition is obviously rarely found in actuality. But it does describe the actions of some markets tolerably well and it provides a bench mark from which to measure the degree of competition that we find in the real world.

1. If you were a retail grocer, what kinds of costs would be fixed for you? Variable? If you were a manufacturer who owned a large computer, would its maintenance be a fixed cost? If you *rented* the computer, would it be?

2. Assume that your fixed costs are $500 a week and that your output can vary from 100 to 1,000 units, given the scale of your enterprise. Graph what happens to fixed costs per unit.

3. Assume that your plant hires 6 men successively, and that output changes as follows:

Number of men	1	2	3	4	5	6
Total units of output per week	100	300	550	700	750	800

What is the marginal productivity of each man? If each worker costs you $100 per week, what is the variable cost per unit as you add men?

4. If you now add fixed costs of $500 per week to the variable cost you have just ascertained, what is the average cost per unit? What is the marginal cost per unit? (Remember, this is figured by dividing the *change in total cost* by the *change in total output.*)

5. Graph the curve of average total unit costs and marginal unit costs. Why does the marginal unit cost curve cross the average unit cost curve at its lowest point?

6. What does average revenue mean and what is its relation to price? What is meant by marginal revenue? Why is marginal revenue the same as average revenue for a competitive firm?

7. Explain carefully why a competitive firm operates between two horizontal curves, one on the demand side and one on the factor supply side.

8. Suppose that the price per unit at which you sell the output of your firm (in the example above) is $1.35. Draw in such a marginal revenue curve. Now very carefully indicate where the MR and MC curves meet. Show on the diagram the output corresponding to this point. What is the approximate average cost at this output? Is there a profit here? Indicate by letters the rectangle that shows the profit per unit of output and the number of units.

9. What will be the result, in a competitive industry, of such a profit? Draw a diagram showing how an influx of firms can change the ruling market price. Will it be higher or lower?

10. Draw a diagram showing how price could drop below the lowest point on the average total unit cost curve, and indicate the loss the firm would suffer.

11. Carefully draw a diagram showing the equilibrium position for the firm. What is the relation of MC, MR, and P at this point? If MC = MR, does this mean that the entrepreneur is now motivated to alter his output? If AC = P, what does this mean as to the movement of firms into or out of the industry?

12. Suppose that you are a druggist, and you know that the least efficient druggist in town makes virtually no profit at all. Assuming that you sell in the same market as he does at the same prices and that you hire factors at the same prices also, what causes could bring about a profit to your enterprise? What would you expect to be the trend of these profits?

13. Would you expect economies of scale from greatly enlarging your drugstore? Why or why not?

14. Do you think as the entire drugstore business expands it enjoys external economies or suffers from external diseconomies? How about the gold-mining business?

15. Is the drugstore business an example of pure competition? Explain carefully in what ways it might qualify and in what ways it might not.

COMPETITION IN THE REAL WORLD 26

Monopoly (and nowadays oligopoly) are bad words to most people, just as competition is a good word. But not everyone can specify exactly what is good or bad about them. Often we get the impression that the aims of the monopolist are evil and grasping, while those of the competitor are wholesome and altruistic, and therefore the essential difference between a world of pure competition and one of very impure competition is one of motives and drives—of well-meaning competitors and ill-intentioned monopolists.

The truth is that *exactly the same motives drive the monopoly and the competitive firm.* Both seek to maximize their profits. Indeed, the competitive firm, placed in a situation in which it must keep careful track of costs and revenues in order to survive is apt to be, if anything, *more* penny-pinching and more intensely profit-oriented than the monopolist who (as we shall see) can afford to take a less hungry attitude toward profits. The lesson to be learned—and it is an important one—is that motives have nothing to do with the problem of less-than-pure competition. *The difference between a monopoly, an oligopoly, and a situation of pure competition is entirely one of market structure—that is, of the number of firms, ease of entry or exit, and the degree of differentiation among their goods.*

MONOPOLY

We have already noted a very precise distinction between the competitive situation, with its numerous firms and undifferentiated goods, and markets in which the number of sellers is few or in which goods are highly differentiated. In the competitive case, as we have seen, each firm caters to so small a section of the market that the demand curve for its produce is, for all intents and purposes, horizontal. By way of contrast, in a monopolistic or oligopolistic market structure there are so few firms that each one faces a distinctly sloping demand curve. That means that each firm, by varying its output, can affect the price for its product.

Another way of describing this difference is to call purely competitive firms, who have no control over their price, *price-takers* and to label monopolies or oligopolies or any firm that can affect the price of its product, *price-searchers.*

"PURE" MONOPOLIES

By examining the economic problems faced by a "pure" monopoly, let us see how such a price-searcher operates. Why do we place the word "pure" in quotes? Because a monopoly is not as easy to define as one might think. Essentially, the word means that there is only *one* seller of a particular good or service. The trouble comes in defining the "particular" good or service. In a sense, any seller of a differentiated good is a monopolist, for no one else dispenses *quite* the same utilities as he does: each shoeshine boy has his "own" customers, some of whom would probably continue to patronize his stand even if he charged slightly more than his competition.

Thus at one end of the difficulty is the fact that there is an element of monopoly in many seemingly competitive goods—a complication we shall come back to later. At the other end of the problem is that even where there is only one seller of a commodity—say the telephone company—there are still *substitutes* for its service. We can send a telegram or write a letter if telephoning becomes too expensive. Hence, before we can draw conclusions from the mere fact that a company provides the "only" service of a kind, we need to know how easy or difficult it is to switch into other products or services.

Evidently the problem of defining a "pure" monopoly is not easily resolved.* Let us, however, assume that we will all agree to call the local power company a monopoly, because no one else sells gas and electricity to the community. In Fig. 26-1 we show what the demand curve of such a monopoly looks like.

LIMITS OF
MONOPOLY

FIG. 26-1

DEMAND CURVE
FOR A
MONOPOLY

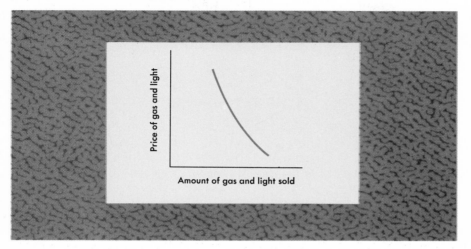

One point is immediately clear. *The monopolistic* firm *faces the same kind of demand curve that the competitive* industry *faces.* That is because it caters to *all* the demand for that particular product, just as does the industrial group of competitive firms. A corollary follows. The monopolist faces a fundamental limitation on his power to control the market imposed by the demand curve itself. Suppose a monopolist is selling quantity *OX* at price *OA* as shown in Fig. 26-2. He would like to sell quantity *OY* at price *OA,* but *he cannot.* He has no way of forcing the market to take a larger quantity of his product—unless he lowers the price to *OB.*†

*How do we recognize a monopoly? Because of the problem of substitutes, there is no very clear sign, except in a few cases such as the "natural" monopolies discussed above. Usually when we speak of "monopolies" we mean (a) very large businesses, (b) with much higher than competitive profits, and (c) with relatively little direct product competition. Not many firms satisfy all three conditions. GM or Standard Oil is a monopoly by criteria *a* and *b,* but not by *c;* Polaroid by *b* and *c* but not *a.* Note, furthermore, that even small businesses can be monopolies, such as "the only gambling house in town" famed in all Westerns.

†What would be the *most* profitable course for the monopolist to follow? It would be to sell his goods at *varying* prices, charging more when the buyer is willing and able to pay a high price. (One could imagine an auction, for example, in which a monopolist doled out his product in this manner.) We call this *discriminatory pricing.* Why does the monopolist not follow it? (1) In some industries it is illegal. (2) It is extremely difficult to carry out, because someone with a low personal demand could buy more than he himself wanted of a good, in order to resell it to someone higher up on the demand curve. If this trading among customers goes on, the final average price will be exactly that established by the demand curve and the supply schedule. Nevertheless, discriminatory pricing is not uncommon in certain fields: antiques, used cars, pawnshops—and perhaps some professional fees.

FIG. 26-2

**DEMAND CURVE
AS A
CONSTRAINT
ON THE
MONOPOLIST**

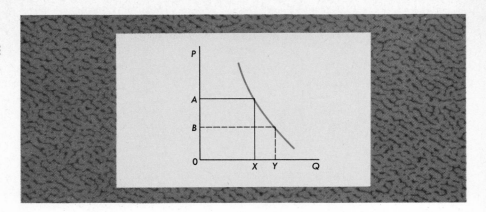

The situation is very similar (on the seller's side) with a *union*. A union can raise the price of labor, since it controls the supply of labor, but it cannot force employers to hire more labor than they want. Hence the question "Can unions raise wages?" must be answered "Yes," insofar as those who continued to be hired are concerned. But until we know the elasticity of the demand for labor, we cannot say if unions can raise the total amount of labor's revenues. (Recall our analysis, pp. 490f.)

There is one thing a monopolist can do, however, that neither a union nor a purely competitive firm can. He can advertise and thus seek to move the demand curve for his product to the right. Advertising does not "pay" for a purely competitive firm selling undifferentiated goods, for such a firm has no way of being sure that *its* goods—and not a competitor's—will benefit: imagine a single farmer advertising "Buy wheat!" But advertising *can* pay for a monopolist who will get all the demand he can conjure up. We can think of advertising as an attempt to sell larger quantities of a good or service without reducing prices, by shifting the demand curve itself. Figure 26-3 shows us this important effect.

FIG. 26-3

**ADVERTISING
AND DEMAND**

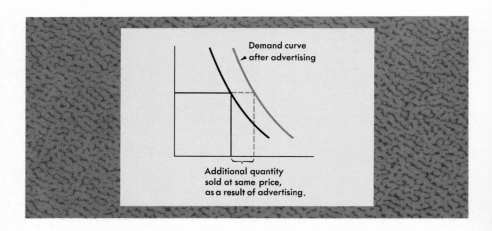

Demand curve
after advertising

Additional quantity
sold at same price,
as a result of advertising.

We have seen in what way the shape of the demand curves faced by monopolists differs from those faced by competitive firms. Are costs curves similarly different?

In general, they are not. We can take the cost profile of a monopoly as being exactly the same as that of a competitive firm. The monopoly, like the competitive firm, buys factors and exerts no control over their prices. A.T.&T. does not affect the level of wages or the price of land or capital by its decisions to expand production or not.* The monopolist, like the competitive entrepreneur, experiences the effects of changing productivity as he hires additional factors, and again like the competitive firm, he shops for the best buy in the factor markets. Thus the same U-shaped average cost curve and the same more steeply sloped marginal cost curve will describe the cost changes experienced by a monopolist quite as well as those of a competitive firm.

It is when we come to the revenue side of the picture that we meet the critical distinction of monopoly. Unlike a competitive firm, *a monopoly has a marginal revenue curve that is different from its average revenue curve.* The difference arises because each time a monopolist sells more output, he must reduce his price, whereas a competitive firm sells its larger output at the same price. Therefore, the revenue yielded to the monopolist by each additional unit will not be as great as that of the preceding unit whose price was higher.

A table may make this clear. Let us suppose we have a monopoly that is faced with an average revenue or price schedule as in Table 26-1.

TABLE 26 · 1

Price	Quantity sold	Total revenue	Marginal revenue
$20	1	$20	$20
19	2	38	18
18	3	54	16
17	4	68	14
16	5	80	12
15	6	90	10

*There is a special situation in which there is only one *buyer,* that we call "monopsony." A large employer who is the only substantial buyer of labor in a small town may be a monopsonist, and his decisions to hire labor or land or capital *will* affect their prices. For the monopsonist, the marginal cost curve is affected not only by the changing productivity of a factor but by its varying price, as more and more of the factor is hired. Because this is a situation infrequently found in the marketplace, we shall not analyze it further here. The principles involved are in no way different from those of monopoly.

FIG. 26-4

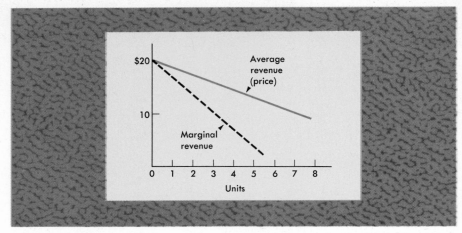

The graph of such a marginal revenue curve looks like Fig. 26-4.

What determines the shape of the marginal revenue curve? Obviously, the change in demand that will be brought about by a drop in price. In turn, this reflects—as we remember from our discussion in Chapter 2—the elasticity of demand which, in turn, hinges on our tastes, the availability of substitutes, and so on.

**EQUILIBRIUM
FOR THE
MONOPOLY**

The next step is obvious enough. We must superimpose the cost profile and the revenue profile to determine the equilibrium position for the monopolist. We can see it in Fig. 26-5.

What will be the equilibrium position? *The monopolist who seeks to maximize profit is guided by exactly the same rule as the competitive firm: he adds factors so long as the marginal revenue they bring in is greater than their marginal cost.* Hence we look for the intersection of the *MC* and *MR* curves on Fig. 26-5. Now if we extend a vertical line down to the horizontal axis, we will discover how much output will be produced (*OX*) at what price (*OA*). (See Fig. 26-6.)

FIG. 26-5

**EQUILIBRIUM
FOR THE
MONOPOLIST**

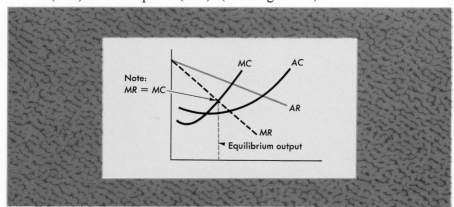

And what will the profit be? As before, profit is the difference between *average* cost and *average* revenue. The intersection of the *MC* and *MR* curves determines in the first place what our output will be; and now, knowing that, we can tell what our average cost and price, or average revenue, will be. Hence we can easily block in the profit of the enterprise. We do this in Fig. 26-6.

FIG. 26-6

MONOPOLY PROFIT

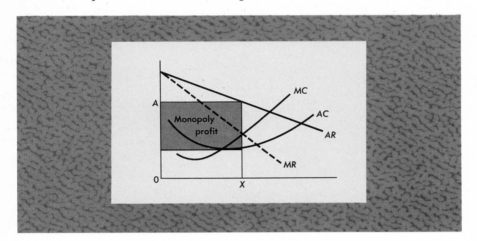

What is the difference between this price and that of a purely competitive market? We remember the formula for the equilibrium price of such a market: Price $= MC = MR = AC$. In the monopoly situation *MC* still equals *MR* (this is always the profit-maximizing guide), but price certainly does not equal *AC*. Whereas the competitive firm is forced to price its goods at the lowest point on its cost curve, the monopolist sells at a price far above cost. Then, too, there is no pressure from "outside" forcing the monopolist to reduce costs. Hence his entire cost curve may well lie above that of a competitive industry producing the same product. It is interesting to note that when hard pressed, some big auto firms (not even monopolies) have reduced overhead expenses by as much as a third. But most of the time, monopolies are not hard pressed.

If this were the case in a competitive market, we know what the remedy would be. An influx of firms would move the supply curve to the right; and as a result, prices would fall until excess profits had been wiped out. But in a monopoly situation, by the very definition of a monopoly, there is no entry into the market. Hence the monopolist is able to restrict his output to the amount that will bring in the high price he enjoys.

Monopoly thus imposes two burdens on society. It sells wares at a *higher price* than that of the competitive firm, and its *output is smaller* than would be the case under competitive conditions. The consumer gets less and pays more for it.

This is not, as we have had occasion to remark before, a full accounting of the "social cost" of monopoly. It is a description of the *economic* difference between the market solution of a competitive and a monopolistic firm. It ignores entirely such matters as power or influence, which may make monopoly politically undesirable, and it omits as well any consideration of the possible usefulness of some monopolies (like the phone company) in providing a unified service or considerable economies of large-scale production.

Finally, we should note that most "natural" monopolies, such as the utility companies or water supply companies or the telephone company, are regulated by public authorities. By imposing price ceilings on these monopolies (usually calculated to allow the companies to earn a "fair return" on their invested capital), the regulating commissions seek to approximate the results of a competitive environment. As Fig. 26-7 shows, its *MR* will be horizontal along the price ceiling, just like that of a competitive firm, and therefore its output will expand.

FIG. 26-7

REGULATION OF MONOPOLY

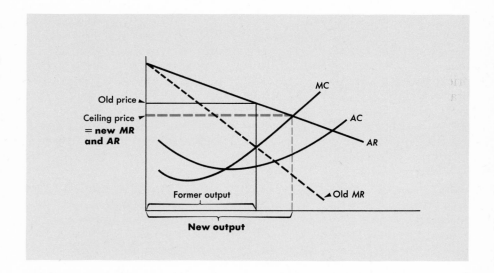

OLIGOPOLY

Monopoly in its "pure" form is a rarity, and unregulated monopoly is rarer still. From our previous study of the American economy, we know that the market structure in which most big corporations operate is not that of pure monopoly, but rather that of oligopoly. In an oligopolistic market situation, a *few* sellers divide the market and typically compete with one another by means of advertising, product differentiation, service, etc., rather than by the classic competitive means of price. (See pp. 122–23.)

What does a typical oligopoly look like under the lens of price theory? On the cost side, it is much the same as a monopolist or a perfect competitor. There is, however, an essential difference between the demand curve of a monopolist and that of an oligopolist. The demand curve for a monopolist, since it comprises the entire demand for the commodity, is the downward sloping curve of the kind with which we are familiar. But the demand curve for an oligopolist, although it is also downward sloping, has a shape that is new to us and quite unusual.

Suppose that you were the president of a large company that, along with three other very similar companies, sold roughly 80 per cent of a certain commodity. Suppose also that a price had been established for your commodity. It yielded you and your competitors a "reasonable" profit, but you and your fellow officers were considering how that profit might be increased.

One possibility that would certainly be discussed would be to raise the price of your product and hope that your customers would continue to be loyal to you. But your company economists might point out that their analyses showed a very elastic demand for your product *if you raised your price, but your competitors did not.* That is, at the higher price, many of your "loyal" customers would switch to a competitive brand, so that your revenues would fall sharply and your profits decline.

Suppose, then, you took the other tack and gambled on that very elasticity of demand by cutting your prices. Would not other firms' customers switch to you and thereby raise your revenues and profits? This time your advisors might point out that if you cut your price, your competitors would almost certainly do the same, to prevent you from taking a portion of "their" market. As a result, with prices cut all around, you would probably find demand highly *inelastic,* and your revenues not larger but smaller.

As Fig. 26-8 shows, you are facing a *kinked* demand curve. In the situation, you might well be tempted to sit tight and do nothing.

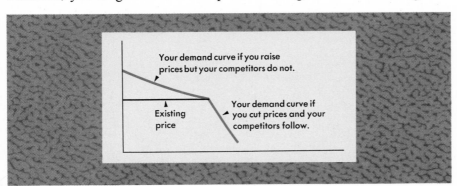

FIG. 26-8

THE KINKED DEMAND CURVE

Your demand curve if you raise prices but your competitors do not.

Existing price

Your demand curve if you cut prices and your competitors follow.

FIG. 26-9

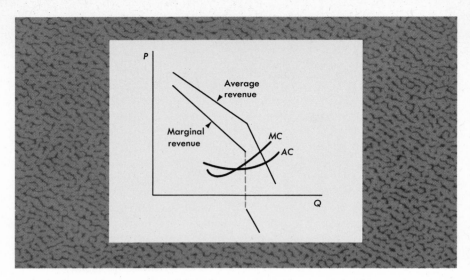

For a very interesting thing happens to the marginal revenue curve that is derived from a kinked demand curve. As Fig. 26-9 shows, we now get two marginal revenue curves: one applicable to the upper, elastic section of the demand curve, and the other to the lower, inelastic section. At the point of the kink, the marginal revenue curve is discontinuous, dropping vertically from the end of one slope to the beginning of the next. *As a result, there is no single point of intersection of the marginal revenue and marginal cost curves.* This means that an oligopolist's costs can change considerably before he is forced to alter his optimum volume of output or selling price.

The kinked demand curve helps explain why oligopoly prices are often so unvarying even without collusion among firms, but it does not really explain how the existing price is arrived at. For once cost or demand conditions have changed enough to overcome oligopolistic inertia, a new "kink" will again appear around the changed price. The kinked curve thus shows what forces affect *changes* in the oligopolistic situation, rather than how supply and demand originally determine the going price.

Price theory, as such, does not shed as much light on how the price of steel or cars or tires or tin cans is arrived at, as it does in a fully competitive industry. But why should this be so? We know in general what the demand curves look like for oligopolistic commodities, and we have a general idea of their supply behavior. Does it not follow therefore that price will be set by the standard supply-and-demand interplay?

THE
MAXIMIZING
ASSUMPTION

The answer—or rather, the lack of a clear-cut answer—causes us to examine another underpinning of classical price theory. We have already looked into the assumptions of pure competition—indeed, in this chapter we are tracing the consequences of failing to meet those assumptions. But the oligopoly problem forces us to confront a second fundamental premise of microeconomic theory. This is the assumption that firms maximize short-run profits.

Under pure competition, as we have seen, such profit maximization has a powerful motive working for it, quite above that of an entrepreneur's desire to get rich. This is the motive of *self-preservation*. Firms that do not constantly equate marginal cost and marginal revenue—the iron rule of maximizing—will simply fail to survive the competitive test. Hence, in the classical model, we can accept short-run profit maximizing as a fair description of reality, as well as a valid guideline for a well-working market system.

Not so, however, with oligopoly or monopoly. To be sure, a great corporation that failed to make any profits for many years would eventually fail, but there is little danger that a large company will go under if it does not make the last dollar—or even the last ten million dollars—of possible profits in any one year or even over two or three years running.

Do the great oligopolistic concerns try to equate marginal cost and marginal revenue, and thus maximize their income?

This is a question that is difficult to answer, by virtue of the very indeterminacy of the oligopolistic equilibrium resting point. We have just seen that a kinked demand curve makes likely a very high degree of oligopolistic inertia. The classic route to higher profits—beating one's competitor on price—tends to be shunned. What we find instead of the single-minded pursuit of gain is a strategic pursuit of long-run growth and strength that may very well lead to short-run decisions *not* to make as much money as possible.

Two factors in particular make the oligopolist's day-by-day behavior difficult to predict in theory. The first is his limited but not insignificant ability to influence the demand curve for his own product. Oligopolies are typically the largest advertisers, for one way in which competition *can* be carried out without disturbing the price structure is by inducing customers to switch brands at the same price.* Thus a considerable degree of oligopolistic success depends not on pursuing the traditional course of profit-maximizing, but on pursuing a successful strategy of sale-enlargement.

Second, the *long-term* considerations that guide the behavior of oligopolies introduces a new element into the profit-maximizing picture that is missing in the competitive case. The entrepreneur of the small

---

*Thus we find a new kind of cost in oligopolistic firms—*selling* cost, or cost incurred, not to hire factors of production and thereby directly to increase output, but to move the demand curve and thereby to increase sales. A competitive firm has no selling costs, because its product is indistinguishable from that of anyone else.

firm lives in a world in which his costs and his demand curve are both subject to change without notice. He must do the best he can, at each moment, to obtain the highest income for himself. The oligopolist, on the other hand, has a considerable degree of control over his future. Since his overhead costs are usually high, he is able to make stringent economies if the need arises. And since he lives in a market situation where he is reasonably sure of not having to face price competition, he plans for the future in terms of improving or changing his product or his advertising or both.

This necessarily introduces into his plans a *time dimension* of much greater depth than in the case of classic competition. And in turn, the ability—not to say necessity—to plan several years in advance gives greater latitude to whatever decisions may be in the best immediate interests of the firm. *Thus profit-maximizing, however valid as a description of the state of mind or aim of the oligopolist, no longer serves, as it does in the competitive case, to describe the exact price and output decisions that we can expect firms to undertake in the face of market pressures.* Oligopolies are, within broad limits, free to follow whatever course—aggressive or defensive—their managements decide is best, and competing oligopolies have often followed *different* courses. Hence microtheory can say relatively little about how the market will impinge on the oligopolistic firm, since its economic pressures are much less imperious than they are in pure competition.

IMPERFECT COMPETITION

We shall return once more to an assessment of the market under the conditions of oligopoly, but we must first finish our review of the marketplace in reality, rather than theory. For oligopoly, although perhaps the most striking departure from the ideal of pure competition, is not the most common departure. Once we pass from the manufacturing to the retail or service sectors where competition is still intense and "atomistic" (i.e., characterized by numerous small units), we encounter a new kind of market situation, equally strange to the pages of a text on pure competition. This is a situation in which there are many firms, with relatively easy entrance and exit, but in which *each firm sells a product slightly differentiated from that of every other.* Here is the world of the average store or the small competitive manufacturer of a brand-name product—indeed, of every seller who can "identify" his product to the public and who must face the competition of many other makers of similar but not exactly identical products.

Economists call this market situation in which there is a tinge of monopoly *imperfect competition* or *monopolistic competition*. How does it differ from pure competition? Once again, there is no difference on the cost side, which is exactly the same for both a perfectly competitive and an imperfectly competitive firm. The difference, again, comes in the nature of the demand curve.

We recall that the special attribute of the demand curve facing a firm in a purely competitive situation is its horizontal character. By way of contrast, *in a market of imperfect competition, the demand curve facing each seller slopes gently downward.* As we have already seen, this is because his good or service is not exactly like that of his competitors, and because he therefore has some ability to raise price without losing all his business.

FIG. 26-10

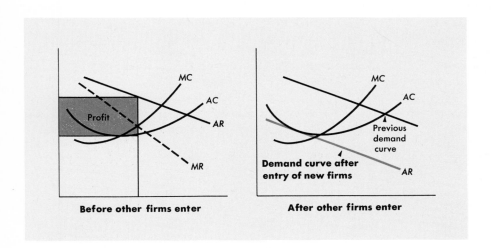

Before other firms enter   After other firms enter

What is the equilibrium position of such an imperfectly competitive firm—say a dress manufacturer? In Fig. 26-10, we show, on the left, an imperfect competitor who is obviously making substantial profits. Note that his best position where $MR = MC$ is *exactly* like that of a monopolist.

But our firm is not a monopolist, and its profits are therefore not immune to erasure by entry into its field. In Fig. 26-10, we show the same firm after *other entrepreneurs have moved into the industry* (with additional similar, although not identical, products) and thereby taken away some of our firm's market and moved its demand curve to the left.

Note that our final position for the marginal dress firm has no more profit than that of a purely competitive seller. On the other hand, because his demand curve slopes, the equilibrium point cannot be at the lowest point on the average cost curve, nor will output have reached optimum size. (Of course, intramarginal firms can be more profitable than the marginal case we have graphed.)

This outcome clearly dissipates economic well-being. The fact that firms are forced to operate to the left of the optimums on their cost curves means that *they have not been able to combine factors to yield their greatest efficiency*—a failure that penalizes factors, once when they are paid too little because their potential marginal productivity has not been reached, and again as consumers when they are forced to pay too much for products that have not been produced at lowest possible cost. In addition, wastage is incurred because the attempt to differentiate products leads in many instances to too many small units—for example, the famous (and all too common) case of four gas stations on one corner.

Inefficient though it may be, just as in a purely competitive industry, monopolistic competition yields the marginal firm in an industry no profit. The entrepreneur therefore feels fully as hard-pressed as would the producer of an undifferentiated commodity. The difference is that a monopolistic competitive businessman has the possibility of *further differentiating* his product, hoping thereby to tilt his demand curve in a more inelastic position. In turn, this might allow him to raise his prices slightly and to squeeze out a tiny "pure monopoly" profit. The result is that we find a tremendous variety of goods in industries in which monopolistic competition is typical—the ladies garment industry being a prime example.*

EXTENT OF
MARKET
IMPERFECTION

How much of the whole market system is imperfect in one sense or another?

Let us begin with pure monopolies. We have seen how difficult it is to define what such a monopoly is, but if we are not too careful about looking for product substitutes, then perhaps we can classify 10 to 20 per cent of output as monopolistic. Nearly all of it is the output of public utilities, regulated by public agencies, or consists of the output of the public sector (for the government is certainly a monopoly, although not a profit-maximizing one).

Oligopolies constitute a more significant category. As we know, they are the predominant form of market structure in important areas of the economy, particularly manufacturing. Yet the degree of oligopoly varies greatly from one industry to another. Within the industrial sector as a whole, about half of the manufactured products sold nationally

---

*Oligopolists as well as monopolistic competitors march to the drums of competition through product differentiation. In the fields of cigarettes, soaps, and breakfast cereals, the market is pretty much made up of three firms, and thirty or forty years ago most grocery stores stocked only about three or four brands of each. But today the shelves holding these products have been expanded again and again as each of the three firms came forward with a new differentiation or one to match a new, highly successful brand of one of its competitor.

are produced by industries in which the top eight firms do at least a third of the business. But this very mild degree of concentration is an average of some industries (bottled soft drinks, sawmills, printing) where the top twenty companies produce only a third of all output, and other industries (autos, cans, cigarettes) where the top *four* companies do up to 90 per cent of the business.

In addition, the problem of measuring or even defining oligopoly is complicated by the question of the market division of sales. For example, the top eight beer and ale companies sell only 28 per cent of the nation's total consumption of beer; but because these drinks are usually produced and marketed within a limited region, the concentration of sales among a few brewers is much greater in any one area, such as New York or Chicago, than it is in the nation as a whole.

It is worth noting the difference between concentration within market areas, however defined, and the over-all concentration of industry discussed in Chapter 6. The emergence of the giant conglomerate corporation has not yet noticeably raised the concentration ratios within most markets, although it is possible that this may happen if the conglomerate movement continues much longer. Hence the growth of the giant multiproduct company poses problems of a political nature, or perhaps of financial speculation, rather than problems related directly to the degree of competition. As of 1968, the texture of the marketplace had not been significantly changed by the emergence of the conglomerate giant, although the structure of American capitalism as a whole had certainly been affected by it.

It is much more difficult, and perhaps even impossible, to measure the extent of monopolistic competition. As we have already discussed, very few industries fully meet the qualifications of pure competition; and even if we remove the proviso of easy entry and exit, not much of America's output is both undifferentiated in character and produced by many firms. Only agriculture, fisheries, and a few other industries comprising perhaps 10 to 15 per cent of national output could then be called purely competitive. Another 30 to 40 per cent resembles pure competition in its numerous firms, but is characterized by differentiated output. Perhaps the same percentage of output is produced in more or less oligopolistic markets.

These estimates should not be taken as more than very rough orders of magnitude. What is important is that market *imperfection,* in one form or another, is the prevailing reality in the micro system of the United States (or any other industrial nation). What significance does this fact have for the effectiveness of that system or for the relevance of the theory that seeks to describe it? These are the culminating questions to which our last chapter will seek to provide some answers.

SUMMARY

1. The motives of monopoly and oligopoly are exactly those of competition. What is different is the *structure of the market* in which these motives give rise to action.

2. The monopoly or oligopoly faces a sloping rather than a horizontal demand curve. It is a *price-searcher rather than a price-taker.*

3. A monopoly is difficult to define narrowly because of the existence of *substitutes* for all commodities. The monopolistic *firm* enjoys the same demand curve as does the competitive *industry,* and is forced to obey the limitations imposed by its demand curve. It can, however, attempt to *shift the curve to the right by advertising.*

4. The cost curves of monopolists and oligopolists are shaped the same as those of competitive firms. However, monopolists face *marginal revenue curves that are not identical with their average revenue curves.* The difference arises because the monopolist must lower his price to increase his sales. Therefore, each additional unit brings in a smaller addition to total revenues than the previous unit brought.

5. Equilibrium for the monopoly (as for the competitive firm) is that output where $MR = MC$. This is the point of maximum profit. AC will not equal P, however, for there is no influx of firms to push prices down to this point.

6. The result of monopoly is twofold: prices will be higher than in competitive firms, and output will be smaller.

7. Oligopoly is a more common market structure than monopoly. It is characterized by a few sellers, rather than one.

8. The oligopolist's *demand curve is typically kinked.* This shape reflects the difficulty of holding his market share if he raises prices alone, and the difficulty of maintaining his price advantage if he cuts price, which will be quickly followed by his fellow oligopolists.

9. Oligopolies often need not obey the dictates of *short-run* profit maximizing. On the contrary, they can plan considerable distances into the future. As a result, *profit-maximizing,* however accurate a description of their goal, *does not lead to the exactly predictable behavior* that it does in the case of the competitive firm.

10. Imperfect or monopolistic competition is used to describe markets in which there are *many sellers selling differentiated products.* The point of difference is the existence of a *slightly sloping demand curve.*

11. Imperfect competition leads to two main results. First, output *does not reach the point of lowest cost* and greatest efficiency, thereby penalizing both consumers and factors. Second, there is a tendency for *differentiation to increase* in the hope of gaining a small profit.

12. The bulk of all markets in industrial countries are *imperfect to some degree.* Pure competition is perhaps as rare as ''pure'' monopoly.

1. In what way, if any, do the motives of a monopolist differ from those of a perfect competitor? In what way does the time span of his decision-making differ? Can this affect his behavior (as contrasted to his motivation)?

2. How would you define a monopoly? Are monopolies necessarily large? What constraints does a demand curve put on the behavior of a monopoly?

3. Suppose that you were the only seller of a certain kind of machinery in the nation. Suppose further that you discovered that your demand curve looked like this:

Price	$100	$90	$80	$70
Quantity of machines sold	1	2	3	4

   What is the average revenue at each price? What is the marginal revenue at each price? Draw a diagram showing the marginal and average revenue.

4. Now superimpose on this diagram a hypothetical cost profile for your business. Where is the point of equilibrium for the monopolist? Is this the same, in terms of MC and MR, as the point for the competitive firm? Now show the equilibrium output and price.

5. Does the equilibrium output of the monopolist yield a profit? What are the relevant costs for figuring profit, average costs per unit, or marginal costs? Show on your diagram the difference between average cost and selling price.

6. Why will a monopolist's selling price not be pushed to the lowest point on the cost curve?

7. What is the difference between monopoly and oligopoly? Between oligopoly and pure competition? Between pure competition and monopolistic (or imperfect) competition? Between the latter and oligopoly?

8. What is meant by the kinked demand curve of an oligopolist? How do you explain the kink?

9. Why does the profit-maximizing assumption lead to such clear-cut results when we speak of pure competition, and to such indeterminate ones for oligopolies? Does the answer have something to do with the time over which the consequences of actions can be calculated?

10. What is a differentiated commodity? Give examples. Draw the demand curve for a farmer selling wheat and that for a toy manufacturer selling his own brand of dolls. What will happen if the doll manufacturer makes a large profit? What will his final point of equilibrium look like if he has many competitors?

11. Compare on two diagrams the equilibrium of the purely competitive firm and of the imperfectly competitive one. Show, by a dotted line, what the demand curve would look like for the imperfectly competitive firm if its product differentiation were removed. Where would its output now be located? What would be its selling price? Would the consumer gain from this?

27

THE MARKET SYSTEM
IN REVIEW

It is time to sit back and review our findings on the market system as a whole. In particular, we want to inquire what light the study of microeconomics throws on the working of the market system in real life.

Let us begin by recalling briefly the nature of the task we undertook. We began our excursion into microeconomics by asking what kind of order could be discerned in the apparent confusion of the marketplace. Did the throng of marketers exert some form of control over the goods and services produced by the firms that sought their business? What principles underlay the various levels of pay which those firms handed over to the marketers when they hired them? What kind of discipline was exerted by the market over the crucial production processes carried on by the firms themselves?

To all these questions, microtheory gave us clear answers within the assumptions of short-run profit maximizing and intense price competition characteristic of the world of atomistic firms it portrayed. Rather than review these answers in specific detail, let us try to summarize the meaning of the market's performance from an over-all point of view.

STRENGTHS OF THE MARKET

Two attributes of the system immediately call themselves to our attention:

1. *The fragmentation of economic power.*
In the world of pure competition, only three forces ultimately direct the workings of the marketplace. One of these is, of course, the willingness and ability of the public to buy the goods and services offered to them. A second is the willingness and ability of the public, as a work force, to offer its services for production. The third is the technological capability of the firm. In this way, *product demand, factor supply, and marginal productivity emerge as the basic controllers of the economic system*—or to put it differently, the psychological desires and dislikes of the public, on the one hand, and the realities of nature and man's ability to control it, on the other.

To be sure, the system requires for its operation another active force—the profit-seeking firm. Note, however, that the firm is singularly devoid of any capacity to influence the background elements we have mentioned. Driven by competition in an environment without shelter, the firm must obey the dictates of the public, both as buyers of goods and as suppliers of factor services, and can in no way impose its own dictates upon the public. Only in the choice of methods of production does it have a free hand, and here, if it does not measure up to average levels of performance, it will not long survive.

Hence, in a world of pure competition, and only such a world, the public becomes the repository of most economic power. This is often called the "sovereignty of the consumer," but it goes beyond that to the joint sovereignty of the consumer and the worker (or factor of production). In this way a society of pure competition comes closer than any other form of economic organization to translating the general ideas of political democracy into economic reality.

2. *The maximization of efficiency.*
In a world of pure competition, as we have seen, output is pushed along each firm's supply curve until the lowest average unit cost is reached. There the firm must maintain its operation. This equation of marginal

cost and revenue, and of price and average cost, is not merely a text-book solution to the problem of equilibrium. Rather, it represents a social solution to the problem of production that gives us the *largest possible volume of output, at the lowest possible prices compatible with existing resources, technology, and the attitudes of the public.*

As we know, this is achieved because the firm must combine its factors of production with one eye on their relative cost and the other on their relative productivities, finally bringing about a mix in which each factor is used as effectively as possible, given its cost. At the same time, each factor is not only assigned to the post that utilizes it most efficiently, but competition in the factor market assures that each factor will be remunerated in full for its contribution to the firm's output. Any firm that fails to pay its factors in accord with their marginal productivities or combines them in a way that lessens their effectiveness will pay the price of seeing its factors bid away to other producers or of simply being undersold on the market. Thus, under the pressure of the system, *the full potential of all human and material resources will be used up to the limits imposed by the willingness and ability of individuals to work.*

We should pay special heed to one aspect of the process by which the competitive market pushes the economic system toward efficiency. One operating rule alone suffices to bring about the whole spectrum of adjustment and coordination by which the system will attain its best results. *That single rule is to maximize profits.* By concentrating on that one criterion of success and not by trying to maximize output in physical terms or by trying to live by a complicated book of regulations, entrepreneurs in a competitive environment do in fact bring the system to a peak of operating efficiency. In other words, profits are not only a source of privileged income, but also an enormously versatile and useful "success indicator" for a system that is trying to squeeze as much output as possible from its given inputs. When we study the operation of a planned economy (Chapter 30), we shall have reason to remember this important point.

WEAKNESSES OF THE MARKET

All these miraculous results of the market describe a system of pure competition. Yet, if there is any certainty in the world in which we live, it is that such a system is an unattainable goal. Merely consider what would have to be done to achieve a market structure in which pure competition would appear. Every giant firm (and many medium-sized ones) would have to be broken into fragments, none large enough to account for a significant fraction of the markets it served. Brand names familiar to every householder and worth millions of dollars to their owners would have to be outlawed, and the faceless output of undifferentiated commodities would have to take their place. All barriers to entry and to factor mobility would have to go: unions, patent restrictions, tariffs, initiation fees, inheritances. Even if it were unambiguously clear that the resulting system would be preferable to our own, it is obvious that such an assault on the present market system would never be tolerated—by the public any more than by the business sector.

And then, would it be unambiguously superior? We have deferred until now a full judgment on the effect of monopolistic imperfections on the market mechanism. Let us try to achieve some perspective on the differences—good as well as bad—that distinguish the marketplace as it exists in reality from that of an ideally pure competitive milieu.

WASTE

The first effect of market imperfections is clear. It represents a departure from the standards of extreme efficiency promised by pure competition. No longer is every firm producing at the lowest point on its cost curve. No longer are profits held to a minimum. No longer is the consumer the undisputed sovereign of the marketplace. In various forms and guises, waste—useless effort or useless expenditure—is introduced into the system.

ADVERTISING

One form of waste is the enormous proliferation of advertising in an imperfect market society. Today we spend over half as much to persuade buyers to choose this or that brand as we spend for all primary and secondary education—indeed, advertising expenditures can be thought of as a vast campaign to educate individuals to be "good" consumers. As we have already pointed out in Chapter 6, some of this expenditure may be necessary to stabilize and solidify consumer demand in an affluent society, and some of it certainly has an important informational function or even an enjoyable aspect. After all, if there were no advertising it would be exceedingly difficult for genuine improvements or for new products to make their way into most households. It is probably fair to state that without the possibility of advertising products, the system would lose a great deal of its dynamism.

Yet not all advertising, by any matter of means, conveys information that is genuinely useful to the consumer or introduces new products. It is difficult to contemplate the battles of aspirins, airlines, soaps (up to 10 per cent of the price of soap is accounted for by selling expense), cars, and cigarettes, without recognizing that much of this represents a wastage of scarce resources, including the resources of very gifted and clever people whose efforts are largely directed toward annulling the work of their counterparts in a different advertising agency.

Waste appears, too, in product differentiation. It has been calculated that the cost to the consumer of annual style changes in cars runs to $5 billion a year or some $700 per car. What the corresponding figures are for other "style" goods, such as the ever-new models of dishwashers and refrigerators, detergents and cosmetics, we do not know. But certainly the prices of many goods could be greatly reduced if a single model were decided on, and all improvements poured into cost reduction. So, too, the resources that must now be spread among competing establishments—the case we mentioned before of "four gas stations"—would be much more efficiently employed in one.

Yet, there are counterarguments. The elimination of brands that assuredly sell the same thing in different packages would leave the question of what policing force would then be left to regulate the one remaining brand. And where product differentiation results in variations in the product itself—and not just in its "image"—one must ask whether the aim of an affluent society is to produce the largest possible quantity of a standardized product at the cheapest possible cost or to offer an array of differing products that please our palates, admittedly at somewhat higher costs. Few consumers in a rich society would prefer an inexpensive uniform to more expensive but highly individualized clothes. From this point of view, even the wasteful parade of car styles has a certain rationale.

Thus, as with advertising, *some* production differentiation plays a useful and utility-increasing function. The question is how much? This is a matter on which it is difficult to form a purely objective judgment, for even if the amount of "useless" product differentiation is relatively small, its impact on the public taste may be disproportionately large. The problem is perhaps particularly acute insofar as much of our "taste" for style seems to be the product of the deliberate advertising efforts of manufacturers. No doubt there is a real aesthetic pleasure in variety, but one doubts that it would take the form of a yearning for "this year's model" without a good deal of external stimulation. Product differentiation thus becomes in part an effort to maximize the public's utilities; but it is also in part an effort to create those "utilities" in order to maximize the producers' profits.

Last, *the wastes of an imperfect market system lie in its inability to push all resources to their point of highest return (and lowest cost).* Every monopoly, large or small, represents a shelter behind which factors are used in lesser quantities than would be the case if the shelter did not exist. Indeed, the whole problem of monopoly is that it prevents the inrush of land, labor, and capital that would take place if there were no barriers to entry.

How serious is the resulting misallocation of resources? Estimates for 1954 give a surprisingly small answer in terms of the aggregate of resources that is blocked out of its point of natural gravitation—perhaps no more than $5 billion—and the effect of transferring this amount of resources would have only a slight effect on the general level of prices. On the other hand, it is also true that profits in monopolistic industries are 50 to 100 per cent higher than those in highly competitive industries: in 1962, for example, the ten largest manufacturing corporations enjoyed profits of 8.7¢ on the sales dollar, whereas the half million corporations doing less than $50,000 of sales each averaged profits of but 3.5¢ per dollar of sales.

GAINS FROM MONOPOLY

Are the higher profits of big business pure waste, like all economic rents? They certainly imply that some prices could be materially reduced. Yet it is difficult to maintain that the high profits of the monopolistic sector have no social utility whatsoever. The handsome factories and offices, the generally more relaxed and generous attitudes toward employees, the growth of fringe benefits and amenities, the prospective transformation of the blue-collar worker into a white-collar salaried employee—all these important evolutionary changes in our economy must also be related to the easier pace and larger earnings of a monopolistic system, rather than to the frenzied pace and penny-pinching attitudes necessitated by a system of full price competition.

More important still, the development of large-scale technologies of low-cost mass production requiring the investment of vast sums, the cultivation of research that cannot possibly "pay off" for years, the restless search for new products that continuously redynamizes the macroeconomy—these attributes of modern capitalism are also by-products of its oligopolistic character and would be impossible to achieve in a regime of atomistic producers.

WASTE AND THE MARKET'S OPERATION

Thus, the economic argument of waste is not a simple issue to assess. The gains and losses are difficult to measure and cannot easily be weighed on the same scale. Perhaps it is more useful to ask whether the presence of waste has seriously impeded the operation of the market as a *system*. And here the answer can be given with more assurance. For the forces of the marketplace, although more slowly and sluggishly, continue to press in the *direction* of pure competition.

The pattern of demand, for example, although clearly to some extent the creature of advertising, still retains an independence (if only in the choice of the advertising it believes) that imposes an ultimate authority over the imperfect market. No firm, however large, feels secure in the "possession" of its customers. In the same way, the mobility of firms and factors is badly impeded by market imperfections, but there is nonetheless visible a long-term circulation of land, labor, and capital both among industries and regions: witness the rise of the computer industry, or the decline of rail transportation before the onslaughts of trucking and air travel. And whereas product competition is much less stringent than price competition, it also exerts a slow winnowing effect, certainly on the product, if not always on its maker.

SIZE AND
INSTABILITY

Thus the forces of self-interest and of a muted competition still prod the economy in the general direction spelled out by microtheory. But the viscosity of the market in the real world, compared with its extreme fluidity in theory, brings further problems in its wake. Specifically, it endangers the capacity of the market for *self-correction.*

We remember that one of the ways in which the market system assured the orderly provisioning of society was through a complicated chain of price signals and quantity responses—a chain that, as we have seen, brought about larger supplies when prices and profits rose, thereby pressing *against* a further price rise or even rolling prices back; and vice versa when prices fell.

These self-correcting market responses were automatically forthcoming in an environment of small competitive firms who "read" price and profit signals in terms of tomorrow's prospects, but they are by no means so reliable in an environment of giant firms who may ignore price changes entirely (for reasons of sheer bureaucratic inertia) or who may interpret them in a perspective of long-run market strategy. American steel firms, for example, were extremely reluctant to add to steel capacity all through the early postwar period, despite urgent price signals to do so, since they figured (erroneously, as it turned out) that the demand for steel would soon be saturated. As a result, we had a steel "shortage," since the industry neither raised its prices to the equilibrium point (for fear of political repercussions) nor produced enough steel to satisfy the quantity demanded at going prices.

Similarly, the self-correcting market of microtheory takes for granted a flexibility of prices as well as outputs. But big firms and big unions are not eager to allow their prices to fluctuate in response to every change in demand—especially not downward. As a result, market imperfections give us the phenomenon of "sticky" prices, whose difficulties we have already encountered in Part Two in dealing with the problem of money supply and general inflation. Thus monopoly elements in the market introduce problems into not only microeconomics but also macroeconomics, by complicating the problem of clearing the market for all goods—that is, making it more difficult to equate the supply of gross national output at *going prices* to the demand for gross national output, without either "gaps" or excesses of demand.

THE MARKET IN PERSPECTIVE

Finally we must revert to an issue we have already touched on in our discussion of oligopoly in Chapter 6, but that returns here in full focus. This is the problem of power.

We do not study power in pure competition because, as we have seen, the fragmentation of decision making effectively removes it as an economic issue. But the problem cannot be side-stepped in the real market. There the existence of large organizations of labor and capital clearly bring economic power into being, both in terms of an ability of these organizations to secure bigger returns than would be forthcoming under pure competition and in terms of the ability of their massed economic strength to exert influences over the social and political life of the community.

Since market imperfections are not new, the problems of economic power are also not new, and we have been engaged for many decades in trying to control both the sheerly economic and the political and social consequences of bigness. The history of our attempts to do so is written in the antitrust laws, the Taft-Hartley Act, other such legislation, and various regulatory agencies of the government.

How successful have been these efforts to control market-based power? There are many contradictory views. To some, who stress the continued growth of very large-scale business, it seems clear that we have not managed to control business power. To others, seeing the emergence of large labor unions, it is labor power that has eluded effective control. And to still others who are most impressed by the growth of big government, the market has seemed the locus for a growth of public power.

What lies behind this confusion of views is a fact of great importance. *It is that power has emerged in every aspect of economic life as the technological drive of modern society has given rise to large organizations in productive, distributive, and regulatory activity.* Business, labor, and government have *all* participated in this organizational growth, whose roots reach down to the changing technical base of our civilization itself.

As a result, the market is no longer a field in which power is fragmented and disappears, but a setting in which business and labor—and to some extent government—establish their bases of operation. Because the market is itself constantly changing, these bases shift, and power structures built on it are never wholly secure—as we see in the slow turnover of corporate giants or the rise and fall of union strength in different industrial areas of the shift in government power from one regulatory agency to another. In all cases, the market becomes, however, a field of activity to be *organized, administered, regulated,* and *controlled,* whether in the name of business, of labor, or of government.

Given the technological momentum of our time and its continuing tendency to encourage organization, it is doubtful that this trend will disappear. We should expect the appearance of power to constitute a major preoccupation of market-based economies for a long while to come.

**DEEPER
WEAKNESSES
OF THE
MARKET
SYSTEM**

As we discuss the departures of the real world from the ideal of pure competition, it is well to remind ourselves that the market is not a perfect system, not even in its most idealized form. Out of the striving for profit under the rigors of a competitive struggle emerge not only benefits but disbenefits for the consumer. The grasping employers of the nineteenth century who sweated their children in the textile mills were excellent "economic men." Extremes of riches and poverty, and the differential attitudes of the market to each—solicitous of the rich, indifferent to the poor—are attributes of market systems that must be put into the balance along with the triumphs of productivity and reductions in cost.

A second problem, emphasized by J. K. Galbraith in *The Affluent Society,* is the tendency of a market society to overlook those activities that are not marketable ventures, such as education or the care of the elderly or low-cost housing or public beautification. The contrast, in Galbraith's words, of "private riches and public squalor" must be counted in the ledger across from the mounting totals of GNP. The slums, just as much as the suburbs, are a product of the market system.

Third, the market is inadequate to deal with the social consequences of some private action. Thus, when Consolidated Edison Company in New York tots up its annual profits, it does not have to enter a charge for several million dollars worth of cleaning bills—although those cleaning bills (paid by private citizens) are a direct consequence of the smoke that pours out of its chimneys in the course of its profit-making activity. The market, in other words, had no mechanism for correcting—or even for allocating—the *external effects* of private action. In the problems of air and stream pollution, traffic congestion, the ugliness of most Main Streets, we see the price that must be paid for this lack of control.

Thus there are serious weaknesses in the market system—weaknesses that transcend the particular difficulties associated with imperfect competition as such. Essentially the weaknesses stem from the fact that the market has no inherent direction, no internal goal other than to satisfy the forces of supply and demand within it. Such a concern for supply and demand would perhaps be an admirable goal if life were still lived in the relatively self-sufficient and largely rural setting of the nineteenth century, and if the extremes of wealth and poverty were limited. But in a world where wealth is still very lopsided, and where men live totally interdependent lives, crowded into enormous concentrations of cities, the inherent defects of the market bring about very serious deformations.

Yet the very absence of any inherent goals within the market system is also a source of strength. It means that the market is actually a *social instrument* capable of being adapted to, and used for, the achievement of many ends. A society that prefers not to alter the existing distribution of its wealth and income must then allow the market to attain whatever results of production and distribution such a pattern of final demand will impose. But a society that wishes to undertake large-scale social improvements or alterations can also use the mechanism of the market to gain its ends.

In that case, needless to say, it must arrange for a transfer of demand from private to public hands: there must be public buyers able and willing to bid resources into new uses, or there may have to be a diversion of income from those who have a great deal to those who have very little. This public transfer of demand is inherently and inescapably a "command" function, although it may be democratically exercised and controlled. But once the transfer has been made, there is no reason why the operation of the system cannot still be entrusted the the free actions of buyers and sellers on the marketplace, and to competitive vying of profit-seeking firms, each seeking in this case to capture some of the public market rather than confining its activities solely to the private market.

Can we arrive at a final judgment of the strengths and weaknesses of the market system?

Perhaps it is clear by now that there can be no single final judgment—that the market has profound weaknesses and huge strengths, and that it is simplistic to try to make a once-for-all appraisal of such a complex and many-sided social institution.

Rather in this last word it seems well to step back from the technical problems of the market and to view it once again in the context of economic history. Then we see the market not merely as an allocatory system but as a social institution—an institution that stands sharply contrasted with its predecessor institutions of command and of tradition.

In this perspective, the strengths and weaknesses of the market take on a somewhat different appearance. They appear now as problems in the historical development of society, problems that must be placed in the perspective of a long economic evolution that is by no means finished.

What does that portend for the future of the market system and for the society in which that system exists? That must be the theme of our final section in which we turn our attention once again to the screen of world history. Before we proceed to that last perspective, however, there is one more section of theoretical teaching that we must add. We cannot follow the larger trajectory of the market system until we have come to understand a whole chapter of economics that we have heretofore ignored: the relation of the American economy to the world about it. Hence, we turn next to a subject that will expand our focus from the problems of a self-contained economy to those of an economy forced to cope with the economic stresses of other economies. We must now learn something about the very important—though to most Americans very unfamiliar—subject of foreign trade. Having traced the rise of the market society and analyzed in some detail how its economic machinery works, we must extend our view to other nations, and then trace the trajectory of the market system as far into the future as we can see.

1. The price system of pure competition yields a world in which *economic power is fragmented. Demand* (based on utility), *supply* (based on disutility and cost), and *productivity are the three underlying forces of the system.* The firm must accept their dictates and can in no way impose its own will upon them. Thus, in a world of pure competition, the public becomes the repository of most economic power. This is the meaning of the *"sovereignty of the consumer."*

2. In a world of pure competition, *efficiency is maximized.* This is because each firm is forced, under the threat of its elimination, to combine factors in the way that will lead to the lowest possible unit cost. At the same time, the market also forces each firm to assign its factors to their point of highest marginal return and to pay them the full value of their marginal contribution to output. The quest for profit thus becomes an instrument for the attainment of efficiency for the society at large.

3. The world of pure competition exists mainly in theory. To achieve it would entail a *massive breakup of large firms, the end of all barriers to economic mobility, the abolition of brand names,* and so on. This is obviously impossible, even if it were desirable.

4. There are several main consequences of the imperfect market that exists. One is waste. We see waste, in part, in advertising, some of which is merely economic effort to nullify other economic effort. Waste is also visible in *product differentiation,* in particular when the "demand" for differentiation is deliberately created. Finally, waste lies in the *failure of the system to push resources to their point of highest return,* because of monopolistic elements in the system.

5. There are some compensating gains from the wasteful elements. Advertising brings *information,* product differentiation brings *variety,* size brings *efficiency* and a more relaxed pace of economic life. And the slow currents of the change that make a market system work are still visible in a reduced but nonetheless effective competitiveness and mobility.

6. Another problem created by imperfection in the market is that of *a lessened capacity of the market for self-correction.* This can result in a failure of the market to clear, in the generation of "surpluses" or "shortages," and in the *sticky prices* that complicate monetary problems.

7. Last, market imperfections pose the problem of *power*—a problem that does not exist under pure competition. The market now becomes the locus in which large units of business, labor, and government contend for influence.

8. Aside from its imperfections, the market even as an ideal system has its weaknesses. Basically, these stem from the fact that the market has *no goal-orientation,* save to the structure of existing demand. In turn, this structure reflects the existing distribution of wealth, with its historical inequalities. On the other hand, this absence of internal orientation means that the *market system is also capable of being utilized for social planning* as well as for the operation of a laissez-faire system.

1. What is meant by saying that the ultimate forces of the pure market are product demand, factor supply, and marginal productivity?

2. What is the meaning of "the sovereignty of the consumer" (and of the worker)?

3. In what way does the market society promote efficiency? How would you define efficiency in terms of pure competition?

4. Make a careful list of all the changes you can think of that would be needed if we were to institute a system of perfect competition.

5. What kinds of advertisements are informational? What kinds are "taste-forming"? Do you think that if there were no ads for cigarettes, smoking would decrease?

6. How much product differentiation do you consider useful? Dress styles? Car models? Laundry soaps?

7. General Motors makes approximately as much profit per car as it pays out in wages per car. Do you think this is intrinsic proof that General Motors earns quasi rents? Monopoly profits? That its costs are lower than those of its competitors? Do you think that the question is answerable? How would you go about answering it?

8. What kinds of actions on the part of buyers and sellers are needed to make a market self-correcting (that is, to enable it to establish equilibrium prices)? In what way do oligopolies or unions interfere with the mechanism of self-correction?

9. What are some of the problems inherent in a "perfect" market? Will a perfect market produce public as well as private goods? How will it deal with the effects of "externalities" such as overcrowding or pollution or traffic congestion?

10. In what way could the market system be used to achieve public goals such as urban rebuilding? Why would it probably be more efficient to use the market as a means of allocating resources to public ends than to have a central direction of resources to the same ends?

four

THE ECONOMICS OF INTERNATIONAL GAIN AND LOSS

THE GAINS
FROM TRADE   *28*

Americans have had the fortune to be extraordinarily sheltered from the currents of international economics that wash against other shores. British students are brought up knowing about exports and imports because a quarter of their national income derives from foreign trade. A Canadian knows about international economics because one Canadian dollar in five is earned or spent beyond Canadian borders. Any educated person in the underdeveloped world will tell you that the future of his country is critically affected by the exports it sells to the developed world and the capital it brings in from that world. Only the United States, among the nations of the West, is generally unconcerned and uneducated about foreign trade, for the general opinion is that we are relatively self-sufficient and could, if we had to, let the rest of the world go hang.

Could we? It is true that only about 6 per cent of our gross national product is sold overseas and only 4 or 5 per cent of the value of GNP is bought overseas. Yet it is worth considering what would happen to our own economy if, by some mischance, its ties with the rest of the world would be severed.

We would feel the impact first in highly selective, but all too noticeable, changes we would have to make in our diet. Coffee and tea, the very mainstays of civilized existence, would no longer be available. Chocolate, the favorite flavor of a hundred million Americans, would be unobtainable. There would be no bananas in the morning, no pepper at supper, no Scotch whiskey at night. Substitutes could be developed for some of these commodities, but judging from our experience in World War II, we might find that they do not taste very good.

More serious would be the loss of certain other products of the world. In the earlier years of the country, we were inclined to treat our natural resources as inexhaustible, but the astounding rate of our consumption of industrial raw materials has disabused us of that notion. Today the major fractions of our iron ore, our copper, and our wood products come to us from abroad. Ninety per cent of the bauxite from which we make aluminum is imported. Ninety-four per cent of the manganese needed for high-tempered steels, all our chrome, virtually all our cobalt, the great bulk of our nickel, tin, platinum, asbestos is foreign-bought. Many of these metals are so strategically important that we stockpile them against temporary disruption, but in a few years the stockpiles would be used up and we should be forced radically to change some of our technology.

Then there would be other losses, less statistically impressive but no less irksome to consumers and industry: the loss of Japanese cameras, of British tweeds, of French perfume, of Italian movies, of Rolls Royce engines, Volkswagen cars, Danish silver, Indian jute and madras. Clearly, shutting down the flow of the imports into America, however relatively self-sufficient we may be, would deal us a considerable blow. One can imagine what it would mean in the case of, say, Holland, where foreign products account for as much as 45 per cent of all goods sold in that country.

But we have still not fully investigated the effects of international trade on the United States, for we have failed to consider the impact of a collapse of our exports. The farm country would feel such a collapse immediately of course, for a fifth of our cotton, almost a quarter of our grains, and more than a quarter of our tobacco go overseas. Mining country would feel it because a fifth of our coal and a third of our sulphur are sold abroad. Manufacturing enterprises in cities scattered all over the nation would feel the blow, as a seventh of our auto production, a quarter of our metalworking machinery and of our textile machinery, a third of our construction and mining machinery could no longer be sold overseas—not to speak of another thirty to forty industries in which at least a fifth of output is regularly sold to foreign buyers. In all, some three to four million jobs, three-quarters of them in manufacturing or commerce, would cease to exist if our foreign markets should suddenly disappear.

Now to be sure, many of those jobs would be replaced by new industries that would be encouraged if our overseas markets and

552

sources of supply vanished. If we could not buy watches or watch parts in Switzerland, we would make more of them here. If we could not sell automobiles to the world, we would no doubt try to use our unemployed skills to make some product or service that could be marketed at home—perhaps one of the items we no longer imported. With considerable effort (especially in the case of strategic materials) we *could* readjust. Hence the question: Why don't we? What is the purpose of international trade? Why do we not seek to improve our relative self-sufficiency by making it complete?

No sooner do we ask the question of the aims of international trade than we encounter an obstacle that will present the single greatest difficulty in learning about international economics. This is the bias of nationalism—the curious fact that relationships and propositions that are perfectly self-evident in the context of "ordinary" economics suddenly appear suspect, not to say downright wrong, in the context of international economics.

For example, suppose that the governor of an eastern state—let us say New Jersey—wanted to raise the incomes of his constituents and decided that the best way to do so was to encourage some new industry to move there. Suppose furthermore that his wife was very fond of grapefruit and suggested to him one morning that grapefruit growing would be an excellent addition to New Jersey's products.

The governor might object that grapefruit needed a milder climate than New Jersey had to offer. "That's no problem," his wife might answer. "We could protect our grapefruit by growing them in hothouses. That way, in addition to the income from the crop, we would benefit the state from the incomes earned by the glaziers and electricians who would be needed."

The governor might murmur something about hothouse grapefruit costing more than ordinary grapefruit, so that New Jersey could not sell its crop on the competitive market. "Nonsense," his wife would reply. "We can subsidize the grapefruit growers out of the proceeds of a general sales tax. Or we could pass a law requiring restaurants in this state to serve state grapefruit only. Or you could bar out-of-state grapefruit from New Jersey entirely."

"Now, my dear," the governor would return, "in the first place, that's unconstitutional. Second, even if it weren't, we would be making people in this state give up part of their incomes through the sales tax, to benefit farmers, and that would never be politically acceptable. And third, the whole scheme is so inefficient it's just downright ridiculous."

But if we now shift our attention to a similar scene played between the prime minister of Nova Jersia and his wife, we find some interesting differences. Like her counterpart in New Jersey, the wife of the prime minister recommends the growing of hothouse grapefruit in Nova Jersia's chilly climate. Admittedly, that would make the crop consider-

553

ably dearer than that for sale on the international markets. "But that's all right," she tells her husband. "We can put a tariff on foreign grapefruit, so none of that cheap fruit from abroad will be able to undersell ours."

"My dear," says the prime minister after carefully considering the matter, "I think you are right. It is true that grapefruit in Nova Jersia will be more expensive as a result of the tariff, but there is no doubt that a tariff looks like a tax on them and not on us, and therefore no one will object to it. It is also true that our hothouse grapefruit may not taste as good as theirs, but we will have the immense satisfaction of eating our *own* grapefruit, which will make it taste better. Finally, there may be a few economists who will tell us that this is not the most efficient use of our resources, but I can tell them that the money we pay for hothouse grapefruit—even if it is a little more than it would be otherwise—stays in our own pockets and doesn't go to enrich foreigners. In addition to which, I would point out in my television appearances that the reason foreign grapefruit are so cheap is that foreign labor is so badly paid. We certainly don't want to drag down the price of our labor by making it compete with the cheap labor of other nations. All in all, hothouse grapefruit seems to me an eminently sensible proposal, and one that is certain to be politically popular."

SOURCE OF THE DIFFICULTY

Is it a sensible proposal? Of course not, although it will take some careful thinking to expose all of its fallacies. Will it be politically popular? It may very well be, for economic policies that would be laughed out of court at home get a serious hearing when they crop up in the international arena. Here are some of the things that most of us tend to believe:

Trade between two nations usually harms one side or the other.

Rich countries can't compete with poor countries.

Cheap foreign labor is a threat to a prosperous nation.

There is always the danger that a country may sell, but refuse to buy.

Are these fears true? One way of testing their validity is to see how they ring in our ears when we rid them of our unconscious national bias by recasting them as propositions in ordinary economics:

Is it true that trade between businesses or persons usually harms one side or the other?

Is it true that rich companies can't compete with poor ones?

Is it true that cheap labor is a threat to a successful firm?

Is it true that one company might only sell, but never buy—not even the services of factors of production?

What is the source of this curious prejudice against international trade? It is not, as we might think, an excess of patriotism that leads us to recommend courses of action that will help our own country, regardless of the effect on others. For, curiously, the policies of the economic superpatriot, if put into practice, would demonstrably injure the economic interests of his own land. The trouble, then, springs from a root deeper than mere national interest. It lies in the peculiarly deceptive problems posed by international trade. What is deceptive about them, however, is not that they involve principles that apply only to relations between nations. *All the economic arguments that elucidate international trade apply equally well to domestic trade.* The deception arises, rather, for two reasons:

1. International trade requires an understanding of how two countries, each dealing in its own currency, manage to buy and sell from each other in a world in which there is no such thing as international money.
2. International trade requires a very thorough understanding of the advantages of and arguments for trade itself.

GAINS FROM TRADE

In a general way, of course, we are all aware of the importance of trade, although we have hardly mentioned it since the opening pages of our book. *It is trade that makes possible the division and specialization of labor on which our productivity is so largely based.* If we could not exchange the products of our specialized labor, each of us would have to be wholly self-supporting, and our standard of living would thereupon fall to that of subsistence farmers. Thus trade (international or domestic) is actually a means of *increasing productivity,* quite as much as investment or technological progress.

GAINS FROM SPECIALIZATION

The importance of trade in making possible specialization is so great that we should take a moment to make it crystal clear. Let us consider two towns, each of which produces two goods, wool and cotton; but Wooltown has good grazing lands and poor growing lands, while Cottontown's grazing is poor but growing is good. Suppose, moreover, that the two towns had equal populations and that each town employed half its people in cotton and half in wool. The results might look like Table 28-1.

As we can see, the same number of grazers in Wooltown turn out two-and-one-half times as much wool as they do in Cottontown, whereas the same number of cotton farmers in Cottontown produce

TABLE 28 · 1

	Wooltown	Cottontown
Wool production (lbs)	5,000	2,000
Cotton production (lbs)	10,000	20,000

double the amount of cotton that they do in Wooltown. One does not have to be an economist to see that both towns are losing by this arrangement. If Cottontown would shift its woolworkers into cotton, and Wooltown would shift its cotton farmers into wool, the output of the two towns would look like Table 28-2 (assuming constant returns to scale).

TABLE 28 · 2

	Wooltown	Cottontown
Wool output	10,000	0
Cotton output	0	40,000

Now, if we compare total production of the two towns (see Table 28-3) we can see the gains from specialization.

TABLE 28 · 3

	TWO TOWNS' PRODUCTION		Gain from specialization
	Mixed	Specialized	
Wool output	7,000	10,000	3,000
Cotton output	30,000	40,000	10,000

In other words, specialization followed by trade makes it possible for both towns to have more of both commodities than before. No matter how the gains from trade are distributed—and this will depend on many factors, such as the relative elasticities of demand for the two products—both towns will gain, even if one gains more than the other.

UNEQUAL ADVANTAGES

If all the world were divided into nations, like Wooltown and Cottontown, each producing for trade only a single item in which it has a clear advantage over all others, international trade would be a simple matter to understand. It would still present problems of international payment, and it might still inspire its prime ministers of Nova Jersias to forego the gains from trade for political reasons that we will examine at the end of this chapter. But the essential rationale of trade would be simple to understand.

Unfortunately for the economics student as well as for the world at large, this is not the way international resources are distributed. Instead of giving each nation at least one commodity in which it has a clear advantage, many nations do not have such an advantage in a single product. How can trade possibly take place under such inauspicious circumstances?

To unravel the mystery, let us turn again to Cottontown and Wooltown, but this time call them Supraville and Infraville, to designate an important change in their respective abilities. Although both towns still enjoy equal populations, which are again divided equally between cotton and wool production, in this example Supraville is a more efficient producer than Infraville in *both* cotton and wool, as Table 28-4 shows.

Is it possible for trade to benefit these two towns when one of them is so manifestly superior to the other in every product? It would seem out of the question. But let us nonetheless test the case by supposing that each town began to specialize.

TABLE 28 · 4

	Supraville	Infraville
Wool output	5,000	3,000
Cotton production	20,000	10,000

But how to decide which trade each town should follow? A look at Fig. 28-1 may give us a clue. The production-possibility diagrams are familiar to us from Chapter 20, where we used them to clarify the nature of scarcity and economic choice. Here we put them to use to let us see the results of trade.

What do the diagrams show? First, they establish the limits that each town could produce if it devoted all its efforts to one product. Since we have assumed that the labor force is divided, this means that each

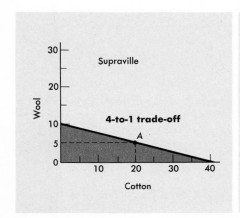
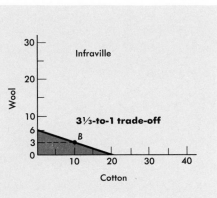

FIG. 28-1

PRODUCTION POSSIBILITIES IN THE TWO TOWNS BEFORE TRADE

town could double the amount of cotton or wool it enjoys when it divides its workers fifty-fifty. Next, a line between these points shows the production frontier that both towns face.* We see that Supraville is located at point *A* where it has 5,000 lbs of wool and 20,000 lbs of cotton, and that Infraville is at *B,* where it has 3,000 lbs of wool and 10,000 lbs of cotton.

But the diagrams (and the figures in the preceding table, on which they are based) also show us something else. It is that each town has a different "trade-off" relationship between its two branches of production. When either town specializes in one branch, it must, of course, give up the output of the other. *But each town swaps one kind of output for the other in different proportions,* as the differing slopes of the two *p-p* curves show. Supraville, for example, can make only an extra pound of wool by giving up 4 pounds of cotton. That is, it gets its maximum potential output of 10,000 lbs of wool only by surrendering 40,000 lbs of cotton. Infraville can reach its production maximum of 6,000 lbs of wool at a loss of only 20,000 lbs of cotton. *Rather than having to give up 4 lbs of cotton to get one of wool, it gives up only 3.3 lbs.* Thus, in terms of how much cotton it must surrender, wool is actually cheaper in Infraville than in Supraville!

Not so the other way round, of course. As we would expect, cotton costs Supraville less in terms of wool than it costs Infraville. In Supraville, we get 40,000 lbs of cotton by relinquishing only 10,000 lbs of wool—a loss of a quarter of a pound of wool for a pound of the other. In Infraville, we can get the maximum output of 20,000 lbs of cotton only by a surrender of 6,000 lbs of wool—a loss of $\frac{1}{3}$ lb of wool rather than $\frac{1}{4}$ lb of wool for each unit of cotton.

COMPARATIVE ADVANTAGE

Perhaps the light is beginning to dawn. Despite the fact that Supraville is more productive in terms of output per man than Infraville in both cotton and wool, it is *relatively* more productive in cotton than in wool. And despite the fact that Infraville is absolutely less productive, man for man, in both cotton and wool than Supraville, it is *relatively* more productive in wool. To repeat, it requires a smaller sacrifice of wool to get another pound of cotton in Infraville than in Supraville.

We call this kind of relative superiority *comparative advantage.* It is a concept that is often difficult to grasp at first but that is central to the reason for trade itself. When we speak of *comparative* advantage, we mean, as in the case of Supraville, that among *various* advantages of one producer or locale over another, there is one that is better than

---

*Why are these lines drawn straight, not bowed as in Chapter 20? As we know, the bowing reflects the law of increasing cost, which makes the gains from a shift in resource allocation less and less favorable as we move from one extreme of allocation to another. Here we ignore this complication for simplicity of exposition.

any other. *Comparatively* speaking, this is where its optimal returns lie. But just because it must abandon some lesser opportunity, its trading partner can now advantageously devote itself in that direction, where its comparative disadvantage is least.

This is a relationship of logic, not economics. Take the example of the banker who is also the best carpenter in town. Will it pay him to build his own house? Clearly it will not, for he will make more money by devoting all his hours to banking, even though he then has to employ and pay for a carpenter less skillful than himself. True, he could save that expense by building his own house. But he would then have to give up the much more lucrative hours he could be spending at the bank!

Now let us return to the matter of trade. We have seen that wool is *relatively* cheaper in Infraville, where each additional pound cost only 3.3 lbs of cotton, rather than 4 lbs as in Supraville; and that cotton is *relatively* cheaper in Supraville, where an additional pound costs but $\frac{1}{4}$ lb of wool, instead of $\frac{1}{3}$ lb across the way in Infraville. Now let us suppose that each side begins to specialize in the trade in which it has the comparative advantage. Suppose that Supraville took half its labor force now in wool and put it into cotton. Its output would change as in Table 28-5.

TABLE 28 · 5

SUPRAVILLE

	Before the shift	After the shift
Wool production	5,000	2,500
Cotton production	20,000	30,000

Supraville has lost 2,500 lbs of wool but gained 10,000 lbs of cotton. Now let us see if it can trade its cotton for Infraville's wool. In Infraville, where productivity is so much less, the entire labor force has shifted to wool output, where its greatly inferior productivity can be put to best use. Hence its production pattern now looks like Table 28-6.

TABLE 28 · 6

INFRAVILLE

	Before the shift	After the shift
Wool	3,000	6,000
Cotton	10,000	—

Infraville finds itself lacking 10,000 lbs of cotton, but it has 3,000 *additional* lbs of wool. Clearly, it can acquire the 10,000 lbs of cotton it needs from Supraville by giving Supraville *more* than the 2,500 lbs of wool it seeks. As a result, both Infraville and Supraville will have the same cotton consumption as before, but there will be a surplus of

FIG. 28-2

**PRODUCTION
POSSIBILITIES
IN THE
TWO TOWNS
AFTER TRADE**

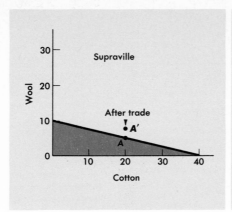

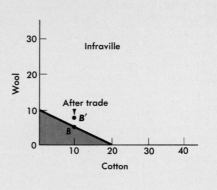

500 lbs of wool to be shared between them. As Fig. 28-2 shows, *both towns will have gained by the exchange, for both will have moved beyond their former production frontiers* (from *A* to *A'* and from *B* to *B'*).

This last point is the crucial one. If we remember the nature of production-possibility curves from our discussion of them in Chapter 20, any point lying outside the production frontier is simply unattainable by that society. In Fig. 28-2, points *A'* and *B'* do lie beyond the pre-trade *p-p* curves of the two towns, and yet trade has made it possible for both communities to enjoy what was formerly impossible.

OPPORTUNITY COST

Comparative advantage gives us an important insight into all exchange relationships, for it reveals a fundamental economic truth previously mentioned only in passing (p. 300). It is that *cost, in economics, means opportunities that must be foregone.* The real cost of wool in Supraville is the cotton that cannot be made because men are engaged in wool production, just as the real cost of cotton is the wool that must be gone without. In fact, we can see that the basic reason for comparative advantage lies in the fact that opportunity costs vary, so that it "pays" (it costs less) for different parties to engage in different activities.

If opportunity costs for two producers are the same, then it follows that there cannot be any comparative advantage for either; and if there is no comparative advantage, there is nothing to be gained by specializing or trading. Suppose Supraville has a two-to-one edge over Infraville in *both* cotton and wool. Then, if either town specializes, neither will gain. Supraville may still gain 10,000 lbs of cotton for 2,500 lbs of wool, as before, but Infraville will gain only 2,500 lbs of wool (not 3,000) from its shift away from cotton. Thus, the key to trade lies in the existence of *different* opportunity costs.

Are opportunity costs usually different from country to country or from region to region? For most commodities they are. As we move from one part of the world to another—sometimes even short distances—climate, resources, skills, transportation costs, capital scarcity or abundance all change; and as they change, so do opportunity costs. That is why trade is more likely to occur between dissimilar producers than between similar ones. There is every possibility for rich countries to trade with poor ones, precisely because their opportunity costs are certain to differ.

But we have not yet fully understood one last important aspect of trade—the *prices* at which goods will exchange. Suppose that Supraville and Infraville do specialize, each in the product in which it enjoys a comparative advantage. Does that mean they can swap their goods at any prices?

A quick series of calculations reveals otherwise. We remember that Supraville needed at least 2,500 lbs of wool for which it was going to offer some of its extra production of cotton in exchange. But how much? What price should it offer for its needed wool, in terms of cotton?

Suppose it offered 7,500 lbs of cotton. Would Infraville sell the wool? No, it would not. At home it can make its own 7,500 lbs of cotton at a "cost" of only 2,273 lbs of wool, for we recall that Infraville traded off one pound of wool for 3.3 lbs of cotton (7,500 ÷ 3.3 = 2,273).

Suppose, then, that Infraville counter-offered to sell Supraville 2,500 lbs of wool for a price of 12,000 lbs of cotton. Would Supraville accept? Of course not. This would mean the equivalent of 4.8 lbs of cotton for a pound of wool. Supraville can do better than that by growing her own wool at her own trade-off ratio of only 4 lbs to one.

We begin to see, in other words, that the price of wool must lie between the trade-off ratios of Infraville and Supraville. Infraville can produce a pound of wool at a cost of 3.3 lbs of cotton, so it properly asks more cotton than that before it is willing to enter into the exchange. Supraville can make a pound of wool at a cost of 4 lbs of cotton, and it seeks a price less than that. Hence, any price ratio between 3.3 and 4.0 lbs of cotton per pound of wool will profit both sides.

Let us put this into ordinary price terms. Suppose that cotton sells for 30¢ per pound. Then wool would have to sell between 99¢ and $1.20 (30¢ × 3.3 and × 4) to make trade worthwhile.* Let us say that supply and demand established a price of $1.10 for wool. Supraville can then sell its 10,000 lbs of extra cotton production at 30¢, which will net it $3,000. How much wool can it buy for this sum? At the going price of $1.10 per lb, 2,727 lbs. Therefore Supraville will end up with the same amount of cotton (20,000 lbs) as it had before specialization and trade,

---

*Needless to say, these prices are used for illustrative purposes only.

and with 227 *more* lbs of wool than before (2,500 lbs produced at home plus 2,727 lbs imported from Infraville—a total of 5,227 lbs). It has gained by trade an amount equal to the price of this extra wool, or $249.70.

How has Infraville fared? It has 3,273 lbs of wool left after exporting 2,727 lbs to Supraville from its production of 6,000 lbs, and it also has 10,000 lbs of cotton which it imported from Supraville in exchange for its wool exports. Thus it, too, has a gain from trade—the 273 lbs of wool (worth $300.30) over the amount of 3,000 lbs that it would have produced without specialization and trade.* In brief, *both* sides have profited from the exchange.

THE CASE FOR FREE TRADE

Would the prime minister of Nova Jersia be convinced by these arguments? Would his wife? They might be weakened in their support for hothouse grapefruit, but some arguments would still linger in their minds. Let us consider them.

1. *"Our workers cannot compete with low-wage workers overseas."* This is an argument one hears not only in Nova Jersia but also in the United States where the competition of sweatshop labor in Hong Kong is often cited at tariff hearings. And indeed, labor in Hong Kong is paid only a fifth of what it is paid here. Will not American labor be seriously injured if we import goods made under these conditions?

There is, of course, no doubt that an American textile worker who loses his job because of low-priced imports *will* be hurt. We shall come back to him later. But note that he would also be hurt if he lost his job because of regular domestic competition. Why do we feel so threatened when that competition comes from abroad?

Because, the answer goes, foreign competition isn't based on American efficiency. It is based on exploited labor. Hence it pulls down the standards of American labor to its own low level.

There is an easy reply to this argument. The reason Hong Kong textile labor is paid so much less than American textile labor is that the *average* wage in Hong Kong is so much lower than the *average* wage

---

*Gains need not be distributed so evenly between the trading partners. If the price of wool had been $1.00, trade still would have been worthwhile, but Supraville would have gained almost all of it. Had the price of wool been $1.19, both sides again would have come out ahead, but now Infraville would have been the larger beneficiary by far. The actual price at which wool would sell would be determined by the supply and demand schedule for it in both communities.

in America. Why is that? Because productivity in Hong Kong industry is so much lower than that in American industry. Thus *it is not the low wage of the Hong Kong tailor that makes it difficult for the American garment worker to compete, but the high wage of American workers in other more efficient American industries.*

To put it differently, the reason that American wages are high is that we use our workers in industries where their productivity is very high. If Hong Kong, with its very low productivity can undersell us in textiles, then this is a clear signal that we must move our factors of production out of textiles into other areas where their contribution will be greater; for example, in the production of machinery. It is no coincidence that machinery—one of the highest wage industries in America—is one of our leading exports, or that more than 75 per cent of our manufactured exports are produced by industries in which the hourly wage rates are above the national average for all manufacturing industries. In fact, all nations tend to export the goods in which their local wages are highest, not lowest! Why? Because those are the industries in which their labor is most effectively employed.

This fact opens our eyes to another. Why is it that the American garment industry is worried about competition from Hong Kong, but not the American auto industry or the electrical machinery industry or the farm equipment industry? After all, the manufacturers of those products could also avail themselves of low wages in Hong Kong.

The answer is that American manufacturers can make these products at much lower cost in America. Why? Because capital is much more abundant in America than in Hong Kong, and capital is needed in large amounts for these manufactures. Thus, if Hong Kong has a comparative advantage over us in the garment trade, we have a comparative advantage over her in many other areas.*

But suppose Hong Kong accumulated large amounts of capital and became a center for the manufacture of heavy equipment, so that it sold *both* garments and electrical generators more cheaply than we. We are back to Supraville and Infraville. There would still be a *comparative* advantage in one or more of these products in which we would be wise to specialize, afterward trading with Hong Kong for our supplies of the other good.

2. *"Tariffs are painless taxes because they are borne by foreigners."* This is a convincing-sounding argument advanced by the prime minister of Nova Jersia (and by some other prime ministers in their time). But is it true? Let us take the case of hothouse grapefruit which can be produced in Nova Jersia only at a cost of fifty cents each, whereas

---

*Newspapers in Southeast Asia carry editorials seeking protection from American imports because, they say, we do not use labor in our production and it is unfair to ask their citizens to compete with our machines that do not have to be paid wages.

foreign grapefruit (no doubt produced by sweated labor) can be unloaded at its ports at twenty-five cents. To prevent his home industry from being destroyed, the prime minister imposes a tariff of twenty-five cents on each grapefruit—which, he tells the newspapers, will be entirely paid by foreigners.

This is not, however, the way his political opponent (who has had a course in economics) sees it. "Without the tariff," he tells his constituency, "you could buy grapefruit for twenty-five cents. Now you have to pay fifty cents for it. Who is paying the extra twenty-five cents—the foreign grower, or you? Even if not a single grapefruit entered the country, you would still be paying twenty-five cents more than you have to. In fact, *you are being asked to subsidize an inefficient domestic industry.* Not only that, but the tariff wall means they won't ever become efficient because there is no pressure of competition on them."

Whether or not our economic candidate will win the electoral battle, he surely has the better of the argument. Or does he? For the prime minister, stung by these unkind remarks, replies:

3. *"But at least the tariff keeps spending power at home. Our own grapefruit growers, not foreigners, have our money."*

In our next chapter we will look into the soundness of this argument. There we will see that the money we pay to foreigners does not leave the country, but ends up in bank accounts in our own banks. A number of things can then happen to these foreign-owned bank accounts, as we shall see, but the single largest use of them must be obvious. Foreigners use them to buy goods from us.

Then there is a second very important consideration. When tariffs prevent inexpensive foreign goods from entering a country, they are depriving the efficient industries of that country from receiving their full share of consumer spending. If American consumers are prevented by tariff from buying inexpensive suits from Hong Kong, they will have to spend more money for suits (whether bought from high-cost American producers or from Hong Kong makers who have paid the tariff), and *they will therefore have that much less left over to spend for efficiently produced American products that do not need tariff protection.*

CLASSICAL
ARGUMENT
FOR
FREE TRADE

Are there no arguments at all for tariffs? As we shall see, there are some important cases in which tariffs make sense—or can at least be justified rationally. But the basic case stands. Economists have always advocated the widest and freest possible trade—not for doctrinaire reasons, but because *trade makes possible maximum production.* Free trade must be considered a means of increasing GNP, not essentially different from technological improvement in its effect on output and growth.

Then, why is the case for free trade so difficult to present when industries are threatened? Again our national bias beclouds our judgment. It was never more charmingly or effectively presented than in this argument by Frédéric Bastiat, a delightful exponent of mid-nineteenth-century classical economic ideals, in a little book entitled *Social Fallacies.* *

In Bastiat's book, Robinson Crusoe inhabits an island with Friday. In the morning, Crusoe and Friday hunt for six hours and bring home four baskets of game. In the evening they garden for six hours and get four baskets of vegetables. But now let Bastiat take over:

One day a canoe touched at the island. A good-looking foreigner landed, and was admitted to the table of our two recluses. He tasted and commended very much the produce of the garden, and before taking leave of his entertainers, spoke as follows:

"Generous islanders, I inhabit a country where game is much more plentiful than here, but where horticulture is quite unknown. It would be an easy matter to bring you every evening four baskets of game, if you will give me in exchange two baskets of vegetables."

At these words Robinson and Friday retired to consult, and the debate that took place is too interesting not to be reported in extenso.

FRIDAY: What do you think of it?

ROBINSON: If we close with the proposal, we are ruined.

FRIDAY: Are you sure of that? Let us consider.

ROBINSON: The case is clear. Crushed by competition, our hunting as a branch of industry is annihilated.

FRIDAY: What matters it, if we have the game?

ROBINSON: Theory! It will no longer be the product of our labour.

FRIDAY: I beg your pardon sir; for in order to have game we must part with vegetables.

ROBINSON: Then, what shall we gain?

FRIDAY: The four baskets of game cost us six hours' work. The foreigner gives us them in exchange for two baskets of vegetables, which cost us only three hours' work. This places three hours at our disposal. . . .

ROBINSON: You lose yourself in generalities! What should we make of these three hours?

FRIDAY: We would do something else.

ROBINSON: Ah! I understand you. You cannot come to particulars. Something else, something else—that is easily said.

FRIDAY: We can fish, we can ornament our cottage, we can read the Bible.

ROBINSON: Utopia! Is there any certainty we should do either the one or the other? . . . . Moreover there are political reasons for rejecting the interested offers of the perfidious foreigner.

*Translated by Frederick James Sterling (Santa Ana, Calif.: Register Publishing Co. Ltd., 1944) p. 203f.

FRIDAY: Political reasons!

ROBINSON: Yes, he only makes us these offers because they are advantageous to him.

FRIDAY: So much the better, since they are for our advantage likewise. . . .

ROBINSON: Suppose the foreigner learns to cultivate a garden and that his island should prove more fertile than ours. Do you see the consequences?

FRIDAY: Yes; our relations with the foreigner would cease. He would take from us no more vegetables, since he could have them at home with less labour. He would bring us no more game, since we should have nothing to give him in exchange, and we should then be in precisely the situation that you wish us in now. . . .

The debate was prolonged, and, as often happens, each remained wedded to his own opinion. But Robinson possessing a great influence over Friday, his opinion prevailed, and when the foreigner arrived to demand a reply, Robinson said to him:

"Stranger, in order to induce us to accept your proposal, we must be assured of two things: the first is, that your island is no better stocked with game than ours, for we want to fight only with equal weapons. The second is, that you will lose by the bargain. For, as in every exchange there is necessarily a gaining and a losing party, we should be dupes, if you were not the loser. What have you got to say?"

"Nothing," replied the foreigner; and, bursting out laughing, he regained his canoe.

THE CASE FOR TARIFFS

Is Crusoe as much of a fool as he appears? Not quite, although his arguments are poorly taken, and Bastiat had little trouble in demolishing them. But in fact Crusoe is groping with ideas that are very important in weighing the gains from trade—interregional as well as international.

MOBILITY

The first concerns the problem of mobility. Explicit in Bastiat's case is the ease with which Crusoe and Friday move back and forth between hunting and gardening. Implicit in the case of Supraville and Infraville is the possibility of shifting men and resources from cotton to wool production. But in fact it is sometimes exceedingly difficult to move resources from one industry to another.

Thus when Hong Kong textiles press hard against the garment worker in New York, it is scant comfort to him to point to the higher wages in the auto factories in Detroit. He has a lifetime of skills and a long established home in New York, and he does not want to move to another city where he will be a stranger, and to a new trade in which he would be only an unskilled beginner. He certainly does not want to move to Hong Kong! Hence, the impact of foreign trade often brings serious dislocations that result in persistent local unemployment, rather than in a flow of resources from a relatively disadvantaged to a relatively advantaged one. If Crusoe had suggested that it was very difficult (perhaps because of the noonday sun) to work in the gardens in the morning when they usually went hunting, Friday would have been harder pressed for a reply.

There is, it should be noted, an answer to this argument—an answer, at any rate, that applies to industrial nations. It is that a government intent on increasing its national productivity should itself bear the costs of relocation and retraining, rather than asking the worker or business-man to shoulder them himself. To the extent that we assist factors in making a transition from a less to a more effective use, we incur a one-time cost in exchange for a lasting benefit. (Incidentally, this argument applies equally well to dislocations originating in domestic adjustments.)

Second, *the argument for free trade rests on the very important assumption that there will be substantially full employment.*

In the days of the mid-nineteenth century when the free trade argument was first fully formulated, the idea of an underemployment equilibrium would have been considered absurd. When Crusoe asks what use they should make of their free time, Friday has no trouble replying that they should work or enjoy their leisure. But in a highly interdependent society, work may not be available, and leisure may be only a pseudonym for an inability to find work. In an economy of large enterprises and "sticky" wages and prices, we know that unemployment is a real and continuous object of concern for national policy.

Thus, it makes little sense to advocate policies to expand production via trade unless we are certain that the level of aggregate demand will be large enough to absorb that production. *Full employment policy therefore becomes an indispensable arm of trade policy.* Trade gives us the potential for maximizing production, but there is no point in laying the groundwork for the highest possible output, unless fiscal and monetary policy are also geared to bringing about a level of aggregate demand large enough to support that output.

Last, *there is the argument of nationalism pure and simple.* This argument does not impute spurious economic gains to tariffs. Rather it says that free trade undoubtedly encourages production, but it does so at a certain cost. This is the cost of the vulnerability that comes from extensive and extreme specialization. This vulnerability is all very well within a nation where we assume that law and order will prevail, but it cannot be so easily justified among nations where the realistic assumption is just the other way. Tariffs, in other words, are defensible because they enable nations to attain a certain *self-sufficiency*—admittedly at some economic cost.

When Crusoe made the argument on his island economy, Friday properly scoffed. But the argument is much more valid for an economy of complex industrial processes and specialized know-how that cannot be quickly duplicated if trade is disrupted. In a world in which the threat of war is always present, self-sufficiency has a value that may properly override considerations of ideal economic efficiency. The problem is to hold the arguments for "national defense" down to proper proportions. When tariffs are periodically adjusted in international conferences, an astonishing variety of industries (in all countries) find it possible to claim protection from foreign competition in the name of national "indispensability."

INFANT INDUSTRIES

Equally interesting is the nationalist argument for tariffs advanced by so-called "infant" industries, particularly in developing nations. These newly-formed or prospective enterprises claim that they cannot possibly compete with the giants in developed countries while they are small; but that if they are protected by a tariff, they will in time become large and efficient enough no longer to need a tariff. In addition, they claim, they will provide a more diversified spectrum of employments for their own people, as well as aiding in the national transition toward a more modern economy.

The argument is a valid one, if it is applied to industries that have a fair chance of achieving a comparative advantage once grown up (otherwise one will be supporting them in infancy, maturity, and senility).* Certainly it is an argument that was propounded by the youthful industries of the United States in the early nineteenth century, and that was sufficiently persuasive to bring them a moderate degree of protection (although it is inconclusive as to how much their growth was ultimately dependent on tariff help). And it is being listened to today by the underdeveloped nations who feel that their only chance of escaping from poverty is to develop a nucleus of industrial employments at almost any cost.

THE BASIC ARGUMENT

Thus there are arguments for tariffs, or at least rational counter-arguments against an extreme free trade position. Workers *are* hurt by international competition; and in the default of proper domestic plans

---

*If every industry must have a comparative advantage in one country or another, how can there be steel industries (or any other) in more than one country? The answer, quite aside from considerations of nationalism, lies in *transportation costs* which compensate for lower production costs in many products and thereby allow a relatively inefficient industry to supply a home market.

for cushioning these blows, modest tariffs can buffer the pains of redeployment. Free trade *does* require a level of high employment; and when unemployment is already a national problem, tariffs may protect additional workers from losing their jobs. Strategic industries and development-stimulating industries *are* sometimes essential and may require protection from world competition. All these arguments are but qualifications to the basic proposition on which the economist rests his case for the freest *possible* trade, but they help to define "possible" in a realistic way.

Nonetheless it may help if we sum up the classical argument, for there is always a danger that the qualifications will take precedence over the main argument.

1. *Free trade brings about the most efficient possible use of resources, and any interference with free trade lessens that efficiency.*

    Note that international trade is in no wise different from interregional domestic trade in this regard. We recognize that we would suffer a loss in higher costs or smaller output by imposing restrictions on the exchange of goods between New York and Chicago. We suffer the same loss when we interfere with the exchange between New York and Hong Kong.

2. *When international trade brings problems of a frictional kind, such as unemployment in an industry that cannot meet foreign competition, the answer is not to block the imports but to cure the unemployment by finding better uses for our inefficiently used resources.*

    Once again, international trade is no different in this regard from domestic trade. When low-price textiles from the South cause unemployment in New England, we do not prevent the sale of southern goods. We try to find new jobs for New Englanders, in occupations in which they have a comparative advantage over the South.

3. *The purpose of all trade is to improve the well-being of the consumer by giving him the best and cheapest goods and services possible. Thus imports, not exports, represent the gains from trade.*

    The whole point of trade is to exchange things that we make efficiently for other things in which our efficiency is less. Anything that diminishes imports will reduce our standard of living, just as anything that blocks a return flow of goods from Chicago to New York will obviously reduce the benefit to New Yorkers of trade with Chicago.

In our last section when we turn to the rise of modern European capitalism and to the troubles of the underdeveloped world, we will see these arguments—and the cost of ignoring them—illustrated not in textbook example, but in reality. At this point, however, let us delay that important chapter of modern history until we have learned something more about the mechanics of international economic relationships.

SUMMARY

1. Imports and exports constitute small but strategic branches of economic activity for the United States. Precisely *the same arguments of economic rationality apply to them as to all purely domestic economic exchanges.* It is mainly the bias of nationalism that hinders us from applying the same reasoning in both cases.

2. The gains from trade essentially arise *from the specialization and division of labor that trade makes possible.* Trade is a means of *increasing productivity.*

3. Trade is obviously advantageous when each of the two trading partners has a clear superiority in the production of one item. It can also be advantageous whenever a *comparative advantage exists*—that is, whenever one partner, although superior to the other in the production of all products, is relatively superior in some. By the logic of the case, the inferior partner must be relatively superior in the production of the others, and output will be increased if each devotes its energies to its favored products.

4. We can tell which product is relatively favored for each trading partner by calculating the *trade off relationship* represented by the productivity curve. This shows us the *opportunity cost* of producing each product in terms of the output of other products that must be foregone.

5. Products must exchange *at prices that lie between the ratios established by the trade off possibilities.* Neither country will accept in exchange a product on terms (that is, at prices) that are less favorable than the terms it has available by devoting its own resources to the production of the item in question.

6. The arguments against free trade often stress the dangers of low-wage competition. This argument overlooks the fact that *low wages are a symptom of low productivity.* Generally it is high-wage (i.e., high-productivity) items that are exported. It also ignores the fact that low-wage countries are generally deficient in capital and have trouble competing with capital-using products from nations in which capital is abundant.

7. *Tariffs are taxes that are borne by domestic consumers.* They constitute a subsidy to a domestic industry that cannot meet competition from abroad.

8. One avoidable cost of free trade is the necessity for *factor mobility.* Government can help bear relocation and retraining costs in cases where free trade imposes severe strains of readjustment.

9. Free trade assumes the existence of full employment, and a *policy of encouraging free trade must be accompanied by one encouraging maximum output.*

10. *National self-sufficiency* and the encouragement of *infant industries* during their early years provide rational arguments for tariffs, although it is not easy to prevent these arguments from being indiscriminately applied.

11. The basic argument for free trade is that it brings about the *most efficient use of resources.* The purpose of all trade is to improve the well-being of the consumer. *Thus, imports, not exports, represent the gain from trade.*

1. Is it true that a colossal nation like the United States can trade with a tiny one like Honduras to the benefit of both? Can it also trade with an industrial, small nation, like Holland? What products do we buy from and sell to each?

2. What do we mean when we say that trade is "indirect production"?

3. Suppose that two towns, Coaltown and Irontown, have equal populations but differing resources. If Coaltown applies its whole population to coal production, it will produce 10,000 tons of coal; if it applies them to iron production, it will produce 5,000 tons of iron. If Irontown concentrates on iron, it will turn out 18,000 tons of iron; if it shifts to coal, it will produce 12,000 tons of coal. Is trade possible between these towns? Would it be possible if Irontown could produce 24,000 tons of iron? Why is there a comparative advantage in one case and not in the other?

4. In which product does Coaltown have a comparative advantage? How many tons of iron does a ton of coal cost her? How many does it cost Irontown? What is the cost of iron in Coaltown and Irontown?

5. Draw a production-possibility diagram for each town. Show where the frontier lies before and after trade.

6. If iron sells for $10 a ton, what must be the price range of coal? Show that trade cannot be profitable if coal sells on either side of this range.

7. What is the opportunity cost of coal to Irontown? Of iron to Irontown?

8. Is it true that American watchmakers face unfair competition from Swiss watchmakers because wages are lower in Switzerland? If American watch workers are rendered unemployed by the low-paid Swiss, what might be done to help them—impose a tariff?

9. Is it true that mass-produced, low-cost American watches are a source of unfair competition for Switzerland? If Swiss watchmakers are unemployed as a result, what could be done to help them—impose a tariff? Is it possible that a mutually profitable trade in watches might take place between the two countries? What kinds of watches would each probably produce?

10. Are the duties on French wines borne by foreigners or by domestic consumers? Both? What, if any, is the rationale for these duties?

11. Do you believe that there should be a tariff on steel products because steel is essential for national defense? Should we refuse to buy low-cost, Russian turbo-generators because the domestic industry needs support?

12. Why do imports represent the gains from trade and not exports?

29 THE PROBLEM OF INTERNATIONAL TRANSACTIONS

We have learned something about one of the sources of confusion that surrounds international trade—the curiously concealed gains from trade itself. Yet our examples of trade have thus far not touched on another source of confusion—the fact that international trade is conducted in two (or sometimes more) currencies. After all, Infraville and Supraville both trade in dollars. But suppose Infraville were Japan and Supraville America. Then how would things work out?

FOREIGN EXCHANGE

The best way to find out would be to price the various items in Japan and America (assuming that Japan produces both wool and cotton, which she does not). Suppose the result looked like this:

TABLE 29 · 1

	United States	Japan
Price of wool (lb)	$1.10	¥ 300
Price of cotton (lb)	.30	¥ 100

What would this tell us about the cheapness or dearness of Japanese products compared with those of the U.S.? Nothing, unless we knew one further fact: *the rate at which we could exchange dollars and yen.*

Suppose you could buy 400 yen for a dollar. Then a pound of Japanese wool imported into America (forgetting about shipping costs) would cost 75¢ (¥ 300 ÷ 400) and a pound of Japanese cotton in America would cost $0.25. Assuming that these are the only products that either country makes for export, here we have a case in which Japan can seemingly undersell America in everything.

But now suppose the rate of exchange were not 400 to one but 250 to one. In that event a pound of Japanese wool landed in America would cost $1.20 (¥300 ÷ 250); and a pound of cotton, $0.40. At this rate of exchange everything in Japan is more expensive than the same products produced in the United States.

The point is clear. *We cannot decide whether foreign products are cheaper or dearer than our own until we know the rate of exchange,* the number of units of their currency we get for ours.

MECHANISM OF EXCHANGE

What determines the rate or exchange? The simplest way to understand it is to follow through a single act of international exchange from start to finish. Suppose, for example, that we decide to buy a Japanese camera directly from a Tokyo manufacturer. The price of the camera as advertised in the catalog is ¥20,000, and to buy the camera we must therefore arrange for the Japanese manufacturer to get that many *yen.* Obviously, we can't write him a check in that currency, since our own money is in dollars; and equally obviously we can't send him a check for dollars, since he can't use dollars in Tokyo any more than we could use a check from him in yen.

Therefore, we go to our bank and ask if it can arrange to sell us yen to be delivered to the Tokyo manufacturer. Yes, our bank would be delighted to oblige. How can it do so? The answer is that our bank (or if not ours, another bank with whom it does business) keeps a regular checking account in its own name in a so-called correspondent bank in Tokyo. As we might expect, the bank in Tokyo also keeps a checking account in dollars in *its* own name at our bank. If our banker has enough yen in his Tokyo account, he can sell them to us himself. If not, he can buy yen (which he will then have available in Japan) from his correspondent bank in exchange for dollars which he will put into their account here.

Notice that two currencies change hands—not just one. Notice also that our American banker will not be able to buy yen unless the Japanese banker is willing to acquire dollars. And above all, note that banks are the intermediaries of the foreign exchange mechanism because they hold deposits in foreign banks.

When we go to our bank to buy ¥20,000, the bank officer looks up the current exchange rate on yen. Suppose it is 385. He then tells us that it will cost us $51.95 (20,000 ÷ 385) to purchase the yen, plus a bank commission for his services. We write the check, which is deducted from our bank balance and added to the balance of the Tokyo bank's account in this country. Meanwhile, the manufacturer has been notified that if he goes to the Tokyo bank in which our banks keeps its deposits of yen, he will receive a check for ¥20,000. In other words, the Tokyo bank, having received dollars in the United States, will now pay out yen in Japan.

Thus the mechanism of foreign exchange involves the more or less simultaneous (or anyway, closely linked) operations of two banks in different countries. One bank accepts money in one national denomination, the other pays out money in another denomination. Both are able to do so because each needs the other's currency, and each maintains accounts in the other country. *Note that when payments are made in international trade, money does not physically leave the country.* It travels back or forth between American-owned and foreign-owned bank accounts *in America.* The same is true in foreign nations, where their money will travel between an American-owned account there and the account of one of their nationals. Taken collectively, these foreign-owned accounts (including our own overseas) are called "foreign exchange." They constitute the main pool of moneys available to finance foreign trade.

THE SUPPLY OF, AND DEMAND FOR, FOREIGN EXCHANGE

But what determines the *rate* at which banks sell the foreign exchange they own? The answer is in no way different from that of all economic analysis of prices. *It depends on the supply of, and the demand for, the commodity in question—in this case, foreign exchange.*

We have already seen how imports give rise to a demand for yen and to a supply (a sale) of dollars, and how the end result of the transaction is an increase in foreign-owned bank deposits in this country. Exactly the opposite is true in the case of exports. Suppose that we were manufacturers of chemicals and that we sold a $1,000 order to Tokyo. In Japan, the importer of chemicals would go to his bank to find out how many yen that would cost. If the rate were 385, it would cost him ¥385,000, which he would then pay to the Japanese bank. The bank would charge his account and credit the yen to the Tokyo account of an American bank with which it did business, meantime advising the bank here that the transaction had taken place. When the appropriate papers arrived from Japan, our U.S. bank would then take note of its increased holdings of yen and pay the equivalent amount in dollars into our account.

Thus, buying and selling goods abroad generates a need for foreign exchange. The same demand for foreign currency (and the same sale or supply of our own) arises when we import *services,* such as transportation or insurance. Every time we fly on Air France, for example, we move dollars from our private bank accounts to the bank accounts of Air France in the United States. These dollars will then be sold for francs. As a result, dollars will go into the American account of a correspondent French bank, while in France, francs will be paid by the French bank to Air France's home office.

In the same way, of course, every time a foreigner flies on an American plane or ships cargo on an American ship or buys insurance from an American company, United States holdings of foreign currency rise abroad, while in this country, banks will take note of their increased foreign deposits and issue dollar checks to the American sellers.

In addition to goods and services, we should note three other regular sources of supply and demand for foreign exchange. The first of these is *travel.* When we travel in a foreign country we need to pay our expenses in its currency, and therefore we have to sell dollars for pounds or pesos or whatever currency we need. When a foreigner travels here, he must, of course, sell his money to get dollars.

Second, we often send gifts of money to friends or relatives in another country or mail pensions to individuals living overseas. These *remittances* supply dollars in exchange for foreign money, just as remittances coming from abroad demand dollars in exchange for foreign money.

Last, we also send and receive large sums of money to transfer dividends or interest or other *income on investments* between countries. When IBM in Italy wishes to transfer part of its profits to the IBM parent company in the United States, lira will move in Italy from its account to the account of an American bank; and in New York, IBM will be able to draw dollars from the local branch of that bank. By way of turnabout, when a dividend on an American security is sent to a foreign holder, dollars will have to travel from America to that country (which is to say, from American-owned bank accounts into foreign-owned bank accounts in America).

The items we have so far discussed are by no means all the transactions that give rise to a demand for, or a supply of, foreign exchange, but they form a group of activities that we call *transactions on current account*. They are, that is to say, part of the everyday business of international exchange, giving rise regularly to a need for foreign exchange both for us and for other countries.

TABLE 29 · 2

U.S.
BALANCE OF
PAYMENTS
ON CURRENT
ACCOUNT

BILLIONS OF DOLLARS (1967)			
Activities that supplied exchange to the U.S. (Transactions that moved foreign currencies from foreign hands into American bank accounts abroad.)		Activities that demanded exchange from the U.S. (Transactions that moved dollars from American bank accounts into foreign-owned bank accounts in the U.S.)	
Exports of merchandise on private account*	$27.2	Imports of merchandise	$26.9
Foreign purchases of U.S. transportation, insurance, and other private services*	3.4	U.S. purchases of foreign transportation, insurance, and other private services	3.5
		Remittances and pensions	1.3
Foreign travel in the U.S.	1.6	U.S. travel abroad	3.2
U.S. income from private investment abroad	7.3	Foreign income from private investments in the U.S.	1.7
Total	**$39.5**		**$36.6**
Net balance	2.9		

*Excludes military and foreign aid and all other items financed by government. See *Survey of Current Business,* March of each year, Table 1, lines 3, 6, 9, minus Table 5, lines 27, 28.

Table 29-2 shows what these actual transactions looked like in 1967.*

The table, which shows us the flows of dollar payments to and from foreigners (by which we really mean, never forget, the flows of dollar payments into and out of foreign-owned bank accounts in America), reveals the forces of supply and demand that rise from the basic transactions of international trade. It is called the *balance of payments on current account.* We will shortly see that there are other balances of payments as well. It should be noted that we include under *exports* only those shipments of goods that were sent abroad through the normal channels of private trade. Exports that were sent as part of foreign aid

*We shall discuss the rather unusual figures for 1968 in a special section at the end of this chapter.

TABLE 29 · 3

U.S.
BALANCE OF
PAYMENTS
ON CURRENT
PRIVATE
ACCOUNT

BILLIONS OF DOLLARS								
	1960	1961	1962	1963	1964	1965	1966	1967
Merchandise*	$+2.9	$+3.2	$+2.1	$+2.4	$+3.9	$+2.0	$+0.7	$+0.3
Transportation, insurance, etc.	0.0	−0.1	−0.2	−0.3	−0.2	−0.2	−0.3	−0.1
Travel	−0.9	−0.9	−0.9	−1.1	−1.0	−1.1	−1.1	−1.5
Remittances	−0.7	−0.7	−0.7	−0.9	−0.9	−1.1	−1.0	−1.2
Income from private investments	+2.7	+3.4	+3.7	+3.9	+4.7	+5.1	+5.2	+5.6
Net balance on private current account	$+4.0	$+4.9	$+4.0	$+4.0	$+6.5	$+4.7	$+3.5	$+2.9

Totals may not add, owing to rounding.
*Does not include military or aid-financed exports.

or military aid are not included here, for reasons that we shall subsequently discuss.

Usually we show only the net figure in the balance of payments, preceded by a plus sign (or with no sign) if the balance is "favorable" to us—that is, if it brings in a net flow of dollars—and with a minus sign if it is unfavorable. The balance of payments of all the items above for the years 1960–1967 is shown in Table 29-3.

It is clear from the figures which way the balance of supply and demand on current account tips. Through most of the 1960's, and indeed for many years before that, foreigners have been spending more dollars within the United States than we have been spending abroad.

It is worth a moment to take note of exactly how this "favorable" balance of current account comes about. In normal years, Europe and the rest of the world are strong net buyers of American goods, although, as we can see, this "merchandise balance of payments" has been slipping in recent years as European productive capacity has enlarged. At the same time, however, our expenditure of dollars for foreign transportation, travel, and remittances has grown steadily larger, so that we are considerable net spenders of dollars for these purposes, especially for travel in Europe and Canada. Finally, we note the mounting stream of net income from private investments—the dividends and royalties earned on America's vast investments overseas. This tips the total balance on current account decisively in our favor.

Thus the international flows of exchange on current private account are very reassuring. Our expenditures in most years have been outweighed by a healthy surplus of expenditures by foreigners. But is the surplus really healthy? Indeed, does not the positive balance of current account mean that the United States is in danger of doing the very thing that so often frightens us: selling or earning so much more than we buy or pay out that we threaten to drain all the money from the rest of the world?

RATE OF
EXCHANGE
AND BALANCE
OF PAYMENTS

The answer to this question—it is a question that has worried many foreigners—hinges on the relation between the rate of exchange and the balance of payments. We have already seen that the rate of exchange establishes the general relation between international price levels. We have seen that the balance of payments reveals the supply and demand for foreign exchange. Now let us put the two together.

Let us suppose, as a first approach to the problem, that goods and services like those above are the only activities that require international exchange (we will soon see that they are not), and let us assume that the rate of exchange, like any other price, is free to move. Then it is not difficult to see that a situation such as we have depicted would soon lead to a new *rate of exchange that would change the level of prices in the U.S. in terms of the prices of other countries.*

For what our figures show is that foreigners will be paying dollars out of their U.S. bank accounts a great deal faster than Americans will be making payments into those foreign accounts. (Similarly, foreigners abroad will be making payments in their own money into the U.S.-owned accounts of their money faster than Americans will be making payments out of those accounts.) The result will soon be a shortage of dollars in the American bank accounts of foreigners and a very large supply of foreign currencies in bank accounts abroad owned by Americans.

APPRECIATION
AND
DEPRECIATION
OF FOREIGN
EXCHANGE

At this point, suppose that a Japanese importer wants to buy another $1,000 worth of American chemicals. He goes to his bank to find out what dollar exchange costs—and has an unpleasant surprise. His banker tells him that exchange is very "tight" at the moment, meaning by this that his own dollar balances in the United States are very low, and that American balances of yen are very high. As a result, the Japanese banker can no longer buy dollars for 385 yen. The bank in this country is now insisting on 390 or 395 or perhaps even 400. Because of supply and demand, the yen had cheapened or *depreciated* in value vis-à-vis the dollar, and the dollar has, of course, risen or *appreciated* vis-à-vis the yen.

Now our importer makes a quick calculation. At 400 yen to the dollar,

578

the $1,000 worth of chemicals costs him ¥400,000 instead of ¥385,000. That is too expensive for the Japanese market. He decides not to place the order.

Exactly the opposite situation would confront an American importer of Japanese goods. Suppose we wanted to buy another camera for ¥20,000. When we went to our bank in this country, we would find our banker very eager to get rid of the yen piling up in his account in Tokyo. Faced with the competition from the bank across the street (which is also trying to get rid of its yen), he will offer us the 20,000 yen not at $51.95 (which is what it cost at 385 yen to the dollar) but for only $51.50 or $51 or even $50, which is what it would cost if the yen slipped to 400 to the dollar.

Faced with this change in exchange rates, our own calculations have to be refigured, especially if we are dealers in cameras. Clearly, the more yen we can get for a dollar, the cheaper will Japanese cameras be, once we price them in American dollars. Thus, just as the depreciation of the yen discouraged the sale of American goods to Japan, it acts to encourage the sale of Japanese goods to America.

The principle is very clear. Movements in exchange rates *always* change the relative price levels of two countries. As a result, one country *always* finds its exports stimulated and its imports made more expensive, while the other country *always* experiences exactly the opposite effect —its exports are discouraged, while its imports are given a boost.

Now let us go back to clear up the business of trade between Infraville and Supraville, once and for all—this time with Japan and the United States again taking the leading roles.

As at the beginning of this chapter, we assume that the prices in the two countries are as shown in Table 29-4.

TABLE 29 · 4

	U.S.	Japan
Wool (lb)	$1.10	¥300
Cotton (lb)	.30	¥100

What happens next?

The first part of the answer depends on exchange rates. We suppose that they are 400 to 1, a rate at which the prices of both iron and wool are *below* the prices of those products in America. As a result, Japan will begin by selling both cotton and wool to us, whereas we will be able to sell nothing to her.

This is however only the beginning of the process. If exchange rates are flexible, they will immediately reflect the fact that the demand for yen is so much greater than the supply. The yen will rise to, say, 300 to 1. At this exchange rate, Japanese wool is now $1.00 in American money (¥300 ÷ 300) but Japanese cotton has gone up to 33⅓¢ (¥100 ÷ 300). Suddenly cotton is *more* expensive than the same product in America. In other words, the pressure of supply and demand on foreign exchange has pushed the exchange rate within the trading range offered by the differentials in opportunity cost of the two countries.

Could the exchange rate continue to rise until the yen was much dearer—say 250 to 1? If it did, not only would Japanese cotton be very much more expensive than American, but even Japanese wool would now be a shade over the United States price (¥3,000 ÷ 250 = $1.20). If the exchange rate swung this far, it would be America that threatened to undersell Japan in everything. But again the very imbalance between the supply and demand for foreign exchange would prevent the threat from happening.

Thus we can see that under the conditions of a freely moving exchange rate, fluctuations in the rate of exchange serve to balance out flows of payments between countries, and in turn these flows tend to stabilize the exchange rate. *Under these conditions no country can ever be only a seller* (*or only a buyer*). Even if it is a land of sweatshop labor, it cannot undersell the world, for the very glut of its exports would raise the international value of its money and in this way set a limit to its exports.

FIXED VS. FLEXIBLE EXCHANGE RATES

The method of establishing international price levels that we have just described is called that of *flexible, or freely fluctuating, exchange rates*. It is the easiest of all means of establishing international prices for the student to understand—but alas for him, it is not the means that is actually used to establish exchange rates between nations.

PROBLEMS OF FLEXIBLE EXCHANGE RATES

Why not? The reasons are not difficult to understand. One of them involves the fact that most international transactions are not concluded immediately across a counter, but extend over weeks or even months between the time that a sale is agreed upon and the time when the goods arrive and payment is due. If exchange rates changed during this period, either the importer or the exporter could be severely penalized. If I agreed to buy a camera for ¥20,000, thinking it would cost $50, and when the camera arrived I found that yen had advanced in price to 300 to 1, so that the camera cost me $67, I would hardly be pleased. And although it is possible to insure oneself to some extent against exchange variations by buying "forward exchange," most traders would rather not deal in exchange rates that are likely to alter over the course of a transaction. More important, international investors who put money overseas for long periods have no way of protecting themselves against changes in rates and are even more concerned about the risks of flexible exchange.

In addition, most monetary authorities fear that fluctuating rates would lead to speculative purchases and sales of foreign currencies just for the purpose of making a profit on swings in their price—and that these speculative "raids" would have the effect of still further aggravating those swings.

There are counterarguments to these fears, and it should be noted that some economists strongly favor flexible or freely fluctuating exchange rates as the best way to arrange international transactions. It will be a happy day for the students of international finance when their recommendations are accepted, for much of the difficulties of learning about international finance will then disappear. The fact remains, however, that the existing system of foreign exchange does *not* allow rates to change freely, and that the system of so-called *fixed exchange rates* seems likely to remain as the world's international monetary system for a long time.

How are exchange rates determined if they are not set by supply and demand? The answer is that exchange rates have been "fixed" in relation to one another by declarations of the governments of all nations. At the center of this fixed relationship is an announced value of one ounce of gold as being worth 35 United States dollars, a price set by the Treasury in 1933. All other countries have declared the value of their currencies in terms of this relationship, so that there is a definite number of francs or pounds or marks that can be bought for a dollar (or for an ounce of gold). *Hence the world operates with rates of exchange that do not fluctuate with supply and demand, but that remain more or less stationary, or change only infrequently.*

Under this system of fixed exchange rates, the U.S. Treasury stands willing to buy all gold offered to it, from foreigners or domestic suppliers, at $35 an ounce. More important, it agrees as well to *sell* gold at $35 an ounce to any foreign government (or the central bank of any foreign government).* Thus all dollar balances held by foreign governments are potentially convertible into gold—a fact that gives rise to many problems, as we shall quickly see.

FIXED EXCHANGE RATES

---

*The Treasury will not sell gold to *American* holders of dollar balances or to foreign *nongovernment* holders of dollars. Within this country, the dollar itself, not gold, is the official "ultimate" money of the country, and it would be wasteful to use our limited gold supply at home when we need it, as we shall see, for international payments.

Now suppose, as before, that the United States runs a surplus in its balance of payments on current account—in other words, that its excess of exports over imports is steadily depleting the dollar accounts of foreign banks. And suppose that the exchange rate could not fluctuate as we have previously imagined. What could then happen?

There are but three possibilities.

One is that trade would simply come to a halt. If the United States undersold the rest of the world on everything, and if the rate of exchange were fixed and there was no way for the world to get U.S. dollars, no one would be able to buy any more American merchandise, whether it was "cheaper" or not. For how could he pay the American seller?

Second, it might be possible to alter the rate of exchange by government decree. If we could make foreign currencies less expensive in relation to American dollars, we could make foreign goods cheaper than American goods. In that way, we could tempt Americans to buy abroad, and thereby make it possible for foreigners once again to buy American goods. We shall look into this possibility later.

Third, we have already hinted above that *currencies might be made available in ways other than current transactions.* This is the very important subject that we must now look into.

GOVERNMENT
TRANSACTIONS

One such transaction may have already occurred to the reader. Not all the exchanges between nations take place between individuals or firms. Governments also need foreign exchange to maintain their diplomatic establishments in other nations or for participation in foreign affairs, foreign aid, debt service, and other such purposes. Much more important, war and military assistance use up large sums of exchange. The United States, for instance, maintains armies in many nations where U.S. soldiers must be fed and supplied with locally bought produce and labor. All these activities, peaceful and otherwise, cost foreign exchange.

Table 29-5 shows us the net result of our government transactions

TABLE 29 · 5

U.S.
BALANCE OF
PAYMENTS ON
GOVERNMENT
ACCOUNT

	BILLIONS OF DOLLARS							
	1960	1961	1962	1963	1964	1965	1966	1967
Net military expenditures	$−2.8	$−2.6	$−2.4	$−2.3	$−2.2	$−2.1	$−2.8	$−3.0
Other government	−0.7	−0.2	+0.5	+0.1	+0.1	0.0	+0.2	+1.1
Balance on government account	$−3.5	$−2.8	$−2.9	$−2.2	$−2.1	$−2.1	$−2.6	$−1.9

divided into two major flows of payments. The first flow, net military expenditures, reveals the drain on the dollar that arises from our overseas military activity. It is "net" because it arises *after* earnings of about a billion dollars per annum from sales of American military equipment to foreign governments. The second flow, "other government," shows us the net result of our foreign aid, our normal diplomatic and other expenditures, and of payments and repayments of government loans.

This second flow must be scrutinized more carefully. We have said that it included foreign aid expenditures, which are gifts of American dollars to other countries. These expenditures have risen from about $2 billion per year in the early 1960's to nearly $3.5 billion in the most recent years. One would think, then, that the "other government" account would show a very substantial outflow of dollars over these years. Instead it shows, in most years, a modest inflow. How can this be?

The answer is that the overwhelming bulk of our foreign aid expenditures does not constitute a dollar drain. Between 80 to 90 per cent of all foreign aid extended by the United States consists of grants or loans *tied to the purchase of American goods.* This means that we are giving away goods for the purpose of economic development by transferring dollars into the bank accounts of foreign governments *on the condition that those dollars be spent in this country.* Hence these expenditures do not in any way affect our balance of payments.

A small portion of U.S. foreign aid is untied, and this portion—10 to 20 per cent of our total aid expenditures—is indeed spent in other nations. This small dollar outflow is included in the "other government" account and would make that account a deficit were it the only item included therein. But the most important component of the "other government" flow comes from other governments steadily paying back their various debts to the United States, and this has resulted in an inflow of dollars on "other government" account.*

Thus, net government expenditures overseas for military and other purposes provide us with one explanation of how dollars can be pro-

*Note that the "official" U.S. balance of payments accounts *include* foreign-aid financed exports in the total of *merchandise* exports. This gives the erroneous impression that these exports earn us dollars, which they do not. In the official balance of payments figures, these "exports" are then offset by an entry for foreign aid that looks as though all foreign aid cost us foreign exchange, which we have seen is not true. In the end, the *net* dollar drain of foreign aid is the same on our basis of accounting as on the official methods, but the false impression of foreign aid "exports" and foreign aid "dollar cost" is avoided. I am indebted to Professor Robert W. Stevens for assistance in preparing these figures. This presentation follows the lines of his article in the *Harvard Business Review,* Nov.-Dec., 1966.

vided to foreign nations to supplement the dollars earned by their direct sales to us. But there is still another very important means of replenishing their dollar accounts. *This is by the movement of capital from the United States to other lands.*

Capital is sent abroad (or can be received from abroad) in several forms. It may travel as additions to American plants in foreign nations, or as additions to their physical assets here. This does not mean that it travels as the actual steel, for example. When investors add to their plant and equipment abroad, what they send is the money. Thus, in order to "export" capital, we must acquire foreign exchange—that is, put dollars into foreign bank accounts here in order to release foreign money abroad (or vice versa if foreigners are exporting capital to us).*

We call this overseas expenditure of American investment funds a shipment of *long-term capital.* We might note that such overseas investment is a normal attribute of a wealthy nation. It was by exports of capital from Britain to the United States that much of our nineteenth-century railroad network was originally financed. By way of turnabout, a good deal of the growth of many European nations since World War II owes its source to American capital invested there. By 1968 the value of American investments in plant and equipment and real estate around the world totaled over $60 billion, whereas foreigners owned some $10 billion of assets in the U.S. From this capital, both American and foreign, interest and dividends flowed in both directions across the oceans. It is because our capital assets are so much larger than those of foreigners that the income from investments in our current accounts showed as a large net source of dollar payments to the United States.

Still another form of long-term capital consists of *financial investments*—purchases by Americans of bonds or stocks from foreigners. In the same way, when foreigners buy American securities, foreign exchange is also involved. In early 1968, American citizens owned roughly $22 billion in foreign securities, and foreigners owned approximately $17 billion of ours.

Last, money also moves from nation to nation as *short-term capital.* This is capital invested by individuals or firms in very liquid foreign securities such as short-term government bonds, or merely held in banks to earn interest. There are several billions of such capital that moves from nation to nation in search of the highest possible return, or as part of the pool of foreign exchange from which international payments are financed.

*There is an all-too-easy source of confusion in the terminology with which we speak of capital movements. Capital going abroad from the U.S. is called a capital "export." This sounds as if it earned dollars for us, like a merchandise export. But we have seen, it does not—*we have to give up dollars to send capital abroad.* Similarly capital coming into the U.S. is called a capital "import" although it increases our supply of foreign currencies. It helps clear up the confusion to think of a capital "export" as actually being the *import of a claim* to foreign assets (which is indeed the reality behind the financial transaction), and to think of capital "imports" as *exporting* claims to American assets.

TABLE 29 · 6

U.S.
BALANCE OF
PAYMENTS

BILLIONS OF DOLLARS	1960	1961	1962	1963	1964	1965	1966	1967
Balance on current account	$+4.0	$+4.9	$+4.0	$+4.0	$+6.5	$+4.7	$+3.5	$+2.9
Balance on government account	−3.5	−2.8	−2.9	−2.2	−2.1	−2.1	−2.6	−1.9
Capital movements								
Long term	−2.2	−2.1	−2.7	−3.3	−4.2	−4.4	−1.5	−2.0
Short term	−1.4	−1.5	−0.5	−0.8	−2.1	+0.8	−0.4	−1.1
Errors and omissions	−0.9	−0.9	−0.1	−0.3	−0.9	−0.4	−0.4	−0.6
Balance of payments (liquidity basis)	$−3.9	$−2.4	$−2.2	$−2.7	$−2.8	$−1.3	$−1.4	$−2.8

(Totals may not add, owing to rounding.)

If we now add capital movements and net government transactions to the American balance on current account, we see a picture very different from the earlier one.*

What we see in Table 29-6 is a complete reversal of the seesaw of supply and demand. Our balance of payments on current account generates a vast overdemand for dollars, but our balance on government and capital account generates an even larger demand for foreign currencies. Thus America does not have a surplus, but a "deficit" in its balance of payments with the rest of the world.

What is the result of this? If the exchange rate were free to move, we know what would happen. The dollar would now be overabundant as the U.S. bank balances of foreigners increased. Hence its price would cheapen. With this cheapening would come a stimulus for American exports and a deterrent for imports from abroad.† The deficit would thus soon be eliminated.

*The reader will notice an item called "Errors and omissions" in Table 29-6. This term is actually a "balancing item," compiled at the end of the balance of payments calculations to assure the bookkeeping equality of debits and credits (see p. 588). The need for the item arises because some kinds of transactions do not get recorded, and thereby throw the totals of payments and receipts out of balance. Smuggling is one such kind of transaction. More important are perfectly legal activities such as the deposit of money by American or foreign travelers in banks in the nations they are visiting. Such items are really transfers of short term capital, and in fact Errors and Omissions can be thought of as mainly composed of just such short-term capital movements.

†Note that it would also be more expensive for an American company to build abroad, since it would cost more dollars to amass the necessary francs, pounds, or whatever. Similarly, investors in foreign securities would find it dearer to send money abroad. Conversely, foreigners would find American investments cheaper. This would set up a corrective tendency in the flow of international capital. Only the government account (which is chiefly determined by political considerations) would be largely unaffected by the changed exchange rate.

But under the system of exchange rates tied to gold, this means of adjustment is ruled out. What then?

GOLD AND RESERVES

The answer brings us finally to consider the role of gold in international finance. We have already encountered gold in our study of the domestic monetary system where we discovered that it now played no role whatsoever in relation to our national money (pp. 325–27). But gold plays a very large role as a medium for the settlement of international deficits.

What happens when dollars pile up in the American accounts of foreign central banks because of an excess of dollar payments over dollar withdrawals? *The answer is that these banks will normally use their large dollar balances to buy gold from the U.S. Treasury, which will be added to their national reserves.** Such a purchase of gold counts as an international transaction like any export, and thus establishes a formal offset to our deficit. At the same time, it reduces the oversupply of dollars and thus takes the "pressure" off the dollar.

A second way of offsetting the deficit is to borrow from the International Monetary Fund, an international institution into which nearly all the nations of the world have deposited both gold and national currencies. Under certain conditions, nations can borrow currencies of which they are short—or gold—and can use these acquired reserves to settle their international deficits.

DOLLAR RESERVES

A third way of meeting the deficit does not require either gold or IMF borrowing. It consists in the willingness of foreign banks to allow

---

*The gold is *not* usually shipped abroad, as one might think. Instead it is trucked to a vault many feet below the street surface in the Federal Reserve Bank of New York, where it is stacked in dull yellow bricks about the shape (but half the thickness) of a building brick. It is possible to visit this vault which now holds some $13 billion of foreign gold, neatly separated into bins assigned to different countries. To see this modern equivalent of Montezuma's treasure is an astonishing sight. Gold may well be, as many have said, a kind of international psychosis, but its power over the imagination, no doubt the result of its traditional association with riches, is still remarkable. It is amusing to note that the Federal Reserve Bank, as custodian of this foreign gold, once suggested to its binholders that they might save a considerable sum if, instead of actually weighing the bricks and moving them from bin to bin whenever gold was bought and sold, both parties agreed to move the gold just on the books, the way bank balances are moved about. All governments demurred. They wanted the actual gold bricks in their bins. Hence, when gold moves from nation to nation to help settle up accounts, it is still actually pushed across the floor of the Fed's vault and carefully piled in the proper bin.

their dollar balances to accumulate without converting them into gold. These rising balances count as an inflow of short-term capital.

We have seen that the meaning of a deficit in the balance of payments is that we make more payments to foreigners for goods, government services, and capital purposes than they make to us, and that this results in steadily growing amounts of dollars in their U.S. bank balances. Ordinarily, these extra-large balances would be skimmed off by using them to buy gold. It is possible, however, for foreign central banks and other official institutions to hold (or invest) their dollars here and to count these dollar balances—all of which *can* be converted into gold—as part of their *reserves*.

Why would foreign countries wish to do that? The answer is that it is profitable. Gold is, after all, an asset that yields a negative return—it costs money to hold it and protect it. Dollar balances, on the contrary, yield positive returns of interest and dividends. By permitting their reserves to remain in dollars, European countries are using American banks as "financial intermediaries," much as individual savers use mutual funds or savings banks as their profit-making depositaries.

In this way the dollar has become an important *reserve currency* for many nations, who count their holdings of dollars much as we count our holdings of gold. In much the same way, within the British Commonwealth, the pound sterling serves as a reserve currency for many Commonwealth members.

When we add the transfers of gold and IMF reserves and the increased official holdings of dollars, our balance of payments deficit disappears, as we can see in Table 29-7.

Does this mean that there is no balance of payments problem after all? Indeed, it does not. By now we must realize that what we mean by the balance of payments is the relationship between the demand

TABLE 29 · 7

FINANCING THE U.S. BALANCE OF PAYMENTS (billions of dollars)

	1960	1961	1962	1963	1964	1965	1966	1967
Balance of payments	$−3.9	$−2.4	$−2.2	$−2.7	$−2.8	$−1.3	$−1.4	$−2.8
Financed by:								
Decrease in gold or in convertible currencies or IMF claims	2.1	0.6	1.5	0.4	0.2	1.2	0.6	0.1
Increase in liquid dollar assets held by foreigners	1.8	1.8	0.7	2.3	2.6	0.1	0.8	2.7

for, and the supply of, dollars for *certain purposes*. That is why we can speak of a balance of payments on current account, government account, capital account, and so on. Each account summarizes our receipts and expenditures for certain categories of international transactions.

When we speak of our "over-all" deficit in the balance of payments, we mean that all dollar payments coming to us from "normal" international transactions are not large enough to cover our dollar outlays for all "normal" purposes. Where did the extra dollars come from? They were received from gold sales or from IMF borrowings or from the willingness of foreigners to accept dollars without being reimbursed in their own currencies or in gold.

MEANING OF BALANCE OF PAYMENTS DEFICIT

This means that it is possible to define our deficit in a number of different ways, depending on what we count as a "normal" international transaction. Suppose, for example, that we want to know how we finance our current and government account and our flows of long-term capital. Then we "draw the line" under those three items, giving us what is called the "basic" balance of payments. If we want to know how we financed all these items, plus flows of short-term capital, we draw it in the manner we have done, to reveal what is called the balance on a "liquidity basis." And there are still other ways of striking meaningful subtotals of our foreign transactions.

Which is the "correct" way? Which is the "true" deficit? The answer depends entirely on the information that we are interested in procuring. The basic balance is useless if we want to see how we finance our short-term capital movements. And the liquidity balance tells us nothing if we want to know the manner in which we finance our long-term capital expenditures abroad.

But suppose we wanted to know how *everything* balanced—not only current and government account and long- and short-term capital, but movements of gold and changes in foreign-held dollars? Then we would draw the line at the very bottom of the table of international transactions—where the net balance is always exactly zero!

Why zero? Because the total balance of payments only shows us *how* all purchases (or sales) were financed. Suppose for example that the sole U.S. transaction were the purchase of one Japanese camera. Our balance of payments would look like this:

Merchandise	−$50
Short-term capital	+$50
Balance	0

The merchandise item of −$50 represents, as we know, the import of a good. And what is the balancing item of +$50? That is the increase in a Japanese-owned bank account in the U.S. that resulted from our payment for the camera. It is listed as a "+" because it really stands for the export of a *claim* on U.S. production, and exports are listed under the + column. (See footnote, p. 584.) Suppose now that the following year we cleared out the Japanese account by sending them gold. If that were the only transaction that year, the Balance of Payments would look like this:

Short-term capital	−$50
Gold	+$50
Balance	0

Here we would have reduced the claim of the Japanese against our production (whence the minus $50), and this would have been offset by the export—always a plus—of $50 in gold. Once again the total of all payments must be zero.

In other words, our over-all balance of payments always balances. But depending on where we draw the line, we can see how we financed (or how foreigners financed) the particular categories of international exchange in which we are interested.

The United States has been running a deficit in both its basic and liquidity balances of payment for over a decade. As a result, we are not too surprised at Fig. 29-1.

THE GOLD PROBLEM

FIG. 29-1 THE CHANGING U.S. GOLD STOCK

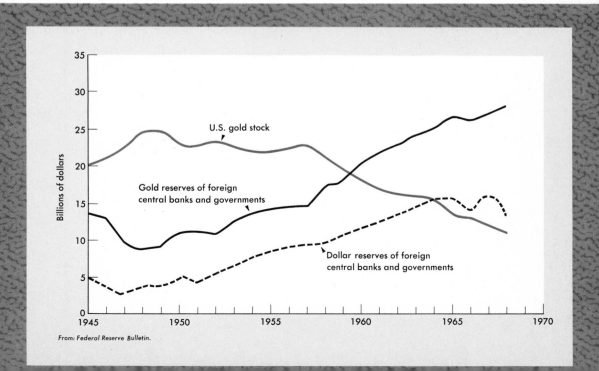

From: Federal Reserve Bulletin.

As we can see, we have lost half our gold stock in fifteen years. But there is something even more serious than that. The dollar reserves of foreign banks and governments are now larger than the remaining gold stock! If those reserves were ever converted *en masse* into gold, our gold supply would be wiped out. In fact, we could not even honor all the existing claims for gold.

It need hardly be pointed out that this would be a major economic catastrophe—not because we would have no gold "behind" our currency, but because we would have cheated foreign nations out of hundreds of millions or billions worth of purchasing power. For if the gold supply ran out, foreigners could no longer repatriate their dollar holdings at a known exchange rate. Instead, their dollar holdings would now have to find their own price vis-à-vis their own currencies; and since dollars are held in very large quantities, this price might be very low.

Take, for example, a Netherlands bank that had allowed $1 million to remain in America, because it was confident that it could always buy gold with it, and thereby get the 3,624,000 guilders which is the official exchange equivalent. Suddenly it would have to turn its dollars into guilders at whatever rate the market brought. The million dollars might be worth only 3 million guilders—or even less.* *Thus countries that had cooperated with us by allowing their dollars to remain here would be penalized.* They would never again allow dollars to pile up in U.S. banks.

Not less important is the likelihood that a world trading slump of violent proportions would probably follow from the sudden inconvertibility of the dollar. Since World War II, the dollar has been *the* unit for settling balances among nations, and its general acceptability has provided a payment means that has helped to sustain the swift rise in world trade since the war. The loss of confidence in the dollar would undo at one stroke the long process of establishing a means of payment that would be as "good" in Europe or Asia as in Latin America or the United States, and it might be a long while before another international unit of payment took its place. In the meantime, many nations would refuse to do business unless they were paid in gold—and since the volume of gold is much smaller than that of internationally held dollars plus gold, the amount of world trade would suffer a terrible collapse.

Now, just because the consequences of a "run" on gold would be so disastrous, it is exceedingly unlikely that the central banks of foreign

---

*We can now see that this possibility of capital loss provides another strong argument against flexible exchange rates. Private investors would be severely penalized if they found their dividends and interest—or the repayment of their capital—depreciated in value because of a change in exchange rates. Of course, there is also the chance of a profit from fluctuating rates. But most investors are first concerned about the *safety* of their investment.

nations would take such a suicidal course of action as to demand their dollar balances in gold. This is not to say, however, that *private* speculators abroad might not take their holdings of dollars and convert them into gold. For many years there has been a perfectly legal market in gold in London and elsewhere, where private individuals could exchange their holdings of dollars or other currencies for gold bullion. The gold they bought was sold to them at the fixed price of $35 an ounce by an international gold pool comprised of the main gold-holding nations. In the pool, the United States, as the largest holder of gold in the world, was committed to providing 59 per cent of all bullion supplied to the market.

In March, 1968, the gold pool suddenly faced a crisis. Alarmed at the shrinkage of U.S. gold reserves, private speculators converged on the London market to convert their dollars into bullion. On the first day of that month, the pool, which had normally sold 3 to 4 tons of gold per day, suddenly found itself obliged to sell 40 tons. A week later the demand had risen to 75 tons. On March 13, it was 100 tons; the next day, 200 tons.

At this rate of drainage, the United States Treasury was being forced to put $1 million of gold into the pool every two to three minutes. Officials in Washington nervously figured that if the gold hemorrhage were not checked, the nation's entire gold reserves would be used up in a few weeks. To prevent such a crisis, the world's central bankers hurriedly convened in Washington, and after a weekend of continuous conferences, announced that the gold pool was to be discontinued and that a new "two-price" system would immediately begin. All *official* holders of dollars (i.e., governments and central banks) would still be able to buy gold at $35 an ounce from the Treasury. But there would no longer be any effort to maintain the price of gold at an "official" level in the private market by supplying whatever gold was needed there at that price. Instead, there would be no sales from any national reserve of gold into the private market, and "private" gold would be allowed to find its own price.*

Since then the two-price system has worked fairly well. Gold on the free market now commands a price of nearly $50 an ounce, but "official" gold is still $35. Moreover, the gold drain from the U.S. Treasury seems, at this writing, to have been stanched and perhaps to have begun to flow back into Fort Knox.

---

*To work, such a system depends on the willingness of central bankers to "play the game." Otherwise they could convert their official holdings of dollars into gold at $35 per ounce, sell the gold in Europe at over $45 an ounce, use the dollars they received once again to buy at $35 an ounce, and so on *ad infinitum,* or at least until the forces of supply and demand had brought the two markets together. A great deal of international monetary cooperation depends on "playing the game." For a scholarly but very readable account of international monetary cooperation, see Henry Aubrey, *Atlantic Economic Cooperation* (Council on Foreign Relations, 1967); and for a very lively and perceptive popular account see "In Defense of Sterling" in *Business Adventures* by John Brooks (New York: Weybright and Talley, 1969).

Meanwhile, the U.S. balance of payments showed such dramatic changes in 1968 that it seems best to discuss it separately. The first quarter of the year began with a deficit of $705 million, a continuation of the gloomy trend of the past, but its last quarter ended with a surplus of $900 million! For the year as a whole, there was a small "favorable" balance of $158 million, measured on the same liquidity basis as in Table 29-6.

Even more surprising were the sources of this dramatic shift. To begin with, our traditionally best dollar-earner, the balance of payments on current account, fell from a plus figure of $2.9 billion in 1967 to a negative figure of $57 million for 1968! This extraordinary decline was primarily the result of a spectacular increase in imports, up $7 billion over the year, an increase that far outdistanced an otherwise healthy rise in exports and investment income.

One would think, with such a fateful change in our most dependable portion of the balance of payments, that the over-all results would have been even more disastrous than in former years. This is particularly true since the net government account was basically unchanged, a small increase in war expenditures being offset by a small decline in "other government." The potential deficit was averted, however, by a truly sensational improvement in the flows on capital account. In 1967, it will be remembered, our capital account was negative to the sum of $3.2 billion: $2 billion of long-term capital and over a billion of short-term capital being invested, net, outside the United States. In 1968 this flow reversed itself, and *over $1 billion was invested, net, in the United States.* This was the result, first, of a sharp fall in U.S. corporate transfers of capital overseas and second, a rush of foreign funds into the American stock market. Foreign purchases of securities rose from $900 million in 1967 to about $1.9 billion in 1968. The effect of the over-all shift in our capital account, a swing of more than $4 billion, was enough to pull the United States balance as a whole to the plus side.

What does this dramatic shift of events signify? We can learn three things from it:

1. *The balance of payments is subject to very rapid improvement or deterioration.*

As we have seen between 1967 and 1968, the United States balance of payments is capable of changes of $3 billion in a single year. This sensitivity is due to the fact that a strong influence on the balance of payments is exerted by flows of short-term capital that can move very rapidly—such as the European money that flowed into the U.S. stock markets in 1968—or by large-scale, but also very fast-moving transactions among governments. One of the reasons for the dramatic change in the U.S. balance, for example, was a $700 million increase in official Canadian holdings of U.S. government bonds under a U.S.-Canadian reserve agreement. The balance, of course, may swing dramatically the other way in another year. A flight of short-term money into European markets or an unwillingness of other governments to accept American government securities might bring as rapid a decline in the American liquidity balance as 1968 brought a rise.

2. *The deterioration in our merchandise balance of payments suggests that we are moving to a new relationship vis-à-vis the rest of the world.*

Part of the tremendous rise in imports in 1968 was due to special factors: a long domestic copper strike that boosted copper imports, for example, and heavy U.S. buying of foreign steel in anticipation of a U.S. strike. But there is no doubt of an underlying trend, visible if we look back to Table 29-3, that suggests a gradual deterioration in the merchandise component of our balance on current account.

Such a trend is actually long overdue. Much of the American export surplus of the 1950's and earlier 1960's was due to Europe's inability to meet heavy production demands, a condition that has now been remedied. But there is a reason even more fundamental than that. We should expect that a nation such as ours, with large amounts of capital invested overseas and a rising inflow of dividends and royalties, would *properly* run a negative merchandise balance on current account. After all, in the normal course of world affairs we know that there must be some rough equating of the inflows and outflows of foreign exchange among countries. If we are to enjoy a steady net inflow of profits and earnings from our capital, we stand in exactly the same danger that we have discussed at various times in other contexts: the danger of "draining" all the foreign exchange of other nations. The only normal way to return this surplus foreign exchange is to buy more than we sell. Thus, as a so-called mature creditor nation, we should expect our normal trade relationship, over the long run, to have a net import balance on goods and services.

3. *The American balance of payments problem is by no means yet solved.*

We have already emphasized how rapidly flows of capital can move in an adverse direction as well as in a favorable one, and now we have added that the likelihood is that our balance of payments on goods and services is apt to worsen. This means that as long as our balance on government account continues to run a large negative figure, we can by no means count ourselves out of the woods. One of the main objectives of our foreign policy over the coming years must be to establish a viable economic relationship between America and the rest of the world.

CURING THE
BALANCE OF PAYMENTS DEFICIT

But it is one thing to say that we must find a viable economic relationship with the rest of the world, and another thing to find the means to establish such a relationship. How shall we deal with the tendency to spend more foreign currencies than we acquire? Or to put it differently, how can we cut down the surplus of dollars that foreigners acquire, over and beyond the amount of dollars they spend?

Basically, there are these possibilities:

1. *The classical medicine.*

One of the remedies one hears is that we must take the bitter purge of the "classical remedy" for balance of payments problems. What is the remedy? Specifically it consists of a stiff application of higher interest rates and a strict diet as far as government spending is concerned. In terms of its objective, it aims to cure the balance of payments problem by *deflating* the economy: forcing down our price level until our exports look more attractive to foreign buyers and until foreign goods become much more expensive for us to buy.

Thus the classical medicine essentially seeks to cure the deficit by boosting exports and cutting imports. Will it work? It may, when a nation is losing out in international markets and must re-establish its competitive position overseas. In a situation such as that of the United States, however, where a balance of payments deficit has persisted despite a very favorable showing on current account, it may do little to remedy the situation. For all the much talked-about inflation in postwar America, prices have risen here less than half as much as in the dozen major trading nations of the world, so that our prices have actually *declined* relative to world prices. This hardly seems an appropriate situation in which to apply the classical medicine.

And then there is another chastening thought. The classical remedy works, as we have seen, by deflating the economy. But there is always the danger that a would-be deflation of costs will tip over into a general contraction of expenditures. In that case, deflation becomes recession, and the "cure" for our balance of payments difficulties consists of unemployment and a slowdown in our real rate of growth. Few Americans are likely to want to pay that price for international equilibrium.

2. *Restraints on capital.*

Still, the problem is there. In some way or other, the excess of dollar payments *must* be reduced. Hence a number of suggestions have been made to reduce the imbalance not by an over-all deflation, but by measures that will serve to discourage American spending abroad on capital account. One of these is the imposition of a tax on the purchase of foreign securities. Another is a general plea to business to defer inessential plans for overseas expansion. A third is the deliberate raising of short-term interest rates at home to attract foreign short-term capital here.

All these measures (which we have taken) aim at restraining the net outflow of American capital. In the short run, there is no doubt that they can help alleviate our deficit on international account. The problem arises when we ask if this is a wise *long-run* policy or not. For there is a useful purpose served when American capital goes overseas—useful not only to the nations to which it brings wealth, but to us as well. Our capital exports soon earn income which returns to us as a "plus" item on current account. In a normal year this investment income from abroad is larger than our capital exports abroad. Thus if we stifle capital exports to save dollars today, we jeopardize a larger flow of dollars to ourselves tomorrow.

3. *Correcting the government overseas deficit.*

The difficulties of taking more than short-term action in the capital market bring us to the next obvious candidate for paring down: the heavy overseas deficit incurred on government account. For the past decade, this government balance has cost us a net deficit of between $2 billion and $3 billion. Here, it seems is a likely cure for the balance of payments problem. What can be done about it?

We have already looked into one often suggested area of "remedy"— reducing our foreign aid expenditures. But we have discovered that the overwhelming bulk of these expenditures does not constitute any dollar drain. If we cut back our foreign aid expenditures, we would cut back on the considerable volume of American production that is transferred to the underdeveloped world, but we would hardly improve our dollar drain at all. The suggestion that the richest nation on earth curtail its aid to the poorest and most miserable for the sake of saving the few hundred millions of dollar drain that is the net "foreign exchange cost" of foreign aid seems like the last and not the first measure to be taken in curing the balance of payments.

What of reducing our military expenditures abroad? That would be a much clearer net saving of dollars, for there is much less linkage between the dollars we spend to sustain troops or bases or actual fighting abroad and the *sale* of American goods to those areas. To the extent that we are able to reduce our overseas committments, not only in Vietnam but in Europe where we still maintain a large and expensive armed presence, we will certainly contribute greatly to the solution of our payments problem. Another means to the same end would be to persuade European nations to bear a larger share of our military costs. The problem in both cases, however, is not an economic one—although it has profound economic consequences. The flexibility of our military budget is based on political considerations about which the economist, whatever his private views, has no professional competence.

4. *Semiflexible exchange rates.*

Finally, might it not be possible to avoid the problem of the deficit altogether by going part way toward flexible exchange rates? We will remember that if exchange rates could move freely there would never be a "deficit" in the first place, since the price of exchange, like any price, would always clear the market. (Indeed, we can now see that a fixed exchange rate creates a problem of "surplusses" and "shortages" exactly the way an arbitrary price floor or ceiling does in a market for goods. See pp. 429–30.)

The difficulty with a freely moving exchange rate, we also recall, was that it posed formidable difficulties for the smooth flow of trade and capital. But suppose we tried to take the best of both worlds by permitting the prices of currencies to fluctuate freely *within fixed limits,* perhaps 5 per cent above or below their "official" rate. That way the normal imbalances of supply and demand could be worked out without requiring a flow of gold, and the instability of the exchange rate would nevertheless be held within reasonably narrow boundaries.

Two problems present themselves for this attractive proposal. The first is that the price of the dollar (or any other currency) would rapidly fall to the floor if it came under speculative attack. At that point we would be back in the same difficulties we are in now. The second problem is that even a small fluctuation of 5 per cent might be sufficient to unsettle world trade. Suppose, for example, that in one year the dollar was 5 per cent below "par" and the German mark was 5 per cent above. In the following year conditions changed, and each currency went the full 5 per cent in the opposite direction. What seems like a movement of only 10 per cent for each currency, considered separately, becomes a swing of 20 per cent when the prices of the two currencies are considered against each other. This might indeed be enough to interfere with the optimum flow of trade or investments.

Thus there is the risk that semiflexible exchanges will prove to be satisfactory only so long as speculative raids or wide swings in exchange rates do not trouble the international scene. But *any* system will work well when things are in basic equilibrium. The trick is to find the means that will work when things are in basic disequilibrium, as in the case of the United States balance of payments deficit.

DEVALUATION

Whatever cure we apply—and over the next decade we will have to apply *some* remedy—all of our proposals so far assume that we can undo the chronic deficit that has plagued our nation. But suppose we cannot? Suppose that we find it impossible to increase our balance on merchandise account, and impossible (or unwise) to restrict the flow of long-term capital abroad, and impolitic to cut back our government overseas spending? What could we do then?

One course of action must be apparent. It is to change the relationship of the dollar to gold, so that the Treasury would ask not $35 for an ounce of gold, but $45 or $75 or any other large sum. Instantly this new exchange rate would make American prices cheaper abroad—it would be the classical medicine painlessly taken. But better yet. With devaluation, our remaining gold stock would immediately be worth a great many more dollars. Therefore, any deficit on the balance of payments could be easily settled by shipping a much smaller quantity of gold. The crisis would be over.

Or would it? We have already seen the problems that would ensue if the United States were unable to meet its obligations in gold at all. But devaluing would in fact be tantamount to very much such a state of affairs. Countries that had held their dollar balances secure in the conviction that they would always be worth so much in gold (and thereby in other currencies), would now find themselves shortchanged by the amount of the devaluation.

The problem, in other words, is that devaluation is a very difficult course for a country to take when its own currency serves many other nations as part of their international reserves. For then, devaluation does not merely affect the value of *our* reserves, but of *theirs* too. Our gold stock is worth more; their dollars are worth less.

But this is not the only difficulty with devaluation. Changing the price of one's currency by fiat is always a two-edged sword. A nation devalues, among other reasons, to increase its exports and to discourage imports. But other nations may not take kindly to this prospect of increased international competition. Hence they may devalue also, leaving international price relationships just where they were.* The era of the 1930's saw a number of such competitive devaluations that brought little in their train but international friction.

Last, we must take into account an effect of devaluation that applies less cogently to us than to nations that are heavily dependent on foreign commerce. It is that *devaluation raises the costs of imports to countries that have devalued.* If the dollar now buys fewer yen, Japanese cameras will cost more. If imports are an important part of that country's standard of living, this means that devaluation will raise domestic prices.

Thus devaluation looks much more attractive superficially than it does on careful examination. This does not mean that it is therefore never useful. There are occasions when it is plain that a nation's ex-

---

*A multilateral devaluation does leave *some* countries ahead of the game—the gold-producers, who now sell their gold for more units of currency of the other nations. Thus multilateral devaluation would in fact make a vast gift to the major gold-producing nations: the Republic of South Africa and the Union of Soviet Socialist Republics.

change rate is hopelessly out of line with other countries, and that none of the milder medicines will suffice to restore a balance of payments. In that case there is a choice to be made. Either trade must be allowed to wither away and fall to the level that the overpriced country can afford, or the difficult step of devaluation must be made, once again putting the country on a competitive footing. Great Britain, for example, after World War II, devalued its prewar pound which was obviously far out of line with postwar realities from $4.00 to $2.80 and then, when it was unable to cure a persistent balance of payments gap that was draining away its reserves, had to devalue again in 1967, from $2.80 to $2.40. Underdeveloped nations on numerous occasions have devalued to bring their inflated price levels back to some sort of parity with world market levels. But it seems unlikely in the extreme that devaluation will be permissible in our own case, where the effects would be so costly to other nations and to our own prestige.

STRENGTHENING THE IMF

A much more promising means of solving the balance of payments problem is a step even more radical than devaluation. It is the suggestion that we go off gold—and onto a new reserve currency to be created and administered by the International Monetary Fund.

The various proposals to create some kind of new international reserve currency are too technical to be discussed here. Many of them envisage the emergence of the IMF as something like a world central bank with the capabilities of increasing or decreasing the reserves of its members, just as the Federal Reserve (or the central banks of other nations) can increase or decrease the reserves of their members.

This would be a far step beyond the present IMF. Today the fund serves only partly as a supplier of international reserves from its holdings of gold and member-nation currencies. It operates mainly as a kind of board of international financial adjustment, by permitting nations to make small changes in the value of their currencies and by giving international approval to larger devaluations (and thereby avoiding the danger of counterdevaluations). To become the world's banker in a more direct way would call for a surrender of national prerogatives that is extremely unlikely to be granted by most nations today.

Yet, in the slightly longer run, there is a strong likelihood that some such system will gradually evolve. Today we see great nations, including our own, placed in situations of the greatest financial embarrassment because they have not learned to do business in a world without gold —or in one tied to gold. Sooner or later the present system, which is cumbersome in the extreme, must give way to some more sensible arrangement. A strengthened IMF, using an international currency reserve that it is itself able to create, is very likely to be the direction in which the international monetary mechanism will gradually evolve. In fact, a recent first step in that direction has been the decision to create Special Drawing Rights for fund members—additions to the IMF reserves that have been created out of thin air (by the concerted agreement of IMF members). Such SDR's, as they are called, are in fact a new kind of international deposit currency which has the prestige and backing of the IMF, and which is therefore just as "good" as gold or dollars.

INTERNATIONAL VS. INTERREGIONAL TRADE

Why does the world have to operate under any of these bothersome and difficult international monetary arrangements?

We may better understand the matter if we go back to our initial paradigm and compare the case of New Jersey with that of Nova Jersia. Suppose that New Jersey had an adverse balance of payments with its sister states—that people in New Jersey were buying many products made outside New Jersey, but producing and selling little in exchange. The immediate effects would be severe. New Jersey checks would constantly be leaving the state, but an equal value of outside checks would not be entering it. Hence bank deposits would fall in New Jersey and rise elsewhere. As a result, money would be relatively scarce in New Jersey and interest rates would rise there. At the same time, because expenditures would be discouraged in New Jersey, wage rates there would fall and unemployment increase.

But correctives would soon appear. Men would leave New Jersey to seek work in New York or Pennsylvania. Money would flow back to New Jersey banks, attracted by higher interest rates. Cheaper wages and prices in New Jersey would serve to tempt capital back into the state. The market mechanism, in other words, would work (although perhaps only slowly) to bring New Jersey back into line with the prevailing price and employment and production levels of the region. To put it differently, New Jersey would tend "naturally" to share in the general economic well-being of its surrounding states.

Why does not this automatic mechanism work as well with Nova Jersia and its sister nations? In part, the answer is that nations, unlike states, are entitled to place *barriers in the way of international movements of labor and capital,* so that an easy shifting back and forth of the factors of production is difficult to achieve. Remember that one of the articles of the Constitution forbids the states from interfering with the movement of commerce across their borders. We have yet to achieve this degree of cooperation in the world. And even if we did, labor and capital are both shy of venturing abroad under different laws and regulations.

The second reason is that Nova Jersia, unlike New Jersey, insists on having *its own currency.* Given that prerogative of sovereignty, the question then arises as to how comparisons of price are to be made at all between countries that have different units of measurement for their commodities.

Thus it is essentially the stubborn reality of nationalism, with its fierce insistence on the separation rather than the joining together of human communities, that imposes the special difficulties of international economics. The world, from an economist's view, is a single vast human community in which he would like to see the powerful agency of the market bring the same salutary results as it does in smaller regions. But his hope is thwarted by the suspicions and jealousies and considerations of national pride and place.

But this last thought serves nonetheless to direct our attention from the technical problems of world trade to the background of the diverse economic structures against which the problems must be worked out. And then the question arises: is the economist justified in hoping to extend the market system to all nations? Can the powerful but subtle forces of supply and demand in fact work their sway not alone within the technically advanced areas of the world, but in the backward ones as well? Is the market imaginable not in the capitalist, but in the socialist economics that now embrace so much of the world?

These are the questions to which our last section will address itself. We must leave technical economics behind now, to resume the narrative of our opening chapters—not merely to bring the "story" of the market system to its contemporary terminus in other parts of the world, but to speculate about the future trajectory of the system whose rise and workings we have come to know so well.

SUMMARY

1. We cannot compare international prices until we know the *exchange rates* of nations' currencies. These are basically determined by the supply and demand for *foreign exchange*.

2. Foreign exchange arises from international transactions. In these transactions importers pay money to banks in their own nations, where this money is transferred to the local accounts of foreign banks. The home office of the foreign bank in turn pays the exporter in the money of his country. *The total of foreign-owned bank accounts in all nations is the sum of foreign exchange.*

3. The transactions that give rise to foreign exchange are of three basic kinds. One is transactions in *current private account* (imports and exports of merchandise, services, travel, remittances, and income on foreign investments). A second is *payments on government account* (regular government expenditures, foreign aid, military). A third is transactions involving *capital account* (long-term and short-term).

4. *A freely moving exchange rate would reflect the supply and demand from these transactions.* If a country tended to spend more abroad than it received from abroad, it would soon run short of foreign exchange, whereas other nations would hold large amounts of its money. As a result its currency would fall in price relative to other currencies. In turn, this would make its imports more expensive and its exports cheaper. The change in prices would then tend to

correct the imbalance of supply and demand. (A surplus of receipts over expenditures would work in just the other direction.)

5. *Under freely fluctuating exchange there can be no balance of payments problem;* however, there are other difficulties involving the *risk of trading or investing loss* or of *speculative raids.*

6. *Fixed exchange rates* are established through the commitment of nations to exchange their currencies for gold on the demand of official holders of foreign balances. The Treasury has agreed to buy and sell gold at $35 an ounce, and nearly all other nations have announced either gold or dollar values for their currencies.

7. Under fixed exchange rates, a disequilibrium in the supply and demand for foreign exchange cannot be remedied by a change in the price of foreign exchange. It must be settled either by the *shipment of gold* or by the *agreement of one country not to demand payment in gold from another but to hold its currency instead.* Foreign nations now hold larger balances in the U.S. than our entire gold stock. Thus the *dollar has become a world reserve currency.*

8. *The over-all balance of payments must always balance*—that is, every transaction must be paid for in one way or another. What we mean by the "balance" of payments is the aggregate of receipts and expenditures for normal international transactions—current private, government, and capital accounts. What our balance of payments shows is *how any difference in receipts and expenditures has been settled*—whether by gold flows or by a rise in foreign-held accounts.

9. A continuation of the gold drain from the United States would pose serious consequences both for trade and for the international economic position of the U.S. The means of remedying the imbalance, however, are not simple. There are six basic ways of doing so.

   - The *"classical medicine,"* or price deflation, carries the risk of recession. In addition the U.S. usually has a very favorable balance on merchandise account.
   - The *deliberate curtailment of capital outflows* penalizes both the world (which needs U.S. capital) and the United States (which will lose the income from its potential foreign investments).
   - A *curtailment of U.S. military spending* abroad necessitates a political decision to alter U.S. foreign policy.
   - *Semiflexible exchange rates* are an attractive possibility—provided that heavy speculation or wide swings of rates do not occur.
   - *Devaluation,* while useful as a means of redressing the trade balance of a small nation, is very difficult for a nation whose currency occupies a reserve status.
   - *Strengthening of the IMF* will be a slow and tentative process.

   Although none is without its difficulties, one or more of these remedies (or new remedies altogether) will have to be applied during the coming years.

10. The basic reason why a smooth-working international finance is so much more difficult to achieve than interregional finance is that factors cannot move freely across national borders and that nations insist on having independent currencies. In the end it is the *political barrier of nationalism* that poses the special problems of international currency.

1. If you wanted to buy a Swiss watch and discovered that it cost 200 francs, what would you need to know to discover if it were cheaper or more expensive than a comparable American watch? Suppose that the price of francs was 20¢ and the American watch $50? What if the price of francs rose to 30¢?

2. If you now bought the watch, to be sent to you, how would you pay for it? What would happen to your bank check? How would the Swiss watch-maker be paid?

3. Suppose that the Swiss, in turn, now decided to buy an American radio that cost $40. He finds the rate of exchange is 5 Swiss francs to the dollar. Explain how he makes payment.

4. Now suppose that the rate of exchange rises for the Swiss, so that he has to pay 6 francs for a dollar. What happens to the price of the radio in Swiss terms? Suppose the rate cheapens, so that he pays only 4 francs? Now what is the price of the radio to him?

5. What are the main categories of the total balance of payments? Why do we divide them into the groups we do?

6. Suppose that the U.S. sold abroad only one product—machines—and that at the going rate of exchange, our machines were more expensive than those of other nations. What would happen if exchange rates were free to move?

7. Suppose exchange rates were fixed. Then what might happen? Could trade simply stop? Might the U.S. devalue (forgetting about its special responsibilities for international payments)? What would be the effect of devaluation on the price of the U.S. machines?

8. What are the difficulties of adjusting the government balance of payments? The balance on capital account?

9. Why is it important to retain our gold supplies for international use rather than using them to back the U.S. money supply?

10. What is actually meant by the balance of payments? Is it possible for the total flows of all international expenditures and receipts to be different? Then why is the balance of payments considered to be a problem?

11. Describe the consequences of a sudden announcement that the U.S. has gone off gold. What would happen at first to the international value of the dollar? Do you think that after a time the dollar might recover its strength? Why?

12. What is there to prevent a country from deliberately subsidizing all its export industries, so that they can undersell the whole world on everything? Assume that the United States tried this policy. Describe carefully what would happen to the balance of payments. What would be the final outcome of the policy?

ADDENDUM:
A NOTE ON THE GOLD STANDARD

The present international monetary mechanism is known as the gold *exchange* standard. It differs in important ways from the pure gold standard under which the world used to operate, and it is useful to know what those differences are.

What was the gold standard? Essentially it was a monetary system that enabled holders of money in any country on the gold standard to exchange it for actual gold at a stated price at any time they wanted to. Thus gold was a domestic monetary reserve (in the sense that Federal Reserve deposits are now), with the difference that, unlike the Fed's deposits, *gold could at any time be demanded by the public.**

The convertibility of ordinary money into gold obviously posed certain problems for the domestic monetary system. But it had its most important effect on the international monetary system. For it permitted anyone at any time to convert his money into gold, ship it abroad, and there convert it back into money of another denomination. That is, an American who wanted to buy gold at the established price could do so, send the gold abroad and sell it there for pounds or marks or francs, at a rate also established and maintained by those governments. Suppose that it took $20 to buy an ounce of gold in the U.S. and that in England the same ounce of gold could be sold to the British Treasury for £4. Then obviously (if we forget about shipping costs, insurance, and other such small charges), $20 was always convertible into £4, or £1 was worth $5.

The gold standard thus provided a means of fixing an exchange rate between countries. But how did this solve the problem of the balance of payments? The method was extremely ingenious. Let us suppose that the United States had a favorable balance of payments—that is, its receipts of dollars from all sources, current and capital, exceeded its use of dollars to buy other currencies. As a result, the demand for dollars would tend to rise, and Britishers or other foreigners going to their banks to purchase foreign exchange would find that £1 would no longer buy $5, but, say, only $4.95.

Now suppose that it costs 4 cents to ship five dollars worth of gold from England to America. Instead of getting less than $4.96 for his £1, a British importer would find it cheaper to take his £1 to the bank, buy the actual gold, send it to the U.S., and there convert it back into $5.

Hence, whenever there was a favorable balance of payments for the U.S., or for any other country, gold would begin to flow into that country. Why? Because foreigners would find it advantageous to pay for goods by

---

*Good little boys used to get $5 gold pieces on their birthdays or Christmas.

actually shipping gold and converting it into the currency, rather than by buying currency directly through a bank.

But that was only the beginning of the gold standard system. As gold now flowed out of England and into, say, America two very important secondary effects were put into motion. In *England the outflow of gold would force the banks to adopt a policy of tight money,* for they would be losing their reserves. In *America the inflow of gold would result in easy money,* for the banks would be gaining gold. Hence, spending in England would be reined in, investment would be curbed, and a business downturn would result, with unemployment and generally falling prices.

In America just the opposite would happen. The inflow of gold would promote easy money, would stimulate investment and output, and would thus lead to a condition of tight labor markets and rising prices.

In this way a favorable balance of payments, by attracting gold would lead to a condition of rising prices; and *an unfavorable balance of payments, by giving rise to a loss of gold, would cause prices to fall in the gold exporting country.* But this would set into motion precisely the changes needed to reverse the original gold drain. As prices fell in Britain and as they rose in America, British goods would look more attractive to international buyers and American goods less so. Hence the demand for pounds would begin to rise and that for dollars to fall. As a result the supplies of the two currencies available for international exchange would again tend toward equality.

The gold standard was thus an extremely effective method of keeping international price levels in line with one another. Any country that was inflationary was "punished" since its exports would decline and it would therefore lose gold; whereas any country that was experiencing a deflation would be helped on its feet because its cheap prices would attract foreign buyers and therefore bring gold (and easy money) into the country.

For many years the international gold standard enjoyed the favor of economists and bankers alike. But during the Great Depression it fell into disrepute. Essentially this was *because the gold standard subordinated the independence of national policy to the rule of the international markets.* The Great Depression saw the birth and development of modern macroeconomic techniques, and even more important than that, the decline of the laissez faire philosophy. But it was impossible for any single government to embark on a policy of economic expansion (with its inevitable consequence of somewhat higher prices) when the gold standard guaranteed that such a policy would result in a flow of gold from the country. For this reason *the gold standard was utterly incompatible with efforts to manage the economy and to maintain a high level of employment by a strong fiscal policy.*

Beginning with England in 1931, one by one the nations of the world "went off" gold. The United States suspended its *domestic* (not its foreign) convertibility in 1933. Today not a single nation practices the old-fashioned gold standard, and although a few economists call for its restitution, there is little practical likelihood that gold will ever again exercise the automatic control over *domestic* economies that it did for nearly one hundred years.

Behind the technical history of the gold standard (which is a good deal more complicated than this summary account) there is an important matter for thought. Like many proposals for monetary reform the use of gold flows to regulate the international economic relations of men represents another instance of an idea that has always attracted some minds: the employment of an "automatic" mechanism to curb the supposed foolishness of human beings. The problem is that gold or any other system is also a creation of men, and its automatic workings are capable of producing as much mischief as their other economic actions. The breakdown of the gold standard warns us that there is no escape from folly, even when folly is disguised as a set of Rules and Regulations designed to keep men from the possibility of error.

SUMMARY

1. The gold standard was a monetary system that enabled holders of money to *exchange currency for gold at any time.*

2. Since gold was convertible into currency and currency into gold in all gold-standard countries, *a fixed relationship of currencies was established among gold-standard nations.*

3. Whenever there was a favorable balance of payment (i.e., a larger quantity of a currency demanded than supplied at its going price), the price of the currency tended to rise. It was soon profitable to convert other currencies into gold, ship it overseas, and reconvert into the currency whose price was rising. As a result, *whenever a nation had a favorable balance of payments, gold tended to flow into its banks.*

4. As a result, *prices rose in the gold-gaining nation,* as its bank reserves rose; and *prices fell in the gold-losing country* where reserves contracted.

5. Thus the gold standard was essentially a *mechanism for keeping international price levels in line. The mechanism by which it worked was gold-induced inflation or recession.*

6. The basic problem of the gold standard was that it *subordinated independent economic policy to the rules of international gold flows.* It was an attempt to superimpose an "automatic" control over economic events that would prove better than the frailties of human judgment. In the end, it merely reflected those frailties.

1. Can you take a $5 bill to any bank and get $5 in gold? Can you get it from the U.S. treasury? Who can get gold under our existing gold exchange system?

2. Under the former gold standard, could you get gold from any bank? Could a Britisher or a German swap pounds or marks for gold? How did this establish rates of international exchange?

3. Suppose that the U.S. was selling much more abroad than it was buying. What would happen to the demand for dollars? Under the gold standard, how would people buy dollars—through their banks or by sending gold over there?

4. As gold flowed in, what would happen to bank reserves? To prices? Why?

5. As gold left countries abroad, what would happen to their prices and why?

6. As prices changed here and abroad (as a consequence of the gold flow) what would happen to our exports and imports?

7. What was the incompatibility between the gold standard and the policies of the New Deal?

five

THE CHALLENGE TO THE MARKET SYSTEM

THE DRIFT
OF EUROPEAN
ECONOMIC HISTORY $\mathcal{30}$

Many chapters back, we focused our narrative of economic history on the rise of modern capitalism in America: and then, to understand better what we had described, we undertook a long theoretical journey, first through macro- and microeconomics and then through foreign trade. But our initial narrative is not yet complete. For the central subject of our early pages was not just the rise of American capitalism, but the emergence of the market system itself, and in describing its development in America we have by no means described it everywhere. That will be our task in this final section of our book. We must follow the fortunes of the market first in Europe and Russia, and then in the underdeveloped world. Then we will hazard a concluding generalization about the market system in the long evolution of economic society.

One thing is immediately apparent when we direct our eyes away from America to the continents of the East, West, and South. It is that the trajectory of economic evolution there has been utterly different

**TRIALS OF
CAPITALISM
ABROAD**

609

from that in the United States. No doubt we recall that when we left the European scene in the early 1800's capitalism was fast becoming the dominant form of economic society. England was the very cradle of industrial capitalism itself; elsewhere on the Continent, if capitalism was not already established, it was clearly waiting in the wings for the last remnants of feudalism to disappear. Moreover, had we looked abroad from America at any time in the nineteenth century, our expectations would have been fully justified. By then, all of Europe was unquestionably capitalist in orientation. And not only Europe. By the end of the nineteenth century, capitalism had reached out to touch most of the other continents of the world. In Asia and Africa, the main European nations had established colonies or spheres of influence that projected the imprint of capitalism into these societies, many of which had barely awakened from an age-long slumber of ancient ways. In South America, as well, capitalism was clearly the main fertilizing influence. Even in reactionary Russia—the last of the great European powers to abolish the legal fetters of feudalism—by the early 1900's, capitalism had succeeded in creating a small but active nucleus from which further growth seemed assured.

Yet what do we find today? To our astonishment, the seemingly unopposed evolution of the world into a capitalist market system has not taken place. In Europe, its original birthplace, capitalism continues to be the dominant economic system; and yet we find that socialist parties either hold power or constitute the main opposition in England, France, Belgium, Netherlands, Italy, Sweden, Norway, Denmark, Germany, and Austria. In Russia, the nucleus of capitalism has been entirely swept away by a communist society. In the huge continents of East and South—in Asia and Africa and South America—we find that the original organizing impetus of capitalism has given way, in many of the most important nations, to a noncapitalist framework of economic organization. China is more communist than communist Russia. India proclaims herself a socialist state. So do Burma, Ceylon, Egypt, Guinea, Syria. Only in South America do we find socialism absent from the official ideologies of political economy; and even there, the example of Cuba and the rumblings elsewhere hardly make it possible to anticipate the kind of capitalist development that we would have expected fifty years ago.

What happened outside America to abort the seemingly assured development of capitalism? A full answer to such a question would require much more than a book in itself, but we can begin to grasp the main picture of evolutionary trends if we follow, first, the factors that caused capitalism in Europe to take on a form different from that in America. From Europe it is not so long a jump, geographically or historically, to Russia; and from Russia we can turn with increased understanding to the so-called underdeveloped world.

What are the reasons behind the turn of events in Europe? They must be sought, to begin with, not in the economic tendencies of European capitalism but in the social and political background whence those tendencies emerged.

Certainly the social background was significantly different from that of America. In the New World, capitalism developed with a population that had, to a large degree, spiritually and physically shed the feudal encumbrances of the Old World; but in that Old World, many of the social outlooks and habitudes of the past lingered on. An awareness of class position—and more than that, an explicit recognition of class hostility—was as conspicuous by its presence in Europe as by its absence in America. In Vienna, in 1847, writes one social historian:

At the top were the nobles who considered themselves the only group worth noticing. The human race starts with barons, said one of them. Then there were the big businessmen who wanted to buy their way into the human race; the little businessmen; the proud but poor intellectuals; the students who were still poorer and still prouder; and the workers who were poor and had always been very, very humble.[1]

The result was a totally different climate for the development of an economic society. Capitalism in America, building on a new and vigorous foundation, was, from the beginning, a system of social consensus. Capitalism in Europe, building on a feudal base, was deeply tinged with class conflict. It was without effort that American capitalism secured the loyal support of its "lower orders"; but in Europe, by the time of the revolutions of 1848, those lower orders had already turned their backs on capitalism as a vehicle for their hopes and beliefs.

Second and no less important in explaining the divergence of American and European economic evolution was the profound difference between the political complexion of the two continents. In America, save only for the terrible crisis of the Civil War, a single national purpose fused the continent; in Europe, a historic division of languages, customs, and mutually suspicious nationalities again and again prevented just such a fusion.

Accordingly, American capitalism came of age in an environment in which political unity permitted the unhindered growth of an enormous unobstructed market, while in Europe a jigsaw puzzle of national boundaries forced industrial growth to take place in cramped quarters and in an atmosphere of continued national rivalry. It is curious to note that whereas Europe was considered "wealthier" than America all through the nineteenth century, American productivity in many fields began to outstrip that of Europe from at least the 1850's, and perhaps

[1]Priscilla Robertson, *Revolutions of 1848* (New York: Harper & Row, Torchbooks, 1960), p. 194.

EUROPEAN
CAPITALISM:
FEUDAL
HERITAGE
AND NATIONAL
RIVALRY

much earlier. For instance, at the Paris Exposition of 1854, an American threshing machine was twice as productive as its nearest (English) rival and eleven times as productive as its least (Belgian) competitive model.[2]

These advantages of geographic space, richness of resources, and political unity were widened by subsequent developments in European industry. Not surprisingly, European producers, like those in America, sought to limit the destructive impact of industrial competition, and for this purpose they turned to *cartels*—contractual (rather than merely voluntary) agreements to share markets or fix prices. Unlike the case in America, however, this self-protective movement received the blessing, overt or tacit, of European governments. Although "anticartel" laws existed in many European countries, these laws were almost never enforced: by 1914 there were more than 100 international cartels, representing the most varied industries, in which most European nations participated.*

Cartelization was undoubtedly good for the profit statements of the cartelized firms, but it was hardly conducive to growth—either for those firms or new ones. By establishing carefully delineated and protected "preserves," the cartel system rewarded unaggressive behavior rather than economic daring; and together with the ever-present problem of cramping national frontiers, it drove European producers into a typical high-cost, high profit-margin, low-volume pattern rather than into the American pattern of very large plants with very high efficiencies. The difference in economic scale is dramatically illustrated by steel. In 1885, Great Britain led the world in the production of steel; fourteen years later her entire output was less than that of the Carnegie Steel Company alone.

As a result, by the early twentieth century, European productivity lagged very seriously behind American. A study by Professor Taussig in 1918 showed that the daily output of coal per underground worker was 4.68 tons in the United States, as contrasted with 1.9 tons in Great Britain, 1.4 tons in Prussia, and 0.91 tons in France. In 1905, the output of bricks per person employed was 141,000 in the United States and 40,000 in Germany; U.S. pig iron production was 84.5 tons per worker in 1909, compared with only 39 tons in Great Britain in 1907.[3] Parts of these differences were attributable to geological differentials, but these, too, were made worse by restrictive business practices. The result was a steady falling-behind in Europe as the twentieth century went on.

The divergence was strikingly noticeable in per capita incomes. In

[2]Thomas Cochran and William Miller, *The Age of Enterprise,* rev. ed. (New York: Harper & Row, Torchbooks, 1961), p. 58.

*In 1939 an estimated 109 cartels also had American participation, since American companies were not prohibited by antitrust laws from joining international restrictive agreements.

[3]Heinrich E. Friedlaender and Jacob Oser, *Economic History of Modern Europe* (Englewood Cliffs, N.J.: Prentice-Hall, Inc., 1953), p. 224.

1911, for example, when per capita income in the United States was $368, the corresponding figure for Great Britain was $250, for Germany $178, for France $161, for Italy $108. By 1928, American per capita income was $541 (in unchanged dollar values), while that of the United Kingdom was only $293; of Germany, $199; of France, $188; and of Italy, $96.[4] While American per capita incomes had grown by nearly 46 per cent, English and French per capita incomes had increased only one-third as rapidly. German incomes rose only about one-quarter as fast, and Italian per capita incomes had actually declined.*

Still another consequence followed from the division of European industry and agriculture into national compartments. To a far greater extent than in America, it made the development of European capitalism subject to the expansion of international trade.

For the division of the European Continent into many national units made international trade a continuous and critical preoccupation of economic life abroad. For instance, a study has shown that in 1913, when manufactured imports provided but 3.6 per cent of United States' consumption of manufactured goods, they provided 9 per cent of Germany's, 14 per cent of England's, 21 per cent of Sweden's.[5] Perhaps even more striking is the degree to which some nations in Europe depended on international trade for the foodstuffs on which they lived: in the five years preceding World War I, for instance, England produced less than 20 per cent of the wheat she consumed and barely over 55 per cent of the meat.[6] We find the same dependence on foreign trade in the export side of the picture. Whereas the United States in 1913 exported a mere fifteenth of its national product, France and Germany exported a fifth, and Britain nearly a quarter of theirs.

Thus, to a far greater degree than America, Europe lived by foreign trade. Here we clearly see the advantage to America of its enormous unbroken market over the fragmented national markets of Europe. All the gains from trade with which we became familiar in Chapter 28 were realized in the swift rise of American productivity; whereas these same gains were denied to Europe. To put it differently, in America, the division of labor was permitted to attain whatever degree of efficiency technology made possible, for in the end virtually all products entered into a single vast market where they could be exchanged against one

[4] *Ibid.,* p. 522.

*We must be wary of placing too much faith in the translation of one income—say £500—into its "equivalent"—$1,200. Until we know the price levels, the living standards and customs of the nations we are comparing, we make such translations strictly at our own risk. But changes *within* a country, from year to year, are, of course, as meaningful in one currency as in another.

[5] *Der Deutsche Aussenhandel* (Berlin: 1932), II, 23.

[6] Friedlaender and Oser, *op. cit.,* p. 206.

another. In Europe, where the need for, and the potential benefits of, a far-reaching division of labor were no less pressing, a tangle of national barriers prevented the optimal specialization of effort from taking place.

Instead, what was visible in Europe was a struggle between the need for international trade as a primary means for advancing productivity, and the retarding hand of national suspicions, rivalries, and distrust. A striking example was provided as recently as the early 1950's by the great cluster of European steel and coal industry near the German-Belgian-Luxembourg borders. Here, in a triangle, 250 miles on a side, was gathered 90 per cent of European steelmaking capacity in a kind of European Pittsburgh. But this natural geographic division of labor had to contend with political barriers which largely vitiated its physical productivity. Typically, German coal mines in the Ruhr sold their output to French steelmakers at prices 30 per cent higher than to German plants; while, in turn, French iron-ore producers charged far higher prices in Germany than at home. As a result, while American steel production soared 300 per cent between 1913 and 1950, the output of Europe's steel triangle rose but 3 per cent during the same period.

BREAKDOWN OF INTERNATIONAL TRADE

Our example, itself, poses a question, however. Prior to 1913, as we have seen, something like a great international division of labor did, in fact, characterize the European market, albeit to nothing like the extent seen in America. By 1913, we will remember, a very considerable flow of international trade was enhancing European productivity, despite the hindrances of cartels and national divisiveness. It was only the beginning of a truly free and unhampered international market, but at least it *was* a beginning.

What brought this promising achievement to an end? Initially, it was the shock of World War I, with its violent sundering of European trade channels and its no less destructive aftermath of punitive reparations, war debts, and monetary troubles. In a sense, Europe never recovered from its World War I experience. The slow drift toward national economic separatism, at the expense of international economic cooperation, now accelerated fatefully. Tariffs and quotas multiplied to place new handicaps before the growth of international trade.

Then came the Depression of 1929 as the final blow. As the Depression spread contagiously, nation after nation sought to quarantine itself by erecting still further barriers against economic contacts with other countries. Starting in 1929, an ever-tightening contraction of trade began to strangle economic life around the world. For 53 grim months following January 1929, the volume of world trade was lower each month than in the preceding month. Between the late 1920's and the mid-1930's, manufactured imports (in constant prices) fell by a third in

Germany, by nearly 40 per cent in Italy, by almost 50 per cent in France. As international trade collapsed, so did Europe's chance for economic growth. For two long decades there followed a period of stagnation which earned for Europe the name of the "tired continent."

Against this background of economic malfunction it is easier to understand the growing insecurity that afflicted European capitalism. During the 1930's serious rumblings were already heard. In England the Socialist Labour Party had clearly displaced the middle-class Liberals as the Opposition. In France, a mildly socialist "Popular Front" government came to the fore, albeit insecurely. Even in Italy and Germany, the fascist dictators repeatedly declared their sympathy with "socialist" objectives—and whereas their declarations may have been no more than a sop to the masses, it was certainly indicative of the sentiments the masses wanted to hear.

Note that the socialist movements were not communist—that is, they were pledged strongly to democratic political principles and envisaged a "take over" through education and persuasion rather than by revolution and coercion. In addition, the socialists sought to convert only the strategic centers of production into public enterprises, rather than to "socialize" all of industry and agriculture. Thus socialism was always a much more evolutionary program than communism. Nevertheless, to the European conservatives of the 1930's, the Socialist leaders appeared every bit as dangerous as did the Socialists' bitterest enemies, the Communists.

By the end of World War II, socialist ideas were clearly ascendant throughout most of Europe. Even before the war was concluded, the Labour Party swept into office in England and rapidly nationalized the Bank of England, the coal and electricity industries, much of the transportation and communications industry, and finally steel. As the first postwar governments were formed, it was evident that a socialist spectrum extended across Europe from Scandanavia through the Lowlands and France to Italy (where the communists came within an ace of gaining power). To many observers, it seemed as if capitalism in Europe had come to the end of its rope.

Yet, European capitalism did not come to an end. Instead, beginning in the late 1940's and early 1950's, it embarked on what is unquestionably its period of strongest economic growth. Indeed, a comparison not only with the past but with United States performance during the same period shows the remarkable change that had come over the Continent.

EUROPEAN
SOCIALISM

RECOVERY OF
EUROPEAN
CAPITALISM

TABLE 30 · 1

**COMPARATIVE
GROWTH
RATES**

	AVERAGE ANNUAL RATES OF PER CAPITA INCREASE				
	France	Germany	Italy	U.K.	U.S.
Pre-World War I (1870–1913)	1.4	1.8	0.7	1.3	2.2
Post-World War II (1948–1962)	3.4	6.8	5.6	2.4	1.8 (1950–64)

Source: M. M. Postan, *An Economic History of Western Europe* (London: Methuen & Co., Ltd., 1967), p. 17.

Note that the nations of Europe not only doubled and tripled their pre-World War I rates of per capita growth, but actually outstripped the contemporary performance of the United States economy by a margin almost as large.

To bring about such results, important changes obviously must have taken place in these economic societies. One of them, it is hardly surprising to learn, was political. The postwar socialist governments quickly showed that they were not revolutionary but reform-minded administrations. Once in power they quickly instituted a number of welfare and social planning measures, such as public health facilities, family benefits and allowances, improved social security, and the like; but they did not engage in sweeping changes. Hence, when many of the socialist governments, facing the exigencies of the postwar period, were voted out again, they bequeathed to the conservatives the framework of a welfare state *which the conservatives accepted*. Harking back to one of the traditional weaknesses of European capitalism, we can say that this represented a conservative attempt to create a social service state which would mend the historic antagonism of the lower classes. As a result, we find today that in most European states, welfare expenditures form a considerably higher proportion of government expenditures than they do in the United States.

The second reason was even more important. This was the rise of a movement within the conservative ranks to overcome a still more dangerous heritage of the past—the national division of markets. This great step toward creating a full-scale Continental market for European producers is called the European Community—or more usually, the Common Market.

**THE COMMON
MARKET**

To some extent, the Common Market was born out of the vital impetus given to postwar European production by the so-called Marshall plan, under which Europe received some $12 billion in direct grants and loans from the United States to rebuild its war-shattered industry. Despite Marshall aid, it soon became apparent that Europe's upward climb would necessarily be limited if production were once again restrained by cartels and national protectionism. To forestall a return to the stagnation of the prewar period, a few farsighted and courageous statesmen, primary among them Jean Monnet and Robert Schuman, proposed a truly daring plan for the abolition of Europe's traditional economic barriers.

The plan as it took shape called for the creation of a *supranational* (not merely an international) organization to integrate the steel and coal production of France, Germany, Italy, Belgium, Luxembourg, and the Netherlands. The new Coal and Steel Community was to have a High Authority with power to eliminate all customs duties on coal and steel products among members of the Community, to outlaw all discriminatory pricing and trade practices, to approve or disapprove all mergers, to order the dissolution of cartels, and to provide social and welfare services for all Community miners and steelworkers. The Authority was to be given direct power to inspect books, levy fines, and enforce its decrees—and still more remarkable, it was to be responsible not to any single member government but to a multinational Parliament and a multinational Court, both to be created as part of the Community. A Council of Ministers was to act as a *national* advisory and permissory body, but even here action could be taken by majority vote, so that no single nation (or even two nations) could block a decision desired by the Community as a whole.

By the fall of 1952, the Coal and Steel Community was a reality, and it lost no time going about its business. At mid-1954, customs duties and discriminatory pricing within the coal and steel "triangle" had been virtually eliminated, and roughly 40 per cent more coal and steel was being shipped across national boundaries than had been shipped prior to the establishment of the Community. Cartels and secret agreements still remain, but the restrictive influence on production was much less than it was formerly.

The success of the Coal and Steel Community led, in 1957, to the next two organizations: Euratom, a supranational atomic power agency, and the Common Market itself, an organization that was to do for commodities in general what the Coal and Steel Community had done for its products. Under the Common Market treaty, a definite schedule of tariff cuts was laid down, envisaging within slightly more than a decade an entirely unimpeded Continental market for Common Market members, with a single "external" tariff vis-à-vis the world. In addition, there were to be a single agricultural policy and, perhaps most imaginative, full freedom for the intermember mobility of both capital and labor.

The Common Market is still in the process of achieving some of these goals, although it is well ahead of its timetable. Already, however, it

TABLE 30 · 2

PER CENT
AVERAGE
ANNUAL
GROWTH IN
REAL GNP

	1950–1960	1961–1966
Common Market	5.9%	4.9%
Rest of Europe	3.1	3.6
United States	3.2	5.6

Source: OECD

has led to a remarkable increase in European trade and production. Trade among member countries has grown from $6.8 billion in 1958 to $24.2 billion in 1967. As a result, the Community's rate of growth has surged ahead, as Table 30-2 shows.

Notice that during the decade of the 1950's, the Common Market's growth was almost twice that of the United States; and although the pace of expansion has slowed somewhat abroad and quickened at home in recent years, it is clear that the doldrums of the European past are well behind us.

The figures, of course, only point to the real changes that have occurred. For the first time the style of life and level of consumption of the European working and middle classes have begun to resemble that of America. The number of autos in use has been growing at the rate of 12 per cent a year; the number of TV sets, at 30 per cent. Not less important, the boom in European trade has led to an even greater boom in world trade. It is encouraging that since 1948 the total value of world exports has risen from $54 billion to over $190 billion, and that the volume of world trade increased at the rate of 6 per cent a year during the 1960's.*

SOCIALISM AND MODERN EUROPEAN CAPITALISM

There is much in these prosperous statistics that reminds us of the general course of affairs in the United States. After its time of trial, European capitalism, like American capitalism, seems to have achieved a high degree of economic success. It is true that socialist parties

*A considerable part of the impetus to world trade must be credited to the spread of more rational—i.e., lower and fewer—tariff barriers. The General Agreement on Tariffs and Trade (GATT) an international body formed in 1947 to work for wider world trade, has succeeded in steadily reducing tariff levels and in dismantling import quotas. It is pleasant to record that the United States has played a major role in this movement. During the 1930's we had the unenviable reputation of being one of the most restrictive trading nations in the world, but our tariff wall has been far reduced since those irresponsible days. Today our average level of duties on dutiable imports is roughly 10 per cent, compared with 53 per cent in 1930; and in addition, a third of all our imports are admitted duty-free. On the negative side, however, it must be noted that we continue to discriminate against imports that affect our manufacturing interests. For example, coffee comes in free, but not instant coffee, so that the underdeveloped nations who would like to process coffee within their own economies are gravely disadvantaged.

continue to constitute a strong political movement in Europe, but the thrust of these programs is no longer directed mainly toward nationalization or other fundamental economic changes, but aims instead at correcting social privileges or at buttressing still further the welfare arrangements that we find in every European country. Equality—social as well as economic—is the present main objective of European socialism, and although equality requires adjustments in the existing distribution of rewards, the socialists do not see it as requiring the destruction of the system by which those rewards are determined.

Yet if socialism has made its peace with modern capitalism in Europe, there is a deeper reason than a mere change of mind on the part of Europe's socialists. The reason is that capitalism in Europe has borrowed a central idea of socialism and adapted it to conservative uses— the idea of *national economic planning.*

CONSERVATIVE PLANNING

For all through Europe we see a reliance on planning that is both greater and more outspoken than anything we have encountered in the United States. In our country, we recall from Chapter 8, we have arrived at a consensus as to fiscal and monetary policy as the proper implements for achieving a stable and satisfactory rate of growth. But in most European nations, there is visible a further commitment to planning as a means of achieving publicly determined patterns of resource allocation as well as adequate rates of growth.

In France, for example, a central planning agency, working in consultation with Parliament and with representatives of industry, agriculture, labor, and other groups, sets a general plan for French growth—a plan that not only establishes a desired rate of expansion, but determines whether or not, for example, the provincial cities should expand faster or slower than the nation as a whole, or where the bulk of new housing is to be located, or to what degree social services are to be increased. Once decided, the plan is then divided into the various production targets needed for its fulfillment, and their practicality is discussed with management and labor groups in each industry concerned.

From these discussions arise two results. First, the plan is often amended to conform with the wishes or advice of those who must carry it out. Second, the general targets of the plan become part of the business expectations of the industries that have helped to formulate them. To be sure, the government has substantial investment powers that can nudge the economy along whatever path has been finally determined. But in the main, French "indicative" planning works as a *self-fulfilling prophecy*—the very act of establishing its objectives setting into motion the behavior needed to realize them.

In England, Germany, the Netherlands, Italy, and Scandanavia, we see other forms of government planning, none so elaborately worked out as the French system, but all also injecting a powerful element of public guidance into the growth and disposition of the resources of their economies. Thus a basic commitment to planning seems to have become an integral part of modern European capitalism. *Note, however, that all these planning systems utilize the mechanism of the market as a means for achieving their ends.* The act of planning itself is not, of course, a market activity; but the realization of the various desired production tasks for industry is entrusted largely to the pull of demand acting on independent enterprises. Thus the market has been utilized as an instrument of social policy, much as we described at the end of Chapter 27.*

EUROPE AND AMERICA

How do we account for the fact that in Europe the evolution into a guided capitalism has evidently progressed much further than in America? In part, the reason is no doubt ascribable to the problems that have racked Europe and have forced upon it a much greater degree of necessary government intervention for survival. The Common Market, for example, would never have been brought into being had Europe not suffered from the effects of economic fragmentation, and the Common Market in turn stimulated and supported the development of purely national planning efforts.

To some extent the difference may be due, as well, to the survival in Europe of those "feudal" (or at least monarchical) attitudes that contrast so sharply with the democratic climate in America. Europeans are used to, and accept, a larger role for public authority in the economic direction of affairs; whereas Americans have traditionally tended to resist and reject such a role. Hence the movement toward planning in Europe has not encountered the fierce ideological opposition it has met in America, where the very word still conjures up fearsome "socialistic" visions to some people.

But these considerations only establish reasons why the drift has moved faster in Europe than in America. What is important is that even in our economy, as we know, the outlines of a guided economy have begun to appear. The winds that have blown the European market systems into a strong commitment to planning are pressing us, albeit more slowly, in the same direction. This does not mean that America is likely to adopt the techniques of French planning. The French system is built around a structure of highly organized private industrial associations that we do not have in this country, largely because of our much more vigorous antitrust attitudes. But in some fashion or other it now seems probable that America will follow in the footsteps of Europe, just as Europe once followed in the footsteps of America.

*Anyone who wishes to learn more about the important subject of European planning should read Andrew Shonfield, *Modern Capitalism* (New York: Oxford University Press, Inc., 1965).

What basic reasons lie behind this drift, and what it portends for the American economy and for the market system in general, are questions we must defer for the moment. For we cannot put these questions into focus until we have looked into another significant drift—in the opposite direction. But to see that striking development we must now examine the rise of a totally different economic structure: the socialist economy of the Soviet Union.

We cannot here recount in detail the history of Soviet socialism. Let us, rather, begin by noting the extraordinarily difficult problem that faced the revolutionary leaders who had secured the victory of "socialism" in Russia in 1917. In the first place, Russia was a semifeudal society in which capitalism was restricted to a small industrial and commercial sector. Second, both production and distribution were highly disorganized in the chaotic situation following the civil war.

Finally, there was little guidance in the official literature of the Communist movement as to how a socialist society should be run. Marx's *Das Kapital,* the seminal work of communism, was entirely devoted to a study of capitalism; and in those few essays in which Marx looked to the future, his gaze rarely traveled beyond the watershed of the revolutionary act itself. With the achievement of the revolution, Marx thought, a temporary regime known as "the dictatorship of the proletariat" would take over the transition from capitalism to socialism, and thereafter a "planned socialist economy" would emerge as the first step towards a still less specified "communism." In the latter state—the final terminus of economic evolution according to Marx—there were hints that the necessary but humdrum tasks of production and distribution would take place by the voluntary cooperation of all citizens and that society would turn its serious attention to matters of cultural and humanistic importance.

In reality, the Revolution presented Lenin, Trotsky, and the other leaders of the new Soviet Union with problems far more complex than this utopian long-term design. Shortly after the initial success of the Revolution, Lenin nationalized the banks, the major factories, the railways, and canals. In the meantime, the peasants themselves had taken over the large landed estates on which they had been tenants, and they had carved them up into individual holdings. The central authorities then attempted for several years to run the economy by requisitioning food from the farms and allocating it to factory workers, while controlling the flow of output from the factories themselves by a system of direct controls from above.

This initial attempt to run the economy was a disastrous failure. Under inept management (and often cavalier disregard of "bourgeois" concerns with factory management), industrial output declined precipitously: by 1920 it had fallen to *14 per cent* of prewar levels. As goods available to the peasants became scarcer, the peasants, themselves, were less and less willing to acquiesce in giving up food to the cities. The result was a wild inflation followed by a degeneration into an economy of semibarter. For a while, toward the end of 1920, the system threatened to break down completely.

To forestall the impending collapse, in 1921 Lenin instituted a New Economic Policy, the so-called NEP. This was a return toward a market system and a partial reconstitution of actual capitalism. Retail trade, for instance, was opened again to private ownership and operation. Small-scale industry also reverted to private direction. Most important, the farms were no longer requisitioned but operated as profit-making units. Only the "commanding heights" of industry and finance were retained in government hands.

There ensued for several years a bitter debate about the course of action to follow next. While the basic aim of the Soviet government was still to industrialize and to socialize (i.e., to replace the private ownership of the means of production by state ownership), the question was how fast to move ahead—and, indeed, *how* to move ahead. The pace of industrialization hinged critically on one highly uncertain factor: the willingness of the large, private peasant sector to deliver food with which the city workers could be sustained in their tasks. To what extent, therefore, should the need for additional capital goods be sacrificed in order to turn out the consumption goods that could be used as an inducement for peasant cooperation?

THE DRIVE
TO TOTAL
PLANNING

The student of Russian history—or, for that matter, of economic history—will find the record of that debate an engrossing subject.[7] But the argument was never truly resolved. In 1927, Stalin moved into command, and the difficult question of how much to appease the unwilling peasant disappeared. Stalin simply made the ruthless decision to appease him not to all, but to *coerce* him by collectivizing his holdings.

The collectivization process solved in one swoop the problem of securing the essential transfer of food from the farm to the city, but it did so at a frightful social (and economic) cost. Many peasants slaughtered their livestock rather than hand it over to the new collective farms; others waged outright war or practiced sabotage. In reprisal, the authorities acted with brutal force. An estimated five million "kulaks" (rich peasants) were executed or put in labor camps, while in the cities an equally relentless policy showed itself vis-à-vis labor. Workers were summarily ordered to the tasks required by the central authorities. The right to strike was forbidden, and the trade unions were reduced to

[7] See Alexander Erlich, *The Soviet Industrialization Debate: 1924–1928* (Cambridge, Mass.: Harvard University Press, 1960).

impotence. Speed-ups were widely applied, and living conditions were allowed to deteriorate to very low levels.

The history of this period of forced industrialization is ugly and repellent, and it has left abiding scars on Russian society. It is well for us, nonetheless, to attempt to view it with some objectivity. If the extremes to which the Stalinist authorities went were extraordinary, often unpardonable, and perhaps self-defeating, we must bear in mind that industrialization on the grand scale has always been wrenching, always accompanied by economic sacrifice, and always carried out by the more or less authoritarian use of power. We have already seen what happened in the West at the time of the industrial revolution with its heavy-handed exploitation of labor; and without "excusing" these acts, we have seen their function in paving the way for capital accumulation.

In much the same fashion, when the Soviet leaders deliberately held down consumption, regimented and transferred their labor forces into the new raw industrial centers, and ruthlessly collected the foodstuffs to feed their capital-building workers, they were, in fact, only enforcing the basic process of industrialization. What was new about the Soviet program was that totalitarian control over the citizenry enabled the planners to carry out this transformation at a much faster tempo than would have been possible had protests been permitted. Under Stalin's iron will, the planners did not scruple to exercise their industrializing power to the hilt.

Without seeking to justify the Russian effort, it is worth pondering one last question. Can rapid industrialization, with its inescapable price of low consumption, ever be a "popular" policy? Will poor people willingly vote for an economic transformation which will not "pay out" for twenty or forty years? * Does rapid and large-scale industrialization *necessitate* a large degree of authoritarian political control? We will return to these problems when we turn to underdevelopment, but we might well begin to think about them now.

THE PLANNING
MECHANISM

A massive industrialization drive requires a determined effort to hold consumption to a minimum and to transfer resources to capital-building, an effort greatly facilitated, as we have seen, by the totalitarian political apparatus. But there is still another question to be considered. How are the freed resources to find their proper destination in an integrated and workable industrial sector?

*We might note in passing that universal male suffrage was not gained in England until the late 1860's and 1870's. Aneurin Bevan has written: "It is highly doubtful whether the achievements of the Industrial Revolution would have been permitted if the franchise had been universal. It is very doubtful because a great deal of the capital aggregations that we are at present enjoying are the results of the wages that our fathers went without." (From Gunnar Myrdal, *Rich Lands and Poor.* New York: Harper & Row, 1957, p. 46.)

Let us remind ourselves again of how this is done under a market economy. There, the signal of profitability serves as the lure for the allocation of resources and labor. Entrepreneurs, anticipating or following demand, risk private funds in the construction of the facilities which they hope the future will require. Meanwhile, as these industrial salients grow, smaller satellite industries grow along with them to cater to their needs.

The flow of materials is thus regulated in every sector by the forces of private demand, making themselves known by the signal of rising or falling prices. At every moment there emanates from the growing industries a magnetic pull of demand on secondary industries, while, in turn, the growth salients themselves are guided, spurred, or slowed down by the pressure of demand from the ultimate buying public. And all the while, counterposed to these pulls of demand, are the obduracies of supply—the cost schedules of the producers themselves. In the cross fire of demand and supply exists a marvelously sensitive social instrument for the integration of the over-all economic effort of expansion.

And in the absence of a market? Clearly, the mechanism must be supplied by the direct orders of a central controlling and planning agency. *In a growing industrial economy, a planning agency must act as a substitute for the market.* Let us reflect for a moment what this entails.

To begin with, it means that the planning agency must provide a substitute for the forward-looking operations of the great entrepreneurs in a market economy. In place of a Carnegie or a Ford, building their plants in anticipation of, or response to, an insistent demand for their products, the planning body must itself set over-all goals and objectives for economic growth. Not the consumer but the planners' own judgment and desires determine the force of "demand." *

Establishing the over-all objectives is, however, only the first and perhaps the easiest part of the planning mechanism. It is not enough to set broad goals and then assume that they will be fulfilled by themselves. We must remember that planning in a totalitarian economy is

---

*In the case of the Soviet Union, the planning authority has typically set its demand goals in terms of Five-Year Plans. The first of these, from 1928 to 1932, had as its basic objective the intensification of industrialization in heavy industry, with special emphasis on electrification; the second took as its main goal the development of transportation and the beginning of agricultural planning; the third plan (1938–1942) was essentially occupied with producing the needs for a war economy; the fourth, from 1946 to 1950, was mainly a plan of reconstruction from wartime damage, with continuing emphasis on heavy industry; a fifth plan, 1951–1955, emphasized a steep increase in output with some stress being given (for the first time) to consumer goods. The most recent plan was by far the most ambitious. A Seven-Year Plan (1959–1965) aimed to increase industrial output by 80 per cent, agricultural output by 70 per cent, and to bring significant increases in housing (a sector long neglected in the interests of industrialization) and in consumer goods, generally. We know that many of these objectives were not met, but there is no doubt of growing emphasis on consumer goods and housing.

not superimposed on a market structure in which individuals take care of the "details" of production according to the incentives of price and profit. In a totally planned economy, each and every item which goes into the final plan must also be planned. Schedules of production are needed for steel, coal, coke, lumber, on down to nails and paper clips, for there is no "automatic" device by which these items will be forthcoming without a planning directive. Supplies of labor must also be planned; or if labor is free to move where it wishes, wage rates must be planned in order to draw labor where it is wanted.

Thus supplementing and completing the master objective of the over-all plan must be a whole hierarchy of subplans, the aggregate of which must bring about the necessary final result. And here is a genuine difficulty. For an error in planning, small in itself, if it affects a strategic link in the chain of production, can seriously distort—or even render impossible—the fulfillment of the total plan.

How is this infinitely complicated planning system carried out in the Soviet Union? It is begun by breaking down the over-all, long-term plan into shorter one-year plans. These one-year plans, specifying the output of major sectors of industry, are then transmitted to various government ministries concerned with, for example, steel production, transportation, lumbering, and so forth. In turn, the Ministries refer the one-year plans further down the line to the heads of large industrial plants, to experts and advisers, and so on. At each stage, the over-all plan is thus unraveled into its subsidiary components, until finally the threads have been traced as far back as feasible along the productive process—typically, to the officials in charge of actual factory operations. The factory manager of, for instance, a coking operation is given a planned objective for the next year, specifying the output needed from his plant. He confers with his production engineers, considers the condition of his machinery, the availability of his labor force, and then transmits his requirements for meeting the objective back upward along the hierarchy. In this way, just as "demand" is transmitted downward along the chain of command, the exigencies of "supply" flow back upward, culminating ultimately in the top command of the planning authority (the Gosplan) itself.[8]

From this description of the tasks of planning, it is obvious that planning is an enormously complex task. Indeed, the very complexity of the task is such that more than one economist in the first days of chaos following the Russian Revolution declared socialism—meaning by this, centralized decision-making—to be "impossible."

[8] For an excellent description of Soviet planning, see Robert W. Campbell, *Soviet Economic Power*, 2nd. ed. (Boston: Houghton Mifflin Company, 1966).

Central planning is not impossible for certain kinds of economic tasks: for "forcing" growth, in particular, it may be more effective than any other means of bringing about the needed allocation of resources. The most recent investigation into Soviet economic performance, for example, indicates that over the period 1929 to 1961, Soviet output rose between 5.2 and 7.2 per cent per annum—roughly twice as fast as the United States' growth over these years.[9] Part of this extraordinary record, to which must be credited Russia's passage from a peasant society to an industrial one, is certainly due to the ability of central planning to bring about tremendously high levels of investment: measured in 1937 prices, investment was pushed from 8.4 per cent of GNP in 1928 to 30.6 per cent in 1961.

The trouble comes when we look to the planning system for its *efficiency* in allocating resources, rather than to its success in forcing total volumes of output. An economy may be very successful in producing larger and larger quantities of steel and electric power, but it may be very unsuccessful in producing the right kinds of steel or in locating its electric power plants effectively or in producing its goods at the lowest possible cost. Sooner or later, such inefficiency will interfere with the rate of growth, and that is exactly what we see in the case of the U.S.S.R. From many indications it appears that the Soviet rate of expansion has been declining in recent years and that the economy is increasingly plagued with difficulties arising from a failure to produce the right goods at the best possible prices. The result is a system that has operated more and more unevenly and awkwardly, as first one and then another of the gears in the great machine jammed.

In 1962, for example, an observer reports:

The Byelorussian Tractor Factory, which has 227 suppliers, had its production line stopped 19 times . . . because of the lack of rubber parts, 18 times because of ball bearings, and 8 times because of transmission components. The pattern of breakdowns continued in 1963. During the first quarter of 1963 only about one-half of the plant's ball bearing and rubber needs were satisfied, and only half of the required batteries were available. One supplier shipped 19,000 less wheels than called for in the contract. In total, they were short of 27 items.[10]

Stories such as these abound in any book describing the Soviet economic system. They should not be taken to mean that Russian planning is a "failure" or that it is on the point of collapse. Taken as a whole, the system continues to produce at good rates. But the bottlenecks do point to deep-seated troubles in running the economy smoothly, even now when industrial needs are still relatively simple and con-

[9] Richard Moorsteen and Raymond P. Powell, *The Soviet Capital Stock, 1928–1962* (Homewood, Ill.: Richard D. Irwin, 1966).

[10] Barry Richman, *Soviet Management* (Englewood Cliffs, N.J.: Prentice-Hall, Inc., 1965), p. 123.

sumers are not yet highly critical. These troubles are apt to exact a higher price as the Soviet economy turns its attention to the more complex and demanding problems of a highly integrated industrial process and a much more demanding citizenry.

What is at the root of the inefficiency of central planning? Essentially the problem is to find a means of guiding the production of individual firms. Do not forget that a Russian factory manager has very little leeway in what he produces or the combination of factors that he uses for production. Both his inputs and his outputs are carefully specified for him in his plan. What the manager *is* supposed to do is to beat the plan, by "overproducing" the items that have been assigned to his plant. Indeed, from 30 to 50 per cent of a manager's pay will depend on bonuses tied directly to his "overfulfillment" of the plan, so that he has a very great personal incentive to exceed the output "norms" set for him.

All this seems sensible enough. Trouble comes, however, because the manager's drive to exceed his factory's quota tends to distort the productive effort from the receivers' point of view. For example, if the target for a textile factory is set in terms of yards of cloth, there is every temptation to weave the cloth as narrowly as possible, to get the maximum yardage out of a given amount of thread. Or if the plan merely calls for tonnages of output, there is every incentive to skimp on design or finish or quality, in order to concentrate on sheer weight. A cartoon in the Russian satirical magazine *Krokodil* shows a nail factory proudly displaying its record output: one gigantic nail suspended from an immense gantry crane. (On the other hand, if a nail factory has its output specified in terms of the *numbers* of nails it produces, its incentive to overfulfill this "success indicator" is apt to result in the production of very small or thin nails.)

PLANS FOR REFORM

What is the way out of this kind of dilemma? A few years ago, a widely held opinion among the Russian planners was that more detailed and better integrated planning performed on a battery of computers would solve the problem. Few still cling to this belief. The demands of planning have grown far faster than the ability to meet them: indeed, one Soviet mathematician has predicted that at the current rate of growth of the planning bureaucracy, planning alone would require the services of the entire Russian population by 1980. Even with the most complete computerization, it seems a hopeless task to attempt to beat the problem of efficiency by increasing the "fineness" of the planning mechanism.[11]

[11] For an interesting glimpse into the Russian change of mind, see *Planning, Profit and Incentives in the U.S.S.R.*, ed. by Myron E. Sharpe (White Plains, N.Y.: International Arts and Sciences Press, 1966).

Rather, the wind for reform in the Soviety Union is now blowing from quite another quarter. Led by economist E. G. Liberman, there is a growing demand that the misleading plan directives of weight, length, etc., be subordinated to a new "success indicator" that will, all by itself, guide the manager to results that will make sense from the over-all point of view. And what is that overriding indicator? It is the *profit* that a factory manager can make for his enterprise!

Note several things about this profit. To begin with, it is not envisaged that it can arise from price manipulations. Factory managers will continue to operate with the prices established by the planners; but they will now have to *sell* their output and *buy* their inputs, rather than merely deliver or accept them. This means that each factory will have to be responsive to the particular needs of its customers if it wishes to dispose of its output. In the same way, of course, its own suppliers will now have to be responsive to the factory's needs if the suppliers are to get the factory's business.

Second, the profit will belong not to the factory or its managers, but to the State. A portion of the profit will indeed be allocated for bonuses and other rewards, so that there is a direct incentive to run the plant efficiently, but the bulk of the earnings will be transferred to the State.

Thus, profits are to be used as an efficiency-maximizing indicator, just as we saw them used in our study of microeconomics (see p. 537). Indeed, to view the change even more broadly, we can see that the reintroduction of the use of profits, implies a deliberate return to the use of the *market mechanism* as a means of achieving economic efficiency. Not only profits but also interest charges—a capitalist term that would have been heresy to mention in the days of Stalin—are being introduced into the planning mechanism to allow factory managers to determine for themselves what is the most efficient thing to do, both for their enterprises and for the economy as a whole.

The drift toward the market mechanism is still new in the Soviet Union, and we do not know how far it will ultimately progress. The objectives of the 1966–1970 Five-Year Plan call for wholesale trade gradually to replace the planned distribution of capital goods, and for the much earlier "freeing" of consumer goods production. As Soviet economist A. Birman has put it: "Only three years ago, no one would have thought that there would be anything but the direct physical allocation of goods. Now economists talk of *torgovat* (trading) instead of *snabzhat* (allocating)." [12]

Meanwhile, the trend toward the market has proceeded much further in a large part of Eastern Europe, and above all in Yugoslavia. There, the market rules very nearly as supreme as it does in Western capitalist countries. Yet the Yugoslavs certainly consider themselves a socialist

[12] From Marshall I. Goldman, *The Soviet Economy* (Englewood Cliffs, N.J.: Prentice-Hall, Inc., 1968), p. 129.

economy. As in the U.S.S.R., profits do not go to the "owners" of the business but are distributed as incentive bonuses or used for investment or other purposes under the over-all guidance of the State. And again as in the U.S.S.R., the market is used as a deliberate instrument of social policy, rather than as a form of economic organization that is above question. Thus, the main determination of investment, the direction of development of consumers goods, the basic distribution of income—all continue to be matters established at the center as part of a planned economy. More and more, however, this central plan is allowed to realize itself through the profit-seeking operations of highly autonomous firms, rather than through being imposed in full detail upon the economy.

How far will this drift toward the market proceed? That is a question to which we will return in our final chapter. What is important to recognize at this juncture is that there is a visible movement toward the market mechanism in every *European* communist nation (we will see shortly why it is only in these nations). One amusing consequence is that we find the same ideological alarm being expressed in these nations as in the United States, as each sees itself in danger of being subverted by the introduction of some elements of the other system.

This convergent tendency of different systems is clearly of great importance in the perspective of economic history. But we cannot deal with it properly until we have surveyed one last type of economic situation that differs as much from Russian socialism* as from American capitalism. This is the situation of economic underdevelopment, to which we next turn.

---

*What is the difference between *socialism* and *communism?* We have already noted one difference in the West, where socialism implies an adherence to democratic political mechanisms, whereas communism does not. But within the socialist bloc there is another interesting difference of definition. Socialism there represents a stage of development in which it is still necessary to use "bourgeois" incentives in order to make the economy function; that is, people must be paid in proportion to the "value" of their work. Under communism, a new form of human society will presumably have been achieved in which these selfish incentives will no longer be needed. Then will come the time when society will be able to put into effect Karl Marx's famous description of communism: "From each according to his ability; to each according to his need."

SUMMARY

1. The development of European capitalism was considerably hampered by a number of factors absent from the American scene. Among these were a *feudal heritage* that brought serious political problems and *severe national rivalry* that prevented economic unification. As a result, productivity in Europe lagged behind that of the United States. Compounding the problem of slow growth was the *breakdown of international trade* following World War I.

2. Capitalism in Europe was seriously threatened by the rise of a *socialist opposition*. However following World War II, conservative parties generally accepted the reformist ideas of socialism and backed large programs of *social welfare and a commitment to national economic planning*.

3. Equally, or more, important was the creation of the *European Community* with its *Common Market*, a successful attempt to revive inter-European trade.

4. Among the many European planning mechanisms, the most elaborate is the French system of *"indicative planning."* A centrally formulated plan is discussed among representatives of industry, labor, and other groups, and in the process of discussion and amendment becomes part of the general expectations of these groups. This leads to the requisite investment needed to bring the plan about. Thus the system works as a *self-fulfilling prophecy*.

5. All the European planning systems *rely on the market mechanism*. While the commitment of the European nations to a guided economy is in most cases greater than our own, a similar drift toward planning is visible in American capitalism as well.

6. The USSR has followed a totally different course. Following the Revolution of 1917, a system of *central planning* was initiated, but it early collapsed. Thereafter a semimarket system was introduced as a rescue measure.

7. Following long debates about how to secure agricultural production to feed workers engaged in industrial projects, Russia under Stalin began a *total collectivization* that used naked force to solve the food transfer problem and the industrialization program.

8. The planning mechanism by which Russia carries out its industrial growth requires the formulation of *highly detailed and accurately interlocked subplans*, any one of which, if wrongly designed or unmet, can wreck the larger one. *Inefficiency* has been the plague of the central planning system, although the system did succeed in achieving its larger objectives.

9. As a result, we see the *introduction of the market mechanism*, using profit-seeking enterprises, into the European communist economics. *The market is being introduced into socialism just as planning is being introduced into capitalism*.

1. Discuss how the fragmentation of a continent can affect the gains from trade. Does the experience of Europe illustrate that the bias of nationalism constitutes the main source of international economic difficulties?

2. In what ways is communism different from socialism? Are these differences merely economic?

3. What is the difference between indicative planning, as we find it in France, and the kind of planning we find in the U.S.S.R.?

4. What is a "self-fulfilling prophecy"? If you were a bank president and said in a speech that you thought your bank would fail, might that provoke behavior that would make your prediction true? Can you think of another example?

5. Imagine that you were in charge of automobile production in Russia. How would you decide how many cars to make? How expensive to make them? What materials to order? What prices to pay for various grades of labor? How to mix land, labor, and capital?

6. How is the transfer of food from country to city accomplished under capitalism? Why was the problem so acute under early Soviet rule? Do you think a program of rapid industrialization can be managed without recourse to coercion of some sort?

7. Do you think that profit-seeking enterprise is compatible with a planned economy? What kind of planning could utilize such enterprises? What kinds could not?

31 THE UNDERDEVELOPED WORLD

We must begin this next to last, and very important, chapter with a sobering realization. It is that our account of the long sweep of Western economic advance has simply ignored the economic existence of four out of five human beings on earth. Mere parochialism was not, however, the reason for this concentration on Western progress. Rather, it was the shocking fact that, taken in the large, *there was no economic progress in the rest of the world.*

This is not to say that tides of fortune and misfortune did not mark these areas, that great cultural heights were not achieved, and that the political or social histories of these regions do not warrant interest and study. Yet the fact remains that the mounting tide of *economic* advance that has engaged our attention was a phenomenon limited to the West. It is no doubt something of an oversimplification, but it is basically true to claim that in Asia, Africa, South America, or the Near East, economic existence was not materially improved for the average inhabitant from the twelfth—and, in some cases, the second—to the beginning of the twentieth century. Indeed, for many of them it was worsened. A long graph of non-Western material well-being would depict irregular rises and falls but an almost total absence of cumulative betterment.

The near end of such a graph would show the standard of living of three-quarters of the human race who inhabit the so-called underdeveloped areas today. Most of this mass of humanity exists in conditions of poverty that are difficult for a Westerner to comprehend. When we sum up the plight of the underdeveloped nations by saying that a billion human beings have a standard of living of "less than $100 a year," and that another, more fortunate, billion people enjoy in a year one-quarter to one-half the income a typical American family spends in a single *month,* we give only a pale statistical meaning to a reality that we can scarcely grasp.*

Why are the underdeveloped nations so pitiably poor? Only a half-century ago it was common to attribute their backwardness to geographic or climatic causes. The underdeveloped nations were poor, it was thought, either because the climate was too debilitating or because natural resources were lacking. Sometimes it was just said that the natives were too childlike or racially too inferior to improve their lot.

Bad climates may have had adverse effects. Yet, many hot areas have shown a capacity for sustained economic growth (for example, the Queensland areas of Australia), and we have come to recognize that a number of underdeveloped areas, such as Argentina and Korea, have completely temperate climates. So, too, we now regard the lack of resources in many areas more as a *symptom* of underdevelopment than a cause—which is to say that in many underdeveloped areas, resources have not yet been *looked for.* Libya, for instance, which used to be written off as a totally barren nation, has been discovered to be a huge reservoir of oil. Finally, little is heard today about native childishness or inherent inferiority. (Perhaps we remember how the wealthy classes similarly characterized the poor in Europe not too many centuries ago.) Climate and geography and cultural unpreparedness unquestionably constitute obstacles to rapid economic growth—and in some areas of the globe, very serious obstacles—but there are few economists who would look to these disadvantages as the main causes of economic backwardness.

Why then are these societies so poor?

*In Iran, for instance, in years of famine, the children of the poor examine the droppings of horses to extract morsels of undigested oats. In Calcutta, 250,000 people have no home whatsoever and live in the streets. In Hong Kong, large numbers of families of four or more live in one bed-space in a squalid dormitory. In Cali, Colombia, when the river rises, the city's sewers run through the homes of the poor. In Hyderabad, Pakistan, child labor employed in sealing the ends of bangles over a kerosene flame is paid eight cents—per *gross* of bangles.

The answer takes us back to an early chapter of our book. These are poor societies because they are *traditional* societies—that is, societies which have developed neither the mechanisms of command nor of the market by which they might launch into a sustained process of economic growth. Indeed, as we examine them further we will have the feeling that we are encountering in the present the anachronistic counterparts of the static societies of antiquity.

Why did they remain traditional societies? Why, for instance, did Byzantium, which was economically so advanced in contrast with the Crusaders' Europe, fall into decline? Why did China, with so many natural advantages, not develop into a dynamic economic society? There are no simple, or even fully satisfactory, answers. Perhaps the absence of economic progress elsewhere in the globe forces us to look upon our Western experience not as the paradigm and standard for historic development, but as a very special case in which various activating factors met in an environment peculiarly favorable for the emergence of a new economic style in history. The problem is one into which we cannot go more deeply in this book. At any rate, it is today an academic question. The dominant reality of our times is that the backward areas are now striving desperately to enter the mainstream of economic progress of the West. Let us examine further their chances for doing so.

CONDITIONS OF BACKWARDNESS

Every people, to exist, must first feed itself; there is a rough sequence to the order of demands in human society. But to go beyond existence, it must achieve a certain level of efficiency in agriculture, so that its efforts can be turned in other directions. What is tragically characteristic of the underdeveloped areas is that this first corner of economic progress has not yet been turned.

Consider the situation in that all-important crop of the East, rice. Table 31-1 shows the difference between the productivity of rice fields

TABLE 31 · 1

RICE PRODUCTION

(100 kilograms per hectare)	
U.S.	34.3
Australia	45.9
Burma	14.8
China (1954)	24.7
India	12.6
Indonesia	16.5
Thailand	14.3
Philippines	11.9

Source: Benjamin Higgins, *Economic Development* (New York: W. W. Norton & Company, Inc., 1959), p. 16.

634

in the main Asiatic countries and those of the United States and Australia as of the later 1950's. (The differences have worsened since then.)

What is true of rice can be duplicated in most other crops.* It is a disconcerting fact that the backward peasant nations which depend desperately on their capacity to grow food cannot even compete in these main products with the advanced countries: U.S. Louisiana rice undersells Philippine rice, California oranges are not only better but cheaper than Indonesian oranges.

Why is agriculture so unproductive? One apparent reason is that the typical unit of agricultural production in the underdeveloped lands is far too small to permit efficient farming. What has been called "postage stamp cultivation" marks the pattern of farming throughout most of Asia and a good deal of Africa and South America. John Gunther, reporting the situation in India thirty years ago, described it vividly. It has not changed since that time.

There is no primogeniture in India as a rule, and when the peasant dies his land is subdivided among all his sons with the result that most holdings are infinitesimally small. In one district in the Punjab, following fragmentation through generations, 584 owners cultivate no less than 16,000 fields; in another, 12,800 acres are split into actually 63,000 holdings. Three-quarters of the holdings in India as a whole are under ten acres. In many parts of India the average holding is less than an acre.[1]

In part, this terrible situation is the result of divisive inheritance practices which Gunther mentions. In part, it is due to landlord systems in which peasants cannot legally own or accumulate their own land; in part, to the pressure of too many people on too little soil. There are many causes, with one result: agriculture suffers from a devastatingly low productivity brought about by grotesque man/land ratios.

These are, however, only the first links in a chain of causes for low agricultural productivity. Another consequence of these tiny plots is an inability to apply sufficient capital to the land. Mechanical binders and reapers, tractors and trucks are not only impossible to use efficiently in such tiny spaces, but they are costly beyond the reach of the subsistence farmer. Even fertilizer is too expensive: in much of Asia, animal dung is used to provide "free" fuel rather than returned to the soil to enrich it.

This paralyzing lack of capital is by no means confined to agriculture. It pervades the entire range of an underdeveloped economy. The whole industrial landscape of a Western economy is missing: no factories, no

---

*Table 31-1 shows only the productive differentials of equal *areas* of land. When we consider that a single American farmer tends up to a hundred times as large an acreage as a peasant in an underdeveloped area, the difference in output *per man* would be much more striking.

[1] *Inside Asia* (New York: Harper & Row, 1939), p. 385.

power lines, no machines, no paved roads meet the eye for mile upon mile as one travels through an underdeveloped continent. Indeed, to a pitiable extent, an underdeveloped land is one in which human and animal muscle power provide the energy with which production is carried on. In India in 1953, for instance, 65 per cent of the total amount of productive energy in the nation was the product of straining man and beast.[2] The amount of usable electrical power generated in all of India would not have sufficed to light up New York City.

SOCIAL
INERTIA

A lack of agricultural and industrial capital is not the only reason for low productivity. As we would expect in traditional societies, an endemic cause of low per capita output lies in prevailing social attitudes. Typically, the people of an underdeveloped economy have not *learned* the "economic" attitudes that foster rapid industrialization. Instead of technology-conscious farmers, they are tradition-bound peasants. Instead of disciplined workers, they are reluctant and untrained laborers. Instead of production-minded businessmen, they are trading-oriented merchants.

For example, Alvin Hansen reports from his observations in India:

Agricultural practices are controlled by custom and tradition. A villager is fearful of science. For many villagers, insecticide is taboo because all life is sacred. A new and improved seed is suspect. To try it is a gamble. Fertilizers, for example, are indeed a risk. . . . To adopt these untried methods might be to risk failure. And failure could mean starvation.[3]

In similar vein, a UNESCO report tells us:

In the least developed areas, the worker's attitude toward labour may entirely lack time perspective, let alone the concept of productive investment. For example, the day labourer in a rural area on his way to work, who finds a fish in the net he placed in the river the night before, is observed to return home, his needs being met. . . .[4]

An equally crippling attitude is evinced by the upper classes, who look with scorn or disdain upon business or production-oriented careers. UNESCO also reports that the many students from the underdeveloped lands studying in the United States—the majority of whom come from the more privileged classes—only 4 per cent were studying a problem fundamental to all their nations: agriculture.[5]

---

[2] Daniel Wit and Alfred B. Clubok, "Atomic Power Development in India," *Social Research,* Autumn 1958, p. 290.

[3] *Economic Issues of the 1960's* (New York: McGraw-Hill Book Company, 1960), pp. 157–58.

[4] *Report on the World Social Situation,* UNESCO, March 9, 1961, p. 79.

[5] *Ibid.,* p. 81.

636

All these attitudes give rise to a *social inertia* that poses a tremendous hurdle to economic development. A suspicious peasantry, fearful of change that might jeopardize the slim margin yielding them life, a work force unresponsive to monetary incentive, a privileged class not interested in production—all these are part of the obdurate handicaps to be overcome by an underdeveloped nation.

Many of these problems, as we anticipated, remind us of the pre-market economies of antiquity. But in addition, the underdeveloped lands face an obstacle with which the economies of antiquity did *not* have to cope: a crushing rate of population increase threatens to nullify their efforts to emerge from backward conditions.

Only a few figures are needed to make the point. Let us begin with our southern neighbor, Mexico. Today, Mexico has a population equal to that of New York State, Pennsylvania, New Jersey, and Connecticut. Thirty years from now, if Mexico's present rate of population increase continues, it will have as many people as the present population of these four states *plus* the rest of New England, *plus* the entire South Atlantic seaboard, *plus* the entire West Coast, *plus* Ohio, Indiana, Illinois, Michigan, and Wisconsin. Or take the Caribbean and Central American area. That small part of the globe has a population of around 70 million. In some thirty years, at present growth rates, its population will outnumber by 30 million the entire population of the United States today. South America, now 20 per cent less populous than we, will be 200 per cent larger than our present population. India will then very likely number a billion souls. China will probably number 1.6 billion.

We have already seen one result of the relentless proliferation of people in the fragmentation of landholdings. But the problem goes beyond mere fragmentation. Eugene Black, formerly president of the International Bank for Reconstruction and Development (the World Bank) tells us that in India a population equivalent to that of all Great Britain has been squeezed out of any landholding whatsoever—even though it still dwells in rural areas.[6] Consequently, population pressure generates massive and widespread rural poverty, pushing inhabitants from the countryside into the already overcrowded cities. Five hundred families a day move into Jakarta from the surrounding Javanese fields where population has reached the fantastic figure of 1,100 per square mile (compare American population density of 50.4 people per square mile).

Even these tragic repercussions of population growth are but side effects. The main problem is that population growth adds more mouths almost as fast as the underdeveloped nations manage to add more food. They cancel out much economic progress by literally eating up the small

[6]Eugene R. Black, *The Diplomacy of Economic Development* (Cambridge, Mass.: Harvard University Press, 1960), p. 9.

surpluses which might serve as a springboard for faster future growth.

Ironically, this population "explosion" in the underdeveloped countries is a fairly recent phenomenon, attributable largely to the incursion of Western medicine and public health into the low income areas. Prior to World War II, the poorer countries held their population growth in check because death rates were nearly as high as birth rates. With DDT and penicillin, death rates have plunged dramatically. In Ceylon, for example, death rates dropped 40 per cent in one year following the adoption of malaria control and other health measures. As death rates dropped in the underdeveloped areas, birth rates, for many reasons, continued high, despite efforts to introduce birth control. In the backward lands, children are not only a source of prestige and of household labor for the peasant family, but also the only possible source of "social security" for old age. The childless older couple could very well starve; as parents or grandparents they are at least assured of a roof over their heads.

Is there a solution for this grim question? Until very recent years, any candid expert could have answered only with a discouraged shake of the head. In the long run there was always the hope that industrialization would eventually bring the lower birth rates characteristic of all urban societies. But the problem was how to reach the long run against the overwhelming tides of population increase.

Today there is a hope. A new technique of birth control known as the IUD (for *intra-uterine device*) has shown brilliant preliminary successes in those areas—mainly Taiwan and South Korea—where it has been introduced. There seems now to be a chance, if the underdeveloped countries apply their full efforts with the assistance of Western *expertise,* that the floodtide can be stemmed, perhaps within another generation. That still leaves the prospect of a Niagara of births to come. But there is new hope that the human torrent can be dammed before it has washed away all possibility of progress.

ROLE OF IMPERIALISM

This gives us a brief introduction to underdevelopment as it exists today. Before we turn to the problem of how this condition can be remedied, we must inquire into one more question. Why did not the market society, with all its economic dynamism, spread into the backward areas?

The answer is that the active economies of the European and American worlds *did* make contact with the underdeveloped regions, beginning with the great exploratory and commercial voyages of the fifteenth and sixteenth centuries. Until the nineteenth century, unfortunately, that contact was little more than mere adventure and plunder. And then, starting in the first half of that century and gaining momentum until World War I, came that scramble for territory we call the Age of Imperialism.

What was this imperialism? It was, in retrospect, a compound of many things: militarism, jingoism, a search for markets and for sources of cheap raw materials to feed growing industrial economies. Insofar as the colonial areas were concerned, however, the first impact of imperalism was not solely that of exploitation. On the contrary, the incursion of Western empires into the backward areas brought some advantages. It injected the first heavy dose of industrial capital: rail lines, mines, plantation equipment. It brought law and order, often into areas in which the most despotic personal rule had previously been the order of the day. It introduced the ideas of the West, including, most importantly, the idea of freedom, which was eventually to rouse the backward nations into a successful effort to overthrow their foreign dependence.

Yet if imperialism brought these positive and stimulating influences, it also exerted a peculiarly deforming impulse to the underdeveloped— indeed, then, totally undeveloped—economies of the East and South. In the eyes of the imperialist nations, the colonies were viewed not as areas to be brought along in balanced development, but essentially as immense supply dumps to be attached to the mother countries' industrial economies. Malaya became a vast tin mine; Indonesia, a huge tea and rubber plantation; Arabia, an oil field. In other words, the direction of economic development was steadily pushed in the direction that most benefited the imperial owner, not the colonial peoples themselves.

The result today is that the typical underdeveloped nation has a badly lopsided economy, unable to supply itself with a wide variety of goods. It is thereby thrust into the international market with its one basic commodity. For instance, in South America we find that Venezuela is dependent on oil for some 90 per cent of its exports; Colombia, on coffee for three-quarters of its exports; Chile, on copper for two-thirds of its foreign earnings; Honduras, on bananas for half of its foreign earnings. On the surface, this looks like a healthy specialization of trade. We shall shortly see why it is not.

Economic lopsidedness was one unhappy consequence of imperialism. No less important for the future course of development in the colonial areas was a second decisive influence of the West: its failure to achieve political and psychological relationships of mutual respect with its colonial peoples. In part, this was no doubt traceable to an often frankly exploitative economic attitude, in which the colonials were relegated to second-class jobs with third-class pay, while a handful of Western whites formed an insulated and highly paid managerial clique. But it ran deeper than that. A terrible color line, a callous indifference to colonial aspirations, a patronizing and sometimes contemptuous view of "the natives" runs all through the history of imperialism. It has left as a bitter heritage not only an identification of capitalism with its worst practices, but a political and social wariness toward the West which deeply affects the general orientation of the developing areas.

Up to this point we have concentrated our attention on the conditions of, and the background to, underdevelopment. Now we must ask, how can an underdeveloped nation emerge from its poverty? How can it put itself on the road to growth?

From what we have already learned, we know the basic answer to this question. The prerequisite for economic progress for the underdeveloped countries today is not essentially different from what it was in Great Britain at the time of the industrial revolution, or what it was in Russia in 1917. To grow, an underdeveloped economy must build capital

How is a starving country able to build capital? When 80 per cent of a country is scrabbling on the land for a bare subsistence, how can it divert its energies to building dams and roads, ditches and houses, railroad embankments and factories which, however indispensable for progress tomorrow, cannot be eaten today? If our postage-stamp farmers were to halt work on their tiny unproductive plots and go to work on a great project like, say, the Aswan Dam, who would feed them? Whence would come the necessary food to sustain these capital workers?

Here is our grim "model" of a peasant economy from Chapter 19 come to life, and we will remember from that model that when consumption could not be cut, growth could not ensue. Still, when we look again at the underdeveloped lands, the prospect is not quite so bleak as that. In the first place, these economies *do* have unemployed factors. In the second place, we find that a large number of the peasants who till the fields are not feeding themselves. They are, also, in a sense, taking food from one another's mouths.

As we have seen, the crowding of peasants on the land in these areas has resulted in a diminution of agricultural productivity far below that of the advanced countries. Hence the abundance of peasants working in the fields obscures the fact that *a smaller number of peasants, with little more equipment—perhaps even with no more equipment—could raise a total output just as large.* One observer has written: "An experiment carried out near Cairo by the American College seems to suggest that the present output, or something closely approaching it, could be produced by about half the present rural population of Egypt."[7] Here is an extreme case, but it can be found to apply, to some degree, to nearly every underdeveloped land.

Now we begin to see an answer to the predicament of the underdeveloped societies. In nearly all of these societies, there exists a disguised and hidden surplus of labor which, if it were taken off the land,

[7]Ragnar Nurkse, *Problems of Capital Formation in the Underdeveloped Countries* (New York: Oxford University Press, Inc., 1958), p. 35, fn. 2.

could be used to build capital. Most emphatically, this does not mean that the rural population should be literally moved, en masse, to the cities where there is already a hideous lump of indigestible unemployment. It means, rather, that the inefficient scale of agriculture conceals a reservoir of both labor and the food to feed that labor if it were elsewhere employed. By raising the productivity of the tillers of the soil, a work force can be made available for the building of roads and dams, while this "transfer" to capital building need not result in a diminution of agricultural output.

This rationalization of agriculture is not the only requirement for growth. When agricultural productivity is enhanced by the creation of larger farms (or by improved techniques on existing farms), *part of the ensuing larger output per man must be saved.* In other words, the peasant who remains on the soil cannot enjoy his enhanced productivity by raising his standard of living and eating up all his larger crop. Instead, the gain in output per cultivator must be siphoned off the farm. It must be "saved" by the peasant cultivator and shared with his formerly unproductive cousins, nephews, sons, and daughters who are now at work on capital-building projects. We do not expect a hungry peasant to do this voluntarily. Rather, by taxation or exaction, the government of an underdeveloped land must arrange for this indispensable transfer. Thus in the early stages of a *successful* development program there is apt to be no visible rise in the individual peasant's food *consumption,* although there must be a rise in his food *production.* What is apt to be visible is a more or less efficient—and sometimes harsh—mechanism for assuring that some portion of this newly added productivity is not consumed on the farm but is made available to support the capital-building worker. We see here the problem that caused the Russian planners such trouble in the early days of Soviet industrialization.

What we have just outlined is not, let us repeat, a formula for immediate action. In many underdeveloped lands, as we have seen, the countryside already crawls with unemployment, and to create, overnight, a large and efficient farming operation would create an intolerable social situation. We should think of the process we have just outlined as a long-term blueprint which covers the course of development over many years. It shows us—as did our earlier model—that the process of development takes the form of a huge internal migration from agricultural pursuits, where labor is wasted, to industrial and other pursuits, where it can yield a net contribution to the nation's progress.

Our model also showed us that capital-building is not just a matter of freeing hands and food. Peasant labor may construct roads, but it cannot, with its bare hands, build the trucks to run over them. It may throw up dams, but it cannot fashion the generators and power lines through which a dam can produce energy. In other words, what is needed to engineer the great ascent is not just a pool of labor. It is also a vast array of industrial equipment.*

How is this equipment obtained? In our model, by expanding the machine-tool—that is, the capital-equipment-building—subsector. But an underdeveloped economy does not have a capital-equipment-building sector. Consequently, *in the first stages of industrialization, before the nucleus of a self-contained industrial sector has been laid down, a backward nation must obtain its equipment from abroad.*

This it can do in one of three ways. (1) It can buy the equipment from an industrialized nation by the normal process of *foreign trade.* Libya, for example, can sell its oil and use the foreign currency it receives to purchase abroad the tractors, lathes, and industrial equipment it needs. (2) It can receive the equipment by *foreign investment* when a corporation in an advanced nation chooses to build in a backward area. This is the route by which the United States got much of its capital from Britain during the nineteenth century, and it is the means by which the underdeveloped nations themselves received capital during their colonial days. (3) It may receive the foreign exchange needed to buy industrial equipment as a result of a grant or a loan from another nation or from a United Nations agency such as the World Bank. That is, it can buy industrial equipment with *foreign aid.*

TRADE PROBLEMS

Of these three avenues of industrialization, the most important is foreign trade. In all, the underdeveloped nations earn from $30 to $40 billion a year from foreign trade. Not all of this, by any manner of means, however, is available for *new* industrial capital. A lion's share of export earnings, unfortunately, must go to pay for indispensable imports—replacements of old equipment, or even food—or to pay interest on loans contracted with the industrialized world.

In addition, another problem plagues the underdeveloped nations in foreign trade. We have seen how international trade is the means by which a great international division of labor can be achieved—that is, by which productivity can be enhanced in all trading countries, by enabling each to concentrate on those products in which it is most efficient.

*An allied problem of no less importance arises from the lack of technical training on which industrialization critically depends. At the lowest level, this is evidenced by appalling rates of illiteracy (up to 80 or 90 per cent) which make it impossible, for instance, to print instructions on a machine or a product and expect them to be followed. And at a more advanced level, the lack of expert training becomes an even more pinching bottleneck. Before its catastrophic civil war, United Nations economists figured that Nigeria alone would need some 20,000 top-level administrators, executives, technicians, etc., over the next ten years and twice as many subordinates. On a worldwide scale, this implies a need for at least 700,000 top-level personnel and 1,400,000 second-level assistants. Not 1 per cent of these skilled personnel exists today, and to "produce" them will be a task of staggering difficulty. Yet, without them it is often impossible to translate development plans into actuality.

With the underdeveloped nations, however, this international division of labor has worked badly. First, as we have seen, their structural difficulties have prevented them from developing their productivities even in their main occupational tasks. Second, most of them suffer from another problem. As sellers of raw commodities—usually only one raw commodity—typically, they face a highly inelastic demand for their goods. Like the American farmer, when they produce a bumper crop, prices tend to fall precipitously, and demand does not rise proportionately. At the same time, the industrial materials they buy in exchange tend to be firm or to rise in price over the years. Thus the "terms of trade"—the actual *quid pro quo* of goods received against goods offered—are likely to move against the poorer nations, who must give more and more coffee for the same amount of machinery.* In 1957 and 1958, when commodity prices took a particularly bad tumble, the poor nations actually lost more in purchasing power than the total amount of all foreign aid they received. In effect they subsidized the advanced nations! As another example, it has been estimated that falling prices have cost the African nations more, in the two decades since World War II, than all foreign funds given, loaned, or invested there.[8]

That is why all the underdeveloped nations are seeking commodity stabilization agreements (not altogether dissimilar from the support programs that stabilize American farm incomes). Recently, the advanced nations of the West have come to recognize the need for some such device if the underdeveloped nations are to be able to plan ahead with any assurance of stability, and agreements have been signed for the international stabilization of coffee prices.

Another possibility lies in the prospect of encouraging diversified exports from the underdeveloped nations—handicrafts, light manufactures, and others. The difficulty here is that these exports may compete with the domestic industry of the advanced nations: witness the problems of the American textile industry in the face of textile shipments from Hong Kong. No doubt, a large source of potential earnings lies along this path, but it is unlikely to rise rapidly as long as the advanced nations refuse to allow the backward ones equal access to their own markets.

A second main avenue of capital accumulation for the backward nations is foreign investment. Indeed, before World War II, this was

LIMITATIONS ON PRIVATE FOREIGN INVESTMENT

---

*It should be noted that not everyone agrees with this argument which has been advanced mainly by Dr. Raul Prebisch, a famous Chilean economist. The argument on the other side claims that the quality of machinery and industrial products is constantly improving, whereas the quality of raw commodities is not, so that the higher prices of industrial goods are offset by their greater productivity when put to use.

[8] Reginald H. Green and Ann Seidman, *Unity or Poverty* (Baltimore, Md.: Penguin Books, 1968), p. 400.

the source of their industrial wealth. Today, however, it is a much diminished avenue of assistance. On the one hand, the former capital-exporting nations are no longer eager to invest private funds in areas over which they have lost control and in which they fear to lose any new investments they might make. In addition, most of the European nations are now busy investing their available capital at home. On the other hand, many of the poorer nations, for reasons that we have already discussed, view Western capitalism with an uneasy eye. They see in the arrival of the branch of a powerful corporation another form of the domination they have just escaped in the past. They scent "imperialism" even when the most equitable terms are suggested. As a result, foreign investment is often hampered by restrictive legislation in the underdeveloped nations, even though it is badly needed. Consequently, not much more than $3 billion to $4 billion a year from all the advanced nations goes overseas as foreign investment in the underdeveloped world.

We must also recognize that the foreign capital that does go into the most backward nations has not been particularly useful in building up an industrial nucleus for further development. Foreign capital tends to concentrate in the extractive industries, such as oil production, ore mining, or plantation agriculture. These investments often form small, self-sufficient enclaves within the underdeveloped world and fail to stimulate the surrounding economy to growth. For instance, the Belgian Union Minière de Haut Katanga, a vast modern mining operation, existed for years in the primitive Congo without shedding any perceptible impetus toward general economic growth. At a later stage in economic development, perhaps at the stage now reached by some South American nations, foreign private capital may play a more dynamic role in the industrializing process, but it is still not yet a major force for advance.

One problem is that Western corporations tend to throw their very considerable local influence toward the support of conservative regimes, which typically lack the boldness or the incentive to carry out the far-reaching changes needed to bring about rapid social advance. Another difficulty is that Western corporations partially offset the growth-producing effects of their investments by draining profits out of the country. In the period 1950–1965, for example, the flow of income remitted from Latin America to the United States was $11.3 billion, three times larger than the flow of new capital into Latin America. In the years 1966–1967, $2.3 billion of income was transmitted to the United States, and only $0.5 billion was sent back to Latin America. This pattern of economic flows should not be misinterpreted as implying that foreign investment is a "negative" influence: the plant and equipment that the West has sent abroad remains in the underdeveloped world, where it continues to enhance the productivity of labor there. But the *earnings* on this capital are not typically plowed back into still more capital goods, so that their potential growth-producing effect is far from realized.

These considerations enable us to understand the special importance that attaches to the third channel of capital accumulation: foreign aid. Surprisingly, perhaps, in the light of the attention it attracts, foreign aid is not a very large figure. International assistance, from *all* individual nations and from the UN and its agencies, does not exceed $6 billion a year (*not* including international military aid). This is no more than 2 or 3 per cent of the total output of the underdeveloped world and only 10 to 15 per cent of its earnings from its export trade.

It is, however, a much larger fraction—perhaps 30 per cent—of the capital formation of the undeveloped areas. Thus foreign aid makes possible the accumulation of industrial capital much faster than could be accomplished solely as a result of the backward lands' export efforts or their ability to attract foreign private capital. To be sure, an increase in foreign earnings or in private capital imports would have equally powerful effects on growth. But we have seen the difficulties in the way of rapidly increasing the receipts from these sources. For the near future, foreign aid represents the most effective channel for *quickly* raising the amount of industrial capital which the underdeveloped nations must obtain.

Foreign aid, particularly from UN sources, is also an extremely important source of *technical assistance* which enables the backward regions to overcome the handicaps imposed by their lack of skilled and trained personnel. For the near term, this may be even more important than the acquisition of the industrial capital itself in promoting growth. Largely because of this bottleneck of skills, it is estimated that the underdeveloped countries could absorb at best $8 billion to $10 billion a year in foreign aid during this decade.

Against these handicaps, can the underdeveloped nations grow? Can the terrible conditions of poverty be relegated to the past? Economic analysis allows us to ask these questions systematically. For growth depends on the interplay of three variables.

1. *The rate of investment that an underdeveloped nation can generate.* As we know, this depends on the proportion of its current effort that it can devote to capital-creating activity. In turn, the rate of saving, the success in attracting foreign capital, the volume of foreign aid—all add to this critical fraction of effort on which growth hinges.

2. *The productivity of the new capital.* The saving that goes into new capital eventually results in higher output.

But not all capital boosts output by an equal amount. A million-dollar steel mill, for example, will have an impact on GNP very different from that of a million-dollar investment in schools. In the short run, the mill may yield a higher return of output per unit of capital investment; in the long run, the school may. But in any event, the effect on output will depend not merely on the amount of investment, but on the marginal capital-output ratio of the particular form of investment chosen.

3. *Population growth.*

Here, as we know, is the negative factor. If growth is to be achieved, output must rise faster than population. Otherwise, per capita output will be falling or static, despite seemingly large rates of over-all growth.

With these basic variables, is growth a possibility for the backward lands? We can see that if investment were 10 per cent of GNP and if each dollar of new investment gave rise to a third of a dollar of additional output,* then a 10 per cent rate of capital formation would yield a 3.3 per cent rate of growth (10 per cent × one-third). This is about equal to population growth rates in the nations with the highest rates of population income.

The trouble is that most of the backward nations have investment rates that are closer to 5 per cent than 10 per cent of GNP. In that case, even with a marginal capital-output ratio of one-half, growth rates would not be enough to begin a sustained climb against a population growth of 2.5 per cent (5 per cent × $\frac{1}{2}$ = 2.5 per cent).

Nonetheless, the outlook is by no means totally black. For many nations, an increase in their present rate of capital formation of 50 to 100 per cent—a difficult but by no means unthinkable goal—should bring them close to, or beyond, the point of cumulative growth. Indeed, economists at the United Nations calculate that there are perhaps twenty countries (whose populations aggregate to nearly half the underdeveloped world) where a great ten-year effort could bring economic development to the threshold of a self-sustaining climb. In none of these countries would anything like a massive alleviation of poverty have been achieved. But the stage would be set for such an advance; the major roadblocks would have been removed; the possibility of a truly large-scale accumulation of capital would be at hand.

SOCIAL AND POLITICAL PROBLEMS

Thus economic analysis makes it possible in theory to foresee a long, slow developmental climb. But this is not yet the end of our analysis. For it is impossible to think of development only in terms of economics.

---

*This seems to be *roughly* what the marginal capital-output ratio of new investment in the underdeveloped areas may be.

As we have seen in the case of Western growth, *economic development is nothing less than the modernization of an entire society.* When we talk of building capital, we must not imagine that this entails only the addition of machines and equipment to a peasant society. It entails the conversion of a peasant society into an industrial one. It means a change in the whole tenor of life, in the expectations and motivations, the environment of daily existence itself.

We have already noted some of the changes that economic development imposes on a society. Illiterate peasants must be made into literate farmers. Dispirited urban slum-dwellers must be made into disciplined factory workers. Old and powerful social classes, who have for generations derived their wealth from feudal land tenure, must be deprived of their vested rights and oriented toward often despised business pursuits. Above all, the profligate generation of life, conceived in dark huts as the only solace available to a crushed humanity, must give way to a responsible and deliberate creation of children as the chosen heirs to a better future.

These changes will *in time* be facilitated by the realization of development itself. A growing industrial environment breeds industrial ways. The gradual realization of economic improvement brings about attitudes that will themselves accelerate economic growth. A slowly rising standard of living is likely to dampen the birth rate in the underdeveloped areas, as it did in the West.

All these changes, as we have said, may take place in time. But it is time itself that is so critically lacking. The changes must begin to take place now—today—so that the process of development can gain an initial momentum. The transition from a backward, tradition-bound way of life to a modern and dynamic one cannot be allowed to mature at its own slow pace. Only an enormous effort can inaugurate, much less shorten, the transition from the past into the future.

COLLECTIVISM AND UNDERDEVELOPMENT

These sobering considerations converge in one main direction. They alert us to the fact that *in the great transformation of the underdeveloped areas, the market mechanism is apt to play a much smaller role than in the comparable transformation of the West during the industrial revolution.*

We will recall how lengthy and arduous was the period of apprenticeship through which the West had to pass in order for the ideas and attitudes, the social institutions and legal prerequisites of the market system to be hammered out. When the industrial revolution came into being, it exploded within a historic situation in which market institutions, actions, customs had already become the dominant form of economic organization.

None of this is true in the underdeveloped nations today. Rather than having their transition to a market society behind them, many of those nations must leap overnight from essentially tradition-bound and archaic relationships to commercialized and industrialized ones. Many of them are not even fully monetized economies. None of them have the network of institutions—and behind that, the network of "economic" motivations—on which a market society is built.

Hence it is not difficult to foresee that the guiding force of development is apt to be tilted in the direction of central planning. Regardless of the importance of private enterprise in carrying out the individual projects of development, the driving and organizing force of economic growth will have to be principally lodged with the government.

Even if the market relationships of free enterprise were more fully developed, much of the initial needs of development are in any event unsuited to private enterprise. Schooling and health, administration and training, the provision of great public works like dams, irrigation systems, basic housing, etc.—the so-called *infrastructure* of the economy— are not projects whose initiation can be left to the profit system. As Wilfred Malenbaum, an authority on Indian development efforts, has put it:

In India, as in other underdeveloped countries, government must not only provide this heavy dose of economic and social overhead investment but must also undertake many specific operations which in the United States, for example, belong distinctly within the scope of the private businessman. The reasons for this . . . stem from the thinness of the supply of entrepreneurs—even in India which is more blessed in this regard than are other poor countries. There is also the difficulty of raising enough funds privately for really big investments like steel mills. Of major importance, moreover, is the fact that there have been decades of relative inaction by the private business sector. . . . [The Indian businessman] is less sensitive to the new as a spur for improving the old. Be that as it may, government will need to fill a broad big business leadership role in India.[9]

POLITICAL IMPLICATIONS

But the outlook indicates more than a growth of economic command. Implicit also in the harsh demands of industrialization is the need for strong political leadership, not only to initiate and guide the course of development, but to *make it stick*. For it is not only wrong, but dangerously wrong, to picture economic development as a long, invigorating climb from achievement to achievement. On the contrary, it is better imagined as a gigantic social and political earthquake. Eugene Black, ex-president of the World Bank, soberly pointed out that we delude ourselves with buoyant phrases such as "the revolution of rising expectations" when we describe the process—rather than the prospect—of

[9]Quoted in Higgins, *Economic Development,* pp. 47–48.

development.[10] To many of the people involved in the bewildering transformations of development, the revolution is apt to be marked by a loss of traditional expectations, by a new awareness of deprivation, a new experience of frustration. For decades, perhaps generations, a developing nation must plow back its surplus into the ugly and un-enjoyable shapes of lathes and drills, conveyor belts and factory smoke-stacks. Some change toward betterment is not ruled out, particularly in health, basic diet, and education; but beyond this first great step, material improvement in everyday living will not—cannot—materialize quickly.

As a consequence, many of the policies and programs required for development, rather than being eagerly accepted by all levels of society, are apt to be resisted. Tax reform, land reform, the curtailment of luxury consumption are virtually certain to be opposed by the old order. In addition, as the long march begins, latent resentments of the poorer classes are likely to become mobilized; the underdog wakens to his lowly position. Even if his lot improves, he may well feel a new fury if his *relative* well-being is impaired. Writing of Mexico, one of the fastest developing nations, the anthropologist Oscar Lewis quotes the findings of a Mexican economist that "in 1955 one-hundredth of the gainfully employed population took 66 per cent of the national income, while the remaining 99 per cent received only 34 per cent; in 1940, the distribution had been exactly the reverse."[11] Lewis warns:

The political stability of Mexico is grim testimony to the great capacity for misery and suffering of the ordinary Mexican. But even the Mexican capacity for suffering has its limits, and unless ways are found to achieve a more equitable distribution of the growing national wealth and a greater equality of sacrifice during the difficult period of industrialization, we may expect social upheavals, sooner or later.[12]

These considerations enable us to understand how, along with a rise in economic standards can come a *rise* in social tensions, and this prospect, in turn, enables us to appreciate the fearful demands placed upon political leadership, which must provide the impetus, the inspira-tion—and, if necessary, the discipline—to keep the great ascent in motion. The strains of the early industrial revolution in England, with its widening chasm between the proletariat and capitalist, are not to be forgotten when we project the likely course of affairs in the devel-oping nations.

In the politically immature and labile areas of the underdeveloped

[10] *The Diplomacy of Economic Development,* p. 9.
[11] "Mexico Since Cardenas," *Social Research,* Spring 1959, p. 26.
[12] *The Children of Sanchez* (New York: Random House, Inc., 1961), pp. xxx–xxxi.

world, this exercise of leadership typically assumes the form of "strong man" government. In large part, this is only the perpetuation of age-old tendencies in these areas, but in the special environment of development, a new source of encouragement for dictatorial government arises from the exigencies of the economic process itself. Powerful, even ruthless, government may be needed, not only to begin the development process, but to cope with the strains of a *successful* development program.

It is not surprising, then, that the political map reveals the presence of authoritarian governments in many developing nations today. The communist areas aside, we find more or less authoritarian rule in Egypt, Ghana, Nigeria, Pakistan, Burma, South Korea, Indonesia, and the succession of South American junta governments. From country to country, the severity and ideological coloring of these governments varies. Yet in all of them we find that the problems of economic development provide a large rationale for the tightening of political control. At least in the arduous early stages of growth, some form of political command seems as integral to economic development as the accumulation of capital itself.

CHALLENGE TO THE WEST

Does this imply that the underdeveloped nations are apt to follow the route of communism?

It is certainly a possibility not to be lightly dismissed. For its political and social ugliness notwithstanding, communism offers a means of achieving the Great Ascent. There is no secret about this means. A communist nation, like a capitalist one, must take its workers from agriculture, must rationalize its agriculture, must import basic industrial equipment, and must relentlessly plow back its increments of output into more capital, more capital, ever more capital. The difference is that communism or total collectivism does the job with little of the handicaps of a free society. Where land is needed, it is simply taken; where workers are required, they are moved; where opposition is encountered, it is suppressed.

As was the case in Russia, all this is likely to be accomplished at a fearful social cost and with huge waste. In communist China, too, millions have been put to death for opposing the regime, and life for the remainder has been regimented to a chilling degree. Yet such an iron hand weighs less heavily on peoples who have never known any form of government other than despotism and who will submit to the yoke of communism if they see a chance of lifting the yoke of poverty from their grandchildren.

This last point is crucial. It must not be forgotten that for all its cruel errors, Russia is still the only peasant nation that has escaped from poverty in the twentieth century, and that China, for all its turmoil, is making a mightier effort to escape than any other underdeveloped country. Communism or iron collectivism *is* a way out of underdevelopment, at least in the beginning, and to see it in any less serious—and in this regard, respectful—light is to underestimate its challenge.

Can the West match that challenge?

We do not yet know. Few if any of the underdeveloped countries *want* to go communist. Their leaders are not blind to the excesses of communism, still less to the burdens of becoming Soviet or Chinese satellites. They are aware that the scale of foreign aid which the Communists can offer is considerably less than our own; and they know that the West has vast resources of men, materials, and money that could be mobilized to speed the great transition and to alleviate its strains.

What they do not know is whether the West is prepared to offer assistance on the scale and for the length of time that would be required to bring these countries through the gauntlet of early development. Nor do they know whether the West is prepared to accept the realities of development as they will likely emerge, bringing to the fore economic structures and political ideologies different from, and sometimes unsympathetic to, both capitalism and democracy.

Perhaps the West itself does not know the answers to these searching questions. It is difficult for us to confront the hard choices that development offers, difficult to swallow the growth of more or less collectivist economies and governments, difficult to abet a process whose initial outcome seems so inimical to our immediate interests.

It would be fatuous to pretend that somewhere, concealed in this picture, is an answer which will solve all problems happily. Rather, the likelihood is very great that the West, quite as much as the underdeveloped areas themselves, will have to make bitter choices and to follow unwelcome paths for many years. Yet, the fact that many alternatives are closed does not mean that none remain. There are degrees of command, political as well as economic, which result in a very different tenor of existence for those who must bear the burden of development and which offer very different possibilities for the future. Nothing could be more disastrous for the West than to overlook these differences and to brand all nonmarket economies or all nondemocratic governments as constituting a single undesirable species. In the mold of economic development is being cast the shape of much of world civilization for the long-term future. On the capacity of the West to overcome its stereotyped conception of other societies, on its capacity to discriminate between mere oppression and purposeful social direction, on its capacity to persevere in the encouragement of development despite inevitable disappointments and failures will depend much of the outcome of this central process of historic change in our time.

S U M M A R Y

1. *Underdevelopment* constitutes the economic environment for the vast majority of mankind. It is ascribable in part, perhaps, to bad climates or inadequate resources, but in the main it springs from the inability of traditional societies to mount sustained programs of investment and change.

2. The main attributes of underdevelopment are *very low levels of productivity*, especially in agriculture where man/land ratios often impose highly inefficient scales of production. No less important, and more difficult to correct, are deep-seated *attitudes of inertia* on the part of the population. And constituting a main obstacle to a development effort are very high rates of *population growth*. (Here the new birth control techniques now offer some hope for the future.)

3. The development effort requires a *shift from consumption to investment activity*. This necessitates a prior increase in agricultural productivity, accompanied by measures that will transfer the food surplus from the peasant cultivator to workers on capital projects. This is an exceedingly difficult task to carry out.

4. In addition to shifting resources from agriculture to capital building tasks, a nucleus of *industrial equipment* must be brought in. This can be done by *international trade*, by *foreign investment*, or by *foreign aid*.

5. The channel of international trade is a difficult one for many backward nations, as a consequence of *imperialism*. Many underdeveloped nations have "*lopsided*" *economies* that sell one raw commodity in markets where demand is typically inelastic. Foreign investment has not produced much capital for the backward nations, partly because of their own suspicions of Western nations, partly because the West has not reinvested its earnings there. *Foreign aid* thus becomes a small but crucial avenue for the transfer of funds and skills. It should be noted that skill is often essential to acquire before funds can be absorbed.

6. Development hinges on three economic variables: the *rate of investment*, the *capital-output ratio* (the size of additional output yielded by net investment) and the *rate of population growth*. Given a 10 per cent net investment rate and a one-third capital output ratio it should be possible to begin growth even against a 3 per cent population increase.

7. The problem is that the economic effort is not detachable from the whole array of *social and political problems*. To mount a development program requires that many traditional institutions and ways be discarded for new and untried ones. This process of change occurred over several centuries in the West, but the exigencies of the population crisis make it necessary to compress it within a few generations today.

8. The result is that the modernization of the backward areas is very likely to require *authoritarian measures*, both political and economic. The strains of maintaining a successful development program, no less than the initial problems of mounting one, are apt to lead to "strong-man" government and collectivist economic measures. In this light *we can see communism as a technique for attempting to bring about the deep-seated changes required for rapid modernization*.

1. In what ways do you think underdeveloped countries are different from the American Colonies in the mid-1600's? Think of literacy, attitudes toward work and thrift, and other such factors. What about the relationship to more advanced nations in each case?

2. Why do you think it is so difficult to change social attitudes at the lowest levels of society? At the upper levels? Are there different reasons for social inertia at different stations in society?

3. Does the United States have a population problem? Will population growth here affect economic or social aspects of life more? Do you think we should adopt an American population control policy? What sort of policy?

4. Review your acquaintance with the model of a peasant economy in Chapter 19. Is this model applicable to China today? Was it applicable to the American Colonies? What differences do population pressure and social inertia impart to the solutions implied by the model?

5. Many economists have suggested that all advanced nations should give about 1 per cent of their GNP for foreign aid. In the U.S., that would mean a foreign aid appropriation of about $8 billion. Actually we appropriate about $2 billion. Do you think it would be practicable to suggest a 1 per cent levy? How would the country feel about such a program?

6. What are the main variables in determining whether or not growth will be self-sustaining? If net investment were 8 per cent of GNP and the capital output ratio were $\frac{1}{4}$, could a nation grow if its rate of population increase were $2\frac{1}{4}$ per cent? What changes could initiate growth?

7. What do you think is the likelihood of the appearance of strong-arm governments and collectivist economies in the underdeveloped world? For the appearance of effective democratic governments? For capitalist economies? Socialist ones? Is it possible to make predictions or judgments in these matters that do not accord with your personal preferences?

32

THE TRAJECTORY OF
ECONOMIC SOCIETY

With this sombre look at the underdeveloped areas we bring to a conclusion our overview of general economic history. Throughout the pages behind us we have followed a majestic theme of economic development in the West, and now at the terminus of our study, this same long process is about to be commenced in the East and South. Thus, from our vantage point, we can see the beginning of worldwide economic development as a genuine watershed in human history. An active and dynamic form of economic life, until recently the distinctive characteristic of the industrial West, is about to be generalized over the face of the globe. The process of diffusion will take generations, but it marks a profound, irreversible, and truly historic alteration in the economic condition of man.

Yet, if the process of economic growth is henceforth to be carried out on a global scale, it is also clear that there will be significant change in the auspices under which this process is likely to unfold. As we have seen, it is command rather than the market system which is in the ascendant as the driving force in the underdeveloped regions. And when we combine the geographic extent of these regions with those in which communism has become firmly entrenched, it seems that command now bids fair to become *the* dominant means of organizing economic activity on this planet, as tradition was not very long ago.

But again there is a difference. During the centuries in which tradition held sway over most of the world, the economies run by the market system were the locus of progress and motion. Today and in the future, one cannot with assurance say the same. For a pre-eminent motive of the rising economies of command is to *displace* the market societies as the source of the world's economic vitality.

Does this mean that economic history now writes finis to the market system? Does it mean that the market, as a means of solving the economic problem is about to be relegated to the museum of economic antiquities, or at best limited to the confines of North America and Western Europe? The question brings to a focus our continuing concern with the market system through history. Let us attempt in these last pages to give an appraisal of its prospects.

THE STAGES OF ECONOMIC DEVELOPMENT

We might well begin such an appraisal by taking a last survey of the array of economic systems which marks our times. It is, at first glance, an extraordinary assortment: we find, in these mid-years of the twentieth century, a spectrum of economic organization which represents virtually every stage in economic history from the earliest and most primitive. But at second look, a significant pattern can be seen within this seemingly disordered assemblage. The few remaining wholly traditional economies, such as those of the Near East or tribal Africa, have not yet begun to move into the mainstream of economic development. A much larger group of underdeveloped nations, in which institutions of economic command are now rising amid a still traditional environment, have just commenced their development efforts and are now coping with the initial problems preparatory to eventual all-out industrialization. Going yet further along we find the economies of iron command, such as China and to a much lesser extent Russia; here we find national communities that are (or recently were) wrestling with the gigantic task of rapid massive industrialization. Finally, we pass to the market economies of the West, to encounter societies with their developmental days behind them, now concerned with the operation of high-consumption economic systems.*

The categorization suggests a very important general conclusion. *The economic structures of nations today bear an integral relation with their stage of economic development.* Acts of foreign intervention aside, the choice of command or market systems is not just the outcome of political considerations, or ideologies and preferences. It is also, and perhaps primarily, the result of functional requirements which are very different at different levels of economic achievement.

INCEPTION OF GROWTH

We have already noted this connection in our discussion of the underdeveloped areas. Now, however, we can place what we have learned into a wider frame of reference. For if we compare the trend of events in the underdeveloped economies with the "equivalent" stage of development in Western history, we see a significant point of resemblance between the two. The emergence of command in the development-minded countries today has a parallel in the mercantile era, when the Western nation also received a powerful impetus toward industrialization under the organizing influence of the "industry-minded" governments of that period.

Thereafter, to be sure, the resemblance ceases. In the West, following the first push of mercantilism, it was the market mechanism that provided the main directive force for growth; in the underdeveloped lands, as we have seen, this influence is likely to be preempted to a much larger extent by political and economic command.

Three main reasons lie behind this divergence of paths. *First, the underdeveloped areas today start from a lower level of preparedness* than did the West in the seventeenth and eighteenth centuries. Not only have the actual institutions of the market not yet appeared in many backward lands, but the whole process of acculturation has failed to duplicate that of the West. In many ways—not all of them economic—the West was "ready" for economic development, as Chapter 3 sought to make clear. A similar readiness is not in evidence in the majority of the backward lands today, with the result that development, far from evincing itself as a spontaneous process, comes about as the result of enforced and imposed change.

Second, the *West was able to mount its development effort in leisurely tempo.* This is not to say that its rate of growth was slow or that strong pressures did not weigh upon many Western countries, arousing within them feelings of dissatisfaction with their progress. Yet the situation

---

*A glance at the back end papers reveals a map keyed to these economic differences. Needless to say, the map gives no more than a subjective interpretation of the extent of Tradition, Command, and Market in the various countries of the world.

was unlike that of the backward areas today. Here immense pressures, both of population growth and of political impatience, create an overwhelming need and desire for speed. As a result, the process of growth is not allowed to mature quietly in the background of history, as it did for much of the West, but has been placed at the very center of political and social attention.

Finally, the underdeveloped countries, who suffer from so many handicaps in comparison with the developmental days of the West, enjoy one not inconsiderable advantage. Because they are in the rear guard rather than the vanguard of history, they know where they are going. *In a manner denied to the West, they can see ahead of them the goal they seek to reach.* They do not wish to reach this goal, however, by retreading the painful and laborious path marked out by the West. Rather, they intend to shortcut it, to move directly to their destination by utilizing the mechanisms of command to bring about the great alterations that must be made.

Can economic command significantly compress and accelerate the growth process? The remarkable performance of the Soviet Union suggests that it can. In 1920 Russia was but a minor figure in the economic councils of the world. Today it is second only—though still a far second—to the United States. If Soviet production continues to gain on American production at the rate of the last ten years, in little more than another generation its industrial output (although not its per capita output) will be larger than our own. Not less important, Chinese growth, until the great famine disaster of 1959–1960, was two or three times faster than India's; and despite political turmoil, China's economic advantage over India still seems substantial.[1]

It is no doubt wise not to exaggerate the advantages of a command system. If it holds the potential for an all-out attack on backwardness, it also contains the possibilities for substantial failure, as in the very badly planned Cuban economy.[2] The mere existence of a will to plan is no guarantee that the plans will be well drawn, or well carried out, or reasonably well obeyed. Nonetheless, these caveats must be set against the dismal record of economies that continue to wallow in the doldrums of tradition, or that undertake the arduous transition into modernity under the inadequate stimulus of halfhearted regimes and half-formed market systems. In this comparison of alternatives, the advantage seems strongly on the side of those backward societies that are capable of mustering a strong central economic authority.

---

[1] See Alexander Eckstein, *Communist China's Economic Growth and Foreign Trade* (New York: McGraw-Hill Book Company, 1966), pp. 45f. For problems of interpreting Russian statistics, see Alec Nove, *Communist Economic Strategy* (Washington, D.C.: National Planning Association, 1959), pp. 38–42.

[2] For an interesting firsthand account of Cuban problems with planning, see Edward Boorstein, *The Economic Transformation of Cuba* (New York: Monthly Review Press, 1968).

Once the development process is well under way, however, the relative functional merits of the market and the command mechanisms begin to change. After planning has done its massive tasks—enforcing economic and social change, creating an industrial sector, rationalizing agriculture—another problem begins to assume ever more importance. This is the problem of efficiency, of dovetailing the innumerable productive efforts of society into a single coherent and smoothly functioning whole.

In the flush period of mid-development, the market mechanism easily outperforms the command apparatus as a means of carrying out this complex coordinating task. Every profit-seeking entrepreneur, every industrial salesman, every cost-conscious purchasing agent becomes in effect part of a gigantic and continuously alert planning system within the market economy. Command systems do not easily duplicate their efforts. Bottlenecks, unusable output, shortages, waste, and a cumbersome hierarchy of bureaucratic forms and officials typically interfere with the maximum efficiency of the planned economy in midgrowth.

What we see here is not just a passing problem which can be easily ironed out. Rather, it expresses the fact that centralized economies of command do not naturally enjoy a congruence between private action and public necessity. By way of contrast, the traditional strength of the Western market system has rested on just this "natural" integration of private behavior and public requirement. As we have seen, this coordination was based on the predictable outcome of gain-seeking individuals in a competitive environment. In such an environment, an "invisible hand," in Adam Smith's marvelous phrase, led men to the very tasks that society desired, and the internal allocation problems of the economy seemingly solved themselves.

More than that, the classical market mechanism solved the economic problem with a minimum of social and political controls. Impelled by the drives inherent in a market society, the individual marketer fulfilled his public economic function without constant attention from the authorities. In contradistinction to his counterpart in a centralized command society, who is often aware of being prodded, cajoled, or even threatened to act in ways that do not appeal to his self-interest, the classical marketer obeyed the peremptory demands of the market as a voluntary exercise of his own economic "freedom."

Thus it is not surprising that we find many of the motivating principles of the market being introduced into command societies. For as these societies settle into more or less established routines, they too can utilize the pressure of want and the pull of pecuniary desire to facilitate the fulfillment of their basic plans.

Economic freedom, as we know it in the West, is not yet a reality, or even an official objective, in any of these countries. The right to strike, for example, is not recognized, and nothing like the fluid consumer-responsive market system is allowed to exert its unimpeded influence on the general direction of economic development. But the introduction of more and more discretion at the factory level argues strongly that the principles of the market society are apt to find their place in planned societies at an appropriate stage of economic development.

Thus our survey of successive stages of development brings us to a consideration of Western economic society—that is, to the advanced economies which have progressed beyond the need for forced industrialization and now enter the stage of high consumption.

From our foregoing discussion, it is clear that the market mechanism finds its most natural application in this fortunate period of economic evolution. Insofar as the advanced Western societies have reached a stage in which the consumer is not only permitted but encouraged to impose his wants on the direction of economic activity, there is little doubt that the market mechanism fulfills the prevailing social purpose more effectively than any other.

Nonetheless, as we noted in Chapter 27, the market is not without its own grave problems, even in this regard. For one thing, it is an inefficient instrument for provisioning societies—even rich societies—with those goods and services for which no "price tag" exists, such as education or local government services or public health facilities.

A market society "buys" such public goods by allocating a certain amount of taxes for these purposes. Its citizens, however, tend to feel these taxes as an exaction in contrast with the items they voluntarily buy. Typically, therefore, a market society underallocates resources to education, city government, public health or recreation, since it has no means of "bidding" funds into these areas, in competition with the powerful means of bidding them into autos or clothes or personal insurance.

A second and perhaps even deeper-seated failing of the market system is its application of a strictly economic calculus to the satisfaction of human wants and needs. As we said before, the market is an assiduous servant of the wealthy, but an indifferent servant of the poor. Thus it presents us with the anomaly of a surplus of luxury housing existing side-by-side with a shortage of inexpensive housing, although the social need for the latter is incontestably greater than the former. Or it pours energy and resources into the multiplication of luxuries for which the wealthier classes offer a market, while allowing more basic needs of the poor to go unheeded and unmet.

These shortcomings, together with those we have examined earlier, such as the problems of oligopoly and general economic instability, and of the absence of any means of coping with the external effects of private action, all have a common attribute. They are indicative of a central weakness of the market system—*its inability to formulate public needs above those of the marketplace.*

So long as the public need roughly coincides with the sum of the private interests to which the market automatically attends, this failing of the market system is a minor one. But in an advanced economic society, it tends to become ever more important. As primary wants become satisfied, the public aim turns toward stability and security, objectives not attainable without a degree of public control. As technological organization becomes more complex and massive, again a public need arises to contain the new agglomerations of economic power. So, too, as wealth increases, pressure for education, urban improvement, welfare and the like, comes to the fore, not only as an indication of the public conscience, but as a functioning requirement of a mature society. And finally, the public stimulus and management of continued growth take on increased political urgency as the passive acquiescence of a poor society is replaced by the purposeful aspirations of a well-to-do community.

We have already paid much attention to the rise of planning in the advanced market societies as a corrective force to deal with just such problems. Now we can go so far as to generalize the economic meaning of this trend. *Planning arises in the advanced market societies to offset their inherent goal-setting weaknesses, just as the market mechanism arises in advanced command societies to offset their inherent motivational weaknesses.* In other words, planning and market mechanisms, in those societies which have begun to enter the stage of high consumption, are not mutually incompatible. On the contrary, they powerfully supplement and support one another.

CONVERGENCE
OF SYSTEMS

What seems to impend at the moment, then, is a *convergence of economic mechanisms* for the more advanced societies. In the planned economies the market is being introduced to facilitate the smoother achievement of established objectives, while in the market economies, a degree of planning is increasingly relied upon to give order, stability, and social direction to the outcome of private activity.

This does not imply that the two major systems today are about to become indistinguishable. The convergence of economic mechanisms may blur, but it is not likely to obliterate, the basic distinctions between them. Nor does the convergence of mechanisms in itself portend profound changes in the larger social structures of socialism and capitalism. Throughout this book we have sought to draw a careful line between the economic substructure and the political and social superstructure. The locus and use of power, the institutions of government, and most important, the actual experience of daily existence in both capitalism and socialism are conditioned by, but by no means wholly traceable to, their underlying economic systems.

Hence a gradual rapprochement of the economic mechanisms should not lead us to hasty conclusions about the rebirth of "capitalism" in the Soviet Union or the advent of "socialism" in the United States. Capitalism and socialism exist not as textbook models but as historic societies, each with its cultural identity, its nationality, its traditions and beliefs. As always before, economic change will have to make its peace with social and political realities, and in this continuing mutual adjustment, the role of economic forces is far from a mechanical one. If anything, the use of economic mechanisms which are functionally apposite to the situation should increase the viability of *both* societies. Socialism and capitalism will then have to adjust their differences in ideology and national purpose shorn of the fond belief that the economic doom of the other is rapidly approaching.

Our analysis has brought us down to the present. But what of the future? In these last pages of our historical survey, let us speculate as to what may lie ahead. For the trajectory of economic development, which has provided us with the framework for our analysis, is itself still unfinished. The curve of scientific discovery continues to rise almost vertically beneath our feet. The tempo of technological improvement, the enormous additions to capital, and the resulting increase in wealth, all point to a future in which the economic environment will be as substantially altered from its present-day condition as that present-day condition is different from economies in a far lower stage of evolution.

In what way is this impending change likely to affect the market system?

The answer brings us back to the opening pages of this book, for it involves the nature of the economic problem itself. We first posed the problem as the need to mobilize and allocate human energies and to distribute the social product in a manner that would assure society of its continued existence. We named survival itself as the basic challenge to the economic system—a choice amply justified by the ragged and hungry condition of mankind over most of history, and even today, over most of the globe.

In the advanced economies of the future this problem will surely recede into the background, as it has already begun to do in the high consumption economies of the present. Although it can never be lost to sight, it will no longer be survival that claims the main attention of society. Nor will it any longer be growth—at least not in the paramount degree to which growth concerns the economies emerging from backwardness or even in the milder degree to which it continues to concern the advanced economies today. Rather, the central problem which is likely to confront the societies of tomorrow is nothing less than the creation of *a new relationship between the economic aspect of existence and human life in its totality.*

CHANGING
NATURE
OF THE
ECONOMIC
PROBLEM

We find one aspect of this problem already close at hand. As the advanced societies do their job of linking science with life, of taking the edge off scarcity, there opens before them a great alternative. On the one hand, the opportunity arises to divert society's energies away from their eternal economic concerns to new areas of human fulfillment—education, the arts and sciences, recreation and personal cultivation, the beautification of the environment. On the other hand, the opportunity also presents itself to occupy the new area of human freedom with the production and consumption of an ever larger volume of ever less-valued goods.

As we have already remarked, a market society does not cope easily with this choice of social opportunities. Its established mechanism continues to direct human energies into the accustomed economic channels. Thus the danger exists that the market system, in an environment of genuine abundance, may become an instrument which liberates man from real want only to enslave him to purposes for which it is increasingly difficult to find social and moral justification.

This is perhaps an aesthetic rather than an economic problem. But the issue goes deeper than one's social preferences. For at the same time that the growing level of mass affluence points to a devaluation of much economic activity, so also does it point to a weakening of the very motivational base on which a market economy rests. As well-being grows, the traditional pressures fade; want and need become less dependable guides for human behavior. We have seen one consequence of this in the rise of advertising as a private means of forming and directing consumers' "demands." Now we can foresee that in a society of very great abundance, not only these cultivated desires but even the basic incentive to maximize income or minimize expenditure may well lose the ability to direct human behavior. In that event, the market system would cease to wield its necessary control over individual action, and society would have to look to some other means of social control to ensure the necessary accomplishment of its basic tasks.

If the growth of affluence itself poses a subtle threat to the functional efficacy of the market mechanism, another danger is signalled by the growth of technology.

For the cumulative impact of technology is radically altering the basic relation on which all economics rests: the relation of man and nature. This alteration is not only evident as in increasing material sufficiency. It is noticeable as well in the changing definition of "work" itself.

Over most of the past, as we have noted, work has been an onerous imperative of existence. The need to work has been the universal prerequisite of social continuity—a prerequisite which crowded out much else of life. Even in the more advanced nations today, work continues to be an inescapable requirement for the majority, although its demands have been incomparably lightened over the years.

This importunate and exhausting predominance of work is certain to be markedly diminished in the not too distant future. It has been many times pointed out, for instance, that today we labor but 60 per cent of the time our ancestors did three generations ago, and that leisure has come to be a preoccupation which rivals that of work. If the present trend of technological advance is maintained, this compression of labor time is certain to continue and may very likely increase. By 1980—certainly by the year 2000—a workweek of 30 hours and a workyear of 48 or fewer weeks are by no means unimaginable.

In the long run, the implications of this trend present the market system with unprecedented problems. For in addition to its various cultural and institutional preconditions, the market system has always taken for granted one self-evident social phenomenon: a mass participation in the economic process. It was the tacit assumption—indeed, the obvious fact—that virtually every family was in some way directly engaged in the economic process which assured a general *dispersion of income* among all members of the community.

But in the highly automated world toward which technology appears to be moving us, this universal participation in the economic process can no longer be taken as an unchallengeable assumption. On the contrary, it is perfectly possible to assume that economic engagement will become the function of a minority rather than of the overwhelming majority, that work will become more of a privilege than a necessity. This view does not forecast a condition of social poverty: on the contrary, it is posited on the greatest social abundance. But whether the market will then provide the mechanism by which that abundance is distributed—or by which access to productive tasks is regulated—is, to say the least, a debatable question.

These speculations take us some distance in the future—precisely how far depends on the rate at which the advanced societies of today realize the revolutionary potential that abundance and technology hold out for them. Yet the implications of a changing economic environment are clear enough. In the foreseeable economies of genuine abundance and technological mastery, the market mechanism is likely to have a declining functional relevance. Both economic and social problems can be divined for which some new form of planning, rather than the market, must provide the answer.

To many of us, this may appear as a disturbing conclusion. Yet its full meaning must be viewed in the light of the long perspective in which we have permitted ourselves to look ahead, to visualize societies at a stage of development wholly different from our own. Then we can see that the declining relevance of the market mechanism is itself symptomatic of a changing relevance of *all* economic control mechanisms. In an environment in which the work of society has been reduced to a small fraction of its present time and in which the social product is very large, the economic problem turns from accumulation—public or private—toward administration. It is man who must then govern things rather than things which must govern man.

It is with such a vista—at once hopeful and problematic—that we leave our historic survey of the market system. Looking not only backward to the past, but forward to the very limit of our historic visibility, we can see the market system itself as groping toward an ultimate transcendence of economics as a fetter on mankind. Over most of history scarcity has imposed its harsh demands on man, forcing him to acquiesce in repressive and cruel social arrangements in order that life might go on. Only recently, first under the market system, later under the system of command, has man begun to work toward a world in which he would be free from want—free, at least, in the sense that the material requirements for a good life no longer lay beyond easy grasp.

Now there can be seen the prospect of a final stage of economic development—a stage in which the making of economic society, as a painful struggle, comes to an end. For the first time, an orderly and generous solution to the economic problem begins to approach within human capability. The great question will then be whether men will use their triumph over nature to achieve a much more difficult victory over themselves.

SUMMARY

1. The spectrum of economic systems in the world corresponds generally to their *stages of economic development.*

2. The inception of growth seems to require a political stimulus. In the West, this was provided by *mercantilism,* after which the market took over the task of growth. The West was favored over the present underdeveloped areas by its ability to mount a *leisurely development,* and by its *vanguard position* vis-à-vis the rest of the world.

3. Today, *command economies* are attempting to push their societies off dead center and to initiate the process of growth. For these tasks, command seems a more appropriate system than the market.

4. *Economies in mid-development,* such as the Soviet Union, are characterized by mixtures of command and market systems. Command is best suited for massive economic and social reallocations, but not to the problems of running a smoothly integrated high-output economy. Bureaucratic inefficiency, and the absence of a congruence between private interest and public requirement, introduce many difficulties into the planning mechanism. Here the market begins to achieve a new relevance.

5. *High consumption economies* are naturally suited to market guidance. However, these economies now suffer from the inability of the market to formulate public needs. *Thus, planning arises in market systems to offset their inherent goal-setting weaknesses, just as the market arises in command systems to offset their inherent motivational weaknesses.*

6. Thus we see a *convergence of systems* in the more advanced nations. However, a convergence of economic systems does not mean that "capitalism" and "socialism" are becoming indistinguishable.

7. Within the most advanced economies we find a further challenge. The problem of *abundance* and of an increasingly productive *technology* is *altering the role of work* and of *participation* in the economic process. If present trends continue, it is possible to foresee a declining effectiveness of the traditional market stimuli and the need for some new system of arranging production and distribution to assure orderly provisioning in the future.

1. How do you account for the simultaneous existence in the world of such radically different economic systems?

2. In what ways was the early growth experience of the West unlike the present growth prospects of the backward world? Do you think these differences will have a substantial effect on the choice of economic systems for the backward countries?

3. Discuss the difference in social goals and priorities between a nation that is just beginning its development and one in mid-development. Between one in mid-development and one at a stage of high mass consumption? What is the relevance of planning techniques for each of these stages of development? Would you expect the techniques of planning to be similar in all stages? What differences would you look for?

4. What is meant by the congruence of self-interest and public requirement in a market system? Is this what we mean by the "invisible hand"? How can this congruence be reconciled with the fact that the market has no means of establishing public priorities?

5. What are the advantages of the market system for economic freedom? Do you think the market system is also productive of political freedom? Draw a scatter diagram showing on one axis the degree of planning and on the other axis your estimate of relative political freedoms for the following nations: Sweden, England, U.S., France, South Africa. Is there much, if any, relationship between the two variables?

6. Do you think there can be a convergence of economic systems without a convergence of social and political systems?

7. If the U.S. continues to grow at 3.5 per cent a year, in about a century average incomes (in 1967 purchasing power) will be between $100,000 and $200,000 per family. How would that affect the working of a market system? What social and economic changes do you think such a trajectory of growth could bring about?

8. Do you think that the economic problem will finally be solved? What sorts of problems might take its place?

STATISTICAL APPENDIX

Gross National Product: Annually, 1929–68 (in billions, rounded)

	1929	1930	1931	1932	1933	1934	1935	1936
Gross national product								
(billions of 1958 dollars)	203.6	183.5	169.3	144.2	141.5	154.3	169.5	193.0
Gross national product								
(current dollars)	103.1	90.4	75.8	58.0	55.6	65.1	72.2	82.5
Personal consumption expenditures	77.2	69.9	60.5	48.6	45.8	51.3	55.7	61.9
Durable goods	9.2	7.1	5.5	3.6	3.5	4.2	5.1	6.3
Nondurable goods	37.7	34.0	28.9	22.7	22.2	26.7	29.3	32.8
Services	30.3	28.7	26.0	22.2	20.1	20.4	21.3	22.7
Gross private domestic investment	16.2	10.3	5.6	1.0	1.4	3.3	6.4	8.5
Fixed investment	14.5	10.6	6.8	3.4	2.9	4.1	5.3	7.2
Nonresidential	10.6	8.3	5.0	2.7	2.4	3.2	4.1	5.6
Structures	4.9	4.0	2.3	1.2	.9	1.0	1.2	1.6
Producers' durable equipment	5.6	4.2	2.7	1.5	1.5	2.1	2.9	3.9
Residential structures	3.9	2.3	1.7	.7	.6	.9	1.2	1.6
Change in business inventories	1.7	−.3	−1.1	−2.5	−1.6	−.7	1.1	1.3
Net exports of goods and services	1.1	1.0	.5	.4	.4	.6	.1	.1
Exports	7.0	5.4	3.6	2.5	2.4	2.9	3.2	3.5
Imports	5.8	4.4	3.1	2.1	2.0	2.3	3.1	3.4
Government purchases of goods and services	8.5	9.2	9.2	8.1	8.0	9.8	10.0	11.9
Federal	1.3	1.4	1.5	1.5	2.0	2.9	2.9	4.9
National defense	—	—	—	—	—	—	—	—
Other	—	—	—	—	—	—	—	—
State and local	7.2	7.8	7.7	6.6	6.0	6.8	7.1	7.0

1937	1938	1939	1940	1941	1942	1943	1944	1945	1946	1947	1948
203.2	**192.9**	**209.4**	**227.2**	**263.7**	**297.8**	**337.1**	**361.3**	**355.2**	**312.6**	**309.9**	**323.7**
90.4	**84.6**	**90.4**	**99.7**	**124.5**	**157.9**	**191.6**	**210.1**	**211.9**	**208.5**	**231.3**	**257.6**
66.5	63.9	66.8	70.8	80.6	88.5	99.3	108.2	119.7	143.4	160.7	173.5
6.9	5.7	6.7	7.8	9.6	6.9	6.6	6.7	8.0	15.7	20.4	22.7
35.2	33.9	35.1	37.0	42.8	50.7	58.6	64.3	71.9	82.3	90.5	96.2
24.3	24.3	25.0	26.0	28.1	30.8	34.2	37.2	39.8	45.3	49.8	54.7
11.8	6.5	9.3	13.1	17.9	9.8	5.7	7.1	10.6	30.6	34.0	46.0
9.2	7.4	8.8	10.9	13.4	8.0	6.4	8.1	11.6	24.2	34.4	41.3
7.3	5.4	5.9	7.5	9.5	5.9	5.0	6.8	10.1	16.9	23.4	26.9
2.4	1.9	1.9	2.3	2.9	1.9	1.3	1.8	2.8	6.8	7.5	8.8
4.9	3.5	3.9	5.3	6.6	4.1	3.7	5.0	7.3	10.2	15.9	18.0
1.9	2.0	2.9	3.4	3.9	2.1	1.3	1.3	1.5	7.2	11.1	14.4
2.5	−.9	.4	2.2	4.5	1.7	−.6	−.9	−1.0	6.4	−.5	4.7
.3	1.3	1.0	1.7	1.3	—	−2.0	−1.8	−.6	7.5	11.5	6.4
4.6	4.3	4.4	5.3	5.9	4.8	4.4	5.3	7.2	14.7	19.7	16.8
4.2	3.0	3.4	3.6	4.6	4.8	6.5	7.1	7.8	7.2	8.2	10.3
11.8	12.9	13.3	14.0	24.8	59.6	88.6	96.5	82.3	27.0	25.1	31.5
4.7	5.4	5.1	6.0	16.9	51.9	81.1	89.0	74.2	17.2	12.5	16.5
—	—	1.2	2.2	13.7	49.3	79.7	87.4	73.5	14.7	9.0	10.7
—	—	3.8	3.8	3.1	2.5	1.4	1.6	.7	2.5	3.5	5.8
7.2	7.6	8.2	7.9	7.9	7.7	7.4	7.5	8.1	9.8	12.6	15.0

667

THE NATIONAL INCOME AND PRODUCT ACCOUNTS OF THE UNITED STATES
Gross National Product: Annually, 1929–68 (in billions, rounded)

	1949	1950	1951	1952	1953	1954	1955	1956
Gross national product (billions of 1958 dollars)	324.1	355.3	383.4	395.1	412.8	407.0	438.0	446.1
Gross national product (current dollars)	256.5	284.8	328.4	345.5	364.6	364.8	397.9	419.2
Personal consumption expenditures	176.8	191.0	206.3	216.7	229.9	236.5	254.4	266.7
Durable goods	24.6	30.5	29.6	29.3	33.2	32.8	39.6	38.9
Nondurable goods	94.5	98.1	108.7	113.9	116.8	118.3	123.3	129.3
Services	57.6	62.4	67.9	73.4	79.9	85.4	91.4	98.5
Gross private domestic investment	35.7	54.1	59.3	51.9	52.6	51.7	67.4	70.0
Fixed investment	38.8	47.3	49.0	48.8	52.1	53.3	61.4	65.3
Nonresidential	25.1	27.9	31.8	31.8	31.6	34.1	33.6	43.7
Structures	8.5	9.2	11.1	11.4	12.6	13.1	14.3	17.2
Producers' durable equipment	16.6	18.6	20.6	20.2	21.5	20.5	23.8	26.5
Residential structures	13.7	19.4	17.2	17.2	17.9	19.6	23.3	21.6
Change in business inventories	−3.1	6.8	10.3	3.1	.4	−1.5	5.9	4.7
Net exports of goods and services	6.1	1.8	3.7	2.2	.4	1.8	2.0	3.9
Exports	15.8	13.8	18.7	18.0	16.9	17.7	19.8	23.6
Imports	9.6	12.0	15.1	15.8	16.6	15.9	17.8	19.6
Government purchases of goods and services	37.8	37.9	59.1	74.7	81.6	74.8	74.2	78.6
Federal	20.1	18.4	37.6	51.8	57.0	47.4	44.1	45.6
National defense	13.3	14.1	33.6	45.9	48.7	41.2	38.5	40.3
Other	6.8	4.3	4.1	5.8	8.4	6.2	5.5	5.2
State and local	17.7	19.5	21.5	22.9	24.6	27.4	30.1	33.0

1957	1958	1959	1960	1961	1962	1963	1964	1965	1966*	1967	1968
452.5	447.3	475.9	487.7	497.2	529.8	551.0	580.0	614.4	652.6	673.1	706.7
441.1	447.3	483.7	503.7	520.1	560.3	590.5	631.7	681.2	743.3	789.7	860.6
281.4	290.1	311.2	325.2	335.1	355.1	375.0	401.3	431.5	465.9	492.2	533.8
40.8	37.9	44.3	45.3	44.2	49.5	53.9	59.3	66.1	70.3	72.6	82.5
135.6	140.1	146.6	151.3	155.9	162.5	168.6	178.9	190.6	207.5	215.8	230.3
105.0	112.0	120.3	128.6	135.1	143.0	152.4	163.1	174.8	188.1	203.8	221.0
67.8	60.9	75.3	74.8	71.7	83.0	87.1	92.9	106.5	188.0	114.3	127.7
66.5	62.4	70.5	71.2	69.7	77.0	81.3	88.3	97.5	104.6	108.2	119.9
46.3	41.6	45.1	48.4	47.0	51.7	54.3	60.7	69.7	80.2	83.6	90.0
17.9	16.6	16.7	18.1	18.4	19.2	19.5	21.0	24.9	27.9	27.9	29.2
28.4	25.0	28.4	30.3	28.6	32.5	34.8	39.7	44.8	52.3	55.7	60.8
20.2	20.8	25.4	22.8	22.6	25.3	27.0	27.6	27.7	24.4	24.6	29.9
1.3	−1.5	4.7	3.6	2.0	6.0	5.9	4.7	9.0	13.4	6.1	7.7
5.7	2.2	.1	4.0	5.6	5.1	5.9	8.5	6.9	5.1	4.8	2.0
26.5	23.1	23.5	27.2	28.6	30.3	32.3	36.9	38.9	43.0	46.2	50.6
20.7	20.9	23.3	23.2	22.9	25.1	26.4	28.5	32.0	37.9	41.0	48.7
86.1	94.1	97.0	99.6	107.6	117.1	122.5	128.9	136.2	154.3	178.4	197.2
49.5	53.6	53.6	53.5	57.4	63.4	64.2	65.2	66.8	77.0	90.6	100.0
44.2	45.9	46.0	44.9	47.8	51.6	50.8	50.0	50.1	60.5	72.4	78.9
5.3	7.7	7.6	8.6	9.6	11.8	13.5	15.2	16.7	16.5	18.2	21.1
36.6	40.6	43.3	46.1	50.2	53.7	58.2	63.7	69.4	77.2	87.8	97.2

Note: 1929–1966 data from U.S. Dept. of Commerce, *The National Income and Product Accounts of the United States*. Later data from *Economic Indicator*. All recent figures subject to minor change from year to year as statistical corrections are made in previous figures.

INDEX

A

Abilities, and earnings, 464–69
Ability to buy (see Demand)
Abundance, problem of, 164, 662
Acceleration principle, 258–60, 388–90
Accelerator, 258–60, 388–90
Accelerator-multiplier interaction, 388–90
Actual and potential GNP, 390–91
Administered prices, 123–24, 528
Advantage, comparative, 556–57, 558–62
Advertising:
    and demand, 125–27, 522
    wastes and gains, 126–27, 539–40
Affluence, 164
Age distribution, 367
Aggregate demand and employment, 366, 373
Agricultural Adjustment Act, 148–49
Agriculture:
    in antiquity, 26–28
    and depression, 136–38
    inelastic demand for, 137, 148–49, 363, 643
    productivity, 137, 149
    proportion of labor force in, 360, 365–66n.,
        383
    and pure competition, 138n., 515
    rationalization of, 640–41
    and technology, 149, 149n., 363
    and underdevelopment, 634–35, 640–41
Aid, foreign, 642, 645
    in balance of payments, 583, 595
Alberti, Leon, 73
Alchian, A., 466n.
Alienation, 99–100
Allen, F. L., 2, 133–34, 135
Allen, W. R., 466n.
Allocation, 14–15, 65, 425–31
American Telegraph & Telephone, debt, 293
Antiquity:
    economic organization in, 25–32
    social justice in, 32–33
Antitrust legislation, 115–17
    restraining effect of, 121
Appreciation of foreign exchange, 578–79
Aquinas, Thomas, 41
Aristotle, 31, 33, 42
Arkwright, R., 78, 78n., 79, 80, 84
Armaments spending, 283n.
Assets and debts, 292–94, 303
    and liabilities, 313
Atomic Energy Commission, 283n.
Aubrey, H., 591n.
Automatic stabilizers, 288–89, 390
Automation, 371–72
Automobile, impact of, 97–98
Autonomous investment, 257–58, 260
Average and marginal relationship, 479, 501–2
Average propensity to consume, 231–32

Average revenue, 504–6, 509, 523–4
Average unit cost curve:
    long run, 510–11
    short run, 497–502
Averitt, R., 118, 118n., 464n., 512n.

B

Backward-bending supply curve, 458
Balanced growth, 393–94
Balance of payments:
    capital movements and, 584–85
    current account, 576–77, 593
    deficit in, 585–86, 587–88, 588–90
    and foreign aid, 583, 595
    and gold standard, 604
    government account, 582–83, 595–96
    in 1968, 592
    over-all, 588–89
    remedies for, 594–99
Bank deposits, creation of, 312–16
Bank loans, 311–14
    and overlending, 319–20
Bank reserves, 309, 311ff.
Banks, commercial, 309n., 309ff.
Banks, money creation by, 312ff.
Bastiat, F., 565–66
Baumol, W., 339
Beard, Miriam, 25, 55n.
Bell curve, 468–69
Beloch, K. G., 29
Berle, A. A., 116–17, 119, 128
Bernstein, P. L., 317n.
Bevan, A. 623n.
Bhagavad-Gita, 16
Bidding for factors, 486–91
Big business (see also Oligopoly, Monopoly)
    emergence of. 114–15
    statistics of, 117–20
Birman, A., 628
Birth control, 638
Black Death, 34
Black, E., 637, 648
Board of Governors (Federal Reserve System), 471
Bonds, refunding, 292–93
Bonds, and savings, 211
Bonds, yield, 321n., 344, 347
Booms, 203, 387, 388–89
Boorstein, E., 657n.
Borrowing, 211
Bottlenecks, 338–40
Boulding, K., 395n.
Boulton, M., 77, 79, 79n., 80
Bourgeoisie, 50, 58, 68, 75
Brooks, J., 591n.
Brown, E. H. Phelps, 469n.
Budget, balanced, 154–55, 161, 291ff. (see also
    Deficit)

federal, 156
Bureaucratization of business, 122–23
Bushmen, 16
Business cycles, 386–90
  causes of, 388
  mechanism of, 388–90
Business debts, 293–94
Business management, 106–8, 121–23
Business savings, 250
Business schools, 162
Butters, J. K., 159n.

C Calvinism, 55–56
Campbell, R., 625n.
Cannon, W., Rep., 161
Capacity, 391–93
Capital:
  assets, 172–73
  deepening of, 398
  defined, 87, 172–73
  emergence of, as a factor of production, 60,
    63–65
  exports, 584n., 584–85
  formation (see Investment)
  goods, 87, 177
  imports, 584n., 584–85
  marginal efficiency of, 261
  movements, international, 584–85
  national, 172–73
  output ratio, 391–93, 646
  and productivity, 87–88, 104–5, 396–400,
    646
  restraints on international movement, 595
  return to, 456ff.
  and saving, 88–89
  services of, 456–57
  stock of, 177
  and wealth, 172–73
Capital formation and growth, 141–43, 382–83,
    640–42
Capitalism:
  American vs. European, 611
  early, and social justice, 84–86
  early industrial, 72ff.
  European, 609–21
  growth process in, 90–92
  and reform, 85
  rise of, 67–68
  and socialism, 618–19, 660–61
Capitalization, 457
Capital output ratio, 391–93, 646
Carlyle, T., 78
Cartels, 612, 612n., 617
Cash balances, 334, 335–37
  supply of, 308
Catholicism, 41–42, 55, 57
"Center," 117ff.
Chamberlain, E. H., 415n.
Checking accounts, 308–9
Child labor, 82–83, 84
China, 650, 657
Choice:
  and economics, 409

of factors, 485–88
  among goods, 418–19
Chrematistike, 33
Church and medieval economics, 41–42, 55–57
Cicero, 31
Circular flow: 204–5
  in macroeconomics, 179, 189, 200–201
  in microeconomics, 412–13, 496
Circularity, 179 (see also Circular flow)
Cities (see also Urbanization):
  in antiquity, 28–29
  in feudalism, 38–39, 50–51
  and monarchy, 53–54
Claims, 173–74, 211–12
"Classical medicine," 594
Clayton Antitrust Act, 116
Clubok, A., 636n.
Coal and Steel Community, 617
Cobwebs, 449–50
Cochran, T., 112, 113n., 115n., 612n.
Coeur, Jacques, 59, 59n.
Colbert, J. B., 68–69
Collective demand, 420–21, 445
Collectivism, 647–51
Collectivization, 622
Collegia, 29–30
Collusion, 124n., 513
Colton, D., 108
Combination Laws, 101
Command:
  and development, 647–51, 655–57
  as economic system, 18–20
  and efficiency, 656–660
  and growth. 90–92, 656–57
Commercial banks, 309n., 309ff.
Commercial revolution, 59–69
Committee for Economic Development, 398n.
Commission on National Goals, 394
Commodity stabilization, 643
Common Market, 616–19
Communism:
  and capitalism, 660–61
  and development, 648–51
  and socialism, 610, 615–19, 629n.
Communist Manifesto, 92
Comparative advantage, 556–57, 558–62
Comparative earnings, 466–71
Compensatory government spending, 152–54,
    284ff.
Competition:
  assumptions of pure, 513–16
  change in, 111–14, 122–28
  as control mechanism, 65–66, 424–25
  cutthroat, 112
  and decreasing cost, 105–6, 112
  emergence of, 65
  extent of pure, 515
  imperfect, 530–33
  international, 553–57, 562–64, 568–69
  as market force, 65–66, 424–25
  monopolistic, 530–33
  nature of, 424–25
  and oligopoly, 123–28, 527–30

among products, 123–24, 126
  pure, 513–16
  and rise of big business, 105–6, 111–28
  role of, in market equilibrium, 424–25
  unstable, 105–6
Complements, 445
Concentration:
  extent of, 117–20, 532–33
  late 19th century, 110–11
  ratios, 120
  stabilization of, 119–28
Confederate inflation, 343
Conglomerates, 119
Congress of Industrial Organizations (CIO), 102
Conspicuous consumption, 108
Conspiracy doctrine, 101
Construction, 243
Consumer durables, 177n., 224
Consumer sovereignty, 67, 124–28, 537
Consumption:
  "bottom," 235, 265–66
  components of, 224
  conspicuous, 108
  flow, 176–77
  function, 229ff., 445–46
  and GNP, 224ff.
  high, 659
  income relationship, 229ff.
  passivity of, 236
  patterns, 224
  and saving, 89, 179, 208, 226ff.
  sector, 222ff.
Control, fiscal and monetary, 156–57, 160–62,
    288–89, 322–24, 348–51
Convergence of systems, 660–61
Corporation:
  behavior, 121–24
  debts, 293–94
  legal form of, 114n., 115
  profits, 123, 126, 256, 541
  rise of, 114–19
  statistics of, 117–20
Cost-reducing inventions, 370
Costs:
  average, 497–500, 501–2
  curves, 499
  decreasing, long-run, 512
  depreciation, 196–97, 199
  fixed, 497–500, 508n.
  and GNP, 202–3
  and incomes, 191–97
  increasing, 411, 512
  long-run, 510–11
  marginal, 497–500, 501–2
  materials, 193–94
  opportunity, 300, 345, 560–61
  and output, 190–91
  per unit, 497ff.
  tax, 194–96
  transportation, 568n.
  variable, 497–500, 510
Coulton, G., 34n., 51n.

Council of Economic Advisors, 163, 163n., 258,
    288, 390
Countervailing power, 126
Crash, stock market, 134–35, 143
Crusades, 51–52
Crusoe, R., 565–66
Cunningham, W., 29n.
Currency:
  domestic, 308–9, 317n., 324–25
  international, 586–87, 597, 598–99
Cycles (business cycles), 386–90

D   Dandolo, 52
Da Vinci, 74
Deane, Phyllis, 76n.
Debit, 310n.
Debts:
  and assets, 292–94
  burden of, 299–301
  corporation, 293–94
  government, 151, 294–301
  gross, 294n.
  internal and external, 296
  as money, 317n.
  perpetual, 298
  private, 292–94, 301–2
  problems of, 296–301, 300–304
  refunding, 292–93
Decreasing costs, 512
Decreasing returns, 478–79
Deepening of capital, 398
Defense expenditures, 162, 283n.
Deficits:
  balance of payments, 585, 587–88, 588–89,
    594–599
  effect on business of government, 153, 300–
    301
  in Great Depression, 152–54
  and losses, 291–92
  spending, 291–304
Demand:
  aggregate, 189n., 199ff., 366, 373–74
  and capacity, 391–93
  collective, 720–21, 445
  curve for competitive firm, 503
  definition of, 417–21, 424
  derived, 471, 482–87
  and distribution of output, 360–61
  elasticity of, 437–43
  and employment, 362f., 366, 373–74
  evolution of, 363–64, 416
  for factors, 466–71, 482–87
  gap, 208ff.
  individual and collective, 420–21, 445
  kinked curve, 527–29
  of monopoly, 520–21
  of oligopoly, 527–28
  and output, 189–90, 199ff., 366, 373–74
  schedules, 419–24
  shifts in, 434ff.
  and substitutes, 444–45
  and supply, 417ff.

Demand-creating technology, 369–70
Demand deposits, 308–9
Demosthenes, 73
Denison, E., 398
Depopulation in Middle Ages, 34
Deposits, creation of, 312–16
Deposits, expansion of, 316–21
Depreciation cost and GNP, 196–97, 199
   and accelerator, 258–60
Depreciation of foreign exchange, 578–79
Depression, Great, 131–44, 146–52, 243, 389n.
Derived demand, 471, 482–87
Destabilizing expectation, 449–51
Devaluation, 596–98
Development, economic, 72ff., 632ff.
   and collectivism, 622, 647–51, 656–57
   and foreign aid, 645
   and foreign private investment, 638–39, 643
   and industrialization, 640–42, 645–46
   and international trade, 642–45
   and market, 647, 656–57
   political and social problems, 646–47, 648
   process, 72ff., 640–41, 646–48, 656–57
   stages, 655ff.
Differentiation of product, 514–15, 530–32, 532n., 540
Diminishing returns, 477–79
Direct taxes, 195
Disarmament, 283n.
Discount rates, 323
Discriminatory pricing, 521n.
Diseconomies of scale, 512
Disinvestment, 178
Disposable income, 224
Dissaving, 233, 265
Distribution:
   as economic problem, 14–15
   of income, 140–41, 159n., 456–71
   market solution to, 488–92
   of wealth, 158, 470
Disutility of labor, 458–59, 468
Diversification, 119–20, 121
Dividends, 218
Division of labor, 10–11, 88, 98–100, 555–56, 613–14
Dodd, S., 113
Dollar, as reserve currency, 586–87, 597
Dues, monetization of, 57–59
Dunham, A., 81n.
Durable consumer goods, 177n., 224

E
Earnings of factors, 456ff., 466–71 (see also Marginal productivity)
Eckstein, A., 657n.
Economic development (see Development)
Economic growth (see Growth)
Economic model, 190
Economic problem, the, 12–15 (see also Scarcity, Tradition, Command, Market)
   changing nature of, 661
Economic rent, 461–65, 510
Economics, approaches to, 7–8

in antiquity, 32–33
medieval, 37–39, 40–43
and scarcity, 11–12
and social organization, 9–11, 15–22
Economies of large-scale production, 104–6, 397–98, 511–12
Edsel car, 125
Education and productivity, 397, 468
Efficiency:
   changing, 410–11
   of factor mix, 490
   and free trade, 569
   loss of in imperfect market, 532, 537
   of market, 537–38, 658–60
   and productivity, 477–82
   in U.S.S.R., 626–28
Eisenhower, D., 394
Elasticity, 437–46
   causes of, 442–43
   defined, 437–38, 438n.
   and expenditures, 440–41
   of factor supply curve, 461–62, 463–67
   of income, 437n.
   and necessities, 443
   and receipts 440–41
   and time, 443–44
Eliot, Chas. W., 114
Employment:
   and aggregate demand, 335–36, 362f., 366, 373–74
   and Depression, 138–40
   distribution of, 359f., 365–66n.
   full, 336n., 336ff.
   and labor force, 358–59
   public vs. private gains in, 374
   and size of business, 118
   and tariffs, 584–87
   and unemployment, 359
   in U.S. (1920s), 138–40
   and wage rise, 374–75
Employment Act of 1946, 154
Enclosures, 61–62
Engels, F., 83n., 85, 92
England and industrial revolution, 75ff.
Engrossing, 40
Entrepreneur, industrial:
   in America, 106–8, 121–24
   rise of, in England, 78–80
Entry into industry, 506–8, 513
Equilibrium:
   change in (macro), 268–69; (micro) 433ff.
   of competitive firm, 505–6
   and industry, 506–10
   defined:
     in macroeconomics, 266ff.
     in microeconomics, 421–24, 505–10
   determination of, 266–68, 270–71
   and employment, 336–37
   of GNP, 266ff., 289–90
   in imperfect competition, 531–32
   and interest rates, 346–47
   long-run, 508–9

of monopolistic competition, 531–32
of monopoly, 524–25
and multiplier, 268–69
of oligopoly, 528–30
in pure competition, 505–10
prices, 421–24
and profits, 509–10
stationary (macro), 200–201
Equipment expenditure, 243
Equities, 211, 241
Erlich, A., 622n.
Errors and omissions, 585n.
European capitalism, 609ff.
European Community, 616–19
European employment, distribution of, 365-66n.
European trade, 616–19
European socialism, 615
Excess reserves, 313ff.
Exchange, foreign, 572ff.
Exchange mechanism (foreign), 572–74
Exchange rate, 572ff.
  and balance of payments, 578–80
  fixed and floating, 580–81, 590n.
  semi-flexible, 596
Executives, corporate, 122–24
Exit from industry, 506–8, 508n., 513–14
Expansion of deposits, 316–21
  limits on, 317–19
Expectations:
  destabilizing, 449–51, 542–43
  and investment, 142–43, 257
Expenditure (see also Demand):
  crucial role of, 199–200
  and output 153, 199–200, 335–36
  and receipts (elasticity), 440; (circular flow)
        200–202, 204
  three streams of, 198–99
  vs. tax cuts, 297–98
Exploitation, 488–89
Exploration, 54–55
Exports, net, 181, 274–76
  and balance of payments, 574–77
  effects of, 274–76
Export sector, 584n., 584–85
Exports of capital, 395–96
Extensive investment, 512
External economies, 512
External effects, 544
Externality of debts, 296

F Factors:
  choice among, 485–88
  costs and incomes, 192–93
  definition of, 63–65, 176n.
  divisibility, 475–76
  earnings, 456ff., 466–71
  historic emergence of, 63–65
  incomes, 455, 456ff., 466–71, 487–92
  market for, 455ff.
  mix of, 476ff.
  and output, 175–76, 477–81
  pricing of, 455ff., 466–71, 487–92

productivity of, 395ff., 474ff.
substitution, 486–88, 490–91
supply curves, 457–71
Factory, rise of, 80–83
Fairs, 38–39
Fallacy of Composition, 274n.
Farm problem (see also Agriculture):
  in Depression, 136–38, 138n.
  New Deal and, 148–49, 149n.
Federal budget, 156–57, 280ff.
Federal defense expenditure, 283n., 283
Federal Deposit Insurance Corp., 311n.
Federal Reserve Banks, 310–11, 320, 322–26
  of New York, 586n.
Federal Reserve notes, 324–26
Federal Reserve System, 156, 309–11, 322–26
Federal Trade Commission, 116, 119
Feudal dues, monetization of, 57–59
Feudalism, 35ff., 611
Final goods, 180–81
Financial demand for money, 344–48
Financial intermediaries, 211
Financial investment, 239–40, 241
Financial wealth, 173–74, 211–12
Firm:
  efficient size of, 476
  equilibrium of, 504, 508–9
  and factor mix, 476ff.
  and industry, 506–10
  theory of, 474ff.
Fiscal drag, 297n.
Fiscal policy, 285ff., 350–51
  and business outlook in Depression, 151–52
  and monetary policy, 350–51
Five-Year Plans (U.S.S.R.), 624n., 628
Fixed costs, 105–6, 112, 497–500, 508n.
Fixed exchange rates, 580–81, 590n.
Flexible exchange rates, 580–81, 590n.
Flexible money supply, 312–16
  and prices, 337–38
Flexible tax rates, 297
Flows vs. stocks, 182
Ford, Henry, 97
Foreign aid, 642, 645
  and balance of payments, 583, 595
Foreign assets, 171, 174, 186
Foreign exchange, 572ff. (see also Exchange rate)
  mechanism of, 573–74
  supply and demand for, 574–80
Foreign investment:
  and balance of payments, 584–85
  and development, 643–45
Foreign trade, 551ff.
  and development, 642–45
  European dependence on, 613–16
  gains from, 555ff.
  and GNP, 274–76, 551–52
  and nationalism, 553–55, 567–70
Forestalling, 40
Fort Knox, 326n.
Fox Bourne, H. R., 80
Fractional reserves, 311

Frederick the Great, 69
Free trade, case for, 562–66, 568–69
French planning, 619
Friedlander, H., 612n., 613n.
Friedman, M., 136n., 229n., 342, 343, 350
Full employment:
    and growth, 390–95
    and prices, 335–36
    and tariff, 566–67
    and underemployment, 336–37, 359

G G.A.T.T. (General Agreement on Tariffs and Trade),
    618n.
Galbraith, J. K., 126, 127, 135n., 544
Gap in demand, 208ff. 285
General Motors, 117n., 123, 464n.
*General Theory of Employment, Interest and
    Money,* 152n.
Gentleman's Magazine, 76
Gerald of Aurillac, 42
Ginzberg, E., 374n.
GNP (see Gross National Product)
Goals, absence of in market, 428, 544–45, 559
Gold:
    and balance of payments, 586ff.
    changing price of, 597
    cover, domestic, 325–27
    crisis (1968), 590–91
    exchange standard, 581n., 603
    and Federal Reserve notes, 325–26
    in Fort Knox, 326n.
    influx into 16th-century Europe, 54
    and international exchange, 581n.
    and international reserves, 586ff.
    and money, 324–26, 581n.
    pool, 591
    problem, 586–99
    shipments, 586n.
    standard, 603–5
    and wealth, 174n.
Gold exchange standard, 581n., 603
Goldman, M., 628
Gold standard, 603–5
Gosplan, 624–28
Gould, J., 122n.
Government:
    antirecession policy, 150–55, 156–57, 160
    and business expectations, 151–52
    deficits, 291ff.
    federal vs. state and local, 280–82
    nondefense purchases, 283–84
    purchases of goods and services, 280–84
    sector, 280ff.
    spending and inflation, 336
    spending in New Deal, 151
    spending vs. tax cut, 297–98
    stabilizers, 152–160
    transactions in international trade, 582–84,
    595–96
Great Crash, 134–35, 143
Great Depression, 131–44, 146–52, 243, 389n.

Green, R., 643n.
Gross investment, 177–78
Gross private domestic investment, 181
Gross National Product:
    actual vs. potential, 390–91
    defined, 180–81, 202–3
    imputed, 184–85
    prospects of, 164
    and quality, 183–84, 384n.
    in real terms, 132, 182, 187n.
    as sum of costs and expenditures, 202–3
    weakness as social indicator, 184–85, 384n.
Growth:
    balanced, 393
    causes of, 395–401
    and command, 656–57
    in early capitalism, 90–92
    European, 616
    full employment, 393
    historic rate, 132–33, 384
    importance of, 394–95, 395n.
    inception of, 381–82, 656–57
    long-run prospects, 164, 384–85
    patterns of, 382ff.
    per capita, 132–33
    potential, 391
    and productivity, 396–400
    rates, 384, 393–94, 395n.
    sources of, 395–99
    stages of, 655ff.
    structural problems of, 381–82
    in underdeveloped countries, 381–82, 645–
    46, 656–57
    in U.S., 132–33, 391, 393, 616
    in U.S.S.R., 626
    value of, 400–401
    variations in rate, 385–86
Guest, R., 99n.
Guilds, 39–40
Gunther, J., 28n., 635

Hammond, J. and B., 81   **H**
Hannaford, J., 438n.
Hansen, A., 636
Hayek, F., 84n.
Heller, W., 297n.
Herodotus, 18
Hill, J., 113
Higgins, B., 634n.
High-consumption economies, 659
Hoarding, 219–20
Hofstadter, R., 115n.
Holding company, 114, 136
Hollingsworth, T., 36n.
Hong Kong, competition from, 562–63
Hoover, H., 133
Household incomes, 192–93
Household sector, 222 (see *also* Consumption)
Huizinga, J., 37n.
Humbertus de Romanis, 55
Huntington, C., 107, 108

Idle resources, 252, 334–36, 336–38 (see also Unemployment)
Imperfect competition, 530–33
Imperfect markets, extent of, 532–33
Imperialism, 638–39
Imports:
  and balance of payments, 574–77, 588, 593
  "danger" of, 553–54, 562–63, 565–67, 569
  importance for U.S., 552–53
  as leakage, 250
Income:
  and costs, 191ff., 197
  differentials, 466–71
  distribution, 140–41, 159n., 456–71
  elasticity, 437n.
  European vs. U.S., 613, 613n.
  and factor costs, 192–93
  maldistribution of, in Depression, 140–41
  marginal utility of, 458–59
  national (defined), 192, 203
  redistribution of, 157–58, 215–17, 296, 341n.
  and rent, 464–65
  taxes, 195, 217–19, 282
  taxes, impact of, 159
  and technological unemployment, 370–71
Increasing costs, law of, 411, 481
Increasing returns, 477–78
India, child mortality in, 9
  wealth of, 172
Indicative planning, 619
Indirect taxes, 195–96, 281–82
Induced investment, 257–60, 388–90
Industrialization, 72ff., 86–92
  economic effects:
    in England, 85–86
    in U.S., 104–5
  forced, 621–23
  and market, 91–92
  and market structure, 110ff.
  origins of, 73ff.
  process, 86–92, 382–83
  social effects:
    in England, 80–86
    in U.S., 95–103
  of underdeveloped countries, 640–42
  in U.S.S.R., 621–23
Industrial revolution, 72ff.
  pace of, 81–82
  social repercussions, 80–86
  stages of, 96
  in theory, 86–90
Industrial technology, 72ff., 95ff.
Industry and firm, 506–10, 531–32
Industry-building inventions, 369–70
Inefficiency in monopolistic competition, 534, 542
Inelastic demand:
  for farm products, 137, 148–49, 363, 643
  for international commodities, 662
Inelasticity, 437–46 (see also Elasticity)
Inelastic supply and price, 437–39, 465–66
Inertia, social, 636–37
Infant industries, 568

Inflation: 338ff.
  confederate, 343
  control of, 348–51
  and employment, 252, 335–36, 340–42
  and government spending, 336
  runaway, 325n., 342–43
  Russian, 342–43
  and service sector, 339–40
  U.S., postwar, 155–56, 340–41
Infrastructure, 648
Injections, 274–77
Inputs, 175ff.
Instability of markets, 447–52, 542–43
Interest:
  costs and investment, 261n., 261–62
  as factor return, 192, 456–57
  and liquidity preference, 344–48
  on public debt, 298–99
  rate and investment, 261–62
  rate and money, 343–48
  rates, 261n.
  and savings, 457
  and usury, 42–43
Intermediaries, financial, 211
Intermediate goods, 176–77, 180
Intermediate products, 176–77, 180
Internal debts, 296
International Monetary Fund, 586, 598–99
International trade:
  breakdown (1930s), 614–15
  and development, 642–45
  in Europe, 613–15, 616–20
  gains from, 555ff., 613
  and GNP, 274–76, 551–52
  and nationalism, 553–55, 567–70
Interregional trade, 599
Intersectoral offsets, 214
Inventions, industry-building, 367–68 (see also Technology)
Inventories:
  behavior of, 241–42, 388–90
  as investment, 178n., 203
Investing, financial, 239–40
Investment:
  autonomous, 257–58, 260
  causes of, 257–60, 260–62
  collapse (in 1929), 142–44, 245
  components of, 241–44
  in construction, 243
  defined, 177–78, 239–40, 243n.
  determinants of, 260–62
  financial, 239–40, 241
  and employment, 368–72
  and equilibrium, 263–73
  in equipment, 243
  and expectations, 257
  extensive, 394–95
  foreign, 575, 584–85
  gross and net, 177–78
  induced, 257–58
  instability of, 142–44, 241–43
  intended, 263–64

in inventory, 178, 241–43
marginal efficiency of, 261
model, 258–60, 262–63
motivation of, 255ff.
net, 178
in occupations, 468
private foreign, 171, 174, 584–85, 643–45
replacement, 178, 196–97, 243, 258–60
and saving, 87–88, 142–44, 262ff.
sector, 239ff.
unintended, 264
in U.S. (1930s), 142–44
Investments, bank, 311–12, 320–21
Isocrates, 28
I.U.D., 638

J Jevons, W. S., 388
Jope, E., 74n.
Josephson, M., 107
Journeymen, 39
Jubilee year, 32
Justice:
in antiquity, 32–33
in early capitalism, 84–86
and market, 428, 491–92
"Just prices," 41–42

K Kaplan, A. D. H., 121n.
Kennedy tax cut, 161, 258, 297
Keynes, J. M., 152n., 230, 285
Kimble, G., 27n.
Kinked demand curve, 527–28
Korean war, 155
Krokodil, 627
Kulaks, 622

L Labor (see *also* Division of labor; Labor force)
demand for, 366, 373–74, 456, 457f.
earnings of, 456–60, 466–70, 490–91
emerges as factor of production, 60–63, 63–65
and minimum wage, 490–91
occupational distribution, 100–101
productivity of, 395–399
reducing supply of, 376–77
saving inventions, 370–72
services of, 457ff.
supply curve of, 358–59, 457ff.
unions, 101–3, 339, 374–75, 522
and wages, 456–60, 466–70
Labor force:
occupational distribution, 100–104, 359ff.
and technology, 100–101
Labor-saving technology, 370–72
Labor unions, 101–3
and wages, 374–75, 522
Laissez faire, 69, 150
Lampman, R., 159n., 471n.
Land:
emerges as factor of production, 60, 63–65
in feudalism, 35–36
return to, 456–57, 460–61

services of, 456–57
supply curve of, 456–57, 460–61
Landes, D., 76n.
Lanzillotti, R., 123n.
Latifundium, 28
Law of diminishing returns, 477–81
Law of increasing costs, 411, 481
Law of variable proportions, 477–81
Leakages, 249–50, 274–77
Leisure, 364, 375–76
Lenin, 621–22
Leviticus, Book of, 32
Lewis, O., 649
Liabilities, 312
Liberman, E., 628
Liquidity preference, 345, 349–51
and interest rates, 344–48
Loans, bank, 311–12, 313–14
Long run:
cost curve, 510–11
defined, 448n.
Losses and deficits, 291–92
Lowe, A., 69n., 452n.
Luddite, 82, 82n.
Luxury goods, 419n.,
and elasticity, 442–43

M Machine tools, 382, 382n.
"Macro," 285n.
Macroeconomics defined, 170, 406
Macroeconomics vs. microeconomics, 446, 485n.
Maine, Sir H., 44
Malenbaum, W., 648
Management, corporate, 121–24
Manorial system, 35–37
breakdown of, 57–59
Mantoux, P., 77n., 78n., 79, 80n., 81n., 82n.
Manufacturing:
and employment, 360–63, 365–66n.
rise of, 73ff.
Marginal capital-output ratio, 391–93, 646
Marginal cost, 482–88, 500–501, 502–10
Marginal disutility, 458–59, 468
Marginal efficiency of capital, 261
Marginal productivity, 477–81
and factor pricing, 489–91
and social justice, 491–92
Marginal propensity to consume, 231–32, 249
Marginal propensity to save, 231–32, 249
Marginal revenue:
of competitive firm, 502–3
and marginal cost, 482–88, 504ff., 523-24
for monopolist, 523-24
for oligopolist, 528
Marginal utility, 418, 442–43, 468
of income, 458-59
Market:
as allocation mechanism, 425–31
in antiquity, 25–33
as capital-building mechanism, 91–92, 647–48, 656–57
challenge to, 124–28, 538–46, 658–63

677

controls over, 149–50, 455
clearing, 422
and distribution, 488–91
and economic development, 647, 656–59,
efficiency, 428, 537–38, 658–59
emergence of, 44–46, 48ff., 59ff.
for factors, 455ff.
and goals, 428, 544–45, 659–60
for goods, 415ff.
and industrialization, 91–93, 647, 656–57,
658–59
interference with, 149–50, 428, 490–91, 545
instability of, 447–52, 542–43
long-run prospects for, 660–64, 658–63
mechanism, 407–13, 425–31
New Deal intervention into, 150
orderly operation of, 447–52, 542–43
and planning, 545, 619–20, 624, 659–60
rationing, 425–31
self-correcting tendency, 423–24, 447–52,
542–43
and social justice, 428, 488–92, 544–45,
659–60
stability of, 447–52, 542–43
structure and degree of competition, 123–28,
513–16, 519–20
structure in U.S., 110–17, 117f., 532–33
tasks, 12–15, 408
and waste, 539, 541–42
weaknesses of, 428, 538–46, 659–60
Market system described, 20–22
and rise of capitalism, 44–46, 67–68
Marshall Plan Aid, 155
Marx, K., 85, 92, 100, 621, 629n.
Mason, E., 118n.
Mass production, 104–6, 397–98, 511–12
Materials cost, 193–94
Maudslay, H., 78, 80, 382n.
Maximilian I, 58
Maximization of profits, 475, 528–30
Means, G., 116–17, 119, 126
Medieval economics, 37–39
Mercantilism, 68–69
and growth, 91, 656
Merchandise items, balance of payments, 574–
75, 593
Merchant, itinerant, 49–50
Mergers, 113–14, 119
Microeconomics defined, 170, 406
Middle Ages, 33ff.
Military spending, 162, 283n.
Mill, J. S., 492
Miller, H., 159n.
Miller, W., 112, 113n., 612n.
Minimum wages, 490–91
Mobility:
of factors, 459–60
of farmers, 138n.
historic emergence of, 65
and tariffs, 566–67
Model, economic, 190
of acceleration principle, 258–59

Modernization, 647
Monarchy, growth of, 53–54
Monetary controls, 156–57, 322–26
Monetary policy, 322–26, 348–51
Monetization: 45, 184
of feudal dues, 57–59
of work, 45, 184, 357
Money:
Confederate, 343
control over, 321ff.
creation of, 312–16
defined, 308–9, 317n., 334n.
and expenditure, 342ff.
as "factor of production," 457n.
financial demand for, 344–48
flexible supply of, 337–38
and gold, 324–26
increasing supply of, 315–21
and interest rates, 343–48
and output, 335–36
and prices, 337–38
quantity, theory of, 331–32
and Russian inflation, 342–43
velocity, 333, 343
Monnet, J., 617
Monopolistic competition, 530–33
Monopoly:
costs, 523
definition, 123, 208, 520–21, 521n.
equilibrium, 524–25
extent of, 520–21, 532–33
gains from, 541
and inefficiency, 525, 540–41
limits of, 521
marginal revenue, 523–24
motives, 519
prices, 525–26
profits, 525–26
regulation, 526
Monopsony, 523n.
Monroe, A., 41n.
Moody, J., 111n.
Moore, B., 76n.
Moorsteen, R., 626n.
More, T., 62
Motives:
economic, of firms, 519
profit, 64–65
Multiplier:
accelerator interaction, 258, 388–89
and automatic stabilizers, 288–89
downward, 251
employment, 252
and equilibrium, 268–69
formula, 246
and government expenditure, 288, 290n.,
295n.
idle resources, 252
and income, 143–44, 246–47
and inflation, 252
and leakages, 249–50, 290n.
and marginal propensity to consume, 248

Mumford, L., 80n., 382n.
Myrdal, G., 623n.

N National Association of Manufacturers, 102
National Bureau of Economic Research, 471
National debt (see Debts)
National Goals, Commission on, 394–95
National income, 192, 203 (see also Gross National Product)
National Industrial Recovery Act (NIRA), 150
Nationalism:
    emergence of, 53–54
    and international trade, 553–55, 599–600
    and tariff, 567–70
National Planning Association, 394–95
Necessities and elasticity, 443
Nef, J., 73n.
Negro incomes, 163
Negro unemployment, 373, 375–76
Nelson, R., 111n.
Net investment, 178
Net national product, 203
Nevins, A., 96, 97n., 104, 104n., 105n.
Newcomer, M., 122n.
New Deal, 148ff.
    and business, 151–52
New Economic Policy (NEP), 622
"New economics," 161, 162
"New Men," 76–80
Nondurable goods, 224
Nonmerchandise items, balance of payments, 575
Normative price theory, 451–52
Nove, A., 657n.
Nurkse, R., 640n.

O Occupational differentials in earnings, 467–71
Occupational distribution of labor force, 100–101
Oeconomia, 33
Offsets to saving, 210–15, 285–86
Ohlin, G., 36n., 50n.
Oligopoly:
    behavior, 121–24, 527–30
    defined, 123, 526–27
    extent of, 117–23, 532–33
    indeterminacy of, 529
    kinked demand curve, 527–28
    marginal revenue, 528
    and power, 126–28, 543–44
    rise of, 105–6, 111–28
    stabilization of, 119–24, 532–34
Open-market operations, 323–24, 348–51
Opportunity cost, 300, 345, 560–61
Orderly market, 447–52, 542–43
Oser, J., 612n., 613n.
Otto, N., 97
Output:
    and cost, 190–91
    and demand, 189–90
    optimum, of firm, 505–6, 506–10, 524–25
    (see also Gross National Product)
    and prices, 335–36
Outputs, 175ff.

Overhead cost, 105–6, 112, 497–500, 508n.
Overlending, 319–20

P Paradox of thrift, 273–74
Participation rates, 355–57
Partnerships, 114n., 117
Peasants:
    in antiquity, 26–28
    in underdeveloped countries, 636–37
"Periphery," 117–18, 123
Perpetual debts, 298–99
Personal income, 224
Personal outlays, 223n.
Phillips curve, 340–41
Physiocracy, 75n.
Pirenne, H., 38, 42, 43
Planning:
    and efficiency, 626–28
    in Europe, 615–20
    in France, 619
    long-run prospects, 662
    and market, 545, 619–20, 624, 659–60
    mechanism, in U.S.S.R., 621–23, 623–29
Pliny, 28
Polanyi, K., 59n.
Political vs. economic problems, 284, 303, 648
Pools, 113
Polaroid Co., 521n.
Popper, K., 9n.
Population:
    in antiquity, 34
    growth in underdeveloped countries, 637–38, 646
    and labor force, 355–57
Poverty, 163–64, 163n.
Powell, R., 626n.
Power:
    of big business, 126–28
    fragmentation of in market, 537
    problem of, 126–28, 543–44
    and wealth in antiquity, 30–31
Power, E., 37n., 61
Prebisch, R., 643n.
Predestination, 55–56
Predictive theory, 451–52
Pre-market economy, 24ff.
Price creep, 340, 341–42, 350
Price leader, 123
Price level, index of, 187n., 332
Prices:
    and allocation, 425–27
    and behavior, 416, 449–51
    of competitive firm, 508–9
    and countervailing power, 126
    determining vs. determined, 463
    and elasticity of demand, 437–42
    and employment, 335–36
    equilibrium, 421–24
    in international trade, 561–62
    monopoly, 525–26
    oligopoly, 124, 125–26, 527–28
    and rationing, 425–31

sticky, 337–38, 542
    target, 123
Price searcher, 520
Price taker, 520
Price theory, 416, 451–52
Product differentiation, 514–15, 530–32, 540
Production, flow of, 174ff.
Production possibility curve, 408–9, 557–58
Production possibility surface, 410
Production problem, 12–14
Productivity:
    agricultural, 137, 149
    of capital, 82, 88, 396–400, 646
    causes of, 87–88, 396–400
    curve, 477–81
    and growth, 86–88, 396–400, 635–36,
        645–46
    and international competition, 562–64
    marginal, 477–81, 483–88
    of mass production, 104–6
    in 1920s, 138–40
    and profit 483–88
    and technology, 87–88, 104–5, 398–99
    and trade, 555
    in underdeveloped countries, 634–35, 640
    U.S. and European, 612–13
Products, defined, 444
Profit motive, rise of, 64–65
Profits:
    of competitive firms, 506, 509–15
    corporate, 123, 126, 140, 256, 541
    and demand, 216–18
    and GNP 216–19
    and investment, 255ff.
    as leakage, 250
    maximization of, 475, 528–35
    monopoly, 525–26
    and quasi rents, 509–10
Propensity to consume, 229ff., 369n., 445
    average and marginal, 231–32
    and equilibrium, 264ff.
    in U.S., 233
Property income, 470–71
Proprietorships, 114n., 117
Protestant Ethic, 55–57
Public goods and market, 544–45
Public sector, 282–85, 302–3 (see also Government)
    growth of, 160
Public works, 151
Pujo Committee, 115
Pump priming, 151–52
Purchasing power (see Demand)
Pure competition, 513–16

Q   Quantity equation, 331–32
    Quantity theory of money, 331ff., 342–43
    Quasi rents, 461–65, 509–10
    Quesnay, F., 75n.

R   Rate of exchange (see Exchange rate)
    Rationing by market, 425–31

Real GNP, 182, 187n.
Real saving, 214
Recession, 204, 387, 388–89
Redistribution of income, 157–58, 215–17
    and inflation, 341n.
    and public debt, 296
Reference cycles, 387
Reformation, 55–57
Refunding of bond issues, 292–93
Regrating, 40
Relief, 151
Religious attitudes to economic activity:
    in antiquity, 32–33
    Calvinist, 55–57
    medieval, 40–43
Remittances, 575
Renard, G., 40n., 42n.
Rent (see also Quasi rent):
    economic, 461–65, 509–10
    imputed, 184–85
    and incomes, 461–65
Replacement investment, 178
Reserve currency, 586–87, 597, 598–99
Reserves:
    bank, 309, 311ff.
    changes in, 322–23
    creation of, 316ff.
    excess, 313
    fractional, 311
    international, 586ff.
    ratio, required, 309, 322–23
Returns, diminishing, 477–79
Returns, increasing, 477–78
Revenue, average and marginal, 504ff.
Richman, B., 626n.
Robber barons, 106–8
Robertson, P., 611n.
Rome, fall of, 34–35
Roosevelt, F. D., 115, 121, 146, 151
Rorig, F., 50n.
Runaway inflation, 325n., 342–43
Runs on banks, 311n.

S   Sales vs. taxes, 194–95, 217, 295
    Saving:
        and capital formation, 88–89, 142–44, 208–
            9, 214–15, 220
        and consumption, 89, 179, 208, 226ff.
        and demand gap, 208ff.
        defined, 208
        deposits, 310
        and development, 88–92, 640–41, 645
        dilemma of, 210
        in early capitalism, 90
        gross, 209
        and growth, 220
        intended, 263–64
        and investment, 142–44, 179, 210–14, 262ff.
        long-run, 228–29
        offsets to, 210–14
        ratio, 226ff. (see also Propensity to consume)
        real and money, 214–15

net and gross, 209
  short-run, 228–29
Savings banks, 309n.
Scale, 475–76
  economies of, 397–98, 511–12
Scarcity, 11–12, 409
Scatter diagram, 234
Schlesinger, A., 135n., 147, 147n.
Schonfield, A., 128n., 620n.
Schuman, R., 617
Schumpeter, J., 2
Schwartz, A., 136n.
Sectors, 198–200
Seidman, A., 643n.
Selling cost, 529n.
Semiflexible exchange rates, 596
Seneca, 29
Serfs, 36–37
Services, consumption, 224
Service sector:
  growth of, 364–65, 371–72
  and inflation, 339–40
Sherman Antitrust Act, 115–16, 121
Shortages, 429–31
  steel, 542
Short-run cost curve, 499, 510
Short-run market changes, 460–61
Size, 114–15, 542–43, (see also Scale)
Skills and earnings, 466–70, 489–90
Slavery, 29–30
Small business, 117–18
Smith, A., 16, 24, 99–100, 658
Socialism:
  and capitalism, 618–19
  and communism, 629n.
  in Europe, 610, 615–19
  in U.S.S.R., 621ff.
Social justice:
  in antiquity, 32–33
  and early capitalism, 84–86
  and market, 428, 488–92, 544–45, 659–60
Social security as transfer, 216
Sombart, W., 56n., 57n., 73n.
Somers, H., 285n.
Sovereignty of consumer, 67, 124–28
Special Drawing Rights (SDR's), 598–99
Specialization of labor, 10–11, 88, 98–100,
    555–56, 613–14
Specificity of factors, 460
Speculation, 135–36, 596
Spending (see Demand)
Spengler, O., 57n.
Stability of market, 447–52, 542–43
Stabilizers, automatic, 160, 288–89, 390
Stalin, 622
Standard Oil Company, 113
Standard Oil Trust, 113–14
State and local expenditures, 281–82
Stationary equilibrium, 200–201
Stevens, R., 583n.
"Sticky prices," 337–38
Stock issues, 240–41, 293n.

Stock market:
  Boom, 133–34
  Crash, 134
  and savings, 211, 241
Stocks (and flows), 182
Structural unemployment, 373, 375–76
Structure of markets:
  and degree of competition, 123–28, 513–16,
    519–20
  in U.S., 110–14, 117ff., 532–33
Substitutes, 442–43
Substitution of factors, 490–91
Sunspots, 388
Supply:
  defined, 417–21, 424
  of factors, 457–71, 486–88
  and prices, 417ff.
  schedules, 419
  shifts in, 434ff.
Surplus, social 30–31
Surpluses in market, 429–31

"T" accounts, 312ff.   T
Taft-Hartley Act, 543
Target pricing, 123
Tariff:
  borne by foreigners, 563–64
  case for, 566–69
  and full employment, 566–67
  and infant industries, 568
  U.S., 618n.
Tastes, 417
  changes in, 434
Taussig, F., 106, 612
Tawney, R., 41, 44, 45, 55, 73n., 83n.
Tax cuts, 161, 258, 297–98
Taxes:
  costs and GNP, 194–96
  direct and indirect, 194–96
  on economic rents, 464–65
  and fiscal policy, 286–91, 297–98
  impact on GNP, 286–87, 289–91
  income, 195, 217–19
  as leakage, 250
  policy, 156, 286–87, 289–91, 297–98
  progressivity of, 287
  rates, 286–87, 297
  vs. sales, 194–95, 217, 295
  and transfers, 217
Technical specificity, 460–61
Technological unemployment, 370–72
Technology:
  and agriculture, 361–62
  and alienation, 99–100
  automation, 371–72
  cost reducing, 370
  demand-creating, 369–70
  and division of labor, 359ff.
  and farm problem, 148–49, 149n., 361–62
  and employment, 367–71
  industrial, 73–74, 95ff.

and investment, 368–69, 370–72
and power, 543–44
precapitalist, 73–74
and productivity, 87–88, 104–5, 398–99
and size of firm, 104–6, 110–114, 511–12
and unemployment, 135, 138–40, 162, 367–72
uneven entry of, 361–62
and urbanization, 98
Terms of trade, 643
Tertiary sector, 364–65, 371–72
Thomas, Elizabeth, 16
Three streams of expenditure, 198–99
Thrift:
  and Calvinism, 55–56
  paradox of, 273–74
Thrupp, S., 42n.
Tight money, 261n.
Time deposits, 310
Time and equilibrium prices, 443–44
Time and oligopolistic behavior, 529–30
Time and specificity, 460
Tolls, 53
Toward a Social Report, 185
Towns, medieval, 38–39, 50–51
  and monarchy, 53–54
Toynbee, A., Sr., 85
Trade:
  European, 613–16
  gains from, 555ff., 613
  policy, 562ff.
Trade-off relationships, 557–58, 558–62
Tradition, 16–18, 634, 655
Transactions:
  demand (for money), 344–45
  volume of, 333n., 334–35
Transfer payments, 215–17, 282
  and taxes, 217–18
Transportation costs, 568n.
Travel, in balance of payments, 575–76
Truman, H., 144
Trusts, 107–8, 113, 115

U Underdevelopment, 632ff. (*see also* Development)
  causes of, 633–39
  industrialization, 640–42, 645–46
  lopsided economies, 639
Underemployment, 336–37, 640
Unemployment:
  combatting, 366–67, 372–77
  defined, 359
  in Depression, 135, 138–40, 154
  and equilibrium, 336–37
  and GNP, 358–59, 366, 373–74
  and price level, 335ff.
  technological, 135, 138–40, 162, 367–72
  in U.S., 135, 138–40, 154, 157, 162, 358, 373
  voluntary, 359
UNESCO, 636
Unions:
  rise of, 101–3

and wages, 339, 522
Unit costs, 497ff.
U.S. Steel, 123
Unstable markets, 447–49, 542–43
Urbanization, 50–51, 98
U.S.S.R.:
  efficiency of, 626–28
  five-year plans, 624n., 628
  growth rates, 626
  history, 621–23
  planning in, 623–29
  reforms, 627–28
Usury, 42–43, 55
Utility, 176, 444
  marginal, 418, 442–43

V Value added, 192, 194
Variable costs, 497–500, 510
Variable proportions, law of 477–81
Veblen, T., 106
Velocity of circulation, 333–34, 343
Vietnam, 283n.

W Wages:
  cutting, 375
  foreign, 562–63
  policy, 374–75
  pressures, 338–40
  and unemployment, 374–75
Walker, Charles, 99n.
War, impact of, 154–55
Ward, Barbara, 91n.
War spending, 162
Waste, 539, 541–42
Watkins, M., 111
Watt, J., 77, 79n.
Wealth:
  distribution in U.S., 158, 172
  financial, 173–74
  in India, 172
  national (U. S.) 171–74
  personal, 173–74, 211–12
  and power, 30–31
Weber, M., 55
Wedgwood, J., 79, 80, 84
Weeks, E., 149n.
Welfare state:
  in Europe, 618–19
  in U.S., 148ff., 157–58
Wilkinson, J., 76–77
Wilson, W., 115
Wit, D., 636n.
Withdrawals, 249–50, 274–77
Women in labor force, 356, 357
Work:
  industrialism and, 99–100
  problem of, 662
World War II, 154–55
Wykes, Thomas, 53

Y Yield, 321n., 344, 347
Yugoslavia, 628–29